The Making of English National Identity

Why is English national identity so enigmatic and so elusive? Why, unlike the Scots, Welsh, Irish and most of continental Europe, do the English find it so difficult to say who they are? *The Making of English National Identity* is a fascinating exploration of Englishness and what it means to be English. Drawing on historical, sociological and literary theory, Krishan Kumar examines the rise of English nationalism and issues of race and ethnicity from earliest times to the present day. He argues that the long history of the English as an imperial people has, as with other imperial people like the Russians and the Austrians, developed a sense of missionary nationalism which in the interests of unity and empire has necessitated the repression of ordinary expressions of nationalism. Professor Kumar's lively and provocative approach challenges the reader to reconsider their pre-conceptions about national identity and who the English really are.

KRISHAN KUMAR is W. R. Kenan Jr. Professor of Sociology at the University of Virginia. His books include *Morris: News from Nowhere* (Cambridge, 1995), *From Post-Industrial to Post-Modern Society: New Theories of the Contemporary World* (1995), *Utopia and Anti-Utopia in Modern Times* (1987) and *1989: Revolutionary Ideas and Ideals* (2001).

Cambridge Cultural Social Studies

Series editors: JEFFREY C. ALEXANDER, *Department of Sociology, Yale University, and* STEVEN SEIDMAN, *Department of Sociology, University at Albany, State University of New York.*

Titles in the series

ILANA FRIEDRICH SILBER, *Virtuosity, Charisma, and Social Order* 0 521 41397 4 hardback

LINDA NICHOLSON AND STEVEN SEIDMAN (eds.), *Social Postmodernism* 0 521 47516 3 hardback 0 521 47571 6 paperback

WILLIAM BOGARD, *The Simulation of Surveillance* 0 521 55081 5 hardback 0 521 55561 2 paperback

SUZANNE R. KIRSCHNER, *The Religious and Romantic Origins of Psychoanalysis* 0 521 44401 2 hardback 0 521 55560 4 paperback

PAUL LICHTERMAN, *The Search for Political Community* 0 521 48286 0 hardback 0 521 48343 3 paperback

ROGER FRIEDLAND AND RICHARD HECHT, *To Rule Jerusalem* 0 521 44046 7 hardback

KENNETH H. TUCKER, JR., *French Revolutionary Syndicalism and the Public Sphere* 0 521 56359 3 hardback

ERIK RINGMAR, *Identity, Interest and Action* 0 521 56314 3 hardback

ALBERTO MELUCCI, *The Playing Self* 0 521 56401 8 hardback 0 521 56482 4 paperback

ALBERTO MELUCCI, *Challenging Codes* 0 521 57051 4 hardback 0 521 57843 4 paperback

SARAH M. CORSE, *Nationalism and Literature* 0 521 57002 6 hardback 0 521 57912 0 paperback

DARNELL M. HUNT, *Screening the Los Angeles 'Riots'* 0 521 57087 5 hardback 0 521 57814 0 paperback

LYNETTE P. SPILLMAN, *Nation and Commemoration* 0 521 57404 8 hardback 0 521 57683 0 paperback

(list continues at end of book)

The Making of English
National Identity

Krishan Kumar

CAMBRIDGE
UNIVERSITY PRESS

PUBLISHED BY THE PRESS SYNDICATE OF THE UNIVERSITY OF CAMBRIDGE
The Pitt Building, Trumpington Street, Cambridge CB2 1RP, United Kingdom

CAMBRIDGE UNIVERSITY PRESS
The Edinburgh Building, Cambridge CB2 2RU, UK
40 West 20th Street, New York, NY 10011-4211, USA
477 Williamstown Road, Port Melbourne, VIC 3207, Australia
Ruiz de Alarcón 13, 28014 Madrid, Spain
Dock House, The Waterfront, Cape Town 8001, South Africa

http://www.cambridge.org

First published 2003

Printed in the United Kingdom at the University Press, Cambridge

Typeface Times (Monotype) 10/12.5 pt   *System* LaTeX 2_ε [TB]

A catalogue record for this book is available from the British Library

ISBN 0 521 77188 9 hardback
ISBN 0 521 77736 4 paperback

To Katya and Kyrill

Contents

Preface   *page* ix

1   English or British? The question of English national identity   1

2   Nations and nationalism: civic, ethnic and imperial   18

3   When was England?   39

4   The first English Empire   60

5   The English nation: parent of nationalism?   89

6   The making of British identity   121

7   The moment of Englishness   175

8   The English and the British today   226

Notes   274
List of references   300
Index   353

Preface

This book could have been entitled alternatively 'the enigma of English national identity'. For it attempts to answer such questions as: why does 'English nationalism' sound so strange to English ears? Why is it – more than in most other cases – so elusive, so difficult to pin down? When – if at all – did it emerge? What is the relation of English national identity to the national identities of those other peoples – the Welsh, Scots and Irish – who share with the English the two islands off the northwestern coast of Europe? Can we separate English from British national identity and, if so, how?

That these questions need to be asked suggests the peculiarity of the English case. It is not so much that English national identity cannot be distinguished by its 'content' – its self-conceived differences, flattering to the national pride, from other nations. This by itself is not unusual. What we call content is in most cases the product of the process by which nations are formed, rather than some qualities intrinsic or special to the nation in question. It is common enough for nations, as for individuals, to develop a sense of themselves by a process of opposition and exclusion. What they are – French, German – is defined by what they are not – German, French. The 'content' of national identity is more often than not a counter-image of what is seen as distinctive in the culture of the other nation or nations.

This pattern is, as Linda Colley especially has argued, probably true for the making of British national identity. British national identity was forged through a series of powerful contrasts with Britain's continental neighbours, particularly but not only France. But the English case shows almost the opposite phenomenon. Not exclusion and opposition, but inclusion and expansion, not inwardness but outwardness, mark the English way of conceiving themselves. The English saw themselves in the mirror of the larger enterprises in which they were engaged for most of their history. They found their identity as constructors of Great Britain, creators of the British Empire, pioneers of the world's first industrial civilization.

No doubt an element of contrast does enter into the story, here as with other nations. The English could see themselves as different from the 'Celts' whom they colonized and in some cases conquered, just as, in even larger measure, they could distinguish themselves from the non-European peoples that made up the Empire. But what is more striking – or so at least this book argues – is the extent of English inhibition in the matter of national self-assertiveness. English rulers and writers, and the political culture they created, saw it as impolitic to beat the nationalist drum, in the face of rule over different peoples and different lands. Hence we do not, in English political writing, find tub-thumping statements of English nationalism. For much of the time, in the society at large, there are virtually no expressions of English nationalism (a different matter from English xenophobia, which is venerable and much remarked on by visitors). There is no native tradition of reflection on English national identity (though many foreigners have felt free to have their say on the English national character).

This native reticence was not modesty; indeed the opposite. The English took pride, as did the Romans of old, in their role as empire-builders. They saw themselves as engaged in the development and diffusion of civilizational projects of world-historic importance. This gave them a nationalism and a national identity of sorts – the type I have called in this book 'missionary' or 'imperial' nationalism and national identity. But it differed from classic nationalism in shifting the emphasis from the creators to their creations. The English did not so much celebrate themselves as identify with the projects – the 'mission' – they were, as it were providentially, called upon to carry out in the world. This did not lessen the extent of self-importance; but it gave it a characteristically different form from that expressed in classic nationalism. Like many other imperial nations such as the Russians, the Austrians and the Ottomans, the English could not see themselves as just another nation in a world of nations.

The problems arise when these projects no longer exist. What happens when empire ends? When industrial supremacy and global power disappear? When the longest-lasting and most significant creation, Great Britain itself, threatens to dissolve and disintegrate? These are the questions facing the English today, made more urgent by the move towards European unity and the calls for a radical pluralization and diversification of English society. Not surprisingly they have been accompanied by an intense debate about English national identity and the future of the English nation. For the first time ever, perhaps, the English have been forced to consider themselves as a nation, as a people with a particular history, character and destiny.

This book is intended as a contribution to that debate. It does so by taking the long look, contemplating the *longue durée*. I have indeed been forced to go back further than I originally intended. The reason for this is a number of important claims, by historians and sociologists, to have discovered English national consciousness flourishing as far back as the eight century – or, if not then, the fourteenth century, or the sixteenth, or the seventeenth, or the eighteenth. Since my own argument is that it is not until the late nineteenth century, at the earliest, that we find a clear concern with questions of 'Englishness' and English national identity – let alone any strong expressions of English nationalism – I have felt the need to confront and as far as possible counter the claims of these scholars.

The form of the book is therefore to a good extent a series of alternating presentations whereby I first discuss and debate these claims, and then present my own account of how I see English identity in the relevant periods. Thus chapter 3 takes on the argument of Patrick Wormald, Adrian Hastings and others that an English national identity was formulated as early as the eight century, the time of Bede, and that by the fourteenth century a fully developed English national consciousness had come into being. Against this I argue, in chapter 4, that the key to English – more properly, Anglo-Norman – identity in these centuries is the construction of 'the first English empire' through the subjugation of the Welsh, the Irish and – though ultimately unsuccessful for the time being – the Scots. This, I contend, the making of the 'inner empire' of Great Britain, sets the pattern and the context in which the English will see themselves, as an imperial rather than a merely national people, in the succeeding centuries.

Chapter 5 confronts another challenging thesis, that of the sociologist Liah Greenfeld, that not only did the English know nationalism in the sixteenth century – though not before – but that they were the pioneers, the inventors of European nationalism. I attempt a detailed refutation of this, especially concerning the role of Protestantism as the basis of a putative English nationalism. In chapter 6 I similarly argue against the view of Hans Kohn that English nationalism came into being in the seventeenth century, during the English Civil War, and in chapter 7, I take issue with Gerald Newman's contention that an English nationalism, formed mainly in opposition to the French, developed vigorously in the second half of the eighteenth century. Against both of these I follow and extend Linda Colley in proposing that the really decisive development of these centuries – especially after the union with Scotland in 1707 – was the rise of an overarching British identity within which Scottish, Welsh and Irish identities nested. English identity, however, remained relatively undeveloped, the English contenting themselves with masterminding the whole enterprise. The same was even truer in relation to the vast overseas empire that England began to create in these centuries – one in which, once again, the other peoples of the British Isles were invited to find a place and an identity.

Chapter 7 advances the view that, despite the continuation of a strong sense of Britishness expressed through an increasingly unified Britain and a common involvement in the British Empire, there was towards the end of the nineteenth

century a 'moment of Englishness'. This was, I argue, largely a cultural movement, responding partly to a sense of the possible decline of empire, partly also
to the strong expressions of ethnic and cultural nationalism in other parts of the
British Isles and on the European continent. If this was English nationalism –
for the first time ever – it took cultural, not political, form.

Chapter 8 considers the current position of both Englishness and Britishness.
It accepts that Britishness is in decline, and that traditional notions of Englishness face challenges not simply from a revived 'Celtic' nationalism but also from
large-scale immigration and the increasing integration of Europe. It argues that
while this has thrown up certain expressions of English nationalism, especially
on the Right, the English remain fatally handicapped by the whole history that
I have traced – a history, that is, of a studied disavowal of nationalism and a
reluctance to reflect on their character as a nation. It is this that makes current
efforts to define English national identity so difficult – even as the need for such
an endeavour becomes ever more urgent.

Throughout the book, I make reference to certain concepts of nationhood,
such as 'ethnic' and 'civic'. I also draw upon my own idea of 'missionary'
or 'imperial' nationalism. Accordingly, chapter 2 lays out these concepts, as
an introduction to the subsequent discussion of English and British identity.
In addition, chapter 1 opens with an account of the central 'English-British'
confusion, as a prelude to the whole inquiry into English national identity. It
includes a glossary of relevant terms, and concludes with new ways of conceiving the English-British relationship, especially in the rise of the new 'British
History' and British Studies.

This chapter thus gives a foretaste of the book as a whole, which follows the
spirit of these approaches in considering English identity in the widest possible
context. English national identity, more even than in the case of other nations,
cannot be seen in isolation. It cannot be understood from the inside out but more
from the outside in. To unravel the enigma of Englishness, we must explore the
long-drawn-out engagement of the English with a variety of peoples stretching
from near neighbours to those thousands of miles across the globe.

It remains to thank the many people and the several institutions that have
given aid, advice, support and encouragement. I began work on this book in
Canterbury, Kent and finished it in Charlottesville, Virginia. At the University
of Kent I was lucky to have around me historians such as Alf Smyth, Peter
Roberts and Hugh Cunningham, who were an invaluable source of sugges-
tions and helpful advice. Other Kent colleagues, Mary Evans, Chris Hann,
Jan Pahl and Frank Parkin, also gave encouragement and provided me with
much material to reflect upon. At the University of Virginia I have benefited
from participation in the British Studies Group convened by Richard Drayton,

and including historians and literary scholars such as Stephen Arata, Alison Booth, Robert Ingram, Alison Milbank, Herbert Tucker and Jennifer Wicke. The University of Virginia also has the splendid Alderman Library, whose well-stocked shelves supplied me with practically everything I ever needed, and whose irreplaceable and perhaps unique LEO section probably did more than anything else to ease the labour of research. To its expert and always efficient staff I owe a great debt. I need also to thank the University of Virginia for awarding me a Sesquicentennial Associateship for the Fall 2001 semester, during which I was able to complete the writing of this book.

Talks to various groups at various universities did much to help me shape my thoughts. I thank the British Studies Group – especially James Cronin and Fred Leventhal – at the Center for European Studies, Harvard University; the Sociology Department – especially David McCrone, Tom Nairn and Lindsay Paterson – of the University of Edinburgh; the Humanities Consortium seminar, organized by Rogers Brubaker and Vincent Pecora, at the University of California at Los Angeles; Anne Nielsen, Yngve Lithman and the students of the Sociology Department at the University of Bergen, where I was a visiting professor for three happy years.

Rogers Brubaker, David McCrone and Tom Nairn deserve more than passing thanks for their constant encouragement and for the wonderful example of their own work. The same can be said of Tariq Modood, who was also responsible for my holding a Benjamin Meaker Visiting Professorship at the University of Bristol in June 2001. This gave me an invaluable opportunity to try out the main ideas of this book in a series of talks to the Sociology Department. For the warmth of their welcome and the constructiveness of their response I am very grateful to all the members of the department, especially Steve Fenton, Steve May, Ruth Levitas, Greg McLennan and Tariq himself.

I want also to thank those whose friendship, support and critical advice have sustained me during the long period of the book's composition. It was good to receive – since I no longer live in England – day-to-day items such as newspaper reports and articles from my sister Shirley Sen Gupta, as well as from my friends Colin Seymour-Ure and – from New York! – Allan Silver. Bernard Crick, whose own work on Englishness puts us all in his debt, has been the kindest and most generous of advisers. At a late stage I was fortunate to meet the inspirer and doyen of the new British History, John Pocock: a formidable figure who nevertheless looked kindly on my amateur efforts. Then there is Katya Makarova, who has lived with this book virtually as long as she has lived with me. In many ways this book began with her, in conversations about English and Russian identity, and the remarkable parallels between them that we both noted. Her thoughts on Russian identity were the immediate stimulus to my own reflections on English national identity and its puzzles.

A special word about Raphael Samuel. His untimely death meant that I had no chance to show him any of this work. Nevertheless, as one who was an early mentor and whose work continued to be a lifelong inspiration, he is of all people the one into whose hands I should have liked most to place this book. Its subject is one that was central to all his writing, as is magnificently clear in his posthumously published *Island Stories.*

I should like finally to thank Jeffrey Alexander, co-editor of the Cambridge series in which this volume appears, both for his receptiveness to the idea of this book and for his support throughout; and Sarah Caro, my editor at the Press, for whose enthusiastic encouragement and critical skills – especially in the reduction of an unwieldy manuscript – I am immensely grateful. Thanks are also due, for skilful copy-editing, to Sheila Kane, and to Hilary Cooper for preparing the index.

1

English or British? The question of English national identity

I am a citizen of a country with no agreed colloquial name.

Bernard Crick (1991aa: 90)

As long as the various peoples lumped together under the heading "English" accept this, let us use it. When they start to object we call them Irish or even Scotch. It really does not matter. Everyone knows what we mean whether we call our subject English history or British history. It is a fuss over names, not over things.

A. J. P. Taylor (1975: 622)

It can be said of the English in Britain, as wags say of the Catholics in Heaven, that they think they are the only ones here.

Conrad Russell (1993: 3)

A natural confusion

'English, I mean British' – this familiar locution alerts us immediately to one of the enduring perplexities of English national identity. How to separate 'English' from 'British'? The reverse problem is nowhere as acute. Non-English members of the United Kingdom rarely say 'British' when they mean 'English', or 'English' when they mean 'British'. On the contrary, they are usually only too jarringly aware of what is peculiarly English, and are highly sensitive to the lordly English habit of subsuming British under English. For them it is a constant reminder of what they perceive to be – rightly, of course, – England's hegemony over the rest of the British Isles.

One has to say immediately though that the problem is not one solely of or for the English. Scottish friends confess, with some embarrassment, that they too sometimes say 'English' when they mean 'British'. Foreigners do it all the time, even though 'Brits', 'Britishers', as well as the more conventional 'British', are readily, if not gracefully, to hand. All this testifies to the imperial reach of the English, both at home and abroad. The confusions of others compound the confusion in the minds of the English, and reinforce them in their bad habits.

But in general it is probably right to say that the elision of English into British is especially problematic for the English, particularly when it comes to conceiving of their national identity. It tells of the difficulty that most English people have of distinguishing themselves, in a collective way, from the other inhabitants of the British Isles. They are of course perfectly well aware that there are Welsh, Scots and Irish, even that there are Manxmen and Jersey Islanders. They make jokes about them, imitate their accents, and call upon them for special effects, as when they lend colour to poverty by portraying it in a Glasgow slum, or amuse themselves by intoning passages from Dylan Thomas's *Under Milk Wood* in a ferocious Welsh accent. But these are particular exceptions to the general rule, which is to see all the major events and achievements of national life as English. Other ethnic groups are brought on in minor or supporting roles.

Though when it is brought to their attention the English are properly uneasy and even apologetic about this practice, they can also on occasion offer a robust defence. Fowler's celebrated view, in his *Modern English Usage*, is likely to strike a chord in the heart of every native Englishman (if not all Englishwomen). It is natural, says Fowler, to speak of the *British* Commonwealth or the *British* navy or *British* trade, and to boast that *Britons* never never shall be slaves.

> But it must be remembered that no Englishman . . . calls himself a Briton without a sneaking sense of the ludicrous, or hears himself referred to as a Britisher without squirming. How should an Englishman utter the words *Great Britain* with the glow of emotion that goes for him with *England*? His sovereign may be Her *Britannic* Majesty to outsiders, but to him is Queen of *England*; he talks the *English* language; he has been taught *English* history as one continuous tale from Alfred to his own day; he has heard of the word of an *Englishman* and aspires to be an *English* gentleman; and he knows that *England* expects every man to do his duty . . . In the word *England*, not in *Britain* all these things are implicit. It is unreasonable to ask forty millions of people to refrain from the use of the only names that are in tune with patriotic emotion, or to make them stop and think whether they mean their country in a narrower or wider sense each time they name it.   (Fowler 1983: 157)

This defence, from the heart as it were, certainly tells us something important about Englishness, and its relation to Britishness.[1] But it describes, rather than explains. Why, given the objective situation of a multinational state, did 'Britain' and 'Britishness' not gain the ascendancy? Why does 'patriotic emotion' attach itself so fervently to 'England' and not to 'Britain'? If 'Britain' sounds – as it does – colourless and boring, why is that so and why on the contrary is 'England' so glowingly sonorous (and not, let it be said, just to the English)? And if neither 'Britain' nor 'England' seems to suit, what else? The mystery is deepened, not diminished, by the accurate observation that *none* of the available names for the United Kingdom will do, for various reasons. We live, says Tom Nairn, in a State

with a variety of titles having different functions and nuances – the U.K. (or "Yookay", as Raymond Williams relabelled it), Great Britain (imperial robes), Britain (boring lounge-suit), England (poetic but troublesome), the British Isles (too geographical), "This Country" (all-purpose within the Family), or "This Small Country of Ours" (defensively-Shakespearian). (Nairn 1994: 93)

As a remedy Nairn proposes, with calculated malice, 'Ukania', a deliberate echo of the 'Kakania' of Robert Musil's famous end-of-empire novel, *The Man Without Qualities* (1930). This was Musil's notoriously satirical (and scatological) coinage for the Habsburg Empire, a baggy, unwieldy domain that also suffered from a plethora of names, and for much the same historical reasons (Austria, Austria-Hungary, 'the Empire', etc.).[2]

We shall return to Austria, and to other imperial and post-imperial nations such as Russia. They have much to tell us, by way of comparison, of the problem of national identity faced by the imperial English. But first we must try to do the best we can with the vexed question of nomenclature. This is of course more than simply about names. It reveals a history and a culture resonant with ambiguities and conflicts. It is a language of power and prejudice as much as it is a reflection of constitutional proprieties.

Britain and the British

In the 'Preface' to his volume in *The Oxford History of England*, A. J. P. Taylor wrote, in his characteristically combative tone:

When the Oxford History of England was launched a generation ago, "England" was still an all-embracing word. It meant indiscriminately England and Wales; Great Britain; the United Kingdom; and even the British Empire. Foreigners used it as the name of a Great Power and indeed continue to do so. Bonar Law, a Scotch Canadian, was not ashamed to describe himself as "Prime Minister of England", as Disraeli, a Jew by birth, had done before him ... Now terms have become more rigorous. The use of "England" except for a geographic area brings protests, especially from the Scotch. They seek to impose "Britain" – the name of a Roman province which perished in the fifth century and which included none of Scotland nor, indeed, all of England. I never use this incorrect term ... "Great Britain" is correct and has been since 1707. It is not, however, synonymous with the United Kingdom, as the Scotch, forgetting the Irish (or, since 1922, the Northern Irish), seem to think. Again the United Kingdom does not cover the Commonwealth, the colonial empire, or India. Whatever word we use lands us in a tangle.

(Taylor 1965: v)

A tangle indeed. Taylor himself, writing the history of 'England' since the First World War, was forced again and again to speak of 'the British' and even to use the despised term 'Britain' ('sometimes slipped past me by sub-editors'). Nor could 'English affairs' for long be kept separate from those, say, of Ireland; while in the account of the Second World War Australians, Canadians, Indians, New Zealanders, South Africans and a host of other members of the British Empire and Dominions crowd the narrative, as when we are told that 'over half the Canadians involved were killed or taken prisoners' in the bungled raid on Dieppe in 1942 (Taylor 1965: 557). How indeed write of 'the Battle of *Britain*' without giving up on 'England' pure and simple? How narrate a central strand of national political life without referring to the *British* Labour Party, whose strongholds were in Wales and Scotland; or discuss a central component of the national culture without reference to the *British* Broadcasting Corporation, headed in its formative years by a Scot? (The abbreviation BBC conveniently helps the English, and many foreigners, to ignore this). As soon as one begins to think seriously about the subject the self-imposed restriction of dealing only with 'English' history dissolves in hopeless contradiction.

Taylor's insouciance is unlikely to be copied in these 'politically correct' days, though actual practice, especially among popular writers, is far less affected. More representative of current scholarly thinking on the subject is a work such as Hugh Kearney's *The British Isles: A History of Four Nations* (1995) or, somewhat differently, Norman Davies's *The Isles: A History* (1999). A similar shift in consciousness is reflected in the decision to replace the old *Pelican History of England* by the *Penguin History of Britain.* Introducing the series, its general editor David Cannadine remarked that it will look 'more critically and more closely at the whole concept of nationhood and national identity', and that it will be 'a three-dimensional history of Great Britain, not a Watfordesque history of Little England' (1995a: 2; see also 1993; 1995b: 16).[3] At a time when a former British prime minister, John Major, could still startle non-English inhabitants of the United Kingdom by declaring that 'this British nation has a monarchy founded by the Kings of Wessex over eleven hundred years ago' (*The Times*, 24 May 1994), such a revision was clearly overdue.[4]

The 'four nations' approach to Britain, and to England, has it own problems, as we shall see. But it is a necessary start to correcting the Anglocentric accounts that have been the staple of standard histories and school textbooks – and not just in England – for over a century. It forces us to consider just what are the meanings of the terms 'English', 'British' and so on which we use so casually and promiscuously. No one can ask of native English speakers that they 'tidy up' their language, that they speak with scholarly precision. That would be absurd – Fowler is right about that. The everyday usages reflect real experiences and real perceptions. They are the result of a real history. But it certainly behoves students of nationhood and national identity to examine carefully what those unselfconsciously used terms connote, what attitudes and assumptions lie buried in them, what historical myths they enshrine or promote.

Britain seems to be the most ancient of the relevant terms.[5] It was first recorded by the Greeks of the fourth century BC as the name of the Celts who lived in western Europe's largest off-shore island. The Romans turned the Greek *Pretanoi* into the Latin *Britanni*, for whose home they then coined the feminine name *Britannia*. The Celts themselves appear to have made no clear distinction between the people and the place. The meaning of the original word evidently referred to the Celtic practice of painting the body.

When the Angles and Saxons invaded the islands in the fifth century AD they did not associate themselves with Britannia or its inhabitants. They called the piece of the island they settled 'Engla-land' and ignored the rest. 'Britain' nevertheless persisted during the Old English period, in various forms (Bretayne, Breteyn, Breoton, etc. – it took its present spelling in the thirteenth century), but thereafter 'was used only as a historical term until about the time of Henry VIII and Edward VI [early sixteenth century], when it came again into practical politics in connexion with the efforts to unite England and Scotland' (*OED*). Despite the union of the crowns in 1603 – James I proclaimed himself 'King of *Great Britain*' – efforts to promote 'Britain' as an overarching identity appear to have had limited success until the Act of Union with Scotland in 1707, which established the united kingdom of Great Britain.

From that time 'Britain' came into common use as a shorthand for 'Great Britain'. It figured widely in official and semi-official encomia to the kingdom, as in William Somerville's 'Hail, happy Britain! Highly favoured isle, and Heaven's peculiar care!' (1735), and, in its most celebrated form, in the panegyric composed in 1740 by the anglicized Scottish poet James Thomson: 'When Britain first, at heaven's command, / Arose from out the azure main...' It was Thomson too who in the same work gave *Britannia* and *Britons* wide currency.

> This was the charter of the land,
> And guardian angels sung this strain:
> 'Rule Britannia, rule the waves;
> Britons never will be slaves.'
> (Thomson and Mallet, *Alfred*, 1740)

'Britons' and 'Britannia' (the Roman female figure with a shield revived by Charles II in 1665 when he put her on a coin in an attempt to reconcile Scots and English) had a success denied to the official efforts in the eighteenth century to replace the old emotive names 'England' and 'Scotland' with 'South Britain' and 'North Britain' within the framework of an overall 'Great Britain' (the later attempt to turn an uncooperative Ireland into 'West Britain' was even less successful). The failure in this respect did not however, as we shall see, prevent the emergence of a strong sense of British identity in this period.

Something of the same lacklustre quality as afflicts 'Britain' has carried over into *British*. 'To identify with "British"', says Bernard Crick, 'is not the same as identifying with the warmth and width of English, Scottish, Welsh or Irish. "British" is a limited utilitarian allegiance simply to those political and legal institutions which still hold this multi-national state together' (*The Independent* 22 May 1993). The majority of English, Welsh and Scots do not think of themselves as 'British'; only a majority of Ulster Protestants do so (see, e.g., Rose 1982: 15). Foreigners use 'British' freely; the British to refer to their trade with other nations, their economy, their armed forces, their legal nationality, the inhabitants of the pre- and non-Anglo-Saxon cultures of the island called Britain, and a few other things besides (see Fowler, above; and cf. Crick 1991a: 97; 1995:173–4). But they rarely use it in relation to themselves in their social, cultural or personal life.

This coldness towards the term 'British' is nowadays highly problematic. With the revival of nationalist movements in Scotland, Wales and Northern Island, and the influx of many hundreds of thousands of immigrants who do not think of themselves as English, Scottish, etc., never can the appellation 'British' appear more necessary, at least if the political and social unity of the United Kingdom is to be preserved. Yet it is those very forces that are making the task difficult.

Britons, Britisher and Brit continue to find some favour, especially with foreign journalists. The *British Isles* similarly does service as a catch-all term to include not just the countries of the United Kingdom but also the Republic of Ireland, the Channel Isles and the Isle of Man. Some scholars, seeking to avoid the political and ethnic connotations of 'the British Isles', have proposed 'the Atlantic archipelago' or even 'the East Atlantic archipelago' (see, e.g., Pocock 1975a: 606; 1995: 292n; Tompson, 1986). Not surprisingly this does not seem to have caught on with the general public, though it has found increasing favour with scholars promoting the new 'British History' (see below).

This is probably the right place to introduce the *United Kingdom*. Although a united kingdom came into being with the parliamentary union of England and Scotland in 1707, the new state (which included the principality of Wales) did not formally adopt the title until the union with Ireland in 1801, which brought into being the United Kingdom of Great Britain and Ireland (after the formation of the Irish Free State in 1921, the United Kingdom of Great Britain and Northern Ireland).

There are some English-speaking groups – contemporary Indians among them – who do refer to 'Yookay' as a country, in the way we might speak of

England, Britain etc. But for the vast majority of the British people the United Kingdom is a term reserved for passports, visa applications and other official purposes. The old British passports referred to one as a citizen of 'the United Kingdom and Colonies'. But few saw or sought a national identity in these official terms. It is noticeable, though, that with current talk of 'the break-up of Britain' and threats to the integrity of the United Kingdom, there has been a rise in references to the United Kingdom in public utterances – for instance, by politicians in radio interviews.

England and the English

For over a thousand years *England* has been the largest and most powerful state in the British Isles. It was always and to an increasing extent the most populous part. In 1801 England contributed just over half of the population of the United Kingdom; today the English make up more than four-fifths (N. Davies 1999: 1153).

It is not surprising that England became, and remains for many people at home and abroad, a synecdochical expression not just for the island of Britain but for the whole archipelago. Macaulay called his great work *The History of England* (1848–61) but it included extensive coverage of Ireland and Scotland, as did W. E. H. Lecky's *History of England in the Eighteenth Century* (1878–90). The French historian Elie Halévy, in his *History of the English People* (1913), similarly and with the same unselfconsciousness included Irish and Scottish history. Walter Bagehot's famous work on the government of Britain is called *The English Constitution* (1867). The OED's report of 1891 on the established usage of the time perhaps underplayed its inflationary tendency: '*England*: the southern part of the island of Great Britain, usually with the exception of Wales. Sometimes loosely used for: Great Britain. Often: The English (or British) nation or state.' In later years the practice has if anything grown, rather than diminished, despite the irritation it causes the non-English inhabitants of the British Isles. Not just in everyday conversation but in journalistic use and in scholarly writing the confusion of 'England' with 'Britain' and 'Britain' with 'England' is so common and pervasive that quotation is largely superfluous (for examples see Kearney 1995: 2; N. Davies 1999: xxvii–xxxix).[6]

'England' is a highly emotive word. When intoned by, say, an Olivier (as in *Henry V*) or a Gielgud (as in *Richard II*), it can produce spine-tingling effects. It has served, in a way never attained by 'Britain' or any of the British derivatives, to focus ideas and ideals. It has been the subject of innumerable eulogies and apostrophes by poets and playwrights. From Shakespeare to Rupert Brooke it has been lauded as the font of freedom and the standard of civilization, a place of virtue as well as of beauty. 'Let not England', urged John Milton in 1643 in pleading for a more liberal attitude to divorce, 'forget her precedence of teaching nations how to live.' Nelson fell at Trafalgar, according to J. Braham's patriotic poem of 1812, for 'England, home and beauty' – a phrase much loved and oft repeated in the nineteenth century. Shakespeare as always supplied the best lines. Despite its familiarity, the following deathbed tribute by John of Gaunt, from *Richard II*, needs to be quoted because of its innumerable echoes in succeeding centuries:

> This royal throne of kings, this sceptred isle,
> This earth of majesty, this seat of Mars,
> This other Eden, demi-paradise,
> This fortress built by nature for herself
> Against infection and the hand of war,
> This happy breed of men, this little world,
> This precious stone set in a silver sea,
> Which serves it in the office of a wall
> Or as a moat defensive to a house,
> Against the envy of less happier lands;
> This blessed plot, this earth, this realm, this England.
>   (*Richard II*, Act 2, Scene 1)

This is truly unbeatable, and could be unpacked at length for what it has contributed to the self-image of the English. Pausing only to note though the usual conflation of 'England' and 'Britain' ('this sceptred isle', 'England, bound in with the triumphant sea', etc.), we might pass on to the nineteenth century and an appreciation by Alfred Lord Tennyson almost as well known and almost as good:

> It is the land that freemen till,
> That sober-suited Freedom chose,
> The land, where, girt with friends or foes
> A man may speak the thing he will;
> A land of settled government,
> A land of just and old renown,
> Where Freedom slowly broadens down
> From precedent to precedent.
>   ('You ask me, why, tho' ill at ease',
>   1842)

There were, as we shall see, many challenges to this self-congratulatory account. But perhaps the most pertinent question was raised by Rudyard Kipling: 'And what do they know of England who only England know?' (*The English Flag*, 1891).

English and *the English* follow England closely in the comprehensiveness of their embrace. As an ethnic adjective, it is often used for 'British', especially by the English who unlike the Welsh, Scots and Irish, have traditionally identified themselves with the Union Jack, the composite flag of the United Kingdom, rather than what is technically their flag, the Cross of St George: thereby symbolically claiming possession of the whole kingdom.[7]

This tendency to inflate the English to take in other groups began very early. When the word 'English' first occurred in Old English, it had already lost its etymological sense, 'of or about the Angles', and was used as a collective expression for all the Teutonic peoples – Angles, Saxons and Jutes – who had settled in Britain in the fifth century. 'With the incorporation of the Celtic and Scandinavian elements of the population into the "English" people, the adjective came in the 11th century to be applied to all natives of "England", whatever their ancestry' (*OED*). For a generation or two after the Norman Conquest state documents distinguished between 'French' and 'English' – i.e., the descendants of the pre-Conquest English – but in practice the distinction soon lost its meaning. So 'English' began its imperialistic career from the very beginning; taking in 'Britain' and the 'British Empire' was a continuation, apparently, of a very old tradition.

The ethnic English, as the core nation of the British Isles and the dominant group of what became the leading industrial and imperial power in the world, have been anatomized ceaselessly by native and other writers. A genre of writing that can be said to have started with Edward Lytton Bulwer's *England and the English* (1833) was powerfully reinforced by the vivid reflections of visitors, such as Ralph Waldo Emerson's *English Traits* (1856), Hippolyte Taine's *Notes on England* (1860–70) and Henry James's *English Hours* (1905). Emerson's and James's accounts continued the tradition of 'travel literature', a favourite form in the seventeenth and eighteenth centuries, in which the writer journeyed through the kingdom and reported on the condition and ways of the inhabitants. Alexis de Tocqueville thus recorded his impressions of his visits in the 1830s in the writings which have been published as *Journeys to England and Ireland* (1958); later distinguished examples of the genre include J. B. Priestley's *English Journey* (1934), A. V. Morton's *In Search of England* (1937) and George Orwell's *The Road to Wigan Pier* (1937). The English have also been the subject of the usual crop of humorous or satirical portraits, many of them not surprisingly by foreigners, such as G. J. Renier's *The English, Are They Human?* (1931), George Mikes's *How to Be an Alien* (1946) and Ranjee Shahini's *The Amazing English* (1948). The Scots, in the form of A. G. Macdonell's comic novel, *England, Their England* (1933), cast an affectionate and not too baleful eye on their idiosyncratic neighbour. But it was the native English themselves who produced the best example of the genre: W. C. Sellar and R. J. Yeatman's wickedly revealing *1066 And All That* (1930) – the best book ever written on the English and their history, or what they take to be their history. With the renewed debates on English identity in the 1990s, the genre revived after a generation or so of disfavour. But, in the more anxious climate of the times, the model now was not so much the satirical type as the more considered national portrait of the kind typified by George Orwell's *The Lion and the Unicorn* (1941): Jeremy Paxman's *The English: A Portrait of a People* (1999) is a good recent example.

It is in and from this kind of writing that attempts are conventionally made to sum up the English 'national character'. With all their pitfalls they are invaluable in helping us understand 'Englishness' and English national identity. My account begins from a different direction but I shall have plenty of occasion to refer to these offerings. To ignore them would be to miss a rich harvest.

'English' as an adjective and noun for a language – *the English language* – has an interestingly parallel history to English as an ethnic description. It exhibits the same striking elasticity. Starting as a group of dialects originally spoken in what is now Denmark and north-eastern Germany, it became after the Anglo-Saxon invasions of Britain the general name for the tongue – 'Englisc' – used from Kent to Edinburgh. 'Englisc' referred, in other words, to the language spoken not just by the inhabitants of the kingdom of England but also by those of the south-eastern part of the kingdom of Scotland. 'Over the centuries a linguistic polarization took place, with the King's English in the south and the King's Inglis (or Scottis) in the north, the two forms so distinct as to be virtually different languages' (McArthur 1985 (3): 29; see also James 1998: 306). English's further conquest took place with its expansion, following that of the English people, into Wales and Ireland. English was now used in four countries, three of which were bilingual between an ever-strengthening English and an ever-retreating Celtic.

From about the fifteenth century onwards, the King's English of the English court, centred on London, was increasingly recognized as 'standard' English, though enormous variation existed in spelling and pronunciation. But with British expansion overseas, starting in the seventeenth century, the English language developed a variety of forms, a number of which gradually emerged as new standard forms (American English, Australian English, Caribbean English, South Asian English, etc.). 'British English', as a language and a literature, has had to compete with these other *Englishes* in the world at large. Even in its home territory, British English, traditionally identified with the speech patterns of the upper and upper-middle classes of south-east England, has in recent years found itself challenged by new or revived varieties, as in Mancunian, Glaswegian and 'Estuary' English, and the English spoken by new immigrant groups such as West Indians and South Asians. With British English embracing all these groups, many of which do not identify themselves as English, English as a badge of a specifically English national identity becomes increasingly problematic.

To turn finally to the group of words formed by the combination term *Anglo-*, as in Anglo-Indian, Anglo-Saxon, etc. They exhibit all the ambiguity and, occasionally, arrogance, involved in the parent terms 'England' and 'English'. At the simplest level, 'Anglo-' is the combining form for 'England' and 'English', whether the people or the language. Thus 'Anglo-Welsh' relations are simply relations between the English and the Welsh. But, following the pattern of 'England' and 'English', 'Anglo-Finnish' relations could be relations either between England and Finland or between Great Britain (or the United Kingdom) and Finland. Similarly with Anglo-American, Anglo-Russian, etc. The offence that the imperial use of 'England' and 'English' causes the Welsh, Scots and Irish is compounded by this multiple meaning of Anglo.

There are further complications. 'Anglo-Irish', for instance, can mean relations between Ireland and England or between Ireland and Britain, as in 'Anglo-Irish talks'. But it can also refer to the group of English settlers in Ireland in past centuries, the group that formed the ruling gentry class and established the English ascendancy in Ireland. For native Irish therefore 'Anglo-Irish' is an emotive term with powerful historical overtones. 'Anglo-Indian' is similarly complex, referring both to relations between India and England (or Britain), and to the sensitively placed Eurasian community in India descended from British fathers and Indian mothers. To add to the richness of the term, Anglo-Indian also refers to those English or British people who spent most of their working lives in India during the British Raj – an 'Anglo-Indian colonel', for example.

Most multifaceted of all is 'Anglo-Saxon'. The *OED* records a complex history, involving multiple confusions, which led to the term being used by 1600 to cover everything 'English' before the Norman Conquest: language, life, people. Secondly, and by an equally expansive route, it has come to be applied to the entire 'culture, spirit, heritage, ethnic type and set of attitudes' (McArthur 1985 (1): 14) associated with the English (or the British) whether at home or abroad. There is an obvious overlap between the two main uses, in the sense that the Anglo-Saxon heritage or Anglo-Saxon attitudes are supposed to be somehow representative of the original pristine culture of the English, especially as that existed before the Norman Conquest, hence *Anglo-Saxonisms*, to refer to plain, pithy, quintessentially English speaking, thinking and doing. Anglo-Saxonism has historically also played an important political role, in the frequent harking back to the supposedly popular democratic assemblies of the Teutonic settlers of Britain, and as the basis therefore for a political ideology of Anglo-Saxonism that frequently had racial overtones. But the larger meaning of Anglo-Saxon or *Anglosaxondom* has equally obviously travelled a long way from its historical base. It has come to occupy a significant place in the political culture of all societies that have a large number of people of English or British descent, and where English is the principal language – the United States, Canada, Australia, New Zealand, South Africa. In this guise it is engaged with debates about dominant ethnicities and multiculturalism, and embroiled in the politics of language and of identity.

British studies: in search of the national identity

In a small volume on the national character published in 1941, George Orwell confessed to some difficulty of nomenclature. 'We call our islands by no less than six different names, England, Britain, Great Britain, the British Isles, the United Kingdom and, in very exalted moments, Albion.' He admitted that 'the so-called races of Britain feel themselves to be very different from one another', and that even the differences between the north and south of England were significant. He consoled himself with the observation that 'somehow these differences fade away the moment that any two Britons are confronted by a European', and still more so, presumably, when an Indian or a Chinaman heaves into view. Armed with the conviction that there was a unified national character, Orwell moved easily between England ('England is the most class-ridden country under the sun', etc.) and Britain ('British democracy is less of a fraud than it sometimes appears', etc.) to conclude with the famous observation that 'England [*sic*] resembles a family . . . a family with the wrong members in control' (Orwell 1970a: 83, 88).

Few scholars today would approach the subject – if they dare approach it at all – with such blithe confidence. Their self-consciousness about the diversity of 'our islands', together with their sensitivity to nationalist feeling within them, render them modest in the extreme, if not actually speechless in the face of such terminological and cultural complexity. But some at least have bravely attempted to grasp the nettle of national identity. Prominent among these have been the historians, for whom perhaps the question is of more urgent practical importance than it is to scholars in other disciplines. In writing the history of 'these islands', what does one call them? What kind of framework does one adopt? To what extent is one dealing with a unitary story – the story of an 'island race', say – and to what extent with separate histories, the histories of 'four nations'?

In 1975 the New Zealand-born historian J. G. A. Pocock, in response partly to what he saw as a growing assertion of English nationalism – he instanced A. J. P. Taylor's volume in the *Oxford History of England* – put in a plea for 'British history'. Noting the lack of a better term that might satisfy the Irish, he meant by British history, he said, 'the plural history of a group of cultures situated along an Anglo-Celtic frontier and marked by an increasing English political and cultural domination' (1975: 605). Though speaking of a 'revival' of British history, Pocock was perfectly well aware that very little along these lines had ever actually been done. For examples he had to turn to the twelfth-century Welsh chronicler Geoffrey of Monmouth's largely fabulous *History of the Kings of Britain* (c. 1136), and William Camden's sixteenth-century *Britannia* (1586), a highly informative survey of the British Isles which nevertheless reads mainly like a guide-book.

In advocating a properly *British* history, Pocock aimed his fire at two main targets. The first was the approach of the John Bull school of English historiography, in which British history was merely English history writ large. ('The history of Britain was merely the history of England as and when it took place elsewhere': Cannadine 1995b: 16). The rejection of this conventionally Anglocentric view also entailed the rejection of its left-wing variant, the 'internal colonialism' approach. Here England was seen as the core imperial nation which had 'colonized' its peripheral regions, 'the Celtic fringe' (see, e.g., Hechter 1999). The largely benign view of England's 'civilizing' and 'modernizing' role was replaced by a more critical account which emphasized dependence, inequality and exploitation in the relations between core and periphery; but it did nothing to shake the impression that British history had been a one-way flow, with England as the fount and origin of all developments.

Pocock by contrast wished to point to the mutual and reciprocal relations between the different parts of the British Isles, such that they have not only created 'the conditions of their several existences but have also interacted so as to modify the conditions of one another's existence'.

[British history], which does not yet exist and must be created, cannot be written as the memory of a single state or nation or as the process by which one came into existence. It must be a plural history, tracing the processes by which a diversity of societies, nationalities, and political structures came into being and situating in the history of each and in the history of their interactions the processes that have led them to whatever forms of association or unity exist in the present or have existed in the past. This calls for a multi-contextual history ... (Pocock 1982: 317, 320)

The admitted difficulty of this undertaking was underscored by a bold extension, implicit in this formulation. British history must not simply be an account of the interaction of the peoples and cultures of the British Isles or 'the Atlantic archipelago'. The British (including the Irish) had also taken themselves and their cultures overseas. They had crossed the Atlantic to colonize the lands that later became the republics of the United States and Canada. They had crossed the world to found societies in its southern half, in Australia and New Zealand. However different they became, these societies were in the first instance British.

They added yet new dimensions to what had conventionally been presented as 'English history'(Pocock 1982: 317; see also Pocock 1992).

No more than in the case of Wales, Scotland and Ireland could these American or oceanic 'British' societies be regarded simply as 'fragments' or 'scions' of the 'parent society', England or – in this case – Britain. This approach, associated particularly with Louis Hartz and his followers (Hartz 1964), was the second target of Pocock's assault. The Hartzian view saw American or Australian society as offshoots of the older British stem; they were related to it as 'fragments' to a monolith, from which they had 'broken off'. Such a conception, argued Pocock, mistakes the nature and development of both 'fragment' and 'monolith'. Both 'fragment' and 'parent society' had to be seen as formed by a dynamic interaction, by an evolving process of 'cultural conflict and creation' (Pocock 1975a: 620). If Britain in some sense came first, its extensions overseas reacted back upon it, modifying it in profound ways just as its continued presence in their lives shaped their evolution.

Recast in the general form of 'British history', much of English and British history could be seen in a new light. Instead of being the story of the evolution and expansion of one nation, it might be possible to see it as the history of 'three kingdoms' (English, Scottish and Irish) or 'four nations' (English, Welsh, Scottish, Irish), all interacting with one another in complex ways. Certain crucial historical episodes, familiar in one aspect, could take on a new appearance. The 'English Civil War' of the mid-seventeenth century now becomes the 'war of the three kingdoms', since 'without rebellion in Scotland, the English Parliament would not have been summoned; without rebellion in Ireland it would not have demanded the king's surrender of the power of the sword' (Pocock 1992: 372; see also 1975a: 602; 1982: 325). Moreover, one might wish also to speak now not just of one but three 'British Civil Wars' convulsing the peoples of the British Isles together with their overseas possessions: that of 1642–46 ('the English Civil War'), that of 1776–83 ('the American War of Independence'), and that of 1911–22 ('the Irish Rebellion') (Pocock 1975a: 606). Using somewhat different terminology, some of these episodes could also be recast as the 'three British Revolutions' of 1641, 1688 and 1776 (Pocock 1980) – or more, according to taste and the task in hand, since the category 'British Revolution' might encompass not just the Irish Revolution of 1911–22 but also a good many of the twentieth-century 'wars of independence' of former British possessions in Asia and Africa.

Whether as a result of Pocock's urging or, more probably, because a number of scholars had already been moving in that direction, there have in recent years been some remarkable changes in the historiography of Britain and its overseas empire.[8] Some have tried their hand at entirely new general histories, notable examples being Richard Tompson's *The Atlantic Archipelago:*

A Political History of the British Isles (1986), Hugh Kearney's *The British Isles: A History of Four Nations* (1995), Jeremy Black's *A History of the British Isles* (1996) and Norman Davies's *The Isles* (1999). Others have re-examined key episodes of British and imperial history, such as the seventeenth-century revolutions (see, e.g., Russell 1987), and the interactions between Britain and its overseas colonies in the 'first British Empire' (e.g., Calder 1981; Bailyn and Morgan 1991b; Canny 1998; Marshall 1998). There has been a magnificent reinterpretation of British nationalism in the eighteenth century in Linda Colley's *Britons: Forging the Nation 1707–1837* (1994); for the same period Gerald Newman essayed something similar for English nationalism in a pioneering work, *The Rise of English Nationalism* (1987). An ambitious and wide-ranging study of British imperialism sought to locate its springs in the culture of 'gentlemanly capitalism' operating at the heart of the British economy, in the financial sector of the City of London (Cain and Hopkins 1993). Students of cultural history have looked at the way the British Empire affected the mentality not just of its subject populations but of the imperial nation itself, the British people (e.g., Mackenzie 1986; Young 1995; Schwarz 1996a). What stands out in all these studies is the impossibility of considering 'England' or even 'Britain' as independent or intelligible units of study. Both are fragments of a larger whole whose boundaries extend to the very limits of the globe.

The historians did not make all the running, though it is fair to say that it is their rethinking of British history that has most made it possible to approach the question of English and British identity in a satisfactory way. Other disciplines have weighed in. In 1975 the American sociologist Michael Hechter published *Internal Colonialism: The Celtic Fringe in British National Development, 1536–1966*; a brave and impressive study, especially considering that Hechter at the time had not set foot in the British Isles. Political science also made sterling contributions. In 1976 Richard Rose (revising a paper of 1970) published an essay, 'The United Kingdom as a Multi-National State' (Rose 1976), which became the basis and rallying point for a wide-ranging programme of work largely under his direction (see Rose 1982; Rose and McAllister 1982; Madgwick and Rose 1982; Bulpitt 1983). Political scientists were also the mainstay of Bernard Crick's stimulating collection, *National Identities: The Constitution of the United Kingdom* (Crick 1991b). Also distinctly political, but strictly unclassifiable in disciplinary terms, were two brilliant contributions from the left-wing thinker and Scottish nationalist Tom Nairn: *The Break-Up of Britain* (1981) and *The Enchanted Glass: Britain and its Monarchy* (1994). Multidisciplinarity was also the hallmark of three major volumes published under the auspices of History Workshop: *Patriotism: The Making and Unmaking of British National Identity* (Samuel 1989a).

Introducing the *Patriotism* volumes, Raphael Samuel noted a critical shift in the thinking of the contributors as their work proceeded. It is as good an indication as any of the new consciousness and the changed approach to the subject.

A late but important element in the shaping of these volumes was the substitution of "British" for "English" in the subtitle. We had started with the second. For History Workshop, as for others, it had all kinds of pleasant connotations. It evoked a people rather than a state, Blake's *Jerusalem* rather than Westminster, Whitehall, or Balmoral. Because of its association with the language, it was umbilically tied to English literature. Because of its subliminal association with the countryside – the "real" England – it conjured up images of rusticity, chronicles of ancient sunlight. "English" is smaller and gentler than "British", and it has the charm, for the historian, of the antiquated and the out of date. "British" was an altogether more uncomfortable term to work with, hard rather than soft and belonging to specific historical epochs rather than the timelessness of "tradition". It is a political identity which derives its legitimacy from the expansion of the nation-state. Its associations are diplomatic and military rather than literary, imperial rather than – or as well as – domestic. Compared with "English" it is formal, abstract and remote. But it allows for a more pluralistic understanding of the nation, one which sees it as a citizenry rather than a folk. It does not presuppose a common culture and it is therefore more hospitable both to newcomers and outsiders . . .   (1989b: xii–xiii)

'Hard rather than soft', 'citizenry rather than a folk', 'hospitable both to new-comers and outsiders'; these expressions strike the note of the new realism, a new sobriety in the face of unprecedented problems both at home and abroad. Gone are the cosy assumptions of 'Englishness', with its sleepy villages and ancestral piles. They have gone because the empire has gone, and so has British economic power. They have gone because the English are not even safe in their homelands, challenged as they are by the rise of Celtic nationalism and by the claims of 'multiculturalism' within English society. And then there is the promise, or threat, of 'Europe'. In whichever direction they look, the English find themselves called upon to reflect upon their identity, and to re-think their position in the world. The protective walls that shielded them from these questions are all coming down.

One consequence of this is that we must, initially at least, lay aside the traditional approaches to English national identity. These have tended to consider the character of 'Englishness' from within, from inside the national culture. They have scrutinized the past and the present for the evidence they offer of 'English traits', of distinctive elements of 'the English character' or 'the English people'. Of such a kind are the famous works of cultural analysis, such as Priestley's *English Journey* and Orwell's *The English People*. Invaluable as they are, they cannot be our starting point. They take for granted the very thing that needs investigation: the wider world within which 'England' and 'Englishness' find their meaning. English national identity cannot be found from within the consciousness of the English themselves.[9] We have to work from the outside in.

It is within the new terrain of 'British studies' that we are most likely to find our most promising leads. But before we come to this, there is a prior task. To speak of English nationalism, or of English national identity, is to use the language of a flourishing branch of social and political theory, that part concerned with the nature and development of nationalism. In recent years there has been an outpouring of new works in the field. It would seem sensible to ask what contribution the new thinking can make to the understanding of our specific subject, English nationalism. Is English nationalism a recognizable variety of nationalism in general? What theory or theories might be appropriate to it?

2

Nations and nationalism: civic, ethnic and imperial

English nationalism – a peculiar thing?

It has been common to query English nationalism, even to deny it. Certainly the term sounds odd in English ears. *Other* nations have nationalism; the English, it has been conventional to say, have patriotism, royalism, jingoism, imperialism – but they do not know nationalism.[1]

This disavowal has been matched, not unnaturally, by scholarly neglect of the subject. If there is no such thing as English nationalism, why bother to study it? Scholars are also human beings, members of cultures and national communities. If a culture denies nationalism, shows a marked indifference even to questions of national identity, it would be eccentric on the part of a scholar or intellectual to devote much time to their investigation. At most one notes the absence of nationalism, then moves on to more important matters. In his trawl through the periodical literature on nationalism written since 1972, Gerald Newman came up with two essays 'in rather obscure journals' dealing with English or British nationalism; for German or Irish nationalism there were more than seventy items apiece (Newman 1987: xviii). So far as books are concerned, there are a number of older volumes on patriotism, and some on 'the English character', but beyond that, especially in the recent period, virtually nothing.[2] Indeed it has been common to remark that until recently there was, in the whole literature on nationalism, only one contribution that dealt squarely with the issue of English nationalism: a short article by Hans Kohn published in 1940.

Newman's own fine work, *The Rise of English Nationalism* (1987), helped to remedy that situation. Hard on its heels came Tom Nairn's *The Enchanted Glass* (1988), a study of 'Britain and its Monarchy' that was at the same time a sparkling account of English national identity, and its problems. Linda Colley's *Britons* (first published 1992) also threw much light on the question of English nationalism. An important theoretical work by Liah Greenfeld, *Nationalism*

(1992), controversially declared sixteenth-century English nationalism to be the world's first, the template and impulse for all later expressions of national consciousness. The three volumes of History Workshop's *Patriotism* (Samuel 1989a) contained, despite its firmly traditional title, much of relevance to both British and English national identity. Perhaps most valuable of all was the collection of essays published by Robert Colls and Philip Dodd under the title *Englishness* (1986) – an examination of a key period, from 1890 to 1920, in the making of English national identity.

So compared with the dearth of the past there has been a good harvest in the last decade or so, for reasons that we shall discuss later. But by comparison with the profusion of new works on nationalism, both as a general phenomenon and in its particular varieties, the crop dealing specifically with English nationalism remains modest indeed. A collection which considered comparatively and historically 'The National Question in Europe' (Teich and Porter 1993), found room for Croatian and Finnish nationalism, but England crept in only under the general rubric, 'The British Isles: Celt and Saxon'. A similar collection focusing on contemporary Europe treated Englishness within the context of 'Britishness' (Jenkins and Sofos 1996: 83–100). An *Encyclopedia of Nationalism* by a noted scholar included an entry on 'English nationalism' – a rare mention – but dealt with it as if Kohn's essay of 1940 had said all there was to say on the subject (Snyder 1990: 88–92). Even the new work on 'British Studies' was less helpful than at first might have appeared. Though recognizing that 'England' was not 'Britain', the tendency of the writers was to emphasize the British dimension of national life and to ignore what was distinctively English. The old practice of making England stand for Britain was reversed, but England now found itself submerged in Britain, and if nationalism was studied, it was Welsh, Scottish and Irish, rather than English, nationalism, that got all the attention.

The scholarly literature is not of course the only possible source of material for reflection. One might, in search of further illumination, go to the writings of non-academics. There is as noted earlier a veritable treasury of writing on Englishness and the English national character by novelists, poets, dramatists, journalists, politicians and independent intellectuals of various kinds. Who could not hope for inspiration from a list that includes Shakespeare, Milton, Defoe, Johnson, Dickens, Lytton, Bagehot, Lawrence, Woolf, Forster, Eliot, Priestley and Orwell?

And yet, from the point of view of a general conception of English nationalism, these contributions turn out to be curiously unhelpful. It is not simply that they are mostly untheoretical; that after all is the strength of this kind of writing. For theory we go to the academics who are paid to do such things. More problematic is the general conviction in this tradition of writing that the English are unique and exceptional. It is their difference from other nations – *all* other nations – that is the cause of comment, whether in celebration or censure. It does not help matters to learn that one way in which the English differ is that they do not have nationalism, in the usual, mostly continental, sense. Nationalism, it is held or implied, is alien to the English tradition. George Orwell observed that nationalism was responsible for those 'ruthless ideologies of the Continent', such as communism and fascism, that had thankfully been rejected by the mass of the English people, if not by the unpatriotic intelligentsia (Orwell 1970b: 31; 1970c: 411). His 'Notes on Nationalism' portrayed it as an all-consuming sickness of the individual and the national mind: 'power-hunger tempered by self-deception' (1970c: 412).

The idea that nationalism is something pathological, something at the same time deeply foreign, is part of the English understanding of it. Hence the unwillingness to accept that there is or can be such a thing as English nationalism. Even those who are prepared to accept the idea of English (or British) nationalism tend to point to its peculiarity. Tom Nairn, for instance, speaks of English/British national identity as 'highly eccentric', and English/British nationalism as *sui generis* or 'heteronomous' by comparison with nationalism elsewhere. Nationalism, he asserts, is 'theoretically alien' to 'England-Britain'. England-Britain does have nationalism – all modern states have it as a matter of necessity – but it is 'a weirdly a-typical formation', a 'non-national nationalism' compounded of anachronistic and archaic traits, of which worship of the monarchy is the principal element (Nairn 1994: 102, 127, 182, 232–3, 335).

The 'peculiarities of the English', as Edward Thompson (1978) attempted to describe them in a famous essay, is a favourite theme of much commentary on English national identity. That this should be so is itself a fit subject for investigation. Nor should we be prepared to dismiss it out of hand, as a simple expression of the natural propensity of nations to think themselves special. There may indeed be something in English history that sets it apart, if not from all nations, at least from many of those with whom it is usual to compare English developments.

But that argument must come later. It is surely prudent to begin with the opposite hypothesis, that England should be considered within the context of the other European and Europe-derived societies of which its history is a part. These too, it must be remembered, often consider themselves special and unique. The Americans think of their nation and history as 'exceptional', indeed as divinely ordained and guided (see, e.g., Bellah 1967); the 'peculiarities of the English' is matched by the German idea of the *Sonderweg*, the peculiarities of German history and development (see, e.g., Blackbourn and Eley 1984); the French are convinced that it was their mission to bring reason and civilization to the modern world, that 'the destiny of France is to be the teacher of mankind'

(Dumont 1994b: 200; cf. Zeldin 1984: 34–5); while, for Russians, we are told, 'their country's exceptionalism is almost a matter of religious dogma' (Lieven 1999: 164).

Such self-absorption, such narcissism, is natural to nations. It is indeed one of the main constituents of nationalism. Nationalism proclaims the unique character and destiny of each and every nation. It is precisely such claims that enables us to treat nations collectively. This is not in any way to deny the individuality or special character of nations. They all have that. It is merely to say that they can, for certain purposes including the claim to exceptionalism or exclusivity, be treated together as possessing certain common characteristics. That after all must be what is meant by considering, as is commonly done, nationalism as an ideology.

Is it right then to speak of 'English nationalism', in the way that we speak of French, German, or Italian nationalism? Are the English guilty of nationalist arrogance and *amour-propre* in asserting that they – virtually alone among western nations – have not experienced nationalism? And if there is such a thing as English nationalism, to what class or category does it belong? Where in the general theory and typology of nationalism does English nationalism fit? It may be that, at the end of our inquiry, we do want to stress certain peculiarities of the English position. But to start off by accepting it at its own estimation is unwise. It would be to lose the opportunity of seeing what light can be thrown on questions of English identity by seeing them within a framework of comparison.

Political and cultural nations

In his book *Cosmopolitanism and the National State* (first published 1907), the German historian Friedrich Meinecke distinguished between 'cultural nations [*Kulturnationen*] and political nations [*Staatsnationen*], nations that are primarily based on some jointly experienced cultural heritage and nations that are primarily based on the unifying force of a common political history and constitution' (Meinecke 1970: 10). A further gloss on the cultural nation saw it as bound together mainly by 'a standard language, a common literature, and a common religion'.

Meinecke was aware of the controversies surrounding this well-known distinction. He was equally clear that they referred to 'ideal types' – as he put it, 'dominant tendencies that seldom appear completely pure and isolated in historical reality' (1970: 11n). Hence it should not surprise us if the categories are fused in particular cases. For instance, a national religion and Church can be a powerful cohesive force 'in former political nations that have lost their statehood . . .' Such cases suggest that 'a cultural nation can be a political nation as well, and we often do not know whether political ties or the ties of religion and church are the stronger in holding it together' (1970: 11).

Meinecke's sensitivity to the historical complexity, and his realization that in many, perhaps most, cases, political and cultural factors support each other, enhance rather than diminish the heuristic value of his analytical distinction. Armed with ideal types, we are in a better position to understand the nature of the forces contending, the relative emphases that might lead to one outcome rather than another, one preference over another.

In the case of nations, the ideal types of political and cultural nation help us to map out the different directions taken on such matters as statehood and citizenship. That is perhaps why, with the recent revival of interest in these concerns, Meinecke's typology continues to seem fruitful to many scholars.[3] In an absorbing study, Rogers Brubaker (1992) has employed this basic distinction to explore how differing traditions of nationhood have shaped and sustained different conceptions of citizenship among the French and Germans. Even more conscious than Meinecke of the dangers of 'bipolar comparisons', he nevertheless shows the extent to which differences of policy and attitude derive from radically different understandings of what constitutes the nation. The French have a political, territorial, state-centred view of nationhood, deriving from the practice of the absolutist monarchy and the ideology of the French Revolution. The Germans, lacking a state for much of their history, turned towards an 'ethnocultural' conception of the nation: the nation was seen as 'an organic cultural, linguistic, or racial community'. The contrast is clearest in the opposing attitudes towards immigrants and the granting of citizenship. The 'state-centered, assimilationist understanding' of nationhood in France is embodied in 'an expansive definition of citizenship', making it possible for second-generation immigrants – Algerians and Moroccans, for example – automatically to become full citizens on an equal footing with other French citizens. The 'ethnocultural, differentialist understanding' of nationhood in Germany makes it remarkably easy for ethnic German immigrants – such as the million or so who arrived from Eastern Europe and the Soviet Union between 1988 and 1991 – to become full German citizens, but remarkably difficult for those of non-German origin – such as the 1.5 Turks living in Germany, many of them born there – to do so (Brubaker 1992: 3; see also Dumont 1986b, 1994b; Kamenka 1973b: 10–11).[4]

If the Meineckean typology can be put to such good use, it might be helpful to elaborate the characteristics of 'political' and 'cultural' nations as ideal-types. The *political nation* is the 'state-nation', rather than, strictly speaking, the 'nation-state'. It is a nation formed, in many cases, 'from the top down', as in France, Spain and Britain where centralizing monarchies accomplished the main work of nation-building as the necessary complement to their state-making (Kiernan 1965; Hont 1994: 217–18). The political nation is, first and foremost, a political (not an ethnic) community. It puts the stress on willed, active citizenship, and on civic participation. It is an artificial, deliberately 'invented' community, brought into being to fulfil certain desired purposes of the political life. It is a 'community of choice', membership of which depends in principle on voluntary inclusion in the political community. Others, foreigners, can join, provided only that they fulfil the residential and civic requirements of membership. Its citizenship law, to put this another way, is the *ius soli*, 'law of the soil'; it is by being born in and inhabiting a certain territory that one receives the rights and incurs the obligation (e.g., to military service) of citizenship.

It was, by common acceptance, the French who during the course of their late eighteenth-century revolution first fully enunciated the principles of the political nation (see, e.g., Kamenka 1973b; Brubaker 1992: 35; Hobsbawm 1992: 18–22; Alter 1994: 9; Dumont 1994b: 201). Britain, Spain, Sweden, the Netherlands and Switzerland are usually added to France as prime examples of political nationhood. So too are the United States and Canada. Given the geographical and historical location of the main examples, Hans Kohn (1944: 455–576) in an influential account labelled this understanding of nationhood 'western' – a characterization that, with qualification, has found favour with several writers (see, e.g., Plamenatz 1973; A. Smith 1986: 138–44; Snyder 1990: 174; Calhoun 1997: 88–9). Besides being western, many of the best-known examples also pre-date 1789, an indication of the importance of early-modern centralizing monarchies in their formation. An important corollary of this view would therefore be that the development of the 'state-nation' preceded, in many important respects, the rise of the ideology of nationalism, since nationalism is, by virtually universal consent, a nineteenth-century invention – a creation largely of the French Revolution (see, e.g., Kedourie 1993: 9; Mann 1995: 45).[5] Once invented, however, nationalism was able to adopt the political nation in its repertory of available models.

The *cultural nation* is the nation-state proper. In this concept, the state arises from the nation, and not the nation from the state. In its general form this concept of the nation also owes its definitive origin to the French Revolution. 'The nation', said the Abbé Sieyès in 1789, 'is prior to everything. It is the source of everything' (1963: 124). But while Sieyès and the French Revolution went on to define this nationhood primarily in political and constitutional terms, theorists in other countries drew a different moral from this stress on the primacy of the nation. Influenced especially by such eighteenth-century thinkers as Immanuel Kant and Johann Gottfried von Herder, they argued that the nation was self-contained and complete. The nation could and should be everything, which meant in principle that there could be nations without states. Nations were living organisms that contained within themselves all the resources for their own growth and development. They were facts of nature, not artificial human constructs; indeed they could be held to be of divine origin. Nationality, said Herder, 'is the language of God in nature' (Barnard 1969: 32); 'in the different nations', said the German historian Leopold von Ranke, 'God gave expression to the idea of human nature' (Meinecke 1970: 206).

The cultural nation represents the apotheosis of nationhood. As opposed to the subjective, voluntary character of political nationhood, the nation as culture is an objective fact. It is not an 'invented' but a 'primordial' entity, existing since time immemorial. One does not join it, one is born into it. One belongs to it as one belongs to one's natural, biological family. Its ties are the ties of blood, if not actually then metaphorically. It is a 'community of fate', not a 'community of choice'. Its principle of membership is the *ius sanguinis* (the 'law of blood'), not the *ius soli* (the 'law of the soil'). Ethnic descent alone gives one entry into the national community, not civic commitment and practice. Racial language is natural to this conception, but race not so much in physical or biological terms as in terms of a common culture and a common ethnicity. The cultural nation is defined by what it considers really binds people together: not the 'superficial' ties of political citizenship but the deep ties of history, language, literature and religion. These are the things, as Herder says, 'filled with the life and blood of our forefathers'. In principle perhaps outsiders could learn to become part of a given culture. In practice cultures are so various, so individual, so separate, so incommensurable, that to become a member of another culture is almost like changing one's skin or even one's species.

It was the cultural, not the political, idea of the nation that had the most successful career in the later nineteenth century. This was largely because there were so many nations without independent statehood, at a time when becoming an independent nation-state was the key to efficient modernization and industrialization (Plamenatz 1973; Gellner 1983). Lacking a state, one was forced to put one's claims as a legitimate nation in cultural, not political, terms. The cultural claim then became the basis for aspiring to political unification and independence. This was the way taken by Germans, Italians, Poles, Czechs, Slovaks, Ukrainians, Serbians, Bulgarians, Romanians and a host of other nations in the Habsburg, Hohenzollern, Romanov and Ottoman Empires in the second half of the nineteenth century. The great concentration of this pattern in the region of Central and Eastern Europe has led it to be labelled 'eastern' nationalism, in contrast to the political nationalism of the west (Kohn 1944: 518–72; Plamenatz 1973: 30–34).[6] It was responsible for much of the history of this part of Europe from the late nineteenth century to the Second World War. In the later twentieth century, following the break-up of Soviet Communism, 'Eastern' ethnic nationalism seemed to have returned to the region with a vengeance.

It is partly this occurrence that has led many scholars to turn once more, with increasing fervour, to the idea of the political nation as the salvation of their current anxieties. Ethnic intransigence and ethnic conflicts threaten to tear apart the political framework of Europe, in the West as much as in the East. There is the spectre of a return of the thirties, with right-wing racism and ethnic chauvinism once more making ground in several European societies (Malik 1996: 9–37). Fascism and Nazism are widely regarded as the pathological but legitimate descendants of the ethnic nationalism that had such a benign beginning in the thought of Herder and Mazzini. What better antidote to such poisonous influences than the open, inclusive, liberal concept of the political nation? So Liah Greenfeld lauds the 'ideal nation' of America, as the ultimate embodiment of the political or civic principle of nationhood (1992: 399–484; see also 1996a: xii). Christian Joppke looks to 'the civic meaning of nationalism', the nation conceived as 'the political community of [equal] citizens', as the best hope for promoting the ideals of citizenship and preserving the liberal legacy of the American and French Revolutions (1994: 554; see also Tamir 1993; Ignatieff 1994: 4, 185–9). Jürgen Habermas, fearful of the prospect of a resurgence of ethnic chauvinism in Germany in the wake of reunification, proposes 'constitutional patriotism', a devotion to the liberal democratic principles of the post-war German state, as an alternative focus for German national identity (1995: 256).

The current concern is understandable, as is the preference for political over ethnic concepts of the nation. This echoes a long-standing liberal conviction, as exemplified in Lord Acton's pointed contrast between a 'merely natural or physical' attachment to the 'race', and an 'ethical' devotion to the 'political nation' (Acton [1862] 1956: 163; cf. Yack 1996: 194; Xenos 1996: 214–15). But before we endorse this position we must consider some problematic aspects of the effort to keep the two apart. Meinecke, we remember, stressed the difficulties of keeping them even conceptually, let alone practically, separate. Are they in the end sufficiently distinct to serve as at least the initial basis of discussion – in our case, the attempt to attach different meanings to 'Britishness' and 'Englishness'?

The ambiguities of nationhood

Current, as well as past, attempts to establish and preserve 'civic nationalism' as both a descriptive and prescriptive category have met with a good deal of scepticism, especially among recent scholars. Proponents of the idea of a purely civic nationhood are, says Bernard Yack, guilty of 'self-congratulation and wishful thinking'. The civic – ethnic distinction 'itself reflects a considerable dose of ethnocentrism, as if the political identities *French* and *American* were not also culturally inherited artifacts . . .' *All* modern political communities, American and British as much as German or Ukrainian, are, says Yack, culturally based. That we choose to emphasize 'politics' in the one case and 'ethnicity' in the other are both expressions of the same misunderstanding. Advocates of civic nationhood, in particular, 'ignore the contingent inheritance of distinctive experience and cultural memories that is an inseparable part of every national political identity'. The very idea of the civic nation, 'with its portrayal of community as a shared and rational choice of universally valid principles', is itself a cultural inheritance derived from the revolutionary pasts of America and France. Similarly, when Habermas, following German reunification, urges his fellow Germans to eschew ideas of the 'prepolitical' community of shared memories and historical experience, and attach themselves instead to the post-war liberal democratic state, he ignores the fact that it is only this community of shared memories – a cultural legacy – that makes German re-unification meaningful and possible in the first place. The German case, says Yack, exemplifies the general rule in all modern societies (as compared say with the classical Greek polis), that their political orders are based not simply on voluntary consent but also on 'contingent communities of memory and experience', that is to say, a cultural inheritance that is not fixed but ever-changing (Yack 1996: 196–7, 199, 203, 209n; cf. also Alter 1994: 10; Motyl 1999: 78).

Yack makes it clear that his strictures apply as much to the proponents of ethnic nationalism as to those of the civic variety. In their case the mistake is to derive national identity from 'some discrete ethnic community' which is held to persist in its more or less pristine form through time. In fact, ethnic identities, like political identities, are 'part of a contingent and ever-changing legacy of shared memories and communal identification'. Culture, rather than ethnicity *per se*, is the fundamental ground of identity (1996: 202). But what might be even more damaging to the case for civic nationalism is the possibility not only that civic nationalism might depend on culture but that it reposes on a decidedly ethnic base. Michael Ignatieff, for instance, one of the most fervent partisans of the idea of the civic nation, nevertheless feels the need to concede that 'the very success of liberal contractualism in Britain and America depended on the ethnic homogeneity of the societies involved . . . To this day, liberal civic nationalism works effectively only in societies that have dominant ethnic majorities (as in France or Britain) or that are so abundant (as in America) that ethnic competition can be contained and attenuated' (1993: 44).

Why, though, exclude America from the list of societies with dominant ethnic majorities? Has it not been common to acknowledge the role of the white Anglo-Saxon majority in creating the national culture that undergirds liberal institutions there? Noting this, Anthony Smith argues that any idea of a separation of, or distinction between, the 'civic' and the 'ethnic' nation is illusory. All concepts of civic nationalism depend, whether knowingly or not, on assumptions about ethnicity, specifically on a 'dominant *ethnie*' model. All states, says Smith, draw 'for their power and solidarity on the mobilized historic culture-community at their core'. It is from the core ethnic community, with its 'memories and traditions, symbols and myths and values', that the people derive the resources for their performance as citizens in the 'civic nation'. 'Though the national state may be "born anew", in Year One of the Revolution, its members and the community they form possess antecedents, a pre-history . . . and hence a sense of shared experience that marks that people off from others and endows it with a feeling of belonging.' Frequently that experience lends to nations the idea of their uniqueness and moral superiority. Formerly religious in character, in the myth of ethnic election, it has now become largely secularized as a belief in the ethnic superiority of the core ethnic community of the nation. Again, we have to see that this is as true of societies that stress civic nationhood as of those that proclaim their ethnic identity. There is 'a sense of national dignity and chosenness that exists in France as much as in South Africa, in the United States as much as in Israel or Japan, in Australia as much as in Sri Lanka' (Smith 1995: 98; 97–115; see also Smith 1986: 129–52; Connor 1994: 90–117, 196–209).

In challenging the idea of civic nationhood, Smith takes as a test case the celebrated example of the emancipation of the Jews in France at the time of the French Revolution. The Jews were supposedly 'emancipated' from their ethnic attachments so that they could be integrated, as 'rational' and secular individuals, into the civic life of republican France. Smith argues that, in abandoning their ethnic ways and becoming full French citizens, Jews were in effect exchanging one kind of cultural identity for another. Jews had to become Frenchmen (Smith 1995: 97; cf. Kates 1989: 213–14; Woolf 1989: 116–18; Hobsbawm 1992: 21; Bauman 1998: 153; Feldman 1998: 174–5). The Dreyfus Affair (1894–1906) brought out this ethnic understanding of French nationhood with striking clarity (see Dumont 1994b).

But we should remember that for much of the nineteenth century, in France as in Britain, Germany and elsewhere in Europe, Jews were able both to be 'themselves' – ethnic Jews – and at the same time to participate widely in the economic, political and cultural life of their societies (see Feldman 1998: 172–3, 177–9; Hyman 1998: 1–80; Benbassa 2000; Sheehan 1999: 26). Moreover, the Dreyfusards, those such as Emile Zola who opposed the racist French establishment in the Dreyfus affair, did, after all, win the battle. The republican principle and the idea of civic nationhood in France were vindicated and, though repeatedly challenged in succeeding years, they have on the whole been maintained (see Brubaker 1992: 2, 138–64; Hazareesingh 1994: 87; Hargreaves 1995; Noiriel 1996).

All students of the subject, from Meinecke onwards, have pointed to the difficulty of maintaining, both in conceptual analysis and in actual practice, a hard and fast distinction between ethnic and civic understandings of nationhood. But the French example, along with other well-known cases such as the American and British, show that the difficulties are not insuperable. The distinction between political and ethnic nationhood, as described by Meinecke, is a real one, available for both theoretical analysis and practical implementation. How true this is, and how much in need of qualification, we shall see in our inquiry into British and English concepts of nationhood. One further consideration is however necessary.

Nations before nationalism, nationalism before nations

One of the most difficult questions, and the source of unending dispute, in the theory of nationalism, is whether we can speak of nations and nationhood before the coming of nationalism as a full-fledged ideology in the nineteenth century. No-one denies that the word nation, in several European languages, predates the rise of nationalism. The medieval universities all had their *nationes*, 'nations', which were guild-like divisions of the student body mainly for the purposes of residence and social life, rather like present-day fraternities in American universities. The University of Paris recognized the 'nations' of France, Picardie, Normandie and England (which included Germans); the University of Prague divided its students into German, Czech and Polish *nationes*; in the University of Aberdeen the 'nations' were regions of north-eastern Scotland, Mar, Buchan, Moray and Angus; in Oxford they were northern and southern England. Then there were the *nationes* of the Conciliar movement in the fifteenth-century church, groupings or parties of like-minded reformers such as the followers of John Wycliffe. In all these cases the use of 'nation' echoed the predominant meaning of *natio* in classical Roman times, as a community of foreigners bound together by similarity of origin and sharing common interests and a common outlook (Zernatto 1944: 352–8; cf. Hertz 1944: 6; Huizinga 1959b: 106–7, 114–15).

This use of 'nation', while quaint-sounding now, creates no theoretical problems. More difficult is the use of such terms, by Dante, for instance, as *nazione fiorentina* or *nazione milanese* in fourteenth-century Italy, the Italy of the city-states. Then there are what have seemed to many people expressions of a distinct national consciousness at various times and places in medieval and early modern history: in the struggles of the Scots against the English in the thirteenth and fourteenth centuries, the time of William Wallace and Robert Bruce (Mackie 1978: 69–84; Webster 1997); in the 'acute consciousness of nationality' evinced by Italians and Greeks in the Fourth Crusade, by Frenchmen and Provençaux in the Albigensian Crusade, by Czechs during the Hussite wars, and by Frenchmen and Englishmen in the concluding phases of the Hundred Years War (Huizinga 1959b: 112; Kamenka 1973b: 5; A. Smith 1992: 55). For some, it is the Jews, from Biblical times through the various diasporas, who seem to sum up the essence of nationhood, with their idea of the chosen people and their sense of a god-given national mission (see, e.g., A. Smith 1986: 117–19; O'Brien 1988b: ch. 1; A. Smith 1994; Hastings 1997: 18).

The difficulty with all these examples is knowing what to make of them. Are they, as some think (e.g., Hastings 1997: 14–17), distinct expressions of national feeling and national identity before the 'age of nationalism' – the era that began with the French Revolution and reached its peak in the later nineteenth century? Or should they be called something else – 'patriotism' (Viroli 1995, Grainger 1986: 11), 'tribal consciousness', 'national pride' or some other form of 'protonationalism' (Kamenka 1973b) – all of which suggest a clear distinction, at least conceptually, between these expressions and true nationalism? Might they not all be seen simply as expressions of ethnicity – for not even the most confirmed 'modernist' denies the existence of ethnic groups and ethnic consciousness stretching right back to the beginnings of recorded history? (Modernists simply deny that 'ethnicity' and 'nationhood' are the same things, or can be reduced to one another.)[7]

The orthodoxy in recent years has been to follow the lead of the 'modernists', those who believe that nationalism is essentially a new thing. As Elie Kedourie put it in a strong statement some time ago: 'Nationalism is a doctrine invented in Europe at the beginning of the nineteenth century' ([1960] 1993: 9; see also Gellner 1983; Hobsbawm 1992). The new doctrine, in this understanding, was the demand that 'state' and 'nation' should be coextensive – in Ernest Gellner's words, 'that the political and the national unit should be congruent' (1983: 1; see also Hechter 2000: 7). Such a demand, it was argued, would have been meaningless in the context of societies of the preindustrial type. It also meant that, for the first time, ideas of nation and nationhood would have to be formulated and elaborated. But that did not imply that, before the enunciation of the ideology of nationalism by late eighteenth-century thinkers, there could not be expressions of what we today might wish to call national sentiments. We might allow, for instance, Gellner concedes, the legitimacy of Tomas Masaryk's tracing of Czech national consciousness back to the Hussites (though equally argue that it was only with the onset of industrialization that nationalism could become a meaningful and indeed necessary project for the Czechs). He also accepts that nationalism generally builds on preexisting inheritances of a cultural kind – such as historical myths and memories – from the pre-nationalist era (Gellner 1983: 55; 1998: 23–4, 90–101).

Similarly the 'primordialists', those who see a more or less continuous history of national expression from the earliest times, do not all deny that something new was introduced around the time of the French Revolution. Anthony Smith, for instance, a leading primordialist, insists on the ethnic roots of nations, and hence a cultural and historical continuity usually played down if not rejected outright by modernists. But he also accepts that the movement from '*ethnie*' to 'nation', and the rise of the ideology of nationalism at the time of the French Revolution, brought in a new world of nation-states that was significantly different from the earlier world of ethnicities (A. Smith 1986: 129–52; 1998: 192–3).

What this seems to mean is that we should accept a degree of plasticity and variability in concepts of the nation, nationhood, and even nationalism. These are large and capacious terms that have to carry a good deal of historical and theoretical baggage: too much so for one scholar, who accuses nationalism of 'ideational paucity' and argues that it only gets some useful meaning when it is employed within the context of more comprehensive ideologies such as liberalism, socialism or conservatism (Freeden 1998). More kindly, other scholars have spoken of the 'ambiguous' nature of the concept (Alter 1994: 1), of the 'kaleidoscopic' forms of nationalism (Hutchinson and Smith 1994: 3), and of the need to see that there is no one 'essential' nationalism but rather a number of nationalisms that bear a 'family resemblance' to one another (Calhoun 1997: 5–6). Hence the common pattern of much of the general writing on nationalism is the construction of typologies reflecting the historical and ideological diversity of the phenomenon (e.g., Alter 1994:16–38; Hall 1995; Hechter 2000: 15–17).

The different varieties of nationalism have to be judged, as always, by their fruitfulness for purposes of inquiry. It is with this in mind that we might introduce a new variety: the type of what we might call 'imperial' or 'missionary' nationalism. To some ears this will sound strange, if not a contradiction in terms. 'Imperialism', says Michael Hechter, 'is not a type of nationalism because empires are purposively multinational' (2000: 9). Quite so. But the case for talking about imperial nationalism as a type of nationalism rests not so much on the nature of empire as a general political form as on the perceptions of particular groups within it. It is these groups that may exhibit 'missionary' nationalism, sometimes to the point of threatening the imperial structures that allow them this sense; and if, as several scholars claim, we can discern nations before nationalism, it may be that here we discern nationalism before nations.

Missionary nationalism

It is well known how the original cosmopolitanism of the French Revolution gave way to an imperialistic, exclusivist, nationalism. Robespierre protested against the nationalism that he thought implicit in the Girondins' 1793 version of the Declaration of the Rights of Man. 'It would seem that your declaration has been drafted for a human herd planted on an isolated corner of the globe, and not for the vast family of nations to which nature has given the earth for its use and dwelling.' The idea of 'national sovereignty' was anathema to him; the only sovereign he acknowledged was 'the human race', seen as divided into local branches – 'nations' – that however remained related as parts of a single organism. In Jacobin thinking, patriotism encompassed both the love of one's own country and a due regard for the like feelings of others in other countries. In this account patriotism (or nationalism) and cosmopolitanism were not opposed but complementary (Hont 1994: 207–19).[8]

We have to see that the revolutionaries were not being hypocritical in their thinking, though we can accuse them if we wish of utopianism. In identifying civilization with the French nation, and specifically the universality of the French Revolution with the mission to carry this message to less fortunate people, they sought to square the circle of universalism and nationalism. As Hazareesingh explains:

The [revolutionary] régime's appropriation of nationalist discourse fed into the revolutionary principle of universalism in both its domestic and external manifestations... The postulate that French material and spiritual values were superior to those of other nations inevitably yielded the belief that these values had to be exported to the rest of the world. Thus nationalist considerations played an integral part in the Republic's efforts to spread the message of the Revolution beyond French borders. Hence the paradoxical conflation, in the justificatory language of the French military adventures of the 1790s, of the principle of nationality with that of political liberation. The messianic message of the Republic assumed both a universalistic and a nationalist character – a symbiosis which was most tellingly illustrated a century later in the Third Republic's ideological justification of its policy of colonial expansion.   (1994: 73).

The French Revolution provides us with a vivid example of 'missionary nationalism': a nationalism that finds its principle not so much in equating state and nation as in extending the supposed benefits of a particular nation's rule and civilization to other peoples. While this can take ethnic form, in the claim for cultural or racial superiority, it is important to see that it is equally compatible with political nationalism. Stuart Woolf has pointed out that what European statesmen of the nineteenth century took from the French experience was not the model of the linguistically or ethnically homogeneous state but the centralized, administrative state. This was especially true of what was thought to be the achievement of the Napoleonic state. Neither Cavour nor Bismarck paid much attention to ethnic nationalism. What mattered to them was the Napoleonic example of imposing legal and administrative uniformity as a way of eliminating 'the dangers of anti-national regional or ethnic identities' (Woolf 1992: 101). What other course indeed was open to a 'united' Germany that excluded millions of Austrian Germans, or a 'united' Italy in which, it is estimated, in 1861 only 2 per cent of the population spoke the official language of the new nation? Well might the former prime minister of Piedmont, Massimo d'Azeglio, make the celebrated remark: 'We have made Italy; now we must make Italians' (Hobsbawm 1992: 44).[9]

The state Napoleon created was not just administrative. It was also imperial. It incorporated many different nations and pursued a policy of centralized nation-building from on top. In doing so it drew upon the power and expertise of the dominant political elites and, in the first place, the dominant ethnic group. But to be successful it had to be sensitive to the diversity of cultures and ethnic groups over which it ruled. It followed the pattern of the political nation – that is, its criterion of membership or citizenship was political, not ethnic – but adapted it to the exigencies of imperial rule.

The Napoleonic state was, like most empires, also missionary. It saw itself as presented with a historic task, to spread the message and the means of French civilization and revolutionary transformation, both conceived in universalistic terms. Not all empires have been proselytizing, and not all conceived their task in such a self-consciously ideological way. But it is difficult to think of any empire, ancient or modern, that was not possessed of some sense of its mission in the world, some conviction that its rule existed in the service of a higher ideal than mere power and advantage. This is clear enough in the case of the Chinese and Roman empires, as also in the various Christian empires of the European middle ages, notably that of Charlemagne and its successors and imitators. In more modern times this has also been true of the Habsburg and Romanov empires, as well as those of the British and French.

Nation and empire

Empires carry a sense of mission that generally goes beyond that of nations. Nations may be convinced that they have a unique contribution to make to the common store of humanity; but that does not entail that they engage in proselytism, or seek to impose a vision on the rest of the world. Imperial nations are prone to just this behaviour. Beyond the sense of their own uniqueness lies the conviction of a global purpose that prompts them to play down mere national pride or the cultivation of national culture. More is at stake than the making of a nation-state.

There is indeed an initial and basic tension between nation and empire. Empire is typically a form of rule in which a symbolic head, the emperor, rules over a series of lands and peoples linked by dynastic connection or allegiance to the emperor. Such were, in modern times, the Habsburg, Hohenzollern, Ottoman and Romanov Empires. These were multinational empires, spanning many lands and nations, and incorporating a wide variety of groups of different languages and different religions. Though there might be occasional attempts at

'Russification' or 'Germanization', the dangers of this are usually quickly realized. Typically, empires make little effort at cultural or ethnic homogenization. To do so would be to strike at the heart of their very being (quite apart from the fact that, as Ernest Gellner stresses, to do so in the conditions of preindustrial societies is both unnecessary and impracticable). Though empires usually have recognizably dominant ethnic groups – Germans, Russians, Turks – to identify the empire with these groups would risk bitter resentment and possibly dissolution. Ruling groups are aware of the need to distance themselves from any one ethnicity, to appear, at least, impartial as between the various peoples that make up the empire.[10]

Nationalism of the nineteenth-century variety is, as statesmen such as the Austrian Chancellor Clemens von Metternich clearly recognized, therefore inimical to empire. Classic nationalism of this type demands that state and nation should be one – the 'nation-state'. Despite the evident fact that the vast majority of nation-states contain more than one nation,[11] the nation-state in principle dedicates itself to the goal, 'one nation, one state'. This does not mean necessarily the drive towards ethnic homogenization. The idea of the 'political nation', as practised, for instance, by France, the United States and Britain, allows for a considerable degree of ethnic pluralism. Quite apart from the fact, though, that it is fairly easy to identify dominant ethnic groups in most of the best-known cases of political nationhood, it is also true that that its main conceptual rival, cultural or ethnic nationalism, has made most of the running in the area beyond Western Europe and North America. Here ethnic homogenization, accompanied by 'ethnic cleansing', has been the stated goal if not, in most cases, the achieved one (Hont 1994: 172–3).

In any case, nationalism of one sort or another has been the main solvent of modern empires. It was nationalism, aided by war, that brought down the Habsburg, Romanov and Ottoman empires during the First World War; and it was nationalism, again aided by war, that destroyed the colonial empires of Holland, France and Britain after the Second World War. In the twentieth century, even more than in the nineteenth, no two principles have appeared more antithetical than nation and empire. The dissolution of the Soviet empire, after 1991, into independent nation-states, has made this plainer than ever.

And yet nation and empire have not always been so opposed. Or rather, perhaps we should say, national identity and empire have not always stood on opposite sides. For it is possible to argue that while nationalism – especially in its ethnic form – is indeed a nineteenth-century invention, a child of the French Revolution, there has existed a sense of the nation for a much longer time. Nationalism and national identity are not, in other words, necessarily the same thing (cf. Keane 1995: 191). By linking state so rigidly to nation, nationalism makes claims to exclusivity and, often, homogeneity that are not a necessary or indispensable part of national identification. There are, as we have seen, other forms of national consciousness, going back to the European middle ages, and even perhaps to Biblical times (see, e.g., Tipton 1972; A. Smith 1994; Bjørn, Grant and Stringer 1994a). It is a mistake to equate all forms of national belonging with the nineteenth-century form, the form that is expressed in the ideology of nationalism.

One kind of national identity is the imperial type, the type I have called imperial nationalism. Empires, though in principle opposed to claims of nationality, may be carriers of a certain kind of national identity which gives to the dominant groups a special sense of themselves and their destiny. Such groups – the 'state-bearing' peoples or *Staatsvölker* – will be careful not to stress their ethnic identity; rather they will stress the political, cultural or religious mission to which they have been called. Hence another name for this kind of national belonging is 'missionary nationalism'.[12]

The key feature of imperial or missionary nationalism is the attachment of a dominant or core ethnic group to a state entity that conceives itself as dedicated to some large cause or purpose, religious, cultural or political. You can get the second element without the first. It is probably the case that all universal empires see themselves as engaged in some kind of 'civilizing' mission, whether or not they are concerned to carry that mission beyond the boundaries of the empire. But they do not always possess, at least for the greater part of their history, a more or less distinct ethnic group that identifies itself with the mission and acts as its principal 'carrier'. Different groups at different times, or a mixture of groups that identify themselves purely with the imperial cause, may take the lead in advancing the imperial mission. They may develop intense feelings of loyalty and emotional attachment to the empire. They can exhibit all the fervour of patriotism, whether expressed towards the persons of the ruling dynasty or its principles. But this is a different matter – or so at least it can be argued – from the case where a single ethnic group, from the inception of the empire to its end, gets its principal identity and sense of belonging in the world from its role as carrier of the imperial mission.[13]

The enigma of English nationalism – the puzzling fact that the English do not think they have nationalism, the confusions of English/British, the current difficulties in trying to define or redefine Englishness and English national identity – can best be approached by considering it as the nationalism of an imperial state. It helps explain the character of English nationalism over many centuries, when the empire (or empires) was in existence; and it helps to explain why questions of national identity have surfaced so urgently in the wake of empire, and why it has been so hard to find convincing answers.

Imperial or missionary nationalism is not of course unique to England, or Britain. It can be found in a number of other famous examples.[14] But like those other peoples that lost empires in the last century – Turks, Austrians, Germans, French, Russians – the English have experienced acute difficulty in establishing a sense of themselves (Brubaker 1996c: 148–78; Lieven 1995: 612; 1998: 268–9). This is the legacy of all examples of missionary nationalism. Who are we when the mission fails, or is aborted? If we have tied ourselves to a star, what happens when the star drops out of the heavens?

Britishness and Englishness

The English were an imperial nation in a double sense. They created a land empire, Great Britain or the United Kingdom, formed by the expansion of England from its southern position at the base of the group of islands off the north-western coast of Europe (the 'East Atlantic archipelago'). And they created an overseas empire, not just once but twice: first in the western hemisphere, in North America and the Caribbean, and later in the east, in India and South-East Asia. At its height, just after the First World War, this empire covered a fifth of the world's surface and incorporated a quarter of its population.

It was Sir John Seeley, in his popular and influential *The Expansion of England* (1883), who gave the first and clearest account of these two inter-related processes, the 'internal' and the 'external'.

In the last years of Queen Elizabeth England had absolutely no possessions outside Europe ... Great Britain did not yet exist; Scotland was a separate kingdom, and in Ireland the English were but a colony in the midst of an alien population still in the tribal stage. With the accession of the Stuart family commenced at the same time two processes, one of which was brought to completion under the last Stuart, Queen Anne, while the other has continued without interruption ever since. Of these the first is the internal union of the three kingdoms, which, though technically it was not complete till much later, may be said to be substantially the work of the seventeenth century and the Stuart dynasty. The second was the creation of a still larger Britain comprehending vast possessions beyond the sea. This process began with the first Charter given to Virginia in 1606. It made a great advance in the seventeenth century; but not till the eighteenth did Greater Britain in its gigantic dimensions and with its vast politics first stand clearly before the world.   (1971: 13).

Seeley charged his fellow countrymen with ignorance of and indifference towards 'this mighty phenomenon of the diffusion of our race and the expansion of our state'. In a famous statement, he remarked: 'We seem, as it were, to have conquered and peopled half the world in a fit of absence of mind. While we were doing it ... we did not allow it to affect our imagination or in any degree to change our ways of thinking; nor have we even now ceased to think of ourselves as simply a race inhabiting an island off the northern coast of the Continent of Europe' (1971: 12–13). Seeley's lectures, originally given to Cambridge undergraduates in the winter of 1881–82, were intended to change that situation; and the book that he produced from them certainly had an enormous impact on the late Victorian public. But it is a signal measure of his failure in a wider context that scholars were still protesting, a hundred years later, at the insularity of English historical writing and English political thinking (Armitage 2000: 16–22).

Seeley wrote at the height of the enthusiasm for empire, just after Victoria had been proclaimed Empress of India (1877) and just before the 'scramble for Africa' vastly extended Britain's overseas possessions. It is not surprising that his account of empire as England's destiny should have been so well received. It is equally understandable why, with the end of empire, his account should have fallen into disrepute and become a source of embarrassment to professional historians.[15]

But Seeley's enthusiasm for empire should not make us ignore the deeper insight that lay in his account. In refusing, unlike so many of his predecessors and even more his successors, to remain within the confines of a narrowly conceived English history, he should be a hero of the new school of 'British' historians, and generally of those who wish to see English developments within the context of a much wider overseas and imperial history (see chapter 1). 'The history of England', he averred, 'is not in England but in America and Asia' (1971: 13). It is particularly interesting that Seeley preferred the term 'Greater Britain' to the 'British Empire'.[16] This allowed him to regard the empire, not as a one-way relation between a metropolitan power and its dependent colonies, but as an organic unity. All British peoples, whether at 'home or 'abroad', were seen as members of single imperial nation. The flow of influence was two-way, even though the English nation was the inspiring and guiding spirit.

It is true that the two empires, 'internal' and 'external', operated in different ways (Seeley was particularly exercised by the relation to India). The thesis of 'internal colonialism' (e.g., Hechter 1999) makes too much of certain formal similarities in the making of the United Kingdom and the British Empire, Great Britain and 'Greater Britain'. But in one important respect they had similar effects. They made meaningless the development of a specifically English national identity. As with Germans in the Habsburg Empire and Russians in the Russian Empire, the English identified themselves with larger entities and larger causes in which they found their role and purpose.

The nature and effect of those identifications is the subject of later chapters. Here one might just sketch some of the major themes. Firstly, there is the story of how, from the time of the Act of Union with Scotland in 1707, political elites attempted to build up a sense of 'Britishness' that might override, or at least accompany, Englishness. The English – along with the Scots, the Welsh and the Irish – were urged to see themselves as part of a large enterprise, a political project, that was catapulting Britain into a leading position among world powers. There was the British Industrial Revolution that brought economic supremacy to Britain and, it was thought, had more of consequence for the world than the contemporaneous political revolution of the French. There were the achievements of the British navy, and the creation of a worldwide British Empire. The empire – especially the 'second British Empire' of the nineteenth century – brought with it a particularly acute sense of Britain's global mission and of its historical destiny, as a liberalizing and civilizing force.

In all this the English could not but be aware of their leading role; by the same token, they were equally aware of the need not to trumpet this as an English achievement, but to see it as a joint effort of all the British nations. No more than the Germans in the Habsburg Empire or the Russians in the Tsarist and Soviet Empires did the English feel the need to beat the drum or blow the bugle. To do so would be in fact to threaten the very basis of their commanding position. When you are securely in charge it is best not to remind others of this fact too often or too insistently. It is insecure nations, such as Germany and Italy after the First World War, who most stridently assert their nationalism.

The claim that what was involved was a British, not merely English, enterprise, was made the more convincing by the fact that it could be tied to a religious cause that had clearly British rather than simply English dimensions. The British nation was 'the Protestant nation', and the British the champions of Protestantism in the world against the menacing forces of a reactionary and benighted Catholicism. This was naturally going to be a sensitive matter with Britain's non-Protestant subjects, notably the Irish Catholics. But the predominance of Protestant subjects, and the strength of Protestant feeling, especially in Wales, Scotland and northern Ireland, meant that for a considerable period Protestantism could serve as a major rallying force and the source of a central component of a unifying British identity.

The decline of religion, a feature common to nearly all modern societies in the past century or so, was therefore likely to throw up a profound challenge to the Protestantism that had underpinned Britishness for so long. The challenge could be, and was, met by a renewed emphasis on such common British projects as British industry and the British Empire. There was also pride in the British armed forces, the British parliament, the British civil service (at home and in the empire at large), and – somewhat shakily at first, but with increasing confidence – the British monarchy. For a significant section of the population, the British trade union and labour movement was also a cause for pride and an important source of identity – one that sometimes, but not for very long, could cut across national attachment. All these things were truly British, not narrowly English, institutions and accomplishments. All groups in the kingdom shared in the labour necessary to sustain them; all shared – no doubt unequally – in the rewards. Never perhaps was this truer than in the two world wars of the twentieth century. Here Britishness – involving not just all the inhabitants of Great Britain but millions of those from 'Greater Britain', as soldiers and subjects – was displayed with a courage and commitment that rightly commanded the admiration of the world.

Nothing sustains a nation, or at least nationalism, like war. Although there have been some occasions in recent times, as during the Falklands war of the early 1980s, when attempts were made to revive a flagging Britishness through war, for obvious reasons this has become increasingly difficult. War is not nowadays a readily available option. And this has occurred in a historical situation where Britishness has come under great pressure. The props underlying it have one by one been knocked away. Religion in general, and Protestantism in particular, has become a minority concern. Those strands of religion in the kingdom that show some vigour – Catholicism, Islam, Hinduism – tend to work against rather than for a common British identity, at least in anything like its traditional form. Empire has gone, and so has industrial supremacy. Britain is no longer a global economic and political power. The attractions of being linked to it are no longer so great. Its constituent nations see other ways of seeking their fortune and making their way in the world. 'Europe', in the form of the European Union, beckons. Previously, as 'the Continent', it was one of the mainstays of British identity as Britain's 'other', as the home of Britain's most implacable political and religious enemies. Now it offers itself as an alternative focus of loyalty and an alternative theatre of activities not just for Britain as a whole but, more threateningly to its unity, for its various component nations.

'I tell you that when you study English history you study not the past of England only, but her future', declared Seeley to his Cambridge students in 1882 (1971: 139). Seeley spoke at a time when he could be reasonably confident that 'the expansion of England' that was the theme of his lectures would continue; that, in the shape of Great and Greater Britain – the dual empire – the framework for British identities and aspirations was more or less firmly set. Now that framework is unravelling, and we can make no such confident predictions about the future identities of the British people. But Seeley was right to insist that for understanding present politics and future prospects, history was the best guide. It is only when we consider how English and British identities were formed in the past that we will grasp the dilemmas facing the English and British today. This will be the task of the chapters ahead.

3

When was England?

One of the most extraordinary aspects of the current scene lies in the number of citizens of the United Kingdom who do not appear to be familiar with the basic parameters of the state in which they live. They often do not know what it is called; they do not distinguish between the whole and the constituent parts; and they have never grasped the most elementary facts of its development. Confusion reigns on every hand.   Norman Davies (1999: xxvi–xxvii)

National consciousness faces the same fate as the bourgeoisie; forever rising in the estimation of historians.   Jeremy Black (1994: 91)

Understanding the United Kingdom in time

Hegel says somewhere that it is only at the time of its dissolution that an entity reveals its principles in their true form and to their fullest extent. Nowhere is this truer than in the case of the United Kingdom. Taken vaguely for granted, unexamined and untheorized, it is only when it is faced by threats from within and without, only when there is talk of 'the break-up of Britain', that serious attention has turned to its character.

On turning in that direction, what scholars have discovered mostly is a conceptual hole. There is a good deal of constitutional history (though not much on constitutional law or constitutional theory); there is some excellent political, social and economic history; and there is sterling work in the history of political thought, though mostly for earlier periods. What is – or has been – almost entirely lacking is any attempt to comprehend the United Kingdom as a whole, any attempt to inquire into its nature and development as a political and cultural entity. There is nothing, for instance, like Fernand Braudel's work on France, nor – perhaps understandably – anything like the outpouring of studies of German culture and the German nation provoked by public debates about Nazism and the Holocaust. Spain and Italy are also better served than Britain in this respect; while, further east in Europe, Russia has for long been the subject of searching inquiries as to its identity and destiny.[1]

It is this gap that, as we have seen in chapter 1, the rise of 'British Studies' is meant to fill. There were indeed some earlier but neglected exemplars (Seeley being one, though his focus was mainly on England). It is often forgotten, for instance, that Arnold Toynbee began his monumental 10 volume *A Study of History* (1934–54) very much at home, with a consideration of 'Great Britain' as a 'test case'. His point was to show how even so solid and long-lasting a national state as Britain could not be considered, in any of the main points of its development, without taking into account influences from the wider Western society of which it was a part. 'Thus English [*sic*] history does not become intelligible until we view it as the history of a wider society of which Great Britain is a member in company with other national states, each of which reacts, though each in its own way, to the common experiences of the society as a whole' (1962a: 23).

This salutary reminder of Britain's European and generally Western character was followed up by a virtuoso treatment of the establishment of the kingdoms of England and Scotland in the early middle ages. The paradoxes and peculiarities of those forms, as they came to be constituted, were traced to the successful responses to the challenge of 'Far Western Christian Civilization', in the case of the Scots, and to that of the Scandinavians, in the case of the English. Both responses, at the point of greatest pressure, released energies that displaced previous centres of power and placed Edinburgh and London at the centre of new configurations (Toynbee 1962b: 190–202).

The hostile, not to say insolent, attitude of most professional historians towards Toynbee meant not only rejection of his overall historical scheme, but also neglect of his treatment of particular episodes, so that, some forty years later, 'British Studies' had to start all over again with the analysis of the complexities that go into the making of Britain and its constituent parts.[2] Much good work has now been done in that direction; we can draw upon this in the necessary task of tracing the development of the various national entities that underlie concepts of Englishness and Britishness. For origins are, as Alexis de Tocqueville pointed out, as important in the lives of nations as they are in the life of the child. 'The circumstances that accompanied their birth and contributed to their development affect the whole term of their being.' Here, he thought, in the beginnings of nations, are to be found the sources of 'national character' (1988: 31–2). Certainly part of the confusion about Englishness and Britishness has to do with an extraordinarily fuzzy conception, on the part of most of the British, of the origins and growth of their nations. The history of national identity, an examination of when and in what form it first crystallized, is a matter of much more than antiquarian interest. It tells us something vital about the nature of that identity, what sustains it and what may contribute to its decline.

It is inevitable that in tracing this we will encounter fierce historical disputes. Nationalism is a powerful force, today as much as yesterday. It has become the subject of intense study in many disciplines. It encourages strong partisanship, scholarly as much as political. Among historians, who have been leading contributors, it is a natural propensity to find the original example of national consciousness in 'their' own period. So, in the case of England, Anglo-Saxon historians find it in the eight and ninth centuries, medievalists find it in the fourteenth, early modernists in the sixteenth, and so on. Nationalism is so important a principle, and so consequential in its effects, that the desire to discover its founding moment and formation in one's own period is difficult to resist. But clearly the period-bound historians cannot all be right; or rather, the likelihood is that they are looking at different things.

We are concerned chiefly with England and English identity, so it is to the making of England and the English that we must turn. This will necessarily, and relatively early, lead us to consider developments in other parts of Britain. But to start with we are dealing with different communities and multiple kingdoms inhabiting the British Isles. When – to adapt a famous phrase about Wales – was England? Adrian Hastings has said that 'one can find historians to date "the dawn of English national consciousness" (or some such phrase) in almost every century from the eight to the nineteenth' (1997: 35). This is a measure of the problem of situating English nationhood and English nationalism in time. We cannot examine every century; but we need to look, however briefly, at some of the principal claims. The first is indeed made for the eight century, at the high point of 'Anglo-Saxon England'.

'Engla Land': the meaning of England and the English in Anglo-Saxon times

It seems to have been the scholarly Northumbrian monk, the Venerable Bede, who in his *Ecclesiastical History of the English People* (731 AD) first spoke of 'the English' (*gens Anglorum*) as a single people. In Britain as a whole Bede identified – 'in harmony with the five books of the divine law' – 'five languages [Latin constituted the fifth] and four nations – English, British, Irish [*Scotti* – the Irish settlers of Argyll and the western Islands], and Picts' (1990: 45). Since Bede's concern was mainly the conversion of the pagan Germanic invaders to Christianity, and the struggle between the competing versions of Christianity – British, Irish and Roman – in Britain, the English could appear unified to him by virtue of their common acceptance of Roman Christianity and their common submission to a single church, based in Canterbury.[3] His history was, as its title made clear, primarily Church history; its purpose moral and prescriptive (cf. Cowdrey 1981: 504). There was no reason therefore to dwell on the fact that the 'the English' were by no means a unified people, being made up of still diverse groups of Angles, Saxons, Jutes and others with distinct ethnicities. More significantly, there was as yet no 'England', but rather, in the territory of south Britain that later came to be called England, a number of competing 'Anglo-Saxon' kingdoms together with significant communities of *Brittones*, the original British inhabitants of much of the island (Smyth 1998b: 25–6). Nevertheless there are scholars, as we shall see, who wish to make Bede's account the basis of their claim that something like an English national identity already existed by the eight century.

'[T]the stubborn refusal of the Northumbrian, Mercian, East Anglian or West Saxon kingdoms to submit to each other unanswerably rebuts the view that "England" was proceeding "logically" towards "unification"... No early Anglo-Saxon king so much as *claimed* to be "King of the English" ' (Wormald 1994: 5). But by the tenth century the kings of Wessex were calling themselves kings of 'Engla land' (the first to do so seems to have been Aethelstan, grandson of Alfred the Great, in 928). Under the onslaughts of the Danes in the ninth century, all the kingdoms of 'the Heptarchy' save that of Wessex had disappeared. Only Wessex, under Alfred (849–99), held out against the 'Great Army' of the Vikings. His successors, proclaiming themselves, like Alfred, 'kings of the English', went on not so much to liberate as to conquer, very much in the manner of the fifteenth-century Castilian *Reconquista*, former territories of the other Anglo-Saxon kingdoms in the north and east, now under Danish rule. They also took Cornwall from the British (thereby leading, by the migration of the defeated British, to the settlement of Brittany in France). As if to lay down a marker for future imperial expansion, Aethelstan called himself not just king of England but *rex totius Britanniae*, king of all Britain; a tenth-century chronicler Aethelweard likewise declared that 'Britain is now called England, thereby assuming the name of the victors'; (Banton 1982: 85; Loyn 1991: 69; Wormald 1994: 6; Smyth 1998b: 39–43; N. Davies 1999: 268–9). A century later another conquest, by William of Normandy in 1066 (representing the last of the Viking raids), put the seal on the unification of England. The great Domesday Book of 1086–87, a grand stocktaking of William's newly acquired possessions, testified to the extent of that unification (though, stopping as it did at the Tees and the Ribble, it did not include the whole of present-day England).

No doubt England by the eleventh century had become one of the most, if not the most, integrated and centralized states in Europe, an achievement usually credited in the main to Alfred the Great. William the Conqueror inherited a well-ordered state with a uniform system of administration, a highly developed structure of royal law, a centralized coinage and an effective system of taxation

(Thomas 1978: 47; Elton 1992: 20–7; Campbell 1995a: 31–5; Wormald 2000). 'The Norman Conquest of England was, up to a point, simply the transfer of an already powerful monarchy into the hands of a man who announced consistently that he ruled as [Edward] the Confessor's nominated heir' (Bates 1990: 68). Or as Patrick Wormald puts it: 'The Norman Conquest cannot have been the *making*, even if it was the saving, of England. England, as its name implies, was made already' (1994: 10; cf. Aylmer 1990: 92; R. R. Davies 1994a: 13; 1995: 11).

But is this the same thing as saying that, by 1066, 'England was a nation-state' (Campbell 1995a: 31; cf. Loyn 1991: 6; Hastings 1997: 42)? A state, perhaps, but a *nation*-state? Campbell admits the difficulties of showing 'a sense of emotional and ideological commitment', a 'nationalist commitment', to the English state. He nevertheless feels that such things as the avoidance of civil war among the nobility, their willingness to take part in the common administration of the kingdom, and the acceptance of a system of 'national' communication by means of royal writs, indicate a relatively high degree of commitment to the state on the part of the upper classes. Then there was the Church, which well before the political unification effected by the kings of Wessex had linked at least southern and midland England (though the existence of a separate metropolitan at York 'could be an impediment to unification'). A further unifying factor was the English monastic movement of the tenth century, which aimed at applying a uniform rule for all reformed monasteries across the kingdom, and which consciously put an emphasis on 'England' as a single entity. In its various forms, 'the Church served to create a background of commitment to king and country'. Finally, there was a common vernacular language, Anglo-Saxon or Old English, and a 'national' literature vigorously promoted by the court of Alfred the Great (Campbell 1995a: 35–40; see also Campbell 1995b: 47; Banton 1982; Foot 1996; Hastings 1997: 39–42).[4]

But this was the Roman Catholic Church, a self-professedly international, ecumenical institution. Whatever its effect in helping to unify the English kingdom during the Anglo-Saxon period, it would not be long before it would be excommunicating English kings and bitterly dividing the kingdom. Generally for the whole period up to the Reformation, the Church was to prove a most unpromising candidate as an ally of nationalism. In many cases, in the name of a higher principle and a different goal, it was to be its most implacable foe. Only with the coming of national churches could religion be seriously annexed to national feeling.

In other respects too the picture of a nationally conscious late Anglo-Saxon England is unconvincing. The unity brought about by the Wessex kings was fragile, and some luck was needed to see it through to William's more definitive unification. For instance, despite its defeat by Wessex and the ravages of the

Danes in the ninth century, a serious attempt was made to resurrect the Mercian kingdom in the following century; and in the mid tenth century the archbishop of York could be found among the supporters of Eric Bloodaxe, the Viking king of York who twice controlled large sections of Northumbria. The rule of a Danish dynasty – Cnut and his successors – from 1016 to 1042 did not necessarily mean the disruption of England's unity: though it might fairly be said that 'the lack of immediate problems underlines the absence of strong national feelings as we understand it: strong kingship mattered as much as the individual dynasty, unity more than Englishness' (Stafford 1984: 129). But Cnut was the ruler of a vast Scandinavian empire with interests that lay well beyond England's borders; his Scandinavian involvements made him the first of England's many 'absentee' kings during the first 300 years of its existence. Moreover, he displaced many English landholders and replaced them with Danes in almost every shire, thus disrupting the continuity of the English governing class and upsetting the always delicate relations between king and nobility (Loyn 1991: 81). Edward the Confessor's reign (1042–66) shows an almost equal degree of turbulence among the aristocracy, with his father-in-law, Godwine Earl of Wessex – one of Cnut's creations – invading the country and reimposing himself by force after his exile by Edward. Moreover the Scandinavian connection continued to have a disruptive effect, as was proved by the fate of Godwine's son, King Harold II, faced with two Viking rivals for the throne of England in the persons of Harald Hardraada and William of Normandy. All in all, the evidence for a 'nationalist commitment' among the upper classes – we know of course virtually nothing about other classes – is extremely shaky. Pauline Stafford seems right to conclude that 'no feelings of nationalism bound the people together' in the tenth century, and that moves towards national unity were offset by 'deep divisions and local loyalties' (1984: 117; see also Stafford 1989: 34–7; Banton 1982: 71–2; Foot 1996: 34). Edgar, king of Mercia and Northumbria, might on reunifying the realm of England in 959 call himself 'king of the English', but a contemporary poet preferred to call him 'ruler of the Angles, friend of the West Saxons and protector of the Mercians' (Stafford 1984: 122).

Faced with the difficulties of showing a clear sense of English national identity in this period, historians of Anglo-Saxon England have tried a different tack. This is where Bede comes in, with a vengeance. In the absence of any real degree of national integration, Bede is credited with the creation of an ideology of Englishness that, once formed, proved highly influential and serviceable to later generations. Patrick Wormald is the most ingenious and eloquent proponent of this view. He begins with the postulate that, in the conditions of the early medieval West, for a state to develop it was necessary, even more than it was to be in the case of later states, that there should be ideological support:

'a state was an "ideological artefact" or in the end nothing' (1994: 10). It was in this crucial respect that England diverged from most of the other states in Europe, who had a much harder time matching their ideologies to their efforts at nation-building. In England's case, if we follow Wormald's argument, success depended upon a happy accident. Bede tells the following famous story, one of the *ur*-texts of later English nationalism:

We are told that one day some merchants who had recently arrived in Rome displayed their many wares in the market place. Among the crowd who thronged to buy was Gregory [the later Pope Gregory the Great], who saw among other merchandise some boys exposed for sale. These had fair complexions, fine-cut features, and beautiful hair. Looking at them with interest, he enquired from what country and what part of the world they came. "They come from the island of Britain," he was told, "where all the people have this appearance." He then asked whether the islanders were Christians, or whether they were still ignorant heathens. "They are pagans," he was informed. "Alas!" said Gregory with a heartfelt sigh: "how sad that such bright-faced folk are still in the grasp of the author of darkness, and that such graceful features conceal minds void of God's grace! What is the name of this race?" "They are called Angles," he was told. "That is appropriate," he said, "for they have angelic faces, and it is right that they should become joint-heirs with the angels in heaven. And what is the name of the province from which they have been brought?" "Deira" [the lower region of Northumbria], was the answer. "Good. They shall indeed be rescued *de ira* – from wrath – and called to the mercy of Christ. And what is the name of their king?" "Aelle," he was told. "Then," said Gregory, making play on the name, "it is right that their land should echo the praise of God our Creator in the word *Alleluia*"   (Bede 1990: 103–4)

It is this experience, Bede says, 'which explains Gregory's deep desire for the salvation of our nation . . . [I]t was through his zeal that our English nation was brought from the bondage of Satan to the faith of Christ, and we may rightly term him our own apostle' (1990: 103, 98). When he became Pope in 592, Gregory remembered his vow to convert the English and in 596 sent 'his servant Augustine and other God-fearing monks to preach the word of God to the English nation', encouraging and fortifying them when their resolve faltered 'at the idea of going to a barbarous, fierce, and pagan nation' (1990: 72–3).

Seizing upon this episode, Wormald argues that Gregory's choice of nomenclature had momentous consequences.

Unlike any other known Latin-speaker in the sixth-century Continent, Gregory the Great invariably described the pagans to whom he despatched his mission as "Angles". As a result, those distinguished by Germanic speech and heathen convictions from Britain's indigenous inhabitants became children of the mother Church of the "English" founded by Gregory's disciples in Canterbury. Anyone laying claim to an ethnic origin on the far side of the North Sea by that token acquired a common Christian identity; so all were "Angelcynn", "of English race". There is thus even more significance than is generally appreciated in the well-known fact that a single English kingdom was anticipated by a single English Church. The very name of "English" was one of its fruits.

(1994: 12–13; see also 1984: 62; Foot 1996: 43)

But ecclesiastical authority by itself would probably not have been enough to instill a sense of a new ethnicity in Britain's Germanic-speaking inhabitants. What made Gregory's innovation so important, argues Wormald, was the interpretation that Bede gave to it in his *Ecclesiatical History of the English People* (the only contemporary work of historiography that so named a future national people). Not only did he take from Gregory the idea that the Canterbury church was the church of the 'Angles', the *gens Anglorum*. He added to it the interpretation, drawn from the Old Testament account of God's dealings with his Chosen People, of the English as latter-day Jews. His *History* recounts the unbridled wickedness of the original Britons, who, proving unworthy of the Roman and Christian civilization offered to them, are justly scourged by the Anglo-Saxon invaders. God transfers his favour to the new race, who will inherit the land flowing with milk and honey that, as Bede describes it at the very outset of his *History*, is the island of Britain. Bede's account is not simply triumphalist. It contains the clear warning that if the English follow the Britons down the same path of sin, they will meet the same fate. But the fundamental association has been made. 'The "*gens Anglorum*" too was a people of the Covenant. Its destiny was indissolubly bound up with its duty to its Maker. And in presenting the Anglo-Saxons with such an image of their past and future, Bede gave their would-be unifiers an impetus that *soi-disant* kings of Tara [in Ireland] could only envy' (Wormald 1994: 14; see also 1983, 1992; and cf. also Cowdrey 1981: 504). It is, concludes Wormald, Bede's influence that helps us to understand the 'ineluctable if startling fact that the words "*Engla-Lond*" and "*Englisc*" were being used in the eleventh century very much as "England" and "English" are used today' (1994: 10; see also Frame 1995a: 8; Hastings 1997: 36–43; R. R. Davies 1997: 19).

There is no reason to question Bede's importance in English (or, for that matter, European) thought and life. He is regularly invoked as 'the father of English history' (more properly, historiography), and his writing has exercised a fascination for scores of scholars throughout the centuries (see Knowles 1962). What has to be questioned is whether he supplies us with a real clue to English identity in the Anglo-Saxon period. We have already noted that his concerns were more theological than sociological or historical in the usual sense. The English Church was a creation of the Roman Catholic Church (as English Reformation historians were to dwell on with anguish), and its chroniclers and commentators, all churchmen, were at pains to fit their accounts of the English Church into the larger scheme of things in which the Catholic Church was implicated. That scheme encompassed the power of the 'universal' Roman Church and the future of Christianity as a whole. Any part of that enterprise had to be considered in that light, in relation to the whole. Given that there was a reasonable degree of ecclesiastical uniformity in certain sections of Britain, it is not so surprising that Bede should have tried to impose some sort of ideological uniformity on the various groups that inhabited those parts: the more so as he was concerned to fend off the challenges from other varieties of Christianity still flourishing in the island, those of the Irish and the despised British (Cowdrey 1981: 509–14). Norman Davies, observing that Bede's 'longings for a future unity...were religious and ecclesiastical, not national', indeed thinks that Bede's preoccupations were as much with the future of Britain as they were with the English (1999: 203). Bede, like the shadowy *Bretwaldas* ('Britain-rulers') that appear in his *History*, was haunted by the memory of the unity of *Britannia*, Roman Britain, in the Roman Empire, and looked forward to its reunification under a new, Christian, Rome. In that sense his purpose was not so much national as imperial (see also Higham 1995; Cowdrey 1981: 504–5). Like several others Davies notes that Bede's *History* not only begins but ends with Britain. The closing lines refer to 'the present state of all Britain [*Britannia*]' and conclude: 'May the world rejoice under [Christ's] eternal rule, and Britain glory in his Faith! Let the multitude of isles be glad thereof, and give thanks at the remembrance of his holiness!' (Bede 1990: 325).

Understanding Bede's purpose is one way of seeing the relation between his work and the English nation that some see imaginatively or ideologically created by it. Ideological creations can live at some distance from the reality they purport to describe. We have no way of judging the reality of English national consciousness from Bede's admittedly virtuoso ecclesiastical history, and some reason to think that they are two quite different things. We have also seen that there is reason to doubt the unity and uniformity of an English nation allegedly constructed, partly on the basis of Bede's vision, by Alfred and his successors.[5]

Finally, a general point about this effort to identify the first 'moment of Englishness'. Not only is there, as we have noted, the natural desire of historians to find the original instance of nationalism in 'their' period. More seriously, there is a carelessness about concepts, a loose and confused use of such terms as 'state' and 'nation', that is at the bottom of much of the disagreement.[6] We might say that an English *state* came into being under Alfred, or under William, but that is not the same as saying that an English *nation* came into being then, or describing the resulting formation as a *nation-state*. Whether we speak of the political or ethnic nation, a nation presupposes a relatively high degree of cohesion and common consciousness among its members, together with a regular and effective system of communication between them. It always entails some sense of a relationship between elites and the commonalty, the ordinary people of the community. A nation composed of elites and expressing only elite-consciousness is not a nation in the accepted sense of the word today (see further on this below).

It is of course notoriously difficult, even today, with contemporary instruments and the records of recent times, to establish with great confidence or any degree of precision the national sentiments of a people. How much more difficult is it with the scanty records of earlier times, such as Anglo-Saxon or late medieval England. But we must nevertheless seek to look for the kind of evidence, insufficient and inadequate as it might be, that will help us discern whether or not it is right to speak of nationhood or national consciousness at any given time. Not every state is a nation, just as not every nation succeeds in forming a state. We need, in assessing the various claims for the origins of English nationalism, to be particularly attentive to just what kind or concept of nation is being invoked, and how far it satisfies the generally accepted meaning of that term. In the case of the Anglo-Saxon period, to 1066, the evidence simply does not seem to be there for accepting a claim of English nationhood, let alone English nationalism. The 'precocity' of English national consciousness is not just remarkable; it is unbelievable.

The English nation from the eleventh to the fourteenth centuries

There is an obvious way to claim a strong assertion of English nationalism in the period after the Norman Conquest. This is to see the common people of England united against the oppressions of their foreign rulers, the Normans. Such was the view of seventeenth-century English radicals in their powerful deployment of the concept of 'the Norman yoke', set against the original liberties of the English people before the Conquest (Hill 1986b). Christopher Hill suggests that 'some theory of this sort may well have had a continuous history since 1066', accompanied by 'folk-memories of Alfred [the Great] as a symbol of national independence' (1986b: 65). Certainly the theory persisted among radicals well into the nineteenth century. But it was not just radicals who held to this view of the relation between Normans and English. There were many other writers who made play with the idea of the Norman yoke. For large numbers of English people it was Sir Walter Scott's immensely popular historical novel *Ivanhoe* (1819) that presented the essential contrast between the free Saxons and the brutal Normans. For those who think about these things at all today, it is likely to be childhood memories of *Ivanhoe*, quite probably in one of the many versions for children's comics that circulated in the first half of the twentieth century, that have supplied the basic impressions of a free and courageous English struggling against Norman tyranny.[7]

Whatever the historical truth that underlies it, the idea of the Norman yoke creates obvious problems for those who wish to see English nationalism strongly developed in the post-Conquest period. For it would mean that we would have to accept the coexistence of two nations, one Norman, one English, one upper class, one embodying the common people. States can exist with a plurality of ethnic groups, but the degree of difference entailed in the stark contrast of English and Norman would have made the Anglo-Norman state unworkable. We would have to accept that there was a more or less permanent state of resentment and rebelliousness on the part of the English, seeking to throw off their Norman overlords and regain their independence.

In fact we know this to be a historical fantasy. The great Victorian historian E. A. Freeman was already protesting, at the end of the nineteenth century, at the *Ivanhoe* view of the Norman Conquest, with its implication of a traumatic break in historical continuity and a deep and virtually unbridgeable divide between 'Normans' and 'Saxons'. The Norman Conquest, he insisted, had to be seen as an episode within an English (not 'Anglo-Saxon') history that began well before the Conquest. By the end of the twelfth century, at the latest, except at the highest levels of society Normans and English were so 'mixed together' that 'it was impossible to tell one from another'. Modern historians have largely concurred in this (A. Williams 1997: 2, and *passim*; Clanchy 1998: 34, 181; Reynolds 1997: 267).

William's kingdom, it is clear, was an English kingdom, and William – among other things – an English king. He called himself 'king of the English', not king of the English and Normans. No more in Norman than in 'Anglo-Saxon' times was England a 'hyphenated' kingdom (Reynolds 1997: 266; 1985: 414). At the same time William imported a French-speaking Norman court, replaced English with Norman appointments at all the highest levels of the Church, and substituted a Norman aristocracy for the English earls and thegns. Latin replaced English as the written language of government, and was even more deeply confirmed than before as the language of religious and intellectual life. French became the spoken language of the elite and all who aspired to belong to it, and French first names became increasingly fashionable among all classes of society (Clanchy 1998: 34–7, 57–73; A. Williams 1997: 98–9, 126–7).

More than that, as duke of Normandy as well as king of England, William began the serious involvement of England in French affairs – an involvement that was to last some 400 years. Until the reign of Henry the Sixth (1422–61) at the earliest, English kings, who were variously also rulers of Normandy, Anjou, Aquitaine, Poitou and numerous other French principalities, were embroiled in conflicts with the French king and other French grandees. Under Edward the Third (in 1340) they claimed the throne of France itself. Not till 1801, in the reign of George the Third, did English and British kings and queens cease to style themselves monarchs of France (N. Davies 1999: 413). In the face of all this, can one do any more than speak of at best an 'Anglo-Norman' identity for the period, say, up to the fourteenth century? What can English identity mean during this period?[8]

Some have claimed that whereas the Norman Conquest did indeed for a while destroy national unity, unity was substantially restored by the late twelfth century (Gillingham 1992: 393–5, 405; Hastings 1997: 43; R. R. Davies 2000: 20, 111). Magna Carta (1215), for instance, is seen as reflecting the community and 'collective solidarity' of the whole realm, the barons, whatever their selfish interests, genuinely and as it were unselfconsciously, representing the people of the whole kingdom (Reynolds 1997: 268–70; R. R. Davies 2000: 202). Simon de Montfort's rebellion against Henry the Third in 1258 has also often been seen as an expression of English patriotism (Elton 1992: 52, 65) – despite Simon's obvious French provenance and political orientation, the fact that he spoke no English, and his known dislike of the English (Clanchy 1998: 129, 192; Pearsall 1999: 89; Reynolds 1999: 11). More persuasively, a renewed sense of Englishness has been attributed to the work of a group of twelfth-century historians, especially Eadmer at Canterbury, John of Worcester, Orderic Vitalis and William of Malmesbury. All were Benedictine monks, of English or half-English origin. They are said to be responsible for reviving the sense of the English, as opposed to the Norman, past, 'for bringing Anglo-Saxon history into existence', relying to a good extent on Bede, and on Asser's *History of Alfred* (Southern 1973: 256; see also Campbell 1986: 209). A similar function seems to have been performed by a group of lay writers, again of mixed English and Anglo-Norman parentage. These include Henry of Huntingdon, Geoffrey Gaimar and Ailred of Rievaulx (A. Williams 1997: 176–86; Gillingham 1995a). 'One has a strong sense', says Adrian Hastings, that in these writers 'national identity is being re-asserted' (1997: 44; cf. Gillingham 1995b: 54–5; R. R. Davies 1995: 12; 1997: 19–20; 2000: 116, 196).

Undoubtedly these historians and commentators appear often as critics of the Normans and champions of the English. They complain of the often cruel treatment of the native English at the time of the Conquest, and of the difficulty faced by those of English blood in achieving preferment in Church and state. 'England', said William of Malmesbury, 'is become the residence of foreigners and the property of strangers; at the present time there is no Englishman who is either earl, bishop or abbot; strangers all, they prey upon the riches and vitals of England' (in A. Williams 1997: 173–4). There is praise of English craftsmanship, and of the beauty and abundance of the English countryside.

At the same time they do not see the Norman Conquest as an unmitigated disaster. Following a by now well-established literary tradition, many of them see it as the just punishment for the sins of the English. There is no nostalgic call for a return to pre-Conquest times, much as some of the Anglo-Saxon kings are admired. William of Malmesbury goes out of his way to censure the rebellions that seek to restore Saxon rule or in other ways undo the Conquest. He cannot understand Edgar Aetheling, the last male representative of the royal house of Wessex, who spurned better offers abroad in order to return to live quietly in his native land. William remarks that 'the love of their country deceives some men to such a degree, that nothing seems pleasant to them unless they can breathe their native air' (A. Williams 1997: 173). In his account of the battle of the Standard (1138), Henry of Huntingdon has the bishop of Orkney appeal to 'brave nobles of England, Norman by birth', and there are frequent references throughout the works of the historians that suggest that they see the English *natio* as an amalgam of English and Norman *gentes*. Recovery of the English past, with due tribute to its accomplishments, was one thing; turning back the clock was another. The English have benefited inestimably from the French connection since, as William of Malmesbury put it, 'the French are unrivalled among western nations in military skill and in polished manners' (Gillingham 1991: 108). The work of the Anglo-Norman historians has in fact plausibly been interpreted as an effort at reconciliation between English and Norman (A. Williams 1997: 186; see also Southern 1970b: 137–8; Gillingham 1995a: 88–9). They wrote in the scholarly language, Latin, for their Norman patrons and upper-class readership. The English are praised, or at least their history rescued, so that they may appear in a better light to Norman aristocrats (the English monks, says Southern, turned 'Old English history into a French romance'). No doubt all this helped the eventual fusion of Norman and English. But it is a quite different matter from seeing the twelfth-century historians as English nationalists.

The plain facts speak against any effort to discern a strong sense of English identity for most this period. Like Cnut before them, English rulers spent the better part of their reigns outside the country – more than half their time, in the case of William the Conqueror, William Rufus, Henry the First and Henry the Second. In his ten-year reign (1189–99) Richard the First spent only six months in England. His successors, John and Henry the Third, spent more time, not out of choice but merely because they were being driven out of their continental lands by their rivals, the French kings Philip Augustus and St Louis. Not that those defeats necessarily limited their ambitions or narrowed their outlook to purely English affairs. The loss of Normandy in 1204, far from chastening the English kings, seems rather to have stimulated even wilder thoughts of conquest and empire.

The consequence of the loss of Normandy was not to confine the English political system within its own shores but to widen the circle to include the king's vassals south of the Loire. Since 1066 this circle had steadily widened beyond England and Normandy: firstly with the struggle between Stephen and the Empress Matilda, then with the accession of Henry II count of Anjou, and now with Richard I and John, counts of Poitou and dukes of Aquitaine. Henry III attempted to widen the circle even further to include the Provençal and Savoyard kinsmen of his wife as well as the Poitevins and Lusignans on his own side of the family. This widening reached bursting point in 1258 with the "Sicilian business", the attempt by Henry III to win the Hohenstaufen inheritance in Italy for his son Edmund as well as having his brother Richard of Cornwall as emperor in Germany. In this network of alliances extending from Spain to Germany and from Scotland to Sicily the king of England stood very far from alone. (Clanchy 1998: 128)

The idea that England 'turned in on itself' at this time seems very far off the mark. 'Foreign' advisers, Poitevins such as Peter des Roches and Peter des Rivaux following upon the earlier Normans and Angevins, proliferated and predominated, stirring occasional protest and even rebellion. But the protesters usually turn out to be another group of 'foreigners', as in the case of Simon de Montfort and his associates. It is a case of 'ins' versus 'outs', rather than one of native English versus foreigner.[9] It is wrong to speak, as is so common, of English kings having 'French interests' in this period. Rather we should say that dukes of Normandy, counts of Anjou, dukes of Aquitaine and the like had 'English interests', in the sense of regarding their kingship of England as a valuable resource in their struggle for territory and status on the European continent (which is why so many of them died, and were buried, in France) (N. Davies 1999: 339).

In virtually every respect England from the eleventh to the thirteenth century was a part of Europe, to an even greater extent than it was at the time of Roman Britain. 'Not only in politics, but in aristocratic social life and culture, in its economic system and its ecclesiastical organization, England was joined to the Continent. It was an integral but subordinate part of a western European order. Never before or since has the union of England with the community of Europe been so all-embracing and so thoroughly accepted as part of the nature of things' (Southern 1970b: 140; cf. Black 1994: 53–75; N. Davies 1997: 330–1). Its architecture was the international Romanesque (Norman) and Gothic style, invented in France. Its courtly language, as much in the thirteenth century as in the eleventh, was French. Its learned language was Latin, the language of scholars and humanists throughout Europe. Its church was part of the Roman church; under the north Italians, Lanfranc and Anselm, archbishops of Canterbury, it turned even more firmly than before in a Roman direction (while, by the same token, another 'foreign'archbishop, Boniface of Savoy, could ally with 'English' elements to resist papal authority). Its great martyr, the Norman, Thomas Becket, was venerated throughout Europe, making Canterbury an international pilgrimage site to rival Santiago de Compostela. Its learning and literature partook of the general 'twelfth-century renaissance' whose centre was France. Culturally, says Richard Southern, twelfth-century England was 'a colony of the French intellectual empire, important in its way and quite productive, but still subordinate' (1970c: 158; see also Kearney 1995: 84–6; Clanchy 1998: 109, 115–18, 182–4; N. Davies 1999: 312–31).

'Englishing the nation'?

The idea of Englishness is clearly problematic for a period of 200 or even 300 years following the Norman Conquest. What kind of a nation is it in which virtually the whole governing class speaks a language different from the common people, and in which the dominant institutions and outlook are firmly international (Galbraith 1972: 49; Reynolds 1999)? Certainly not a modern nation – or better, perhaps, not a nation in the modern sense. The disjuncture between state and people – common of course in premodern societies – is only too evident. This is presumably why few students of English nationalism have homed in on this period to discover the origins of English national identity.

Things take a markedly different turn with the fourteenth century. It is then, according to a reading that has venerable origins, that England comes into its own as a nation. The rupture between state and people is healed. Some of the signs are traced back to the thirteenth century, some seen as expressing themselves more fully in the fifteenth. But there is an impressive body of opinion that finds in these late medieval centuries clear evidence for the formation of something like an English national identity. Geoffrey Elton speaks for them all when he says that in these years an English nation, across all its ranks, became a reality.

The long years during which the kingdom of England stood on the margins of a power structure centred upon the Continent of Europe were over; for both its rulers and its people, the realm once again occupied the middle point. Moreover, its people now very definitely thought of themselves as one and as English. The English nation, speaking English throughout its social ranks, had unquestionably arrived, and the Poitevins and Savoyards thrown out by the rebellion against Henry III were the last foreigners to claim power within the land. Even the Church ceased to import Frenchmen and Italians to fill bishoprics ... Before long, the rapidly increasing self-consciousness of the nation produced a characteristic mixture of tolerant superiority and grim xenophobia, both nourished by experiences in war and politics. While in the twelfth and thirteenth centuries the people of England had generally looked to France for civilization, learning and the good life, by the middle of the fourteenth they knew that all things were done best in England.

> (Elton 1992: 69–70; see also 51–2, 110–11; and cf. Keeney 1972: 96–7; Thomas 1978: 47–8; R. R. Davies 1994a: 18; 2000: 158; Black 1994: 98–9; 2000: 101–3; Turville-Petre 1996: 1–26; Hastings 1997: 47–51; Clanchy 1998: 173–89)

What, according to its proponents, accounts for this 'Englishing of the nation' (Elton 1992: 52) by the fourteenth century? The list of factors appears no less formidable for being essentially familiar. There is the loss of most of their French possessions by the English kings, allowing them to focus their attention on their English realm. There is the establishment of Parliament with its two Houses, Lords and Commons, as a regular organ of consultation, and as a representative institution of the whole nation. There is the growth of the English common law, with its own corps of common lawyers trained at the Inns of Court, and an increasing reliance on native treatises such as those of Glanvill (*c.* 1187) and Bracton (*c.* 1270). This in turn aided the centralization and nationalization of justice, as common law came to supersede local customary law, and the king's court to replace local courts. War too, it is claimed, contributed to the growth of national feeling. In the wars against the Welsh and the Scots, and above all in the wars against the French, English kings came to rely on the levy of all free men, and not just their feudal vassals, to supply their armies. 'Common service in warfare made men aware that they were part of something larger than their local community, and stimulated emotional attachment to the king and the country' (Keeney 1972: 90). The long bow, the main instrument of English victories at Crécy (1346) and Agincourt (1415), itself becomes a tool of nation-building, 'absolutely vital for both the construction and the achievement of English late medieval nationalism, whipped up particularly by the exertions of the Hundred Years War' (Hastings 1997: 48).

In the Church too there were strong national currents. John Wyclif argued for a national Church, and his criticism of the papacy and some of the central tenets of the Catholic faith led to the heretical movement of the Lollards, 'the first English Reformers'. The Lollards believed that Holy Scripture should be accessible to everyone; their tracts were written in English and they produced an English Bible – one of the several translations attributed to Wyclif – in the 1390s (Hudson 1982; but see also Aston 1965). Here we encounter what, for some, is the most impressive evidence of the growth of an English national consciousness in the fourteenth century: the triumph of the vernacular and the establishment of a distinctively English literature and culture, one in which the English could take pride. By the fourteenth century, English was established as the common language of all classes; in the next century William Caxton's new printing press took it to all the corners of the kingdom. England had developed its own centres of learning to rival those on the Continent; the Oxford of Wyclif and William of Occam was a match for Paris, Pisa or Bologna. English Perpendicular, 'the most purely English style ever practised' (Hastings 1997: 48), saw out the Gothic in a blaze of glory, as in the (fifteenth-century) chapels of King's College, Cambridge and Westminster Abbey. English literature came into its own with such distinctive works as the Wyclif Bible, William Langland's *Piers Plowman* (1367–86), John Gower's *Confessio Amantis* (1390), and such anonymous works from the second half of the fourteenth century as the *Cloud of Unknowing, Sir Gawain and the Green Knight* and *Pearl* and *Patience*. Above all there is Chaucer, whose 'Prologue' to the *Canterbury Tales* (1387) is seen 'as the best literary expression of national maturity to be found in the fourteenth-century English renaissance', offering 'a thoroughly horizontalist portrait of the nation' (Hastings 1997: 47). Chaucer was, says Turville-Petre, 'the first writer in English explicitly to claim status as national poet', boldly declaring at the end of his *Troilus and Criseyde* (1385–88) that he hoped his work would help surmount the 'so gret diversite in Englissh' (Turville-Petre 1996: 216). The whole phenomenon is widely regarded as 'the triumph of English'. 'For anyone who speaks English', says Basil Cottle, 'the most exciting thing about the period is not the drums and tramplings of the futile war with France, or the sorry strife of peasants, or the divisions of religious sectaries, but the redemption of our language' (1969: 15; cf. Aylmer 1990: 95; Black 1994: 68–9; R. R. Davies 1997: 11–12).

This is all standard stuff, and a good deal of it is undeniable. What is questionable in it, however, touches directly on the subject of national identity. This is particularly so in the areas of language and literature, which are central to the claims for Englishness in this period. 'A common language', says Turville-Petre, 'is a powerful fact of that sense of belonging and (literally also) of being understood that is at the heart of nationalism.' *Ergo* the triumph of the English language is also the triumph of English nationalism. 'The use of English... becomes a mark of those who share national identity with us' (1996: 19, 21).[10] Let us leave aside for the moment Ernest Renan's reminder, with the example of England and America, that a common language can divide as much as join (1990: 16); or Vivian Galbraith's comment that William of Malmesbury 'breathes nationality, and in excellent Latin' (1972: 50).[11] What we also have to note is the very incomplete hold of English in the fourteenth century. English – Middle English – may have become the most generally spoken language; but in literature and the culture generally Latin and French continued to have the greater prestige, and to be employed for most important matters of church and state. Royal and aristocratic libraries were still overwhelmingly stocked with works in Latin and French. Latin remained the language of the Church, French that of the law courts (despite attempts to legislate for the use of English in pleading). French was still the courtly language, the language of chivalry and romance (Salter 1980: 77; Coleman 1981: 18–19; Hussey 1994: 96–9; R. R. Davies 1997: 3; N. Davies 1999: 426).

This suggests a distinct class basis to the new works in English, both on the part of writers and the audiences to which they directed their works. It has been suggested that Langland, Gower, Chaucer, the *Gawain* poet and others who chose to write in the vernacular did so as representatives of a new middle class who were urging a new ethic of private responsibility and public rectitude, a call to bring practice in line with the ideals of Christian ethics (Coleman 1981: 15–17, 273–6). This may be so, but no-one suggests that this class was in any way dominant (the middle class, we know, is always rising), and their moralizing approach to their upper-class patrons and masters in fact testifies to their subordinate status. We have too often allowed ourselves to read literary history backwards. Just because Chaucer and the others have conventionally come to be seen as the founders of the English literary tradition, we have too readily assumed a prominence and a popularity during their time for which there is little evidence (cf. Hilton 1989: 43). Indeed it seems that even the English that emerged as 'standard English' was shaped less by the poets than by the clerks of Chancery, the government bureaucrats of the fourteenth century, operating under very different influences and with very different purposes from the poets. It was this Chancery English, the language of bureaucrats and businessmen, that was generally to be diffused by Caxton's printing press in the next century. 'The shape of standard English has been determined most crucially not by the poets, the schoolmasters, or the lexicographers but by the men with power' (Cable 1984: 94; see also Hussey 1994: 102–3).

The poets themselves are not a clear-cut case. Gower's main works are equally in Latin, French and English; and J. H. Fisher has properly reminded us of Chaucer's European dimension:

Born into a family with a French name, married to the daughter of a Flemish knight, living in an Anglo-French court, serving in capacities that required him to write daily in French and Latin, Chaucer was bicultural and bilingual to a degree that it is hard for us to comprehend.   (in Hussey 1994: 99–100; cf. Salter 1980: 73–6)

More serious is the appropriation of Chaucer as 'the poet of a particular kind of Englishness', not all of it benign (Pearsall 1999: 86). Chaucer has commonly been seen not just as 'the father of English literature' but, especially in the *Canterbury Tales*, as expressing a certain bluff Englishness, full of boisterous good humour, common sense and a healthy dislike of foreigners – even when they come from no further afield than Norfolk. This view of Chaucer as a poet of Englishness is in the main a nineteenth-century invention (Pearsall 1999: 94–6; Collette 1989: 121–3). It depends on reading very much through the distorting lens of nineteenth-century nationalism. Discarding this reveals a very different Chaucer. The distinguished medievalist Derek Pearsall says that the 'idealisation of Chaucer as the poet of Englishness has little or no basis in his poetry . . . Of national feeling or a sense of national identity – whether it has to do with ideas of national or racial history, with England as a land, with ideas of national character, or with opposition to some hostile national other – I find little or nothing in Chaucer... [T]here is no English poet who is *less* interested in England as a nation' (1999: 86, 90, 99). Chaucer indeed saw himself as a Europeanist. His use of English was a self-conscious attempt to emulate the achievements of France and Italy in creating a literary culture in the vernacular. This was a distinctly European project whose aim was the creation of vernacular literatures as the common property of all the educated classes of Europe (Salter 1980: 79; Pearsall 1999: 93). Such literatures, based on common European literary models, were for cultural elites who shared a common humanistic outlook. They were not about or for 'the nation'. As Elizabeth Salter says, Chaucer's use of English is 'the triumph of internationalism' (1980: 79).

The complexities of nationhood in this period are interestingly revealed in an early attempt to annex Chaucer for a nationalist project in the early fifteenth century. Henry the Fifth is one of the iconic figures of English nationalism, especially as viewed through Shakespeare's presentation of him. The real Henry did indeed make a special effort to promote the English language. He encouraged the use of English in the Chancery, so that by the end of his reign English was the norm in Chancery documents. He set the poet John Lydgate to the translation of Guido delle Colonne's epic Latin poem, the *History of the Destruction of Troy*, on the grounds that there should be an English version of the greatest story of antiquity. The English ambassadors to the Council of Constance (1415) were instructed to use the English tongue (apparently as a strategic move to increase England's share of voting power at the Council). And Chaucer was acclaimed by several poets, including Lydgate, as the founder of the English language (Genet 1984; Fisher 1992; Patterson 1993; Pearsall 1999: 91–2).

But what was the context of this impressive promotion of the national language? Henry the Fifth was, like most of his predecessors, engaged in a war with the king of France, to whose throne he lay claim. Undoubtedly the stress on English was meant to integrate the very mixed groups that fought against France under the banner of St George. But more importantly Henry wished to ensure that the identity of the English nation, as expressed through its language, was symbolized and concentrated in his own person. The 'king's English' was to be taken literally. It was to be the language in and by which an individual showed his attachment to the monarch as a personal ruler. It was in no sense an expression of the nation, if by that we mean – as overwhelmingly became the case in the era of nationalism – the people. Henry the Fifth was neither appealing to nor attempting to create a sense of English nationalism, whatever Shakespeare may seem to suggest. He was seeking to bolster the sense of personal allegiance to himself as king, much like other medieval rulers (Genet 1984: 75; Patterson 1993: 84–7).

The outcome of Henry's campaigns reveal how wrong it would be to see Henry or other English rulers of the time as engaged in 'proto-nationalist' activity. Henry felt that there was a divine providence leading him to the throne of France, and events seemed to bear him out. After the great victory at Agincourt (1415) Henry went on to conquer the whole of Normandy. He forced the French king, Charles the Sixth, to recognize him as his heir, and he sealed his triumph by marriage to Charles's daughter, Catherine of Valois. Only his early death from dysentery stopped him from continuing the conquest of the kingdom that, like many of his predecessors, he regarded as rightfully his. He passed on this legacy to his successor, Henry the Sixth, who duly succeeded to the French throne, only to lose it along with most of England's French possessions in the closing stages of the Hundred Years War. But the tragedy of Henry the Sixth's reign should not make us forget how traditional his concerns were, nor the extent to which they reflected the continuing European ambitions of English kings (see, e.g., N. Davies 1999: 405–22). England in the fifteenth century remained part of dynastic Europe. English rulers wished to be more than simply kings of England; and while they might use national feeling to aid their designs, it would have made no sense to stress an exclusive English nationalism (see Genet 1984: 75–6).

The English case reinforces what have traditionally been given as reasons for the absence of nationalism in the Middle Ages (Kohn 1944: 78–115; Galbraith 1972: 46–7).[12] In premodern societies, elites and masses remained distinct entities, the former supranational, the latter sub-national. Dynastic politics, played out by actors who effectively belonged to a common European ruling class, inhibited the growth of national consciousness. Manorial and regional loyalties remained strong, making it difficult for most ordinary people to conceive of the nation, much less become attached to it. Latin and French continued to be the dominant languages for most expressions of learning and cultivated enjoyment among the educated classes; as late as 1516 Thomas More was still writing his *Utopia* in Latin, the language also of most of the works of Erasmus. The fifteenth-century Italian Renaissance, ramifying throughout Europe, intensified this internationalism not simply in learning and literature but also in painting, music and architecture.

Most importantly, there was the Catholic Church. The Church continued to make and, where it could, enforce its universal claims – claims recognized by most reformers up to and including Luther in his early years. As a matter of survival it was certainly capable of playing national politics, as in its struggles with the German Emperors and especially during the period of the Avignonese popes (1309–77) and the Great Schism (1378–1417) (Deansley 1954: 179–91; Southern 1970d: 156). But it never renounced its transnational and indeed transmundane mission. Whatever their differences with the papacy, no Christian thinker or statesman could have disagreed with the position as stated by St Thomas Aquinas: 'Though one distinguishes people according to diverse dioceses and states, it is obvious that as there is one Church there must also be one Christian people' (in Hertz 1944: 115; see also Coulton 1972). Medieval Europe was Christian Europe, the Europe of western Christendom. The Catholic Church stood for a unified Christian community. No European ruler denied this, English rulers least of all. Though Wyclif might tinker with the idea of a national church, English kings remained unimpressed. They supported the Roman Pope during the Great Schism, and Henry the Fifth worked for the restoration of papal power at the Council of Constance, subsequently establishing good relations with Pope Martin V. Later Lancastrian kings continued the policy of partnership with Rome. 'Between the healing of the Schism and Henry VIII's change of heart (1417–1534) nothing was further from the minds of English kings than any break with Rome; from Rome's point of view, they were the only reliably faithful sons among the rulers of Europe' (Elton 1992: 97).

Historians in recent years have appeared anxious to discover the stirrings of nationalism in whatever period they happened to specialize. There is evidently some kudos to be gained in this. Perhaps there is also the feeling that the further back in time a nation's identity can be traced, the stronger and more resilient that identity. Whatever the reasons, we need to resist the attempt to impose anachronistic readings on the past. As far as England is concerned, we can certainly see the signs of a growing sense of nationhood in the fourteenth and fifteenth centuries. This has to be distinguished not only from ideological nationalism, as the nineteenth century came to understand that, but also from a fully-fledged sense of the nation, the feeling shared by rulers and ruled alike of belonging to a common political community.

4

The first English empire?

Britain is now called England, thereby assuming the name of the victors.
> Aethelweard, *Chronicon*, 10th century (in Banton 1982:85)

This, the most noble of islands, 800 miles long and 200 broad, was first called Albion, then Britain and is now known as England.
> Henry of Huntington, 12th century (in Gillingham 1995: 52)

Crossing the deep sea, he [Henry the Second] visited Ireland with a fleet, and gloriously subdued it; Scotland also he vanquished, capturing its king, William...He remarkably extended the kingdom's limits and boundaries [until they reached] from the ocean on the south to the Orkney islands in the north. With his powerful grasp he included the whole island of Britain in one monarchy, even as it is enclosed by the sea.
> Gerard of Wales, 12th century (in R. R. Davies 1990: 78)

The English and others

The historian A. J. P. Taylor once argued that the unification of Germany in the nineteenth century was brought about not by nationalist forces but through a series of wars against other countries – Denmark, Austria, France. The substance of German unity and German national consciousness was not, as the liberals claimed, a deep sense of German culture but the deposit of wars and conflicts that forged a Germany confident of its strength and eager to expand its power. Prussia, which of all the German states had the least interest in German nationalism, was the agency through which Germany achieved this self-definition as a 'crusading' power, charged with the mission especially of civilizing the East (Taylor 1945: 114–5).

The perception that ethnic or national identity is more a matter of exclusion and opposition than of some more or less unchanging cultural 'essence' has become a commonplace of recent years. An influential formulation was that of

Frederick Barth's, with his insistence that it is 'the ethnic boundary that defines the group, not the cultural stuff that it encloses' (1969: 15). Such an approach, seeing ethnicity or nationhood as interactional or relational, the product of conflicts over boundaries and the work of 'boundary maintenance', has found favour with a large number of scholars (see Eriksen 1993: 37–58). As Richard Jenkins summarizes this view, 'the production and reproduction of difference *vis-à-vis* external others is what creates the image of similarity internally, *vis-à-vis* each other' (1997: 12). In a stimulating study of the growth of French and Spanish national identity, Peter Sahlins has drawn attention to the role of border communities in defining and establishing national identities through local struggles over jurisdictions and territorial boundaries.

In the French-Spanish borderland, it is this sense of difference – of "us" and "them" – which was so critical in defining an identity. Imagining oneself a member of a community or nation meant perceiving a significant difference between oneself and the other across the boundary. The proximity of the other across the French-Spanish boundary structured the appearance of national identity long before local society was assimilated to a dominant center.   (Sahlins 1989: 9; see also 270–4)

At the same time Sahlins points to the fluidity and flexibility of collective identities. Inhabitants of the Catalan community of the Cerdanya – shared between France and Spain – in the eastern Pyrenees were perfectly capable of recognizing and participating in a shared culture. Marriages and economic relations flowed across state boundaries; Cerdans could play the 'French' or the 'Spanish' card depending on their own interest. As John Armstrong has said, 'the boundary approach clearly implies that ethnicity is a bundle of shifting interactions rather than a nuclear component of social organization' (1982: 6). The content of ethnic or national identity can change from time to time depending on who is regarded as the other against which one defines oneself.

The Barthian approach to ethnicity can be complemented by the Freudian, which stresses opposition between familiars in the construction of identity. Here the key thing is the mixture of nearness and distance in the relationship. Freud spoke of the 'narcissism of minor differences', and remarked that 'it is precisely communities with adjoining territories, and related to each other in other ways as well, who are engaged in constant feuds and in ridiculing each other – like the Spaniards and Portuguese, for instance, the North Germans and South Germans, the English and the Scotch, and so on' (1963: 51). 'The near in blood, the nearer bloody', as Shakespeare says – an insight well appreciated by Ottoman sultans who preemptively put their brothers to the sword on acceding to the throne. How near the relationship has to be is clearly variable, stretching from near neighbours to distant communities linked by common rule. But clearly there has to be some awareness that the other is in some important respects like oneself, or else the comparison becomes meaningless as well as unnecessary. It is precisely this recognition of a common kinship between himself and the African cannibals he observes that leads Conrad's Marlow, in *The Heart of Darkness*, to shudder with horror.

Over the centuries the English have had a variety of neighbours, both near and far, with whom to compare themselves and against whom to assert their distinctness. Different groups at different times have provided, as foils, a striking array of self-images of the English whose only constant feature is English superiority. Thus in relation to the wild and lawless Irish the English have seen themselves as rational and restrained. As against the canny, tight-fisted Scots they are open and generous (even, in festive mood, a little 'Irish'). Confronted with the cunning and calculating Welsh they are plain-speaking and direct. Looking across the Channel to the priest-ridden and autocratically governed French, the English congratulated themselves on their freedom and tolerance. German pomposity and militarism were contrasted with English simplicity and individualism. Italian irregularity and irresponsibility could reflect back to the English their own prudent conduct and care for the future. With the peoples of the British Empire a new range of oppositions opened up, many of them employing the conventional contrast of 'civilized' and 'barbarian', but drawing also on the theme of the innocent and child-like native to whom the English could bring the benefits of their superior development and maturity.

There is, in other words, no 'Englishness' by itself. One can draw up elaborate lists of English characteristics, and it can be fun to do so. Moreover, as we noted in chapter 1, they can be instructive and revealing in all kinds of ways. But the very examples above show how inconsistent such self-portraits tend to be, how one-sided and misleading. They are baffling because they tell us nothing about how they are formed. They leave out of the picture the pressures that have given it shape and colour. In order to understand English identity at any time we need to consider the context in which it is defined. It is a context in which, among other things, the English encounter other peoples.

Geoffrey of Monmouth and the Britons

Chief among those other peoples are the 'Celtic' (not only, and not entirely) peoples of the British Isles. If a sense of Englishness was developing in England in the medieval and early modern period, it was not so much the result of internal developments in the direction of a common culture as of a common consciousness in relation to England's nearest neighbours (cf. Elton 1986: 73; Hilton 1989: 41; R. R. Davies 1995: 8; Collinson 1997: 38 n.14; Clanchy 1998: 180). Such a consciousness was slow to develop. It was not in the first instance a matter of popular feeling. Royal and dynastic ambitions led the way, as so often in the early development of national feeling in Europe. But by the sixteenth century England's intentions towards its neighbours stood starkly revealed. Their fate was to be part of Greater England. In recognition of this, English kings and their spokesmen appropriated the ancient name of Britain: a cruel irony, given that the destiny of the original British was for them to be obliterated and absorbed by the English invaders of their land. England got its identity by asserting its primacy, first in Britain, later in the world. By that time English ascendancy was sufficiently assured for England's global role to be played out under 'British' auspices. But before the turn to world empire, there was the matter of the 'internal' empire of Britain. English identity was originally made by a series of encounters, frequently brutal, with the neighbouring peoples of the two British islands. These encounters resulted in the near-complete dominance of the isles by the English, to the point where English and British became synonymous. But in the process the English too were changed. What was Englishness in the sixteenth century was not the same in the eighteenth century; it could even become 'Britishness', thereby revealing a changed sense of national identity, and a different conception of the relation between the English and others.

We have already noted the English imperialism implicit in Bede's formulation of the peculiar destiny of the English people. Anglo-Saxon kings also sometimes called themselves kings of Britain, though being hardly in command of England itself this was little more than wishful thinking. Another text, of the twelfth century, is more important because it was accompanied by decisive action on the part of English kings. This is Geoffrey of Monmouth's *Historia Regum Britanniae, History of the Kings of Britain* (*c.* 1136). This 'strange, uneven and yet extraordinarily influential book' (Thorpe 1966: 9) had a remarkable history.[1] Not only did it, through its tale of King Arthur and Merlin the magician, inspire a whole genre of European romantic literature, but it also, through such adaptations as the French *Roman de Brut* (1155) of Robert Wace and the English *Brut* (c. 1200) of Layamon, together with fourteenth- and fifteenth-century versions, popularized the whole idea of Britain and British history. 'It was this book', says Denys Hay, 'which, by diffusing the legendary history of Britain . . . did more than any other single influence to make men conscious of the term Britain' (1955–56: 57).

The irony was that this epic, the first and most influential, of *British* history, was appropriated by the English as their story, the history of their legendary exploits. The breathtaking nature of this substitution is evident from the barest recital of the matter of Geoffrey's *History*. Geoffrey, a twelfth-century Welsh monk, tells of the coming of the Britons to an island in the 'West Ocean' in the twelfth century BC, under the leadership of Brutus, great-grandson of the Trojan Aeneas. For nearly 2,000 years, under such kings as Leir, Cassivelaunus,

Cymbeline and Arthur, son of Utherpendragon, the British occupy 'the best of islands ... from sea to sea'. Though conquered by the Romans, they come to co-exist with them and to receive from them the inestimable benefits of Christianity (though the first Christian emperor of Rome, Constantine, is satisfyingly shown as having British origins). With Roman help they see off the attacks of Picts, Scots, Irish and Saxons. But with the withdrawal of the Roman legions even the valiant exploits of Arthur and his knights cannot save them from the increasingly ferocious invasions from the Continent. Eventually under their last king, Cadwallader, they are overwhelmed by the 'odious race' of Angles and Saxons in the seventh century AD. Geoffrey's *History* ends tragically with the British divided into two nations: one made up of the Britons who crossed back over the Channel and settled in the Armorican peninsula (Brittany); the other made up of 'a few little pockets of Britons who had stayed behind, living precariously in Wales, in the remote recesses of the woods. From that time on the power of the Britons came to an end in the islands, and the Angles began to reign' (Geoffrey of Monmouth 1966: 282). The Britons had to accept their fate, as just punishment for their sins. But the time will come when Merlin's prophecy will be fulfilled:

The mountains of Armorica shall erupt and Armorica itself shall be crowned with Brutus' diadem. Kambria shall be filled with joy and the Cornish oaks shall flourish. The island shall be called by the name of Brutus and the title given to it by the foreigners shall be done away with.   (Geoffrey of Monmouth 1966: 175)

Nothing could be plainer. This is a British epic in which the villains are the Saxons, the ancestors of the English. More particularly, it is the tragic story of the Welsh, for Geoffrey disclaims any intention of telling the story of the Picts, Scots or Irish (1966: 123–4). 'As the foreign elements around them became more and more powerful, they were given the name of Welsh [*Gualenses*] instead of Britons: this word deriving either from their leader Gualo, or from their Queen Galaes, or else from their being so barbarous'. The Welsh are a pathetic remnant, 'degenerated from the noble state enjoyed by the Britons' (1966: 284). But as Britons they have had a glorious history. Under Arthur they ruled all of Europe. Geoffrey's purpose is to rescue the British /Welsh from the oblivion into which their history has fallen, and to counter the growing tendency among the learned Anglo-French world of the twelfth century 'to write off the Britons as barbarians, as brutish creatures without a history' (Gillingham 1990–91: 110; cf. Leckie 1981; R. R. Davies 2000: 40).

But how was it then that 'the English appropriated to themselves the heroic exploits of a British race whose Welsh descendants they were rather less inclined to honour'? How was it that Geoffrey's 'British History – or Brut tradition, as it was also known – came to form the basis of an English national epos which, continued, expanded and elaborated by a host of medieval chroniclers, helped to underwrite – however paradoxically – the continuity of English experience and the antiquity of English kingship' (Mason 1987b: 61)? Scholars are unclear about the precise mechanisms, just as they are about Geoffrey's intentions (see Gillingham 1990–91: 100–4); but certain pointers are persuasive. Firstly, as William Leckie (1981: 104–7) shows, twelfth-century Anglo-Norman historians enthusiastically acclaimed Geoffrey's *History* but interpreted it not, as he intended, as a rehabilitation of the British contribution to the island's history but as the justification of the passing of dominion from the Britons to the Saxons (see also Johnson 1995b: 129; R. R. Davies 1995: 6; 2000: 41–9). The Welsh are clearly described as 'barbarous' at the close of the *History*, while their inveterate enemies the Saxons by contrast are seen as restoring just that peace and prosperity that the Britons had originally brought to the island: 'The Saxons . . . behaved more wisely. They kept peace and concord among themselves, they cultivated the fields, and they rebuilt the cities and castles' (Geoffrey of Monmouth 1966: 284).

Twelfth-century historians therefore partly interpreted Geoffrey's enterprise in the spirit of the Norman–English reconciliation that they were attempting in their own works. But the more important thing was the interpretation of the Norman kings and their followers as the rightful legatees of the rule over the whole island enjoyed by the ancient Britons. Geoffrey's *History* could be read as 'the legitimation of serial invasion and conquest' (Pearsall 1999: 89) – first the Britons, then the Saxons, then the Normans. The Britons' enemies after all were the Saxons, not the Normans. The new Norman rulers, having defeated the Saxons, could see themselves as the avengers and legitimate successors of the Britons, and thereby entitled to rule the whole of Britain 'from sea to sea', as had the Britons. Geoffrey's patrons were members of the Anglo-Norman elite, and it would be surprising if he had not wished to please them in some way. He dedicated his *History* to Robert, earl of Gloucester, the natural son of Henry the First, and explicitly asks his patron to consider the work as his own, 'as the work of one descended from Henry, the famous King of the English'. Robert, with his wit, wisdom, learning and 'innate talent in military affairs', effectively becomes co-author. His military talents in particular complement, as it were, this intellectual product, with the result that now 'our island of Britain hails you with heartfelt affection, as if it had been granted a second Henry' (Geoffrey of Monmouth 1966: 51–2). It would be difficult to imagine a plainer indication that, as Geoffrey sees it, the torch of British rule is being passed on to the Norman kings (Thorpe 1966: 10; Frame 1995a: 8; Clanchy 1998: 12).

But perhaps the most important thing was simply that Geoffrey had presented a portrait of a united Britain, a Great or Greater Britain unified by great kings such as Arthur and inhabited by a single people, the Britons. The destiny of

Britain seemed plain; whether under Saxons or Normans, its future was to be once more a united kingdom. Since the English were by the twelfth century already the superior power in the island, it seemed natural for them to argue that they should take the lead in this task (R. R. Davies 2000: 35–53).

At any rate, for whatever reasons and by whatever route, the facts are clear enough. By the late twelfth century, and increasingly throughout the later centuries down to the sixteenth and beyond, Geoffrey of Monmouth's *History of the Kings of Britain* is being used to justify English claims to rule over the whole of Britain. In some adaptations, Arthur – king of all Britain – can appear as an English king and the Britons as English (with, in one version, the Saxons being cast as Saracens) (Turville-Petre 1996: 76–89, 125–7; Gillingham 1990–91:103 n.23); in others, the hint – it is only that – in Geoffrey's *History* that the English king has precedence over those of the other British domains is magnified to far-reaching claims for English suzerainty (Ullman 1965: 258–63; Mason 1987b: 62). The most celebrated use of Geoffrey's book was that of Edward the First in making his claim to English overlordship of Wales, Scotland and Ireland. In 1301, in pressing his claims to Scotland, Edward declared on the authority of Geoffrey's *History* that just as Locrinus (the eldest son of Brutus, to whom Brutus had bequeathed Loegria-England), was supreme over his brothers (who had received Kambria-Wales and Albany-Scotland), so the English ought to be supreme over all British peoples (the Scots countered by declaring that the threefold division of Britain between Brutus's three sons justified Scottish independence).[2] English kings thereafter regularly invoked the Brut legend in their arguments for English hegemony over Britain, especially in relation to the Scots (Mason 1987b: 62–3).[3]

Celts and English

But, just as with Bede, books are not enough. If Bede's *History* needed Alfred to give it substance, so Geoffrey's *History* might not have had the influence it did had it not been accompanied by massive action on the part of English kings. English kings needed historical justification for their enterprises, and Geoffrey's account was of critical importance in this. But equally important was English determination to make their claims a reality by decisive action. Between the twelfth and sixteenth centuries English kings engaged in a wide-ranging and largely successful effort to bring the whole island of Britain under English rule, or at least English influence. The English also crossed the sea to the adjoining island of Ireland and laid the basis of incorporation there also. The British Isles were being thoroughly Englished. The process was formally completed by the acts of union with Scotland in 1707 and with Ireland in 1801, but well before those dates English influence and power were evident in every part of the isles.

Not surprisingly, this had an important effect on the way the English conceived themselves, their sense of national identity and national destiny.

Rees Davies has emphasized that English claims to British supremacy were long-standing, and that 'the historical mythology of English overlordship of the British Isles...had an almost immemorial resonance to it' (R. R. Davies 1990: 4). These claims go back at least to the Wessex dynasty, and so pre-date the Norman Conquest. But there is no doubt that a new and decisive phase of the story of England in Britain began with the coming of the Normans, and especially with the Anglo-Norman expansion of the twelfth century. The Normans did not simply conquer England. They went on to conquer Wales and Ireland as well, and if, as English kings, they did not quite succeed in Scotland, they can surely be said to have ensured that Scotland would never again be free of English influence.[4]

We need first to consider briefly how things stood in the non-English parts of the isles before the encounters with the English. I begin with the Welsh, who were the first to feel the force of English expansion and who ended up more completely absorbed by the English than any of the other Celtic groups. The fate of the Welsh can seem especially tragic. The residues of the original inhabitants of Britain, the people who could claim to be the most truly British, they found themselves dispersed into separate communities (Welsh, Cornish, Breton), driven into a small corner of the island and fighting an increasingly losing battle for survival. Even their name, as Geoffrey of Monmouth pointed out, was an insult. The Welsh themselves struggled to maintain the name of Britons, or alternatively *Cymru* or *Cymry*, a word that meant 'people of the same region' and could be applied equally to the land; Gerald of Wales preferred to use the name of their legendary kingdom, Kambria, founded by Brutus's son Kamber. But to the English, and increasingly to themselves, they were Welsh and their country was Wales (*Wallia*): both demeaning words derived from a generic German word for anything foreign – *Wealh* in its Anglo-Saxon form (R. R. Davies 1987: 19; 1995: 8, 18; Smyth 1998b: 28). Thus in their very name the Welsh accepted that they were someone else's creature, living on the sufferance of a foreign power – 'aliens in their own land', Gwyn Williams calls them. In the passage from 'Britons' to 'Welsh' a new reality was born. '*Britain* continues to govern the imagination of the Welsh but is banished from their reality. The realities of fewness and fragility have their own logic. *Wales*, as a political entity, comes into existence as a junior partner in a *Britain* run by England' (G. Williams 1985: 41, 58).

Up to a point they had only themselves to blame for this condition. Despite a well-defined ethnic and territorial identity, they were incapable of achieving political unity (R. R. Davies 1987: 3–20, 461–2; Frame 1995a: 9). There were certainly attempts at establishing a united kingdom of Wales, the last and most important coming in the mid-thirteenth century when by the agreement of the Welsh barons Llywelyn ap Gruffudd assumed the title of prince of Wales, *princeps Wallie* (1258), and had it confirmed by treaty with the English in 1267, thus becoming the first Prince of Wales to be 'legal' in English eyes (R. R. Davies 1987: 308–15; G. Williams 1985: 83). But that triumph was as short lived as previous efforts at unification. Welsh magnates and princelings were unwilling to accept the overall authority of any one of their own for very long. Hence they found themselves helpless in the face of superior English power.

Ireland's situation was only a little less precarious. Here too, Irish kings had tried to achieve Irish unity but with little success. Ireland remained fundamentally a series of small kingdoms – Ulaid, Connacht, Leinster, Meath, Munster – ruled by leaders who occasionally tried to assert their rule over the whole island by claiming the title of 'high king'. This was a title traditionally associated with the early medieval (fifth to sixth centuries) rule of the Uí Néill royal family from their base in Tara, a site (in Meath) which acquired legendary status in Irish history (N. Davies 1999: 180). Increasingly in later centuries such rule came to depend on control of Dublin. In the tenth century Brian Boru of Munster succeeded in conquering much of Ireland and briefly enjoyed the position of high king. He was defeated in 1014 by the usual combination of insiders (other Irish) and outsiders, the outsiders being in this case the Vikings. The most sustained efforts at unity were made by twelfth-century kings such as Turloch O Connor of Connacht and Muirchertach O Mac Lochlainn of Cenél Eógain, who were able to maintain their positions as high kings for some decades. But, as with the Welsh, such overlordships were generally shortlived and transient, undermined by outside intervention and by internecine struggles among the Irish kings (Frame 1995a: 8–9, 108–12; R. R. Davies 1995: 19–20). The Irish, who had never been conquered by the Romans, and who in the early middle ages developed a flourishing artistic and religious culture that was one of the brightest in Europe, through their own political weakness were unable to withstand the power of the English when conquest began in earnest in the late twelfth century.

Ireland, separated by the sea, and Wales, separated by the great eight-century earthwork, Offa's Dyke, had clear-cut boundaries with England. They helped to shape Irish and Welsh identities, even though they were no barriers to English expansion. Wales and Ireland were at least geographical expressions. The same could not be said of Scotland. Its borders with England were not finally settled until the thirteenth century. More to the point, it contained such a diversity of ethnicities and territories as to make any definition of Scottishness problematic for centuries. Scotland was indeed 'one of the strangest conglomerates anywhere in Europe' (Kiernan 1993: 3; cf. Grant 1994: 76; Broun 1994: 37; Frame

1995a: 10; R. R. Davies 1995: 14–15). Four contrasting and conflicting groups –
Picts, Irish, British and English (Angles) – struggled for supremacy. Later
Viking invaders and Norman settlers added further elements to the cauldron.
Eventually the Irish – the *Scotti* – were to give their name to the kingdom, but
in the process their own character was radically changed, and their legacy was
ambiguous in the extreme.

It is easiest, in a very complicated story, to follow the fortunes of the Irish,
since they were the eventual victors. Sometime in the first half of the first
millennium, from their base in Dál Riata in north-eastern Ireland the Irish
people known as the Scots set up a parallel kingdom of Dalriada on the north-
western coast of Caledonia, in the area corresponding to the modern Argyll
('the Eastern Irish'). There they came into contact and conflict with the Picts,
another Celtic people (probably) about whom little is known except that they
were brave fighters who had held off the Romans and who, as the rulers of
most of the territory north of the Forth, did not readily concede their lands
to the Scottish immigrants. Conflict, accompanied by a considerable degree
of mixing, between the two groups took place for several centuries, with the
Picts occasionally regaining control of Argyll (it was from a Pictish king that
in the sixth century the Irish monk St Columba received the island of Iona and
from there began the evangelization of the Picts). Eventually a Dalradian king,
Kenneth Mac Alpin, with assistance from the Vikings, defeated the Picts in 839
and forcibly and finally united the two kingdoms.

His actions were to have a lasting effect. It is Mac Alpin who, as if to emphasize the permanence of his intentions, is said to have brought the 'Stone of
Destiny' from his western homeland, Kintyre, and installed it for his inaugura-
tion in the abbey at Scone, near Perth. The symbolism of this was that Scone
became the ceremonial centre of the Pictish monarchy. Placing the Stone there
marked the decisive passage of power from the Picts to the Scots. Thenceforth
all Scottish kings were inaugurated in Scone Abbey (though the Stone itself was
removed and taken to Westminster by Edward the First in 1296). It was from
that time too that the joint kingdom began to call itself *Scotia*, Scotland. The
Pictish language, and the Picts as a distinctive people, gradually disappeared, as
Picts intermingled with the Scots; Scots-speaking Irish (Gaelic) now ruled all
the territory north of the Forth (Mackie 1978: 16–19; W. Davies 1984: 65–70;
Duncan 1984: 131–6; Broun 1994: 39–48; N. Davies 1999: 182–92).

The Scots then had to deal with the Britons of Strathclyde, the British
kingdom in south-west Scotland that at its height included Cumbria down to
the Wesh border. The Britons shared power with the Scots and Picts in the early
medieval period and at times, as in the seventh century during the reign of Owen
Map Bili, achieved dominance over them. Thereafter their power declined, diminished by the Scots to the north and the Angles to the south. In the eight

century the advance of the Northumbrian Angles drove a wedge between what now became the purely northern British kingdom of Strathclyde and the southern British region of Cumbria. In the next century the Britons of Strathclyde succumbed to the Scots. In a confused situation the Scottish king, Donald II (r. 889–900), expelled Eochaid, the last British king of Strathclyde, and banished the British aristocracy, who sought refuge in north Wales. Scottish kings installed themselves in Strathclyde. Donald II was the first Scot to be called 'King of Scotland', thereby asserting Scottish rule over a wide territory both north and south of the Firth of Forth.

Scottish involvement with the Germanic Angles was more complicated and more consequential. The Anglian kingdom of Northumbria, though not always united, at its height stretched all the way from the Humber to the Forth. In the early centuries Northumbria was dominated by two rival dynasties, one based in the more northerly kingdom of Bernicia with its capital at Bamburgh, the other in the kingdom of Deira with its capital at Eboracum (York). By the eight century the Bernician dynasty was in charge of the whole kingdom. They defeated the British tribal kingdoms of Rheged and Gododdin in the south-eastern lowlands of Caledonia, and in the 630s Edwin, king of Northumbria, occupied the capital of the Gododdin, Dunedin (later Edinburgh – though not, it appears, named after Edwin as is sometimes thought). Northumbrian advance north of the Forth was checked in 685 by a crushing defeat at Dunnichen (Nechtansmere) at the hands of the Picts. Anglians never again advanced beyond the Forth. One consequence was a permanent dividing line in the future Scotland between the 'Lowlands' – the land south of the Forth, Germanic in language and culture – and the 'Highlands', the lands north of the Forth which, as the territory of the Scots, was Gaelic-speaking and Celtic in culture (Mackie 1978: 20–21; N. Davies 1999: 184–89).

The Scottish attempt to advance south of the Forth was strongly resisted by the English, in the guise now of an expansive Wessex monarchy, but, helped by the Danish and Viking invasions, the Scots eventually prevailed. In 945 the English king, Edmund, recognized Scottish rule in Strathclyde and ceded Cumbria to the Scottish king, Malcolm the First, in return for a promise of aid against the Vikings. In 960 the Anglian stronghold of Edinburgh fell to the Scots. The disasters of the reign of Aethelred the Unready (978–1016), with England yielding to the Danes, provided a further opportunity for Scottish gains. Malcolm the Second advanced into Bernicia, defeated the English at Carham in 1018, and carried the Scottish border to the Tweed. He was halted there by Cnut and his Danish army in 1027. The Scottish kingdom remained plagued by feuds (the Shakespearean Duncan – Macbeth – Malcolm episode, typical of the times, was still to come), and English pressure was far from over. Scottish domains now included Lothian – the region between the Tweed and the Forth that was formerly part of Northumbria – whose English inhabitants possessed a language and culture very different from their Celtic rulers. But Malcolm the Second could claim descent from the single royal family whose branches had ruled Scotland since the late ninth century (when the Scottish kings succeeded to the ancient British throne of Strathclyde). He had established and shakily united a Scottish kingdom whose limits (with the exception of Viking possessions in the north and west) were now those of modern Scotland (Mackie 1978: 30–1; Duncan 1984: 136–9).

Of the three Celtic peoples of the British Isles, only the Scots managed to create a strong and united kingdom (R. R. Davies 1995: 20). They were therefore the only people able to resist for a time the relentless advance of the English over the whole area. Even this conceals a more complicated story. But the further account of the forming of the Scottish nation, as of the fates of Wales and Ireland, is best given from an English angle.

Conquest and colonization: Wales

The stories of Wales and Ireland are relatively simple to tell: they are tales of conquest and colonization by the English. 'By 1415 Wales had been conquered, finally and irreversibly' (R. R. Davies 1987: 461). The Welsh, as the descendants of the ancient Britons, always seemed to bring out a peculiar degree of animosity in the English. In Bede's *Ecclesiastical History of the English People* the Irish and the Picts are seen as knowing their place, and keeping to it, in the rightful pattern of peoples of Britain. They live in peaceful co-existence with the English. The Britons (i.e., the Welsh) however 'have a natural hatred for the English'. They are sinful and rebellious, and so 'are opposed by the power of God and man alike, and are powerless to obtain what they want. For, although in part they are independent, they have been brought in part under subjection to the English' (Bede 1990: 324). By their very wickedness, in Bede's account, the British people 'served as a foil which made the identity of the English people it resisted stand out in high relief' (Cowdrey 1981: 507; see also Smyth 1998b: 31). The Britons deserve their chastisement at the hands of the English.

Bede as so often was prophetic. Anglo-Saxon pressure on the Britons was relentless, driving them back into the fastnesses of Wales and Cornwall. The Danish and Norwegian invasions of the ninth and tenth centuries threatened not just the Anglo-Saxons but, from Irish bases, the Britons of the west. Welsh kings were forced to seek the assistance of the English. At Wye in 927, Hywel Dda, high king of Wales, made formal submission to Athelstan, king of England. That act has been seen as marking the end of Welsh independence and the beginning of its incorporation in a Britain dominated by England (G. Williams

1985: 58). But more correctly perhaps it should be seen as the first step of the incorporation of Wales into England itself.

The Normans continued and completed what the Anglo-Saxons began. Within a few years of the Conquest Norman knights were ravaging the borders of Wales and setting up Marcher lordships there that allowed them to control great swaths of eastern and southern Wales. In 1093 Rhys ap Tewdwr, 'the last king of Wales', was killed by Normans at Brecon. Norman settlers established themselves in the Marches, built great castles, imported their customs and their religion, Roman Christianity, and intermarried with the local Welsh aristocracy (one of the most famous chroniclers of the times, Gerald of Wales, was descended from Norman lords and a Welsh princess). The Welsh March became a new border within Wales itself, establishing virtually two cultures, two civilizations: the one in the uplands of the north and west, Welsh-speaking, parochial and economically backward, the other in the lowlands of the south and east, Anglo-Norman, increasingly English-speaking, open to European influences and economically dynamic (G. Williams 1985: 62–5; R. R. Davies 1987: 82–107; N. Davies 1999: 282–3). Even if Wales was to remain independent, it would do so as a nation divided by a massive fault-line – one, of course, clearly visible even today.

But it was not to remain independent. Gradually but inexorably, in the twelfth and thirteenth centuries, it was brought into submission to England. Henry the First (1068–1135) curbed the power of the Marcher lords, made Carmarthen a royal lordship, and imported Flemings into Dyfed, transforming the agrarian economy. But in the English Civil Wars after his death the Welsh and Marcher lords were able to regain a substantial degree of independence. Henry the Second (1133–89) mobilized a massive expedition whose aim, it was said at the time, was 'to destroy all Welshmen'. Failing in this endeavour, Henry settled for a peace in which the Welsh princes took an oath of fealty and homage to him. But much of the necessary work was done. Most of southern and eastern Wales – the old kingdom of Morgann-Gwent (replaced by Monmouth and Glamorgan), much of Powys and Dyfed-Deheubarth – passed permanently under Norman control. Only Gwynedd in the north, home of the old high kings, remained to carry the torch of Welsh independence.

Gwynedd held out for a considerable time, periodically rallying other Welsh lords to the cause. One of its princes, Llewellyn ap Gruffud, in 1267 forced the English king to acknowledge him as Prince of Wales. But this was during the English 'time of troubles' caused by Simon de Montfort and his followers (Llewellyn indeed married Montfort's daughter). Edward the First (r. 1272–1307), having as heir already defeated Montfort in 1265, on succeeding his embattled father Henry the Third in 1272 quickly moved to reverse English losses in Wales and to deliver the *coup de grâce* to Welsh hopes for independence. In two campaigns – 1276–67 and 1282–83 – he crushed Llewellyn ap Gruffudd and annexed his principality to the English crown. By the Statute of Rhuddlan (1284) English law and institutions were imposed on Wales, especially in 'Welsh Wales', the lands of Llwellyn's principality (the Marcher lordships generally retained their own law and administration). English-style shires were created in the north, and English common law and English courts introduced for criminal cases. English settlers were brought into chartered boroughs from which the Welsh were excluded. A ring of powerful new castles was erected at all strategic sites in the north – still today the most visible reminders of English dominance. In 1301 Edward had his eldest son pronounced prince of Wales. In what was to become a long-lasting tradition, the principality became an appanage of the heir to the English throne. Wales was to be considered in effect a testing-ground for the future king of England, a place to practice and learn the skills of royal rule (G. Williams 1985: 88–93; R. R. Davies 1974: 20–1; 1987: 355–76; N. Davies 1999: 369–71).

There was one last Welsh rally under Owain Glyn Dwr (Owen Glendower), who in 1400 claimed the title of prince of Wales and with the help of the French, and certain disaffected English lords, took Harlech and Aberystwyth and convened a Welsh parliament (1404–5) – the first and last in Welsh history. But the Lancastrian King Henry the Fourth recaptured the lost towns and once more, and finally, brought the Welsh into submission (though Owain himself escaped to become the stuff of Welsh legend and inspiration, a second Arthur) (G. Williams 1985: 106–12; R. R. Davies 1987: 443–56).

The coda to the story has its own piquancy. With the accession of Henry Tudor (born at Pembroke Castle and of Welsh descent) in 1485 as Henry the Seventh, it could be held that the tables had been turned. The Venetian envoy wrote to his government that 'the Welsh may now be said to have recovered their former independence, for the most wise and fortunate Henry VII is a Welshman...' Welsh writers, especially of the Elizabethan period (and ignoring Elizabeth's own avowal that she was 'mere English') enthused over the Tudors as one of their own; and the Tudors were not above responding in kind, making great play with the red dragon of Wales in their heraldry and pageantry, and drawing upon ancient British history in their struggle with Rome (Roberts 1972: 49–51; 1998: 14–16, 25–33; G. Williams 1985: 117; Kearney 1995: 153; N. Davies 1999: 445–6).

In fact the Tudors did little for Wales; far from it, they tightened the screws. When the break with Rome led the English state to feel it had to secure its realm more firmly, it responded by confirming royal rule in Wales with the backing of stronger parliamentary authority. The Acts of Union of 1536 and 1543 completed the 'anglicization' of Wales that had started with the Edwardian statute of 1284 and continued steadily thereafter. In particular, they abolished the Marcher lordships and extended to the whole of Wales the English shire system already established in North Wales. In effect the principality expanded to take in the whole country. The 'dual power' in Wales – Marcher lords in south and east, English kings in the northern principality – finally came to an end. The 'shiring of Wales' meant that, for the first time in its history, there was now a uniform pattern of administration throughout the whole principality: a pattern based on English common law and English justices of the peace. Parliamentary representation was accorded, one member for each county and one for each set of boroughs. Moreover, there was an effort to speed up the process of cultural integration and assimilation that had in any case gone a long way among the Welsh gentry. The Welsh were included in the changes brought in by the Henrician Reformation, thus becoming officially Protestant and Anglican. The Acts of 1536 and 1543 also enjoined that English was to be the sole language of administration and of the law courts, and that knowledge of English should be a prerequisite for office-holding. The 'sinister usages and customs' of Wales were all to disappear (Roberts 1972: 53–4, 60–1; G. Williams 1985: 119–20; R. R. Davies 1997: 15; Noonkester 1997: 264–5).[5]

The Tudor legislation was more in the nature of a tidying-up than a new departure. The integration of Wales with England had been going on apace since the eleventh century. Military conquest and political annexation had been accompanied by slower yet deeper changes at the social and economic levels. The growth of towns, many with English settlers; the extension of cultivated land at the expense of pasture; the rise of an anglicized Welsh gentry with extensive connections to England; the reform of the Church in Wales and a tightening of the control of Canterbury; even the very renaming of the Welsh so that most ended up with anglicized surnames – all pushed Wales closer to England and away from historic ties to Ireland and the western sea-ways of Britain. These changes preceded the Acts of Union and continued apace in the centuries beyond them. Only the Welsh language and Welsh literature – but this was to prove important in the future – remained to remind the Welsh of their distinctiveness as a people. In most other respects the Welsh had long ceased to be independent. When, at the Council of Constance in 1415, the French delegate raised the question of recognizing Wales as a 'separate nation' (*natio particularis*), the English spokesman confidently and in most respects accurately replied that 'the whole of Wales was peacefully obedient in spiritual matters to the archbishop of Canterbury and in temporal matters to his most serene majesty the king' (R. R. Davies 1987: 464; and generally 462–4; Kearney 1995: 126–7; Frame 1995b: 74).

Conquest and colonization: Ireland

The conquest and colonization of Ireland had nothing of the clear-cut quality of the Welsh case. Justified, as it was with Wales, by the idea that the people were backward and barbarous and needed civilizing (Gillingham 1993), it encountered greater resistance and for a time its success hung in the balance. Eventually the English were to prevail; but the society they created in Ireland was fundamentally divided and, unlike Wales, never fully integrated into the English system. Moreover, not only did the division between 'natives' and 'foreigners', fatally confirmed later by religious differences, last longer than in Wales, there was also the phenomenon of an Anglo-Norman aristocracy that showed repeated tendencies to 'go native' and oppose the English crown as Irish patriots.

Henry the Second's invasion of Ireland in 1171 – 'the English conquest', the event that changed Irish history for ever – was set in motion, as so often, by internal Irish struggles. Dermot Mac Murrough of Leinster had designs on the high kingship held by Rory O'Connor of Connacht. Driven out of Ireland by his enemies in 1166, he sought the help of the English king. With Henry's somewhat guarded encouragement he made his way to Pembroke where he enlisted the help of Richard de Clare, second earl of Pembroke, a military adventurer commonly known as 'Strongbow'. Strongbow, currently out of favour with Henry, was offered Dermot's daughter in marriage and the succession to the Leinster kingship in return for military assistance. Accompanied by a troop of Norman knights, Dermot crossed back over to Ireland and was restored to his kingdom in 1167. In 1170 Strongbow himself arrived in Ireland with a large force. He conquered Dublin and Waterford and, on Dermot's death in 1171, succeeded him as king of Leinster. Alarmed by these developments, Henry in 1171 decided to invade Ireland himself. To the Irish therefore, Dermot has always been the Vortigern of Irish history, the man who let in Ireland's enemies and brought about its ruin.

Henry forced the submission of most of the Irish kings and awarded the 'lordship of Ireland' to his son John in 1177. When, on succeeding his brother Richard in 1199, John became king of England, the lordship of Ireland was fused with the kingdom of England, there to remain until – in accordance with Henry the Second's original plan – it was declared a separate kingdom by Henry the Eighth in 1541 (the English king thereby becoming the head of two kingdoms) (N. Davies 1999: 340–6).

In the wake of the Anglo-Norman conquest of Ireland, Norman knights – 'the English' – poured into Ireland in the late twelfth and thirteenth centuries. They became large landowners, earls and dukes. They gave to Ireland a host of famous names: de Lacey, de Courcy, de Braose, de Barry; the ubiquitous 'Geraldines', earls of Kildare and Desmond and dukes of Leinster, who were descendants of Strongbow's ally Maurice fitzGerald; the fitzStephens, descendants of Maurice's half-brother, Robert fitzStephen. These families and their followers were those who came to be known as 'the Old English', to distinguish them from the 'New English' who came with the plantations of the early seventeenth century. This was to be a significant dividing line among 'the English in Ireland'. Not only did many of the Old English remain Catholic after the Reformation, but in the centuries before that they intermarried with the native Irish aristocracy, often adopted Irish ways, learned the Irish tongue, and in time came to see themselves as having an 'Irish' interest different from that of their English counterparts. The establishment of a separate Irish Parliament in Dublin in the early fourteenth century gave them a powerful weapon with which on occasion to oppose the English crown (Frame 1993: 100–1; Lydon 1995: 112–14). All this put the English in Ireland in a predicament characteristic of many colonial societies: foreigners to the natives, but at the same time distinct and different from their fellow-countrymen across the water. As it was famously put – according to Gerald of Wales – by Maurice fitzGerald in 1171 when he was besieged in Dublin, and doubtful of Henry's assistance, 'just as we are English to the Irish, so we are Irish to the English' (Gillingham 1993: 35; Hastings 1997: 80–1; cf. Frame 1977: 30–1).

The Reformation, and the coming of the New English, in the sixteenth century, added a new twist to the Irish story. Up to that time it seemed clear that, however much the newcomers adopted Irish ways, there were two peoples in Ireland, the English and the Irish (Frame 1993; Lydon 1995). Henry the Second had not been able to subdue the whole of Ireland. The English held most of the south-east, but in the north-west Irish families such as the O'Donnells and the O'Neills were able to retain much of their authority and to rule according to traditional 'brehon' Irish law. Repeated fighting at times restricted the English community to the Pale around Dublin. An attempt was made to fortify the English presence by emphasizing the distinction between the English and Irish communities, and to discourage the adoption of Irish ways by the English. By the Statutes of Kilkenny (1366) the English were prohibited from adopting a wide range of Irish customs and manners. The preamble to the statutes complained that 'many English . . . foresaking the English language, fashion, mode of riding, laws and usages, live and govern themselves according to the manners, fashion, and language of the Irish enemies; and have also made divers marriages and alliances between themselves and the Irish enemies aforesaid' (Lydon 1995: 106; see also Frame 1977: 28; 1993: 96; R. R. Davies 1997: 13). The difficulty of enforcing these statutes was shown by the marriage of the Leinster king, Art Mac Murrough, to an Anglo-Irish heiress. The confiscation of her inheritance for this act by the English government in 1391 led to Mac Murrough's rebellion, which the English were unable to put down until Mac Murrough's death in 1416 (Frame 1995a: 214–15). Such episodes were typical. The English were in Ireland; but Ireland was not English (Frame 1977: 18; 1981).

The Anglo-Norman conquest of Ireland, unlike that of Wales, remained incomplete at the end of the fifteenth century. Not only did Irish chiefs retain considerable power in the north, aided by Scottish kings who regarded Ireland as part of their legitimate sphere of influence. The Anglo-Norman magnates themselves established a high degree of autonomy, making themselves practically independent of the English king. Southern Ireland was dominated by the fitzGeralds of Desmond and Kildare and the Butlers of Ormond. Though never denying their feudal allegiance to the English king, they often saw themselves as an independent Anglo-Norman bloc with their own interests and outlook (Frame 1977; Kearney 1995: 131–6). This situation complicated the role of 'the Irish' as a foil to the English, as an element in the making of English national identity. For what if 'the Irish' included not just the native Irish but English settlers who had gone native?

Anglicization by stealth: the Scottish case

If conquest and colonization fit, as a first approximation, the fate of the Welsh and Irish, that of the Scottish presents at first glance a very different story. Here was a country that, despite formidable English pressure, was able through the agonizing 'Wars of Independence' (1296–1371) to resist English power and maintain its status as an independent kingdom. Scottish kings of the fourteenth and fifteenth centuries freely made treaties, often anti-English treaties, with foreign powers; their Church was acknowledged as independent by the Papacy (so that, for instance, in the Great Schism, they took different sides from the English); they had their own parliament, their own laws and law courts; their writers exploited the Brut legend to construct a national history more venerable, more ancient and more continuous than that of the English (Mason 1987b; Bruce and Yearley 1989).

But who were these Scottish kings who so flaunted their independence? What was the character of their laws and institutions? In what language did their writers tell the national story? The answer to all these is: fundamentally English, as long as we remember that 'English' from the eleventh to the fourteenth centuries included at the elevated levels of church and state French or Anglo-Norman culture. Scottish kings were Norman kings; Scottish laws and institutions were largely modelled on English ones; the language of the Scottish court, Scottish writers, and a good part of the Scottish nation was, when it was not French, a variety of English. England did not really need to conquer Scotland, though it tried. Its culture and institutions shaped Scottish evolution from an early date. Scotland may have appeared, in its own eyes, to have escaped the fate of the Welsh and the Irish. But it was an illusion. Scotland was as decisively anglicized as these others: more so, in fact, as the Scottish elite steadfastly refused to admit it and so the Scots did not create a strong counter-identity as developed among the Welsh and Irish in reaction to English rule (Frame 1995b: 70–4). The Scots, after all, had their own 'Celtic fringe' to deal with. What took place in Scotland therefore can best be described as assimilation by stealth. The Scots were not conquered by the English; they 'Englished' themselves. This did not stop both sides developing national stereotypes and using them as foils to each other. But it complicates the story of 'English imperialism'.

The Scots, as we saw, defeated and/or absorbed the Picts and Britons. They then expanded southwards in the tenth century to take in the former Northumbrian region of Lothian south of the Forth (Edinburgh was captured in 954). This was inhabited by Angles and Scandinavians, speaking a variety of the German language called 'Inglis' and later, with the advent of the Scots, 'Scottis' (a hybrid tongue, with a strong admixture of Scandinavian, described as 'a sort of Anglo-Danish Creole' by Ewart James (1998: 306)). The Scots took over not just the language but a good deal of the culture and customs of the Lothians, in a spectacular example of a conquered people 'taking its conquerors captive'. Let Arnold Toynbee, who gives the best description of the process, tell the story:

The culture of the conquered territory exercised such an attraction upon the Scottish kings that they made it the seat of their kingdom and came to feel and to behave as though Lothian were their ancestral homeland and as though their native Highlands were an outlying and alien part of their dominions. In consequence, by an historical paradox, the eastern seaboard of Scotland, from the northern shore of the Firth of Forth to the southern shore of the Moray Firth, was colonized, and "the Highland line" was pushed back steadily farther towards the north-west, by settlers of Anglian origin from Lothian under the auspices of rulers of Celtic origin and at the expense of a Celtic population who were the Scottish kings' original kinsmen and who had once conquered the Lowlanders under the leadership of these very kings' forefathers. By a consequential and not less paradoxical transference of nomenclature, "the Scottish language" came to mean the Teutonic dialect spoken in Lothian, the *ci-devant* march of the Anglian principality of Northumbria, instead of meaning the Gaelic dialect spoken by the original Scots who had first brought the Scottish name into Britain in a migration from the north-west corner of Ireland to Argyll during the post-Hellenic Völkerwanderung.

(Toynbee 1962b: 191; cf. R. R. Davies 1990: 13–14; N. Davies 1999: 301)

A rich paradox indeed, and one which was to be made even more remarkable by the activities of the Scottish kings from the eleventh century onwards. In what seems an almost precise parallel to the pattern of England's development, Anglicization in Scotland was followed by and mixed in with Normanization. Alternating between bouts of aggression and acts of subservience towards England – the basic pattern established by Malcom the Third Canmore (r. 1058–93), Macbeth's nemesis – the primary process was nevertheless one of the increasing influence of England on Scotland. A marked change in the significance of the pattern was brought about when, under Malcolm and Margaret's youngest son, David the First (r. 1124–53), Normans were invited to settle in Scotland and their influence became paramount at the Scottish court. Margaret, sister of the English pretender Edgar the Aetheling, apparently knew no Gaelic and had filled the Scottish court with her English friends. She was responsible for partly Anglicizing the Scottish monarchy. Her son David took it much more firmly in a Norman or Anglo-Norman direction.

David's elder sister had married Henry the First of England, in one of a series of carefully arranged dynastic marriages between Malcolm and Margaret's offspring and the English kings and their nobility. Henry had David, as 'David fitzMalcolm', brought up at the English court, and equipped him with a fully Anglo-Norman education, an Anglo-Norman earldom, and an Anglo-Norman wife (R. R. Davies 1990: 50). On succeeding to the Scottish throne David returned the compliment by embarking on a comprehensive Normanization of his court and country. Norman families such as those of de Brus, de Moreville and fitzAlan were given vast estates, and Normans were encouraged to settle in the country, spreading as far north as the Moray Firth. The Norman pattern of administration was adopted, with the establishment of royal burghs and sheriffdoms. So too was the Norman custom of the royal minting of coins, David being the first Scottish king to do so. The legal system was systematized on the basis of Anglo-Norman common law. Under David's enthusiastic patronage, monasteries of the new French Cistercian order spread throughout Scotland, their wealth and splendour best exemplified by Melrose Abbey. Norman French was the language of David's court, which under him and his successors, especially William the Lion (r. 1165–1214) and his wife Ermengarde de Beaumont-le-Maine, became the centre of a thriving continental Norman culture (Duncan 1975: 133–51, 174–81, 214–15; Barrow 1980: 117; Sellar 1988; R. R. Davies 1990: 6; 1996: 10; 1997: 7; 2000: 160–6; Kearney 1995: 80, 97–100; Frame 1995a: 26–9, 51).

Hence it was not at all surprising that the Scottish nobles should have turned to the English king, Edward the First, to resolve the succession dispute that had arisen on the death of Margaret 'Maid of Norway' in 1290 (Mackie 1978: 62–8; Frame 1995a: 160–5). Edward had indeed arranged the betrothal of Margaret Maid of Norway to his eldest son when she succeeded to the Scottish throne in 1286. Her death at the age of seven, after four nominal years as queen of Scots, precipitated the succession crisis in which the contenders for the Scottish throne accepted Edward's claim to overlordship of Scotland and agreed to abide by his arbitration. That subsequent events destroyed the harmony between England and Scotland, leading to the 'Wars of Independence', is undoubted. What has to be scrutinized is how far these can be seen as 'national' wars of independence, and what was the nature of the 'Scottishness' that supposedly triumphed in those wars.

For who were the main protagonists in the succession dispute, 'the Great Cause'? John Balliol, Edward's chosen candidate, who was king of Scotland from 1292 to 1296, was a descendant of Guido de Bailleul, a companion of William the Conqueror. The Balliols held lands in Normandy, England and Scotland. Their main English base was at Barnard Castle in County Durham. It was the marriage of John's father – John Balliol the First, founder of Balliol College, Oxford – to Dervorguilla, an heiress of Galloway and descendant of King David the First, that gave the Balliols a powerful Scottish base and a claim to the Scottish throne. Thus a Norman family with strong English connections – though, as it turned out, no lickspittles of the English king – became Scottish kings (Stringer 1994b: 34, 43–4; N. Davies 1999: 373).

The Bruces, main rivals of the Balliols, had equally impeccable Norman roots. Robert the Eight de Bruce, king of Scotland from 1306 to 1329, victor at the great battle of Bannockburn (1314) and legendary 'patriot king', was a descendant of the French baron Robert the First, sire de Bréaux and also a companion of William the Conqueror. The family's English seat was at Skelton in Cleveland. Robert the Second had been a friend of David the First at the English court, and was rewarded with the estate of Annandale in Dumfriesshire. So the Bruces established their Scottish base, and one of them married a descendant of David the First, thus establishing their claims to the Scottish crown. But they continued to maintain their English allegiance as well, fighting with Henry the Third at the battle of Lewes, and accompanying Edward the First on crusade. It was this service that led them to expect Edward's support in the succession dispute. Like John Balliol, therefore, Robert de Bruce 'was born into the heart of the Francogenic Anglo-Scottish aristocracy' (N. Davies 1999: 376; see also Frame 1995a: 165).

The Balliols and Bruces were typical of much of the Scottish aristocracy of the later middle ages. Starting often from bases in northern England, they acquired lands in Scotland and became active in Scottish politics. Such was the case not just of the Balliols but also of great families like those of Robert de Ros and Eustace de Vescy – English lords who married into the Scottish royal family – and Willima de Forz, who like John Balliol the First married a Galloway heiress, Christiana (in fact sister to Dervorguilla). Similarly, on their side, Scottish kings and Scottish landowners acquired holdings in the north of England. A dense network of cross-border landholdings, marriages and social ties developed in the Anglo-Scottish Borders, leading to a 'cross-Border society' in which national identification, Scottish or English, was low or blurred (Stringer 1994b: 42–50; 1995: 87–8; cf. Hay 1975: 83; Frame 1995a: 11, 58–60).

Hence, when the 'Wars of Independence' came in the 1290s they had the character more of a civil than of a national war in the Border region. And what was true of the Border region was true of the two countries as a whole. Both had aristocracies which were largely of Anglo-Norman character. Thus it can be said truly that 'what occurred in the years following 1294 was not a conflict between "England" and "Scotland"... but a struggle for power within the Norman ascendancy' (Kearney 1995: 101). 'The Bruce' and William Wallace – probably, by his name, a descendant of the Strathclyde Britons – might have become Scottish national heroes. The Declaration of Arbroath (1320) might sound to modern ears as a ringing declaration of Scottish national identity and Scottish nationalism (Grant 1994: 68–73; R. R. Davies 1994b: 130). But we need to remember what was the Scotland that fought for and gained its independence. It was one in which the English element was already dominant, in language, laws, religion and culture. Already by the fourteenth century the line was being drawn between the civilized, prosperous and English-speaking society of the Lowlands, and the backward, barbarous Gaelic-speaking society of the Highlands (Jones 1971: 158; Grant 1994: 76–7; R. R. Davies 1997: 8). Scotland's divided inheritance, which persists to this day, was in the process of being formed. But there was no doubt which was the dominant half.

'It is almost as if there are two Englands and one of them is called Scotland' (Campbell 1995a: 47). James Campbell's remark aptly sums up the paradox of Scotland's extraordinary evolution. A land of five peoples – Picts, Britons, Irish, English, Norse – each with their own language; the further addition of the Normans with their own language: all this gives way by the fourteenth century to a basically Anglicized country with a Celtic fringe. As Archibald Duncan says, Scotland's southward expansion and absorption of Anglo-Norman culture ensured that 'Britain was not to be two countries and cultures, one English England, the other Gaelic Scotland, divided at the Forth, but two English countries each with a dissident Celtic culture, the Gaels in Scotland, the Welsh under English rule' (1984: 136; cf.; Kiernan 1993: 5; Stringer 1995: 93; R. R. Davies 1997: 7–8). The English may not have formally defeated the Scots, and a new twist was to be added in 1603, when a Scottish king became king of England; but though Scotland may seem to have escaped the fate of the Welsh and the Irish, it did so only by capitulating the more completely to its southern neighbour (Aylmer 1990: 94; R. R. Davies 2000: 170–1). The more lasting conquests are those achieved without the conquered being aware of the fact.

The first English empire?

'A large part of medieval and modern "British" history can be seen as a process of conquest and forcible Anglicisation, extending of course to Ireland as well as Wales and Scotland.' So says Gerald Aylmer (1990: 94; cf. R. R. Davies 2000: 142–71), and it is impossible to deny the charge in general, though the degree of force in Scotland was always less than that in Wales or Ireland. What is more contentious however is the claim that such anglicization amounted to imperialism. The argument is that what was created by England in the middle ages was formally similar to the empire constructed by the English (and then British) overseas, from the seventeenth to the nineteenth centuries. The 'First British Empire', then, or 'First English Empire', is not so much, as is conventionally held, the eighteenth-century North Atlantic empire, as the empire created by the medieval Anglo-Norman kings, 'an English empire of the British Isles' that reached its apogee in the reign of Edward the First (1272–1307) (R. R. Davies 1994b: 128; see also 1990: 126–8; 2000: 4–30; cf. Elton 1992: 69–75; Kearney 1995: 116; Hastings 1997: 55). The conquest and colonization of Wales and Ireland, the attempted conquest and to good degree anglicization of Scotland, are seen as formally similar to the conquest and colonization of the overseas possessions in North America and the Caribbean, and later in India and the Far East. A stronger variant of this view would see in this 'first English empire' not simply a similarity to later expressions of empire but the very source of them. The English, it is claimed, learned and practised their imperialism first within their neighbouring territories, the 'Celtic fringe'; here was developed the appetite for empire that later found more extensive opportunity for its expression. Empire began at home (Hechter 1999: 75–6; Corrigan and Sayer 1985: 11, 15–16; Kearney 1995: 139; see also Armitage 2000: 6–7, 26–9).

The evidence for the imperial nature of the medieval English kingdom is indeed impressive. By 1400 English rule extended to the whole of Wales and more than half of Ireland, with native Irish lords in the remaining half repeatedly doing homage to English kings. Even Scotland in these years seemed destined to be brought under English rule, or at least to become an English dependency. Anglo-Norman writers, such as William of Malmesbury, William of Newburgh and Gerald of Wales, were already writing of the Welsh, Irish and Scots as rude, barbaric and backwards, thus beginning – some 400 years before it is conventional to date this attitude – the stereotyping and stigmatizing of the 'Celts' that was to become so long-standing an English posture (Jones, 1971; Gillingham 1992, 1993, 1995b; R. R. Davies 2000: 113–41).[6] English expansion could therefore take on the character of a 'civilizing mission' – a view encouraged and promulgated by such agencies as the Roman Church, whose pope, Adrian the Fourth, in 1155 issued the bull *Laudabiliter* to Henry the Second giving him permission to take possession of Ireland so that he could reform its 'rough and ignorant people' and extirpate their 'filthy abominations' and 'enormous vices' (Jones 1971: 167, 170; Frame 1995a: 36–7; R. R. Davies 1974: 19; 1990: 21–3, 111–15; 2000: 34, 114–19). What indeed could be more imperialist and 'triumphalist' than the behaviour of Edward the First, 'hammer of the Scots', conqueror of Wales and lord of Ireland?

He marked the end of the native principality of Wales by carrying off relics, which were ceremonially received in Westminster Abbey, and by impaling the head of Dafydd, the brother of Llewellyn ap Gruffydd who had been executed after a state trial in 1283, at the Tower. He built into the walls of Caernarfon castle bands of stone of contrasting colours in imitation of the walls of Constantinople and placed imperial eagles over the main gateway. He publicly stripped John Balliol of his kingship, and carried the Scottish regalia, royal records, and Stone of Destiny into England. When he died in 1307, the Gaelic *Annals of Connacht* described him as "king of England, Wales and Scotland, duke of Gascony and lord of Ireland".

(Frame 1995a: 142–3; cf. R. R. Davies 1988b: 11; 2000: 22–9)

Moreover politics, culture and society in the British Isles all carried a stamp typical of imperial systems, at least those of the kind later established by the British elsewhere. Wales and Ireland had the pattern of 'parallel societies' common in colonial societies: two peoples, settler and 'native', living side by side according to their own customs and governed by their own laws (R. R. Davies 1974: 12–13; 1994a: 17; 1996: 4; 2000: 145–50). Wales had its 'Welshries' and 'Englishries'; in Ireland the plea of the 'exception of Irishry' indicated the difference between the legal status of the native inhabitants and that of 'the English in Ireland'. This parallelism suggests a symmetry that is however as misleading as in other cases of empire. The English communities in Wales and Ireland were privileged. They had the best land and occupied the most important cities. Their language and culture were proclaimed as superior, and they had the means to demonstrate this. Their laws and their administrative systems overrode native ones, where these were allowed to persist. To be governed by their laws and to have the protection of their courts was indeed a privilege eagerly sought by many a native lord or city-dweller, who needed to obtain a certificate of 'denizenship' to enjoy the same rights as the English community (Jones 1971: 168–9; Frame 1993; 1995a: 179–87; Lydon 1995; R. R. Davies 1990: 116–17; 1993: 6–7; 2000: 161).

All this might well lead one to think of Wales and Ireland as 'colonies', and to consider the relation of the English to the Welsh and Irish as similar to that of the English to the native Americans of North America or the Indians and Africans of the nineteenth-century empire (G. Williams 1985: 89; Kearney 1989: 155; Kiernan 1993: 6–9; Gillingham 1993: 36–7; R. R. Davies 1974: 13; 1994b: 126). There is even a parallel, in the increasingly troublesome behaviour of the English community in Ireland, with other English settler communities in North America and Africa who came to resent the overbearing ways of the metropolitan power. There is a structural similarity in the position of all 'middle nations', such as the English in Ireland and Wales and the English colonies in North America, that leads to a characteristic alternation between passionate identification with the 'mother-country' and an equally powerful revulsion when they feel themselves ignored or mistreated (cf. R. R. Davies 1988b: 14; Frame 1995a: 197).

But the parallels must not be pushed too far. If there was a 'first English empire' in the middle ages – and there seems no reason to deny that – it had peculiarities that set it apart from later instances of empire. For one thing it was radically incomplete. Scotland may have been anglicized but it was never conquered; the terminology of colonialism seems 'wholly inappropriate' in its case (Stringer 1995: 92). Ireland remained for long a divided society, with important areas controlled by native chieftains; even when these were subdued, the Anglo-Irish lords often acted as if their possessions were owing to their private conquests rather than to royal grants (Frame 1977). Such was to an extent the situation even in Wales, the most completely conquered of the Celtic lands. Marcher lords up to the sixteenth century regarded their territories as their own private domains, ruled by laws and customs different from those of the rest of the principality. We tend to forget how much the conquest of Britain was the result of private initiative and *conquistador* ventures; in this respect Strongbow in Ireland was typical (R. R. Davies 1990: 68; 1993: 6).

The English conquest of Britain was slow, piecemeal, largely unplanned and often the result of local initiative and local invitation. It was Welsh, Irish and Scottish lords who in the first instance turned to England for assistance and support. That, in a familiar way, they usually got more than they bargained for is true but does not affect the main point. 'English power was extended within the British Isles as invitations were issued (by native rulers), opportunities seized and challenges met. There was little that was co-ordinated about what happened' (R. R. Davies 1994b: 123; see also 1990: 3, 47–8).

English kings – with the possible exception of Edward the First – were for most of the medieval period not interested in the conquest of the British Isles. Their sights were set on continental empires and crusading triumphs; they wished to emulate Charlemagne or Frederick Barbarossa, and at times they came close to doing so. Hence the slow and fragmentary character of the spread of English power in Britain and Ireland (R. R. Davies 1990: 67, 111; 1994b: 130–1; 2000: 12, 18, 192). The nature of medieval English rule, it has been suggested, was more of a composite than a unitary character, reflecting the unevenness of its spread, its dynastic quality and the existence of several political communities, such as those of Gascony and Ireland, with their own representative institutions (Frame 1993: 101; 1995a: 186–7, 222–4; 1995b: 77, 82). This approach, often applied as we shall see to a later period of British development, has much to commend it for the earlier period, and once more draws attention to the peculiar nature of the 'first English empire'.

There is no need to deny, in all this, that English national identity gained much of its definition and contours from the contrast with the 'barbarous Scots', the 'wild Irish' and 'the lazy and fatuous Welsh'. The allegedly brutish, treacherous, lawless and immoral Celt was a stereotype which for long provided the English with a reassuring self-image (Jones 1971: 171). Nor should we overdo the contrast with other systems of empire. The later British empire, J. R. Seeley famously said, was acquired 'in a fit of absence of mind' (1971: 12); and if that too is an overstatement, it rightly reminds us that many of the later European empires were, like the first English empire, also the result of haphazard growth and opportunistic seizures of the moment. The idea of England's 'internal' empire, and in general the thesis of 'internal colonialism', continue to offer illuminating parallels and insights, not least those that touch on the national identities of the various peoples of the British Isles (see, e.g., R. R. Davies 1996: 16; 1997: 16–18).

The reason for insisting nevertheless on the differences between the first and later English empires is that it helps us to make sense of one of the central problems of English national identity, namely the relation between Englishness and Britishness. If the 'internal' empire were so much like the 'external' empire, it would be difficult to explain how it became the basis for a common British enterprise in the creation of a truly British society and an unequivocally British, not English (overseas) empire. The fact is that, despite the real degree of English conquest and colonization during the middle ages, the peoples of the British Isles did not come to regard themselves in the long run as colonizers and colonized. The English, or at least their culture, may have ruled the roost; but the peoples of Wales, Scotland and Ireland came to play an active and at times predominant part in the development of what became an increasingly integrated *British* society. Partly because of the incomplete and long-drawn-out nature of English colonization, partly because English elites realized the necessity of incorporating other British groups in government and administration, British society became a blurred patchwork of ethnic groups in which the distinction between the dominant group and others became increasingly difficult to see (something similar happened in the Habsburg and Romanov empires). A British identity came to supervene on that of English, Scottish, Welsh and, to a degree, Irish. Such a superimposition did not efface other ethnic identities but it did come to qualify them in important ways. To the outside world especially the face that was turned towards it was increasingly not English but British.

Sir George Clark said that 'the history of the British Isles is not a mosaic but a painting in which the colours run into one another and overlap' (1971: 5). This is an apt image for the development of the British Isles, both in general terms and specifically in relation to the blurring of ethnic identities within what became the United Kingdom. The main part of that story must await a later chapter. What we must see though is how early the blending and overlap began. Subject populations began the slow march through English institutions that amounted to a virtual colonization in reverse. In Wales, in the wake of Glyn Dwr's rebellion and seizing the opportunities offered by the devastation of the Black Death, the Welsh squirearchy regrouped and began to take over rich lands in both north and south. Powerful Welsh families, such as the Herberts in the south-east and the Dynevors in the south-west, challenged and in many cases replaced the Marcher lords and took an active part in the Wars of the Roses. Welsh families also moved into previously restricted English towns, many of which were now depopulated by the plague. A dense network of trade with English regions produced an increasingly integrated economy. Welsh merchants invaded neighbouring English trading cities, such as Bristol, becoming part of the mercantile patriciate. 'Towns, manors, professions lost their English monopoly . . . By the end of the [fifteenth] century the bureaucracy of colonialism had been taken over by the colonized' (G. Williams 1985: 115; see also R. R. Davies 1987: 425–9; Grant 1995: 104). Nor did the enterprising Welsh restrict themselves to their native land. In a pattern that was to become familiar with other Celtic groups, they made their way to London, often rising high in the royal administration (Elton 1986: 75; Jenkins 1998: 232). The great house of the Cecils had Welsh origins (as Seisyllts), as did the branch of the Cromwell family (which changed its name from Williams) that produced Oliver Cromwell (G. Williams 1985: 121). Ultimately, of course, with the Tudors, descendants of Owain ap Maredudd ap Tudur, the Welsh took over the English throne itself.

So too, just over a century later, did the Scots, in the person of the Stuart king, James the Sixth and First, king of Scotland and England and energetic proselytizer of the 'British' idea. The Scots least fit the model of a colonized people. Despite renewed efforts by the English kings after Edward the First, the Scots managed to hang on to their independence and, with the English embroiled in the Wars of the Roses, give it a firm monarchical and aristocratic basis in the fifteenth and sixteenth centuries (Grant 1987, 1995). Admittedly this was a highly anglicized court and aristocracy; in that sense, the Scots could be said to be the most truly colonized of the Celtic societies – their own 'Celtic fringe' adding an exotic touch (Grant 1988; R. R. Davies 2000: 170). But the same could be said of the United States of America in the first century of its existence and, despite its undeniably 'English' character, no-one denies its independence. Scotland to a good extent went its own way, though never without an awareness of its powerful neighbour to the south. It developed its own political and religious institutions, its own national ideologies and its own historiographical traditions (Mason 1987b; Frame 1995a: 187–97; Ferguson 1998: 36–95). Though the main feature of all of these was to emphasize Scotland's difference from and independence of England, thereby conceding once more a dangerous dependence on England as a point of reference, they sufficiently laid the foundations of an autonomous political and cultural existence. 'By the sixteenth century there was even less chance than in 1296 that Scotland could be incorporated into an English state; when it did come to have the same monarch as England, it was as a *partner*, in a dynastic union' (Grant 1995: 107). Since, to a greater extent even than the Welsh, the Scots after the union poured into England and overran the administration of the new British state, there were not a few English to complain that it was the Scots who were taking over England, rather than the reverse.

Ireland comes the nearest to the colonial model, and indeed has been so regarded by many commentators. Most often this refers to Ireland's condition after the plantations of the sixteenth and early seventeenth centuries, the Cromwellian repression during the civil wars, and the defeat at the battle of the Boyne (1690) (see, e.g., Kiernan 1993: 9; Hadfield and Maley 1993: 1–15). But for many Ireland was decisively colonized at the time of the twelfth-century invasion. As the Irish historian J. A. Watt puts it, medieval Ireland

became a country to which Englishmen of all levels of society, save the very highest, emigrated and settled in large numbers, expropriating the lands and towns of the indigenous population, building a new society in the image of the one they had left. It was also a society which the home government retained and maintained as a dependency, exercising firm control over the policies and personnel of the overseas administration it had established and continued to develop. Thus medieval Ireland fulfils the strictest criteria semantics can impose on the word "colony" . . .'

(in Gillingham 1993: 37; see also, but with many qualifications, Frame 1981)

But even Ireland had its peculiarities, so far as its colonial status went. There was the role of the independent native Irish chieftains, who until Tudor times maintained strong connections with Scotland and who at various times could also link up with disaffected Anglo-Irish lords in opposing the English king. There was the fact that, after 1541, Ireland was a separate kingdom, under an English king, it is true, but with its own Parliament at Dublin. Above all, there was the Anglo-Irish community itself which, in the persons of such magnates as the Butlers of Ormond or the fitzGeralds of Kildare and Desmond, was at times almost a law unto itself. The Anglo-Irish lords were proud of their Englishness and looked down on the native Irish. But that did not stop them from asserting themselves against the English crown, in pursuit of their personal ambitions, nor in taking on a considerable measure of 'Gaelicization' in their manners and outlook (Frame 1977: 24–32). It took a fresh wave of colonization and harsh measures on the part of the English state to subdue Ireland. Then, indeed, from the eighteenth century onwards, its condition did resemble classic colonialism. But even then the persistence of the Anglo-Irish gentry, who at times carried the torch of Irish patriotism, and at the same time continued their social and marital mingling with the English gentry and aristocracy, prevented the emergence of a clear-cut distinction between metropolis and colony. Equally complicating was the existence after the seventeenth century of a powerful non-gentry Protestant sector in the north which looked to England to protect it against the Catholics of the south. All of these overlapping ties inhibited any attempt by the English state to treat Ireland as a simple colony.

Practically everything in the relations between England and its Celtic dependencies, and in the structure of those dependencies themselves, can be found somewhere or other, at some time or other, in the history of imperialism, including the later history of British imperialism. To question the concept of the 'first English empire' is not to deny the essentially imperial character of the British Isles as it emerged from the middle ages. But not all empires are the same. England's first imperial venture, by its contrast between the English and other peoples, and an enforced contact between them, certainly helped in the formation of an English national identity. But not only were several additional developments necessary before anything like a clear sense of English national identity – let alone English nationalism – could emerge. There were also features of the first English empire that actually delayed that outcome. Among these was the possibility for Englishness to be transmuted into, or at least overlaid by, something else. Englishness could become Britishness. But it would take a second, and even a third, empire to give that possibility full expression.

5

The English nation: parent of nationalism?

The birth of the English nation was not the birth of a nation; it was the birth of the nations, the birth of nationalism. England is where the process originated.
Liah Greenfeld (1992: 23)

FLUELLEN Captain MacMorris, I think, look you, under your correction, there is not many of your nation –
MACMORRIS Of my nation? What ish my nation? Ish a villain and a bastard and a knave and a rascal? What ish my nation?
Shakespeare, *Henry V*, Act 3 Scene 3

But here I am in Kent and Christendom.
Thomas Wyatt (1503–42) (in Hammond 1996: 25)

A sixteenth-century nationalism?

The rise of a school of British historians – James Campbell, Susan Reynolds, Patrick Wormald, John Gillingham, Rees Davies and others – proclaiming the existence of medieval English nationalism has been a lively feature of the contemporary scholarly scene. If their arguments do not convince – for reasons advanced in the preceding chapters – this is not to say that the challenge has not been stimulating. It has forced us to reconsider the meaning of nationalism. It has put in front of us a case that, were it to turn out as they present it, would be a remarkable example of precocity – yet another instance of that English tendency to go it alone. They raise again, that is, the whole question of 'nations before nationalism'; were their strong expressions of national feeling and a real sense of nationhood before the coming of the ideology of nationalism in the nineteenth century? It is a question that clearly will not go away. Nor of course is it simply a historical question. It has profound theoretical implications. If a sense of nationhood can be found flourishing in twelfth-century England – not to mention the time of Alfred the Great – then much of what we have

89

come to think about nationalism would require profound reconsideration. The hallowed association of nationalism with modernity and industrialism would certainly need fresh scrutiny. So too would the idea that it required a certain democratizing impulse – still best symbolized by the French Revolution – for nationalism to arise.

The medieval world was at once too cosmopolitan and too particular, too international and too local, to give rise to a strong sense of nationhood. That traditional view, associated with Hans Kohn (1944) and several other scholars of his generation, has been given powerful support by the work of recent sociologists and historians such as Ernest Gellner (1983) and Eric Hobsbawm (1992). It is the basis of the rejection, in the previous chapters, of the idea that anything like a real sense of English nationhood or English nationalism – the very word is anachronistic for any period before the nineteenth century – existed or could exist in the medieval period, from the seventh or eight to the fourteenth or fifteenth centuries. However strong and well defined the English *state* became, that is a different matter from arguing that a complementary sense of common *nationhood* also developed. The English – along with the dependent Welsh and Irish – could proclaim fervent allegiance to an English king (who might turn out to be Welsh or Scottish); they could, on occasion, display strong xenophobic feelings (of a kind to be found almost everywhere, at any time); some of their intellectuals could spin genealogical histories that demonstrated England's greatness and glorious destiny. That does not mean that the English people saw themselves as an 'imagined community' (Anderson 1991), as a horizontally integrated group of like-minded individuals occupying the same cultural and political space.

Did they do so in the sixteenth century? Did the century of Shakespeare and Spenser, of the Protestant Reformation and the Anglican Church, of deeds of derring-do by English heroes such as Drake and Raleigh, inaugurate English nationalism? That has been the claim of a number of scholars, though the basis for doing so varies considerably. Most generally there is the argument that England shared in a wave of sixteenth-century nationalism. This has been advanced especially by E. D. Marcu (1976). Not just England, says Marcu, but Spain, Portugal, Italy, France and Germany experienced an upsurge of nationalist feeling that, though 'dressed in . . . contemporary style' and expressed in 'contemporary vocabulary', differed 'in no essential way from any later kind' (Marcu 1976: 9, 87).

We shall come to England in a moment. But it will help the discussion if we dispose, however briefly, of some of the other examples. With Spain and Portugal, whatever national feeling we can discern is linked, in almost every case, to the idea of empire – in most cases, world empire. This is true, by

Marcu's own admission, of most of the major writers – such as Camões and Cervantes – that he considers. Camões in his epic poem *The Lusiads* (1572) mourns Portugal's decline in relation to Spain, for it is Portugal, not Spain, that was intended by destiny to 'make humanity forget Assyrians, Persians, Greeks and Romans'. Cervantes, a prisoner of the Moors in Algiers, calls upon the Spanish kings to liberate all Christians everywhere and to create a global Christian empire (Marcu 1976: 19, 26). None of this should be surprising. Portugal and Spain were the two leading imperial powers of the early modern period. Their ambitions, fuelled by the great voyages of discovery, were ecumenical. They wished to restore, on a grander scale, the Roman Empire in its Christian form. To see themselves simply in national terms, as Portuguese or Spanish, would have appeared grotesque and ignoble (Koenigsberger 1975: 169–72; Pagden 1995: 29–62).

Italy and Germany were alike, at once too little and two big to be nation-states. Both contained major international powers in their midst, in the former case the Papacy, in the latter the Holy Roman Empire. Neither Papacy nor empire, with their global ambitions, were or could be interested in nationalism ('Rome was not the center of Italy but of the world': Gilbert 1975: 22; cf. Kiernan 1965: 35). At the same time there were few other forces to create a sense of Italian or German unity. It is true that there were thinkers such as Machiavelli or Guicciardini who dreamed of expelling the foreigner from Italy. But the reality was that Italy was divided into distinct regions each more or less under the control of foreign powers, France or the Habsburgs. Even had the Italian princes wished to pursue a policy of unification – and there is scant evidence for such a desire – they were not free to do so. Italians were caught between the universal aspirations of the Papacy and the manoeuvrings of a fragmented and largely powerless polity: not surprisingly, the dominant form of political thought in this period was utopianism (Gilbert 1975: 31; Martines 1980: 322–31; Breuilly 1993: 3–5).

As for Germany, there was some cultivation in the sixteenth century of the idea of a common German culture based on Germany's tribal past (Krieger 1975: 79–82). But, if the Italian states were too weak to control their destiny, the German principalities and bishoprics were too independent and too self-interested for any kind of German unity to be seriously contemplated – a move that was in any case at odds with the thinking and policies of the empire. As with Italy, but in a different constellation, supranational force combined with political fragmentation to inhibit any real development of national consciousness.

What of France in the early modern period? Here is the country that, along with England, is usually taken as having achieved the highest degree of statehood by the sixteenth century. In parallel with this, it has become common to claim in the general literature on nationalism, the French also achieved nation-hood. Thus Joseph Llobera writes that 'there is little doubt that by the end of the medieval period the idea of France had found expression in a single state . . . and in a sense of national identity' (1994: 57–8; cf. Marcu 1976: 57–71).

But in what did this sense of national identity consist? Undoubtedly, by the consensus of all students of the period, in the identification of France with the monarchy (Church 1975: 43–4). Louis the Fourteenth's famous quip, *l'état, c'est moi*, expresses precisely and concisely this equation. For nation – or, as the writers of the period preferred it, *patrie* – read state, and for state read monarch. When French writers praised France, and traced its origins and growth to greatness, it was its kings that they celebrated. Kings are, said the jurist Jérôme Bignon in a dedicatory epistle to Henry the Fourth, the 'true creatures of heaven, the dearest children of god and the first-born of his Church . . . It is through you, Sire, that we live and enjoy our comforts. It is to you that we owe our peace, our liberty and our lives' (in Church 1975: 50–1). This is the authentic voice of royalism; this is the 'crown-centred patriotism' that was the *leitmotiv* of the period and that reached its apogee in the reign of Louis the Fourteenth (Church 1975: 55–6; cf. Kohn 1944: 187–95; Greenfeld 1992: 102–33).

But royalism or 'crown-centred patriotism' is not nationalism. That became clear in the early eighteenth century when French thinkers increasingly began to distinguish the French *nation* from the king-centred *state*. The disasters of the later years of Louis the Fourteenth's reign themselves precipitated this new awareness. There was a need to separate the French people from what was increasingly seen as a despotic and obscurantist monarchy (Church 1975: 60–5; Kohn 1944: 204–8; Greenfeld 1992: 154–72; Breuilly 1993: 88–90). Enlightenment thinkers set the stage for the discovery, in the course of the French Revolution, that the nation, not the state, was the embodiment of the French people, and that the only legitimate state was the 'nation-state' (Palmer 1940; Godechot 1971).

The absence of nationalism in the French case – often seen as paradigmatic – suggests that we treat all claims of sixteenth-century nationalism with caution. National sentiment, such as it was, had to contend with ideals and attractions of a vastly superior kind. As Orest Ranum writes, in introducing an incisive collection of studies dealing with this question:

Whether expressed by revolutionary Englishmen, *thèse-royaliste* Frenchmen, or Brunswickian Germans, the elements of national consciousness appear so overladen with religious and constitutional presuppositions and principles that it is difficult to assert that national consciousness held a primordial place in early-modern political cultures . . . [National consciousness] rarely if ever manifested itself overtly in an age still dominated by court politics, localism, and imperial-papal universalism . . . The persistence of local consciousness and the attractiveness of universal ideals of Christendom, even among those living in Protestant cultures, are indications of the boundaries of national consciousness.   (1975b: 12; cf. Anderson 1974: 38–9; Breuilly 1993: 75–6).

Was England an exception to this general sixteenth-century pattern (Hastings 1997: 119)? Did it run counter to the political culture of the age, not just to exhibit but actually to *invent* nationalism? This is the striking claim that has been made in recent years.

England: the first nation?

It used to be common, in an older historiography, to see nationalism rampant in sixteenth-century England. The Victorians, who are responsible for most of our myths, began the fashion. The suppression of 'over-mighty' subjects by the Tudors, the break with Rome, the thwarting of Popish plots at home and abroad culminating in the defeat of the Spanish Armada, the securing of the Protestant religion and the Protestant state: all these aroused the fervour of patriotic Victorians in an age of ascendant nationalism. Particularly strong was the adulation of Elizabeth the First, the Virgin Queen, mother only of her people, the first English monarch to give her name to an age. Elizabeth was seen as having created a uniquely strong and loving bond between crown and people, enabling – for the first time – the English nation from top to bottom to think and act alike. 'The greatness of the Queen', said J. R. Green in his influential *Short History of the English People*,

rests above all on her power over her people. We have had grander and nobler rulers, but none so popular as Elizabeth. The passion of love, of loyalty, of admiration which finds its most perfect expression in the "Faery Queen" [of Spenser], throbbed as intensely through the veins of her meanest subjects. To England, during her reign of half a century, she was a virgin and a Protestant Queen; and her immorality, her absolute want of religious enthusiasm, failed utterly to blur the brightness of the national ideal. Her worst acts broke fruitlessly against the general devotion.   (1893: 374)

While Green saw the bond between Queen and people as the essential national principle in Elizabethan England, the enthusiasm of John Anthony Froude was fired by the daring discoveries and overseas ventures of the Elizabethan mariners and explorers. It was in Froude, even more than in Seeley, that the identification of England with its overseas possessions and its imperial destiny found its most eloquent spokesman (Burrow 1983: 231–50; see also Armitage 2000: 100–01, 183–4). For Froude, Richard Hakluyt's sixteenth-century narratives of the explorers and voyagers of his time, *The Principal Navigations, Voyages and Discoveries of the English Nation* (1598–1600), were 'the Prose Epic of the modern English nation' (1876: 446). And they recounted the achievements not, as of old, of heroic kings and princes, but of 'the common people'.

[A]s it was in the days of the Apostles, when a few poor fishermen from an obscure lake in Palestine assumed, under the Divine mission, the spiritual authority over mankind, so, in the days of our own Elizabeth, the seamen from the banks of the Thames and the Avon, the Plym and the Dart, self-taught and self-directed, with no impulse but what was beating in their own royal hearts, went out across the unknown seas fighting, discovering, colonizing, and graved out the channels, paving them at last with their bones, through which the commerce and enterprise of England has flowed out over all the world.

(1876: 447)[1]

Froude forgives Elizabeth her 'despotism' because 'she was the people's sovereign', and because 'it was given to her to conduct the outgrowth of the national life through its crisis of change'. 'The work was not of her creation; the heart of the whole English nation was stirred to its depths; and Elizabeth's place was to recognize, to love, to foster, and to guide' (1876: 455–56).

Later historians, as we shall see, have taken a more critical view of Elizabeth, and a more cautious approach to the idea of sixteenth-century English nationalism. But the tradition has continued among some scholars – not to mention in popular presentation – of seeing the sixteenth century as the birth-time of the English nation, in essentially the form in which it has persisted to this day (see e.g. Rowse 1943: 54–60; 1957). Neville Williams, in his biography of Elizabeth, treats her reign as that 'during which the people of England attained a true national consciousness' (1972: 9; cf. Strong 2000: 174). Geoffrey Elton, having previously, as we have seen, discovered the English nation fully formed by the mid-fourteenth century (1992: 69), has to concede that the work was not yet quite done, that 'the English nation-state was by no means yet safely constructed'. It was the Tudors and their successors who supplied the final essential building blocks (1992: 112).

Sixteenth-century 'pride of nationhood', says Elton in another account, easily turned into popular chauvinism and contempt for other nations. 'Nevertheless a peculiarly fortified kind of selfawareness... pervaded the thoughts on national identity even among the more distinguished members of the nation' (1986: 75). What particularly forged this powerful sense of English nationhood was the combination of a monarchy, the Tudor monarchy, that deliberately sought to unite all the groups in the kingdom, and a parliament that, without seeking to set itself up as a rival to the crown, acted as a genuinely national forum for the expression and redress of grievances:

By making laws for the whole realm that demanded obedience from the whole realm, Parliament testified to the existence of a single nation, membership of which overrode sectional or local attachments. By making laws for sectional or local interests, Parliament directed these potentially separatist and disruptive concerns towards an instrument of government of which all members of the nation were deemed to be a part. And so that national self-consciousness of 16th-century Englishmen, loudly enough voiced in speech and writing, found practical entrenchment not only in the monarch and his glory but also in the Parliament and the laws it made for all.

(1986: 81–2; cf. Seton-Watson 1977: 7–8)

But it is an American sociologist, Liah Greenfeld, who has advanced the most radical claims concerning an alleged sixteenth-century English nationalism. The English of the sixteenth century, maintains Greenfeld, not only had but invented nationalism. 'The original modern idea of the nation emerged in sixteenth-century England, which was the first nation in the world (and the only one, with the possible exception of Holland, for about two hundred years) . . .' (1992: 14). When, in refusing to accept Henry the Eight's claim for supremacy in the English church, Sir Thomas More appealed to the idea of the unity of Christendom, he was thinking in 'pre-nationalist' terms that were already outdated, in England at least. He could not understand that for those who judged and condemned him, 'being Englishmen . . . was no longer incidental to their allegiances, as it was for him, but had become the very core of their being . . . By 1600, the existence in England of a national consciousness and identity, and as a result, of a new geo-political entity, a nation, was a fact' (1992: 30).

What is the evidence for such a view? Greenfeld first makes the bold claim that in sixteenth-century England 'the nation was perceived as a community of free and equal citizens' (1992: 30). Partly this follows, for her, from the supposedly changed meaning of 'empire' contained in the famous preamble to the 1533 Act in Restraint of Appeals, in which it is asserted that 'this realm of England is an empire . . . governed by one supreme head and king' (Elton 1960: 344). The king now claimed not just, as in the past, temporal, but in addition spiritual authority; 'empire' now meant full and untrammelled national sovereignty. 'The adoption of this novel meaning of "empire", as an independent polity . . . was of crucial importance in the evolution of the first nation' (Greenfeld 1992: 34; cf. also E. Jones 2000: 33–4). Greenfeld sees shifts in the meaning of other key terms, such as 'country', 'commonwealth' and 'nation'. Together with 'empire', all came in the sixteenth century to be synonyms for 'the sovereign people of England'. National sovereignty came to be understood not simply as the sovereign power of the king but increasingly as that of the people (1992: 31–5).

Underlying this shift to the idea of the sovereign people Greenfeld discerns massive social changes. There was unprecedented social mobility. The old nobility, 'the over-mighty subjects' of the later middle ages, was extinguished by the Tudors, substantially by 1540. In its place stepped a 'new aristocracy' recruited from 'people of modest birth but remarkable talents', an aristocracy 'open to talent'. The 'idea of the nation – the people as an elite' – appealed to the new aristocracy. It legitimated their position as a service aristocracy, an aristocracy not of birth but of talent and education dedicated to the common good of the community. 'In a way, nationality made every Englishman a nobleman...' Thus was created the crucial bridge from the old idea of England as a royal patrimony to the idea of England as a 'commonwealth' (Greenfeld 1992: 47).

The change in character and consciousness at the top of English society was accompanied, argues Greenfeld, by corresponding movements at the middle and lower levels. Enclosure of the commons and the sale of monastic lands following the dissolution of the monasteries gave ample opportunity for the lesser gentry and more prosperous yeomen to increase their holdings and evolve into a solid squirearchy. Here was a new middle class, wealthy and increasingly well educated, mingling in the universities and Inns of Court with younger members of the aristocracy, themselves now expected to be educated for state service. 'Upper status categories became very broad, binding together people from what previously would have been very different walks of life.' The openness of the social structure once more encouraged the idea of a unified people sharing a common purpose. 'The idea of the nation appealed to the constantly growing middle class, no less than it did to the new aristocracy. It justified the de facto equality between the two in many areas.' The gentry joined the younger sons of the nobility in the House of Commons, and both began to demand a greater share of power for Parliament as the embodiment of the nation. 'The power of the Parliament and national consciousness thus fed on each other, and in the process both grew stronger' (1992: 49–50).

All this mobility and merging gave a dynamic, democratic impulse to English society as a whole. 'The commitment to the idea of the nation on the part of the most active and articulate segment of the English population signified a profound change in political culture' (Greenfeld 1992: 31). Greenfeld argues for a rise both in the notion of individual human rights and in the concept of citizenship as the political expression of those rights. Nation, people and Parliament came to be linked in a single discourse of citizenship (1992: 44–5, 420, 426). More than that, the stress on individuality, 'a commitment to one's own and other people's human rights', meant that in the English case 'love of nation' implied 'the exaltation of oneself as a human being – a free, rational individual – and therefore the exaltation of human dignity, humanity in general' (Greenfeld 1992: 31; see also 487).

One might overlook this embarrassing display of Anglophilia as an exaggerated expression of Greenfeld's zeal to promote the Anglo-Saxon concept of civic nationhood – a concept she sees as ultimately more fully realized 'by Englishmen on the other side of the Atlantic', in the new United States of America, in what was 'a direct continuation of the process begun in England in the sixteenth century' (1992: 401). Certainly this elevated view of sixteenth-century English nationhood is not supported by any evidence that she cites – and indeed is somewhat undermined by the copious evidence of English xenophobia – 'strong anti-alien feeling' – and contempt for other peoples that she *does* cite (1992: 42–3; cf. Loades 1992: 298). But this account of nationalism is important for showing what Greenfeld means by the term, and gives us some criterion by which to assess her claims for sixteenth-century English nationalism. Moreover, it has to be said that in other respects Greenfeld gives us the most systematic statement of the case for considering the sixteenth century as the birth-time of English nationalism. Hers is a sensitive and scholarly account, based on an impressive range of primary and secondary sources.[2]

It is also, at least in this part of her presentation, a very familiar account; so familiar as to make us immediately uneasy. In fact Greenfeld's picture of the political and social changes in Tudor England substantially replicates that offered by the eminent English historian A. F. Pollard in a short but influential work published nearly a century ago, entitled *Factors in Modern History* (1907). There Pollard, going against the prevailing Whig tendency to scold the Tudors for holding up the progress of parliamentary government, painted by contrast a glowing picture of a dynamically rising middle class expressing itself through its national organ, Parliament, and allied to a monarchy that identified itself with the nation. The alliance between the middle class and the national state was the battering ram that destroyed the universalism of the Catholic Church and the hierarchical order of feudalism, the twin pillars of the Middle Ages. Although Pollard saw these factors at work in a number of European countries, it was in sixteenth-century England that they found their most concentrated expression (1907: 22). Like Greenfeld, then, Pollard sees in the joint outlook of the new middle class and the 'New Monarchy' the triumph of the principle of nationality – not only but especially in Tudor England (1907: 26–78; and see also Rowse 1943: 46).

Pollard's lead was followed by a group of mainly left-leaning historians – R. H. Tawney, Christopher Hill, Lawrence Stone, and others. Under the general heading of 'the rise of the gentry', they purported to show the development of a class that, formed under the patronage of the Tudor monarchy, and employing new capitalist methods and techniques, was powerful enough by the middle of the seventeenth century to challenge the crown directly in the English Civil War.[3] Capitalism, rather than nationalism, was the main concern of these historians. Nevertheless, they accepted that the national state, especially as represented by Parliament, played an indispensable part in the rise to power of this new class. Liah Greenfeld has thus been able to draw extensively on the researches of this group to support her account of the social changes that gave rise to the new consciousness of the nation in sixteenth-century England. Though not mentioning Pollard, she has also drawn on another venerable text, Lewis Einstein's *Tudor Ideals* (1921: 187–96), for her picture of an increasingly patriotic literary and political culture in Tudor England (see, e.g., Greenfeld 1992: 47–50, and 500–1ns).[4]

The familiarity and venerability of Greenfeld's account are not, of course, by themselves the issue. What matters is its accuracy. Here her reliance on an older picture does turn out to be a serious problem. The first thing that has to go, in the light of work done over the past half-century, is the idea of a 'new aristocracy' drawn from humble men of talent and dedicated to public service. People of humble origin, such as Thomas Cromwell, did indeed rise from the ranks, and the Tudors did indeed ennoble a number of 'new men', such as Cromwell himself, John Russell and the Cecils (MacCaffrey 1965: 54). But these were additions to, not a replacement of, the old aristocracy. The old aristocracy had to change its ways, and this it did by becoming a more cultivated and educated aristocracy, fit to take up state service (see, e.g., Hexter 1961c; MacCaffrey 1965: 62–3; Wrightson 1982: 191–3). But it did not become a service, still less a servile, nobility, along the lines of that of Russia or Prussia in the eighteenth century. While willing to serve, and by no means hostile to newcomers, it preserved a good deal of its independence and its traditional aristocratic culture, both of which frequently put it in opposition to the crown. This could be seen not just after the Restoration of 1660 but right up to the end of the eighteenth century (Clark 2000a: esp. 14–42; Clark 1986: 33–4; see also P. Williams 1979: 428–36; Wrightson 1982: 23–7; Bernard 1992; A. G. R. Smith 1997: 182–3; Nicholls 1999: 13).

Even more battered is the thesis of 'the rise of the gentry', or of a new middle class challenging the ascendancy of the aristocracy. This has been debated more intensively than practically any other topic in English history. The upshot has been the decisive rejection of the principal claim. Once more it has been easy to concede that the Tudor period was one that allowed for a high, though not necessarily exceptional, degree of social mobility. The literature on 'social climbing', and the sneers against newcomers, are vivid evidence of this. But social mobility into the middling or higher ranks did not give rise to a consciousness of class, of a sense of the opposition of one interest and ideal to another. There was no 'new middle class' that linked its fortunes to the 'new monarchy' in a common front against the old aristocracy. Those who had successfully advanced out of their class were only too eager to embrace the customs and outlook of the class that had the unchallenged claim to power and prestige, the landed aristocracy (Hexter 1961d; see also Wrightson 1982: 30–1; Guy 1988: 36; Heal and Holmes 1994; A. G. R. Smith 1997: 185; Nicholls 1999: 13–15).

But the absence of a 'social revolution' in Tudor England is not the only, or the most serious, problem in Greenfeld's argument for sixteenth-century English nationalism. More important is her whole discussion of political authority, and the nature of the bond between monarch and people. For it is central to her argument that in Tudor England – for the first time anywhere – the idea of the nation emerged as an idea of the sovereign *people*, the people as an 'elite', and that the role of the Tudor monarchy was to enable that to happen by its own identification with the people. Greenfeld goes out of her way – even more than Pollard – to stress the novelty of this idea, and its importance as the constitutive principle of all nationalisms, whatever their particular differences.

At a certain point in history – to be precise, in early sixteenth-century England – the word "nation" in its conciliar meaning of an elite was applied to the population of the country and made synonymous with the word "people." *This semantic transformation signaled the emergence of the first nation in the world, in the sense in which the word is understood today, and launched the era of nationalism* ... As a synonym of the "nation" – an elite – the "people" lost its derogatory connotation and, now denoting an eminently positive entity, acquired the meaning of the bearer of sovereignty, the basis of political solidarity, and the supreme object of loyalty ...

National identity in its distinctive modern sense is, therefore, an identity which derives from membership in a "people", the fundamental characteristic of which is that it is defined as a "nation". Every member of the "people" thus interpreted partakes in its superior, elite quality, and it is in consequence that a stratified national population is perceived as essentially homogeneous, and the lines of status and class as superficial. This principle lies at the basis of all nationalisms and justfies viewing them as expressions of the same general phenomenon.   (1992: 6–7. Greenfeld's emphasis)

It is necessary to follow Greenfeld along one further line of argument to consider the startling implications of her claim that the English invented nationalism in the sixteenth century. The nation does not simply mean 'the elite people', the people as elite. That would allow kings and emperors, not to mention more modern dictators, to argue that they embody the people or nation – a not uncommon claim. Greenfeld will have none of that. The nation as the people means popular government; it means democracy.

The location of sovereignty within the people and the recognition of the fundamental equality among its various strata, which constitute the essence of the modern national idea, are at the same time the basic tenets of democracy. Democracy was born with the sense of nationality. The two are inherently linked, and neither can be fully understood apart from this connection. Nationalism was the form in which democracy appeared in the world, contained in the idea of the nation as a butterfly in a cocoon.   (1992: 10)

Greenfeld accepts that 'not all the people of England were actually included in the nation in [the] first century of its existence'; and she regrets that, with the further development of nationalism, as the idea of the nation moved from the people as sovereign to the people as unique, so 'the original equivalence between it and democratic principles was lost' (1992: 31, 10). But with this further extension of her argument about the general character of the nation we get some measure of the vastness of her claims about sixteenth-century England. What she seems to be saying is that, in their invention of the nation, the English also and simultaneously invented the idea of the modern democratic nation-state.

Nearly all recent historians of Tudor England as well as nearly all theorists of nationalism explicitly or implicitly reject this position as anachronistic. In her enthusiasm for the Anglo-Saxon idea of civic nationhood, and her concern to show its transference in a pristine state to early America, Greenfeld seems to have felt the need to wish it onto early modern England so that the Anglo-Saxon variety can appear the pure type, the prototype, of all nationalism. All other instances of nationalism – in France, Germany and Russia – are seen by her as reactions, in the spirit of *ressentiment*, to the first English example (and so necessarily distorted, deviations from the pure English type). But then why did it take – by her own account – 200 years or so for the English example to be copied (1992: 14)? What was happening to the idea of nationalism in the meantime? And how do we explain that it is the English (or British), not the French, who in the eighteenth century seem to express the greatest degree of *ressentiment*, in their complaints as it happens at the dominance of French culture? Many of these puzzles become clearer if we acknowledge that it was not the English who invented nationalism (whatever might be said about liberalism), and certainly not in the sixteenth century. Whatever signs of change we find in Tudor England – and these are in some spheres momentous – they do not add up to a declaration or celebration of English nationalism.

Greenfeld herself says that 'in the sixteenth century English nationalism centered on the figure of the monarch' (1992: 50). This extraordinary admission in no way stops her in her tracks, or even causes her to pause to reflect. She continues blithely: 'The Crown, for its part, favored nationalism, occasionally bolstered it with official measures which greatly enhanced its respectability, and in general lent it the sort of support it needed to develop' (1992: 50). Among those official measures she lists the Act of Appeals as an example of Henry the Eighth's support for 'the growth of national consciousness' among his subjects (not, we should note, *citizens*). It was 'Henry's aim and expressed wish to imply in its application to England that England was a sovereign polity separate from the rest of Christendom' (1992: 51).

But why then does the equally emphatic assertion of sovereignty at about the same time by the French crown, and the developing strength of Gallicanism in the French Church, not amount in that case to an assertion of French nationalism – an absence that Greenfeld's whole account of sixteenth-and seventeenth-century France is at pains to show (1992: 91–133)? It was after all in Jean Bodin's France, not Henry the Eighth's England, that the most striking claims for state sovereignty were made in the sixteenth century.[5] It is clear that there can be declarations of state sovereignty that do not involve an appeal to 'the nation' or to the national principle. In France such declarations were carried out in the name of the king. That is why French historians – in agreement here with Liah Greenfeld – have been so reluctant to see nationalism in France in the early modern period. In the seventeenth century, says Henri Hauser, 'the idea of nationality was eclipsed by the idea of the state'; the concept of *patrie* 'resulted from the dissociation of the idea of the king from the idea of the nation' (in Church 1975: 44; see also Greenfeld 1992: 103, 128). Patriotism, loyalty and dedication to the *patrie*, therefore, meant loyalty and dedication to the monarch as the embodiment of the *patrie*; France and its king were one. Until this equation was broken, until, in the eighteenth century, France came to be identified with its people – the 'nation' – there could be patriotism but not nationalism. The difference was made clear in the famous statement in article 3 of the Declaration of the Rights of Man and the Citizen of 1789: 'All sovereignty resides essentially in the Nation.' No longer could any king, however glorious and god-like, assert that '*l'état, c'est moi.*'

In sixteenth-century England it was the same as in sixteenth- (and seventeenth-) century France, at least as concerns state and nation.[6] This is the almost universal consensus among contemporary historians of the period. The state was the monarchy, and not just in a symbolic but in a real practical sense. 'The monarch', says David Loades, 'was the keystone in the arch of government: the shaper of policy and the maker of decisions' (1997b: 9; see also A. G. R. Smith 1997: 121). When Sir Thomas Smith, in his *De Republica Anglorum* (1583), declared that the monarch was 'the life, the head, and the authority of all things that be done in the realm of England', he was, says Mark Nicholls, uttering words that 'no contemporary would have questioned' (1999: 11; see also Ferguson 1965: 387–91; McLaren 1999: 198–234). Nor could there be anything more traditional than Sir Thomas Smith's view, in his other celebrated treatise *A Discourse of the Commonweal of This Realm of England* (1581), that the state was Aristotle's household writ large, and that its economy was essentially a household economy (Wood 1992: 153–4).

What seems clear is that far from having the character of a modern nation-state – let alone a 'proto-democratic' one – the Tudor state is best seen as a patrimonial one, in Max Weber's sense (Weber 1978, II: 1006–69; Coleman and Starkey 1986; Slavin 1993). That is to say, its principle is personal. The state is the king's domain. Its officers are his household servants, its offices his to give away to favourites or to sell to the highest bidder. The extension of its power is seen as the expansion of his power. Its claims flow as much from the feudal notion of royal suzerainty as from the modern notion of state sovereignty, though it is clear that in the Tudor period the one was passing into the other.[7] Parliament has a place, but more as a site of traditional patronage and interest-group bargaining than as the forum of 'legitimate opposition', in the modern sense, to the crown.

Not only was the Tudor monarchy personal, it was deeply elitist and aristocratic. There is no hint of that 'sovereignty of the people' that Greenfeld appeals to, no idea that the state derives from or reposes upon 'the nation'. 'Tudor monarchy', says David Loades, 'rested upon an unwritten understanding between the monarch and the "political nation"' (1997: 4). The political nation included the great nobility and the gentry, and it could also include royal officers of middling rank, but with the exception of London it largely excluded the governing elites of the towns and, more emphatically, the great bulk of tradesmen, artisans, yeomen farmers and labourers (Guy 1988: 45; Loades 1997b: 5). If we agree to call the upper ranks 'gentlemen', they constituted around 2 per cent of the English population in the sixteenth century (Wrightson 1982: 24; A. G. R. Smith 1997: 182–3; Nicholls 1999: 14). At most, if we include the wealthier merchants and lawyers, the political nation at the end of the sixteenth century might be said to amount to about 4 per cent (P. Williams 1979: 421–8). But it was not so much the precise quantity as the particular concept of the political nation that makes it so difficult to see any correspondence between state and nation – understood as 'the people' – at this time. Membership of the nation was effectively restricted to a small section of the community that alone was thought capable of political activity. Though Elizabeth made great play with the love that the people bore her, it is clear that she generally addressed her remarks to the only class that mattered, the 'gentlemen of the counties' that she called upon to kiss her hand in her famous 'golden speech' to Parliament in 1601. As Michael Mann says, the 'nation' in Elizabethan England was a *class*, the small class of nobility and gentry that constituted the political nation. 'Naturally this did not include the masses . . . they were excluded from the political nation' (1986: 463). In this sense Montesquieu spoke for England as much as for prerevolutionary France when he spoke, in a celebrated passage, of the traditional assembly of the 'the nation, that is, the nobility and the bishops; the common people were not taken into consideration' (1949, II: 102; see also Zernatto 1944: 361; Hobsbawm 1992: 73–4; Gellner 1996: 104–5).

The case for an alleged sixteenth-century English nationalism rests on very precarious foundations. Socially and politically the requisite changes do not seem to be there. A small political class under a virtually deified monarch continued to represent the nation. While its members might on occasion be stirred to express nationalist, or at least patriotic, sentiments – though usually directed at the crown rather than the country – this was not generally the case for the bulk of their fellow countrymen. We know that even the supposed popularity of Elizabeth the First, which so struck the Victorian imagination, was a carefully constructed propaganda device on the part of her statesmen, aided and abetted by the queen herself (Yates 1975: 29–87; Fletcher 1982: 311–12; Haigh 1988: 144–62; Strong 2000: 173–200). Popular identification with the English nation – even as symbolized by the person of the monarch – was far more low-key than we are apt to imagine from accounts, both at the scholarly and popular levels, which derive largely from Victorian sources.[8] 'A man or woman born and raised in Tudor England', says Mark Nicholls, 'would acknowledge that he or she was an Englishman or Englishwoman, but the acknowledgement would not, perhaps, be accompanied by any quickening of the pulse' (1999: xvii; cf. Fletcher 1982: 317). Gloriana, 'Good Queen Bess', 'England's forgotten worthies', the supposed popular rejoicing at the exploits of Drake, Frobisher, Hawkins and Raleigh as they singed the Spaniard's beard, all have the usual mixture of myth and truth, of spontaneous and staged expression, of genuine patriotism and age-old xenophobia (Furtado 1989: 44; Cressy 1990). What they cannot be allowed to do is paint a picture of English nationalism, of a nation linked by the horizontal ties of nationhood rising above the ties of class, region and religion. But we need to look at religion, the most important force of the age, in more detail.

The Protestant nation

Social and political changes are only some of the conditions that for Liah Greenfeld lead to the rise of English nationalism. More consequential are religious changes. Henry the Eighth's break with Rome 'opened the doors to Protestantism, perhaps the most significant among the factors that furthered the development of the English national consciousness' (1992: 51). England was the Protestant nation. A series of momentous developments produced an entirely new consciousness. There was firstly the printing of William Tyndale's English Bible, whose impact 'was unprecedented in its character and extent', and which 'tied Henry, or rather England, to "the back of a tiger"' (1992: 51; cf. Hammond 1996). The existence of a vernacular translation of the Bible was important because 'the major independent contribution of Protestantism to the development of English nationalism . . . had to do with the fact that it was a religion of the Book'. Of central significance was the rediscovery and rehabilitation of the Old Testament in Protestant theology. For it was there 'that one found the example of a chosen, godly people, a people which was an elite and a light to the world because every one of its members was a party to the covenant with God'. For thousands of ordinary Englishmen, armed with the new English Bible, the Old Testament 'provided them with the language in which they could express the novel consciousness of nationality, for which no language had existed before. This language reached all levels of society and was, as a result, far more important in its influence than the language of Renaissance patriotism known only to a small elite' (1992: 52; cf. J. Clark 2000b: 272)).

There is immediately an awkward problem with this first part of the argument. As Greenfeld herself notes, 'the printed English Bible was a comparatively late addition to the vernacular translations of the book'. The first English translation of a part of the Bible appeared in 1525, and only in 1538, after much opposition, was a vernacular Bible, Tyndale's Bible, actually printed in England. In France, Italy and Holland, vernacular translations had existed much earlier, since the 1470s; in Germany a German Bible had been printed as early as 1466, and new vernacular versions had appeared regularly ever since. Yet, says Greenfeld, 'nowhere did the availability of the vernacular Bible have the effect it had in England' (1992: 53). How so? Why did the English Bible stimulate national consciousness when the French, Italian and even German Bible – in the country that launched the Protestant Reformation – failed to do so?

Greenfeld falls back on an argument that has a baffling degree of circularity. The role of Protestantism in general and the English Bible in particular, in the development of English national consciousness, apparently has to be seen against the fact that 'nationalism predated the Reformation and most likely contributed to its appeal in England' (1992: 52). So we have to assume the existence of nationalism, as an already accomplished fact, in order to understand the impact of Protestantism in furthering English nationalism. But we have already seen the shakiness of the case for English nationalism on other, non-religious, grounds. So Protestantism will have more or less to go it alone, in making the case.

The same problem of circularity afflicts the specific argument concerning the significance of the English Bible. The Protestant emphasis on the religion of the Book was not just important in spreading the idea of the chosen people but, even more, thinks Greenfeld, in stimulating literacy. It made people want to read; and the availability of a vernacular Bible brought such a possibility within the reach of ordinary people. But why then was it the *English*, rather than other Protestant peoples such as the Germans, who had their national consciousness raised by a reading of the Bible in the vernacular? Here again we have to fall back on a prior condition. Because of 'secular developments – the general state of flux in the social structure in England and the change of attitude towards education', literacy, it turns out, 'was exceptionally widespread in sixteenth-century England... The English, therefore, and in contrast to other societies, were not satisfied with the availability of the vernacular Bible, but actually read it' (1992: 53–4). The effect of this widespread reading of the Bible in English, supported after the accession of Elizabeth by the official authorities, is considered by Greenfeld to be nothing short of revolutionary. It nurtured a 'novel sense of human... dignity', it 'opened a new, vast terrain to the possible influence of the national idea and at once immensely broadened the population potentially susceptible to its appeal' (1992: 54).[9]

It is clear is that an incredible amount hinges on the supposedly greater literacy of the English, which, once granted, leads on to the dizzying development of national consciousness – alone in Protestant Europe – brought on by the Protestant Reformation in England. Unfortunately for her view of literacy in this period Greenfeld relies on the picture of a Tudor/early Stuart 'educational revolution' presented by Lawrence Stone (1964) which, at least as she interprets it, has been shown to be misleading for the very groups that are crucial to her argument. Undoubtedly, education for the aristocracy and gentry developed greatly during the sixteenth and seventeenth centuries; undoubtedly too, Protestants and especially Puritans stressed the necessity of Bible reading for salvation. But the fact remains that as late as 1642, after decades of Puritan propaganda and hundreds of Puritan publications, more than 70 per cent of adult males in England – and 90 per cent of women – were still illiterate. For the preceding century, David Cressy estimates that by the time of Elizabeth's accession (1558) the illiteracy rate was 80 per cent for men and 95 per cent for women (1980: 72, 176; cf. Stone 1969: 101; A. G. R. Smith 1997: 199, 451). So there had been some improvement in the ability to read and write, but hardly enough to warrant Lawrence Stone's description of it as an 'educational revolution', certainly so far as it affected the mass of ordinary English people (Wrightson 1982: 190; A. G. R. Smith 1997: 200). Puritan exhortation to read was all very well; but it came up against the facts of social structure and social inequality that severely limited the ability of the great mass of the English population to follow that admirable advice. It is indeed impossible to argue that, at least in the sixteenth century, the English people had a higher level of literacy than the peoples of Protestant Holland or Protestant Germany, or indeed of Catholic France, Spain or Italy (see Cipolla 1969: 54–61; Burke 1979: 251–2; Kamen 1984: 210–11; Gawthrop and Strauss 1984: 32).

Greenfeld appears to be on firmer ground with the second of her main claims concerning Protestantism and English national identity. Here she refers to the role of the Marian exiles, the radical Protestants who, returning to England after Elizabeth's accession and relying upon her favour, seized the initiative and proposed transforming England into a truly godly country under Protestant auspices. The persecution of Protestants under Mary, says Greenfeld, and its bloody but short-term character, ensured 'a long-term identification between the Protestant and the national causes, which immensely strengthened nationalism and was, perhaps, the most important contribution of religion to its development' (1992: 55; cf. Loades 1982).

The crowning expression of that identification, according to Greenfeld, was John Foxe's *Book of Martyrs* (1554–83). This massive compilation of the sufferings and martyrdom of a vast range of victims – most particularly English Protestants during Mary's reign – at the hands of 'Romish Prelates' became enormously popular during Elizabeth's reign and for centuries beyond. In 1571, at a time of crisis during the revolt of the Catholic northern earls and the Pope's bull excommunicating Elizabeth, convocation decreed that the *Book of Martyrs* be set up along with the Bible for all to read in churches and other public places, 'where in some instances it remained until quite recent times' (Haller 1963: 13, 221). By the end of the seventeenth century something like 10,000 copies had been printed, together with numerous abridgements and abstracts – 'more, it is safe to say, than any other book of similar scope except the Bible' (Haller 1963: 14).

The importance of Foxe's book to English historiography and English self-conceptions has always been recognized (see, e.g. Burrow 1983: 247–8). It was however the distinguished Tudor scholar William Haller, in his *Foxe's Book of Martyrs and the Elect Nation* (1963), who most clearly and influentially proclaimed the nationalist significance of Foxe's contribution. Englishmen in general in the reign of Elizabeth, says Haller, accepted the book as 'an expression of the national faith second in authority only to the Bible and as an unanswerable defence of England's ideological position in the contemporary struggle for national independence and power'. It supplied

a history of the Church and the nation, seen by the light of what was taken to be the truth of revelation . . . Thus the Book of Martyrs set moving in English life a body of legend which was thought to make clear how and why the situation in which the nation presently found itself had come about, and so to justify whatever course the nation, as represented by the queen, might take in its own defence and for the accomplishment of its destiny.   (1963: 14)

The critical events of Elizabeth's reign – the Catholic plots centred on Mary Stuart, leading to her execution, the rising and suppression of the northern earls, the massacre of the Huguenots in France on St Bartholomew's eve, above all the threat posed by and the defeat of the Spanish Armada – were all seen in the light of this apocalyptic, providentially directed history. Later editions of the *Book of Martyrs* added the providential deliverance of the English nation from the 'Gunpowder Treason' of 1605, together with an account of the further sufferings of Protestants at home and abroad that once more were seen as the prelude to a final deliverance from the Antichrist (1963: 222, 227; see also Cressy 1990, 1994).

Foxe's book generally followed the apocalyptic pattern that was common in Reformation Europe but, argues Haller, it laid out a special role for England.

Conditions in England – the fact of its being an island [*sic*] placed as it was on the map of Europe, the stage it had come to in the development of its institutions, the emergence of London as a metropolitan centre, the character of the people, the state of their language, the genius and personality of their ruler – all this meant not only that England would follow a course peculiar to itself but that Protestantism would there follow a course peculiar to England.   (1963: 242–3)

The continuing crises of Elizabeth's reign, despite the restoration of Protestantism after her accession, fuelled the sense of urgency and expectation among the returned Marian exiles, and convinced them that God had reserved for England a special role in the ordering of his dispensation (Haller 1963: 245; see also Pocock 1975b: 108–9; Hastings 1997: 58–9; N. Davies 1999: 468, 502–5; E. Jones 2000: 50–60).

Greenfeld, not surprisingly, follows Haller closely if not always elegantly, as is clear from her summary of Foxe's *Book of Martyrs*:

The message of the book was that England was in covenant with God, had remained faithful to the true religion in the past, and now was leading the world in the Reformation, because it was favored in His sight. Being English in fact implied being a true Christian; the English people was chosen, separated from others and distinguished by God; the strength and glory of England was the interest of His Church; and the triumph of Protestantism was a national triumph.   (1992: 61)

It is in this context that we are asked to understand the famous utterances: Bishop Hugh Latimer's exclamation, on learning of the birth of a son to Henry the Eighth, 'thanks to our Lord God, God of England! for verily he has shown himself God of England, or rather an English God'; Bishop John Aylmer's marginal note to a passage celebrating England's plenty and prosperity, 'God is English'; Elizabeth's reference to herself as the 'nursing mother of Israel'; John Lyly's 'so tender a care hath [God] always had of that England, as of a new Israel, his chosen and peculiar people' (Haller 1963: 87, 245; Marcu 1976: 77–80; Greenfeld 1992: 60). The national self-congratulatory and apocalyptic note apparently reaches a climax in the writings of John Milton during the seventeenth-century civil war. In *Areopagitica* (1644) Milton apostrophized the English Parliament as the governors of an exceptional nation, 'a nation not slow and dull, but of a quick, ingenious and piercing spirit, acute to invent, subtle and sinewy in discourse'.

Yet that which is above all this, the favour and the love of heaven, we have great argument to think in a peculiar manner propitious and propending towards us. Why else was this nation chosen before any other, that out of her, as out of Zion, should be proclaimed and sounded forth the first tidings and trumpet of Reformation to all Europe? . . . Now once again . . . God is decreeing to begin some new and great period in his church . . . what does he then but reveal himself to his servants, and as his manner is, first to his Englishmen?

(Milton 1990: 608–9; see also Haller 1963: 240–1; Firth 1979: 232–7; Hastings 1997: 57; Greenfeld 1992: 76)

The seeming complacency of that last line is characteristically immediately undercut by Milton: 'I say, as his manner is, first to us, though we mark not the method of his counsels, and are unworthy' (1990: 609). And there is much else in *Areopagitica* and others of Milton's writings to shatter any idea of him as an uncritical English nationalist. But there is no need to deny that he along with several other Puritan writers saw England as the elect nation, chosen to head the fight against Antichrist and lead the way into the millennium. The question is what we are to make of this common opinion – common, at any rate, to Puritan thinkers of the late sixteenth- and early seventeenth-century and radical Protestant sects during the civil war (see, e.g., Walzer 1968: 290–6; Lamont 1969; Hill 1970; McGregor and Reay 1986). Is this English nationalism? Did sixteenth- and early seventeenth-century Protestantism, whether or not it took millennial form, elaborate a view of the English nation such that we are entitled to speak of the rise and 'entrenchment' of a 'modern, full-fledged, mature nationalism' in England in this period (Greenfeld 1992: 70)?

Protestantism and nationalism

One of the first reasons for doubting this is that the idea of the English as an elect nation is an old idea – one, moreover, borrowed from elsewhere. By this is not of course meant the Old Testament origin of the idea but something much nearer home, in time as well as space. Among European nations, as Joseph Strayer (1971) has shown, the first to develop the idea of the elect nation was France. In an effort to strengthen the power of the Capetian monarchy, publicists during the reign of Philip the Fair (1285–1314) developed the idea of the French king as 'the most Christian king' and his kingdom of France as the land of the greatest faith and piety, especially favoured by God. This conception was effectively deployed against the claim of the Papacy under Boniface VIII to spiritual authority over all temporal rulers. In seeking to heal the breach between the Papacy and the French king, Pope Clement V, in his Bull *Rex gloriae* (1311) drew upon these by now familiar claims concerning the French king and people to give papal sanction to the concept of the holy kingdom and the chosen people: 'The King of Glory formed different kingdoms within the circuit of this world and established governments for diverse peoples according to differences of language and race. Among those, like the people of Israel ... the kingdom of France, as a peculiar people chosen by the Lord to carry out the orders of Heaven, is distinguished by marks of special honor and grace' (Strayer 1971: 312–13; cf. Fawtier 1960: 95). The idea was sufficiently popular and well established for Jeanne d'Arc to call upon it in rallying the French against the English in the Hundred Years War (Strayer 1971: 313; see also Kirkland 1938–9; Armstrong 1994: 85).

Every nation, probably, at some point in its development thinks of itself as especially favoured of God. As we have seen, some commentators claim that Bede did as much for the English people as early as the eighth century.[10] The fact that the French did so in the fourteenth century has not led many theorists, nor indeed many French historians, to argue that the French invented nationalism at this period of their history.[11] That proud boast is reserved for the French at the time of their great eighteenth-century revolution. What gives the French case significance from the point of view of English nationalism is that the idea of the English as the elect nation seems to have been borrowed directly from the French, and for much the same purposes of elevating the monarchy and establishing its independence of the Papacy. John McKenna (1982) has shown how the English kings of the fourteenth and fifteenth centuries, anxious as always to emulate the superior ideology and civilization of the French court, deliberately promoted the idea of the English kings as endowed, like the French kings, with the mystical attributes of regality (anointment with the holy oil at their coronation, miraculous power to cure the king's evil, etc.). At the same time they seized upon the corresponding idea of their people, the English people, as the godly, chosen people. The chancellor's opening address to the Parliament of 1377 matched precisely for the English king and kingdom the French doctrines of the French king as 'the most Christian king', sent by God as his vicar or legate, and of France as the new Israel. The great victories over the French at Crécy (1346) and Poitiers (1356) must have made this *translatio* appear especially apt and satisfying.

And thus you have what the Scripture tells us, "*Pacem super Israel*", peace over Israel, because Israel is understood to be the heritage of God as is England. For I truly think that God would never have honored this land in the same way as He did Israel through great victories over their enemies, if it were not that He had chosen it as His heritage.
(McKenna 1982: 31)

From this time 'the persuasive analogy between England and Israel' and the concept of the elect nation became favourite themes of tracts and sermons, in the pulpit and in Parliament. A new English 'political theology' developed that, modelled on the French, claimed that power and primacy in the West had now passed to England, as God's chosen. (McKenna 1982: 27, 30; see also Hastings 1997: 59–60; Collinson 1997: 21–2; J. Clark 2000b: 270).

This account – of the early introduction, at second-hand, of the idea of the elect nation – clearly bears on the argument of Greenfeld and others that English Protestantism was principally responsible for the creation of English nationalism in the sixteenth century. Firstly, we find that the idea is originally not English at all, but medieval French. Neither Greenfeld nor theorists of nationalism generally are inclined to discern nationalism in France in the period in which the idea of the elect nation was quite clearly stated. Secondly, we find the idea emerging strongly though imitatively in fourteenth- and fifteenth-century England, at a time when England was not merely still Catholic but was widely regarded as among the most religiously orthodox countries in Europe (E. Jones 2000: 33).

The problem for Greenfeld and others of her persuasion is obvious. How can English Protestantism, and its particular version of the elect nation, be held responsible to a unique degree for English nationalism when the relevant political theology was already alive and well in pre-Protestant England – without, it seems, giving rise to any great development of nationalism? The idea of the Protestant nation might, it is true, fortify English nationalism if that had developed independently on a different basis, socially and politically. But that, as we have seen, was not the case, and we have also seen that Greenfeld herself stresses that Protestantism was 'the most significant among the factors that furthered the development of the English national consciousness'. 'The role of religion in the development of English nationalism . . . was much greater than that of a facilitating condition, because it was owing to the Reformation, more than to any other factor, that nationalism spread as wide as it did in the sixteenth century' (1992: 51, 53). The finding that what Protestantism proclaimed so insistently, at least in the relevant Puritan utterances, was not distinctive to it but can be found at other times and in non-Protestant cultures must surely throw considerable doubt on the whole argument of a close link between Protestantism and English nationalism.

It is not just the earlier history of certain key Protestant ideas that creates difficulties for Greenfeld's thesis. It is also the character of English Protestantism itself, what is claimed for it and in particular its employment as the central unifying feature of English nationalism. Protestantism had to play this role, argues Greenfeld, because in a religious age nationalism could not stand on its own. 'At this period the existence of a separate entity such as a nation was not self-evident. It was problematic and needed justification.' Enter Protestantism:

It was only natural that at the time of the centrality of religion in every sphere of social existence, nascent nationalism was clothed in religious idiom. Furthermore, because of the association between the Reformation and English national identity, Protestantism not only provided the yet voiceless nationalism with a language, but also secured it a sanctuary and a protection which it needed in order to mature. In short, though Protestantism cannot be said to have given birth to the English nation, it did play the crucial role of a midwife without whom the child might not have been born.   (1992: 62–3)

Once more, as often in Greenfeld's account, the direction of causality is uncertain and unclear. Here it seems as is if she is borrowing Marxist language and lacing it with a little Weber. Protestantism is the decent 'cover' or ideology for the rude beast, nationalism, which has its own independent principle and is developing under its own steam, but for the moment needs the clothing of religion. At best they walk hand in hand, owing to the correspondence of Protestant individualism with the 'rationalist' individualism developing in sixteenth-century England, thus rendering Protestantism 'a perfect ally for the nascent national sentiment'. So far so Marxist. Then there is the Weberian twist: Protestantism may not have caused nationalism, but no Protestantism, no nationalism. The continuation also follows Weber, here converging with Marx, that once nationalism was established it could dispense with its religious cover and run free (Greenfeld 1992: 66).

But even if we allow that Protestantism played a largely justificatory role, was it capable of doing so? Did it have that national, unifying effect that is required of it? Here Greenfeld seems to be forgetting one of the most obvious facts about the Protestant Reformation. The Reformation, far from unifying the nation, drove dagger-like incisions into it – in England just as much as on the Continent. The English nation was divided from end to end – more so perhaps than ever before or since. The state might, after 1558, officially support the Protestant settlement, but there were millions of English Catholics who regarded themselves as loyal and patriotic Englishmen and Englishwomen, and Elizabeth at least was not one to inquire too deeply into their religious convictions. 'Her Majesty', as her Lord Keeper Francis Bacon said, does not like 'to make windows into men's hearts and secret thoughts' (Haigh 1988: 37). Moreover, far from wishing to put herself at the head of a Protestant crusade on behalf of English nationalism, Elizabeth infuriated her Puritan supporters by refusing to pursue Catholics at home and abroad, until reluctantly forced into action by the plots around Mary Stuart and the threat of the Spanish invasion.

Nothing could be more misleading than Greenfeld's portrayal of Elizabeth as the Protestant queen, the arch-symbol of the Protestant nation; nor, in its Protestant understanding, her claim of 'the triple identification of the nation, godliness, and the queen' (1992: 64–5). As Christopher Haigh says, 'Elizabeth wanted to be queen of the English, not queen of the Protestants . . . She tried to comprehend Catholics within the nation' (1988: 36–7). She frequently visited her Catholic nobles, checked the increase of Protestant preaching in the Church of England, and resisted attempts to abolish Catholic vestments and church ceremonies, preferring her priests to look and act as clergymen of 'the old religion'. The two masters of her Chapel Royal, the great composers Thomas Tallis and William Byrd, were known Catholics. Eventually the Elizabethan equipoise broke down. Englishmen divided fiercely on religious lines, and fought each other in a bitter civil war in which Protestants of different kinds were pitted against each other. But that, even more than the divisions of Elizabeth's reign, should make it plain how doubtful it must be to connect Protestantism directly with English nationalism. What kind of nationalizing force is it that fragments, rather than unites, the nation?[12]

Not only did Protestantism drive a wedge between its increasingly intolerant adherents and those of their fellow countrymen who refused to conform. There was also a central ambiguity, or ambivalence, within Protestant doctrine itself that made the equation of nation and Protestantism hard to sustain. This particularly applied to the Calvinist doctrine of 'the elect' – the concept, as we have seen, that for Haller as well as Greenfeld most powerfully hitched Protestantism to English nationalism. For who were the elect? Haller, in his study of Foxe's *Book of Martyrs*, conjoined it in the very title of his book with 'the nation'. But as several scholars have pointed out (e.g., Fletcher 1982: 309; E. Jones 2000: 54), Foxe nowhere in his book talks about 'the elect nation'. He works, as Katharine Firth (1979: 106–10, 242–52) has most systematically shown, within an apocalyptic tradition that is international or global in the fullest sense of the word. 'Foxe's conception of the true Church is international and mystical, identifying the Church as the congregation of the elect' – *wherever* they are to be found, inside or outside England (1979: 108). 'He claimed no special destiny for England. No national church was the Church of God, rather, all nations were called by him ... Foxe explicitly denied that God had elected one church or nation above another; his Church was wherever the true faith was believed' (1979: 252; see also Christiansen 1978; Hadfield 1994: 57–8). The elect or the saved exist in relation to the damned on a universal plane. This can set them off from the damned within their own nation, or, equally, it can link them with other members of the elect in other nations. But there is no special significance in the nation itself, as a particular political collectivity – how could there be, in so cosmic a theology as Protestant apocalyptic thought? That is why Milton, who also works within this tradition, was able to identify the elect first with the English nation, then, when incensed by the efforts of the Presbyterians to take over the Republican state, simply with the select and superior group of right-minded people *within* the nation. Later, when England came to be threatened by foreign enemies, Milton shifted his position back again to seeing England as the elect nation (E. Jones 2000: 54–5; see also Firth 1979: 237).

When the seventeenth-century Puritan divine Richard Baxter thanked God that he was born in England, this was not an expression of national feeling. It was an expression of gratitude that he had been born in the land of the True Church, and that consequently the salvation of his soul might be possible there (Weber 1998: 166). What mattered was religion, not nation (here Baxter precisely reverses Greenfeld's order of priority). Protestant apocalypticism recognized the role played by particular nations in the fulfilment of the Apocalypse of St John, but it would not have occurred to them to reserve that honour for one nation alone. As David Loades says;

it would be a mistake to suppose that either Bale [Foxe's teacher and fellow-exile] or Foxe postulated a unique dispensation of providence for England. In arguing that God had vouchsafed a particular providence to their fellow countrymen, they were not denying the equally authentic vision of their German or Swiss friends . . . As long as the protestant vision of England retained its eschatological priorities, that is well into the seventeenth century, it is proper to speak of *an* elect Nation, but not of *the* Elect Nation.
    (1982: 303–4; author's emphasis; see also Prestwich 1985; Facey 1987; Collinson 1997: 24–5; Claydon and McBride 1998b: 10–15; J. Clark 1994: 47–8; 2000b: 270; Armitage 2000: 78–9)

'Every hill is Sion, every river is Jordan, every countrie Jewry, every citie Jerusalem.' So wrote the Calvinist George Widley (Collinson 1982: 230). It is the authentically international voice of apocalyptic Protestantism. The True Church found its believers scattered over the globe; following different paths they would converge on the single goal, god's Celestial City. It was the only place that mattered; by comparison England, however elevated its role in the minds of English Protestants, was a small thing. The nation could at best be a carrier; it could never contain the essential principle in itself.

Politically speaking, the internationalism of the Protestant movement was always a difficult matter to put into effect. Puritans in England were repeatedly frustrated by the unwillingness, first of Elizabeth, then of James the First, to help fellow Protestants abroad by the practical measure of armed support (see, e.g., Patterson 1982; McGiffert 1982). But to most Protestants the international character of their struggle was never in doubt, any more than it would have been to the believing Communist of the twentieth century, whatever the role of this or that country as the promoters of the international movement. What went on in Geneva, Bohemia, the Netherlands, France or Scotland mattered profoundly to Protestants in England, as they showed by their readiness to give material aid and to risk their lives in assisting their co-religionists in those countries (Hexter 1961e: 33; cf. Schama 1988: 93–96). The great struggle against the Papacy was seen in the light of an international crusade – *all* Protestants against the Pope, the Antichrist. Since Antichrist was embodied in an international power, the Catholic Church, it was only natural that the Christian forces of righteousness should also have an international character. Anti-popery became the organizing principle of a whole view of the world, the expression of a struggle on a global scale for the soul of all mankind (Lake 1980, 1989).

In 1581 the staunch Protestant William Charke wrote: 'He that smitheth our religion wounded our commonwealth . . . Religion and policie are, through God's singular blessings, preserved together in life as with one spirit; he that doth take away the life of one doth procure the death of the other' (in Loades 1982: 297). No one in that age of religious strife would have doubted that religion and politics were inextricably connected, that religion needed the protection of the state as much as the state needed to be legitimated by religion. Nor, as a more general matter, is it necessary to deny that religion and nationalism can be linked, as several contemporary examples, for example Bosnia and Northern Ireland, make plain.

But there is an inherent tension between religion and nationalism (see on this Hobsbawm 1992: 67–71; Greenfeld 1996b; Asad 1999).[13] Religion always strives towards cosmopolitanism and universalism. Certainly in sixteenth-century Europe, in England as much as elsewhere, Protestantism was far too many-sided to be squeezed into any national form. In opposing the international Catholic Church, Protestantism was bound to think and act in equally international terms. The seventeenth-century 'wars of religion' therefore took on an inescapably international character, whether in the form of the Thirty Years War on the Continent or the 'English Civil War' that drew in from the start warring religious groups in Ireland and Scotland as well as England.

The relationship between Protestantism and English nationalism was therefore always going to be a tense one, as tense as is always the relationship between religion and nationalism (contemporary Iran provides a vivid example of this). Indeed, as we shall see, Protestantism was rather more successful in supplying an identity for a *British* national identity than for a purely English one. But in the sixteenth century at least its relationship to Englishness was at best ambiguous, at worst resentful and hostile. The English state did not always seem to be on the side of the true Church, not, at least, enough to satisfy the most ardent Protestants. And when it came to the choice, religion took precedence over nation. Bishop Aylmer may have thought that 'god is English'; but this marginal remark is accompanied by the stern reminder to his compatriots that 'you fight not only in the quarrel of your country, but also and chiefly in defense of his true religion, and of his dear son Christ' (in Marcu 1976: 79).

Literary Englishness

There is one final strand to Greenfeld's argument that the sixteenth century saw the development of a full-grown English nationalism. This is the contribution of the writers, thinkers and scientists of the time. She notes 'the nationalism of Elizabethan literature, striking in its omnipresence and intensity'. This secular vernacular literature was the culmination and

conspicuous expression of the national consciousness and identity coming of age in England ... Everything English became an object of attention and nourished a new feeling of national pride ... It was another, perhaps the last, among the long strings of developments which collectively led to the firm entrenchment of modern, full-fledged, mature nationalism in England already at the end of the sixteenth century.

(1992: 67, 70)

Who were these literary nationalists? They were historians such as Holinshed and Camden; playwrights such as Marlowe and Shakespeare; poets such as Spenser and Drayton; prose writers such as Lyly and Nash; social and political commentators such as William Harrison and Sir Thomas Smith. 'The new feeling of patriotic love grew into a passion and was expressed in poetry with exuberance and deep lyricism heretofore reserved for the sphere of intimate personal relations' (1992: 67). In addition, Greenfeld wishes to add the achievements of English science to the list of patriotic and nationalist endeavours. The English, she says, unable to compete with the French and Italians in classical learning, embraced modernity as the sphere of their cultural specificity and superiority, and science as the emblem of that modernity. Science became the activity which expressed the national temperament at its best and highest, creating an atmosphere highly conducive to its further progress.

> It was the importance of science for the English national identity and the function it performed for the cultural image of England that created the state of public opinion favorable to its cultivation, encouraging to those who had the abilities to devote to it, and causing many Englishmen who knew very little about the substance of scientific knowledge to stand in reverence before expressions of scientific creativity. It was nationalism that raised science to the apex of occupational prestige and ensured its institutionalization.
>
> (1992: 80)

No one doubts that, at some stage of its development, science came to find a peculiarly congenial home in England, and that Englishness – at least in one of its faces – came to be associated with the sceptical, empirical temperament normally thought favourable to science. But when did this take place? Certainly not in the sixteenth century, as Greenfeld's own account makes plain. Departing from the century of the putative formation of English nationalism, Greenfeld in fact wanders freely into the succeeding century, citing the cases of famed scientists such as Bacon, Harvey, Boyle, Newton and Halley. The nationalist fervour accompanying 'England's self-definition as the scientific nation' climaxes for her in the foundation of the Royal Society (1660), as expressed especially in Thomas Sprat's patriotic and propagandistic *History of the Royal Society* (1667) (Greenfeld 1992: 82–3).

But in what way is a late seventeenth-century text evidence for sixteenth-century English nationalism? How do seventeenth-century scientists express the scientific temperament that is assumed to accompany the rise of English nationalism in the preceding century? Let us leave aside the obviously international connections and correspondences of English scientists in the seventeenth century; let us ignore the well-known fact that Newton spent more time tracing the Beast of the Apocalypse than he did in his work on gravitation and mechanics. The fact remains that if science is to be seen in nationalist perspective – a particularly dubious assumption at *any* time, and especially so in this period – then it is not until the late seventeenth century that it can be allowed any serious part in the story of English nationalism. It was only then that the 'Moderns' achieved victory over the 'Ancients', only then that the English might in any sense come to be associated with a particularly modern turn of mind, scientific or otherwise. Before then, and especially in the sixteenth century, not only was science in England undeveloped by comparison with France, Italy or even Poland and Bohemia, but English culture generally shared in the internationalism that was the hallmark of Renaissance humanism.[14] To claim science for the cause of nationalism is probably unwarranted in any country before the nineteenth century; in sixteenth-century England, and for most of the seventeenth century, the connection lacks all credibility.

Matters are not so straightforward in the case of the more narrowly defined literary culture cited by Greenfeld. Here the claim of a specifically literary Englishness has also been made by a number of other writers, most notably Richard Helgerson (1992) in his study of 'the Elizabethan writing of England'. In such disparate works as Spenser's *Faerie Queene*, Coke's *Institutes of the Laws of England*, Camden's *Britannia*, Speed's *Theatre of the Empire of Great Britain*, Drayton's *Poly-Olbion*, Hakluyt's *Principal Navigations of the English Nation*, Shakespeare's history plays, and Hooker's *Laws of Ecclesiastical Polity* – all written by men born within a few years of one another, from 1551 to 1664 – Helgerson finds 'an experiential and structural model of national self-writing', an articulation of 'a national community whose existence and eminence would then justify [the writers'] desire to become its literary spokesmen'. 'Never before or since have so many works of such magnitude and such long-lasting effect been devoted to England by the members of a single generation . . . To men born in the 1550s and 1560s, things English came to matter with a special intensity both because England itself mattered more than it had and because other sources of identity and cultural authority mattered less' (1992: 1–3; see also Hadfield 1994; McEachern 1996; Strong 2000: 186–7). Such men – poets, playwrights, lawyers, churchmen, 'chorographers' and cartographers – belonged to different (though overlapping) 'discursive communities', but together they laid 'the discursive foundations' of the nation-state.

In the same eight years and largely though their efforts, England was mapped, described, and chorographically related to its Roman and medieval past; the voyages of the English nation were gathered and printed, and an ideological base was laid for England's colonial and mercantile expansion; English history was staged before thousands by newly founded professional acting companies performing in newly constructed playhouses, and a national dramatic literature was provided with its most enduring works; and, finally, a church of England was established, challenged, and defended with unprecedented authority and sophistication. The men who accomplished these tasks engendered (even as they gendered) a national cultural formation that has not only survived for the last four centuries on the British Isles but has served as a sequentially engendering paradigm for nations throughout the world.   (1992: 299–300)

This is a formidable claim, and Helgerson substantiates it with flair and subtlety. But a full reading of his book quickly dispels any idea that the national discourse so constructed evinces an uncomplicated celebration of the English nation. There is some, but not an overwhelming amount, of that 'national pride,' 'patriotic love' and 'passionate devotion' to the nation that Greenfeld (1992: 67–9) finds to be the predominant character of Elizabethan writing. What Helgerson discerns in fact is a deeply divided literary intelligentsia whose competing visions and allegiances quite fairly reflect the mixture of medievalism and modernity that made up the substance of Elizabethan England. There are those, such as Spenser, Shakespeare and Hooker, who lean towards the state and monarchy, evoking a traditional social order at whose apex is the crown. And there are those, such as Drayton, Coke and Hakluyt, who seem to evoke, in a more populist and inclusive mode, the spirit of the nation, of the people as a whole. In the civil wars of the seventeenth century we might say that these two visions came into open and brutal conflict (and there was no clear victory for either). In Elizabeth's time, partly owing to the queen's own consummate statecraft – and stagecraft – the balance between them was held. 'Elizabeth's presence on the throne kept categories from closing, allowed for an open exchange between a still dynastic state and a discursively subdivided nation' (Helgerson 1992: 298). What this means though is that 'state' and 'nation' remained distinct and distinguishable entities. 'State', the political ruling class, emphatically did not derive from 'nation', the people. The hybrid form 'nation-state', which came to define the aspirations of all nationalists, did not figure in the conception of any significant Elizabethan writer. It may be permissible to speak of Elizabethan patriotism – an attachment to the land, and the ruler as the embodiment of the land, but 'Elizabethan nationalism' sounds as anachronistic as it in fact is.

Of course, this is a complex matter, as the case of Shakespeare immediately suggests. For many people, the Shakespeare who puts the exquisite paean to England in the mouth of John of Gaunt (*Richard the Second*, Act 2, Scene 1), or who gives Henry the Fifth such tingling patriotic speeches, such as that during the battle of Agincourt (*Henry V*, Act 3, Scene 1), epitomizes the essence of Englishness (e.g., Hastings 1997: 56–7). Did not Jane Austen's Henry Crawford regard Shakespeare as 'part of an Englishman's constitution'(*Mansfield Park*, ch. 34)? As with Chaucer, it took the Victorians to put the seal on Shakespeare's status as the quintessential distiller of the national genius. As Green put it in his *Short History of the English People*:

Nowhere is the spirit of our history so nobly rendered. If the poet's work echoes some-times our national prejudices and unfairness of temper, it is instinct throughout with English humour, with our English love of hard fighting, our English faith in goodness and in the doom that awaits upon triumphant evil, our English pity for the fallen.

(1893: 433)

It is indeed, as Green implies, Shakespeare's history plays that are made to carry the burden of English nationalism. *Henry the Fifth*, in particular, as Peter Herman says, 'has the potential to become an exercise in English nationalism and many critics, as well as audiences, have taken it that way' (1995: 206). There was no doubting its nationalistic potential in the film version, starring Laurence Olivier and set to stirring music by William Walton, made during the dark days of the Second World War (see Armes 1978: 167–8; Lewis 1995). But as Herman as well as other critics have shown, *Henry the Fifth* is no simple endorsement or idealization of the monarch, seen as the shining emblem of the nation. Rather it – as well as several others of the history plays – questions at various points the myth of Tudor legitimacy and in general reflects the disturbances and distrust of authority that were widespread in the 1590s (Herman 1995: 224–5; see also Guy 1988: 447–9; McEachern 1996: 83–137). There is indeed no comforting assertion of English superiority or triumphant nationalism to be found anywhere in Shakespeare – and, as for the 'elect nation', there is not even 'the slightest hint of a nationalism Protestantly inclined' (Hastings 1997: 57).

All of this of course is exactly what one would expect from a writer so long celebrated for his 'negative capability', his many-sided and disinterested anatomy of the human condition. Who are the Shakespearean protagonists? In the great tragedies, a Scottish king, a British king, a Venetian Moor and a Danish prince. Elsewhere there are Italians galore (Leontes, Prospero, etc.), and several Spaniards and Portuguese (not to mention diverse ancient Greeks and Romans). English protagonists are conspicuous largely by their absence, save in the case of the dubiously English kings – hardly in most cases, as Shakespeare portrays them, exemplars of the truly English virtues. None of this seems to make of Shakespeare a promising candidate for the role of early English nationalist.[15]

What might – cautiously – be said about Shakespeare's social and politi-cal attitudes in fact points away from any kind of nationalist identification, at least in the modern populist sense. Helgerson has plausibly argued that one of Shakespeare's goals as a player-poet of relatively humble origins was to elevate the theatre in social esteem, to put plays on a par with the poetry and litera-ture of university-educated writers and other clients of courtly and aristocratic patronage. In doing so he had to break the current and customary association of the theatre with the groundlings and the great unwashed. The popular the-atre was tainted with barbarism. To be accepted it had to be civilized, that is, lifted to the level of high society. This involved not just the mechanics of the-atre production – the building of well-equipped, permanent theatres such as the Globe – but also the plots of the plays themselves. In the history plays, as Helgerson shows, Shakespeare came to represent the nation not by the ordinary people – artisans, peasants, fools and clowns – but by its upper-class members, its kings and nobles. Respectability, for the theatre and its practitioners, was achieved by amputating the nation, separating its upper from its lower half. This involved both 'a redefinition of the nation and of the place the common people...occupied in that nation' (Helgerson 1992: 215).

Whatever subversive potential Shakespeare's plays contain – which they undoubtedly do – is undercut by the stronger and more dominant theme. It is this theme that has impressed itself on the national mind through the centuries.

Shakespeare has stood, as he still stands today, for Royal Britain, for a particularly anachronistic state formation based at least symbolically on the monarch and an aris-tocratic governing class...In response to a complex set of conditions that included the artisanal identity of the theater itself, Shakespeare helped establish the new genre of the national history play and then gave that genre a singularity of focus that contributed at once to the consolidation of central power, to the cultural division of class from class, and to the emergence of the playwright – Shakespeare himself – as both gentleman and poet.   (1992: 244–5)

Thus did Shakespeare become England's 'national poet'. But the nation he represented was one that found little room for the majority of the people of England.

In brief summary: neither socially, politically nor culturally did sixteenth-century England display the features that would lead us to expect the develop-ment of nationalist feeling. There was not that drawing together of the classes, nor any fundamental moves towards democratization, that might lead people to think of themselves as belonging to one nation. Religion could sometimes supply the principle of unity, but it could equally divide and fragment, and in the period of the Reformation its divisive quality was somewhat more evident than its capacity to unite, at least at the national level. There were democratic currents in the literary culture, but these were overlaid and to a good extent stifled by powerful countervailing attitudes that stressed the monarchical qual-ities of the English state and society. At best, what emerged, and persisted for many centuries to come, was a fundamental split between the 'high' culture of the society and the popular or mass culture. Both could and did develop energetically. There was frequent interaction between the two levels, often of a creative kind. But the separation of the two, in the context of a highly specific and restrictive notion of the 'political nation', made it difficult to elaborate a truly national idea. Only in exceptional periods, until the coming of egalitarian and democratic ideologies, was it possible to overcome the division and see the English as a united people sharing a common way and destiny.

It would probably not be too much of an exaggeration to say that most people in sixteenth-century England, as in the rest of Europe, thought of themselves as either locals or cosmopolitans. No doubt localism was still the dominant sentiment for the mass of the people, though it was beginning to change for the 'middling sort' (Wrightson 1982: 222–8; Loades 1997b: 147–58; 1997a: 264–7).[16] But there were those – Catholics as much as Protestants, jurists as well as poets and playwrights, priests as well as aristocrats and monarchs – who saw themselves as having simultaneously international or cosmopolitan as well as national or local affiliations and identities. This is something difficult to grasp in an age of nationalism, though perhaps less so now in an increasingly post-national age. But when the poet Thomas Wyatt declared his relief at being at home, the places that came to his mind as expressing that fact were not 'England' but 'Kent' and 'Christendom'. That, with its fusion of localism and cosmopolitanism, is perhaps a measure of the distance that separates the age of nationalism from the age of the Tudors.

6

The making of British identity

The Isle within itself hath almost none but imaginary bounds of separation, without but one common limit or rather guard of the Ocean sea, making the whole a little world within itself, the nations an uniformity of constitutions both of body and mind, especially in martial processes, a community of language (the principal means of civil society), an unity of religion (the deepest bond of hearty union and the surest knot of lasting peace).

> King James the Sixth and First, 1604 (in Rowse 1957: 315)

Countries are not laid up in heaven; they are shaped and reshaped here on earth by the strategems of men and the victories of the fortuitous. But once they take root and are bolstered by the habits and mechanics of unity and by a common mythology, they soon acquire an image, if not of immemoriality, at least of almost inevitable and organic development.

> R. R. Davies (2000: 54)

One nation divided

The seventeenth century has always seemed an unpromising time to look for expressions of English nationalism, which is probably why we do not hear of many claims to find it there. Its principal characteristic, in England as elsewhere, is conflict and division. It is the period of the Thirty Years War, of rebellions and revolutions in practically every major European country. 'These days are days of shaking', declared an English preacher in 1643, 'and this shaking is universal: the Palatinate, Bohemia, Germania, Catalonia, Portugal, Ireland, England' (in Trevor-Roper 1965: 59). The sixteenth century, for all the struggles of the Reformation and Counter-Reformation, succeeded in absorbing its strains and preserved intact the courtly aristocratic society with which it began. The seventeenth century did not absorb its strains; instead it was transformed by them. At its end, says Hugh Trevor-Roper in a celebrated account, 'intellectually, politically, morally, we are in a new age, a new climate. It is as if a series of rainstorms has ended in one final thunderstorm which has cleared the air and changed, permanently, the temperature of Europe' (1965: 62–3; cf. Clark 1960a: ix).

The point about the seventeenth-century conflicts is that they did not simply set state against state, nation against nation. In fact this may even have been the lesser phenomenon. What struck all contemporary observers, and have continued to preoccupy historians since, were the massive fractures *within* societies. European societies were convulsed by revolutions and rebellions in which parliaments and estates rose against courts and kings, religious communities fought each other for confessional supremacy, and classes came into open conflict with each other (Clark 1960a: 306–24; 1960b: 121–60; Aston 1965; Forster and Greene 1970; Kamen 1984: 258–91). England was the storm-centre of this Europe-wide crisis. In a violent civil war at mid-century, the English executed their king, abolished their monarchy, removed the upper chamber of their Parliament, and disestablished their national Church. All of these were restored in 1660, and have remained a part of the English (later British) state ever since. It is even unclear how much change there was at the political and social levels, though the change in the intellectual climate is unmistakable. But no-one can doubt the extreme bitterness and vehemence that seized the English population in this period. After the return of the kings and bishops, a significant section of the English population felt itself alienated from all the main centres of power and influence. For over a century religious nonconformists and political radicals – often the same people – withdrew into their own enclaves, pursuing their lives as best as they could in a society dominated by other groups and values. English society faced no great challenge from them, nothing comparable to the great conflicts of the period before 1660. But they were a lasting testimony to the divisiveness of those conflicts and the long legacy they left behind. 'God is dashing England against England . . . Christian against Christian . . . The English against the English' – such was the anguished cry of the Puritan preacher Jeremiah Whitaker in the midst of the Civil War (in Collinson 1997: 33).

Such divisions were bound to affect any concept of the nation as an equal, unified people. Even Liah Greenfeld, convinced as she is that the English invented such a concept in the sixteenth century, is somewhat at a loss to account for its fortunes in the following century. According to Greenfeld, the idea of the nation developed in the Tudor period was a radical, indeed 'inherently revolutionary', one. Its emphasis was popular. The nation is the people, free and equal. Such a concept, she thinks, could continue to find powerful expression in the seventeenth-century Civil War, though at the cost of denying membership to certain sections of the English population: all those groups identified with 'the Court' (cf. the abbé Sieyès' denial of membership of the French nation to the French aristocracy in 1789). But, as Greenfeld uneasily sees it, its course became increasingly rocky after the Restoration of 1660. The nation ceased to be identified with 'the people' – a radical, rational and 'idealistic commitment' – and came instead to be identified with 'the land, government, and ways of England' – a conservative, 'emotional attachment'. 'England' became not its people but its king, its constitution, its territory, its national idiosyncrasies and eccentricities. 'In Restoration England, tired of the revolutionary striving to attain the ideal, people found comfort in the thought that their destiny was not of their making, but was instead inherent in the "soil and climate", and were eager to be satisfied with the status quo' (1992: 401). Reversing the trend of the Civil War, 'Court' – an 'updated particularism, clothed in nationalist rhetoric' – triumphed over 'Country' – 'the original ideals of English nationalism' (1992: 400; see also 73–7). The English left it to their brethren across the Atlantic, in the new nation of America, to carry the torch of popular nationhood, and to bring its principles to a triumphant fulfilment.

This account of English political developments in the seventeenth and eighteenth centuries at least has an air of plausibility lacking in Greenfeld's characterization of Tudor England. But it makes even more incredible her discovery of an original English nationalism in the sixteenth century. Technological inventions, we know, can have a chequered career; but what kind of social invention is it that, once discovered and proclaimed to the world, can disappear so comprehensively from the land of its birth? More tellingly, how to explain the fact that the principle of nationalism, invented according to Greenfeld in the sixteenth century, by her own account goes underground everywhere for the next two centuries, to re-surface finally only in France in the late eighteenth century, when the French 'discovered' and elaborated the English principle of nationhood (Greenfeld 1992: 14, 156–8)? What parallel is there to such a historical process in modern times? There is something suspicious about so elusive and evanescent a creature, one that can come and go quite so easily. What is more convincing, of course, and is in accord with the view of most students of nationalism, is to discount this first reported sighting of nationalism and to see that, in England as much as elsewhere, it is not until the time of the American and French Revolutions that ideas of nationhood in the modern sense begin to gain ground.

The principal obstacle to this view remains, not the implausible idea of a sixteenth-century English nationalism, but the possible expression of a distinct national consciousness during the Civil War of the mid-seventeenth century. This would still have to come to terms with the awkward and undisputed fact of its suppression or muting after 1660. The argument would have to turn on some notion of a lost or buried tradition that was later revived. This is, as a general phenomenon, by no means unfamiliar or unpersuasive. Popular politics and popular culture are full of such forgettings and rememberings. Certainly the concept of popular sovereignty seems to have made a decided appearance during the Civil War, though it took above two centuries more, with many twists and turns, appearances and disappearances, for it to become a practicable reality in England. Moreover, it might be said that it never really disappeared, for, whatever its fate in England, it crossed with the dissenters and radicals to America, to be kept alive there and to reappear in the country of its origin at the time of the American War of Independence.

Can the same be said of the concept of the nation? Did nationalism, as an idea and a force, emerge alongside doctrines of popular sovereignty during the English Civil War? So it has been claimed by a number of scholars, though significantly most of them prefer the term 'patriotism' to nationalism. Liah Greenefeld and Adrian Hastings, as the most committed believers in early English nationalism, not surprisingly find fresh material for their thesis in the movements and writings of the period. For them, the new and distinctive thing is the gradual recession of the religious character of the national idea and the assertion of a more self-consciously secular and democratic nationalism. Monarchy and religion – 'earlier indispensable allies' – dropped away as central justifying elements of the nation. Though religious language persisted:

it was no longer religion, but the national idea based on the liberty of the rational individual, which united people. [There was] a switch in the relative centrality of the specifically religious and secular national loyalties... The Revolution helped to disentangle the issues historically associated with the idea of the nation but not essential to it and made it clear that nationalism was about the right of participation in the government or the polity – it was about liberty, and not monarchy or religion.

(Greenfeld 1992: 73–4; cf. Hastings 1997: 60–1)

Others have concurred, though more cautiously, in this finding of what seems the spirit of democratic nationalism in the Civil War (Fletcher 1982: 316; Furtado 1989; Hill 1989a: 5–7, 1989b).[1] But the most impressive testimony to the importance of the English Revolution in the development of nationalism comes from Hans Kohn, the great student and historian of the national idea. Dismissing the notion of a Tudor nationalism – if anything England was, he argues, at that time behind the Continent in 'the awakening of a national consciousness' – Kohn sees the seventeenth century, and in particular 'the Puritan Revolution', as the time when the English made their decisive contribution to the growth of nationalism. The revolution 'lifted the people to a new dignity, of being no longer the common people, the object of history, but of being the nation, the subject of history, chosen to do great things in which every one, equally and individually, was called to participate. Here we find the first example of modern nationalism...' (1940: 80).

This national awakening was partly constructed out of a legendary past of freedom and equality – a reassertion of 'Saxon' liberties stifled by 'Norman' conquerors – but more importantly it represented an 'immense surge towards the future, towards a new nationalism represented at that time by the English, destined, however, for the whole of humanity... The new nationalism was fundamentally liberal and universal, carrying a message for all mankind and implying (if not always granting) the liberty and equality of every individual' (1940: 81).[2]

But then comes a fundamental twist. This democratic message was carried on the back of religion. The Puritan Revolution, says Kohn, 'in spite of its profound national and social implications, was fundamentally a religious movement'. It was a synthesis of 'Calvinist ethics and a new optimistic humanism'. But the Calvinism is the more important force, as is clear from the enunciation of a familiar idea: 'Being a Calvinist revolution the new nationalism expressed itself in an identification of the English people with the Israel of the Old Testament' (Kohn 1940: 79). Indeed most of Kohn's evidence for his argument of a seventeenth-century English nationalism comes from statements of this central idea that were more emphatic versions of similar statements made in Tudor times. It is clear that Greenfeld has simply transposed Kohn's thesis one century back. Where she draws upon Aylmer and Foxe, Kohn turns to Milton and Cromwell. Similar too is the appeal to the significance of Protestantism as a religion of the book – 'England became the people of a book, and that book was the Bible' – and to the inspiration especially of the Old Testament. The 'religious nationalism' of the English people was experienced as 'a revival of Old Testament nationalism'. 'The three main ideas of Hebrew nationalism dominated the consciousness of the period [of Cromwell and his generation]: the chosen people idea, the covenant, the messianic expectancy' (Kohn 1940: 81–2; see also 1944: 155–83).

Compared to Greenfeld, Kohn at least gets the emphasis right. His stress on the messianic fervour aroused during the mid-seventeenth-century conflict, as compared with sixteenth-century thought, squares well with current scholarly opinion. English apocalyptic thought, as Katharine Firth has shown, in the writings of Bale, Foxe and others was a measured and moderate thing in Tudor times. There was little discussion of the future: 'the promise of the New Jerusalem was wrapped in mystery' (1989: 252). God preserved his Church among a small number of the elect scattered throughout the world, who were expected to endure their suffering in the expectation of joy in the life to come. For some, as for Foxe, the reign of Elizabeth raised the hope that, with the establishment of the Reformation, the Church might be perfected in the world as a whole. But Foxe denied, as we have seen, any special destiny for England, nor did he believe that the English had arrived at some perfected state. 'England reformed was neither a Utopia nor a millennial kingdom . . . Bale and Foxe loved their country but neither believed it to be or presented it as the elect nation with an apocalyptic destiny' (Firth 1979: 252).

Apocalyptic thought in England received a fresh impetus in the first half of the seventeenth century as a result partly of the Thirty Years War on the Continent, which brought a flood of Protestant refugees to England. Among these were such figures as the German Samuel Hartlib, who, together with his friend John Dury, played an important role in spreading the millenial and utopian ideas of such thinkers as Johann Valentine Andreae, John Henry Alsted and John Amos Comenius among the English. The effect was to place England (or Britain) at the centre of an unfolding drama in which the future of the world was to be played out. As Firth writes:

Both at home and abroad the conviction grew that Britain had a special role to play in the defence of the Protestant faith. On her soil the New Reformation might come to pass. A utopian vision nurtured abroad and set in a millenarian context found its way into Britain and there worked upon the native apocalyptic tradition, giving it a new life and direction . . . The tradition of exiles and scholars was seized by a new chiliastic doctrine and from it was forged a weapon for social revolution and civil warfare.

(Firth 1979: 253–4; and generally 204–41; see also Trevor-Roper 1984b; Christiansen 1978; Hill 1990)

There is now general agreement that millennialism played not just an incidental but a central part in the English Civil War. From learned thinkers such as Joseph Meade and Samuel Hartlib to Ranters and Fifth Monarchy Men, from Gerard Winstanley and the Diggers to Milton and Cromwell, from Muggletonians and Familists to Seekers and Quakers, there existed a profound conviction that the prophecies of the Book of Revelation were on the point of fulfilment, that the final battle had opened up between the forces of Christ and Antichrist. 'As the landmarks of the old order were thrown down one by one – bishops, the House of Lords, monarchy, Parliament itself – many people were led to believe that these must be the upheavals foretold in Scripture to herald the world's end or its transformation' (Capp 1986: 165; see also Lamont 1969; Hill 1973; McGregor and Reay 1986). More generally, there has been a marked return in current historiography to the view of the English Civil War as fundamentally about religion, rather than, say, about class or even constitutional liberties. As John Morrill, one of the principal exponents of this view puts it, 'the English civil war was not the first European revolution: it was the last of the Wars of Religion' (1993b: 68). Religion, say McGregor and Reay (1986: 3), 'was both the legitimizing ideology of the rulers and . . . the revolutionary idiom of the ruled'.[3]

The problem all this poses for both Greenfeld and Hastings, as well as Kohn, is obvious. For Greenfeld and Hastings there is an absence of that secularizing tendency that they claim to discern in the seventeenth century, and especially during the Civil War. Their English nationalism therefore has to hold on to its religious clothing a little longer than they would like, to disappear mysteriously in the placid waters of the 'long eighteenth century'. For Kohn, the problem is more complex, since he explicitly accepts the religious basis of the 'Puritan Revolution'. English nationalism in the mid-seventeenth century, he says, is 'religious nationalism'. The question to be put to him then is how to see nationalism in a religious garb. It is not simply that nationalism as we have come to know it defines itself in defiantly secular terms – indeed substitutes itself as a secular religion in the place of all other religions. This may not matter so much in a world of nation-states, where nationality has already been asserted as the indispensable requirement of legitimacy, and where religion can appear simply as an ally of nationalism (as in modern Ireland or nineteenth-century Poland). But it matters profoundly in a world, such as that of the seventeenth century, where men and women fought and died for religion, and where national feeling was subsumed in a wider context that took into account the fate of religion as the overriding concern.

The examples of Milton and Cromwell, whom Kohn takes as his principal examples of the expression of English nationalism, both show this difficulty. We have seen that Milton's view of England as the elect nation was a severely qualified one. He placed his hopes on England only in so far, and for so long, as England promised to be the agency of the higher values in which he believed. Kohn himself says that 'his main concern remained the liberty of man, the autonomy of the rational being', in pursuit of which goal he found England at times sadly lacking, even in the midst of revolution. Kohn remarks on 'the Catholic temper of Milton's nationalism', and quotes him in a way that shows the immense gap that separates this kind of 'nationalism' from most later varieties.

Nor is it distance of place that makes enmity, but enmity that makes distance. He therefore that keeps peace with me, near or remote, of whatsoever Nation, is to me as far as all civil and human offices, an Englishman and a neighbour; but if an Englishman forgetting all Laws, human, civil and religious, offend against life and liberty, to him offended and to the Law in his behalf, though born in the same womb, he is no better than a Turk, a Saracen, a Heathen.   (Kohn 1940: 85)

Milton's essential cosmopolitanism comes out repeatedly. In a Commonwealth state paper which he drafted in 1655 he proclaimed that 'since God hath made of one blood all nations of men...on earth...all great and extraordinary wrongs done to particular persons ought to be considered as in a manner done to all the rest of the human race' (in Hill 1989a: 6). For Milton, the English had led the world with their revolution, but it was in no sense a revolution for them alone. It was not a national but an international revolution, the first stage of a total transformation of the world. We need to take Milton's millenarianism and utopianism – as those of many other men and women of his time – seriously, and not see in it some sort of ideological cover for a more basic English nationalism or imperialism. It is from such a perspective that we should understand the famous passage in which Milton sees the whole world eagerly watching the English Revolution, as a portent of the coming liberation of the whole of mankind.

> I seem to survey, as from a towering height, the far extended tracts of sea and land, and innumerable crowds of spectators, betraying in their looks the liveliest interest, and sensations the most congenial with my own ... Surrounded by congregated multitudes, I now imagine that, from the columns of Hercules to the Indian Ocean, I behold the nations of the earth recovering their liberty which they had so long lost; and that the people of this island ... are disseminating the blessings of civilization and freedom among cities, kingdoms, and nations.   (in Kohn 1940: 86; cf. Hill 1989b: 163)

It says much for the fairness and scrupulousness of Kohn's account that it is he himself who quotes many of these passages, though they tell against the strict argument of his account that England pioneered nationalism in the course of its revolution. A similar scholarly impartiality informs his portrait of Oliver Cromwell. Cromwell he sees as 'the typical Englishman', the man who 'more than any other awakened the consciousness of the English people as the chosen people'. He 'completely identified the English people with ancient Israel; English nationalism was born in the great decisive hour of its history by repeating the experience of the chosen people, of the covenant, of the battles fought for the Lord' (1940: 87–8, 89–90).

Of Cromwell's attachment to England, and his belief in its mission under God's guidance, there is no doubt. The English, he said, are 'a people that have had a stamp upon them from God; God having, as it were, summed up all our glory to nations, in an epitomy, within these ten or twelve years last past'. There are numerous rhapsodic speeches where he proclaims his belief that the English are to God 'as the apple of his Eye', that God has a special care for them and watches solicitously over their affairs. 'The dispensations of the Lord', he declared in 1654, 'have been as if he had said, England, thou art my first-born, my delight amongst the nations, under the whole heavens the Lord hath not dealt so with any of the people round about us' (Hill 1970: 147; see also 217–50). More prosaically he can also say simply, 'We are English, that is one good fact' (Hill 1970: v).

But no more than Milton does Cromwell believe that God's purpose works exclusively for the English nation, nor that the battles are battles on behalf of any one people. Kohn himself says that 'the cause for which [Cromwell] fought was indeed supra-national, the ideal of what he deemed true Protestantism and of the universal concern of humanity and liberty' (1940: 88). It was this that allowed him to move, quite self-consciously it seems, from praise for the English as the promoters of this cause to a sense of the godliness of all the peoples of Britain as inhabitants of this blessed isle. It was Britain, and not just England, that was furnished with 'the best People in the world'. The God 'that hath watched over you and us', he told a Parliament in 1653 that contained Irish and Scottish representatives, 'hath visited *these Nations* with a stretched out arm; and bore His witness against the unrighteousness and ungodliness of man, against those that would have abused such *Nations*' (in Kohn 1940: 90; my emphases). It was not just the English but their righteous neighbours in the isles that also had 'a good Eye' to watch over them.

Cromwell even extended his embrace to the Irish, whose resistance he crushed so ruthlessly, declaring that if they could free themselves from the tyranny of their priests they too 'may equally participate in all benefits, to use liberty and fortune equally with Englishmen' (Hill 1970: 120). Mindful of the massacres of Drogheda and Wexford we can, if we wish, see this as hypocrisy, as the Irish have always done. But it is also entirely consistent with Cromwell's belief that England was struggling on behalf of the whole world, and not just the English, for civilization and liberty; that all the peoples of the world had a right to this inheritance; and that the English would, and should, enjoy God's favour only so long as they continued in this divinely ordained task. As Sir Charles Firth put it, 'religious rather than political principles guided his action, and his political ideals were the direct outcome of his creed' (1953: 468). Of 'the two greatest Concernments that God hath in the world', said Cromwell, 'the *one* is that of Religion . . . and also the Liberty of men professing Godliness (under the variety of forms amongst us) . . . The *other* thing cared for is the Civil Liberty and Interest of the Nation, which . . . is, and I think ought to be, subordinate to a more peculiar Interest of God' (C. Firth 1953: 475; cf. Greenfeld 1992: 75). Religion, the 'Interest of Christians', came first, the 'Interest of the Nation', second. Like Milton's, Cromwell's identification with England was conditional, not absolute; nothing could have been further from this attitude than nationalist pride, or the modern patriotic belief in 'my country right or wrong'.

Hans Kohn has said that English nationalism 'has always been and still is closer than any other nationalism to the religious matrix from which it arose'. He notes too that 'it never made the complete integration of the individual with the nation the aim of nationalism; it always put a great emphasis upon the individual and upon the human community beyond all national divisions' (1940: 92). How far this is any species of nationalism, and how far it sums up the English legacy, are both moot points. But Kohn is as sensitive here as he is throughout his account of seventeenth-century 'English nationalism' to the peculiarity of the English case. The English Civil War – the only real candidate at this time for the putative job of creating English nationalism – was an astonishing event. It unleashed a flood of ideas in the world that, in various forms, were to play an important role in the American and French revolutions of the next century. In that sense – especially perhaps in its proclamation of the sovereignty of the people – it may be said to have made a contribution to the doctrine of nationalism.[4] But in its own time, and judged by its own character, it could not be the bearer of the national idea. It was indeed, as Kohn says, 'a primarily religious revolution' (1940: 91), a Protestant or Puritan revolution in which ideas of individual liberty were mixed in complex ways. Both of these features militated against a clear enunciation of the principle of collective identity which conceived a people as a nation, in a world of nations. The English Civil War was at once too international and too individual, too much concerned with the fate of religion and the question of personal salvation, to embrace such an exclusive and self-limiting conception.

For the Jacobins of the French Revolution, and despite the misgivings of Robespierre and others, the internationalism of the French Revolution could be allowed to retreat into a national shell (re-emerging as French imperialism). This was possible because the idea of the nation had been germinating in French thought for much of the eighteenth century (Palmer 1940; Godechot 1971). The sovereign French people would teach the world liberty, by force if need be. For the Puritans of the English Revolution, no such escape was possible. They couched their message in millennial, almost cosmic, terms. When the millennium did not come, when ideas of Christian brotherhood and freedom were repressed by the very people who should have been promoting them, the Revolution had nowhere to go. For it was, as Cromwell said, 'God's revolution' (Firth 1953: 472), and 'the invention of men', which for Cromwell was 'dross and dung in comparison with Christ', could no more determine its fate than human contrivance the movement of the heavens.

Towards Great Britain

'If Charles I had been king of England only', says Geoffrey Elton, 'there would have been no rebellion or Civil War' (1992: 156; cf. Ellis 1988: 46). The British dimension to the Civil War reminds us that it was not only religion that proved an obstacle to the development of English national consciousness. In the seventeenth century England did not stand alone. With the accession of James the Sixth of Scotland to the English throne in 1603, England became part of a multiple monarchy of three kingdoms. James the First of England was also, separately and simultaneously, king of Scotland and king of Ireland (Ireland having being converted from a 'lordship' to a separate kingdom, reserved to the English crown, in 1541). Multiple kingdoms or 'composite states' were the source of conflict and instability throughout Europe in the seventeenth century, most notably in the case of the Spanish monarchy with its Portuguese, Italian and Netherlandish possessions (Koenigsberger 1986: 12–21; Greengrass 1991; Elliott 1992; J. Wormald 1992: 189–90; 1996: 150; Russell 1995; Reeve 1999: 296). Some of the causes were constitutional, but the most significant causes were differences of religion. In this respect, and as the source of its deepest conflicts, the multiple monarchy of the British went further than its continental counterparts. As Conrad Russell says:

> though there were other cases in Europe in which one king presided over two religions, I am aware of none in which a single king presided over three [Anglicanism, Scottish Presbyterianism, Irish Catholicism]. Moreover, Britain appears to be a unique case of multiple kingdoms all of which were internally divided in religion, and in all of which there existed a powerful group which preferred the religion of one of the others to their own.   (Russell 1987: 398; see also 1990b: 27–9; 1995: 136–7; Morrill 1996: 10–12)

Under the cautious and conciliatory rule of James the First, this volatile and unstable mixture was contained. The incautious and headstrong Charles the First, together with his advisers Laud and Strafford, ensured that it would explode (Trevor-Roper 1984d: 454–6). In their drive to impose religious uniformity in all three kingdoms, they stirred up rebellion in Scotland and Ireland. Whether this can be considered the main cause of the 'English Civil War' remains hotly debated, but no-one denies that the rebellions were the immediate cause of Charles's need, following the eleven-year period of personal rule, to turn to the English Parliament in 1640–41 (Russell 1987: 406; 1990b: 12–13). He thereby unleashed all the pent-up religious and constitutional grievances in that body and was faced with a third rebellion, this time in England. Moreover the three-kingdom character of the Civil War was marked throughout. All three kingdoms intervened constantly in each other's affairs. English and Irish troops were called upon to impose Charles's will in Scotland in 1640; the English and Scots moved against the Irish rebels in 1641; the Irish intervened in England in 1643; the Scots invaded Ireland in 1642, and they repeatedly invaded England, in 1640, 1643, 1648 and 1651. Under Cromwell, the English retaliated with crushing force against all their enemies, securing the defeat of the Scottish and Irish rebels and the subjugation of Scotland and Ireland in 1649–51. In the Commonwealth and the Protectorate, for the first time ever, England, Scotland and Ireland were ruled as a single country, under a single legislative and executive authority in London (an arrangement which ended with the Restoration of 1660). Truly the Civil War cannot be regarded as an exclusively English affair, either in its causes, course or consequences (see Russell 1990b: 218; 1991; Trevor-Roper 1984c; Levack 1987: 109–21; Morrill 1993c, d, e, 1995a, b: 26–38; Pocock 1996; D. Smith 1998:105–96).

The Civil War indicated in the clearest possible way that England's future lay, in good part, beyond itself. Together with other events – the Protestant Reformation in Scotland, the Ulster plantation in Ireland, the union of the Scottish and English crowns, the overseas settlements in the New World – it highlighted the British aspect of the seventeenth century, one that increasingly drew attention away from a purely English self-awareness to a realization of England's destiny in a larger framework (Ellis 1988; Morrill 1995b; 1996). The 'British idea' resurfaced. The unfinished imperial project of Edward the First, to create a British kingdom of which England would be the centre, once more began to attract attention. Even more far-reaching was the inception of the other empire, the 'external' empire across the seas – with Ireland in more ways than one a stepping-stone. With dreams of an English continental empire fading, the way was clear to look elsewhere – westwards across the ocean to North America and the Caribbean and, not very much later, eastwards towards India and Asia.

First, the matter of Great Britain. When James the Sixth of Scotland became also James the First of England in 1603, he ardently desired to form a 'perfect Union' between the two countries. He would, he announced, not style himself king of England and Scotland, but 'King of Great Britain'.[5] The royal and merchants ships of 'South and North Britain' were instructed to fly the new British flag, the Union Jack (named after James-Jacques). Moreover he would strive for a union not just of crowns but of laws and beliefs, of hearts and minds. After his death, his son Charles commissioned the painter Rubens to commemorate his father in a fitting manner. Rubens responded with a magnificent idealization of James's vision. On the ceiling of Inigo Jones's newly built banqueting hall, the artist showed England and Scotland as two women, each of whom holds a crown over the head of a new-born baby, symbolizing Great Britain, while the goddess Minerva joins the two crowns. At the centre, enthroned, sits James, the begetter not just of the vision of a united kingdom but of this precise image of it as a new-born, still developing, child.[6]

James strove in vain. His hopes were wrecked on the mutual antagonisms of his Scottish and English subjects – the Scots, with reason, regarding the English as harbouring imperialist designs, the English looking down on the Scots as boorish and backward (J. Wormald 1992, 1994, 1995, 1996; Levack 1987: 8–9, 32–41, 193–4; Russell 1995: 144–5). The situation was not helped, from an English point of view, from the perception that it was the Scots – whose king it was after all who was succeeding to the English throne – who were taking over the English rather than, as it had long been natural for the English to assume, the other way round.

Yet despite the underlying suspicion, born of age-old enmities stretching back to the time of Edward the First, England and Scotland had enjoyed good relations for long stretches of time since the conflicts of the thirteenth and fourteenth centuries. There were several attempts to heal the breach, not all equally thoughtful or tactful. In 1503 the marriage between James the Fourth of Scotland and Margaret Tudor, daughter of Henry the Seventh – the marriage of 'the thistle and the rose' – opened the possibility of long-term peace and dynastic unity between the two realms. Undeterred – or perhaps inspired – by renewed war between the two countries and the crushing defeat of the Scots at Flodden (1513), it was precisely this prospect that the Scottish theologian John Mair (or Major) powerfully laid out in his *History of Greater Britain* (1521). Mair looked forward to the creation of a British monarchy through a series of dynastic marriages culminating in rule by a single person. 'All men born in Britain are Britons', declared Mair; they share a common geography and are the common heirs to the whole island's history (Hay 1955–6: 63; Williamson 1983: 36; Mason 1987b: 66; 1994b: 162–7; Dawson 1995: 89).

Throughout the sixteenth century there was talk of union in both countries, though what this might mean could differ considerably. The Protestant Reformation in England brought added urgency to the need to secure the northern half of the island, and to break Scotland's attachment to the 'auld alliance' with France (Morgan 1996). In the 1540s, in the episode known as 'the rough wooing' from its high-handed and violent methods, Henry the Eighth and after him the Protector Somerset sought (unsuccessfully) to secure a marriage between Edward Prince of Wales and the infant Mary Queen of Scots, as a step towards union under a Protestant British monarch. In his proposal of 1548 Somerset urged the abandonment of the names 'England' and 'Scotland' and the union of the two kingdoms as 'one empire' under 'the indifferent old name of Britain'; he also referred to 'Great Britain' – its first use, apparently, in contemporary politics. So would they 'make of one Isle one realm, in love, amity, concord, peace, and charity' (Bindoff 1945: 200–1; see also Williamson 1983: 36; 1999: 145–6; Mason 1987b: 67–71; 1994b: 170–8; Merriman 1995: 115–17; Armitage 1997: 39–40; 2000: 36–46). Though the plan foundered, discussion of it caused the name 'Great Britain' to acquire general currency after the mid-century, so that when James adopted it fifty years later his choice of terms at least occasioned no great surprise. In the meantime, the Reformation had also triumphed in Scotland, so that one enormous stumbling block to unity was removed. Scotland's Protestant revolution of 1560, aided by the English, provoked 'euphoric outpourings on the subject of the unity of the island of Britain', particularly north of the border (Dawson 1995: 90; see also Williamson 1983: 40–2; 1999: 143–9; Ellis 1988: 45; Kidd 1993: 21–2; Hirst 1996: 212; Brown 1999: 250). Differences over church organization and liturgy were, for the time being, suppressed in celebration of a common Protestant culture. James therefore inherited an English throne in a climate that was in many ways highly favourable to his dream of a united kingdom (Hay 1955–6: 64–5; Williamson 1983: 44–51; Ellis 1988: 46–7; Merriman 1995: 111; J. Wormald 1996: 151; Macinnes 1999: 35).[7]

Nor, in his new realm, was he alone in promoting the case for 'Great Britain'. There were several in England who shared his vision. The antiquarian Sir Robert Cotton – like several English landowners, of Anglo-Scottish descent – substantially repeated the arguments of John Major in favour of union, demonstrating the antiquity of the name 'Britain' and arguing for the basic similarity of the two kingdoms. Sir Francis Bacon, scholar and statesman, also appealed to the idea of Britain, calling for 'one just and complete History of both nations' to be written, so that 'this island of Great Britain, as it is now joined in monarchy for ages to come', should equally be 'joined in history for times past' (Bindoff 1945: 206–10; J. Wormald 1992: 179). The failure of James's attempt at a 'true' or 'perfect' union did not stop the idea of Great Britain preoccupying several writers of the time, as for instance Michael Drayton in his *Poly-Olbion* (1613) and John Speed in his *Theatre of the Empire of Great Britain* (1611). After the Restoration of 1660 it even enjoyed quite a vogue. Charles the Second, though not taking the title 'King of Great Britain', clearly wished to encourage a greater sense of a common British identity among his subjects. It was he who in 1665 introduced the female figure of Britannia on coins of the realm, thus providing a useful character for pamphleteers and ultimately, after the union of 1707, a symbol to be celebrated in song and verse. Britannia symbolized not just the unity of Britain but also recalled the glories of classical Greece and Rome, with their associations of liberty, maritime supremacy, and imperial destiny. James Thomson's popular 'Rule, Britannia', set to music by Thomas Arne in Thomson and Mallet's masque *Alfred* (1740), drew generously on these themes (Furtado 1989: 49; Dresser 1989: 30; Armitage 2000: 119; N. Davies 1999: 1148–9). The concept of Great Britain was thus familiar and even popular when it came to be adopted, formally and finally, with the union of 1707.

In truth, as Cotton and Bacon both pointed out, there was much that the two kingdoms shared in common – religion, language, laws and geography. An Anglo-Scottish aristocracy, going back to medieval times, was beginning to be an important component of the aristocracies of both countries, supplying an important bridge. Most importantly, the two nations now shared a king. The English might feel that the Scots were too Protestant, the Scots that the English had a tendency to backslide in matters of religion (McEachern 1996: 194–5). Fundamental suspicions and long-standing prejudices dogged Anglo-Scottish relations for generations, even after the union of 1707. But there was certainly much in the nature of the two kingdoms to suggest that should they attempt a full union, there were many things working in favour of integration – unlike, say, the case with Ireland, with its Catholic majority and memories of brutal English conquests stretching back to medieval times.

Scholars have disagreed sharply over the amount of convergence and divergence between the two societies preceding and accompanying the Act of Union of 1707. For some, such as Mark Goldie, 'the Union sponsored convergence; it was not sponsored by it' (1996: 222; cf. J. Wormald 1992: 192–3; 1996: 155; Trevor-Roper 1992: 291–2; Brown 1995, 1998; Kidd 1998). There was much to suggest divergence in the second half of the seventeenth century. Scots retained bitter memories of the forced Cromwellian union of 1654, and were likely to view any future union with England through that experience. The Covenanter Revolution had entrenched Presbyterianism deeply in Scotland's religious consciousness, so that the Restoration of 1660, with its reimposition of episcopacy in Scotland as well as England, occasioned greater resentment north of the border than in the south. Covenanter rebellions in the 1660s and 1670s were severely repressed, and in the 1680s south-west Scotland suffered military occupation and religious persecution. Politically too, Scotland diverged considerably from England. Its Parliament had less power and authority and the crown's rule was more absolutist in character – a resource that James duke of York, the Catholic heir to the throne, showed every intention of employing, to the consternation of both Scottish and English Whigs (Harris 1999: 270–1). At the same time, Scots were conscious that their monarchy had migrated to London, leaving Scotland bereft of the courtly patronage that had been a significant source of sixteenth-century Scottish Renaissance culture. Scottish law also, emphasizing its continental and Roman character, increasingly came to insist on its difference from English common law. Finally, there were significant differences in social structure, with Scottish society dominated by a small landed elite overseeing a vast peasantry – a 'backward' condition that was a favourite subject for English caricatures of the Scots.

Seen from a wider perspective, however – a bird's eye rather than a worm's eye view – the differences between the two kingdoms after 1660 might not seem so much greater than those within them. They could appear no greater, for instance, than those between Anglicans and nonconformists or between Whigs and Tories in England. Moreover, as even scholars like Goldie admit, there was nothing in the whole British Isles to compare with the divide between Lowlanders and Highlanders in Scotland, thus providing a common 'civilizing mission' for English and Lowland Scots alike (Goldie 1996: 228–9). Again, Scottish law and procedures had far more in common with England – from whose practice they derived – than they had, say with France or Spain. Above all, there was that most important bond between the two nations: the shared inheritance of Protestantism, and the need to defend it against the threat of a Catholic reversal, specifically in the form of French domination of Europe (Robertson 1994:

228–9, 236–7; Pincus 1995). It was this, in the troubled negotiations of 1705–07, that supplied the overriding motive for union and the urgent ground of action. From the time of James the Second's expulsion in 1688, union was in the air as the obvious solution to the problem of securing the Protestant succession and maintaining the Protestant character of the two societies. But rarely can a marriage have taken place in less immediately propitious circumstances.

Historians in recent years have tended to emphasize the factional, conflictual and crisis-ridden nature of the union of 1707.[8] When a union did seem, for strategic and prudential reasons, inescapable, there were calls by such Scots as Andrew Fletcher of Saltoun for a 'federal' rather than an 'incorporating' union (Robertson 1987; 1994: 239–46; 1995c: 203–10; Brown 1998: 238–40). Fletcher was to become a legendary influence on Scottish thought, and his writings were to be a source of inspiration to many later generations of Scottish nationalists. But the circumstances of the time, smoothed by liberal doses of English gold and adroit English patronage, favoured the all-out 'incorporating' Unionists. Moreover the settlement of 1707 seemed generous in other than mercenary ways. Scotland was to remain independent in matters of religion, education, legal institutions and local government. It was to have forty-five seats in the House of Commons, despite the fact that its land tax assessment was one-forty-fifth that of England's; it was also to have sixteen peers in the House of Lords. There was to be free trade between the two countries, including trade with the colonies. Above all, the Protestant succession would be secured; and most Scots realized in any case that the English would never allow a Stuart restoration north of the border. The prospect of a civil war in Scotland accompanied by an English invasion weighed heavily with many in casting their lot for an incorporating union (Robertson 1995b: 34; 1995c: 204, 211; Devine 1999: 10, 16). The earl of Roxburghe's summary of Scottish motives is often quoted as the most judicious statement of why the Scots accepted union in 1707: 'trade with most, Hanover with some, ease and security with others, together with a general aversion to civil disorders' (in Goldie 1996: 245). It is a compelling assessment, pointing to both the reasons for success in the years to come as well as the causes of persisting tension between the two countries.

Britons: Welsh and Irish

'May we be Britons, and down go the old ignominious names of Scotland, of England!... Britons is our true, our honourable denomination.' So wrote the Scottish earl of Cromarty – echoing the words of Protector Somerset in 1548 – in putting the case for union before 1707. By adopting the 'mother name' of Britain, he argued, Scots and English could sink their differences and, without giving up their separate identities, construct an overarching British identity that would draw them together in all important matters (Richards 1991: 67). Other Scottish supporters of union, such as John Arbuthnot and William Seton, urged that by sharing in the more developed character of English trade and industry, the Scottish economy and Scottish society would be modernized, so that the disabling differences between the two societies would be removed. Each would then contribute their distinctive qualities to the new joint enterprise, to their mutual advantage and progress. What would emerge would be a new entity, with its own principles of development (Robertson 1987: 210; 1994: 243–4; 1995c: 221; Kidd 1993: 38–41).

Were the Scottish unionists right? Did a British identity, not necessarily effacing but rather adding to existing ones, emerge in the eighteenth century? Were there, in other words, *Britons*? What was the basis of their Britishness? How did it relate to their Englishness – or their Scottishness, Irishness or Welshness? What in general was the character of ethnicity and nationhood in the new state formed in 1707 – the united 'Kingdom of Great Britain', expanded in 1801 to the 'United Kingdom of Great Britain and Ireland'?

A glance from the periphery can, as often, illuminate the central process. Wales, 'England's oldest and oddest colony' (Jenkins 1998: 216), and the Welsh are usually the least discussed, in considerations of eighteenth-century Britishness. Yet in many ways they were the exemplary Britons. That is, they manifested a profound loyalty to the dynasty and the reformed religion without at the same time giving up their sense of their distinct Welshness. The idea, long advanced by Welsh nationalist historians, that the Welsh gentry were comprehensively anglicized, leaving the Welsh torch to be carried by the common people, does not stand up to rigorous scrutiny (Jenkins 1995, 1998; Roberts 1972, 1998; Bradshaw 1998: 80–1; cf. G. Williams 1991: 150–1). A common Welsh consciousness could be found in all ranks of society. From Tudor times until well into the nineteenth century, Welsh elites – especially the clergy – were active in patronizing, promoting and themselves cultivating the Welsh language, Welsh bardic poetry, Welsh harp music and Welsh antiquarian and genealogical studies.

Moreover, unlike the case in Ireland or the Scottish Highlands, the Welsh language received the inestimable boon of becoming the language of Welsh Protestant Christianity. There was a Welsh Bible and a Welsh Book of Common Prayer, and the official recognition of Welsh as the language of worship, well before the end of the sixteenth century, 100 years before the reluctant printing of the Bible in Irish Gaelic and 200 years before the Scots had a translation in vernacular Scots Gaelic (Roberts 1972: 64–6; Jenkins 1995: 122–3; Hastings 1997: 86–7; Bradshaw 1998: 78–9). Borne aloft on this decisive development, the Welsh language thrived as no other vernacular apart from English in the British Isles. In 1700 at least 90 per cent of the people of the twelve Welsh counties spoke Welsh; not until the early twentieth century did the proportion fall below 60 per cent – 'a pattern of survival far superior to that of either Irish or Scottish Gaelic' (Jenkins 1998: 215). In the absence of independent political and legal institutions, language and the culture it enshrined encapsulated Welshness. Indeed the word *iaith* signified both 'language' and 'nation' (Roberts 1998: 13).

But such cultural distinctiveness did not lead to a demand for political separation or the assertion of an independent national identity. For the whole period from the mid-sixteenth to the late eighteenth centuries there were no distinctively Welsh risings or insurrections, no distinctive Welsh politics at all (Jenkins 1998: 214–15; Roberts 1998: 35; Bradshaw 1996: 40). A high degree of cultural dissimilarity coexisted equably, it seems, with an equally high degree of political stability and willing acceptance of the Welsh position within the English and later British state. Philip Jenkins notes the 'curious paradox' of seventeenth- and eighteenth-century Wales, 'being perhaps the most thoroughly "other" and "Celtic" society in the British Isles, yet one so assimilated in political terms as to be essentially indistinguishable from any English region' (1998: 216).

Such a condition did not evolve spontaneously, of course. It was based on the decisive English conquest and partial colonization of Wales in the middle ages. Over the centuries Welsh elites had made their peace with England, by the familiar methods of accommodation, assimilation and integration. But the accession of the Tudors to the English throne heralded a new phase in Anglo-Welsh relations. The Tudor legislation of 1536 and 1543, by merging the Principality and the Marches of Wales, and by the comprehensive extension of English law and administration to the region, effectively created a new constitutional as well as cultural entity. The Welsh 'could now be said to inhabit a land united for the first time in history'; modern Wales, and Welsh identity as we know it, are sixteenth-century creations (Roberts 1998: 11).

The coming of the Tudors stimulated both a vigorous revival of Welsh culture and a more complete accommodation to the English regime. Here, according to Welsh publicists, was a Welsh dynasty on the English throne, fulfilling the prophecies of Merlin that a descendant of Arthur would one day restore the Britons to the throne and reunite all the peoples of Britain. Moreover, had not Arthur's empire encompassed more than the island of Britain, taking in large parts of the western hemisphere? In a far-reaching move, it was Welsh antiquaries, such as John Dee and Humphrey Lhuyd, who in the wake of the union with England coined the phrase 'the British empire', and argued that the Tudors had inherited a historic claim to the new-found lands in the west through the succession from King Arthur and Prince Madoc – the latter, according to Lhuyd, being the twelfth-century Welsh prince who, long before Columbus and the Spaniards, had crossed the Atlantic and discovered America (G. Williams

1991: 123–5; Roberts 1998: 29–30; Armitage 1995b: 57–8; 2000: 46–7, 105–7). It satisfied both Welsh pride and English ambitions that British legends and Welsh mythology should so helpfully justify the claims made for England's destiny in the New World.

Welsh and English interests also chimed nicely in the Reformation settlement of the sixteenth century. Not only did the Welsh gentry share, along with their English counterpart, in the monastic spoils, thus sweetening the union with England and – combined with the liberal distribution of crown offices and ecclesiastical benefices to local elites – binding them by the strong ties of material interest to the Tudor dynasty and its Protestant successors (Jenkins 1998: 227; Roberts 1998: 15; Bradshaw 1998: 75–6). Welsh antiquarians were also assiduous in showing that the Reformation represented the vindication and triumph of the ancient Celtic Church. The Reformation was seen 'not as an innovation but as the restoration of an authentic proto-protestantism which the British church had possessed before it was swamped by Roman and monastic pollution' (Jenkins 1995: 126). In Wales as in England, 'Protestantism came to be accepted as the final triumph which providence had ordained for a Celtic church whose virtues had been prematurely eclipsed' (Roberts 1972: 69; see also Bradshaw 1996: 52; 1998: 80–1; Kidd 1999: 99–121). While for the English this British heritage had to be awkwardly squared with the 'Gothic' and Anglo-Saxon inheritance – the source, after all, of the Roman pollution – for the Welsh there was no such problem. The Protestant Reformation could be seen as the revival and continuation, after an unfortunate hiatus of some centuries, of the authentic religious tradition of their British forebears. No wonder that the Welsh became ready converts to Protestantism, nor that Wales in the seventeenth and eighteenth centuries became a bastion of loyalist sentiment and High Church Anglicanism (Jenkins 1995). For the British state based on the Protestant faith, the Welsh were model citizens, model Britons. 'Wales . . . became the first region of the British Isles to develop an ideology of "British" unity based on loyalty to the monarchy and the protestant cause. It was the "Ancient Britons" who were the harbingers of modern "Britishness" ' (Jenkins 1998: 216; cf. G. Williams 1982: 194–5; Roberts 1998: 31; Bradshaw 1998: 110).

The eighteenth-century Welsh indeed seem to hold all the key elements of the standard British package: cultural particularism combined with a commitment to the wider British political culture of Protestantism, dynastic loyalism and imperialism. The practice, revived by the Tudors, of conferring the title of 'Prince of Wales' on the heir to the throne and making Wales his appanage, gave the Welsh a figure on whom to focus their particular concerns while at the same time linking them firmly to the dynasty. Welsh writers and publicists of the period laid joint claim to the English inheritance of liberty, property and constitutionalism, to the extent even of more readily referring to Magna Charta than to such Welsh 'national' concepts as the Celtic Church or 'the Saxon yoke'. They were prepared to call themselves equally and simultaneously 'Welsh', 'English', 'Britons' and 'patriots' – 'an ideological contortion that is made possible only by the dynastic loyalty which subsumed Welshness under "Britishness" ' (Jenkins 1998: 230). Clearly it was not difficult, in Welsh eyes, to be both Welsh and (new) British, the precise focus depending on particular concerns and contexts.

To turn to Ireland, England's other 'colony', is to be faced at first glance with a situation almost the exact opposite of that of Wales. For were not the Irish conquered and colonized even more brutally than the Welsh? In what ways might they be willing to accept a British identity? Even if the medieval conquest was incomplete, there seems no such uncertainty about later English and British attempts. Ireland might have its own parliament (since 1264), and even be proclaimed a separate kingdom (in 1541). But the reality of English rule, aided and abetted by Scots and Welsh, seems only too evident. The Irish kingdom was reserved to the English crown; the lord deputy who governed Ireland on behalf of the crown was always an Englishman sent from England; and the Irish Parliament was, especially since Poynings' Law of 1495, subject to English royal control (and, after the Declaratory Act of 1720, to British parliamentary control).

From the middle of the sixteenth century – beginning ironically under the Catholic rulers Mary the First and Philip the Second – the English began the fateful policy of plantation in Ireland (Foster 1989: 59–78; Canny 1993: 57–80; Bradshaw 1998: 96–8; Ohlmeyer 1998; Barnard 1998; Armitage 2000: 49–60). Despairing of subduing the Gaelic chieftains, and seeking to offset the power of the often Gallicized English families of Anglo-Norman descent (the 'Old English'), English rulers granted lands to English and, after 1603, Scottish settlers. Irish resistance – as with the great rebellion of Hugh O'Neill in the Nine Years War (1594–1603) – was dealt with severely. O'Neill's rebellion convinced James the First's government that the northern Gaelic stronghold of Ulster must be crushed once and for all. English and Scottish settlers poured into Ulster after 1609, almost entirely displacing the native Irish and ensuring that Ulster would henceforth become the bastion of Anglo-Scottish loyalist Protestantism – the home base of the 'New English'. Plantations continued in the first half of the seventeenth century throughout the island, culminating in a new wave under Cromwell after the crushing of the Irish rebellions in the 1640s and 1650s. With this renewed English conquest the Gaelic landowning class was virtually extinguished and Old English power drastically curbed. Land transfers reduced the landholding of native and Old English communities from about two-thirds (in 1641) of the total area of Ireland to barely one-fifth by 1688 and, with renewed confiscations after 1690, to a mere one-seventh by 1704 (Foster 1989: 115; Morrill 1993e: 109; Barnard 1998: 312).

Differences of religion filled out this picture of conflict and division. The Reformation failed in Ireland; not just the native Irish but the bulk of the Old English remained Catholic, militantly and defiantly so. Resistance to the state-sponsored Reformation fused the two historically antagonistic communities, native Irish and Old English, into a new ethnic community, the Catholic Irish (Foster 1989: 30; Canny 1993: 55–7; Lynch 1994: 135; Hastings 1997: 80–8; Bradshaw 1998: 48–72, 110; Caball 1998; Clarke 1978). A permanent wedge was driven between the predominantly Catholic population and the Protestant minority, the New English, who dominated Irish society from the late seventeenth century. Ireland, from the point of view of the English, remained a danger zone, harbouring potentially rebellious recusants who were only too willing to connive with England's enemies. This became especially apparent at the time of the Revolution of 1688. James the Second, deposed in England, found refuge among the Catholic Irish. It was from Ireland that, with French support, he sought to win back his crown; it was in Ireland that he was crushingly defeated by William the Third at the Battle of the Boyne (1690).

James's defeat set the seal on the 'Protestant Ascendancy' in Ireland that had commenced with the Cromwellian conquest of the mid-century. Old English and Old Irish political cultures were both virtually eliminated. From now on there were only two cultures in Ireland: New English – the culture of the dominant Protestant power-holders – and 'New Irish' – the culture of the disfranchised and embittered Catholic population (Morrill 1993e: 112; Asch 1993b: 161; Bradshaw 1998: 111; Kidd 1998: 323–4 n.10). Ireland, it appears, and as has so often been stated, had all the hallmarks of a classic colony.[9] The Irish, unlike the Welsh, seem to be highly unlikely candidates for embracing a British identity.

But even in the unpromising case of Ireland the idea of a common British identity can be made to seem plausible, if it is not pushed too far. Once again the colonial analogy can mislead as much as it can illuminate. For what kind of colony was it that was, like Ireland, a kingdom, with its own parliament? 'Do not', asked the Protestant Irish leader William Molyneux rhetorically in his *The Case of Ireland . . . Stated* (1698), 'the Kings of England bear the stile of Ireland among the rest of their kingdoms? Is this agreeable to the nature of a colony? Do they use the title of Kings of Virginia, New England and Maryland?' (in Bartlett 1990: 15; cf. Pittock 1997: 132). However determined and dependent, Ireland had a constitutional and institutional separateness that paradoxically allowed it – like Scotland – to be both different and at the same time to share in a common British culture.

The important thing to remember is that the Protestants in Ireland, though undoubtedly a minority and undoubtedly in control of the majority Catholic population, thought of themselves as Irish, while at the same time looking to Britain for that wider identity that was necessary to securing their place in Ireland. We tend to forget, firstly, how large a minority the Protestants were. Only 2 per cent of the population of Ireland in 1600, New English Protestants made up around 30 per cent by 1700 (Foster 1989: 14; Hill 1995: 274; Barnard 1998a: 323). It is impossible for such a large section of the population to regard themselves as an 'embattled minority' for any length of time. Adaptation and acclimatization are the inevitable results of such a prolonged presence in a new land (as the English and others in North America equally showed at about this time). This brings in the second factor, time. By the eighteenth century Protestants had been in Ireland long enough to become a group distinct from their fellow Protestants in England and Scotland, the countries of their origin. The 'New English' might be called such by others, but for them they were Irish as much as English or British: so much so that by the end of the eighteenth century they were declaring themselves Irish 'patriots', and calling for a radical degree of independence from the British Parliament (Hayton 1987; Canny 1987; Asch 1993b; Bartlett 1990, 1995; Leersen 1997a: 294–376; Ford 1998: 212; Barnard 1998b: 212–13).

How this came about illustrates the evolving character of Britishness in the new state formed by the union with Scotland in 1707. More even than the Scots – many of whom were distinctly cool at the prospective union – Irish Protestants in the late seventeenth and early eighteenth centuries showed themselves eager to dissolve the regnal and parliamentary boundaries and to unite with England. The recent reign of James the Second, the brief return of Catholics to power in Jacobite Ireland, and the unsettling terms of the Treaty of Limerick (1691), which seemed too indulgent towards the Catholics, all made them anxious to bind themselves more firmly to England and the Protestant succession (Hill 1995: 275–7; Kelly 1987: 240–4; Smyth 1993; 1996: 246–9; 1998). William Molyneux rightly claimed in the dedication to William the Third of his *The Case for Ireland ... Stated*, that 'your majesty has not in all your dominions a people more united and steady to your interests, than the Protestants of Ireland' (Hill 1995: 284; see also McBride 1998: 243–4). Molyneux, in his enthusiasm, even went so far as to make the implausible claim that ' 'tis manifest that the great body of the present people of Ireland, are the progeny of the English and Britains [Britons], that from time to time have come over into this kingdom' (Hill 1995: 280). This passage has been much debated, but one clear intention seems simply to have been to affirm the unshakably British identity of the Irish Protestants (Smyth 1993: 789–90). It is striking that especially during the crisis of 1688–91, when the Catholic threat was at its greatest, both English and Scots in Ireland stressed their common British identity (Smyth 1996: 253).[10]

Denied the union they had desired, Irish Protestants up to the mid-eighteenth century still continued to draw the parallel with Scotland and call for Ireland to be included in 'the family of Britain', as Charles Lucas put it in a work of 1756 (Hill 1995: 291; Kelly 1987: 244–5). Their calls went unheeded by a British Parliament that saw no immediate need for union and which contained strong commercial interests hostile to Irish competition. Resentful at English indifference, and increasingly conscious of their Irish character, Irish Protestants in the later eighteenth century sought legislative independence from the British Parliament. But, in turning away from union, it was still arguments from English political culture upon which they drew, and it was still Molyneux who was the source of inspiration and support. For Henry Grattan, Molyneux's distant successor as Protestant spokesman, it was Magna Carta and the rights guaranteed by England's 'ancient constitution' that were the basis of Ireland's claim to an independent parliament. It was 'as the descendants of free-born Englishmen' that the Protestants of Ireland – like the American colonists – asserted their entitlement to English liberties, and hence legislative independence.[11]

Grattan's movement for an independent Irish parliament – achieved in 1782 – was accompanied by the repeal of many of the penal laws against Irish Catholics; in 1788 he declared he had set a people free. Grattan's hope – like that of more radical Protestants such as Wolfe Tone, founder of the United Irishmen – was for a united Ireland in which Protestants and Catholics alike would find an equal place.[12] Unlikely as that prospect might have seemed at the time, it reminds us that the birthplace of Irish nationalism was in the Irish Protestant culture of the eighteenth century – the culture to which, of course, Jonathan Swift, Edmund Burke and other Irish 'patriots' belonged. Bishop Berkeley, another famous product of Protestant Ascendancy culture, in his early years was wont to refer to the Irish people as 'natives'; it was not long before he began to talk of 'we Irish'. 'Those who in the 1690s', says Roy Foster, 'called themselves "the Protestants of Ireland" or even "the English of this kingdom" could see themselves as "Irish gentlemen" by the 1720s' (1989: 178; cf. Smyth 1993: 789; Bartlett 1990: 12; Barnard 1998b). 'Ireland is now their home', wrote one Irish Protestant pamphleteer in 1739, 'and they look upon themselves as principals' (Bartlett 1995: 83). The 'English in Ireland', as they had been called since the time of Henry the Second, were fast becoming the Irish in England (or Britain) – a people with their own identity within 'the free empire of Britain', as the Dublin corporation claimed in 1791 (Hill 1995: 294).

Although resistant to a parliamentary union with Britain, the Dublin corporation still saw Irish identity in strictly Protestant terms. Ireland, it declared, was 'a Protestant nation enjoying a British constitution' (Hill 1995: 294; cf. McBride 1998: 260). And of course Irish nationalism with a Protestant face was always going to be an ambivalent, conflict-ridden thing. Dean Swift as much as Edmund Burke saw their futures in England rather than Ireland; and England, or Britain, was always to be a point of reference for the Anglo-Irish gentry. Many Irish landowners relied on office-holding in the British state to supplement their incomes. In 1783, 37 per cent of the 150 Irish peers were employed in the royal household, central government, the foreign and colonial service or full-time service in the army (Foster 1989: 174). Social and cultural connections complemented these material interests. The country estates of the Irish gentry were modelled on English lines; so too were the social life and Georgian architecture of the capital, Dublin (Foster 1989: 185–94; Bartlett 1990: 12). Many Anglo-Irish resided in England and married English brides, as they had done since James the First's time (Canny 1987: 202; 1991: 54; Morrill 1993e: 87–8). Strong ties bound together the Irish and English gentry: both recognized, whatever the English jibes at their country cousins, that they formed part of one ruling class (Connolly 1992: 103–44; Claydon 1999: 127).

So Irish Britishness was always qualified, in a way not true of the Welsh; the majority Catholic population saw little to celebrate in the connection with Britain, both before and after union, though some did indeed think that a closer union might help offset the power of the Protestant Ascendancy at home (O'Brien 1993: 38; Connolly 1995: 203–7; Bartlett 1998: 273). After the failure of the 'patriots' in the 1780s and 1790s, and under the pressure of the threats posed by the French Revolution, Irish Protestants settled for union with Britain in 1801. This in time actually made Catholic Emancipation easier; but with the growth of Protestant evangelicalism in Ireland in the early nineteenth century it was now too late too bring about the secular and non-sectarian Irish nationalism – more properly 'constitutional patriotism' – that Grattan and the patriots had striven for (Bayly 1989: 197; Asch 1993b: 186–7; Whelan 1995: 238–47; Hastings 1997: 91).

Irish nationalism from Daniel O'Connell onwards took on an increasingly Celtic and Catholic character (Boyce 1995: 123–53). But that had the effect of making the Irish Protestants less Irish and more British. In the nineteenth century the Anglo-Irish joined their Welsh, Scottish and English brethren in the joint enterprise of empire, Protestantism and 'the civilizing mission'. 'After the Union the Ascendancy was largely content to accept a British or imperial identity, reinforced by a new sense of mission ... An ideology of British cultural superiority closely connected with evangelical Protestantism gave substance to imperial unity' (Asch 1993b: 189–90; cf. Bartlett 1990: 25; 1995: 87; Bebbington 1982: 502; McBride 1998: 261). Eventually, with the secession of the bulk of Ireland in 1922, that Britishness was reduced to its Ulster redoubt. But the very fierceness and fervour of British commitment there today among the Ulster Protestants are an echo of the very real degree of Britishness that prevailed on a wider scale in Ireland at an earlier time. If we cannot say that Ireland shared in a British identity to the same extent as the Welsh, Scottish and English, a significant proportion of the Irish did indeed see themselves as Britons, as they still do (cf. Pittock 1997: 132–3).

North Britons

'We are', wrote the Irish Protestant Captain O'Hara sadly to his son in 1766, 'a people made rather for copies than originals' (Bartlett 1990: 25). He was remarking on the dependence of the Irish Protestant community on English models and its inability, as he saw it, to forge an independent identity for itself. But perhaps Captain O'Hara was unduly gloomy; or perhaps he had too rigid an idea of identity. To contemporaries on the British mainland, and to subsequent commentators, there was an undeniable distinctiveness to the Irish Protestants. No-one could mistake Dean Swift or Edmund Burke for the average, or even the exceptional, Englishman. At the same time, it was clear how much they were both indebted to the legacy of English culture.

This mix was typical of the evolving British identities of the eighteenth century. One could both retain one's distinctiveness in ethnic or even national terms and, at the same time, share in the new British identity made available by the newly created British state. There is nothing unusual in this combination – one might even say that something like it has been the norm for most people, for most of the time. This is not necessarily to embrace extreme post-modernist doctrines of 'multiple identities'. There *are* limits to the number of identities that any one person can carry at any one time, nor can they all have equal saliency. But this does not confine the individual to the straitjacket of one exclusive identity, national or other, nor does it preclude the emergence of new identities, sometimes with remarkable speed. Eric Hobsbawm has said that 'national identification and what it is believed to imply, can change and shift in time, even in the course of quite short periods' (1992: 11). This is exactly what happened in eighteenth-century Britain, and continued into the nineteenth century and beyond. The creation of a British state by the Act of Union with Scotland in 1707; its extension to Ireland by the incorporating union of 1801; and, throughout, the construction of a British overseas empire that drew together all the peoples of Britain and Ireland in its administration and defence; all these supplied the building blocks for a new British identity that increasingly came to supplement and, at times, suppress the other, older identities that persisted alongside. Add to this the fact that it was precisely in this period that the ideology of nationalism was, for the first time in any real sense, gaining ground in Europe and its dependencies, and it becomes clear why Britishness, as a new national identity, came upon the scene at a most propitious time.

It was something of this kind that Linda Colley argued in her pioneering study, *Britons* (1994). A new British identity, she claimed, emerged in the period between the Act of Union of 1707 and the accession of Queen Victoria in 1837. Linking the peoples of England, Scotland, Wales and Protestant Ireland – Irish Catholics along with Catholic Scottish Highlanders always remained problematic within this definition – it rested on a common experience of constitutional monarchy, economic opportunity and empire. Above all, argued Colley, it rested on religion, specifically the Protestantism that was shared by the vast majority of Britons. It was in the mirror of Protestantism that Britons saw themselves, and it was by virtue of that self-image that they defined the crucial 'Other' as Catholic civilization and the powers that supported it. Britishness was therefore a militant identity, forged in the promotion of Protestantism at home and abroad and in its defence against what was seen as the threats posed by the most powerful contemporary Catholic power, France, with whom Britain was repeatedly at war during the eighteenth and early nineteenth centuries. 'Protestantism was the foundation that made the invention of Great Britain possible' (Colley 1994: 54).

> More than anything else, it was this shared religious allegiance combined with recurrent wars that permitted a sense of British national identity to emerge alongside of, and not necessarily in competition with older, more organic attachments to England, Wales or Scotland, or to county or village. Protestantism was the dominant component of British religious life. Protestantism coloured the way that Britons approached and interpreted their material life. Protestantism determined how most Britons viewed their politics. And an uncompromising Protestantism was the foundation on which their state was explicitly and unapologetically based.   (Colley 1994: 18; see also 1992: 314–23)

There should be, one would have thought from this and other passages, little doubt that Colley was not arguing that a British identity effaced other identities. She speaks of persisting 'organic attachments' to England, Scotland and Wales, and of the 'profound cultural and historical divisions' (1992: 53) between them. She mentions locality – 'county and village' – and social class as rivals to national identity (see also Colley 1994: 16–17; and 1992: 315–16, 325; 1986: 116). All this should have endeared her to those who are chary of assertions of exclusive identity. Yet a careless reading of her book has led several scholars to oppose her main thesis on the grounds that she seems to privilege a British over other attachments, as if these were completely erased in the creation of the new British identity (see, e.g., Clark 2000b: 263, 274–5). Moreover, some argue, even if a British identity came into being, it had little of the quality of genuine nationalism. There might be a 'British patriotism', says Colin Kidd, but 'it was unable to tap deeper historical roots of national consciousness. It was modern and fragile in comparison with Englishness and . . . Scottishness'

(1993: 206). 'Lacking any sustenance from an historic British ethnic identity it seems not to have met deeper atavistic needs' (Kidd 1998: 342). Britishness, says Bernard Crick, was (and is) 'highly and sensibly utilitarian, not emotionally nationalistic'. It existed 'in a narrow and specific context', related to the British *state* but 'not to a national culture or national identity, unless that culture or identity is seen in much narrower terms than is usually meant by nation or nationalism' (Crick 1995: 172–3).[13] Britishness, in this view, simply cannot be understood in the same terms as Englishness or Scottishness.

But is it really so difficult to understand commitment and loyalty to a British monarchy, a British Parliament, a British navy, a British army, a British empire? Is the British national anthem less rousing than those of other nations? Does the British Union Jack not evoke 'emotionally nationalistic' feelings? Might not a common British Protestantism – especially in a situation of threat and danger – inspire a spirit of dedication and sacrifice? When 'Britannia' ruled the waves – as she most certainly did for a century or more – was that not an occasion for national – even nationalist – pride? It does not seem to advance analysis greatly to call all these feelings merely 'patriotic loyalty' to 'the British state', reserving the term nationalism for some sort of deeper attachment to a 'national culture' (Crick 1995: 172). This is to see all nationalism as essentially ethnic or cultural nationalism, and to deny any reality – or at least equality – to its civic forms.

We have seen the difficulty of maintaining the distinction between the two, but we have also seen how fervently it can be championed, and how important the consequences can be of holding to one or the other (see chapter 2, above). We may, if we wish, call British nationalism 'civic' or 'political', by contrast with English or Scottish 'cultural' nationalism. Certainly Britishness was more closely attached to certain political and constitutional forms – monarchy, parliament, a system of common laws, the empire – than in those other cases. But not only is this mainly a matter of emphasis: it is impossible to think of Englishness, for instance, without reference to the legally established Church of England, just as it is impossible to think of Scottishness without reference to the Scottish Kirk and the Scottish courts. It also mistakes the nature and extent of possible commitment and allegiance – an 'emotional' as much as 'a pragmatic, utilitarian sense of obligation' (Crick 1995: 173) – that can be elicited by political forms and political activities. The ritual and ceremony that attend monarchy and parliament, for instance; the fervour that can be aroused in national wars – British, not English, 'Your *Britain*, fight for it now', in the slogan of a famous series of Second World War posters; the glory – and profit – that can come from military and imperial pursuits; the sense of a civilizing, Christianizing mission – all these indicate the potential for a powerful British identity that was fully capable of matching and at times surpassing other identities.

It will be necessary to look at some of these things more carefully, to sub-
stantiate this claim. Once again, it helps to start first with a non-English nation,
in this case Scotland. We have already considered Welsh and Irish Britishness.
How far did the Scots also become Britons – 'North Britons', in eighteenth-
century parlance? How did their Britishness relate to their Scottishness? Why
was it that when George the Third claimed to 'glory in the name of Briton', he
found himself accused of saying that he was a Scot (Kidd 1993: 205–6)? How
was it that it was a Scot, James Thomson, who wrote the wildly popular 'Rule
Britannia', in effect a rival British national anthem to the official 'God Save the
King/Queen'?

We have seen that the Scots were, both before and after the sixteenth-century
Protestant Reformation, the foremost proponents of 'the British idea' (see
Williamson 1983; Mason 1987b, 1994b; Dawson 1995). One might have expected therefore that, despite the reluctance shown by some Scots to the union
of 1707, of all the British peoples the Scots would have been the most loyal
and committed Britons, the most willing to take on the new identity. Yet it is
just this, partly in reaction to Colley's argument, that has been resoundingly
denied by a significant band of recent historians and sociologists, many but by
no means all Scottish. 'The superimposition (or forging) of a British identity',
says Jim Smyth, 'was a project (or process) flawed at its inception' (1998:
319). The union, says Colin Kidd, was not founded on 'any sense of common
Britishness . . . Not only was [it] not accompanied by any ideological consensus,
but there was no real attempt to build a bridge between English and Scottish
nations to create a common British Revolution culture.' Not the sense of a unifying British identity but 'the politics of the closet' sealed the union. 'Britain
remained an uninspiringly underimagined community. Contemporary construction of British nationhood lacked a compelling ethnic or historical vision' (1993:
49–50; 1998: 333–5). There might be a British state and a British Empire, but,
according to this view, their impact on feelings of national identity were severely
qualified. 'The Scots in the eighteenth century', says Bernard Crick, 'did not
come to think of themselves as "Britons" except when singing patriotic songs'
(1995: 172; see also Bindoff 1945: 216; Szechi 1991: 123; Wormald 1992: 191,
193; 1996: 155, 170–1; Robertson 1994: 225, 248).

There has always been a contrary view, the view restated by Colley: that the
union encouraged and enabled a real sense of Britishness to emerge among
the peoples of Britain in the eighteenth century (see, e.g., Hay 1955–6: 65;
1975: 89; Goldie 1996: 220). There is also the fact that the union, born in
such apparently unpromising circumstances, has already lasted for nearly three
centuries. This fact disturbs some of the sceptics, such as Jenny Wormald,
for whom the long persistence of the union is an anomaly, a mystery still
to be explained. She ponders on 'the passive but stupendous power of this

ill-defined but deeply embedded British fact of life' (1992: 194). What she does not seem able or willing to accept is that this 'British fact of life' may have had real consequences for the thoughts and feelings of the people of Britain.

The problem as so often has been the belief in an 'either-or' model: either Britishness or Scottishness, Britishness or Englishness, etc. Nothing in what we know about ethnic or national identities should compel us to accept such a model. Modern-day Indians, for instance, work happily with local (town or village), state or provincial, and all-India identities that often involve the use of three or even four languages (see, e.g., Khilnani 1998: 150–95). This has been the common experience of many peoples at all times, most of whom have lived in 'composite' or multilayered states or empires. It is the modern insistence that we have one overriding national identity that is the anomaly, not the acceptance of multiple identities (which is not to say, with the post-modernists, that we can or do change our identities like a suit of clothes).

Mark Goldie seems to come nearer the truth of the matter when he says that during the eighteenth century, 'Scotland acquired a complex dual identity, a civic Britishness overlying a Scottish cultural identity' (1996: 222; cf. Trevor-Roper 1992: 296). Keith Brown similarly asserts that 'the challenge of becoming British without ceasing to be Scottish was one that the Scots of the eighteenth century were well equipped to meet' (1998: 258; cf. Janet Smith 1970: 108–9; Smout 1989: 5; 1994: 107; Paterson 1994: 43; Devine 1999: 29–30). This seems a fair statement of the question, though it perhaps exaggerates the fixity of the pre-existing Scottish identity and understates the extent to which it was modified by the increasing overlay of Britishness. In what way, then, were the Scots – as with the Welsh and the Irish Protestants – able to carry this dual identity, to be both Scottish and British at the same time? All students, even those hostile to the nationalist historiography that portrays the Scots as essentially and stubbornly Scottish throughout all the political changes of the eighteenth and nineteenth centuries, accept the importance of the persistence of Scottish autonomy in matters of religion, law and education. The loss of a Scottish Parliament in 1707, says Hugh Trevor-Roper, might be, and was, a cause of lament for the 'lesser nobility' whose 'social theatre' it was. But for most Scots Parliament did not – unlike the case of Ireland – occupy a central position in the national consciousness. They could accept its loss with equanimity, even with relief. What mattered, and what they had no intention of giving up, were their law and their Church, 'the twin palladia of the Scottish nation'. 'The lawcourts and the General Assembly of the Kirk were the real native institutions of Lowland Scotland, the guardians of its national identity.' If they could keep these, the Scots did not mind losing their 'costly and feeble' Parliament (1992: 293–4).[14]

Brian Levack has argued that the union of 1707, whereby the Scots preserved their distinctive national institutions, resulted in a state 'unique in Europe', a 'quasi-federalist' state without the usual attributes of the unitary state. 'It had one parliament and one central administration, but it encompassed two systems of national law and two state churches.' The new British state was thus both unitary and 'pluralistic'; it was 'qualitatively different from both the English and Scottish states out of which it was fashioned'. It could also be described as a 'multinational state, one in which the historic English and Scottish nations retained their own identities'. It 'did not create anything that resembled a united British nation' (1987: vi, 23; cf. Wormald 1992: 194, on 'the anomaly of Scotland'). It was, in other words, far from the 'perfect union' that James the First had sought. The Treaty of Union established a British state, not a British nation. This state 'failed to inspire the type of British national consciousness that James hoped to inculcate' (1987: 204–5). As a result, Scotland and England were not fully integrated and, given English political and economic predominance, Scotland inevitably became a 'satellite' of England. 'In a certain sense, the Treaty of Union, by preserving a Scottish nation, has either created or perpetuated forces that have worked towards its modification or repeal' (1987: 222; see also 12–14, 23–6, 65–6, 100–1, 136–7, 167–8, 178–9, 204–5).

In 1709 Daniel Defoe, an ardent unionist, admitted that at the time of union 'the people cryed out they were Scots Men, and would be Scots Men still, they condemn'd the name of Britains [Britons], fit for the Welsh Men, who were made the scoff of the English after they had reduc'd them' (in Smyth 1998: 319). This antagonism on the part of the Scots was matched by some well-known expressions of Scottophobia in eighteenth-century England, as in the 1740s when a Scotsman, William Murray (later Lord Mansfield) was appointed solicitor-general, or in the anti-Bute agitation of the 1760s, when John Wilkes was able to stir up what David Hume called a 'rage against the Scots' as part of his campaign against the policies of Lord Bute, the first Scotsman to be appointed a British prime minister (Levack 1987: 205–6; Janet Smith 1970: 109; Smout 1989: 8; Richards 1991: 99–100; Colley 1994: 105–17; Evans 1994a: 147–8; Kidd 1996: 381; Devine 1999: 27–8, 30).

But perhaps we should not take isolated expressions of native English xenophobia – which, as we have seen, has a long history – as either an index of strong English nationalism or of a deep-seated resistance to accepting Scots as fellow Britons.[15] As for Defoe's utterances, it needs to be pointed out that he thought Scottish antipathy to the union would be a passing affair. The two nations would in time come together in a common British identity. In his *History of the Union of Great Britain* (1709) he looked forward to the formation of a new national identity, 'a New National Interest', predicated upon England's and Scotland's common Protestant past and potentially shared commercial future.

In his vision, 'the new British nation needed to embrace its providentially ordained and historically inevitable role as champion of a free, Protestant, and commercial world order' (Penovich 1995: 233, 241; see also Kidd 1998: 337–8). There is indeed considerable evidence that Defoe's optimism was not misplaced. As Colley claims – in terms that effectively reprise Defoe – an overarching British identity did develop in the eighteenth century. It is wrong, or at least misguided, to oppose to this the persistence of distinctively Scottish institutions. For one thing, their distinctiveness can be exaggerated. For another, their persistence was no barrier to the growth of an alternative or additional identity that was a fitting response to Scottish and English experience in the eighteenth century.

The example of law and legal institutions well illustrates this. The Scots did indeed take pride in their law courts, their legal profession and their traditions of law. But how far did this separate them from English law and English legal culture? The original Davidian revolution of the twelfth century substantially Anglicized Scottish law, as we have seen (chapter 5). Later Scottish law did introduce greater elements of Roman and canon law than in the case of England, but many commentators from both sides of the Border continued to remark on the 'close similarities' between English and Scottish law (Levack 1987: 76–85; Cairns 1995: 247). It was this that lead James the First to declare, perhaps hyperbolically but not necessarily inaccurately, that 'there is a greater affinity and concurrence between most of the ancient laws of both kingdoms than is to be found between those of any two other nations' (in Levack 1987: 76). The union of 1707 preserved the separation of laws, but this did not, for a number of reasons, prevent their convergence. One was simply the desire of the Scots themselves to 'modernize' their society, which meant essentially copying English law. As John Cairns puts it:

From 1707 onwards, Scots lawyers turned to English law as a means of developing Scots law, because it was readily accessible, and the law of a neighbouring "well governed realm" . . . Of course, they continued to draw on more familiar Roman and civilian legal systems; but, as the eighteenth century progressed, English law came more and more to be seen as an ideal system, as the law of a commercial country, as lawyers came to be concerned with improvement in the laws . . . "Anglicisation" was thus not necessarily imposed *as such* on Scots law, but to some extent willingly adopted as modernisation.
(1995: 267; see also Phillipson 1987: 227)

The desire to catch up with the more advanced nation of England was one factor that slowly undermined the distinctiveness of Scots law and procedures. But another was in a sense more fundamental, though perhaps because of its very obviousness rarely acknowledged by those keen to emphasize Scottish separateness. The fact is, after all, that, with the abolition of the Scottish Parliament,

Scotland no longer had any independent source of law-making. It was as subject as any other part of the united kingdom to the authority and sovereignty of the British Parliament – a Parliament, based in London, in which though the Scots were generously represented in proportion to their population, they were clearly always going to be subject to an English majority. In addition, the British House of Lords, in which the Scots had only sixteen peers, now had ultimate jurisdiction over all Scottish law suits. To the surprise, it seems, of both sides in the union negotiations, a 'notable feature of Scottish litigation after 1707 was the popularity of appeals to the House of Lords' – a consequence of 'the confused and unsatisfactory nature of litigation before the [Scottish] Lords of Session that left Scots law indeterminate' (Cairns 1995: 246, 266–7; see also Levack 1987: 98).

Thus though the union formally preserved Scottish law, this could only apply with real effect to the sphere of private, not public, law. The public law of the land, in Scotland as elsewhere in the kingdom, was the law made by the British Parliament. Even Scottish private law was not left entirely to the Scottish lawyers and Scottish courts. The Union Treaty allowed Scottish law to be altered 'for evident utility of the subjects within Scotland' – a massive enabling clause that gave the British Parliament a power which though selectively exercised was as effective in the threat as in the execution (Cairns 1995: 248).

In all important areas of public law – in the laws regulating trade, customs and excises, for instance – uniformity was imposed, even where this involved setting up entirely new bodies, such as the Scottish Court of Exchequer (Cairns 1995: 250–1). It was made very clear almost immediately after the union of 1707 that it was the British state, acting according to its own determination of its interests, that would decide how far legal uniformity should go. Thus in the wake of the abortive Jacobite rising of 1708 the English law of treason, and English criminal procedure for the prosecution of treason, were introduced in Scotland – 'a process that resulted in the virtual imposition of English law on Scotland' (Levack 1987: 99; Cairns 1995: 252; Devine 1999: 18). Other major legal changes followed the suppression of the Jacobite rebellion of 1745 – for instance, the abolition of heritable jurisdictions (the private courts of landowners) and the military land tenures of the clan chieftains (Lenman 1981: 1; Noonkester 1997: 268; Devine 1999: 46). In 1815, after much debate, the Scots were made to accept trial by jury in civil cases (it already existed in criminal cases).

Such fundamental changes in laws and procedures made it clear that Scottish legal independence was severely qualified. Brian Levack, whose whole account of the Anglo-Scottish union is intended to emphasize its incompleteness and the 'pluralist' British state that emerged, nevertheless has to admit that in the area of law what developed was a 'limited pluralism'. He even suggests, without fully accepting so stark a view, that Scottish legal independence was a fiction. 'One can argue that the Treaty deprived Scotland of all effective sovereignty and allowed England to control the country without having to assume the obligation of supervising the Scottish judicial system' (1987: 99; see also Lenman 1981: 1; Szechi 1991: 122, 124–5; Smout 1994: 110; Kidd 1997: 111–2).

What of the Church (or Kirk) of Scotland, that other 'palladium' of Scottish national identity? How effective was it in preserving a sense of Scottishness after the union of 1707? The two Acts of Security appended to the Treaty were designed to ensure that the new British state would encompass two separate and independent national churches. The constitutional provision for independence was stronger in the case of the Scottish church than in the case of Scottish law. This reflected both Scottish demands and, it appears, relative English indifference. No attempt was to be made to dictate to the Scots in matters of religion. The consequence was that, with the exception of pockets of Catholicism in the west and the north, an uncompromising Calvinism held sway over most of the land. Episcopacy declined. Dissent and nonconformity never gained the strength that they did in England after the Restoration. A somewhat dour Presbyterianism came to be the hallmark of Scottishness in the eyes of many observers.

But the very fact that the English Parliament was willing to concede what would have been unthinkable half a century before shows that perhaps religion was ceasing to be quite the badge of national identity that it had earlier aspired to be. Or if not religion *per se*, perhaps any particular variety of it, or at least any particular variety of Protestantism. By the Toleration Act of 1689 the English Parliament considerably modified, without completely abolishing, the penalties against Dissenters. Catholics remained firmly excluded from civic life; in that sense the English state continued to proclaim its adherence to one national religion. But it was clear from this Act that the Church of England, though remaining the state church, would now have to compete with other churches and denominations for the allegiance of English Protestants (as the rise of Methodism was to demonstrate spectacularly in the latter part of the eighteenth century). The English state remained staunchly Protestant, but to be a member of the English state, to be an English citizen, one did not now have to be a member of the English Church. The same principle could be applied to the new British state. There would not be a single, uniform, British Church, to which all Britons must belong. Political union could be separated from religious union. In the negotiations preceding the union, religion was kept firmly off the agenda. Partly this was because it remained contentious; but partly also it was because to the English commissioners it was no longer of such importance to insist on religious unity or uniformity. It was taken for granted by both sides that the Scots would keep their own church. The issue that had been the single largest obstacle to union throughout the seventeenth century was not even discussed (Levack 1987: 134).

The British state did not completely withdraw from intervening in Scottish religious affairs. In 1712 it used its undisputed parliamentary sovereignty to extend toleration to Scottish Episcopalians, and to permit lay appointment of ministers and church officials – acts that were not likely to allay Scottish apprehensions that, despite the Acts of Security, the British Parliament aimed to destroy the independence of the Scottish Presbyterian Church and perhaps even renew the attempt to impose religious uniformity throughout the kingdom (Devine 1999: 19; cf. Szechi 1991: 127). This never happened; but Scottish fears were in a number of other ways well founded. One was the clear signal that the British state, in pursuit of its interests, was prepared to tread on the religious susceptibilities of its citizens and risk antagonizing opinion in sensitive quarters, in Scotland as much as Ireland (in the latter case it was toleration of Catholics that alarmed Irish Protestants) (cf. Kidd 1997: 116). Another, and more dangerous, was what seemed to be the secularizing tide flowing outwards from South Britain. The policy of toleration did not amount to an abandonment of religion. The settlement in 1701 of the British crown on the Protestant Hanoverians, in the teeth of controversy and despite the stronger hereditary claims of the Catholic Stuarts, showed how important religion remained in English as much as Scottish eyes. But toleration, as a principle of state, certainly indicated a loosening of the ties that bound citizens to a national church. One could be British while being either or neither Anglican or Presbyterian. For the Scots, with their sense that the maintenance of the Presbyterian religion was critical to Scottish identity, such a policy of religious pluralism was deeply threatening. It seemed to be a prelude to a general secularization of life – a secularism that, to the alarm of many, seemed also to characterize English philosophical and political thought in the later seventeenth and eighteenth centuries. Since English thought – in the form especially of Bacon, Newton and Locke – was to have a profound effect on the eighteenth-century Scottish Enlightenment, such a secularizing influence was a further indication that the Scottish Kirk might not be as unalterably central to Scottish life as it and its supporters hoped and claimed (Chitnis 1976: 156–73; Phillipson 1981, 1987; Allan 1998: 188–95; Devine 1999: 68, 72–7).

Britishness and Englishness

Thus the two bastions of Scottishness, the Law and the Church, do not appear quite as impregnable or impermeable as the proponents of the idea of a separate Scottish identity wish to claim. They seem to have been forced to yield to pressures and influences that heavily diluted their distinctiveness and weakened their efficacy. But did those influences lead in a *British* or an *English* direction? If the full expression of a distinct Scottishness was mitigated by extraneous forces, did these point to an increasing Anglicization – thus merely continuing a centuries-old trend – or the creation of a new British identity? Was the effect of union not, as many hoped, the beginning of a new shared enterprise between all Britons, at home and abroad, but rather – as many others had always feared – the extension of English imperialism, Edward the First's ambition finally realized?

This is, in effect, what has been claimed by Colin Kidd, one of the foremost students of British ethnicities in this period. Kidd agrees with Colley that Scottishness was substantially modified after the union. Scottish nationalist historiography is wrong to deny that the union had a profound effect on Scottish identity, forcing it to abandon its independence and isolation. The historic form of Scottish patriotism, tied to the ancient Scottish monarchy and aristocracy, and to memories of a proud history of independence from England, could not survive the increasing realization that, compared with much of the rest of Western Europe, Scotland was a backward and undeveloped country.

But, says Kidd, what increasingly developed was not so much, as Colley claims, a new kind of British identity, but rather an 'Anglo-British' identity in which the English element was primary. 'Britishness, couched in predominantly English terms, was tantamount to Anglo-Britishness.' North British identity was 'anglocentric'. This was because England was what Scotland needed to be. 'English society provided a model for liberal modernity.' A new type of Scottish patriotism developed, an 'Anglo-British patriotism', based no longer on what were increasingly seen as an antiquated social structure and obsolete political traditions but on superior English models. Not an oppressive feudal aristocracy, of the old Scottish type, but an 'improving' aristocracy and a dynamic entrepreneurial middle class, as in England, seemed to be the ideals to aim for. Not Scottish autocracy and absolutism but the parliamentary constitutionalism and individual liberties won by the English seemed to be the wave of the future, one in which Scotland must share on pain of being condemned to backwardness and obscurantism. Full participation in the English polity and economy was Scotland's best hope for a happy and successful future. The union had now made that possible, and the opportunities this offered were to be seized, not despised from the perspective of a provincial and outmoded Scottish patriotism. 'From the 1750s, an English-oriented North Britishness was firmly established in Scottish culture. There was a consensus in favour of Union and the benefits of *de facto* incorporation within the English constitution. Scots felt a measure of pride, but a greater sense of relief, that Scottish institutions were becoming attuned to the rhythms of English prosperity and civil liberty.'[16]

There is an undoubted plausibility in this account. Scotland, as we have seen, had long been subject to English influences, at least since the comprehensive Anglicization of Scottish institutions that took place under David the First in the twelfth century. Scots retained their political independence against repeated English assaults, but cultural and ideological influences could not be so firmly held at bay. There were always thinkers and statesman, especially from the sixteenth century onwards, who saw great benefits to Scotland in a closer union with England, not least because of English achievements in politics, law and commerce. Once union was agreed, it was increasingly seen by the Scottish intelligentsia as an opportunity to modernize Scotland by sharing in English practices. Scots retained their sense of cultural distinctiveness – at least in certain spheres, such as religion and literature – but felt no sense of shame in abandoning many traditional Scottish ways that now were condemned as obstacles to 'improvement' – in manner and morals as much as politics and commerce (Kidd 1996: 365–6; Janet Smith 1970: 110–11; Clive 1970: 239; Pocock 1983: 128; Phillipson 1987; Szechi 1991: 129–30; Devine 1999: 29).

This was a familiar picture throughout the British dominions. Britishness, whether among Scots, Welsh, Anglo-Irish or North American colonists, always contained a core of Englishness (Kidd 1999: 250–86; see also Breen 1997: 26–9). Given English predominance in the British Isles since medieval times, this was always likely to be the case. English state power, English economic and imperial expansion, and the force of English legal and constitutional ideas, were bound to give England a commanding role in all areas of British development. Where 'nationalist' or 'patriotic' protests against English domination took place, these too were as likely to be couched in the terms of English political discourse – Magna Carta, the 'rights of free-born Englishmen', etc. – as in those of any non-English traditions. This was as true for Scots as for Irish Protestants and American colonists (Kidd 1996: 377–81; see also Phillipson 1970: 126; J. C. D. Clark 1994: 296–381).

All this can readily be admitted while at the same time seeing, and showing, that Britishness was not and is not mere Englishness, Englishness writ large.[17] Indeed, in the eighteenth, nineteenth and twentieth centuries it is more difficult to discern a primary Englishness than it is to distinguish Scottishness, Welshness or Irishness. Englishness is overlaid with Britishness, to an extent surpassing that of these others. Or perhaps we might better say, Englishness and Britishness are so interfused as to be virtually indistinguishable. While England undoubtedly exerts the major force in the direction of the kingdom, it is in turn radically affected by its interaction with the other parts and by the process of integration that took place with increasing force after the 1707 union with Scotland. England, as we shall see more fully in chapter 7, had its own reasons for playing down its distinctiveness in the multinational kingdom and far-flung empire in which it played so central a role. But in any case the evolution of a genuinely British society gave it little choice. Increasingly the culture, the social structure and the economy of the united kingdom became British – as British as the parliamentary state that governed it, the monarch that headed it and the great overseas empire that it constructed.

Culture and religion: the Protestant nation

What – to take culture first – would eighteenth-century 'English' culture be like without the Irishmen Jonathan Swift, George Berkeley and Edmund Burke? How can eighteenth-century 'English' poetry, 'English' drama or the 'English' novel be considered without mentioning the Irish poet Oliver Goldsmith, the Irish playwright Richard Sheridan or the enormously influential and widely admired Irish novelist Maria Edgeworth? What is the 'English Enlightenment' without the Scottish Enlightenment, the contribution of that great galaxy of talents that includes David Hume, Adam Smith, Adam Ferguson, John Millar, William Robertson and James Hutton?[18] What is 'English' architecture without the Scot Robert Adam, the most celebrated and influential architect of his generation in Britain? Nor should we forget the importance in the development of the novel of the Scottish novelist Tobias Smollett, or the popularity in England as much as Scotland of James MacPherson's 'Ossian' and the Scottish 'national poet', Robert Burns. It was indeed the Scots who pioneered the scholarly study of English literature: the first chair of English literature anywhere in the world was founded in 1762 at the University of Edinburgh. The influence of English thought and learning on the Scots and Irish is well known, and many of these latter felt the need to make their way to London, for the full exercise of their talents. But it is clear that the Scots and Irish returned the favour with interest, in the process ensuring that what the eighteenth century witnessed was neither an Irish nor Scottish nor English but a truly British Enlightenment (see Chitnis 1976; Smout 1980: 614; Phillipson 1981, 1987; Weinbrot 1993; Colley 1994: 123; Leersen 1997a, 1997b; Pittock 1997: 135–8; Murdoch 1998: 95–104; Devine 1999: 64–83; Porter 2000).

The nineteenth century continued the pattern. There was a common British culture that included, from Scotland, the novelist Sir Walter Scott, the philosopher James Mill, the political economist John McCulloch, the reforming lawyers Henry Brougham and James MacKintosh, the social critic and sage Thomas Carlyle, the ardent bourgeois propagandist Samuel Smiles, the physicist James Clerk-Maxwell and a host of other outstanding scientists, technologists and physicians. Influential journals such as the *Edinburgh Review* – described as 'a kind of Delphic oracle' by one of its frequent contributors, Carlyle – not only provided a platform for many of the major writers and thinkers of nineteenth-century Britain but, as a reforming 'whig' journal, had a considerable impact on the practical politics of nineteenth-century Britain (e.g., the passing of the 1832 Reform Act). Its Edinburgh rivals, the *Quarterly Review* and *Blackwood's Magazine* (during the nineteenth century known as *Blackwood's Edinburgh Magazine*), supplied an equally lively and combative Tory counterpoint, while also fostering some of the best literary talent of the century (for general studies, see Collini, Winch and Burrow 1983: 23–61; Harvie 1993, 1994; Chitnis 1986; see also Patterson 1994: 60). And who can imagine British culture without Robert Louis Stevenson, Arthur Conan Doyle and John Buchan?

The Irish contribution to British culture rose to a glorious peak in the 'Irish Revival' of the late nineteenth and early twentieth centuries. The writings of Oscar Wilde, W. B. Yeats, James Joyce, J. M. Synge, Sean O'Casey and George Bernard Shaw, while sometimes stressing Irish separateness and opposition to England, nevertheless drew on the whole heritage of English literature and are inconceivable without it (Foster 1989: 14–15). The fact that so many of the writers were of Irish Protestant background emphasized the British, rather than native Irish, inspiration. This too explains the ambivalence that many of them felt about Irish nationalism: respecting the aspiration, but regretting the narrowness, and the potential loss of the rich cultural legacy of Britishness (Pittock 1997: 133).

There was another cultural bond, of a different kind, that brought together the peoples of the united kingdom of Britain and Ireland. This was the bond of religion, the religion of Protestantism. This is for Colley, as we have seen, the strongest bond, the essential foundation of Britishness in the eighteenth and first half of the nineteenth centuries. It is an argument that has been much debated, from a variety of perspectives (e.g., Claydon and McBride 1998a; McLeod 1999; J. C. D. Clark 2000b). One criticism is the evident exclusion of the Irish – and English and Scottish – Catholics. In the English and Scottish cases (and even more the Welsh one) one may say, cruelly, that this does not matter so much. Catholics were a significant minority, and made many important contributions to the culture and economy of the kingdom, but they *were* a minority, and there are many cases in both the ancient and the modern world where the dominant culture flourished through the exclusion, and at the expense, of minorities, despite the vital contribution made by those minorities to the cultural and economic life of the host societies (the position of the Jews in European societies being perhaps the best-known example). Catholics were second-class citizens, thought of and treated as aliens and potential traitors, until and beyond the Catholic Emancipation Act of 1829. After the failure of the Jacobite Rising of 1745, and the subjugation and depopulation of the Scottish Highlands, they lost their last principal stronghold on the British mainland.

To all intents and purposes, Britain in the eighteenth and nineteenth centuries was a Protestant island.

The same of course was not true of 'John Bull's other island', Ireland. Here Catholics were the great majority, suffering even greater deprivation and discrimination than their coreligionists on the British mainland. Britishness, certainly in so far as it turned on Protestantism, was always likely to exclude them, and even to define itself against them. The British state's culpability in the great potato famine of the 1840s, in which Ireland lost a fifth of its population through death or emigration, marked the decisive turning point. Henceforth the Catholic majority could see its future only in an independent Ireland.

Things had not always seemed like that. In the late eighteenth century the British state, in the interests of national security and the augmentation of its armed forces, made distinct overtures to the Irish Catholics (as well as to Scottish Highlanders). Irish Catholics joined with Irish Protestants in providing recruits for the massively expanded armed forces and in policing and administering the empire (though Catholics generally remained at the lower levels (Bayly 1989: 127; Cullen 1989: 230, 234; Connolly 1995: 203; Black 1998: 71; Bartlett 1998: 264). The Irish Catholic presence in the East India Company militias was particularly high. The Company made a deliberate policy of recruiting Catholic Irish – it had after all Hindus and Muslims among its troops – and Catholics were a high proportion of the Irishmen who made up 48 per cent of the Bengal army between 1825 and 1850 (Bayly 1989: 127). Nor were Irish Catholics seen simply as cannon-fodder for the British army. There were moves to incorporate them into the full panoply and practice of the British Empire, both the 'internal' empire – 'the British Empire in Europe' – and the overseas empire. Irish merchants were active in the trade to North America and the British West Indies as well as in the English market (Bayly 1989: 81–2). Leading Irish Protestant gentry, such as the first Baron Wellesley (brother of Sir Arthur Wellesley, the first duke of Wellington), who was lord-lieutenant of Ireland in the 1820s and had himself married a Catholic, opposed Protestant triumphalism and urged the full assimilation of Catholics into Irish civic life. In the early part of the nineteenth century there was popular Catholic support for the St Patrick's Day celebrations, which were the occasion for the display of viceregal pageantry and the patriotic praise of British heroes such as Nelson and Wellington (Bayly 1989: 113; Connolly 1995: 198).

So even Catholic Ireland was not wholly excluded from the evolving British identity of these years. Combined with efforts to rein in the Protestant Ascendancy, there were in the later eighteenth and the first part of the nineteenth centuries real reasons to hope that the Irish – both patriots and peasants, soldiers and savants, Catholics and Protestants – would share in the pan-Britannic enterprise of empire and world commerce (Bayly 1989: 12). That this was not to be so represents the major failure of 'the British idea'.[19] Protestantism cannot wholly be blamed for this failure. But it certainly fuelled much of the prejudice against the Irish that lead to repeated acts of injustice and oppression, and to the conviction on the part of the Irish Catholics that there was no future for them in Britain. The struggle over Catholic Emancipation in 1827–29 – a struggle that split the political nation and in the eyes of some contemporaries threatened civil war – seemed to prove the point. It showed the extent to which the social order remained identified with the Protestant religion. The defence of 'the Protestant constitution' in 1829, as Jonathan Clark has shown, aroused far greater passions than the struggles over electoral reform in 1832. Indeed electoral reform, producing a more representative Parliament in tune with the popular anti-Catholic temper, was urged by some politicians as a means of punishing those sections of the political elite that had sold the pass in 1829 (Clark 2000a: 501–26; see also Colley 1994: 324–34; Wolfe 1998: 295).

Some have argued that it was not simply Catholicism that was the divisive force in Britain. Protestantism itself could divide as much as unite the kingdom. Colley's thesis, they argue, fails to acknowledge that. She sees a unified Protestantism linking English, Scots, Welsh and Irish Protestants. She does not consider the bitter conflicts arising out of the splits within the Protestant camp. The established Anglican Church in England, Wales and Ireland confronted a host of 'Old Dissenters' – Presbyterians, Congregationalists, Baptists, Quakers and Unitarians. Later there was the explosive rise of 'New Dissent', particularly Methodism, which took yet more people away from the Anglican Church. The established Presbyterian Church of Scotland was likewise embroiled in conflicts with its dissidents, the Episcopalians (not to mention the Catholics of the Highlands). Dissenters in all parts of the kingdom suffered penalties akin to those afflicting Catholics, and could face a like degree of hostility, as shown for instance in the Sacheverell riots of 1709–10, or in 1791 when the Birmingham mob burned down the home of the prominent Unitarian Joseph Priestley and wrecked several Dissenting chapels (Haydon 1993: 245–52; Pittock 1997: 39–41; Black 1998: 59). There were good reasons therefore why in the eighteenth century, at least, dissenters could not be counted upon for whole-hearted patriotism or unconditional loyalty to the state (Stafford 1982: 381–4).

In this sense 'church' and 'chapel' marked lines of opposition, not convergence, within Britain. Competing regional and even national identities could crystallize around whichever branch of the Protestant family happened to be dominant there – Presbyterianism in Ireland (Ulster) and Scotland, Methodism in Wales. Protestant divisions complemented the primary division between Protestants and Catholics. They completed the picture of religious disunity in the united kingdom. There was a British monarch, a British Parliament, a British economy, a British empire; but, as Keith Robbins says, 'there was, after all, no British Church' (1995: 190; see also Bebbington 1982; Thompson 1993: 378; Robbins 1993b; Claydon and McBride 1998b: 17–26; Black 1998; Clark 2000b: 262, 272–4).

But how common is it, in the relation of religion to national identity, to find absolute congruence? How often do we find one religion firmly and exclusively attached to a particular national identity? The cases of Catholicism linked to Irish and Polish identities, say, are impressive but, on a comparative view, also rare. The norm is for religion to divide rather than unite populations in relation to the nation. There are, in practically every case we care to consider, religious minorities who find themselves at odds with the dominant religion of the population. 'National religions' are usually the religions of dominant groups declaring themselves to be the nation (see van der Veer and Lehmann 1999: esp. 3–14).

But that does not prevent religion acting as a unifying force, especially where one's own religious differences are regarded as relatively minor by comparison with greater differences elsewhere. Islamic societies are often divided, for instance, between Sunni and Shi'ite Muslims, but that has not stopped their populations from acting together forcefully on occasion against perceived threats from non-Muslim sources, Christian, Jewish or merely 'Western' and secular. Hinduism has many sects that often forget their differences when confronted with Muslims. Anglo-Irish Protestants, who were mostly Anglicans, regarded the Presbyterians of Ulster with suspicion and hostility, but that did not hinder them from stifling their differences in the face of what was perceived as the common threat coming from the Irish Catholics.

What all these examples point to is the unifying force of religion in the face of threats from outside. It is with religion as with war. Distinctions that on other occasions lead people to oppose each other pale by comparison with the greater differences displayed by the enemy – 'the Other', to use the fashionable term. Groups sink their differences in recognition of the needs of the common struggle. Where war and religion overlap, this phenomenon is strengthened – as in the medieval Crusades, or the seventeenth-century wars of the Reformation and Counter-Reformation. Here, we may say, what seems at stake is not merely the survival but the soul of the nation.

It is in this perspective that we should judge the contribution of Protestantism to British identity in the eighteenth and for much of the nineteenth centuries. The essential common feature of Protestantism, the thing that gave it its unifying power, was its anti-Catholicism (Haydon 1993; O'Brien 1993: 37; Black 1998: 60–1). It helped that, since the sixteenth-century Reformation, the two powers that most threatened first English and then British independence were Catholic: first Spain, then France, both of whom were seen as having pretensions to 'universal monarchy' (Pincus 1995).[20] Memories and myths of the defeat of the Spanish Armada, elaborated in numerous popular texts and prints in the seventeenth and eighteenth centuries, supplied one ingredient of the potent anti-Catholic creed. So too did other vivid reminders of the heroic days of Protestantism and the fight against the Spanish-led Counter-Reformation. The anniversary of the date of Elizabeth the First's accession continued as a day of national celebration; innumerable cheap editions and revisions of Foxe's *Book of Martyrs* were avidly consumed; riotous celebrations accompanied the burning of the pope's effigy on the Fifth of November (Haydon 1993: 28–47; Colley 1994: 18–36).

France, Britain's main rival for economic and imperial preeminence in the eighteenth and nineteenth centuries, was the other Catholic bogey, more suited to the period (Newman 1987: *passim*, esp. 74–84, 123–56). In a series of major conflicts – the War of the Spanish Succession (1702–13), the War of the Austrian Succession (1740–48), the Seven Years War (1756–63), the War of American Independence (1775–83), and the French Revolutionary Wars (1793–1815) – Britain found itself fighting for its global position and sometimes for its very survival against France. France became the emblem of all that was hated and feared from a Catholic power, the more so as it was seen as actively engaged on the side of the Catholic (Jacobite) interest within Britain itself. Such feelings, born of religious animosity, could paradoxically survive the removal of the religious threat. The formal stripping of Catholicism and monarchy from the French state, during the French Revolution, did little to abate a popular Gallophobia that had been deeply ingrained by past fears and rivalries; quite the opposite, in fact. During the Revolutionary Wars, men from all classes and regions of Britain (and Ireland) rallied to the defence of the Protestant Church (against French atheism) and the Protestant monarchy (against French republicanism) (Colley 1994: 283–319; see also Allan 1998: 197).

The French were known supporters of the Stuart pretenders, James Edward and Charles Edward, both ardent Catholics. The fear of France was thus closely connected to the fear of Jacobitism: perhaps the central political fact of eighteenth-century Britain, at least until 1745, and at popular levels for a considerable time afterwards. Nothing mobilized anti-Catholic feeling – or indeed any other kind of feeling – more powerfully than the threat of a Jacobite restoration and the reimposition of Catholicism by a Stuart dynasty. In the Jacobite risings of 1715 and, even more, 1745, there were *grandes peurs* comparable to those of the French Revolution. By 1745 the majority of Scots were as hostile to the return of the Stuarts as the Welsh and English (Irish Catholics remained strangely passive in both risings) (Hayton 1995: 289). The crushing of the rebellions, and in particular the comprehensive pacification of the Scottish Highlands that followed the failure of 'the Forty-five', were British, not English, accomplishments. What united Protestant Britons of all varieties was a deep-seated and fervent anti-Catholicism. Anti-Popery, says Paul Langland, was an 'expression of national unity . . . In truth it provided the decisive argument against the legitimate line of Stuarts, as it had done ever since 1689. There were many diverse reasons for opposing the Young Pretender in 1745 . . . But the one thing which almost all Englishmen and most Scots shared was detestation of his religion' (Langland 1992: 202; see also Haydon 1993: 76–116, 130–63; Colley 1994: 72–85; Allan 1998; Devine 1999: 17, 31–47).

Nor should we forget, in the context of anti-Catholicism, Catholic Ireland. Ireland was capable of keeping the anti-Catholic flame burning when both Jacobite threats and the fear of French power receded. Indeed Hugh McLeod claims that 'for nineteenth-century British Protestants, the supreme embodiment of the Catholic Other was not France but Ireland' – an Ireland despised for its poverty and backwardness, and feared as a potential source of rebellion and of succour to Britain's enemies. On both counts, as McLeod notes, 'the main basis of British attacks on the Irish was an objection to their religion'. It was Catholicism that was responsible for Irish drunkenness and fecklessness, Catholicism that made Ireland a possible stepping-stone for foreign invaders (McLeod 1999: 47; see also Haydon 1998: 34; McBride 1998: 238). Catholic Irish immigrants to England and Scotland in the nineteenth century faced prejudice and vilification generally reserved for non-European and non-Christian peoples (McLeod 1999: 54–5; see also Curtis 1968; Gillley 1978; Bebbington 1982: 502; Robbins 1993b: 91–2, 99–100; Devine 1991; 1999: 486–500; Evans 1994b: 203–6; Kidd 1997:116–17).

What impresses one, in examining the various manifestations of anti-Catholicism, is the flexibility and elasticity of Protestantism as a unifying agent. It is wrong to treat British Protestantism according to the canons of theological consistency and organizational uniformity, at least in so far as we consider its cultural and political significance. That has been the principal error of Colley's critics. British Protestantism was a Broad Church – as broad and vague as the Anglicanism that so often was its target, in the doctrinal and organizational disputes within Protestantism. Protestants of all hues shared certain basic values and understandings; they thought they knew who the main enemies were and where the real threats lay. In this they could appear at times culpably confused. During the anti-Catholic Gordon riots of 1780 in London – precipitated by an eccentric Protestant Scottish nobleman, Lord George Gordon, and preceded, we should remember, by similar riots in Glasgow and Edinburgh – some of the crowd were called upon 'to go to such a house, as there were *Catholics* there'. 'What are Catholics to us?', they replied; 'we are only against *Popery*' (Haydon 1993: 13; see also 258–9; 1998: 39). But it would be wrong to see this merely as muddled understanding. 'Anti-popery' was the popular cry, familiar from popular iconography and from innumerable outbreaks of popular protest.

It summed up well enough what Protestants of all churches and denominations thought they were up against.

Despite its internal differences, then, Protestantism did provide an essential, perhaps the essential, constituent of British identity, at least until the second half of the nineteenth century.[21] 'An uncompromising anti-Catholicism remained central until about 1860' (McLeod 1999: 44).[22] Churches and chapels, Sunday-schools and day schools, cartoons and caricatures, poetry and literature, all contributed to the creation of a dominant Protestant culture and consciousness in Britain (Bebbington 1982: 501–2; Paz 1992; McLeod 1999: 50–3). Moreover, Protestantism could be combined in all sorts of ways with other vaunted British accomplishments, in politics, commerce and empire. In a typical combination, lasting well into recent times, a comprehensive and self-congratulatory Protestant image was set against an equally comprehensive and unflattering Catholic image. Protestant nations were free, independent, tolerant and prosperous, friendly to and thriving on commerce and constitutional liberties. Catholic nations were sunk in despotism, dogma and poverty, the prey of power-hungry monarchs and superstitious priests. The contrast was particularly effective when applied to empire. Britain's success in its rivalry with France, and the allegedly more liberal character of its colonial administration, were attributed in large part to the adventurousness and spirit of independence bred by its Protestant character (Armitage 2000: 143–5, 162–3, 173–4, 196–7; Bebbington 1982: 502–3; Haydon 1998: 34–5; Allan 1998: 197; McLeod 1999: 51–2).

There is perhaps one other point to consider. Why was it that Protestantism was able to act as the bond of national identity in the eighteenth century when, as we have seen, it was incapable of doing so at the time of the Reformation, in the sixteenth century? Partly this was because the entity to which it was attached – Britain – was more plural, more 'international' or multinational, than the single entity of England. It was difficult to see England by itself as '*the* Protestant nation', '*the* elect nation', in a world of other equally combative and energetic Protestant nations. But the composite entity of Britain and Ireland, with their different kinds of Protestant populations, could more plausibly shoulder the burden of missionary Protestantism, the more so when this entity could be seen as the core of a worldwide empire through which Protestant culture could be diffused on the widest possible scale.

The shift towards a narrower, more national, identification was also made possible by a change in the character of Protestantism itself, and of the anti-Catholicism that it engendered. Protestantism since the second half of the seventeenth century had lost something of its theological severity and ideological fervour. It had shed – without ever completely abandoning, as repeated revivals made clear – much of its millennialism, its sense of a cosmic struggle against the

Antichrist. Anti-Catholicism did not abate, but it began to lose its theological character and to take on instead 'political and cultural associations'. It came increasingly to be identified with the struggle against certain characteristics thought to be inherent in Catholic cultures – arbitrary power, absolutism, dogmatism, domination by priests (Pincus 1995: 53–4). The consequence was a change in the way England and Britain perceived their roles as bastions of Protestantism. No longer were they engaged in an international crusade to spread the Protestant light. Rather they were now bulwarks against the menace of an expansionist Catholic civilization bent on world domination. This more modest conception allowed for a more national, even insular, interpretation of Protestantism's mission in the world (Kidd 1998: 328–9; Pincus 1995: 58–62; 1998).

Some mitigating of the crusading zeal there might be, at least in the strict sense of wishing to convert the whole world to Protestantism. But a more generalized and diffuse Protestantism nevertheless could still form the substratum of a missionary desire to spread the fruits of Protestant freedom and enlightenment. In the burgeoning commercial civilization and expanding overseas empire of eighteenth- and nineteenth-century Britain, the tropes of Protestantism could easily be subtilized into the more directly cultural and political themes of liberty, prosperity and progress.

Society, economy and empire

Britishness was not just a cultural and religious phenomenon, it was also a fact of social and economic structure. First one has to recognize that the ruling class in the British Isles was, from the eighteenth century onwards, truly British rather than simply English.

This continued a pattern that had begun earlier, under the rule of the Stuarts. Then it was that wealthy landowners began to intermarry with heirs and heiresses from the adjacent Stuart kingdoms, acquire titles in more than one realm, and become assimilated into the political and cultural life of more than just the country of their birth. If London, as the seat of the court, was the inevitable magnet, this did not mean that metropolitan upper-class social and political life was not itself affected by the presence of Welsh, Irish and Scottish grandees, such as the second earl of Antrim, or James, third marquess and first duke of Hamilton. The Abercorn branch of the Scottish Hamiltons indeed well illustrates the increasingly British nature of the aristocracy even before the union. They maintained a court presence in England, retained a strong interest in Scotland, and were well established as major Irish landowners who had married into the Anglo-Irish aristocracy. Equally British – rather than English or Anglicized – in character were the Boyle earls of Cork, the Butler earls of

Ormond and the fitzGerald earls of Kildare (Brown 1995: 223–4, 227–32; 1999: 247; Morrill 1995b: 24–6; 1996: 27; Harris 1999: 268–9).

The eighteenth century, in the decades following the union of 1707, multiplied these cases many times over. Linda Colley dates the most impressive waves of convergence in the making of a British ruling class to the decades of the late eighteenth and early nineteenth centuries. It was at this time that the peripheral 'Celtic' elites of Britain were decisively integrated into the governing structure of Britain and its empire.

> In the wake of the loss of the American colonies, these Celtic élites amalgamated with their English counterparts far more extensively than before, reinvigorating the power structure of the British empire and forging a unified and genuinely British ruling class that endured until the twentieth century ... Particularly in the last quarter of the eighteenth and in the first quarter of the nineteenth centuries, there was, throughout the British Isles, a consolidation of the top personnel into a new and far more integrated upper class. The formerly separate landed establishments of England, Wales, Scotland and Ireland gradually fused, their members intermarrying, acquiring estates scattered throughout the kingdom, competing for office at home and in the empire, adopting similar lifestyles and forms of expenditure, and laying claims to be the guardians of a "national" – in the sense of British – culture.
>
> (1994: 156, 193; see also 1986: 98, 104; Thompson 1971: 10–11; Jenkins 1983; G. Williams 1985: 148–9; Bayly 1989: 83–4; Cullen 1989: 232–3; Szechi 1991: 128; Connolly 1992: 103–44; Murdoch 1998: 131–2; Devine 1999: 25)[23]

In the leading public schools and universities, in court, in Parliament, in the armed forces, in imperial administration, nobility and gentry from all parts of the kingdom mixed and mingled, creating a common society and a common culture. While 'Anglicization' is one way of describing this process, it is a misleading and one-sided account. The parts, to quote John Pocock's famous statement about British history, 'interacted so as to modify the conditions of one another's existence' (Pocock 1982: 317). This was as true in the sport and recreation of the British aristocracy as it was in its social and political life. The English aristocracy of the eighteenth century had been cosmopolitan – that is, French – in its outlook and pursuits. Those pursuits, like those of most European aristocracies, tended to be heavily urban: gambling, gossiping, visiting, dining, drinking, dancing and whoring. Town houses, theatres, taverns, ball-rooms, casinos and clubs, in London and Bath, were the central institutions. Country life was looked upon as tedious and boring, fit only for country bumpkins of the type of Fielding's Squire Western. On the continental Grand Tour that became obligatory for the young nobleman, the countryside was a meaningless interlude between the stops at the great cities – Paris, Rome, Naples (Beckett 1986: 347; Newman 1987: 14–18, 35–44; Lieven 1992: 152; Colley 1994: 170; Armstrong 194: 86–7).

The British aristocracy of the nineteenth century, by contrast, carved out a style of life for itself that was not only distinctly native but became the model for the European aristocracy as a whole. The emphasis shifted from town to country. Aristocratic life centred on the large country estate and involved typically outdoor pursuits: horse-breeding, fox-hunting, grouse-shooting, deer-stalking, salmon-fishing (Thompson 1971: 136–50; 1988: 267–70; Beckett 1986: 347–9; Lieven 1992: 152–3). While there were general European currents, such as the movement of Romanticism, promoting this change, it was also directly related to the increasing integration of the British upper classes. Many of the new pursuits had a clear Irish or Scottish provenance, as is obvious from contemporary prints and caricatures. The hunting, shooting, fishing squire of popular lore is more a British – Irish or Scottish – than an English type. Shooting trips to the Scottish Highlands became a favourite aristocratic sport, snobbishly preferred to the continental Grand Tour that was increasingly favoured by the bourgeoisie. The same was true of the preference for the Lake District and North Wales, and the taste for landscape and the 'sublime' that went with them. Together with the heroic and military virtues – often following classical models – inculcated by the big public schools, a new model of aristocratic culture emerged in the nineteenth century. Foreigners might call this 'English', as do too many of the accounts of the aristocracy of this period (e.g., Thompson 1971; Becket 1986); but any examination of its features and its practitioners will show that it was unquestionably British (Colley 1994: 164–93; Evans 1994a: 151).

A British ruling class does not by itself necessarily make a British nation, or create a sense of British national identity.[24] But we know enough of 'hegemony', in the Gramscian sense, to recognize the power of ruling structures and 'dominant ideologies'. The eighteenth- and nineteenth-century British ruling class, fundamentally aristocratic, emerged as one of the most powerful of modern times, in control of the world's leading economy and the world's greatest empire. Unlike other European aristocracies, it did not collapse in 1914. It can even be argued to be still in existence, though now undeniably sharing power with a middle class which in many ways has adopted its own outlook and manners (Mayer 1981: 88–95; Wiener 1981). At any rate, through its institutions, its ideas, the appeal of its values and way of life, it spread an ideal of Britishness whose force has by no means vanished even in these days of challenge to a united kingdom of Great Britain.

There was, in any case, more than a British ruling class to sustain the idea of Britishness. There was, with gathering force in the late eighteenth and early nineteenth centuries, a maturing British economy, fired by an astonishing British Industrial Revolution. It is no longer possible, as it used to be, to speak of the 'English Industrial Revolution' – always a misnomer, as was clear even in the earliest accounts. All investigations reveal a picture of full participation by all parts of the united kingdom, Welsh, Irish and Scottish to some extent even greater than English. If there were disparities and inequalities, they lay more within the different segments of the kingdom – creating backward or undeveloped 'regions' – than between them (Hudson 1992: 101–32; Richards 1991: 113; Murdoch 1998: 76–8, 96–97). Nowhere is the model of 'core-and-periphery', England and the 'Celtic fringe', more distorting than in the case of industrialization and its significance for national identity.

We are familiar with the 'dark satanic mills' of the North of England. Tocqueville and Engels wrote eloquently and passionately of Manchester, and the paradox of so much misery amidst such wealth. But what of Glasgow, Belfast and the industrial towns of South Wales? Who are their chroniclers? Foreign observers seem to have been as anglocentric as the English themselves. Yet, on a dispassionate view, the driving force of the Industrial Revolution came not just from the industries of Lancashire and the West Midlands, but also the textile mills, coalfields, engineering works and shipyards of Clydeside; the linen and shipbuilding industries of Ulster; and the iron, steel and coal industries of south Wales (Smout 1980: 618–22; Lenman 1981: 124–8, 164–5; Berg 1985: 204–7; G. Williams 1985: 143–5; Szechi 1991: 129; Wagner 1993: 152; Evans 1994b: 194–5). And what would the Industrial Revolution have been without the great inventors and innovators? The English were prominent enough – Darby, Davy, Kay, Arkwright, Cartwright, Cromton, Cort and many others. But we should not forget that many of the great names are those of people who came from the 'peripheral' nations, Scotland in particular producing a chain of brilliant inventors and engineers: James Watt, Thomas Bell, Alexander Cochrane, William Symington, John Macadam, Thomas Telford, Robert Napier (Ashton 1961: 58–93).[25] Their inventions and the processes these created – from steam power to modern road-making and ship-building – were, it is clear, not simply 'peripheral' but absolutely central to the Industrial Revolution; they 'belong to *British* economic history, not to Scotland alone' (Smout 1980: 613). They sprang from a scientific and intellectual culture that centred on Glasgow and Edinburgh and that, for more than a century, was a vital nursery of technical and industrial innovation in the British economy.

The British economy, in the nineteenth century, moved into the centre of the world economy, of which it was the principal creator. Here too it is important to see that the part played by Wales, Scotland and Ireland was not just as some provider of raw materials and cheap labour, colonial-style, but as nerve-centres of the new world economy (Smout 1980; Landsman 1994). The industrial complexes of Clydeside and South Wales were the control points from which trade and manufacture flowed out to the world, carried in part by the trade routes of the British Empire. Glasgow, 'Second City of the Empire', was the centre of the trade in North American tobacco; and as Glyn Williams puts it for Wales:

The incredible world empire of south Wales coal is familiar. But this was much more than a simple matter of coal export. South Wales capital, south Wales technology, south Wales enterprise, south Wales labour not only fertilised whole tracts of the world from Pennsylvania to the Donetz basin; they were a critical factor in world economic development... At the height of the First World War, Stanley Jevons, professor of economics, could envisage a post-war British global hegemony centred entirely on south Wales.

> (1982: 196–7; see also 1985: 141–8, 221–3; Morgan 1982: 125–6; Evans 1991: 95–6; J. Davies 1994: 383–4, 402–6; Smout 1980: 617; Bayly 1989: 81–2; Pittock 1997: 84)

Some periphery, we might say. The Industrial Revolution was a pan-Britannic achievement. All parts contributed to it – unequally, just as its impact was uneven. But the lines of division, both in terms of causes and effects, were not between England and the Celtic parts. The Industrial Revolution added its vital – perhaps indispensable – contribution to the making of Britain as a unified system. The parts were now more tightly drawn together, the economy confirming – with all the force of material need and interest – the integration already growing apace in the realm of politics, culture and imperial expansion. In the process the configuration changed, some parts rising to a new prominence, others declining. But they were parts of the same system; the people who made and experienced the Industrial Revolution were, whether they were fully aware of it or not, becoming Britons.

A British Industrial Revolution and a British economy produced a British working class and a British labour movement. This too, for large numbers of men and women, was a source of identity, 'British' no less for being class based (Colley 1994: 323, 336–42; 1989; Cunningham 1981: 7–18). The British labour movement was indeed one of the most profoundly British of institutions, linking groups across the kingdom in a common struggle and in common defence of their rights (Colley 1986: 111–13; Smout 1989: 11–12; Davies 1994: 375–81; Murdoch 1998: 143–7). In the face of a *British* ruling class, of course nothing other than a British movement would have made sense. Celebrated accounts tell us of 'the making of the English working class', yet cannot – how could they? – ignore the enormous influence on English workers of the Welsh-Scottish reformer and socialist visionary Robert Owen, or the leadership of the Irish Chartists James Bronterre O'Brien and Feargus O'Connor.[26] In the later nineteenth century Welsh and Scottish radicals again took the lead, producing the first British Labour Party leader in Keir Hardie and the first Labour prime minister in Ramsay MacDonald, to say nothing of the charismatic Liberal leader David Lloyd George. In the twentieth century the British labour movement was to be one of the strongest bulwarks of Britishness, absorbing elements which might otherwise have been attracted to the nationalist parties.

There is finally the empire, and the military and bureaucratic apparatus that went with it. Practically all commentators agree that, whatever the ratios of participation in other British institutions, in the British Empire the English were equalled or outnumbered by Scots, Welsh and Irish. Indeed it has been common to assert that the non-English Britons, especially the Scots, participated in the empire out of all proportion to their native populations (Dilke 1868: 511; Colley 1994: 126–32; Armitage 1997: 63). Not all profited equally – Irish Catholics did not usually find themselves at the upper levels of the military or of colonial administration. But the empire was the theatre where all Britons displayed themselves; where, especially in relation to non-white and non-European cultures, they found a common identity and a common purpose. For Scottish, Irish and Welsh elites especially, a 'British imperial consciousness... steadily undermined parochial patrician commitments' (J. C. D. Clark 1989: 226)

The Scots, as Sir John Seeley noted (1971: 105), had already shown their enthusiasm for empire in British North America. The loss of the American colonies, accompanied as it was by an even greater surge of expansion eastwards, far from diminishing rather increased the British as opposed to the English character of the empire. Irish peers, such as Richard Wellesley, governor-general of India, led the way in developing the grand viceregal style of the empire, just as his more famous brother Arthur, first duke of Wellington, became the most celebrated of British military heroes ('Arthur Wellesley and his brothers, of course, effectively created Britain's Second Empire in Asia' (Bayly 1989: 127)). The great statistical surveys of north and south India (1798–1815) were conducted by a Scots administrator, Francis Buchanan (Bayley 1989: 111, 125). The imperial army and police, largely scorned in the first half of the nineteenth century by English workers, were disproportionately drawn from 'the younger sons of small peasant holdings in the Highlands of Scotland, Ulster and southern Ireland', in addition to Indians and other colonial peoples. After the crushing of the 1745 rebellion, the Scottish Highlands, with the encouragement of the great Highland magnates such as the dukes of Argyle and Athole, became a prime source of recruits for some of the most famous British regiments, such as the Black Watch. Highlander courage and prowess in fighting became legendary in the British army. In 1830 Scots accounted for 13.5 per cent of the British army as a whole (20 per cent in 1815), and as many as one in four regimental officers. The Irish presence was even stronger, Irish recruits representing in 1830 about 43 per cent of British crown forces; in the Bengal army from 1825–50 they made up nearly 48 per cent (Bayly 1989: 126–7; Richards 1991: 88; Colley 1994: 126; Pittock 1997: 129–30; Devine 1999: 27).

The British ruling class, already increasingly integrated in 'Britain's Empire in Europe' (i.e., the United Kingdom), ramified out in ever widening circles with the growth of the overseas empire in the nineteenth century. With the opportunities provided by empire it could now expand its ranks beyond the aristocracy and gentry. It could include the sons of the commercial classes, such as Sir Thomas Munro, governor of Madras, son of a ruined Glasgow tobacco trader; or scions of even poorer groups, such as Lachlan Macquarie, governor of New South Wales, a tenant farmer's son from the Isle of Mull. But as in the United Kingdom itself, gentry and aristocracy predominated in the governing structures of empire, in the army and the colonial service. Once again though what is striking is the extent of the representation of Irish and Scottish peers and lesser gentry alongside their English counterparts. Thus the Moiras, leading Irish peers, were to be found at the highest levels of the Irish, British and Indian services; also prominent in both domestic British and imperial service were Irish gentry families such as the Wellesleys, the Macartneys, Castlereaghs and FitzMaurices. From the Scottish Borders came the Elliots, the Edmonstones, Eliphinstones and Maitlands, all of whom achieved high office in the imperial army and administration (the Elliots, as the Lords Minto, supplied a governor-general and a viceroy of India, a governor-general of Canada, and a younger son as governor of Newfoundland, besides several lords of the Admiralty and assorted ambassadors). Scots, already active in the Atlantic empire, also went on to make a speciality of India: by the middle of the eighteenth century, a third of the East India Company's army officers were Scotsmen, and Scots made up a large part of the marine, medical and other civilian administration. The pattern continued in the nineteenth century (Bayly 1989: 134–6; Richards 1991: 89–98; Szechi 1991: 128; Wagner 1993: 158–9; Colley 1994: 126–8; MacKenzie 1993: 723–8; 1998: 221).

The Scots, everyone agrees, were of all the British nations the most prominent in the British Empire. Imperial service became 'a focus of specifically Scottish national pride. The appointments pages of the Edinburgh *Blackwood's Magazine* became an inventory of the expansion of the British empire' (Bayly 1989: 136; see also MacKenzie 1993; 1998: 223; Wagner 1993: 154–5; Murdoch 1998: 109–10). During the American and French wars the Scots, as if to prove their essential Britishness, were the most loyal and supportive of all the king's subjects (Lenman 1981: 56–72; Cullen 1989: 241; Richards 1991: 99; Wagner 1993: 153–7; Colley 1994: 140–1; Murdoch 1998: 71). Glasgow and Dundee were virtually imperial cities, their trade and industries closely bound up with the empire. Thomas Lipton of Glasgow, the 'king's grocer', became a household name throughout the empire with his chain of grocery shops. Scottish religious missionaries were everywhere in the empire, some such as David Livingstone and Mary Slessor achieving fame throughout the Western world (Forsyth 1997: 7–8). Scottish schools and colleges became models for similar creations in all corners of the empire. In educational ideas, statistics, botanical and agricultural expertise, Scots were acknowledged to have had 'a formative role in the construction of the colonies' (Bayly 1989: 136; see also Richards 1991: 86; Porter 1999b: 236).[27]

The empire, especially after the loss of the American colonies, ceased to be predominantly English and increasingly offered to all the peoples of the United Kingdom the opportunity to participate in a common enterprise, as more or less equal partners. 'The English had been able to regard the heartland of their first empire, the American colonies, as peculiarly their own, pioneered by their own ancestors... In contrast, in terms of those who won it, those who governed it and those who settled it, the Second British Empire would... be emphatically British' (Colley 1994: 144; see also Bebbington 1982: 502). 'The Empire was the key to British unity', agrees Murray Pittock (1997: 135); empire allowed the inequalities that obtained within the United Kingdom to be ironed out on a wider stage. Taking the example of the Scots, the outstanding imperial nation, Linda Colley argues that empire compensated for the feeling of inferiority experienced by the 'peripheral' nations within the British Isles. 'If Britain's primary identity was to be an imperial one, then the English were put firmly and forever in their place, reduced to a component part of a much greater whole, exactly like the Scots, and no longer the people who ran virtually the whole show. A British imperium, in other words, enabled Scots to feel themselves peers of the English in a way still denied them in an island kingdom' (1994: 130; see also Richards 1991: 96–7, 101–6; Mackenzie 1993: 738; 1998: 229–31; Devine 1999: 289; and, for the Welsh, G. Williams 1985: 141). The British Empire was the integument that, even more than the integration produced by an increasingly British mainland society, tightly meshed the parts of Britain together.

A British nation?

But if there was, self-evidently, a British imperial state, was there also a British *nation*? Were there, by the end of the eighteenth century, *Britons*, people who shared a sense of a common consciousness and a common identity despite admitted differences of region within the British Isles? Doubts have frequently been expressed on this score, as we have seen. Reaffirming this, John Reeve declares roundly that, while we can speak of a British state, 'Britain is certainly not a nation' (1999: 308). David McCrone similarly says that the peoples of Britain acknowledged British *citizenship*, a British 'state identity'; but in their nationhood – in the 'cultural' as opposed to the 'political' realm – they remained diverse, as Welsh, Scottish and Irish nations. 'Britishness sat lightly on top of the constituent nations as a kind of state-identity' (2000: 121; see also 2001: 98; and cf. also Robertson 1994: 248; Morrill 1995b: 9–13; 1996: 16–17; Murdoch 1998: 151).

'State and nation' is a well-known distinction; but perhaps too much has been made of it. It is similar, if not identical, to the distinction between 'civic' and 'ethnic' concepts of nationhood; and we have seen (in chapter 2), the difficulties of separating these two, in theory as well as in practice. The attempt to distinguish a British state from a British nation suffers from the same kinds of ambiguities and overlaps. The British state involves, at a minimum, a British monarchy, a British Parliament, British political parties, a British judiciary and British legal system, a British civil service and British armed forces. Increasingly these were expressed in the context of the British Empire. Groups from all classes and regions of Britain participated in this British imperial state. Is it so difficult to imagine them developing a British consciousness and outlook, especially in relation to outsiders and actual or potential rivals for power and influence (Colley 1992: 316)? Comparable cases exist in the Roman, Ottoman and Russian Empires; and here it has not proved difficult to discern, certainly among ruling groups, a distinct identity based on the institutions of empire (Kumar 2000). For many, simply the experience of armed service – as 'the school of the fatherland' – and war, in which Britain was engaged for so much of the eighteenth century, would have been powerful 'nationalizing' forces, as we know them to have done in several cases (e.g., Weber 1976: 292–302).

But the case for a British identity does not turn simply on common political or military institutions. There were, as we have seen, also a unified British ruling class, an integrated British economy, and a British labour movement linking all parts of the kingdom. Culturally, the inhabitants of the United Kingdom overwhelmingly spoke the same language (a rare thing in any multinational state). They shared, in the main, the same religion, however diversified internally. Scientific, intellectual and literary culture increasingly spanned the whole of the British Isles, linking its practitioners in a dense network of interconnected circles of influence and interest (Strong 2000: 415–31). Such were the building blocks of Britishness. It is difficult to imagine what more might be needed to provide a common national consciousness – again, so far as this can be said to occur at all, and to be recognized as such.

All arguments for national consciousness or national identity rest on shaky and questionable evidence; there simply is no way of showing incontrovertibly that such a thing exists in any given case or even, precisely, to say what that might mean (Brubaker and Cooper 2000). But that is not a sufficient reason for dismissing it as a meaningless or unusable concept, or to deny that it points to a real phenomenon. Like identity in general, it allows us to deal with certain questions and to describe certain attitudes and behaviour which cannot readily be comprehended in any other way (as Stuart Hall argues, 1996: 2). Certainly, if we can talk about English or Scottish or Irish national identity, we should be entitled to speak of British national identity. The kind of institutions and experiences that give rise to the former seem amply in evidence also in the latter case. It may be helpful in some contexts to be reminded that, as Peter Scott says, 'Britain is an invented nation, not much older than the United States' (in Colley 1992: 309). But all nations are invented, and 200 years is a long time (leaving aside the much longer existence of the idea of Britain). If we can speak of the German or Italian nations, with their much shorter histories, it is surely not difficult to think of the British nation in similar terms.

It is the English who seem to have the greatest difficulty in speaking about or grasping the consciousness of Britain and Britishness. For them, Britain has mostly been, in a very general sense, 'England'. Not so the other inhabitants of Britain. For them, Britain has been the defining experience of the last 200 years, or even longer. It has made then what they are. Whatever else they may be, they are also Britons, members of the British nation. As Gwyn Williams emphatically puts it:

The existence of a historic British nation, dominated by but qualitatively distinct from the English polity, is a central fact in the modern history of these islands. The history of the Scots and of the Ulster Protestants is inconceivable without it. The history of the Welsh is totally incomprehensible without it.

(1982: 195; see also 1985: 141; Landsman 1994: 259)

'Welsh identity', Williams further remarks, 'has constantly renewed itself by anchoring itself in variant forms of Britishness' (1982: 194). So too, we may say, have Scottish and Irish identities. What of English identity? What were the implications for Englishness of this British entity? How did the English see themselves in the mirror of Great Britain and the British Empire? The paradox is that, having to a good extent made these things, the English, unlike the other British nations, found it curiously difficult to define their own role within them – at least as that relates to their national identity.

The moment of Englishness

The English, of any people in the universe, have the least of a national character; unless this very singularity may pass for such.

David Hume ([1741] 1987: 207)

Nations are what their deeds are. Every Englishman will say: We are the men who navigate the ocean, and have the commerce of the world; to whom the East Indies belong and their riches; who have a parliament, juries, etc.

G. W. F. Hegel ([1830–31]1956: 74)

The stream of World-History has altered its complexion; Romans are dead out, English are come in ... To this English People in World-History, there have been ... two grand tasks assigned: the grand Industrial task of conquering some half or more of this Terraqueous Planet for the use of man; then secondly, the grand Constitutional task of sharing, in some pacific endurable manner, the fruit of said conquest, and showing all people how it might be done.

Thomas Carlyle ([1840] 1971: 202, 205)

It will be found that the modern character of England, as it has come to be since the Middle Ages, may ... be most briefly described on the whole by saying that England has been expanding into Greater Britain.

J. R. Seeley ([1883] 1971: 64–5)

English nationalism: the dog that did not bark?

Scottish intellectuals and scholars have for long been exercised by the question, why no nationalism in nineteenth-century Scotland? Scotland was – and is – a small country, dominated by its richer and more powerful neighbour to the south. Why, in 'the springtime of nations', when so many other nations in similar situations were fervently embracing nationalism, did the Scots not do so? Why did they not imitate the Irish, or the Czechs or the Norwegians, all of whom were peoples who sought to liberate themselves from rulers regarded as oppressive and alien?[1]

Because the English are so incurious about and indifferent to their own nationalism, a similar question is rarely asked about English nationalism. England was not of course in the same situation as Scotland or any other of the small nations of Europe. On the contrary it was at the very centre of what was becoming the richest and most powerful country in the world. Nevertheless the nineteenth century stimulated nationalism practically everywhere, even among those, such as the French and Russians, who could by no means be held to be inferior or dependent nations. Why did the English not feel the same prompting? Why, even more than 'Scottish nationalism', does it sound strange to speak of 'English nationalism' in this period?

We shall see that England was not immune to the currents of nationalism flowing through Europe, though it seems to have taken a long time for them to wash ashore. There was a 'moment of Englishness', if not English nationalism in a full-bodied and full-blooded form, at the end of the nineteenth century. But it is noticeable that this has largely escaped the attention of scholars, mainly because they have responded to what has seemed the evident absence of nationalism in nineteenth-century England. There is indeed by now a considerable literature on British ethnicities and identities, especially under the aegis of the new 'British history'. But not only does this relate mainly to Welsh, Irish and Scottish, rather than English, identities, it is also heavily skewed towards the medieval and early modern period. As John Wolfe has said, 'it is ... a curious historiographical paradox that recent historians of nationalism and national identity in Britain have concentrated their attention primarily on the seventeenth and eighteenth centuries while the nineteenth century has been relatively neglected'. It is a paradox because it was in the nineteenth century that nationalism 'in the generally received sense of the word ... established itself as a major ideological force on the European and world stage'. Present-day historians have here only continued the indifference shown by nineteenth-century English commentators themselves. Wolfe records that a computer search of the British Library *Catalogue of Printed Books* suggests that only *one* British publication before the 1860s – Hugh McNeil's pamphlet *Nationalism in Religion* (1839) – contains the word 'nationalism' in its title (Wolfe 1998: 292, 297 n.18).

There is indeed at least one major study that not only purports to analyse 'English nationalism' in this period but, casting its historical net some way backwards, also argues that the English actually invented nationalism, sometime in the late eighteenth century and before the French caught up with them in the course of their great revolution. In 1987 the American historian Gerald Newman published a provocative and engaging book with the title *The Rise of English Nationalism*. Its intention was to show the existence of a full-fledged English nationalism in being by the late eighteenth century. England, Newman argued, was not, as it liked to think of itself, exceptional. It had not escaped the swelling currents of nationalism sweeping through all the European nations at about the time of the French Revolution. Indeed it had to a good extent anticipated them, not to say contributed materially to their formation. English nationalism, Newman remarkably claimed, 'far from being non-existent, was probably the earliest and strongest on earth, and one of the most successful' (1987: 160; see also xxii, 49–60).

How had this come about? Newman drew upon a wide range of cultural sources, in literature, caricature, painting and literary and cultural criticism, to show the rise of what he portrayed as a profoundly nativistic response to rampant cosmopolitanism. As with other countries, he argued, so in England an alienated and embittered intelligentsia reacted against the Frenchified cosmopolitanism of its native aristocracy, accusing it of being responsible for widespread corruption and national decay. In the eyes of artists and writers such as William Hogarth, Tobias Smollett, Henry Fielding and Richard Cowper, the English aristocracy stood condemned for infecting the manners and morals of the native English with the fashions and frivolity of Paris. Berating this, these artists went on to fashion an ideology of English nationalism which, they alleged, derived from the lives of the ordinary English people. This ideology rejected aristocratic cosmopolitanism and championed instead the supposedly native English qualities of sincerity, simplicity, innocence, honesty and plain-dealing. All this, claims Newman, took place in the second half of the eighteenth century, starting around 1750. 'By 1789 the making of English nationalism was over' (Newman 1987: 227; see also 127, 145).

If Newman is right, Colley must be wrong and – on the argument of the last chapter – so must I (not to mention those such as Liah Greenfeld and Hans Kohn who see the rise of English nationalism in the sixteenth and seventeenth centuries). Rather than Britishness and British identity, what developed in the eighteenth century, for the first time ever, was a vigorous English nationalism.

Fortunately, at least for the sake of the argument, Newman is not right. Or, to put it another way, in the context of our concern it is impossible to judge his thesis by the evidence he adduces. This is largely because he fundamentally confuses English and British, Englishness and Britishness. Page after page is littered with this confusion.[2] It clearly does not occur to Newman that this matters, that distinguishing England from Britain, in the century in which the British state was formed and British identity actively promoted, might be critical to his argument. It is one thing to draw upon Wilkite Scottophobia, and this Newman duly does (1987: 176–82).[3] It is quite another to cite, as self-evidently and uncomplicatedly concerned with Englishness, Scottish writers such as Tobias Smollett and James Thomson, or Irish writers such as Oliver Goldsmith and Edmund

Burke (1987: 60, 93–4,133–5, 228–9). In a particularly egregious example, the Scottish inventor James Watt's proud appeal to his fellow-countrymen – that, if they think he merits the accolade, they may say of his invention '*Hoc a Scoto factum fuit*' ('This was made by a Scot') – is quoted in the context of a discussion of a peculiarly English concern with boldness and originality in the arts and sciences. Unmoved by this clear statement of Scottish patriotism, Newman sees Watt as an exemplar of 'the Sincere Ideal' beloved of the *English* nationalists (Newman 1987: 149–53).

In examining Newman's account, it becomes clear in fact that he is not dealing with nationalism at all, English or other, but essentially with the development of a strand of English moralism that has alternately been seen as the source of the glories of the English literary tradition and the bane of its underdeveloped social science (Kumar 2001). The frequent references to 'primitivism', 'uncorrupted virtue' and 'innocence' in the literature of the period he discusses, moreover, point to a type of thinking very common in eighteenth-century literature and social thought not just in England but in Western Europe as a whole. 'Degeneration' and 'corruption' were its basic tropes. It was the kind of thinking best exemplified in Rousseau, and found also in several of the thinkers of the Scottish Enlightenment, such as Adam Ferguson. While it is perfectly possible – and indeed common – for themes of regeneration and recovery to be found in nationalist ideology, such themes cannot simply be equated with nationalism; they are often to be found, after all, among thinkers concerned with the renewal of empire, as in the later Roman and Austrian Empires.

In the nostalgic harking back to 'Old England' and 'the England of Elizabeth' in the moralizing literature of the eighteenth century, one sees, not the signs of a nascent English nationalism, but an early revolt against modernity, associated with the new-fangled ways being imported from Paris by a fashion-loving aristocracy. It was to feed partly into the romantic movement, with its interest in Gothicism and the medieval. But it also expressed a deep-seated anxiety about individual character and public morality. The true response to this was not English nationalism but Methodism and the Evangelical movement, the great forces that transformed public life in the late eighteenth and early nineteenth centuries.

The idea of English nationalism in the eighteenth century is anachronistic (cf. Evans 1995: 232). This is not because the idea of the nation did not exist then; it was, as everyone agrees, actively in the process of formation at this time. It is simply that it was an irrelevance to English life and English thought, in the current conditions of England's existence. There was no English nationalism, just as there was no Scottish nationalism, because there was no need for it. The reasons in both cases were the same. The English and the Scots, as well as the

Welsh, were implicated at the deepest levels in social structures and political systems that directed their attention away from their own ethnic identities. They were parts of wider entities – Great Britain, the British Empire – which actively engaged them and in which they could find an identity. The same was not true of the Irish, at least not in the same way and to the same degree; hence the rise of Irish nationalism in the nineteenth century.

But for the English too the case was not quite so straightforward. Scots and Welsh – and Protestant Irish – while developing strong British identities, were also generally aware of themselves as being distinctively Scottish, Welsh, Irish. Dual identities were normal for them, as they have been for many peoples in multinational states (Spain, Belgium, India, etc.). For the English, as for other imperial peoples such as the Russians, it was not so easy, as we have seen (chapter 3). There was a basic asymmetry in the relation of the different peoples of the British Isles, both to Great Britain and to 'Greater Britain', the British Empire. Scots, Welsh and Irish played a central and far from 'peripheral' role in their evolution. But they were always aware – despite frequent Scottish protestations of equality – that they were junior partners, that Britain and the empire were fundamentally English creations. Hence the maintenance – one might almost say, as compensation – of their particular ethnic identities.

The English too were conscious that Britain and the empire were their creations. But rather than assertive, this made them cautious about insisting on their national identity. When you are in charge, or think you are in charge, you do not go about beating the drum. But that then leaves a certain difficulty about expressing your own national identity. That has been the English dilemma ever since the ideology of nationalism emerged in late eighteenth-century Europe. Nationalism gave many peoples the language of a more or less exclusive collective identity. For the English this exclusivity was precluded by their role in the larger structures of which they were part. To have embraced nationalism, at least in its accepted from, would have been impolitic in the extreme. By stressing English superiority, and reminding the other British peoples of their more dependent role, it would have threatened the unity and integrity of the very structures that the English had so painfully constructed.

Compared with the Scots, Welsh and Irish, therefore, the question of national identity was different for the English. There was certainly some felt need to express the part the English played in the scheme of things. But it could not take the form of conventional nationalist pride. The English could not simply celebrate themselves. English identity had to find objects other than the English nation on which to fasten. The obvious ones, the ones in which English identity could be subsumed, were the two 'English empires', the empire of Great Britain and the British overseas empire.

England and the 'British Empire in Europe'

In 1768 the Anglo-Irish writer Oliver Goldsmith published a book entitled *The Present State of the British Empire in Europe, America, Africa and Asia*. The first 200 pages concerned England, Wales and Scotland. The empire, it is clear, was not just British overseas possessions; it was also Britain itself, the entity created by England over the course of several centuries. Contemporaries were given to calling this the 'Empire of Great Britain' or the 'British Empire in Europe', to distinguish it from the British empire elsewhere. But the parallels are clear. Whatever the differences between the two empires – and of course they were enormous – they shared an ideology that emphasized the two key features of empire that, by analogy with Rome, had emerged in the early modern period: full sovereignty within the territorial boundaries of the realm, and rule over a multiplicity of peoples and territories (Bayly 1989: 77–81; Pagden 1995: 11–28; Kidd 1999: 77; Armitage 2000: 24–60).

The English had of course attempted to create an earlier British empire, under Henry the Second and Edward the First (see chapter 5). Their failure at that time is instructive in helping us to understand their greater success in the eighteenth and nineteenth centuries. Rees Davies, in his *The First English Empire*, explains that failure as in part owing to the rigidity and inflexibility of the medieval English state. The English state's 'precocious' centralization and developed legal codification made it intolerant of diversity, incapable of absorbing or adapting to different systems. Confronted with the 'otherness' of Welsh, Scottish and Irish cultures, the English stone-facedly insisted on the imposition of their own system and culture. No concession was to be made in the interests of creating a unified British community, no justification for rule offered other than in terms of conquest. 'The ideology and mythology of English power and success remained defined in exclusively English terms [and] little real attempt was made to create a pluralistic pan-British mythology or to explain English dominance other than in terms of right and power, English right and English power' (R. R. Davies 2000: 88; see also 111–12, 191–203).

One cannot suppose that eighteenth-century English statesmen pored over their medieval history in an effort to avoid past mistakes. No doubt there were many circumstances, not all of them known to them, that propelled them along a different course. But a different path they did take. England was as dominant, in fact even more so, in the Britain that was created from the sixteenth to eighteenth centuries as it was in the medieval empire. But, especially after the union with Scotland in 1707, the English did not take so high-handed an attitude towards the other peoples that shared the British Isles with them. Whatever the English may have felt and said privately, in public there was a much greater sensitivity towards the claims of other British cultures. There were the well-known exceptions, in the areas especially where Catholicism predominated – Ireland and the Scottish Highlands. But not only did intolerance towards Catholics abate in the nineteenth century (allowing, for instance, the rise of quite a strong movement of Catholic Unionism in Ireland in the late nineteenth century (Pittock 1997: 132)). There were, also, strong considerations of statecraft that led English statesmen to mute any assertion of English dominance or superiority. They had, as Bernard Crick has said, 'a clear and politic sense of the diversity of the United Kingdom'.

> They took for granted that the main business of domestic politics...was holding the United Kingdom or "Britain" together. They were ruthless in maintaining English political dominance; but on the whole, let numbers, wealth and territorial advantage take care of that. They had little desire for cultural hegemony, and they viewed Scottish and Irish culture either with cynical tolerance or with a romantic attraction.
>
> (Crick 1991a: 91; see also 1995: 171)

The development of a 'state-cult *English* nationalism', Crick rightly says, would in these circumstances have been 'counterproductive' (1995: 171). Certainly the English political elite made no attempt to do so in the eighteenth and nineteenth centuries. Quite the opposite: they went in instead for a species of 'positive cultural politics' (Crick 1995: 171). This applied especially to the monarchy. There seems to have been a quite deliberate policy to emphasize its British, not to say imperial, character. On a famous occasion, in 1822, George the Fourth – the first Hanoverian monarch to visit Scotland – was persuaded to appear at the old royal palace of Holyroodhouse in Edinburgh dressed in a kilt. The occasion was expertly stage-managed by Sir Walter Scott, who was probably responsible for the crowning moment when the king solemnly invited the assembled dignitaries to drink a toast to 'the chieftains and clans of Scotland' (Trevor-Roper 1984c: 29–31).

The recuperation of the once despised Highland culture was indeed going on apace in these years, prompted by MacPherson's 'Ossian' and furthered by the popularity of Scott's *Waverley* novels and Landseer's paintings (Trevor-Roper 1984; Robbins 1995: 12–13; Pittock 1997:153–9; Devine 1999: 231–43, 292–3). Queen Victoria also played her part. Requested by her prime minister, Lord Melbourne, to 'spend an appreciable part of the year' in Scotland, she took to the task with enthusiasm. She dressed her children in plaid, cultivated Scottish music, and developed a genuine fondness for the Highlands and Highlanders ('such a chivalrous, fine, active people'). In 1847 she and Albert, who shared her liking for things Scottish, acquired Balmoral Castle in the Grampian Highlands (Albert himself designed the Balmoral Tartan). Balmoral became the queen's favourite residence. Her statesmen were required to visit her there, and after Albert's death it was to Balmoral that she turned for consolation, virtually shutting herself away there for many years. Balmoral was to continue in favour with many of the queen's descendants, especially George the Fifth and Elizabeth the Second. It spread the taste for Scottish lairdship among the British aristocracy, and did much to fix the Scottish Highlands as one of its principal playgrounds. (Cannadine 1984: 118–19; MacKenzie 1993: 730; Robbins 1995: 172–4; Cannon and Griffiths 1998: 572–4; Devine 1999: 293).

Victoria was also careful to make several tours of Wales and Ireland, as did her son Edward, Prince of Wales. The title of Prince of Wales, reserved for the eldest son of the monarch, was indeed an important symbol of the monarchy's Britishness. Instituted in the bad old days of Edward the First, it had over the centuries become a means of showing the crown's concern for its Welsh subjects. Not all holders of the title had taken their duties seriously (one of the most famous, Edward the Black Prince, never even visited the Principality). But there was a greater awareness and sensitivity among nineteenth- and twentieth-century monarchs and their advisers.

A celebrated instance of this came in 1911, when George the Fifth was persuaded by the chancellor of the exchequer, David Lloyd George, to re-institute the ceremony of the Investiture of the prince of Wales. This was done at Caernarvon Castle with great pomp and pageantry, in medieval style (as was done with the equally celebrated Investiture of Prince Charles at Caernarvon in 1969). Lloyd George even coached the Prince, Edward (the future Edward the Eighth), in Welsh, so that he could speak a few words of the language of his Welsh subjects at the Investiture (Charles achieved better results in 1969). The revived, or reinvented, Investiture, served many purposes. These were troubled times, with labour unrest, threatened rebellion in Ireland, the disestablishment of the Welsh Church, and Germany offering a growing challenge to Britain's power abroad. The rituals of royalty were called upon to perform their time-honoured function of integrating and celebrating the nation. But undoubtedly one of the aims, especially in the eyes of Lloyd George, was to reaffirm the monarchy's commitment to Wales and the Welsh people. The Investiture, with all its pomp and panoply, was a declaration to the world that the monarchy was not English but British (Morgan 1982: 124; Cannadine 1984: 133–4; Nairn 1994: 220–34; Evans 1994b: 208).[4]

We have been speaking above of 'the English elite', but this is misleading. The elite was, as we have seen, becoming British in the course of the eighteenth century. Increasingly in the nineteenth century this showed itself not just in the character of the monarchy but also in that of the country's leading statesmen. At the beginning of the century we find such figures as the Irish peer Viscount Castlereagh, one of the architects of the Irish union of 1800 and, as foreign secretary in Lord Liverpool's government, principal negotiator of the coali-tion against Napoleon and Britain's chief representative at the congresses that re-shaped Europe after Napoleon's defeat in 1815. At the end of the century we find two Scotsmen, the earl of Rosebery and Sir Henry Campbell-Bannerman, leading the Liberal Party and both going on to become prime minister. In between come such notable statesmen as the Irish peer Viscount Palmerston, fiery foreign secretary and prime minister, and the Scottish earl of Aberdeen, also foreign secretary and prime minister.

Perhaps the politician who best expresses the British dimension of politics in the nineteenth century is the Liberal leader William Ewart Gladstone. Scottish by descent on both sides, he was born in England and had an English upbringing and education. But Scotland remained a central interest throughout his life. He was passionately involved in Scottish Church politics, and became rector of both Glasgow and Edinburgh universities (not quite matching Rosebery, who added the rectorship of Aberdeen to these). Unlike some of the other statesmen forced to visit Victoria at Balmoral, Gladstone was content, enjoying the walks and the surrounding countryside. His election for the Scottish constituency of Midlothian in 1879, following an emotional campaign, represented a kind of homecoming.

But nor was Wales neglected. Gladstone married into a Welsh family, and his home at Hawarden, in north-eastern Wales, became a treasured retreat for study and reflection (it was where he chose to die, at the ripe old age of 89). He regularly holidayed at Penmaenmawr on the north Welsh coast. He attended eisteddfodau, and took a keen interest in Welsh language and culture. Truly, as Keith Robbins has said, 'no other Victorian politician could emulate Gladstone's personal binding of the British body politic' (1995: 106; see also 112).

Radical politics, too, had a strongly British character, perhaps even more so than in the case of more conventional party politics. Trade unionism began with the efforts of an Irishman, John Doherty, and a Welshman, Robert Owen. Irish and Welsh radicals held leading positions in the Chartist and other working-class movements of the first half of the nineteenth century. The Irishman Daniel O'Connell had already, by 1830, taken the movement for the repeal of Irish union into the British Parliament. In the later nineteenth and early twentieth centuries radicals, many of them from the 'Celtic fringe', increasingly invaded parliamentary politics. There was Charles Parnell, Irish Home Ruler and leader of the Irish party in parliament; the Scottish Labour leader Keir Hardie, who sat for the Welsh constituency of Merthyr Tydfil from 1900 to 1915; David Lloyd George, Manchester-born but bred in Wales, to which his Welsh family took him at the age of two. Exclusively Welsh-speaking in the early years of his life, Lloyd George went on to become a crusading Liberal Home Secretary and then prime minister, 'the first British Prime Minister whose mother tongue was not English' (Robbins 1995: 113).

These were the leaders, the political elite. But at every level of politics and society, Britishness was stamping itself on the character of the nation. We saw the eighteenth-century origins of this in chapter 6. In the nineteenth century it gathered pace, as Keith Robbins (1995; 1998: 262–93) has most extensively shown. Britain's industrialization, the first of its kind in the world, catapulted it to world power. At the same time it brought in its train a host of urgent new issues, to do with class, community, work, poverty, public health and urban life generally. British intellectuals and statesmen struggled to make sense of this unprecedented social revolution. In the 'Blue Books' that scrutinized poverty and child labour; in the novels of Dickens, Disraeli, Gaskell and Eliot; in the social and cultural criticism of Thomas Carlyle, John Stuart Mill, Matthew Arnold and John Ruskin, British society was subjected to a powerful and wide-ranging anatomy (Williams 1963; Kumar 1995).

In such a situation, national identity was not and could not be a major concern. Or rather, national identity at the level specifically of Englishness would have seemed to many petty and irrelevant. The English were at the centre of a world-wide empire and worldwide economy. They were the principal managers of a polity and society that included not just English but Welsh, Irish and Scottish. Many of these latter were coming to play an equally central role in the affairs of British society. British society itself, at all its levels and in all its parts, was face to face with a series of problems the like of which the world had never known. The urgent need was to understand these problems, to find a language adequate to their nature, and to devise policies to deal with them.

Nationalism had little to offer in this task, either in the way of exhortation or of analysis. The English were not oppressed. They did not need to establish their own state, in the face of alien rulers (whether those 'aliens' were ethnically different, or the native ruling class considered as alien). If they had to mobilize to deal with the challenges that faced them, the only meaningful level at which to do this was Britain, not England. Even those who felt themselves the victims of the vast social changes sweeping across Britain, even those, the urban workers and the agricultural labourers, who felt that they did not share in the new power and prosperity, realized that to resist and to reshape the new order they would need to organize at the level that reflected the new British realities. The labour movement was British from the start, and has remained so even when other groups have been questioning their British loyalties.

It is for this reason that it is so hard to find expressions of English national-ism in the eighteenth or nineteenth centuries – whether in political and social thought, literary and artistic culture, or popular movements (cf. Mandler 2000: 225–36; 2001: 121, 136). There is no equivalent, in England, to the nationalist theory of a Herder or a Fichte; no English Grimm or Savigny; no searching of the national soul, as is to be found in nineteenth-century Russian literature; no nationalist poetry of the type exemplified by the Polish poet Adam Mickiewicz; no nationalist movements of the kind found throughout continental Europe in the nineteenth century. Clearly not all of these are equivalent expressions of nationalism; they reflect very different conditions among the varying peoples. But they do share a common concern with 'the nation', with the question of what it is and how it is to find its place in the world. Even the French, who like the English might be thought to be sufficiently powerful and self-confident not to need nationalist solace, increasingly came to be preoccupied with nationalist questions. Having, in the course of their great eighteenth-century revolution, elevated the nation above all other forms and groups, they were forced by the succession of revolutions and changes of regime in the nineteenth century to inquire with a deepening a sense of urgency into the nature of nations in general and the French nation in particular (see, e.g., Renan [1889] 1990; Dumont 1994a).

Nothing of the kind is to be found in England. English writers and thinkers seem unconcerned by these questions. Even in the rare instance when we do seem to find an example of such an interest, it often turns out to be about something else. Such is the case, for example, with Edward Lytton Bulwer's *England and the English* (1833). Far from being the study of national character that its title seems to promise, it is much more like William Hazlitt's *Spirit of the Age* (1825) or Thomas Carlyle's 'Signs of the Time' (1829). Bulwer is concerned, as they are and as his editor Standish Meachem says of him, with 'a frame of mind' (Bulwer 1970: ix) – with the new materialism and utilitarianism of the age, with the clash between aristocratic and middle-class values, with the state of education and morality in the nation. It is a kind of national stocktaking at a crucial period in the country's history: vivid in its portraits, and valuable as a source of the varying attitudes to be found to the great questions of the time. But, despite chapter headings with titles like 'View of the English Character', and sub-sections on such matters as 'Courage of the English', there are virtually no reflections in the work on national character or national identity as we should understand them.[5]

The English did of course take great pride in what they saw as their achievements: the defeat of France in the Seven Years War, and then again in the Napoleonic wars; the protection of constitutional liberties and the rule of law; the astonishing expansion of trade and commerce; England as 'the workshop of the world', the envy and exemplar of all other nations. The English too could look upon the United Kingdom as their creation, just as they saw themselves as being at the heart of the overseas empire. Never mind that this overlooked the contribution of other British peoples; there were plenty of Mr Podsnaps to contemplate with complacency these peculiarly and uniquely 'English' accomplishments. Moreover, on any objective view, it was impossible to deny the leading role played by England in many of these developments.

But the very momentousness and magnitude of these achievements stilled a simple English nationalism. The English might be their architects, but recognition of this could not take the form of merely English self-congratulation. This would have been to lessen the importance and significance of these things. To see them in the terms of contemporary nationalism would have been to reduce them to an intolerably mundane level. It would have been to put the English on a par with Serbians and Romanians, Poles and Hungarians. The English sympathized with these, and their struggles for national independence, but they themselves were after something much loftier. The English saw themselves as the heirs of the great builders of the past – of Alexander and his empire, of the Romans and their empire. These were creators of whole civilizations, world empires. Their aspirations were thoroughly cosmopolitan. Though their creations might be initiated by a particular people and be named after them, they could never be reduced to that people. The Roman Empire was never an empire simply for the Romans. No more was the empire created by the English, whether in Britain or the world beyond, simply an English possession. It expressed English striving, and it gave the English a central role to play. It bestowed on them a sense of missionary purpose. But such a missionary or imperial identity was a far cry from that of contemporary nationalism, which indeed was engaged precisely in destroying such conceptions.

It is in this context that we need to understand what has often been taken as an expression of arrogant English pride, English nationalism in its most blatant form. The English, as we have seen (chapter 4), have from the time of Bede and the Anglo-Saxons tended to refer to the whole of Britain as 'England', and have often substituted 'English' where justice as well as plain fact cried out for 'British', if not 'Welsh', 'Scottish' or 'Irish'. No doubt it is fair to regard this as in some sense an expression of English imperialism (see, e.g., Wormald 1994). But it is not an expression of English *nationalism* – not, at least, in any conventional meaning of that term. Were that so, we would not find so many non-English members of the United Kingdom being quite so content to employ 'England' and 'the English' as a short-hand expression for the whole of the United Kingdom and its inhabitants – even, on occasion, for the empire as a whole.

Here, for instance, is a Scottish member of parliament, David Scott, addressing the House of Commons in 1805:

We commonly when speaking of British subjects call them English, be they English, Scotch, or Irish; he, therefore, I hope, will never be offended with the word English being applied in future to express any of His Majesty's subjects, or suppose it can be meant as an allusion to any particular part of the United Kingdom.

(in Colley 1994: 162; see also Cunningham 1986: 294)

Of course there have been many, then and since, who did object to this casual and seemingly thoughtless substitution of England for Britain, let alone the

British Isles as a whole. These days we are much more sensitized to the offence this is likely to give, and much more likely therefore – unless we follow the example of A. J. P. Taylor – to avoid this usage. But the important point is that a Scotsman like Scott did not consider it offensive, nor indeed as being in the nature of an assertion of English superiority. It is almost as if it carried a neutral connotation.

It is, I believe, with this understanding that we must consider Admiral Nelson's famous exhortation at the battle of Trafalgar – in the same year, 1805, as Scott's remark – that 'England expects every man to do his duty'; or Willam Pitt the Younger's only a little less celebrated remark, in his last public speech in 1806, that 'England has saved herself by her exertions and will, as I trust, save Europe by her example' (quoted N. Davies 1999: 734). Norman Davies calls Pitt's remark 'inexcusable', but he himself acknowledges that 'the people at that period who might have been expected to insist on "British" where "British" was due were the very ones who willingly acquiesced' (1999: 734). Nelson was perfectly well aware of the number of Irish and Scottish sailors aboard HMS *Victory*, just as Pitt, who had championed Catholic emancipation and actively sought Irish recruits for the armed forces, knew very well the contribution made by all Britons, and not just the English, to the struggle against Napoleon. The use of 'England' in both cases reflected a relatively well-accepted sense that the part could stand for the whole, without any necessary suggestion that it was the chief or only part. More importantly, it could indicate a belief that England and Britain were now so interfused that the use of one for the other could not possibly matter. Sir John Seeley, who in his *The Expansion of England* uses England and Britain interchangeably, justified this practice on the grounds that 'in these islands we feel ourselves for all purposes one nation' ([1883] 1971: 43).

Empire and English identity

Great Britain was one theatre within which the English could find a role for themselves. Englishness modulated into Britishness. No more than the Scots or Welsh or Irish did the English lose a sense of their distinctiveness. But there was a difference. The other British nations clung to their national identities as a kind of compensation for, or counterweight against, the predominant role of the English in the United Kingdom. They were Britons, but also clearly Scots, Welsh and Irish. Eventually, when the United Kingdom seemed to lose its vigour and utility, this could issue in full-blown Irish, Scottish and Welsh nationalism.

For the English it was never going to be so easy. Ruling the roost, they felt it impolitic to crow. Especially at the intellectual and ideological level – the level at which nationalism has usually been elaborated – there was no felt need to formulate a statement of English nationalism. The pressure, whether or not consciously felt, went in the opposite direction. For good political reasons the English suppressed the assertion of their own separate identity. They waxed eloquent on Parliament, the monarchy, the courts, the 'Condition of England'. But there were almost no attempts to bind these together into some kind of profile of English national identity, or an assessment of English national character. The nearest thing perhaps was some such work as Walter Bagehot's *The English Constitution* (1867). Far wider than its title suggests, this is a magnificent dissection of English political culture. But it makes no attempt to turn this into a statement about the English people *as* a people, having a particular character and destiny.

If Great Britain was one pole of attraction leading to the muting or suppression of English nationalism, 'Greater Britain', the British Empire overseas, was another. In many ways this was an even more powerful suppressant of English national identity. If the English could find an identity as the creators of Britain, how much more alluring the role as makers of the greatest empire the world had ever seen. Repetition has made that achievement sound stale; guilt, and the loss of empire, have made the English themselves reluctant to dwell on it in recent times. It takes an American historian to state the obvious.

> It remains a matter of historical fascination that a relatively small archipelago off the coast of Europe not only could become the first "modern" nation-state but could transform itself into a vast global empire, ultimately making it seem as if the affairs of this proverbial workshop encompassed world history itself.
>
> (Noonkester 1997: 251; cf. Bailyn and Morgan 1991a: 31)

In his 1852 essay 'England's Forgotten Worthies', celebrating the Elizabethan mariners who were responsible for England's first venture into empire, James Froude imagined the young Walter Raleigh, with his half-brothers the Gilberts, rowing down to the port of Dartmouth and 'listening, with hearts beating, to the mariners' tales of the new earth beyond the sunset' (1876: 479). Charles Kingsley made use of a similar image of the young Raleigh (Houghton 1957: 211), and in 1870 Sir John Everett Millais memorably represented the scene in his painting 'The Boyhood of Raleigh'. Millais's painting was one of the most popular of the Victorian period; and copies of it could still be found hanging in many an English home in the first part of the twentieth century. In the seaman's tense finger, pointing westwards towards the Indies, and the young Raleigh's brooding eyes, Millais evoked a prophetic vision of an English empire of and beyond the seas (Strong 1978: 11; Burrow 1983: 231–2).

Froude and Kingsley, together with John Seeley, were among the most influential writers in defining England's destiny in imperial terms in the second half of the nineteenth century (Houghton 1957: 121–3; Burrow 1983: 231–85).

But already in the 1840s, in his *Chartism* (1840) and *Past and Present* (1843), Thomas Carlyle was hailing the English as the new Romans, and their task as the civilizing of the world. 'Romans are dead out, English are come in' ([1840]1971: 202). Carlyle generously included the Russians in this world-historic venture. They, like the Romans and the English, are also a 'silent' people, doers and workers rather than, like the French, ineffectual prattlers and theorists. The Russians were doing the work of civilization in Asia. But they were doing it largely as a military operation, 'drilling all wild Asia and wild Europe into military rank and file'. The English conquest of the world certainly made use of arms – Carlyle was not squeamish about the use of force – but above all it did it through the overwhelming superiority of England's trade and industry (an achievement of English workers as much as their masters, Carlyle was at pains to remind his readers). England's Epic, 'unsung in words, is written in huge characters on the face of this planet, – sea-moles, cotton-trades, railways, fleets and cities, Indian Empires, Americas, New Hollands; legible throughout the Solar System!' ([1843] 1910: 221).

Seeley saw one significant aspect of this imperial system when he described it as 'an extension of English nationality'. 'Greater Britain', he said, is not properly speaking an empire at all but 'a vast English nation' (1971: 40, 63). This was consistent with his view that the empire was essentially a union of English-speaking peoples, peoples of English or British stock. In principle, he argued, 'if Greater Britain in the full sense of the phrase really existed, Canada and Australia would be to us as Kent and Cornwall...When we have accustomed ourselves to contemplate the whole Empire together and call it all England, we shall see that here too is a United States. Here too is a great homogeneous people, one in blood, language, religion and laws, but dispersed over a boundless space' (1971: 54, 126).

Here then was one way for the English to see themselves: as the creators of a worldwide system in which they as it were gigantically replicated themselves, carrying with them their language, their culture, their institutions, their industry. Here, on an even broader canvas than Great Britain, was a plane on which to portray themselves in their world-historic role. As put by the writer Charles Adderley, the founding of Anglo-Saxon colonies was inspired by the generous and altruistic desire of 'spreading throughout the habitable globe all the characteristics of Englishmen – their energy, their civilization, their religion and their freedom' (in Houghton 1957: 47). If this was a matter of pride – and for Seeley and others it clearly was – it would have been both ludicrous and insulting to describe it in the terms of English nationalism. There was a grandeur in this conception, and just about enough reality, to lift it well above the nation-state level that was the usual object of European nationalism. This was a vision of the English at the opposite pole of the Little Englandism of Victorian Liberalism.

It saw the English less as a people than as the seed of a mighty race embarked on a mission to remake the world in its own image. Ultimately, as Seeley was prepared to contemplate with equanimity, the English outside England would be not simply more numerous but also in all probability more industrious and prosperous than those in the home country. Such, to a degree, had been the fate of the Roman Empire; such one should expect of all peoples who construct not a nation-state but a 'world-state' (or, as Seeley pointed out, thinking of the first British Empire, in the case of the English not just one but 'two world-states' (1971: 231; see also 14–18)).

Seeley's conception of the empire was clearly partial. It was of a predominantly white empire. His hope was that some sort of accommodation might be reached between the empire proper, the 'Colonial Empire', the empire as England writ large, and what 'may be called an Oriental Empire', rule by conquest, as in India, over a heterogeneous group of peoples many of them differing in fundamental respects from the culture of the rulers (1971: 239–40). But for others it was just this heterogeneity that gave England its great opportunity to fulfil its mission in the world. Here a different conception of empire came into play. Instead of the 'Greek' model – essentially Seeley's model – whereby groups of emigrants go off to colonize distant, often empty or sparsely populated lands, this conception appeals to the 'Roman' model, according to which a 'higher' or more 'advanced' people take it upon themselves to conquer and civilize peoples of a very different kind from them. In the first case, the colonies, being virtually replicas of the home society, spun off from its body, are more or less autonomous and self-governing. In the second case, the imperial people must exercise some kind of 'tutelary' authority over the disparate peoples under its rule. With some oversimplification, the Greek model could be applied to the first British Empire, that of the North American colonies; the Roman model to the second empire, that created in Asia and Africa (Doyle 1986: 54–103; Pagden 1995: 126–55; Armitage 2000: 29–36; and cf. Hobson 1988: 6–8).

What the Roman conception of England's mission allowed in was the idea of progress, one of the dominant ideas of the age. The non-European peoples of the empire could be conceived as child-like, undeveloped and backward in that rationality that led the West to make its great leap forward. Now it was the duty of Western powers to exercise a beneficent and tutelary despotism over these people to supervise and promote their advancement. The law of progress held that, though progress was inevitable and universal, there would always be backward civilizations that would require a helping hand. For such civilizations, as liberals such as John Stuart Mill argued, a 'vigorous despotism' could be the means of bringing them on to maturity. Hence the great emphasis on education in liberal thinking about the empire, as in Macaulay's celebrated (or notorious) 1835 Minute on Indian Education, in which he argued that the aim should be 'to form ... a class of persons, Indians in blood and colour, but English in taste, in opinion, in morals, and in intellect' (Mehta 1999: 15; see also 83–4; 70–4; Clive 1975: 342–99).

The English, through the empire that they saw as their creation, could and did take pride in being in the forefront of this mission to educate and elevate the human race. The British Empire, declared Lord Rosebery in 1884, is 'the greatest secular agency for good the world has seen' (in Faber 1966: 64). In 1912 Lord Hugh Cecil summarized Britain's vocation in the world as 'to undertake the government of vast, uncivilised populations and to raise them gradually to a higher level of life' (in Paxman 1999: 69). One can find innumerable instances of utterances of this kind from the lips of statesmen and the pens of writers in the nineteenth and early twentieth centuries (see, e.g., Faber 1966: 38–40, 63–5). And though the English were careful on the whole to stress the British, and not simply English, character of this noble and heroic task, undoubtedly there was a feeling that the English could stake a particular claim to having carved out the empire in the first place, and to have sustained it thereafter. Thomas Hughes's wildly popular *Tom Brown's Schooldays* (1857) was written to celebrate 'the Browns' of England – those typical middle-class families that 'in their quiet, dogged, homespun way ... have been subduing the earth in most English counties, and leaving their mark in American forests and Australian uplands. Wherever the fleets and armies of England have won renown, there stalwart sons of the Browns have done yeoman's work' (Hughes 1986: 18). Macaulay, typically, made even more grandiose claims for the English as the agents of progress. The English, he said,

have become the greatest and most highly civilised people that ever the world saw, have spread their dominion over every quarter of the globe, have scattered the seeds of mighty empires and republics over vast continents of which no dim intimation had ever reached Ptolemy or Strabo, have created a maritime power which could annihilate in a quarter of an hour the navies of Tyre, Athens, Carthage, Venice and Genoa together, have carried the science of healing, the means of locomotion and correspondence, every mechanical art, every manufacture, every thing that promotes the conveniences of life, to a perfection which our ancestors would have thought magical, have produced a literature which may boast of works not inferior to the noblest which Greece has bequeathed to us, have discovered the laws which regulate the motions of the heavenly bodies, have speculated with exquisite subtilty on the operations of the human mind, have been the acknowledged leaders of the human race in the career of political improvement.

([1835] 1907a: 121)

Empire, industry, progress, science, civilization – all these terms were fused in a singular *mélange* impossible to separate into its particular components. And, even more inseparably connected, there was Englishness, the core of the whole world-transforming movement. It is obvious indeed, from the statements above, how easy it would have been to turn these perceptions into an assertive statement of English nationalism. We do get many comments that seem to have this flavour, as when Charles Kingsley in *Westward Ho!* speaks of its hero, the seaman Amyas Leigh, as the 'symbol... of brave young England longing to wing its way out of its island prison, to discover and to traffic, to colonise and to civilise, until no wind can sweep the earth which does not bear the echoes of an English voice' (1947: 12). What is remarkable, then, is that these perceptions did not lead to a strong current of English nationalist thought. If the English were singled out, it was because they were seen as spearheading a movement that had general European and indeed world dimensions. They were indeed to be congratulated for their leading role; but they were not the only ones playing a part in what was seen as the general progress of mankind towards an unprecedented era of peace and prosperity. Writers like Thomas Buckle and Herbert Spencer, who were known throughout Europe and beyond for their accounts of this general progress of society, had no time for anything so narrow, provincial and petty as English nationalism. What they were charting was no less than the fate and future of human society itself; and while the West had taken the lead, no special accolade was to be accorded to any particular nation for its part in what was seen as a general Western achievement (see Bury 1955: 334–49; Burrow 1966).

Thus it was that the Great Exhibition of 1851 in London's Hyde Park was widely greeted not simply as a monument to English or British industrial prowess, but as proclaiming the triumph of industrialism *in general*, as a way of life pregnant with promise for the whole of humankind. Its full title, significantly, was 'The Great Exhibition of the Works of Industry of all Nations'. The aim of the exhibition, declared the *Edinburgh Review*, was 'to seize the living scroll of human progress, inscribed with every successive conquest of man's intellect'. *The Times* saw it as marking 'a great crisis in the history of the world', foreshadowing an epoch of universal peace. The opening day of the exhibition, it said, was 'the first morning since the creation that all peoples have assembled from all parts of the world and done a common act' (all quotations in Bury 1955: 329–31). Albert the prince consort, the moving spirit of the Exhibition, in introducing it to the public sounded the same note of common endeavour and world solidarity. It will show, he said,

that we are living at a period of most wonderful transition, which tends rapidly to accomplish that great end to which indeed all history points – *the realisation of the unity of mankind*... The Exhibition of 1851 is to give us a true test and a living picture of the point of development at which the whole of mankind has arrived in this great task, and a new starting-point from which all nations will be able to direct their future exertions.

(In Bury 1955: 330; see also Briggs 1965b: 23–4, 43–51)

In the Crystal Palace that housed the Exhibition, the British half was divided into raw materials and industrial applications; the other half, devoted to the exhibits of other nations, followed no such order, and exhibits were classified by nation. The British contribution, in other words, was 'universal', that of other nations merely 'national'. The introduction to the catalogue of the Exhibition spelled out the message that the Exhibition was at once a British achievement and at the same time a gesture of internationalism and goodwill to all: 'Other nations have devised means for the display and encouragement of their own arts and manufacture; but it has been reserved for England to provide an arena for the exhibition of the industrial triumphs of the whole world' (in Milbank 2000: 12–13). The characteristic and conventional substitution of 'England' for 'Britain' here unwittingly makes the point. 'Other nations' have and need the comforts of nationalism; for England, working on a far grander plane, industrial greatness and imperial power supply both the motive and the opportunity for a much more elevated role.

Imperialism is not nationalism, though the former can contain the latter and at times be reduced to it.[6] This is what, in a climate of increasing anxiety and intensified competition between nations, seems to have happened in the late nineteenth and early twentieth centuries. But in England, as in comparable countries such as Austria and Russia, for much of the better part of the nineteenth century imperialism trumped nationalism. For the English in their empire, as for the Austrians and Russians in theirs, empire offered an identity that lifted them above 'mere' nationalist self-glorification. Joseph Conrad, in his *Heart of Darkness* (1902), saw and explored well enough the corruptions, both political and personal, of empire. He wrote at a time when such perceptions, in the midst of an increasingly strident and boastful imperialism, were becoming relatively common among educated people. But, in a pointed remark, he seems to excuse England, because in the part of the world where they rule, the large part coloured red on the maps of the world, 'one knows that some real work is done' there (Conrad 1995: 25). Conrad says no more about this 'real work', but it seems plausible to relate to it to an earlier observation in the novel, a famous comment on European imperialism by the narrator Marlow:

The conquest of the earth, which mostly means the taking it away from those who have a different complexion or slightly flatter noses than ourselves, is not a pretty thing when you look into it too much. What redeems it is the idea only. An idea at the back of it; not a sentimental pretence but an idea; and an unselfish belief in the idea.

(Conrad 1995: 20)

Whether or not the novel goes on to undermine even this defence of empire is an open question. But, taken with what seems to be Conrad's more sympathetic attitude towards the British Empire, it seems possible to say that in his eyes as in those of the empire's defenders the English and the British were indeed working with an 'idea'. Perhaps this was no more than an ideal, self-flattering to the national psyche but incapable of realization in the real world of national interests and international rivalries, not to mention personal greed and ambition. That might well be the consensus today. But we have to accept that at the time many thought differently. For the British generally, the empire was a force for good in the world. It was the means whereby all peoples – or at least many of them – might share in the material progress and moral enlightenment that were, so it was felt, increasingly characterizing Western nations. For the English specifically, there was the sense that – not necessarily by choice or desire – they were centrally placed in the accomplishment of this task. When William Huskisson spoke of planting 'in every quarter of the globe . . . the seeds of freedom, civilization and Christianity', he equated that undertaking with bringing to the lands of the empire 'English laws and English institutions' (in Noonkester 1997: 283).

It was not a task that, at least to the best or most thoughtful minds, lent itself to tub-thumping celebration of ethnic nationhood. 'Englishmen of the best kind', says A. P. Thornton, 'talked little of their superiority to others, they were content to assert that superiority in action. They did talk a great deal, however, of their responsibility to others, and among these others was generally included world interests as a whole' (1968: 240). On an imperial power, said Frederick Lugard, reposed a dual mandate: a mandate of trusteeship towards the subject people, and a mandate of responsibility to the civilized world. A failure to discharge one's duty in either respect deprived one of the right to imperial rule. What Lugard, governor-general of Nigeria, said of the African territories of the British Empire was repeated with relation to other parts of the empire by Balfour, Cromer, Curzon, Milner, the Chamberlains, the Churchills and a host of other statesmen (Faber 1966: 68–85; Thornton 1968: 78–82, 240–2, 409–12). *La mission civilisatrice* or 'the White Man's Burden' was, it is true, invoked by a number of other nations in the age of European imperialism; and England was no exception to the relative degree of hypocrisy involved in this (see, e.g., Hobson 1988: 113ff.; Rich 1990: 12–13). But if hypocrisy, properly speaking, means saying one thing and doing another *without consciousness of the discrepancy* between them, then the hypocrisy of English or British imperialism was no bar to the suppression of a narrowly conceived nationalism.

There is one further point. When the British wound up their empire in the 1950s and 1960s, it was common to remark how little difference it seemed to make to the ordinary people of the country. The British, having acquired the empire in a fit of absence of mind, seemed to have given it up with equal insouciance. Empire therefore cannot have penetrated very deeply into the national psyche. It cannot have been an important constituent of national identity. David Miller reflects the opinion of many commentators when he says that an imperial ideology 'may have been the sustaining ideology of that relatively small section of the upper-middle class who made careers out of imperial administration, but for the bulk of the population the colonial empire remained a somewhat remote entity' (1995a: 159; see also Judd 1996: 426; MacKenzie 1999a: 291). George Orwell had earlier declared that 'it is quite true that the English are hypocritical about their Empire. In the working class this hypocrisy takes the form of not knowing that the Empire exists' (1970a: 80).

These familiar observations are wide of the mark. They are the kinds of conclusions that one might come to from depending on unreliable and superficial sources such as opinion surveys and casual conversation. It may be true that the ordinary English or British people say little and know less about the British Empire. That does not mean that empire may not have penetrated the culture – and therefore those people – deeply, at levels and in ways that people themselves may not be conscious of. We know that this is true of such phenomena as race and class, and indeed nation. Why not empire? Certainly, recent research is uncovering a vast sub-stratum of images, sounds, stories and sentiments that puts empire at the centre of both popular and high culture in Britain, from the eighteenth to the mid-twentieth centuries. Speaking simply of the period before the First World War, Antoinette Burton notes 'the traces of empire that were everywhere to be found "at home" ... in spaces as diverse as the Boy Scouts, Bovril advertisements, and biscuit tins; in productions as varied as novels, feminist pamphlets, and music halls; and in cartographies as particular as Oxbridge, London, and the Franco-British Exhibition' (2000: 138–9).

Such everyday items, the stuff of 'banal nationalism' (Billig 1995), are what fills the unreflecting consciousness. They are neither noticed nor remembered until we are reminded of them, often forcibly as in times of conflict or war. But they are there, waiting to be activated. With the passage of time, no doubt, generations that have grown up without empire will lose that reservoir of sentiments and images which kept alive, at however subconscious a level, the experience of empire. But for the British this may still be too early. Certainly there is a continuous history right through to the 1950s that kept the fact of empire strongly present in the national culture. And since the formal end of empire there is the presence in Britain of many people – of African, Caribbean and South Asian descent – from the former British Empire who serve as persisting and powerful reminders. At any rate for the period we are concerned with – the nineteenth and early twentieth centuries – the position is clear. As Burton says, 'empire was ... not just a phenomenon "out there", but a fundamental part of English culture and national identity at home, where the fact of empire was registered not only in political debate ... but entered the social fabric, the intellectual discourse and the life of the imagination' (2000: 139; see also Mackenzie 1999a, 1999b; Hall 2001).[7]

The English people were, as far as nationalism went, one of Carlyle's 'silent people', along with the Romans and Russians. There was no epic of English nationalism. There was no celebration of the English race, or the English way. There was however considerable satisfaction expressed, and pride taken, in England's leading role as an agent of civilization and progress. This was not nationalism, though it could be taken as a substitute for nationalism. It was a view of the world, and of their place in it, taken by those who felt that history had thrust a certain destiny upon them, and that they had a duty to fulfil it. It was indeed in the nineteenth (rather than in the sixteenth) century, that the English and, more generally, the British, could see themselves as an 'elect nation', called to carry out a particular, God-given, mission in the world (cf. Bayly 1989: 140–1). Only when this sense failed them, only when they had serious qualms about it, did they turn inwards towards themselves, and begin to ask themselves who they were.

The need for nationhood

It was common for the English in the nineteenth century to compare themselves with Rome. Like the Romans, the English had built up a worldwide empire, larger even than that of Rome. Like the Romans, their pursuit was not simply, and perhaps not even mainly, to build up their own power. As they saw it, they like the Romans were engaged in a mission to spread law and civilization across the globe. This implied a certain attitude towards the other peoples with whom they came into contact, and whom they conquered. While it was clear that, as the leaders and initiators, the English like the Romans were superior, this did not mean that other peoples in time could not share in the level of civilization of their imperial rulers. Indeed this was the very goal of the imperial mission, its very *raison d'être*. All inhabitants of the empire were to be equal subjects, or citizens. The pride of those who asserted *civis Romanus sum* was to be matched by those who could claim *civis Britannicus sum*, and protection correspondingly afforded to them; the *Pax Romana* was to have its equivalent in the *Pax Britannica*. Nationalism and racism were therefore both tempered in the halcyon years of empire, in the period following the loss of the American colonies and the rebuilding of an even mightier empire in all corners of the globe.[8]

But Rome carried another message as well. Its very power and imperial reach had corrupted it. It had declined into a despotism. It had increasingly to rely on a diet of 'bread and circuses' to keep its population docile. The aristocratic and intellectual classes increasingly withdrew from politics and public life, leaving the vacuum to be filled by a new class of unprincipled and power-hungry adventurers. A moral rot set into the heart of empire, leading by slow degrees to decline and fall. Before Rome – or at least its western half – fell to the barbarians, it had collapsed inwardly, spiritually and morally bankrupt.

It was this tragic and melancholic aspect of the history of the Roman Empire that increasingly haunted the minds of Englishmen in the late nineteenth century. We are inclined to mistake the time that was the high-point of the British Empire. We are apt to place it in the late nineteenth and early twentieth centuries, at the height of the imperialist scramble and the expression of fervent imperialist ideas. Was this not when Britain came to occupy a fifth of the earth's land surface and to govern a quarter of its population? Was this not when it outshone Rome in its imperial splendour, symbolized by such events as Queen Victoria's Diamond Jubilee of 1897, Edward the Seventh's coronation of 1901, and George the Fifth's Durbar in India in 1911? Was this not, as one commentator put it on the occasion of Edward's coronation, when 'the Imperial idea blazed forth into prominence, as the sons and daughters of the Empire gathered together from the ends of the earth to take their part', and all processed to the stately tunes of Elgar's *Imperial March* and *Coronation Ode* (in Cannadine 1984: 125; see also Cannadine 2001: 106–12)?

We should remember Hegel's warning, that ideas and ideologies are most fully elaborated at the time when their subjects, as practical concerns, are on the point of dissolution. Such may be the case with the British Empire.[9] 'It remains a widely held view', says David Cannadine, 'that Victoria's jubilees and Edward's coronation mark the high noon of empire, confidence and splendour. But others, following the mood of Kipling's "Recessional", regard them in a very different light – as an assertion of show and grandeur, bombast and bravado, at a time when real power was already on the wane' (1984: 125–6; cf. Jenkyns 1981: 334–7; Hyam 1999: 50).[10] Christopher Bayly (1989) has persuasively argued that the 'meridian' of empire was not, as conventionally held, the late nineteenth but the late eighteenth and early nineteenth centuries, the time when Britain already far outstripped its rivals in territory and global influence, and when the institutions of empire were established with an ease and confidence never again available to British rulers. By the late nineteenth century Britain's rivals – France now joined by Germany, Russia, the United States, Japan – were growing more powerful as well as more numerous. Britain's economic predominance came under threat; its naval supremacy was no longer unquestionable; its global power was challenged in both East and West. All this, for the British, 'betokened a world of fear, tension and rivalry which had not existed in the balmy days of Palmerston' (Cannadine 1984: 126; see also Faber 1966: 65–7; Thornton 1968: 77–8; Clarke 1970: 30–161; Porter 1987: 33–81; MacKenzie 1999a: 280).

For the English, as opposed to other Britons, the change was especially traumatic. They were at the heart of the imperial enterprise, the chief architects of empire. The loss of their unrivalled freedom of action, the checks and reverses expressed by such experiences as the disastrous campaigns in Afghanistan, the death of General Gordon at Khartoum, and the struggle with the Boers in South Africa, led to a severe questioning of their missionary role as an imperial people. They seemed to be heading in a difficult, dangerous and morally untenable direction.

Probably it was the Boer War, more than any other event of this time, that destroyed for ever the confidence that Englishmen of all classes and persuasions had had in their empire. J. A. Cramb, in his *Origins and Destiny of Imperial Britain*, written during the Boer War, likens the destiny of Britain to 'the Nemesis of Greek Tragedy', and remarks: 'There is perhaps not a single heart in this Empire which does not at moments start as at some menacing... sound, a foreboding of evil' (in Jenkyns 1981: 336). The morally indefensible nature of the aims of the Boer War, the manner of its conduct, with the employment of the first 'concentration camps', the defeats by a much smaller, less well-equipped but braver and more idealistically inspired force – all these produced a growing revulsion among many thinkers and statesmen. The hysterical rejoicing in Britain at the relief of Mafeking (1900) can be seen less as an expression of jingoistic pride than as an outburst of gratitude that the disasters of the war had not been total. 'It was not the bugle-call of imperial effort that was being sounded, but the first, raucous, notes of its swan-song' (Faber 1966: 66; see also Hyam 1999: 50).

J. A. Hobson's celebrated *Imperialism* (1902), compiled from articles written during the Boer War, was one of the most influential and widely discussed of the many critiques of empire that appeared in this period. It struck a chord not just with liberals and socialists but with several conservative thinkers as well (Hobson 1988: 11). In his passionate denunciation of imperialism as class-based, parasitic, financially crippling and morally ruinous, Hobson drew the by now familiar comparison with the fate of Rome. The Roman Empire, he argued, like the British had in its later stages gradually been taken over by a 'moneyed oligarchy', which displaced the traditional aristocracy. This oligarchy, dependent on a mercenary colonial army rather than home forces, had steadily sucked the moral and material life away from the empire, both in the home territory and in the colonial dependencies. The lesson for the British Empire was plain to see (Hobson 1988: 366–7, 136, 247–8; see also Freeden 1986, 1988; Owen 1999).[11]

Declining confidence in empire chimed well with general ideas of 'decadence', 'degeneration' and the 'crisis of European culture' that were so popular with European artists and intellectuals of the *fin-de-siècle* – in England as much as on the Continent (Nordau [1892] 1993; Masur 1966; Pick 1989; Hennegan 1990: 188–209). No doubt these too were responsible for the more inward turn, the self-questioning, that we find in English cultural life at the end of the nineteenth century. But there was also a more positive stimulus to national self-awareness. The last third of the nineteenth century was the period, as Eric Hobsbawm has shown (1984, 1992: 101–30), when nationalism for the first time became a truly mass force. In doing so it changed its character in significant ways. No longer simply 'a principle of nationality', a more limited and restricted idea elaborated by liberal intellectuals such as Mazzini, it now claimed a trans-forming universality. 'Henceforth *any* body of people considering themselves a "nation" claimed the right to self-determination which, in the last analysis, meant the right to a separate sovereign state for their territory' (Hobsbawm 1992: 102). Moreover, unlike the more political or civic concept of nationhood that generally held sway in the first half of the century, the mass nationalism of the second half was more emphatically ethnic and cultural. The soul of a nation was seen to lie essentially in its language, its religion, its culture, its folkways and folklore, its history and traditions. Finally, nationalism, regarded for much of the earlier period as befitting mainly 'stateless societies', nations without states like the Germans and Italians, or Czechs and Poles, or Serbs and Bulgarians, now came to be seen as a proper object of concern for estab-lished nation-states, such as France, Britain and America. They too now felt the need to put out the flag, to cultivate national sentiment and to look to national monuments and national rituals (Hobsbawm 1992: 102–4; see also Mommsen 1978).

The effects of these developments on Britain were bound to be complex. After all, there was already a strong and still developing British identity in being, made all the more elevated and attractive by being linked to empire. How would nationalism, in its more pronounced ethnic form, affect this complex? It is interesting that Hobsbawm (1984), in his account of the 'production' or invention of nationalist traditions and rituals in late nineteenth-century Europe, occasionally mentions Britain – in the context of rituals of royalty, for instance – but barely refers to England, or indeed any of the other constituent nations of the British Isles. This suggests that nationalist currents were, in part at least, absorbed by the entity of Britain, which continued to provide an adequate focus for collective identity for the bulk of its inhabitants. This was especially so if nationalism, as many insisted, had to take on an imperialist character, if only those nations that were also or became empires had a future, 'since the possession of an empire was an essential precondition for the free development of one's own national culture in time to come' (Mommsen 1978: 126). In an empire that was so comprehensively British rather than simply English, the type of nationalism that was most likely to be satisfied would be British rather than English. As Joseph Chamberlain put it in his Rectorial address at the University of Glasgow in 1897, the desire for the consolidation and further extension of the

British Empire was an 'entirely popular sentiment not confined to individuals of classes, but identified inseparably with the national character of Britain' (in Mommsen 1978: 126).

Yet, in the end, this was not entirely satisfactory, or at least no longer so. British nationalism had, it is true, symbols that could command intense feelings of loyalty, most obviously the monarchy. But was the British monarchy not 'foreign', shown most clearly in those great gatherings of European royalty in the late nineteenth century when the German, Russian and other foreign relatives of the British monarchs were on display?[12] Moreover, no matter to what degree English, Scots, Welsh and Irish submerged their identities in a common Britishness, for how long could it fail to be recognized that Britain was ultimately a multinational entity? The danger was that a British identity would come to seem what many have claimed it always was anyway, simply a civic or political identity that overlay deeper cultural differences. That had not been the perception for much of the eighteenth and nineteenth centuries. But it was what seemed to be implied by the development, for the first time in any serious form, not merely of Irish but of Scottish and Welsh nationalist movements in the late nineteenth century (Foster 1989a: 431–60; Boyce 1995: 228–58; Harvie 1995: 15–24; Devine 1999: 292–8; Morgan 1982: 90–122; G. Williams 1985: 226–51; J. Davies 1994: 416–21, 454–7).

Irish nationalism had begun earlier, following classic European patterns of resentment and the demand for national independence. Now, with the failure of Home Rule under Gladstone, it became distinctly more 'ethnic', taking the form of an intensive cultural – Gaelic – revival. It also became more radical and indeed revolutionary. This was certainly not the case with the Welsh or Scottish movements, though both contained radical elements. What marked those, and what they shared with Irish nationalism, was the rediscovery, or reinvention, of a native culture and a national history, of a more or less 'Celtic' kind. This not only gave a new definition to Welshness, Irishness and Scottishness. It also asserted an essential difference from the dominant people of the United Kingdom, the English.

This might be one spur to English nationalism, as it is today. If others reject you, it is natural to play up your strengths, and to take pride in precisely those things that distinguish you from those others. In the English case this was un-likely to lead to any form of political nationalism, given England's undoubted predominance in the kingdom. Nor, with very few exceptions, did Welsh or Scottish nationalists at this time call for the break-up of the United Kingdom. Their nationalism was cultural, not political. That squared with the new em-phasis on ethnicity generally in European nationalism in the last third of the nineteenth century. Every nation had a national 'soul', a distinctive cultural heritage that marked it out from all others and which it was its duty to cultivate and further. If not just Slavs and Scandinavians, but even Scots, Irish and Welsh, their British brethren, were discovering their national souls at this time, did it not behove the English to do likewise?

There were other, more negative, reasons why English nationalism should receive a boost in this period. They relate to the things that, up to now had inhibited or suppressed expressions of English nationalism – or, to put it more correctly, had made it unnecessary. The idea of the Protestant nation, and the long struggle against France, had been the building blocks of Britishness. They had minimized other national differences – English, Scottish, Welsh – in the face of a common enemy, and in defence of a common religious identity.

'We no longer hate the French', declared Edward Lytton Bulwer in 1833 (1970: 38). This was undoubtedly premature, and justified largely by the fact that Bulwer dedicated the first book of his *England and the English* to 'His Excellency, the Prince Talleyrand'. France remained the bogey for some time still to come. The British continued – with reason – to regard the French as their principal rivals for industrial and imperial supremacy right until the end of the nineteenth century (Clarke 1970: 108–16; Colley 1992: 321). But by that time it was also clear that other rivals – Germany, Russia, Japan, the United States – were now on the scene, and likely to appear even more threatening than France in the future. At the very least, Francophobia would no longer serve, either for Englishness or Britishness, as an effective tool. Children's nurses might continue to scare their charges with the threat that 'Boney will get you', but serious thinkers and statesmen were aware of challenges from altogether other directions, ideological as much as national.

An obvious fact about many of these new challengers was that they were not Catholic – indeed, in the case of Germany and the United States, they were predominantly Protestant. How to play the Protestant card of British national identity against such 'Others'? But there was also a deeper factor at work that undermined the importance of Protestantism in the make-up of the national identity. Not only did Catholics cease to be the main enemy, and anti-Catholicism generally decline in Britain in this period, but religion in general declined. Just as Britain came to be affected by the currents of ethnic nationalism sweeping through Europe, so also it was subject to the same secularizing currents that were flowing throughout Europe in the later nineteenth century (Chadwick 1990; Colley 1992: 328; 1994: 332–4; McLeod 1999: 54–65). Religion did not cease to have a relation to national identity – it is difficult to imagine that this could ever be the case, at least in some sense of the word 'religion'. But not only did religion slacken in its intensity, at least so far as its traditional forms were concerned; it became more diffuse, so making difficult the identification of the nation with any particular form of religion. In particular, it made it increasingly difficult to tie a British identity specifically to Protestantism.

Faltering confidence in empire; the decline of religion, and the identities it had sustained; changing perceptions of the national enemy; the rise of cultural and ethnic nationalism; all these worked to undermine the primacy of the British identity that had been established in the wake of the Unions of 1701 (Scotland) and 1801 (Ireland), following upon that much earlier incorporation of 1541 (Wales). Not that British identity by any means collapsed; far from it. But there was room now for the expression of other forms of nationalism in the United Kingdom. Specifically, there was room, and a felt need, for some expression of English national identity.

The discovery of Englishness

In a lay sermon given at Balliol College in 1898 under the title 'The Nation as an Ethical Ideal', the master, Edward Caird, asserted 'our claim' to be 'a *chosen people*, with a special part to play in the great work of civilisation and of Christianity':

> It was in this country... that a great movement towards political freedom was first initiated; indeed it was carried to a considerable point of advance, when it was hardly begun in any other country ... [T]here was from an early time at once greater liberty for individuals and a more ready reaction of the opinions of the people upon government. At the same time, with this freedom of the individual and as the complement of it, there has gone a great facility of association ... It is perhaps not too much to say that this country first showed to the modern world the immense power that lies in the associated action of free citizens, and proved that its greater vitality, its combination of subordination and independent initiative, makes it more than a match for the mechanical drill of despotism.
>
> (in Stapleton 1994: 41)

Caird was a Scotsman, but his subject was England and the English – one of the several interventions by Scotsmen in the making of Englishness in this period. Here he gives a classic statement of what came to be called 'the Whig interpretation of history', the tendency, as its anatomist Herbert Butterfield wrote, 'to emphasize certain principles of progress in the past and to produce a story which is the ratification if not the glorification of the present' (Butterfield [1931] 1951: v). In another work, *The Englishman and His History* (1945), Butterfield traced this tendency specifically in the case of the writing of English history. But whereas the earlier work had been severe with the tendency it analysed, this later work, written in the concluding stages of the war against Germany, now saw something to praise in it. It might be mistaken in its historical method, and the findings based upon it. But it was right in emphasizing that the English had found the secret of progress through a peculiarly blessed inheritance, blending past and present in an orderly evolution:

Let us praise as a living thing the continuity of our history, and praise the whigs who taught us that we must nurse this blessing – reconciling continuity with change, discovering mediations between past and present, and showing what can be achieved by man's reconciling mind. Perhaps it is not even the whigs that we should praise, but rather something in our traditions which captured the party at the moment when it seemed ready to drift into unmeasurable waters. Perhaps we owe most in fact to the solid body of Englishmen, who throughout the centuries have resisted the wildest aberrations, determined never for the sake of speculative ends to lose the good they already possessed; anxious not to destroy those virtues in their national life which need long periods of time for their development; but waiting to steal for the whole nation what they could appropriate in the traditions of monarchy, aristocracy, bourgeoisie and church.

(Butterfield 1945: 138–9)

Here was the Whig interpretation of history applied to England and appropriated as the national tradition, made virtually identical with the actual history of England. All – Whig and Tory, Liberal and Radical, democrat and imperialist – could subscribe to it.[13] Such an understanding also formed the basis of Caird's paean to English development. It was in fact in the later nineteenth century that the Whig interpretation of English history was given the form in which it came to figure in English national consciousness. As Butterfield showed, the elements of that historical myth were already firmly in place by the end of the seventeenth century. They included the idea of the antiquity and independence of the House of Commons; the 'myth of *Magna Carta*', as the foundation of the liberties of all free-born Englishmen; the belief in a tradition of constitutional rule, which limited monarchy, stretching unbroken from the Middle Ages through to the seventeenth century; and the theory of primitive Teutonic freedom and of the 'Norman yoke' that had attempted, unsuccessfully, to stifle it (Butterfield 1945: 69).

This classic version of the Whig interpretation of English history represented all these things as having been there, so to speak, all the time. It was a story of ancient and immemorial English freedom that, though it had had at times to be defended against attempts to usurp it, had been a constant of English history. What the nineteenth century – building on Burke and the writers of the Scottish Enlightenment – did was to temporalize or historicize this myth (Burrow 1983: 11–35; see also Butterfield 1945: 80–1; Trevor-Roper 1979: 12). It gave it the form in which it entered the school textbooks and turned it into a central element of the English tradition, 'part of the landscape of English life, like our country lanes or our November mists or our historic inns' (Butterfield 1945: 2). In the historical writings of Macaulay, Stubbs, Froude, Freeman and Green, English liberties were seen, not as a once-and-for-all achievement or inheritance, but as a story of steady, continuous and cumulative growth and expansion, broadening out from precedent to precedent. English history was conceived as 'a single progressive drama' (Burrow 1983: 295). The timeless elements of the seventeenth-century Whig myth were recast in dynamic form, as an ascending series of instalments leading to greater and greater degrees of freedom: Magna Carta, Lancastrian Constitutionalism, the break with Rome, the Civil War, the Glorious Revolution, the opposition to George the Third, the 1832 Reform Act – to name some of the principal episodes picked out by Whig historians (Blaas 1978: 10). To these constitutional matters Seeley added the theme of England's destiny as an imperial power. All these were what made English history, and so England, special and unique.

Progress and continuity, or progress with continuity, were the watchwords of English history, according to the nineteenth-century version of the Whig inter-pretation. English society, in this new evolutionary perspective, was therefore capable of change and improvement. The face of the nation was turned from the past towards the future. England's inheritance had allowed it to avoid the fanaticism and bitterness, born of countless revolutions and civil wars, that had disfigured the politics of its continental neighbours. This fortunate legacy had enabled it to become the richest and most powerful country in the world. So the English would continue to grow and prosper, the envy and exemplar of other nations.

Among the Whig historians, the medievalists William Stubbs and Edward Freeman were the principal exponents of the theory of the 'free' Anglo-Saxons and the primitive Teutonic democracy that, it was held, had prevailed in England in Saxon times and had since continued to be the bedrock of English constitu-tional liberties (Burrow 1983: 126–228; Briggs 1985). Here was a component of the Whig myth that could detach itself and become a free-standing element in England's understanding of itself. The rise of Teutonism or Anglo-Saxonism as a component of English national identity marked the culmination of a mo-mentous shift in English national mythologies. For over 500 years, from the twelfth to the seventeenth centuries, and despite repeated attempts to puncture its historical accuracy, Geoffrey of Monmouth's *History of the Kings of Britain* (c. 1136) held sway (MacDougall 1982: 7–27; Burrow 1983: 108–9). Here the Britons, and by an ingenious translation the English, were seen as an imperial people, the descendants of Brutus, grandson of Aeneas the founder of Rome. Geoffrey's mythical history tied England firmly to Rome, living in its orbit, conquered by it, and occasionally ruling it, as through the 'British' emperor, Constantine the First, who was also ruler of Britain and whose mother Helen was said to be British.

The Reformation, and the break with Rome, made this mythology problem-atic. There was a need now to demonstrate non-Roman origins, to show in particular that the English Church had always enjoyed an independent exis-tence from Rome. One strategy, employed by scholars from Scotland as well as

England and Wales, was to go back to the Celtic roots of British Christianity, and to argue that the foundations of the pure English Church were to be found in the beliefs and practices of the Celtic Christian Churches before the coming of Augustine and the submission to the Roman Papacy. Given the all-British nature of Protestantism, and the ambitions of the Church of England to become a British Church and to represent all British Protestants, this solution generally proved satisfactory in the sixteenth and seventeenth centuries. (Jenkins 1995: 126; Kidd 1999: 99–122).

But to nineteenth-century Englishmen, as well as to some before them, this was still unsatisfactory. It put too much emphasis on the Celtic as opposed to the Anglo-Saxon origins of the English Church, and of English culture generally. The awkward problem for them was that it was precisely under the Anglo-Saxons, it seemed, that Rome had acquired its ascendancy in England. Bede's *Ecclesiastical History of the English People* was the great monument to that. The ingenious solution was to draw upon the writings of certain Protestant reformers and antiquarians, such as John Bale and Matthew Parker, who had argued that the original Anglo-Saxon Church was independent, pure and uncorrupted; only much later in its history did it fall under the thralldom of Rome and suffer corruption. In this view:

the English Church was initially independent from Rome and remained more faithful than any other to the spirit of Christ; the introduction of Roman forms by St Augustine began a period of decline which accelerated rapidly from the time of Hildebrand; the reform movement beginning with Wyclif and reaching its climax in the sixteenth century stood for a restoration of primitive purity and thus continuity with the early church.

(MacDougall 1982: 34–35; see also Horsman 1976: 387–8; Kidd 1993: 13; 1999: 106–8)

Aided by the enthusiasm for Anglo-Saxon laws and ways shown by antiquarians such as William Camden and Richard Verstegen, the way was now clear for the emergence of a full-blown Anglo-Saxon ideology. Geoffrey of Monmouth's Roman-oriented British saga, with its homage to Virgil's similar mythical hymn to Rome in the *Aeneid*, could give way to a purely English tradition, based on the Anglo-Saxons and drawing its inspiration from Tacitus's portrait of a hardy, independent, simple but free people in his *Germania*. 'The Saxons were to replace the Britons, just as King Alfred replaced King Arthur as the model king' (Burrow 1983: 109).

The idea of the primitive democracy of the Saxons, a constituent part of the original Whig formulation of the seventeenth century, became central to the vision of nineteenth-century Whig historians such as Stubbs, Freeman and Green (McDougall 1982: 91–103). But there was a subtle change. Instead of a concentration, as in the previous Whig version, on the 'high politics' of

Parliament, with its aristocratic and gentry connotations, there was now a focus on the institutions of 'the people'. Late nineteenth-century Anglo-Saxonism, influenced by the work of German historians and folklorists such as Justus Möser, Friedrich von Savigny and Jacob Grimm, put the stress on race, language, custom and culture, rather than the formal institutions of the state. It was the popular, local institutions of the hundred, the shire, the folk-moot and the village community that fired the imagination of English scholars. It was these that were the true expressions of the 'folk-spirit' of the English race. It was here, not so much in 'the High Court of Parliament', that the true genius of the English people for establishing free institutions showed itself. Parliament in fact, the assumed central symbol of the state, was no more than the outgrowth and development of the original primal cell of Teutonic society, the *mark*-community or self-regulating township. As J. R. Green wrote in his deliberately named *Short History of the English People* ('a history, not of English Kings or English Conquests, but of the English People'):

It is with a reverence such as is stirred by the sight of the head-waters of some mighty river that one looks back to these tiny moots, where the men of the village met to order the village life and the village industry, as their descendants, the men of a later England, meet in Parliament at Westminster, to frame laws and do justice for the great empire which has sprung from this little body of farmer-commonwealths in Sleswick.

(1893: 4)

In the Anglo-Saxon myth, argues McDougall, 'the concept of race is central' (1982: 2). Without a doubt, Anglo-Saxonism could and did take racial form, in the physiological and biological sense in which we have come to understand that term. In a famous pronouncement Joseph Chamberlain declared: 'I have been called the apostle of the Anglo-Saxon race, and I am proud of that title ... I think the Anglo-Saxon race is as fine as any on earth' (in Judd 1996: 145). But racial Anglo-Saxonism rarely connoted 'Little Englandism', or attached itself to a narrow English nationalism. On the contrary, it was expansive, including all people of English blood or descent. It referred to a whole civilization or way of life; it included not just England, but the United States, Canada, Australia, New Zealand and other territories where English people had settled. 'I refuse', said Chamberlain, 'to think or to speak of the USA as a foreign nation. We are all of the same race and blood. I refuse to make any distinctions between the interests of Englishmen in England, in Canada and in the United States ... Our past is theirs – their future is ours ... We are branches of one family' (in Judd 1996: 145; see also Gott 1989: 97). It was a sentiment of which Cecil Rhodes and Alfred Milner, other leading Anglo-Saxonists, heartily approved. It was also, as we have seen, the central idea of Seeley's view of English history. In so far as Anglo-Saxonism can be linked to other ideologies, the principal one must surely be imperialism, not nationalism in the strict sense (Horsman 1976: 387; but cf. Melman 1991: 592).

But that did not prevent its becoming a core component of the developing sense of Englishness in this period. For while it might be expansive in one direction, it was crucially restrictive in another. Once it had been decided that the Celts were not, as had once been thought, Teutons, the way was clear for making a sharp distinction between the Anglo-Saxon inheritance and that of the Celts. Only the English, and perhaps the Scottish Lowlanders, were the heirs to the freedom and manly qualities bequeathed by the Anglo-Saxons; Welsh, Irish and many Scots were excluded from that fortunate legacy. A strong strain of anti-Celtic rhetoric marked late nineteenth-century Anglo-Saxonism, whether in the scholarly work of Freeman or the more popular writing of race theorists such as the Lowland Scot Robert Knox (following in the footsteps of another anti-Celt Lowlander, Thomas Carlyle). Celts, whether in Wales, Ireland or the Scottish Highlands, were seen as fanatical and unruly, idle dreamers who were responsible for the disorder and backwardness of their societies (Curtis 1968; Horsman 1976: 391–2, 399, 405–07; Burrow 1983: 191–2; Swift and Gilley 1989). Thus considered, the future of England might seem to lie in a returning to itself, to its true Saxon nature, and in getting rid of the Celtic elements it had so unwisely acquired in the course of its expansion. Such arguments were to resurface, at a time of greater stress for the English, in the later twentieth century. In the earlier period what they mainly stressed, reversing a long-standing tendency, was English exclusiveness, a sense of difference from the other nations of the United Kingdom.

At the very least, Anglo-Saxonism attached a special merit to being English, to belonging to a people not just peculiar but privileged, blessed by its inheritance and its mission in the world (Simmons 1990; Barczewski 2000). Moreover, it addressed the English people in a particular way. Late nineteenth-century Anglo-Saxonism acted primarily as the vehicle of a sense of the English people as a whole, as a *Volk*. Its tendency, that is, was inclusive, unlike the older theory of the 'Norman yoke' that had mainly addressed the 'popular classes', the oppressed and exploited (Melman 1991: 577–8; Mandler 2000: 239; cf. Hill 1986b: 118). In this aspect its predominant thrust was democratic, or at least populist. It did much to turn the Whig account of English history in a democratic direction, to make it take in, as earlier constitutional accounts had failed fully to do, the ordinary English people. As John Burrow says, 'the traditions of Westminster Hall and St Stephen's Chamber might be esoteric . . . but anyone who spoke the English tongue and came of stock not palpably immigrant had as good a claim as anyone else to those of the shire-moot and township, to the English Conquest of England and the freedom brought from the German woods' (1983: 108; see also Melman 1991: 582; Mandler 2000: 243).

All over Europe at this time the 'folk' were being discovered – and where necessary, invented – by earnest scholars. They were investigated and explored, their lore and language, their songs and dances, their customs and stories, collected and written down. England was no exception to this folk mania. It was in this period that Cecil Sharp was collecting and publishing English folksongs, an activity that he explicitly associated with a national purpose. 'Our system of education', he wrote in his *English Folk Song* (1907), 'is, at present, too cosmopolitan; it is calculated to produce citizens of the world rather than Englishmen.' Music in elementary schools, if it were based on English folksong, would 'refine and strengthen the national character' (quoted in Howkins 1986: 77). As Alun Howkins shows, Sharp's ideas quickly became the orthodoxy of English musical education. By 1914 the Board of Education was instructing teachers of music that 'the music learned by children in elementary schools should be drawn from our folk and traditional song'. It was not, its circular continued, 'always realised how strong and vital a tie between the members of a school, a college or even a nation may be formed by the knowledge of a common body of traditional song' (in Howkins 1986: 78).

Sharp was part of a whole 'English Musical Renaissance' that took place in the late nineteenth and early twentieth centuries, much of it based on English folk music (Howes 1966; Marsh 1982: 72–89; Crump 1986; Howkins 1989; Bashford and Langley 2001). Percy Grainger – Australian by origin – joined Sharp in the revival of English folk music, making English folk tunes the basis of many of his compositions, and arranging traditional English folk songs in the forms in which many of them came to be widely known. It was English folk song, too, that apparently 'more than anything' enabled Ralph Vaughan Williams 'to shake off the influence of idioms' acquired during his period of formal academic study, and set him on the course that led him to become perhaps the most English of composers (Scholes 1942: *sv.* 'Vaughan Williams'). His setting of the Tudor folk-song 'Greensleaves', and the ballets *King Cole* and *Job*, are good examples of this Englishness – the immensely popular 'Greensleaves' in particular coming, through numerous uses in films and commercial advertising, 'to represent England and Englishness' (Howkins 1989: 94). Gustav Holst – of Swedish descent – also sought in his music to give the English a sense of themselves, most characteristically perhaps in such works as his operas *The Perfect Fool* and *At the Boar's Head* – the last a comedy in which Falstaff is made to move to the strains of English folk tunes. Then there is Edward Elgar, who to the outside world has always been 'the English composer' – more perhaps because they know of no other than because of any qualities of Englishness that they discern in his work. But those qualities are of course deeply there – especially seen in such works as the symphonic poem *Falstaff*, the overture *Cockaigne*, the *Coronation Ode* and *Imperial March*, and most masterfully in the *Enigma Variations*, several of whose movements such as 'Nimrod' have come to be taken as peculiarly expressive representations of English national types. Finally we should note the popularity among English composers of this time of composing 'Rhapsodies' evocative of particular English regions, and based usually on folk melodies from the region. Vaughan Williams composed a 'Norfolk', Holst a 'Somerset' rhapsody, both based on local folk-songs. Delius's *Brigg Fair* is subtitled 'A Lincolnshire Rhapsody'. John Ireland's *Mai-dun* evokes the Wessex of Thomas Hardy, while George Butterworth, active in the folk music revival, based his *A Shropshire Lad* on the folk-based melodies from his own song-settings of A. E. Houseman's poems. The typical features of all these works was to display the moods and character of these regions by a musical evocation of particular scenes and sounds: the mist of a May morning, the mellow sunshine of an autumn evening, rustic songs and dances.[14]

It must be clear, even from this brief account, how important the English countryside was in this burst of musical creativity at the turn of the century. The influence of Elgar's beloved Malvern Hills is well known (Crump 1986: 167), but the English countryside was an inspiration to practically every important composer of this generation. Nationalism in music as in other spheres – all inspired by the movement of Romanticism – was throughout Europe accompanied by a renewed interest in the countryside: not just in its folk music, but in the characteristics of landscape, and in the forms of (a rapidly vanishing) rural life. In England in the early nineteenth century this had taken the form of enthusiasm for wild, solitary areas, such as the Lake District, the Welsh mountains and the Scottish Borders and Highlands. These were the favoured haunts of the early Romantic poets, Wordsworth, Byron, Coleridge; they were celebrated not just in Romantic poetry and painting but in the Gothic novels of Ann Radcliffe and the historical novels of Walter Scott. They were part of the discovery, not merely of England, but of Britain (see Chamberlin 1986: 116–30; Trumpener 1997: 3–157).

A marked narrowing of focus took place in the later nineteenth century. No longer was wilderness praised, whether of the British or English variety. English writers and poets of the later nineteenth century discovered the 'south country', the lush downland landscape of the southern counties of Kent and Sussex, Wiltshire and Somerset, Hampshire and Dorset (Wiener 1981: 50; Howkins 1986: 62–4; 2001: 151; Taylor 2001: 134–6). These regions – the heart of the old Anglo-Saxon kingdoms – became the emblem of a certain kind of 'Englishness' that was later, and up to this day, to decorate postcards and tourist posters. It is the face of England best known to the foreign tourist. It is a land of small towns and cathedral cities set among green rolling hills, interspersed here and there with the ruins of an old castle or abbey; sheep dot the countryside; small streams meander through it. It is perfectly caught in Frank Newbould's painting 'The

South Downs', which was chosen to stand for the nation in the series of posters put out during the Second World War under the general heading, 'Your Britain [*sic*], fight for it now', and has become one of the most reproduced images of England.[15] The choice of scene showed how strongly the 'south country' had imposed itself on the national consciousness, to the point where it was endlessly reproduced as an image of 'timeless' England. England, in this image, *was* 'the south country'. It was cut off not just from Britain but from much of the rest of England, the England of the Midlands and the North.

In his highly influential book *The Condition of England* (1909), the journalist and Liberal politician C. F. G. Masterman noted that 'four-fifths of [the English] people have now crowded into the cities'. The whole point of his book was to take stock of the new urban and industrial England that had emerged in the nineteenth century. And yet when it came to evoking 'the spirit of England', Masterman too fell back on the English countryside, one moreover that took its main features from the southern landscape.

Nature still flings the splendour of her dawns and sunsets upon a land of radiant beauty. Here are deep rivers flowing beneath old mills and churches; high-roofed red barns and large thatched houses; with still unsullied expanses of cornland and wind-swept moor and heather, and pinewoods looking down valleys upon green gardens; and long stretches of quiet down standing white and clean from the blue surrounding sea.   (1960: 161)[16]

It was the type of countryside celebrated in the poems and writings of W. H. Hudson, Richard Jefferies, Edward Thomas, Hillaire Belloc, George Sturt and, during the First World War, a number of war poets such as Edmund Blunden and Rupert Brooke associated with the 'Georgian' movement (Williams 1973: 182–96, 248–63; Wiener 1981: 54–64; Howkins 1986: 74–82; Brooker and Widowson 1986: 130–3). Despite the author's intention, it was also the aspect of the countryside seized upon by the popular imagination in its reading of Thomas Hardy's 'Wessex' novels. Hardy wrote, to a good extent stoically and dispassionately, to show change in the English countryside, the ebbing of the age-old rural way of life and the coming of new ways; there was, from his point of view, as much bad as good in 'old England', and real gains to be made from modern life (M. Williams 1972; R. Williams 1973: 197–214). His public responded by wallowing in rural nostalgia, fed by innumerable popular renderings and adaptations of his stories. Hardy became the 'the English rural annalist *par excellence*' (Brooker and Widdowson 1986: 120; see also Wiener 1981: 52–3; Widdowson 1989). Hardy's 'Wessex', decked out with old agricultural implements and actors in country smocks, became part of that essential 'Englishness' that was put on show for tourists to the West Country, but it was also an important part of their own image, and of their own national culture, that the English themselves absorbed in the closing years of the nineteenth century.[17]

What was perhaps even more remarkable was the elevation of the southern English countryside to literally utopian status. This was the achievement of William Morris, in his utopia *News from Nowhere* (1890). Morris was a committed socialist, indeed a self-styled Communist and follower of Karl Marx. But, despite Marx's own strictures on 'the idiocy of rural life' and the need to avoid nostalgia for the preindustrial past, it was precisely to such a past that Morris seemed to look in his vision of a future communist society. The society of *News from Nowhere* strongly recalls fourteenth-century England, the golden age of the artisan, as Morris saw it, and one of the peaks of English civilization. The new society rehabilitates the handicraftsman. It does without factories and large-scale, power-driven machinery. It has abolished large towns and cities, and reverted to cities and villages on a medieval scale and pattern. Above all it adopts what can only be described as a religious attitude towards the countryside. The climax of the novel takes the form of a boat journey up the River Thames, following virtually its whole length from London to its source in the upper reaches, the place where Morris had his own country home, Kelmscott Manor (Morris 1995: 165–209). The countryside around the river is minutely and lovingly described. It is made clear that it is this countryside itself, the way it looks and sounds, the work done in it, that is the heart of the good society. And this is, self-evidently, southern England, the countryside of the Thames valley that Morris so loved and that he was to feature repeatedly in his other pictures of a desirable world (Kumar 1994).[18] Morris, like Hardy, would have been horrified by his legacy, the turning of his vision into a nostalgia for the Middle Ages and the production of costly hand-made articles for wealthy consumers. But there is no doubt of his role in putting a certain version of the English countryside at the centre of the new definition of Englishness (Faulkner 1992; Kumar 1998).

The 'south country' celebrated by the poets and writers was not just the home of humble artisans and countrymen – in fact at this time a fast-disappearing class, it was also the region of some of the grandest country estates – Blenheim and Beaulieu, Woburn and Longleat – of the English gentry and aristocracy, and the site of the major royal parks and palaces. It had, in other words, an unmistakably class character. It ignored the industrial cities and conurbations of the Midlands and the North with their large working-class populations (Taylor 1991: 150–1; 2001: 136–7). It ignored even London, the centre of the nation's politics, commerce and culture. Cities, especially large modern cities, had no place in the image of Englishness that was created. The essential England was rural. It was there, not in the cities, that the English virtues were seen at their best and most typical. Cowper's 'God made the country, and man made the town' sums up, even more than in its own time, the intense anti-urbanism of late nineteenth-century English artists and intellectuals, all the more deeply felt because country life was so unmistakably disappearing.

All this goes to show that the Englishness of this time was not merely a class phenomenon. It went deeper, affecting all classes. Masterman had said, in his *The Condition of England*, that 'never, perhaps, in the memorable and spacious story of this island's history has the land beyond the city offered so fair an inheritance to the children of its people, as today, under the visible shadow of the end' (1960: 161). This was the significant phenomenon – the celebration of rural life not, as in the eighteenth century, when it was thriving, but at the moment of its demise, when only a small minority of the English people could be said to be engaged in country life in any real sense.[19] In vain did D. H. Lawrence expostulate:

> The Englishman still likes to think of himself as a "cottager:" – "my home, my garden". But it is puerile. Even the farm labourer today is psychologically a town-bird. The English are town-birds through and through, today, as the result of their complete industrialization. Yet they don't know how to build a city, how to think of one, or how to live in one. They are all suburban, pseudo-cottagy . . .   (1950: 121)

But the English persisted in their stubborn attachment to the country. Scholars have indeed traced a significant movement of 'anti-industrial' feeling in this period, a comprehensive rejection of the Industrial Revolution and all it stood for, the urban-industrial way of life (Wiener 1981: 41–72; Marsh 1982: 1–23). This is truly an extraordinary phenomenon, in the society that pioneered the Industrial Revolution and became the first industrial society in the history of the world. But there is no doubting the shift in perception when we compare the early with the late nineteenth century. In the earlier period we encounter a real engagement with the new world of industrialism, some of it unashamedly celebratory. There is Turner's euphoric painting, 'Rain, Steam, Speed'; artists such as Philip de Loutherbourg and J. C. Bourne depicted the great achievements of engineering, in iron bridges, iron ships and railways; writers such as Carlyle, Dickens, Disraeli and Gaskell grappled with the novel problems of an industrial society.

At the end of the century there is a distinct turning away from all this. Certainly there were writers like H. G. Wells and George Gissing who continued to confront the realities of a modern industrial society. But many of the writers and artists who came to typify the late Victorian or Edwardian turn of mind – Thomas Hardy, William Morris, E. M. Forster, the pre-Raphaelite painters, as well as a host of poets, musicians and architects – preferred to look elsewhere for their material. Frequently they found it, and their hopes for a cultural and spiritual renewal, in the countryside. At the close of Forster's *Howard's End*, as Helen Schlegel contemplates with horror the 'creeping' expansion of London and wonders if it is a portent of things to come, her sister Margaret reassures her that old country places like Howard's End will not disappear, and may even be the source of regeneration:

Because a thing is going strong now, it need not go strong for ever...This craze for motion has only set in during the last hundred years. It may be followed by a civilization that won't be a movement, because it will rest on the earth. All the signs are against it now, but I can't help hoping, and very early in the morning in the garden I feel that our house is the future as well as the past.   (1941: 316)

Pastoralism, or a rural ideology, is a very old thing in English literary culture, as Raymond Williams (1973) has been at pains to stress. But he too admits that it takes on a new intensity in the late nineteenth century, when the rural way of life was beginning to disappear. What is equally striking is its appearance in the social and political thought of this period. ' "Back to the Land" ', said Lord Milner in 1911, 'is a watchword which, in some form or another, is beginning to appeal to serious men of every hue of political thought' (in Howkins 1986: 68). In a literal sense that was not true – one has only to think of H. G. Wells and the Fabians, who poured scorn on the back-to-the-land, 'simple-lifer' philosophy of John Ruskin, Edward Carpenter and their followers. But Milner was correct in discerning the influence of a more diffuse pastoralism in the political thinking of this time. More precisely put, and of course linked to it, was a wide-ranging 'Englishing' of political thought in this period. What 'serious men of every hue of political thought' discovered was that their thinking was intrinsically English, and could be tied to one or more central strands of the English tradition.

One is not surprised to find this in conservative thought. With its stress on notions of continuity, deference and hierarchy, it could summon up reassuring memories of 'Old England' and the glories of the English past. As the self-proclaimed party of tradition and custodian of the national culture, it did not prove too difficult for the Conservatives, under Disraeli and his successors, to seize the high ground of patriotism and empire – though not without some awkwardness in combining their essentially southern English electoral base with their claim to stand for Great Britain and the British Empire (Smith 1967: 101–3, 160–61; Blake 1972: 124; Cunningham 1986; Evans 1994b: 201).

It is, however, more surprising to find this strand of English nationalism in liberal thinking, with its strong Cobdenite internationalism, its opposition to empire, and its suspicion of any kind of state patriotism and jingoism. But such 'Little Englandism', in the hands of Hobson, Hobhouse and Hammond, could be and was presented as a species of patriotism; it was the imperialists, with their lust for conquest and expansion, who were imperilling the true traditions of English life and England's claims to greatness (Wiener 1981: 60–1; Grainger 1986: 140–66; Gott 1989: 96–7; Green and Taylor 1989: 106–8). More positively, liberalism in these years – the 'New Liberalism' as it came to be called – claimed the national inheritance in two ways. Drawing upon the seventeenth-century tradition of Independency, and on the deep springs of the Nonconformist conscience, which had always led the movement for reform, the English Idealists under T. H. Green transformed late nineteenth-century liberalism. Their ethical philosophy countered traditional liberal individualism with the claims of the community, and the need to put the collective power of society at its service. In general, the Idealists always stressed the importance of patriotism to the practice of citizenship. Secondly, liberal thinkers such as F. W. Maitland, J. N. Figgis and Ernest Barker rescued the pluralist tradition of English associational life, the wealth of group-life expressed in colleges, churches, chapels, co-operative societies, mercantile corporations and trade unions. These voluntary organizations were seen as the life-blood of the new liberal-democratic society, and a necessary counterweight to the growing power of the state.

The two influences in the New Liberalism nicely balanced each other, and each in turn could be seen as deriving from some long-standing tradition of English life. So successful was this remoulding of liberalism in these years that it constituted itself virtually the national philosophy. The Conservative Party might more successfully wave the patriotic flag, but its own philosophy and practice, as that of other groups, increasingly had to come to terms with the new liberalism. 'Liberalism became Englishness. The principles of a party established themselves as a major element in the self-image of a people' (Smith 1986: 255). Liberalism became 'central to English self-understanding', a position that, despite the eclipse of the Liberal political party itself, it maintained well into the twentieth century, and perhaps still does (Stapleton 2000: 257; see also Smith 1986; Colls 1986: 35–7; Freeden 1986; Hirst 1994: 26–40; Mandler 2001).

Associationist thinking – under the label 'Guild Socialism' – spilled over into the ideas of early socialist writers, such as G. D. H. Cole and Harold Laski (Hirst 1994: 101–11); while the collectivism of the Idealists found its way into Fabian thought, the Fabians simply arguing that they, and the new Labour Party, were better carriers of the collectivist spirit than the old Liberals. In such a way did English liberalism show its capaciousness, its ability to influence and absorb many varieties of political thought (though the Conservatives had to wait for new men like Harold Macmillan, and the 'third way' of the 1930s, to transform themselves in the fittingly liberal way). Nevertheless there is still something quaint and revealing in the extent to which early English socialism also laboured to present itself in the national colours. Here was a social philosophy, after all, even more international than liberalism, even more contemptuous of nationalism, seen generally by socialists as a bourgeois doctrine designed to infect the international proletariat with 'false consciousness' and to deflect it from the class struggle.

Yet from the 'hearty patriotism' of H. M. Hyndman, founder of the Social Democratic Federation, through to the worship of the English countryside of the Marxist William Morris, founder of the Socialist League, there was a conscious effort on the part of socialist thinkers to link up with specifically English traditions, to show that they were as patriotic – were indeed the true patriots – as Englishmen of any other political stripe. Hyndman's harking back to the Tory radicalism of William Cobbett, and the belief in the fifteenth century as the 'golden age' of the English labourer, was matched by Morris's celebration of the fourteenth century as the high point of English artisanal freedom and creativity, and his appeal to the spirit of 'fellowship' that had characterized English medieval life (Morris here drawing on the same tradition of associationalism as had inspired the pluralists and Guild Socialists.) Both wished to indicate that, however indebted they might be to continental ideas for the theory of socialism, there were strong native traditions that made it possible to elaborate a distinctly English socialism. A similar stress on Englishness was present in the writings of Robert Blatchford, author of the popular and significantly named socialist tract *Merrie England* (1893). The 'basis of Socialism', said Blatchford, was that 'England should be owned by the English, and managed for the benefit of the English...We want England for the English' (1976: 91). Blatchford's socialist weekly *The Clarion* extolled the importance of healthy country pursuits, and he was responsible for setting up numerous cycling and rambling clubs among workers – one more testimony to the far-reaching power of the English rural ideal (Wiener 1981: 118–23; Yeo 1986: 310–13; Colls 1986: 36–7; Kumar 1998; Stapleton 2000: 257–60; Howkins 2001: 151).

What was perhaps even more important than the Englishing, in their various ways, of the main varieties of political ideology was the elaboration of an overall tradition of political thinking that was said to be distinctively English. To a good extent this drew upon the generosity of the Whig or liberal tradition, in its nineteenth-century form, but it broadened out to become a whole philosophy of the English way of thinking and doing. Its central belief was a thoroughgoing distrust of 'system' or theory, and a preference for truths gained by experience or won by painstaking investigation of the empirical world. This could apply in the natural sciences as much as in the moral or social sciences, as is well exemplified in Charles Darwin's painfully long-drawn-out observations of the natural world and his almost pathological unwillingness to offer generalizations. Generally this empiricism applied to all spheres of English thought and culture. Its cult of the concrete and its repugnance to systematic theory, deriving from Francis Bacon and powerfully fed by English Romanticism, led to the

English preference for feeling over intellect, poetry over philosophy, literature and history over social and political thought (Thompson 1978: 61–4; Simpson 1993; Kumar 2001).

Taken with the cultivation of folk-song and the celebration of the cosy southern landscape, this might suggest a certain unworldliness, a certain escapist quality to the Englishness that was being defined at this time. No doubt that element was there, a certain strain of English poetic whimsy has continued to mark the national culture, captured at its best by the Ealing film comedies of the later 1940s. But such echoes of English romanticism have been matched – perhaps in some way inspired – by the equally proverbial stress on English pragmatism and hardheadedness. 'By the English way of looking at things', noted the French observer Taine in the 1860s, 'a tree must be known by its fruits, and theory judged by practice. A truth has no value unless it leads to useful applications in practice' (1958: 248; see also Emerson [1856] 1966: 52). It had not always been like this. English thought of the sixteenth, seventeenth and even eighteenth centuries could match that of any country in Europe for boldness of speculation and piercing visionary insight. Thomas More and William Blake are as much part of the English inheritance as Francis Bacon or Jeremy Bentham (it was the English, we should remember, who invented utopia). But by the mid-nineteenth century Taine's observation had become conventional. And by the end of the century a quite distinctive picture of English thought and philosophy, selectively interpreted, was being drawn. English thought, it was claimed, is empirical, concrete, individualist, utilitarian. It is exemplified at its most characteristic in such thinkers as Francis Bacon, Thomas Hobbes, John Locke, Jeremy Bentham, John Stuart Mill and Charles Darwin (T. H. Buckle and Herbert Spencer, with their taste for 'system', are by this reckoning very 'un-English'). It eschews the wild abstractions and futile speculations of continental – and Celtic – thought.

It was the historians, constitutional theorists and political writers of the late nineteenth century – Stubbs, Freeman, Green, Maitland, Bryce, Dicey, Barker – who were most responsible for setting out this view of the English tradition. They did so by a pointed contrast with the European Continent, seen as afflicted with political instability and rampant authoritarianism in direct proportion to its rationalizing propensity and fondness for abstract thought. It was indeed in the political and constitutional realm that the most important lessons were drawn. Continental thought, influenced by Roman law and Catholic theology, had no place for custom and local traditions, for the slow cumulation of changes that came by trial and error and were embodied in the precedents of common law. Centralization and bureaucracy – and their corollary, violent revolution – were the consequences of the rational, systematizing way of thinking of continental societies. Compared with the map of old France, said Stubbs, with its record of historic communities, 'the map of modern France is a catalogue of hills and rivers, a record of centralization, codification, universal suffrage, government by policemen' (in Burrow 1983: 141). Maitland spoke of France as the country 'where we may see the pulverising, macadamizing tendency in all its glory, working from century to century reducing to impotence and then to nullity, all that interferes between Man and the State' (in Burrow 1983: 141). Bryce compared the revolutionary tradition of modern France with 'the respect for law and wish to secure reforms by constitutional rather than violent means' which he saw as 'the habits ingrained in the mind and will of Englishmen' (in Smith 1986: 255). Freeman contrasted the 'bit-by-bit reform' of the English with the 'magnificent theories and . . . massacres in the cause of humanity' of the continentals (in Burrow 1974: 266). In an all-embracing comparison of 'Teutonic' and 'Keltic' traditions, which pointed to the tainted inheritance of British as much as continental Kelts, the medievalist Goldwin Smith wrote the melancholy fate of the French:

The Teuton loves laws and parliaments, the Kelt loves a king. Even the highly civilized Kelt of France, familiar as he is with theories of political liberty, seems almost incapable of sustaining free institutions. After a moment of constitutional government, he reverts, with a bias which the fatalist might call irresistible, to despotism in some form, whether it be that of a Bonaparte or that of a Robespierre.   (in MacDougall 1982: 97–8)

Bentham had scornfully dismissed abstract theories of 'natural law' and 'the natural rights of man' as 'nonsense on stilts'. English thinkers of the later nineteenth century – ignoring the seminal contribution of native English thinkers to this supposedly continental tradition – enthusiastically embraced this position. They rejoiced in the fortunate inheritance that, after the regrettable interlude of the seventeenth-century Civil War, had allowed England to resume its time-honoured course of peaceful evolution and incremental change. This they attributed to a native habit of thought that had rejected pure rationalism and system-building in favour of observation and experience, and that looked to simple, concrete liberties rather than the grand design of human liberation as the goal of political striving. Thus had England avoided the disasters that had convulsed the Continent, leading continental societies on a ceaseless but unavailing search for stability. English life in contrast exhibited an enviable continuity.[20]

Englishness as history, language and literature

The great medieval historian R. W. Southern has written of an 'imaginative appropriation' of the past that took place at the end of the nineteenth century, when earlier modes of historical interpretation – classical, biblical and prophetic – were rejected and historians sought to uncover the spirit of the past as a bundle of experiences possessing an 'emotional cohesion' (1973: 243–4). Not only professional historians – he instanced Stubbs and Maitland, and might have added Freeman and Green – showed this disposition; poets and novelists such as Rudyard Kipling and Henry James showed it even more. Southern quotes a passage from James's novel *The Tragic Muse* (1890), describing the feeling which comes over the Englishman Nick Dormer when he looks over the landed estate which he would never inherit. What came over him, says James, was

simply the sense of England – a sort of apprehended revelation of his country. The dim annals of the place appeared to be in the air (foundations bafflingly early, a great monastic life, wars of the Roses, with battles and blood in the streets, and then the long quietude of the respectable centuries, all cornfields and magistrates and vicars) and these things were connected with an emotion that arose from the green country, the rich land so infinitely lived in, and laid on him a hand that was too ghostly to press and yet somehow too urgent to be light.   (in Southern 1973: 245)

The 'imagined country' of James's England, it is not too difficult to see, was not so very different from the image of England that was being cultivated in the wide-ranging discovery of England that took place at this time. From the elements of that discovery we could construct a composite portrait – interesting as much for what it leaves out as for what it puts in – as follows: a country of cathedral cities and small towns and villages set in the 'southern' countryside, to include Cotswold towns, Brooke's Grantchester and Shakespeare's Stratford; the ancient colleges of Oxford and Cambridge; 'vernacular' domestic architecture, much of it newly minted, in the half-timbered 'Tudor' or gabled Queen Anne style; village life centred on the green, the pub and the church, all cosily clustered together – a complex often recreated anew, as in the model villages of Port Sunlight and Bournville, the new 'Garden Cities' such as Letchworth, and rural suburbs such as Bedford Park in London. Wedded to the Whig view of English history, with Parliament playing the role of tutelary agent, such a cultural complex could exhibit both timelessness and gradual, progressive, evolution.

The historians had, in the second half of the nineteenth century, produced the necessary texts for this understanding of England's inheritance – Green's *Short History of the English People*, in its many revisions and reprints, being perhaps the work that most fully and most successfully popularized the new scholarship. But just as important was the communication of this national history in a disciplined way – the professionalization and institutionalization of history teaching itself, in the schools and universities. This too was an accomplishment of these years (Heyck 1982: 120–54; Collini 1993: 216–21). The Royal Historical Society was formed in 1868 and in 1886 came the *English Historical Review*, in what can be seen as a clear parallel to the rise of a distinctly nationalist historiography in France and Germany after 1870 (Robbins 1993c: 3–5).

These were scholarly enterprises, for the professionals and university re-searchers; what was more significant for the dissemination of the new history was the founding in 1906 of the Historical Association, together with its journal *History*. As conceived by the founder A. F. Pollard, these were to be concerned above all with the teaching of history, in the schools and universities; and it was clear from the start that such a pedagogy was to have a strongly nationalist or patriotic flavour. An early Association pamphlet of 1909 by a Miss Mercier declared that 'teachers of history should interpret the national character, the national ideals, and educate their pupils in the ethos of their own race. Nations, no more than individuals, can afford to dispense with their own peculiar charac-teristics' (in Robbins 1993c: 7). A more vigorously patriotic purpose had been urged in 1901 by C. H. K. Marten, provost of Eton and a future tutor to the young Princess Elizabeth. History teaching in the schools, he proclaimed, 'may and should provoke patriotism and enthusiasm: it should help to train the citizen or the statesman: its study should lead to right feeling and right thinking'. One may be pardoned for thinking, he continued, 'that no people has a nobler or more inspiring story...Our history has a continuity which is lacking in that of many other countries. We have no cataclysms like the French Revolution of 1789' (in Soffer 1987: 85 n.22; Samuel 1989c: 12).

J. R. Seeley, in his 1869 Inaugural Lecture as Regius Professor of History at Cambridge, had announced the new role of history when he said that history 'is the school of statesmanship...the school of public feeling and patriotism' (in Collini, Winch and Burrow 1983: 226). While this did not make history-teaching necessarily nationalistic in a crude sense – and Seeley himself was free of that – it did move history away from its earlier concern with the demon-stration of general, universal, truths (the attitude of *historia magister vitae*) to a much stronger focus on national history and the inculcation of knowledge and respect for one's own nation. Certainly the Whiggish text-books produced for the schools in the first third of the twentieth century strongly reflected the patriotic, sometimes markedly jingoistic, purpose (Samuel 1989c: 10–14). The route from the average school history text-book to the brilliant parody of Sellar's and Yeatman's *1066 and All That* (1930) was a relatively short and direct one.

The propagation of the Whig interpretation of English history was paralleled in these years by what Stefan Collini has nicely called the 'the Whig interpre-tation of English literature' (Collini 1993: 342–73). If the Whig interpretation of history celebrated England's historical and political distinctiveness, indeed its uniqueness, the Whig interpretation of literature proclaimed a distinctive tradition of English literature that could also be said to constitute the cultural soul or essence of the English nation. These were the years, to put it differently, which established what we now call the 'canon' of English literature. English culture, at its deepest level, is seen as created by a series of great 'national' poets, dramatists and novelists. Their writing embodies values, whole ways of life, which express the aspirations of the national culture at its best and most characteristic. It is hardly too much to say that English literature came to take on a religious function, far exceeding in importance the vapid Anglicanism that passed for the national religion. Urged on by critics and moralists such as Matthew Arnold, its study and dissemination were conceived in missionary terms (Baldick 1983: 18–85; Collini 1993: 360).

Literature, at least since the seventeenth century, had always played a central role in English cultural life. It had long outclassed, say, music and painting. Now it was put on a national pedestal as the first deity of the English nation. For many people, literature – not Parliament or the monarchy – *was* England, the noblest and most heartfelt expression of the English people. Collini has suggested that this installation of literature, and critical debates about it, as the symbolic badge of English nationhood might be related to the absence of the kinds of conflicting moral and political ideologies that sharply divided other European societies. The uniquely consensual moral and political climate, at least since the early eighteenth century, stilled those debates that led to other kinds of definition of national identity and – as it were by default – elevated literature to a central place in national discourse (Collini 1993: 345–8). Literature did not replace politics – the Whig tradition was still dominant here, and remained a key denominator of national identity. But in the absence of serious political dissension, literature became the arena in which questions of national identity and the health of the national culture could be, and were, most fiercely debated.[21]

The late nineteenth century laid out a series of markers that, for the first time, aimed at establishing what was at once peculiarly English about English literature and, at the same time, laid the claims to its greatness. Among the most important were a number of verse anthologies that put together, within the covers of one book, what was said to be a representative selection of the works of the best and most typically 'English' poets through the ages. Palgrave's *Golden Treasury of English Verse*, whose declared object was to produce a 'true national anthology', first appeared in 1861, and for long held the field. A somewhat similar function was later fulfilled by Sir Arthur Quiller-Couch's *Oxford Book of English Verse* (1900), which by 1939 had been reprinted twenty times and sold half a million copies. Then there was the 'English Men of Letters' series launched by Macmillan, under the general editorship of John Morley, in 1877. The series 'bore all the marks of a consciously designed national monument' (Collini 1993: 355). The selection of writers included philosophers and historians such as Locke, Hume, Gibbon and Macaulay, together with what is the by now familiar list of poets, novelists and other men of letters starting with Chaucer, through Shakespeare, Spenser, Milton, Swift, Pope, Johnson,

Wordsworth and Coleridge, and concluding with the great Victorian poets and novelists. 'Right from the start', says John Gross, the series 'was accorded semi-official status ... No comparable series has ever come so close to attaining the rank of a traditional British [*sic*] institution' (1973: 122–3). On inspecting the works of those put in – and considering the writings of those left out, such as Charlotte Brontë – it is possible to see that the editors consciously selected writers who seemed to embody certain distinctively 'English' qualities. These included sincerity, individuality, concreteness and a sense of the richness and diversity of life. The implicit contrast was with the formalism and classicism of much continental literature, especially that of France (and, even more implicitly, the despotism and proneness to revolution that went with those characteristics of thought).

The 'nationalizing' of their literature was one way in which the English, somewhat belatedly, caught up with the nationalism of other European cultures; the nationalizing of their language was another, no less important. For 'it is at least arguable that the establishment of a "single" language was the necessary prerequisite for the institution of a national literary tradition which in turn became the "true" bearer of the language' (Dodd 1986: 18). Like most European languages, English had for long existed in a multitude of forms. Pronunciation, spelling, forms of speech, even grammar could vary from place to place, and from class to class. When, under the first four Georges, even the king might speak the English language as a foreigner, and aristocrats from Scotland, Ireland or the North of England brought their regional accents into the Palace of Westminster and the drawing-rooms of Mayfair, it was difficult for anyone to lay down at all convincingly what the 'true' English was.

All this was to change in the second half of the nineteenth century (Dodd 1986: 15–19). The public schools then began their function, still going strong, of standardizing speech and accent on the model of those of the southern gentry, with their various outposts in the Church, the Bar, Oxbridge, London society and the great country houses. In the philological studies of the period the English language was purified and purged of its 'regional dialects', and the pronunciation and speech patterns of the metropolitan south were deemed the national form of speech. The great monument to this activity was the *Oxford English Dictionary on Historical Principles*, begun, characteristically, by a Scot, James Murray, in 1879. Murray's stated object was to capture 'the genius of the English language'; he presented his undertaking as 'a great national project' (Collini 1993: 352–3). In his *Dictionary* the English language was, in its form, spelling and pronunciation, for the first time ever thoroughly nationalized and standardized. The English nation had acquired the linguistic face it was thereafter to show to the world. For those within the nation who persisted in the use of other forms, eccentricity, perversity, ignorance and uncouthness were the terms now used to account for their speech. Moreover, there was a close, even symbiotic, link with the national literature that was also identified in these years. For what largely made the national language was its employment in certain forms by the great names of English literature (circularity, as always, being an inescapable part of this process of definition). The study of the national language could therefore proceed largely through the study of literature – once more showing the preference for the expressive rather than the technical or theoretical mode in English culture.

Just as the new historical consciousness had to be communicated by a distinct pedagogy in the schools and universities if it were to have its desired effect on national identity, so too the new literary consciousness had to go beyond the small group of critics and editors into the wider body of the nation. English language and literature, properly studied and understood, had to find their place in the national educational system if they were to play their part in defining the nation. This too was accomplished in these years, though not without some stiff resistance (Gross 1973: 186–209; Baldick 1983: 59–85; Doyle 1986: 92–102; 1989). Strong scepticism and hostility towards the teaching of 'modern', 'easy' subjects such as English literature had to be overcome in the universities.

London had led the way, with a chair in English Language and Literature at University College since the 1820s; and English literature was a central concern at the new Working Men's College founded in 1854 by F. D. Maurice and F. J. Furnivall. But for long they stood alone, and it was not until the 1880s that the citadel of higher education at Oxford and Cambridge was breached. In 1885 Oxford established the Merton Professorship of English Language and Literature (a separate Merton chair simply in English Literature was instituted in 1903), and in 1893 set up an English Honours School. Cambridge resisted for longer, confining itself to the study of the English language as part of the Medieval and Modern Languages Tripos until 1911, when it established the Edward the Seventh Professorship of English Literature. An independent English School did not come until 1917, but when it did it had a stronger literary inflection, less contaminated by the study of English language, than at Oxford. Victories were also quickly recorded in the new civic universities, and in the university extension system, the Mechanics' Institutes and the Working Men's Colleges (as both advocates and critics pointed out, English literature was a particularly suitable subject for the teaching of artisans and for the new women students now entering the universities). So far as the schools were concerned, much of the pressure came from the English Association, founded in 1906 'to promote the due recognition of English as an essential element in the national education'. 'By 1920', says Brian Doyle, 'English in a substantially adapted form when compared with "English Language and Literature" or "English and History" [the titles of many older chairs] had come to be seen by public administrators, politicians, educators, academics and "men-of-letters" not only as a necessary constituent of a modern national system of education, but even in many cases as its most essential core element' (1986: 92).

The climactic moment, by general consent, in this movement to establish English at the centre of the national curriculum came with the Newbolt Report of 1921, on *The Teaching of English in England*. The Newbolt Committee, which had been set up at the instigation of the English Association and which strongly reflected its thinking, took as its aim 'the development of a system of education centred upon a national consciousness, based upon the native language and literature' (Baldick 1983: 95). The First World War had revealed the importance of the canon of English literature in sustaining morale and instilling patriotic pride – many a soldier carried a copy of the *Oxford Book of English Verse* in his knapsack (Fussell 1977: 155–90; Brooker and Widowson 1986: 120–1). It seemed to confirm the status of literature as 'the privileged location or bearer of national consciousness' (Collini 1993: 364). The Newbolt Report heavily underscored the point:

It is only quite lately that we in England have begun to have the definite consciousness, which the French gained in the age of Louis XIV, that we have a great and independent literature of our own which need not lower its flag in the presence of the greatest on the earth ... Our language and literature are as great a source of pride and may be made as great a bond of national unity to us as those of France are, and have long been, to the French.   (in Collini 1993: 366; see also Baldick 1983: 92–98; Doyle 1986: 102–11)

Doubts have been expressed concerning the effectiveness of the Newbolt report in shaping the study of English literature in the universities, but few doubt its major role in influencing the role and purpose of the study of English, as a 'School of national culture', in the elementary and secondary schools (Baldick 1983: 92–8; Doyle 1986: 111; 1989: 68–9; Collini 1993: 365–8). This sector of education, after all, as was shown by France in the same period, was the place that mattered in the creation of a national consciousness; and there too, as the Newbolt Report pointed out, French language and literature had been made 'an indispensable instrument of national culture' (in Collini 1993: 366; and see Weber 1976: 303–38). English schools followed suit. Generations of English schoolchildren were, in the years succeeding Newbolt, to have their sense of England and Englishness formed through the study of the great works of English literature. Whether or not this also succeeded in the further aim, as hoped by Newbolt, of uniting the classes – 'culture unites classes' – it seems undeniable that it accomplished it main purpose of providing an enduring image of England that, in times of crisis (as in the Second World War), could again and again be called upon to rally the English in attachment to and defence of their country.

Englishness identified

In *Englishness Identified* (2000), his sparkling survey of English manners and the English character from the mid-seventeenth to the mid-nineteenth centuries, Paul Langford notes that it was only in 1805 that the word 'Englishness' seems to have entered the national vocabulary. The innovator, one William Taylor of Norwich, was accused by contemporaries of 'employing words and forms of construction which are not sanctioned or not current in our language', and indeed Taylor seems to have invented the term in conscious imitation of the 'Deutschtum' of early German Romanticism (Langford 2000: 1–2). Langford's own work makes it plain that while many distinguished foreigners, from Voltaire to Herzen, commented acutely and often amusingly on the English character, the English themselves seem to have shown little self-consciousness during this period (see also Buruma 1998). First England, and then Britain, might have come to occupy an increasingly important role in the world in these years, but the English, preoccupied with immense and novel ventures, seem to have felt neither the need nor the desire to engage in introspective speculations as to their own nature as a people.

It was only when these enterprises began to falter, only when new commercial rivals threatened Britain's industrial supremacy and faith in the empire began to waver, that a degree of English self-consciousness began to emerge. This is the 'moment of Englishness' that I have tried to describe in this chapter. English intellectuals and artists – historians, political theorists, literary and cultural critics, composers, poets and novelists – for the first time began an inquiry into the character of the English people as a nation – as a collectivity, that is, with a distinct sense of its history, its traditions and its destiny.

The exercise was strictly limited and low-keyed, in what we might call a typically English way. There was no English Mazzini or Kossuth, no group of nationalist intellectuals who devoted themselves to the systematic investigation and construction of the idea of their nation, no committee of scholars appointed to purify and police the national language and literature. All these things were found elsewhere, on the European Continent and increasingly in other parts of the world, in the second half of the nineteenth and the early twentieth centuries. In the case of England, we have to piece together the project of English nationalism from developments and initiatives that occurred to a good extent in isolation, and frequently with a marked unawareness of and indifference to what was taking place at the same time in other spheres.

Nevertheless, a picture of Englishness does emerge. It is possible to put together a quite comprehensive view of England and the English from the elements that we have surveyed, however briefly, in this chapter. Moreover, what is even more important in some ways, it is possible to show why, in the perspective of the whole of English history, that it was only now that there arose a felt need, in some cases urgently felt, to give some definition to Englishness (which still seems a better term than to speak of the rise of 'English nationalism'). Once that definition was attempted, however, it was done with a force and a persuasiveness that has given it astonishing staying power (as we shall see in chapter 8). Diffuse and imprecise it might be, by comparison with some powerful contemporary attempts to define the French, the Italian, the Irish, the Polish or the German nations. But those very characteristics might be among the reasons why the Englishness identified at the end of the nineteenth century continued, and continues, to serve to a good extent as the image the English still have of themselves.

8

The English and the British today

The British nation and the British state are clearly entering a process of dissolution, into Europe, or the mid-Atlantic, or a post-imperial fog. Britain has begun its long march out of history.   Gwyn Williams (1982: 190)

Who knows what vigour Englishness might exhibit if for the first time in many centuries the English find themselves speaking for only England?
                                                              Paul Langford (2000: 319)

For many people, members of minorities and of the majority alike, the existing images of Britishness do not embrace the new mix of cultures and communities that exist today. We need to reform and renew conceptions of Britishness so that the new multiculturalism has a place within them.
                                                              Tariq Modood *et al.* (1997: 359)

I think it is a great Error to count upon the Genius of a Nation as a standing argument in all Ages; since there is hardly a spot of ground in Europe, where the Inhabitants have not frequently and entirely changed their Temper and Genius.   Jonathan Swift (in MacDougall 1982: 77)

Forever England

In December 1991 Britain signed the Treaty of Maastricht and so committed itself, in principle at least, to a European Union. The move caused consternation in several quarters, not least among Tory supporters but also among 'Little Englanders' on the Labour left. It seemed to herald the loss of British parliamentary sovereignty and the end of British independence. At the Conservative Party conference in the following year the then prime minister, John Major, sought to reassure the Tory disaffected.

I will never, come hell or high water, [he declared,] let our distinctive British identity be lost in a federal Europe ... If there are those who have in mind to haul down the Union

Jack and fly high the star-spangled banner of the United States of Europe, I say to them: you misjudge the temper of the British people! . . . And to those who offer us gratuitous advice, I remind them of what a thousand years of history should have told them: you cannot bully Britain.   (*The Guardian*, 10 October 1992)

'Britain' being less than 300 years old, there was some annoyed muttering among the pedantic at this show of ignorance, and some suspicion among others that the prime minister might have some entity other than Britain in mind. But worse was to come. A few months later, in a speech given on the eve of St George's Day, Major returned to the theme of national identity. Warming to his earlier emphasis on longevity and continuity, he declared that Britain would survive for a long time 'in its unamendable essentials'. 'Fifty years from now, Britain will still be the country of long shadows on county grounds, warm beer, invincible green suburbs, dog lovers and pools fillers and – as George Orwell said – "old maids cycling to Holy Communion through the morning mist" ' (*The Guardian* 23 April 1993).

'The speech was manna from heaven for the satirists' (Paxman 1999: 143). Commentators, satirical or serious, were quick to pounce on a number of things about it. Firstly, that the saint it commemorated was the patron saint of *England* (there is, as it happens, no patron saint of Britain). Secondly, that its references all seemed quintessentially English. Scotland, Northern Ireland and most of Wales know nothing of county cricket, nor do warm beer or dog lovers readily conjure up recognizable images of the culture of those places. More familiarly, it was noted that Major's 'unamendable essentials' did not simply carry a 'Made in England' stamp but involved a further degree of social and cultural exclusion. The selected features were predominantly masculine – 'he evokes beer and cricket, not sweet sherry and needlepoint' – and they ignored the lives of many people outside the middle-class 'Middle England', that they evidently celebrated. 'Major mentions the suburb, but not the inner city; the cricket ground, but not the football stadium; the dog lover but not the unemployed. This evoked nation is empty of motorways, mine-shafts and mosques' (Billig 1995: 102; cf. Giles and Middleton 1995: 5).

At any rate, the puzzling 'thousand years of history' that Major's Britain had earlier laid claim to now seemed to make more sense. It was really England, not Britain, that was the bearer of the proud identity invoked – as was evident also in the many coded references in the patriotic speeches of Margaret Thatcher (cf. Cannadine 1995b: 13).[1] This became even clearer in a speech in the following year when Major declared that 'this British nation has a monarchy founded by the Kings of Wessex over eleven hundred years ago, a Parliament and universities formed over seven hundred years ago, a language with its roots in the mist of time . . . This [nation] is no recent historical invention: it is the cherished creation of generations' (*The Times* 24 May 1994). Once more there was bewilderment mixed with outrage. To the chagrin of Scots, Welsh and Irish, a monarchy of allegedly Anglo-Saxon descent, an English Parliament and the two ancient English universities were, it seemed, to be taken as the central and revered pillars of the 'British nation'. There was, as Lord Jenkins of Hillhead delicately put it, 'some rather curious history' here. For one thing, 'I'm not sure many parts of the United Kingdom regard their monarchy as being descended from Wessex' (*The Independent* 26 May 1994). As for the supposed antiquity of the British nation, Peter Scott had crisply pointed out a few years earlier that 'Britain is an invented nation, not so much older than the United States' (Scott 1990: 168).

It had been common in the past for the English – and others – to say English when they should properly have said British. There had been repeated attempts, at least at official levels, to break this habit, not least during the two world wars (e.g., Cunningham 1986: 294). Government propaganda posters during the Second World War carried the clear slogan, 'Your Britain – Fight for It Now.' These efforts met with mixed success, but they at least indicated the consciousness that language had lagged behind social and political reality. Now, in a period when the United Kingdom was experiencing unparalleled stress and English identity seemed in crisis, English politicians such as Margaret Thatcher and John Major – both of whom seemed almost caricatures of a certain kind of 'Middle England' Englishness – reverted to the bad old ways, but with a twist. They reversed the old form of words but preserved its substance. They said the politically correct 'Britain', but by it they meant England.

The Englishness of Major's Britain was especially brought out in the pointed quotation from George Orwell's famous evocation of England in 'The Lion and the Unicorn' (1941). As well as 'old maids biking to Holy Communion through the mists of the autumn morning', Orwell's impressionistic sketch of the national culture included 'solid breakfasts and gloomy Sundays, smoky towns and winding roads, green fields and red pillar boxes' (1970a: 74–5). Just a little later T. S. Eliot, the expatriate American, was offering 'Derby Day, Henley Regatta, Cowes, the twelfth of August, a cup final, the dog races, the pin table, the dart board, Wensleydale cheese, boiled cabbage cut into sections, beetroot in vinegar, nineteenth-century Gothic churches and the music of Elgar' ([1948] 1962: 31). His fellow poet John Betjeman, in a BBC broadcast of 1943, had offered much the same fare but at more elaborate length and with a much more clearly revealed loathing of modernity:

For me, England stands for the Church of England, eccentric incumbents, oil-lit churches, Women's Institutes, modest village inns, arguments about cow-parsley on the altar, the noise of mowing machines on Saturday afternoons, local newspapers, local auctions, the poetry of Tennyson, Crabbe, Hardy and Matthew Arnold, local talent, local concerts, a visit to the cinema, branch-line trains, light railways, leaning on gates and looking across fields...If it were some efficient ant-heap which the glass and steel, flat-roof, straight-road boys want to make it, then how could we love it as we do?

(in Paxman 1999: 151)

It is clear that John Major was tapping a rich vein of commentary on the national character. Most evidently he harks back to Stanley Baldwin, like him a Conservative prime minister and like him the self-consciously created epitome of a certain kind of Englishness. Son of a wealthy Worcestershire ironmaster, grandson of a Scottish grandfather and a Welsh grandmother, Baldwin turned his back on all of these and presented himself, with great success, as the quintessential country-loving Englishman, a kind of English country squire. 'To the public he seemed to embody the English spirit and his speeches to sound the authentic note of that English character which they so much admired and so seldom resembled. Pipe-smoking, phlegmatic, honest, kind, commonsensical, fond of pigs, the classics and the country, he represented to Englishmen an idealised and enlarged version of themselves' (Blake 1972: 216; see also Wiener 1981: 100–2; Grainger 1986: 324–5, 358–61; Rich 1989a: 36–40; 1989b: 500–1; Miller 1995a: 89–93; Stapleton 2000: 264–5).

Baldwin could, on occasion, use the appropriate 'British' form – he was after all three times prime minister of Britain – but he made clear his repugnance towards the practice. In his famous address, 'England', to the Royal Society of St George on 6 May 1924, he declared that, mindful of whom he addressed, 'the first thought that comes into my mind as a public man is a feeling of satisfaction and profound thankfulness that I may use the word "England" without some fellow at the back of the room shouting out "Britain". I have often thought how many of the most beautiful passages in the English language would be ruined by that substitution which is so popular today' (1926: 1). Disdaining his role as prime minister of Britain, Baldwin addressed his audience as an unrepentantly proud and patriotic Englishman. 'The Englishman is all right as long as he is content to be what God made him, an Englishman, but gets into trouble when he tries to be something else.' The English are praised for their cheerfulness, calmness and perseverance in times of crisis; for their kindness, and their 'profound sympathy for the under-dog'; for their 'diversified individuality', and their love of 'character' and eccentricity. In his peroration, in which he asked what England stands for and what it most means to him, he expressed a fear that the essential England might be under threat, as 'her fields [are] converted into towns'. But he reassured himself, and his audience, that there was an England that spoke to English men and women of all classes, one that would persist through all changes. It was here that he delivered himself of the credo that was to become famous, and of which echoes are to be found throughout the literature of Englishness in the twentieth century (up to and including John Major).

To me, England is the country, and the country is England. And when I ask myself what I mean by England, when I think of England when I am abroad, England comes to me through my various senses – through the ear, through the eye, and through certain imperishable scents . . . The sounds of England, the tinkle of the hammer on the anvil in the country smithy, the corncrake on a dewy morning, the sound of the scythe against the whetstone, and the sight of a plough team coming over the brow of a hill, the sight that has been seen in England was a land . . . The wild anemones in the woods in April, the last load at night of hay being drawn down a lane as the twilight comes on . . . and above all, most subtle, most penetrating and most moving, the smell of wood smoke coming up in an autumn evening . . . These things strike down into the very depths of our nature . . . These are the things that make England.   (Baldwin 1926: 6–7)

Many scholars have pointed to the intense desire for quietness and serenity in Britain after the trauma of the First World War (see, e.g., Rich 1989a: 38; Light 1991; Winter 1996). For the English at least, that sense of longing seems to have been best satisfied by turning their backs on the squalor of urbanism and industrialism, and contemplating instead the 'timeless' life of the English countryside. They shared Baldwin's belief, fervently expressed in a BBC broadcast of 1933, that 'the country represents the eternal values and the eternal traditions from which we must never allow ourselves to be separated' (in Wiener 1981: 100). In the interwar period, English men and women from every walk of life poured out of the cities into the countryside, hiking, rambling and cycling. They were aided, as the bicycle had aided similar pilgrims in the 1890s, by the new developments in transport, especially the long-distance coach and the private motor car. Further assistance came in the form of a stream of guidebooks and magazines – John Betjeman's *Shell Guides*, Batsford's *Face of England* series, J. Robertson Scott's *The Countryman* – on the countryside, explicitly linking it to the English heritage and the English national character (Lowerson 1980: 260–4; Wiener 1981: 72–80; Stevenson 1984: 390–2; Lowenthal 1991; Trentman 1994; Miller 1995a: 99; Matless 1998: 62–100; Howkins 2001: 152–3). 'Never before', as H. V. Morton wrote in his popular travel-book, *In Search of England*, 'have so many people been searching for England' (1927: vii).

Morton was a left-wing socialist, but like the conservative Baldwin he too endorsed, though with more qualification, the view that England was the country and the country, England. He mourned the decline of agriculture and the neglect of the countryside, and warned: 'History proves to us that a nation cannot live by its towns alone' (1937: ix). This striking convergence across the political spectrum illustrates how powerful was the rural nostalgia that overtook England in this period.[2] It represented both a persistence and an intensification of the vein of Englishness, discussed in the last chapter, that was uncovered in the years before the First World War. The countryside featured strongly, as it did then, but there was also a stronger emphasis now on the quieter, private, ordinary, 'unofficial' England.

A book that struck a deep chord with the English public was a series of meditations, *Soliloquies in England* (1922), published by the Spanish-American philosopher George Santayana. Marooned in Oxford during the war, he put his time to good use in exploring the 'south country' that surrounds Oxford. Santayana was distressed by the signs of war that he could not ignore – 'the constant sight of the wounded, the cadets strangely replacing the undergraduates' – but found a Wordsworthian relief and consolation in the countryside. 'Nature and solitude continued to envelop me in their gentleness, and seemed to remain nearer to me than all that was so near' (1922: 1). Santayana noted his father's reverence for the British polity and British power, but feels that 'behind it lay something like an ulterior contempt, such as we feel for the strong man exhibiting at a fair'. This was not the England that Santayana himself responded to. 'We should none of us admire England today, if we had to admire it only for its conquering commerce, its pompous noblemen, or its parliamentary government ... There is, or was, a beautifully healthy England hidden from most foreigners; the England of the countryside, and of the poets, domestic, sporting, gallant, boyish, of a sure and delicate heart' (1922: 3).

This is the voice of Baldwin, and of a host of other commentators in the interwar period. It can be found in such well-known works as J. B. Priestley's *English Journey* (1934), with its praise of 'little England' and dislike of 'red-faced, staring, loud-voiced Big Englanders' who 'want to go and boss everybody about all over the world' (1977: 389).[3] It is also found in Philip Gibbs's *England Speaks* (1935), which inveighs against 'this machine age' that is killing the true England of 'quiet places where there are still English meadows not yet taped out by the jerry builders' (in Giles and Middleton 1995: 34). And there are similar accounts by Edmund Blunden, H. V. Morton and Arthur Mee (Giles and Middleton 1995: 73–103). Even students of English historiography have noted, in the interwar writings of popular historians such as G. M. Trevelyan, H. A. L. Fisher, Arthur Bryant and Ernest Barker, a move away from the 'high politics' of traditional accounts of English history, and a concern instead with social and cultural history, with the everyday lives of ordinary people. Englishness was seen to inhere in the practical, individualistic, even eccentric and amateur style of English craftsmen, inventors and industrialists through the ages. As with the nineteenth-century Whig historians, this was considered to have protected England from doctrinaire politics, seen at its worst now in the totalitarian schemes of Italy, Germany and Russia (Hernon

1976; Collini 1993: 338–40; Bell 1996: 18; Stapleton 1994: 154–76; 2000: 265–7).

Alison Light has discerned in the 1920s and 1930s a 'privatisation of national life', 'a move away from formerly heroic and officially masculine public rhetorics of national destiny and from a dynamic and missionary view of the Victorian and Edwardian middle classes in "Great Britain" to an Englishness at once less imperial and more inward-looking, more domestic and more private' (1991: 8; see also Samuel 1989d: xxii–xxviii; 1999b: 82; Rich 1989a: 36–40; Stapleton 1994: 154–6; 2000: 263–4; Waters 1997: 210–12). She sees in this a certain 'feminization' of the national culture, and finds it especially well exemplified in the themes and characters of novels by popular women writers of the interwar period, such as Ivy Compton-Burnett, Agatha Christie and Daphne du Maurier. 'Whilst the women of the middle classes might be seen to adopt many of the codes of what had been the model of an imperial masculinity [reticence, reserve, etc], that idiom could at the same time become a new kind of Englishness: it could "feminise" the idea of the nation as a whole, giving us a private and retiring people, pipe-smoking "little men" with their quietly competent partners, a nation of gardeners and housewives' (1991: 211).

It was not just the women writers of the period who were enamoured of this image of Englishness. The cult of the amateur and the eccentric, the distaste for posturing and pomposity on the 'continental' model, the love of home and hobbies, are everywhere. We find it portrayed in the immensely popular drawing of the national character done by 'Pont' for *Punch,* with its focus on 'love of animals', 'domestic life', 'social sense', rural and sporting pursuits, travel (Pont 1940). We find it hilariously displayed in A. G. Macdonell's long-lasting novel about the English, *England, Their England* (1933). The English, as shown by Macdonell, retreat to the country as often as possible, and reserve their enthusiasm for cricket, football and golf. What goes on in the pub interests them far more than what goes on in Parliament. They have no taste for, or expertise in, international affairs. The most admired figure in the novel is an eccentric and talkative engineer who embodies all the old English genius for practical skills and mechanical contrivances. But 'rural England is the real England' (1949: 77). The novel ends on a mystical note in the very English city of Winchester, with a dream-like evocation of 'the muted voices of grazing sheep, and the merry click of bat upon ball, and the peaceful green fields of England, and the water-meads, and the bells of the Cathedral' (1949: 223).

What was presented in these various forms in the interwar period was Englishness, not English nationalism. The English, after the horrors of the First World War, shrank from nationalism. The outbreak of the war itself was widely attributed to the triumph of the principle of nationalism. 'It is…pretty clear to anyone who marks the influence of nationalism during the last fifty years', wrote the constitutional theorist A. V. Dicey, 'that a sentiment which seemed to Mazzini and Cavour almost wholly good, contains in it a good deal of possible evil' (in Rich 1990: 24; see also Rich 1989a: 35). President Wilson's use of the principle of nationality to regulate the postwar settlement was viewed with misgiving by the British, a misgiving they felt fully vindicated by the increasingly menacing developments of the 1920s and 1930s in central and southern Europe. If the 'moment of Englishness' at the end of the nineteenth century represented some sort of catching up with continental nationalism, the English now hastened to disavow it. The Englishness that was defined in the interwar period was almost wholly indebted to that earlier moment, but it saw itself in a quieter, more introspective mode. There might be some complacency, and an air of self-congratulation at their good fortune, but there was no beating of the national drum. That, after all, was what was going on so loudly on the Continent, with devastating results.

Against the mass nationalist hysteria of the Fascist and Nazi rallies, the English championed the good sense, resourcefulness and courage of the ordinary 'little chap', the Charlie Chaplins of this world. These, during the Second World War, were the heroes of Dunkirk, of J. B. Priestley's 'Postscript' talks on the BBC, of Orwell's and Barker's writings on the English character. They dominate the pictures celebrating ordinary English life and ordinary English people in the popular magazine *Picture Post*. They are the silent, unsung, firefighters and other workers during the Blitz of Humphrey Jennings's documentary films *London Can Take It* and *Fires Were Started*. Together with the country squire, representative of the heart of old England, they appear in Michael Powell and Emeric Pressburger's mystical celebration of the Englishness of the English countryside and the English cathedral city in *A Canterbury Tale*. After the war they find another incarnation in the good-hearted irreverence and whimsicality of the Ealing comedies, such as *Kind Hearts and Coronets* and *Passport to Pimlico*. In all these ways the Englishness of the interwar period found its climax, suitably expressed in the calm fortitude and cheerful stoicism of 'the people's war', and its hopeful aftermath in the 'the people's government', the new Labour administration.[4]

The persistence of Britishness

But the Second World War was fought by the British, not just the English. And not just British from the British Isles, but British from the Dominions of Canada, Australia, New Zealand and South Africa; and British from the colonies and dependencies of Asia, Africa and the West Indies. *Picture Post*, in its issue of July 1949, inveighed against the 'colour bar' that flourished in Britain, and pointed to the huge contribution that the 'coloured population', in Britain and from overseas, had made to the war effort (Hopkinson 1970: 255–60).

Troops might march off to the front singing 'there'll always be an England', but those troops contained contingents of Scots, Welsh and Irish who peaceably, as in the past, allowed the old confusion to pass (though the king and queen were scrupulous in their use of the correct forms). The Ministry of Information, in its 'Programme for Film Propaganda', stressed the need for films to convey 'British life and character' and 'British ideas and institutions'; there was also strong urging of the need for 'publicity about the British Empire'. The latter was triumphantly accomplished in Powell and Pressburger's *49th Parallel*, in which a band of Nazis are defeated by an intrepid collection of representative Canadians (including a French Canadian) (Aldgate and Richards 1986: 21–43).

The move from 'England' to 'Britain' and back again was frequent and common, suggesting that by this time the two were so merged in the minds of inhabitants and commentators alike that they did not notice the confusion nor feel the need to explain it. Winston Churchill – half American – was seen by many both at home and abroad as the epitome of Englishness, 'the embodiment of John Bullishness', as one commentator put it; his speeches were resonant with echoes of Shakespeare, Milton and the King James's Bible. Yet he did more than anyone else to portray the struggle as a 'Battle of Britain', and indeed of and for the British Empire. It was 'the sea-girt islands of Britain' that he proclaimed to be the last bastions of freedom against the hordes of barbaric Huns. J. B. Priestley also presented himself as the very type of the bluff, plain-speaking Yorkshireman. Yet in his wartime 'Postscript' broadcasts he generally spoke of the British people as a whole, as when he declared that 'the true heroes and heroines of this war, whose courage, patience and good humour stand like a rock above the dark morass of treachery, cowardice and panic, are the ordinary British folk.' For Priestley the qualities of the nation – kindness, humour and courage – were not just English virtues but the property of all those who shared a common inheritance ('the kindness of England, of Britain, of the wide Empire forever reaching out towards new expressions of freedom'). Finally there is the actor and broadcaster Leslie Howard, who was extraordinarily popular not just in Britain but in Canada and America. Shot down by German fighter planes in 1943, his death was the occasion of an outpouring of grief on both sides of the Atlantic. Howard – son of a Hungarian Jew – was 'the Englishman's Englishman', a role he portrayed to perfection in such films as *The Scarlet Pimpernel*, *Pimpernel Smith*, *Pygmalion* and *The First of the Few*. But he made it clear in all his lectures and broadcasts that what was at stake was 'the destiny of Britain', and indeed of all English-speaking peoples. It was 'the British soul', he told Americans, that responded in sympathy with the principles of American freedom. In his documentary film *From the Four Corners*, soldiers from Australia, New Zealand and Canada are shown the sights of London, culminating in Westminster, the mother of parliaments. The sights and what they symbolize celebrate their shared heritage as Britons. It was this breadth of concern that might explain why, as an obituary notice in the *Manchester Daily Despatch* noted, Howard had a fervent following not just in North America but all over the British Empire (on all these, see Aldgate and Richards 1986: 44–75).

It is evident that for much of the twentieth century Britishness flourished alongside, and perhaps to a good degree overlapped, Englishness (cf Marquand 1995: 279). There were many good reasons for this, obvious when stated but often forgotten. The British Empire might arouse criticism from Little Englanders and left-wingers, and there were many signs that its future was uncertain. But in terms of size and population, it reached its greatest extent in the years following the First World War, when it covered a fifth of the world's land surface and incorporated a quarter of the world's people. It was not until after the Second World War that, with increasing speed in the 1950s and 1960s, the empire dissolved. But that end was not foreordained, nor its speed foreseen in the first half of the century (Lloyd 1996: 282). For much of the century empire was a central presence in the life of the British people.

The impact of empire on identity is always difficult to assess. In the twentieth century empires everywhere came under attack, their legitimacy challenged, their gains to the imperial powers questioned. The British Empire was subjected as much as any other to these strains. The imperial mission, and an identity that derived from it, was more difficult to sustain. Yet there are a hundred indications that empire continued to play a key part in British consciousness. In stories, poems, comic-books, photography, films, plays; in the great imperial exhibitions (such as the Wembley Exhibition of 1924, for which London's great Wembley Stadium was built); in the pageantry and spectacle of imperial monarchy; in the annual celebration of Empire Day; in the participation of troops from all parts of the empire in two world wars; in the presence of peoples from the empire within the United Kingdom itself: in all these ways the British were daily reminded that they were an imperial people (Cannadine 1984: 149; Mackenzie 1984: 256–8; 1999b; Stevenson 1984: 46–53; Williamson 1990: 45–6; Lloyd 1996: 284; Samuel 1999b: 86–92).

The economy too remained resolutely British (and indeed for much of the time imperial), more so than ever before. Imperialism and global rivalry knit the industrial parts of Britain together even more tightly than in the nineteenth century. In the post-1945 era, much of the economy was integrated under great national, all-British conglomerates – the British Coal Corporation, British Gas, British Steel, British Rail, British Shipbuilding, British Leyland motors. The national airline was British Airways, the telephone system – hived off from the

Post Office in 1981 – British Telecom. Moreover, all regions of the kingdom shared in the ups and downs of the trade cycles. Unemployment during the Great Depression devastated the coalfields of South Wales as much as those of Clydeside, and the shipbuilding industries of Belfast as much as those of Tyneside. Likewise all areas shared in the post-Second World War boom, thus hiding the realities of an antiquated industrial system. When, in the 1970s and 1980s, the chickens began to come home to roost, it was 'the collapse of British power', and 'the illusion and reality of Britain as a great nation' that were the titles that grabbed the headlines (Barnett 1972, 1984). Though the unlovely term 'Englanditis' was coined by some to describe the ailment from which Britain suffered, it was clearer to most that the cause was properly designated 'the British disease', an affliction compounded of indifference to technical and scientific education in particular and a deep-seated antipathy to industrial culture in general (Wiener 1981: 126–54; Kumar 1988; Williamson 1990: 189–93). While it might be true that these attitudes were more to be found in English culture than in the culture of Britain as a whole, the integration of the economic, political and indeed cultural system ensured that the old 'condition of England' question had now to be re-framed as a 'condition of Britain' question.

If the industrial system was British, so too, and largely as a consequence of this, was the labour movement. It is hard to overestimate the importance of this factor in sustaining a British identity in the twentieth century. Nationalist movements had begun their careers in the British Isles in the late nineteenth century. In Ireland this had resulted in the separation of the bulk of Ireland from Britain in the 1920s. But the Welsh and Scottish nationalist movements were weak, and indeed remained so until the 1960s. There are a number of reasons for this, but among them must be placed the integrative role of the trade unions and the Labour Party.

Chartism and early trade unionism were, as we have seen, both British, as was, even more clearly, the Labour Party (here more or less inheriting the Britishness of the Liberal Party) (see Robbins 1995: 114–17, 120–2). Of the 'Big Four' early leaders of the Labour Party, three – Keir Hardie, Bruce Glasier and Ramsay Macdonald – were Scots (the fourth, Philip Snowden, came from the North of England). At the end of the twentieth century Scots reappeared among the leadership in the persons of John Smith and Tony Blair.[5] Wales had always been important, a stronghold of Labour from the 1920s. It provided safe seats for many Labour politicians – from Keir Hardie to Michael Foot – and supplied some prominent figures, such as Aneurin Bevin and Neil Kinnock. From as early as the end of the nineteenth century, indeed, a familiar feature of the British political scene was established, by which the Conservatives were reduced largely to an English – even a southern English – base, while the

Liberal and later the Labour parties came to depend on Welsh and Scottish support (Cunningham 1986: 293–4; Robbins 1995: 113).

Labour occasionally flirted with Home Rule for Scotland and Wales, but its leaders knew that to take and keep power it would have to remain a resolutely British party. The extension of the suffrage in 1918 to all men over 21 (and again in 1928 to all women over 21) changed the face of British politics. Henceforth Labour, whether or not in office, was a power in the land. Its nationalization policies and the creation of a welfare state after 1945 – more or less accepted by the Conservatives until the 1980s – gave it a vast and far-reaching influence in every corner of British society. Together with its powerful ally, the all-British Trades Union Congress, it ensured that nationalist parties would be marginalized for much of the century. Wales and Scotland, it had always been admitted, did disproportionately well out of the welfare state. Welsh and Scottish workers were well aware that their power, status and standard of living were more likely to be promoted by a powerful labour movement, covering the whole of Britain, than by relatively small nationalist parties. If Britishness and British identity held their own in the twentieth century, much of this must be attributed to the power and influence of labour.

There was, for much of the twentieth century, another, equally novel, power in the land, and this too was determinedly British. The British Broadcasting Corporation (which received its charter in 1927) from the start conceived itself as 'the voice of Britain'. The Scotsman John Reith, its first and most influential director-general, held to a firm British and indeed imperial ideal. The BBC, the world's first national public-service broadcasting organization, saw itself as standing above party, region, sectional nationalism and anything that threatened the unity and integrity of Britain and the British Empire. Its goal, as defined by Reith, was a high-minded national culture taking in all classes and regions of Britain, and spreading as far as possible to all corners of the British Empire. The 'National' programme, inaugurated in 1930, and its wartime complement, the 'Forces' network, were relentlessly centralist, opposed to regional particularism and dialectical speech. The aim was, quite literally, to get the whole of the British nation to speak with one voice (see Reith 1924, 1949: 134–6; LeMahieu 1988: 141–54; Curran and Seaton 1991: 131–50; Samuel 1999c: 176–7).

There have been innumerable criticisms of the BBC, on the grounds of class, gender, race, regional (i.e., metropolitan) and ideological bias. But few would deny that at critical points in the twentieth century the BBC did indeed stand for Britain, most notably during the dark days of the Second World War. More diffusely it became, through its news broadcasts, its wide coverage of the arts, both popular and high, its broadcasts of the great sporting events, its Promenade concerts, its Christmas Day broadcasts by the king to the nation and the empire, and its use to make announcements of national importance, the most representative of national institutions, more so than Parliament and perhaps only a little less so than the monarchy (Scannell and Cardiff 1982; MacCabe and Stewart 1986; LeMahieu 1988: 227–8; Curran and Seaton 1991: 151–77; Samuel 1999c: 178–85). The coming of television, that most classless of media, if anything enhanced the BBC's reputation as the voice of the nation, the nation 'speaking to itself'. Even commercial television – ITV – when it came in the 1950s, was not allowed to follow the fragmented American model but was forced into the national mould marked out by the BBC (Smith 1973: 57). It was the view of a respected political journalist, Andrew Marr, that at the end of the twentieth century the BBC was 'still more important in keeping these islands glued together than any political party' (*The Independent* 8 April 1995).

The BBC cemented its role as the voice of Britain by its close association with the most esteemed national institution, the British monarchy. Begun with the royal broadcasts of the interwar period, it continued with the televised coronation of Queen Elizabeth the Second ('the First', to stony-faced Scotsmen) and such other major royal events as the Investiture of the Prince of Wales and the wedding of Charles and Diana. All drew large audiences, and proclaimed not simply the BBC's official status as guardian of the national culture but the continuing popularity of the monarchy all over Britain (Cannadine 1984: 139–60; Billig 1992; Nairn 1994: 19–22; Chaney 2001).[6] Since the time of Victoria, the royal family had striven to show its British character. In the late twentieth century, marked by the fragmentation and dissolution of so many British institutions, it appeared to many, despite its many trials and tribulations, perhaps the sole surviving British institution to command appreciable loyalty and respect.

The Englishness that was defined before the First World War, and that persisted after it, was mostly a cultural rather than a political phenomenon. It was an affair of English history, English intellectual and political traditions, English literature and the landscape of England. It did not attempt to erect a political movement of English nationalism, even though such political movements were emerging all over Europe, including parts of the British Isles. If we want to use the terms of an earlier discussion, we can call this Englishness a form of ethnic or cultural nationalism, by comparison with a British 'civic' nationalism. But while helpful in some ways, this is also misleading on a number of grounds. For one thing, cultural nationalism, as in countries such as Germany and Italy, often had distinct political ambitions and could give rise to powerful nationalist movements that had the creation of an independent state as their goal. For another, as we have seen, the ethnic–civic distinction is unstable and breaks down repeatedly, conceptually as well as in practice. While Britishness might be seen to have a civic rather than an ethnic character – a point emphasized particularly by Scottish and Welsh nationalists – it has over the centuries developed a set of institutions, symbols and traditions that can lead to a form of emotional identification remarkably similar to that evoked by ethnic nationhood. The line between culture and politics, here as so often, is hazy and erratic.

The rise of political nationalism among the English during this period would in any case have been rather extraordinary. It might have been possible for the Irish and, with less reason, the Scots and Welsh, to claim 'oppression' within the United Kingdom, and to seek to separate themselves from the 'dominant' English. Such a course was hardly open to the English, though there were occasional grumbles to the effect that the English were subsidizing the more 'backward' and less enterprising Celtic regions. The English were not exclusively in charge of Britain and the British Empire – far from it – but they had been the principal creators of those entities and had for long derived their sense of themselves from their part in them. It would have seemed strange for anyone to propose that the English should seek to withdraw from the United Kingdom and set up their own independent English state, as thoroughgoing nationalists.

What is novel is that such calls do not now sound as outlandish as they would have done as little as twenty or thirty years ago. It might still be stretching things too far to say that a true form of English political nationalism has emerged, that 'England for the English' has become a rallying cry with which to go the polls or take to the streets – at least with any realistic chance of success. What is striking though is the fact that such things can be talked about now, and that there are people for whom such an outcome would not be unwelcome. A muted, quiet cultivation of Englishness has persisted for much of the twentieth century alongside a more public and arguably, as in the past, a more dominant Britishness. In a world of superpowers, in a world more insistently global than ever before, it would seem that the future lay with the larger entity, with Great Britain rather than with Little England. That was certainly the opinion of nearly all serious observers up to the last quarter of the twentieth century. What now may have brought it into question, or at least into debate? Why is Britishness on the defensive, assailed by various forms of ethnic nationalism, including an English variety? Has a political English nationalism finally come of age?

The break-up of Britain?

A stream of books, newspaper articles and television series in recent years has proclaimed the 'death of Britain'. *The Day Britain Died* (2000) was the title of a major BBC TV series presented and then published as a book by the chief political correspondent of the BBC and former editor of *The Independent*, Andrew Marr. Another journalist, the broadcaster Gavin Esler, presented a BBC Radio 4 series in 2000 under the more open title 'Brits', but, as he said in a lecture about it, his pressing concern too was 'is the UK really RIP?' (Esler 2001: 8). 'Yes' was the emphatic response of the veteran commentator Tom Nairn in his book *After Britain* (2000). Nairn, 'a celebrated iconoclast of things British', as the book-jacket blurb rightly put it, had more reason than most to feel vindicated by what seemed to be the turn of events. As early as 1977, in what can now be seen as the pathbreaking prelude to the current debate, he had published the seminal *The Break-Up of Britain* ([1977] 1981). Responding partly to the revival of Scottish nationalism, partly to what appeared a profound crisis in the British state and the British economy, Nairn argued there that the ramshackle and antiquated structures of British society were incapable of holding Britain together for much longer. Now, nearly a quarter of a century later, he could feel that the prognostications of that earlier work were being borne out. The United Kingdom, as hitherto constructed, was on the point of collapse. 'Farewell Britannia' was the valediction that he pronounced in a lecture at the London School of Economics (Nairn 2001).

Nairn and Marr are both Scots, and it is the pressure from a powerfully revived Scottish nationalist movement that has been a principal agency of the movement towards a constitutional resettlement in Britain. In 1998, more than a hundred years after Gladstone had unsuccessfully tried to introduce the concept of Home Rule into British politics, the Labour government of Tony Blair passed, with remarkably little opposition, acts which enabled the setting up of a Scottish Parliament and a Welsh Assembly. Northern Ireland, which had had its own parliament for over fifty years – from 1920 to its abolition during 'the Troubles' in 1973 – also had a substantial measure of devolution restored by the Belfast Agreement of 1998, which set up a Northern Ireland Assembly as part of a proposed wider Irish settlement. Together these acts of devolution have been described by a well-known political scientist, Vernon Bogdanor, as 'the most radical constitutional change this country has seen since the Great Reform Act of 1832... They seem to imply that the United Kingdom is becoming a union of nations, each with its own identity and institutions' rather than, as the Royal Commission on the Constitution put it in 1973, 'one nation representing different kinds of people' (2001: 1, 287; see also Osmond 2001: 113).[7]

Devolution, the revival of nationalism in Scotland and (to a lesser extent) in Wales, and the ever-pressing need to solve the Northern Ireland question, have been one set of forces threatening the traditional unity and integrity of the United Kingdom. They have thrown into question the hallowed supremacy of the Westminster Parliament, and so the whole constitutional arrangement by which Britain has been governed for the past three centuries. New constitutional patterns now seem possible, such as regionalism and federalism, of a kind that up to now have only existed as paper schemes dreamed up by a few theorists (Banks 1971; Kendle 1997; Burgess 1989; Bogdanor 2001: 44–50; Nairn 2001).

They suggest, at least potentially, a new set of identities within the British Isles, and new kinds of relations between the different peoples making up the once United Kingdom.

Something similar is intimated by the second major development affecting traditional British identities: Britain's entry into the European Union, and the possibilities and prospects that this implies. For many centuries, since around the time of the Protestant Reformation, England and then Britain have defined themselves to a good extent against 'Europe', that is, the European Continent. The preservation of English/British identity against the machinations of 'Brussels bureaucrats' and more vaguely specified threats from unsalubrious European religious and political traditions has become the last-ditch stand of Little Englanders of both left and right in Britain. By the same token, Britain's entry into Europe has been hailed by many other commentators as a heaven-sent opportunity for the British to renegotiate their identities, both among themselves and in relation to other peoples, in Europe and beyond. 'Europe of the regions' has been one popular slogan, suggesting a federation of regional entities throughout Europe that would have the satisfying effect of dissolving hardened and outdated national identities, and making possible perhaps the construction of an overarching European or even cosmopolitan identity (see, e.g., Harvie 1991, 1994b; Coombes 1991; Sharpe 1993; Jones and Keating 1995; Bradbury and Mawson 1997; Castells 1998: 326–34). Like the radical measures of devolution in Scotland, Wales and Northern Ireland, Britain's commitment to the European Union signifies a significant loss of the parliamentary sovereignty that has been the central pillar of the British constitution. With that gone, or at least severely qualified, what alternative configurations might be possible, with what implications for the collective identities of the varying groups within Britain?

A third development has made, according to many accounts, even fuzzier the already 'fuzzy frontiers' of British identity (Cohen 1994: 5–36). Britain has always been a country of immigrants, if on a more long-drawn-out pattern than America. Celts, Romans, Saxons, Danes, Scandinavians and Normans have poured over the land. Later came Jews and Huguenots and a new wave of Celts in the Irish. Later still, peoples from the British Empire and Commonwealth, whites from Australia, Canada and South Africa, blacks and Asians from Africa, the Caribbean, India, Pakistan, Bangladesh and Hongkong.

It is those latter, the blacks and Asians, who have provided the dominant challenges to existing identities. Despite the fact that they make up no more than about 7 per cent of the total British population, and are outnumbered by recent white immigrants, it is they, not those other immigrants, who are thought of and for much of the time treated as 'aliens' by the dominant white majority (Runnymede Trust 2000: 372; Alibhai-Brown 2001: ix). It is as if the earlier groups of (mainly white) immigrants have wished to halt the longstanding and on the whole successful process of assimilation and integration, to say 'thus far and no further'.

Why should that be? Undoubtedly racism, the view that whites and non-whites occupy different universes, has, as in the United States and elsewhere, been part of the answer. But an equally important part may have to do with the fact that the traditional British and English identities are under pressure for the other reasons that we have described, and at the same time. Each cause acts to reinforce the other. Nationalist movements in Scotland and Wales force the English to ask questions about themselves, while at the same time leading to more rigid conceptions of Scottishness and Welshness. 'Europe' threatens some people in all parts of Britain, the English probably more than others (Weale 1995). This vulnerability in turn leads to a greater fear of 'swamping' and 'dilution', the sense that some hard-won and precious identity, long preserved, is now under attack from alien influences. The natural response is to man the barricades and pull up the drawbridge – even if, as so often, the more dangerous enemies are within the walls.

At the same time there are others who, as with Europe, see opportunities rather than threats. For them, the arrival in Britain of people of different races and cultures opens up the prospect of a transformation of identities that can only be welcomed. Some of these visions can be dizzying. For those of a post-modernist way of thinking, the presence of so many diverse cultures within society allows for a 'pick and mix' attitude that might mean not simply more variegated but also more provisional, constantly changing, identities. All kinds of exotic hybrid and 'hyphenated' identities seem to be on offer, and it would be the worst kind of 'essentialism' to resist the opportunities for free individual expression that such cultural resources offer (see, e.g., Dodd 1995; Caglar 1997; and generally for the perspective, Hall 1997; Modood and Werbner 1997; Werbner and Modood 1997).

Not all commentators of the optimistic school take so exuberant a view of the possibilities (satirically explored many years ago by Nigel Dennis in his novel *Cards of Identity* (1955)). But most are at least pleased to see what they discern as the dissolution of the old, crusty, backward-looking British and English identities. They celebrate the new hybrid, multicultural Britain, humming with new kinds of food, music, clothes, literature, religions, marriage patterns, family styles and, potentially at least, a new politics. These are not, it is emphasized, cultures or communities of separation, sitting uneasily side by side, as in the old pluralism. Rather they are genuinely new constructs, creative and hybrid forms that bode well for the future health and vitality of British culture. Such was the view combatively put forward, for instance, by the Ugandan-born Yasmin Alibhai-Brown (the unfamiliar kind of hyphenated surname being itself significant), in her much-discussed book, *Who Do We Think We Are?* (2001). In a somewhat darker but still hopeful key, it was the picture of the new Britain that emerged in Zadie Smith's dazzling first novel, *White Teeth* (2001). A somewhat similar view, emphasizing the complexities and conflicts both personal and social, is presented in the work of Hanif Kureishi, in the screenplay for the film *My Beautiful Laundrette* (1984) and the novel *The Buddha of Suburbia* (1990).

How far does this all portend the 'break-up of Britain' – or, as it has been expressed in other accounts, the 'unmasking' or the 'unravelling' of Britain (McCrone 1997; Samuel 1999d)? What does it mean for the identities of the different British peoples – Scottish, Welsh, Irish, English and those who might prefer to call themselves 'Black British', or 'British Asians' or even 'British Muslims'? It is the English – the mainly white English – who are the principal subject of this book; and so it is their situation that will concern us the most. But that situation is, as it always has been, partly a reflection of the situation of their British co-nationals. So we need first to consider, however briefly, how things stand with them.

The Welsh, it is fairly clear, have little interest in breaking up Britain. Separatism has hardly ever, if at all, been on the agenda of Welsh nationalism (E. Williams 1989; Cohen 1994: 9–10; Bogdanor 2001: 146–50). The early translation of the Bible into Welsh allowed the Welsh, uniquely among Celtic speaking groups in the British Isles, to preserve their language and to develop a literature based on it. The main concern of Welsh nationalism has been to preserve and extend the Welsh cultural heritage. Hence the struggle to keep Welsh language instruction in the schools, to have their own universities which would study the Welsh past and Welsh culture, and to ensure that they had their own voice in the new media of culture and communication such as radio and television. In all this they have been triumphantly successful, as they were also in the related field of religion, where the disestablishment of the Anglican Church of Wales in 1920 – when less than a quarter of the Welsh population professed to belong to it – left the field clear for the overwhelmingly more popular Nonconformist churches.

Nowhere else in the British Isles has nationalism been so clearly and so closely cultural (Nairn 1981: 196–215; Bogdanor 2001: 144). Even political aims have been smuggled in under a cultural cover, as in the successful insistence that Welsh be a qualification for official employment, thus more or less ensuring that all Welsh official posts would be filled only by Welshmen and Welshwomen. The aim of Welsh nationalism, its underlying motive, was succinctly stated by Saunders Lewis at the founding of the Welsh nationalist party, Plaid Cymru, in 1926: 'Not independence. Not even unconditional freedom. But just as much freedom as may be necessary to establish and safeguard civilization in Wales' (in Nairn 1981: 214).

The Welsh have remained, as they have been since the Reformation, loyal Britons. Socially and politically they have been more integrated into the United Kingdom than any other non-English people. Loyal Tories in the eighteenth century, they became bastions of Liberalism and Labourism in the nineteenth and twentieth centuries. But in all cases the ties were to national British political parties, not to local Welsh nationalist ones such as Plaid Cymru. Material ties have cemented this cordial relationship (originating, as more fiery nationalists occasionally remind the Welsh, in brutal Anglo-Norman conquest). Welsh agriculture and industry have been wholly tied to the British economy and the British market. Deindustrialization has hit them as much as other parts of Britain, further enhancing the sense of a shared fate. The Welsh know that, while globalization and foreign investment might give them some new jobs and industries, they are not likely to succeed economically by detaching themselves from Britain. They know too – at least the better-informed among them do – that Welsh local government and social services are heavily subsidized by the English taxpayer (Rose 1982: 138). Together with the absence of any key natural resource, such as North Sea oil in the case of Scotland, the Welsh lack both a lever and a material incentive to break away and go it alone.

The Welsh are therefore likely to be satisfied, for the time being at least, with the granting of their own National Assembly (an offshoot, in any case, of the more pressing demands of the Scots). It is a weaker body than the Scottish Parliament, in that it has only executive but not legislative powers, and it lacks the power to raise revenues (Bogdanor 2001: 209–13, 254–64). This is consistent with the more moderate, less separatist thrust of nationalism in Wales hitherto compared to Scotland. However, we know from what small acorns mighty oaks do grow. The genie is now out of the bottle, to change the metaphor. The British government has implemented more radical measures of devolution than ever were attempted before. It has accepted practical, if not principled, limitations to the sovereignty of the British Parliament. Who knows on what future occasion the Welsh may not demand what the Scots now have? Who knows what circumstances might not make them willing to engage in a joint effort to bring about the final demise of the British state and the United Kingdom (see, e.g., Bogdanor 2001: 200; Osmond 2001: 109–10)? That time may be some way off now. But there has been a fundamental change in the political climate. The English are well aware of that. The Welsh example, modest as it might still appear, is a warning that the English too may need to set their house in order.

The Irish of Northern Ireland present the English with a different sort of challenge, though oddly enough perhaps a lesser one so far as national identity goes. The reason why this may sound odd is of course that Northern Ireland has been the central preoccupation of the British state for the past thirty years (for Ireland as a whole, we can perhaps say for the past 300 years) (see Whyte 1990; Boyle 1991; Davey 2001). Since the beginning of 'the Troubles' in 1969, there has been barely a year when Northern Ireland has not made the news, not infrequently of the headline kind. A resolution of its problems, especially of the wide-ranging nature contemplated in the 1998 Belfast Agreement, ought surely therefore to have significant consequences for English conceptions of themselves and their place in the United Kingdom.

So indeed it may well do, but not in the same way as the challenges coming from the Scots, the Welsh or the Black and Asian British. For in the case of these peoples, the challenge is fundamentally ethnic. The English are forced to define themselves in response to attempts by others to distinguish themselves, on grounds of culture and even race, as clearly as possible from the English. That is not the case with the majority of the Northern Irish, the Protestant people of Ulster. Here the problem is the extent to which the Protestants have sought to identify themselves as closely as possible with the British mainland, to the point almost of denying that they had any distinctive ethnicity at all.

With the Northern Ireland Catholic minority, there is of course an ethnic difference. But this is so large, and so longstanding, that it does not really constitute a challenge to the English. As far as they are concerned, the Northern Irish Catholics belong ethnically and spiritually with the Irish Catholics of the Republic of Ireland.[8] Whether they find a tolerable place in a reconstituted Northern Ireland, or in a reunified Ireland, or in some 'Council of the Isles', they have ceased to play, except vestigially, their historic role as 'the Other' of English (though perhaps not British) national identity. The dominant feeling among most informed people in England is rather sympathy for their sufferings at the hands of the Protestant majority. But they are not a mirror to the English.

Nor, but for other reasons, are the Ulster Protestants. Of mixed English and Scottish descent, they have long ceased to think of themselves as 'English', as they did up to the middle of the eighteenth century. But since the early twentieth century, and especially after the secession of the rest of Ireland in 1921, they have come to insist ever more strongly on their Britishness. That was why they resisted the idea of a separate Parliament for Ulster, as proposed in the 1920 Government of Ireland Act. As Sir Edward Carson, the Unionist leader, told the House of Commons in 1919, 'Ulster has never asked for a separate Parliament. Ulster's claim has always been of this simple character: "We have thrived under the Union; we are in sympathy with you, we are part of yourselves" ' (in Bogdanor 2001: 61). To accept a separate Parliament, Unionists feared, would be to cut themselves off from mainland Britain, and deprive them of equality with other British citizens represented in the Westminster Parliament.

A separate Parliament was imposed on Ulster – mainly, it seems, because the British government hoped that this would solve the Irish question, perhaps by acting as a stepping-stone to a united Ireland of the future – and in time Ulster Protestants came to find it an invaluable tool of their rule of the province. But they continued to protest their unshakeable Britishness, and to resist any attempt to be defined as Irish, even 'Northern Irish'. Their hostility to the Republic, and their exclusion of Catholics from all positions of power and influence in Ulster, gave them a standing cause for holding to this identity. Their Protestantism and their loyalty to the British crown were for them the badges of their essential Britishness, at a time when other British citizens seemed to be showing a shameful uncertainty on both counts.

But, in the face of repeated attempts by British governments to bring about some kind of power-sharing in Ulster, and the suspicion that the ultimate aim was a sell-out in the form of a united Ireland, some kind of Irish definition began to seem attractive to at least some Ulstermen. That after all had been the response of late eighteenth-century Irish Protestants, the Protestants of Grattan's Parliament, reacting to a similar story of neglect and pressure by the British government. It was also the response of Protestants such as the Yeats family in late nineteenth-century Ireland (Foster 1989b: 14). Moreover, it was becoming clearer, in the last part of the twentieth century, that one of the most effective ways to assert yourself and to make claims on the British government was by defining yourself as an ethnic group. Ethnicity was the name of the game. Scots, Welsh, Afro-Caribbeans, Muslims and Hindus were all doing it. Even the Cornish revived old claims to separate treatment.

One way, therefore, for the Ulster Protestants to defy both calls for the unification of Ireland and the increasing attempts of the British government to push them into a settlement with an embattled Catholic population was to insist on their separate identity (Cox 1989). They had after all been in Ireland for over 350 years. They had evolved their own way of life, based to a good extent on the Presbyterian religion. They were indeed the most religious people in the kingdom – a 1990 survey found that only 12 per cent of the Northern Ireland population described themselves as having no religion, compared with 34 per cent in mainland Britain. They were also significantly more conservative than other peoples in the kingdom on moral issues (Cox 1989: 39; Boyle 1991: 70–1). Ulster Protestants saw themselves as hardened by conflict, a tougher and more virile people as compared to the more cosseted peoples of the mainland. If they were pushed too hard, if the British government abandoned them, they could go it alone, as they had been prepared to do in 1914 ('Ulster will fight, and Ulster will be right'). Paisleyism – the outlook of Dr Ian Paisley and his Free Presbyterian Church – best sums up this quintessentially Ulster Protestant identity (Bruce 1987; see also Cox 1989: 35–6).

Secession remains an option open to the Ulster Protestants, though with the resounding support for the Belfast Agreement – from both Northern Protestants and Catholics – as shown in the 1998 referendum it seems increasingly unlikely (Bogdanor 2001: 108; Davey 2001: 86). In any case the attempt to establish a distinctively Northern Irish ethnicity seems to have had very limited success. In the 1990 British Social Attitudes Survey, 66 per cent of Ulster Protestants described themselves as 'British', and only 27 per cent described themselves as 'Ulster' or 'Northern Irish'. Significantly only 4 per cent described themselves as 'Irish', compared with 20 per cent in 1968 – a measure, perhaps, of declining confidence among Protestants in their ability to stand alone and an increasing reversion to the old British identity (see, e.g., Trimble 1989: 47–8). Moreover, on several indicators of social and political attitudes – towards class, state intervention, egalitarianism – Northern Ireland Protestants revealed themselves to be remarkably like their other British compatriots (Boyle 1991: 70–1).

The Ulster people therefore do not present the English with the usual contrasts that draw forth an answering affirmation of identity. They are both too bothersome and too much the same. Ever since the creation of the Irish Free State in 1921 the British government has been trying to get rid of the Northern Irish, or at least the Northern Irish problem. For decades after the separation Northern Ireland was left to its own devices. Only with the outbreak of 'the Troubles' in the late 1960s did the British government turn reluctantly to the affairs of the province. Polls in recent years, especially since the onset of the Troubles, have repeatedly shown that the people of mainland Britain would be heartily pleased if Northern Ireland were to go its own way, with their blessing (Marr 2000: 81; Nairn 2001: 67). This is not the stuff of identity-creation. The English think of the Ulster Protestants not as the alarmingly different 'Other' who both threatens and challenges them but as a political nuisance that too often disturbs their peace. They are not like the barbaric Celt of old, or the French and Germans of more recent times. They are more like the disorderly and delinquent members of the same family who should either be disciplined for their own good or shipped off to some remote colony.

With the Scots things are different again. The Scots indeed present the English with perhaps their greatest challenge. The British state was created by the union with Scotland in 1707. Scots shared equally in the development of the state and in the evolution of the British identity that went with it. They were also partners in the creation of empire. Their economy reflected, as much as the English, this dual British and imperial context. If the Scots were to secede from the union, this would affect England more seriously than any other current development (only Europe perhaps might have equal impact). This is why much of the current commentary on the 'break-up of Britain' focuses so much on the Scots (e.g., Nairn 2000; Marr 2000). A Britain without Scotland not only deprives the United Kingdom of its very *raison d'être*; it forces the English to consider more deeply than ever before who they might be, if they are not the founders and guardians of a British state and a British society.

Not that the secession of Scotland is in any way imminent or inevitable, whatever Scottish nationalists might hope or say. Opinion among Scots on this issue has fluctuated widely in recent years (McCrone 1992: 212–14; Lloyd 1999; Harvie 1999; Marr 2000: 68–71). Most Scots seem inclined to give the new Scottish Parliament a chance (and some awkward early episodes in the Parliament's history have made some of them feel that it would be wise to hold on to the British connection for some time longer, at least). But what is undoubted is the steady growth in Scottish national consciousness. This is partly shown by the rise in support for the Scottish National Party (the SNP), from 5 per cent of the Scottish vote in the 1966 election to 20 per cent in the 2001 election, well ahead of the Conservatives (15.6 per cent) and Liberal Democrats (16.4 per cent) (*The Independent* 9 June 2001). The SNP is now clearly second only to Labour in Scotland, a remarkable rise for a party that until the 1960s was regarded largely as a refuge for cranks and extremists. At the same time Scots since the late 1980s have shown a clear preference for Scottishnesss over Britishness – certainly as compared with expressions of national identity among the Welsh and English (McCrone 1992: 24; 2001: 102–3; McCrone *et al.* 1998: 631; Davidson 2000: 200–1).

Scottishness was not, as we have seen, buried by the union with England in 1707, despite the rise of a powerful British identity. It was kept alive by the retention of autonomous religious, legal and educational institutions after the union. Later, the evolution of the Scottish Office, and the practice of leaving Scottish affairs mainly in the hands of Scottish MPs at Westminster, meant that the distinctiveness of Scotland as a political unit was substantially recognized both at the executive level of government and in the way in which Parliament conducted its business (Paterson 1994: 103–31; Bogdanor 2001: 111–16). A heaven-sent fillip to Scottish nationalism was given by the discovery and exploitation, in the 1970s, of North Sea oil, claimed by nationalists as Scottish oil. Under the slogan 'rich Scots or poor British' Scottish nationalists argued that that the British state would use the oil profits mainly to offset the balance of payments deficit rather than make the necessary investment in Scottish industry. An independent Scotland would be able to apply the oil profits to urgently needed projects to renew the Scottish economy. North Sea oil was the device whereby Scottish nationalists were able to put Scottish national identity on a firm material base, complementing and to an extent offsetting the vague cultural mishmash – 'kailyardism' and 'tartanry' – that had served up to then to define Scottishness (Nairn 1981: 131, 191; McCrone 1992: 31; Harvie 1995: 183–7; Bogdanor 2001: 125–6).

Finally, there is the European Union, which offers to Scotland, as to other parts of the United Kingdom, the chance to go it alone. Scots had for long complained at being on the periphery of the British state, remote from the centre of power and influence in London. Britain's entry into the European Union threatened to increase that sense of remoteness. Brussels, via London, was even further away than London itself. A direct connection with Brussels, and independent representation there, would give the Scots the chance to influence European Union policy in their favour. Moreover, since the rules of the European Community forbid the imposition of tariffs on the goods of member states, the Scots would not be shut out of British markets. An independent Scotland would therefore continue to enjoy one of the principal advantages of membership of the United Kingdom – one of the very things, in fact, which had led to union of 1707 in the first place – while being free of what many now perceived as its stifling burdens (Bogdanor 2001: 127).

David McCrone has well summarized Scotland's current condition, balanced precariously between an acceptance of autonomy within a reconstituted United Kingdom and a determination to search for outright independence beyond it.

Scotland is renegotiating its place in the Union, and even considering whether the "marriage of convenience" which it represented should hold at all. The Scots had gained considerable economic and political influence within the imperial framework, but that was long gone. The ideological support systems of unionism, imperialism, and Protestantism no longer functioned as they had done. Scotland's economy had been transformed and reoriented towards Europe and a post-imperial world. The new variable geometry of territorial power involving the European Union, the British state, and Scotland was becoming more significant, reflected in the fact that, like the Welsh, Scots saw in Europe a new Union to augment or even replace the older British one.   (2001: 106)

Englishness embattled

What, to David McCrone, seems Scotland's opportunity, is England's predicament. To those who think that Scotland – and Wales and Northern Ireland – should determine their destinies for and by themselves, the loosening of the historic ties that bound them to the United Kingdom is a welcome development. Protestantism – except in Northern Ireland, where it thrives on sectional conflict – is a largely spent force, as is religion in general for the majority of the inhabitants of the United Kingdom.[9] Empire has gone. With it has disappeared not just the imperial administration but the imperial economy, in both of which all peoples of the kingdom shared. The deindustrialization of Britain, wiping out whole sections of regionally concentrated British industry, has added to the disintegrating effect of this loss. Globalization in general and the European Union in particular now make it possible for the different parts of the kingdom to attempt to make their own separate contracts with the global economy, as the example of Ireland has demonstrated spectacularly in recent decades. The coming into being of the European Union itself, and Britain's entry into it, have knocked away another central plank of British identity. No longer, or at least with nothing of the same force, can Europe or any part of it play its historic role of 'the Other'.

These and similar developments may seem liberating to the non-English parts of the United Kingdom, or at least those among them who have chafed at the ties that bind, and especially at what they have seen as the oppressive force of English predominance. But England – may it not also feel liberated? May it not think it might be better off without 'the Celtic fringe', much of which it feels it has subsidized with hardworking English taxpayers' money? If small nations like Scotland (population 5 million) or Wales (3 million) think they can go it alone, there should surely be less problem for the English, whose population of 50 million makes up 85 per cent of the UK's total, and who own the greater part of the resources of the kingdom (Rose 1982: 30; Davies 1999: 958).

And yet, with some important exceptions, the situation has not been seen like that. The English have not on the whole rejoiced at the possible departure of their erstwhile British brethren. They have not sought to grasp the opportunity to go it alone, unshackled by links to troublesome and resentful nationalists. For them, rather, these developments are threatening. They are the source of a profound crisis of identity. For they reverse the very things by which the English have built up a sense of themselves over the centuries. It was by creating and maintaining the 'inner empire' of Great Britain that the English secured their position and established their dominance in the British Isles. It was in the expansion of their overseas empire that they saw themselves, like the Romans of old, renewing the civilizing mission in the world. Protestantism fortified them in that sense, and allowed them to join with other Protestant nations in the struggle against the reactionary forces of continental Catholicism and absolutism.

All of these things provided the English with an identity – what I have called in this book a missionary or imperial identity – that not so much suppressed as made it unnecessary to ask searching questions about the English themselves, their particular history, culture and traditions. England was – or at least so it saw itself – too big for these merely ethnic or narrowly national questions. Great Britain and 'Greater Britain' were causes nobler and more demanding by far than the establishment of a conventional 'nation-state'. What happens when these causes exist no longer? How do the English then see themselves? The walls that encircled the vacant space of Englishness have, one by one, crumbled. The English have been forced to ask themselves the kinds of questions that other nations have engaged in for a long time. Not surprisingly, not having a tradition of inquiry of this kind, they have found it difficult to find satisfying answers.

Nevertheless the striking thing is that nationalism has finally caught up with the English. It has done so because the things that held it at bay are no more. In the late nineteenth-century 'moment of Englishness', the empire and Great Britain were still going concerns, apparently set for an indefinite future. Now one has gone and the other may be going. For the first time ever the English have had to turn the mirror directly to themselves, to see who they are and where they may be going.

The evidence for this is clear to anyone who has been in England during the 1990s and the early years of the new millennium, whether as native resident, interested observer or casual visitor. There has been a massive and unprecedented inquiry into the national soul. It has taken the form of grand historical inquiries, such as Linda Colley's *Britons* (1992/94), Adrian Hastings's *The Construction of Nationhood* (1997), Raphael Samuel's multivolume *Theatres of Memory* (1994, 1999a) and Norman Davies's *The Isles* (1999). The works of these and other historians, such as Jonathan Clark (e.g., 2000b), have – in a way perhaps common in France or Germany but decidedly uncommon hitherto in England – been the subject of newspaper editorials (e.g., *The Times* 1997) and fierce debate in the commentary and correspondence columns of newspapers and magazines (e.g., Davies 1998; Harvie 1999). There have been articles galore on Englishness and Britishness in the newspapers and magazines (e.g., Wright 1994, 1996; Barker, 1997; Worsthorne 1999a). For the benefit of both its home and overseas readers, the *Economist* brought out a special edition entitled 'Undoing Britain?' (1999); a well-known British journalist living in America did not need the question mark as he assured his American readers in a prominent magazine that 'the abolition of Britain' was real (though 'there'll always be an England') (Sullivan 1999). The constitutional changes heralded by devolution received arresting treatment in Anthony Barnett's *This Time: Our Constitutional Revolution* (1997). Television weighed in with major series such as Simon Schama's *A History of Britain* (2000–01) and Andrew Marr's *The Day Britain Died* (2000). The possible contribution of black and Asian British to the redefinition of national identities also received considerable attention, notably in Yasmin Alibhai-Brown's *Who Do We Think We Are?* (2000/01) and the Report of the Runnymede Trust on *The Future of Multi-Ethnic Britain* (the Parekh Report) (Runnymede Trust 2000).

As in the past, commentators often treated 'English' and 'British' together. In many cases this was now deliberate, a recognition that the distinction was especially problematic for the English and that there was now an urgent need to acknowledge it. But it was also striking how many of the inquiries were specifically directed to questions of England and Englishness. The magazine *New Statesman and Society* devoted a whole special issue to 'England, Whose England?' (*New Statesman* 1995). Channel 4 television sent journalists Peregrine Worsthorne (white) and Darcus Howe (black) on their personal odysseys in search of Englishness. The same Worsthorne debated Englishness with another black journalist, Trevor Phillips, in *Prospect* magazine (Phillips and Worsthorne 1996). Jeremey Paxman's urbane inquiry *The English* (1999) became a best-seller, and there was also a lively response to Simon Heffer's combative *Nor Shall My Sword: The Reinvention of England* (1999). Accusing the English of narrowness and timidity in the face of the promise of Europe, Stephen Haseler stirred things up with his *The English Tribe* (1996). A similar charge featured in Edwin Jones's *The English Nation: The Great Myth* (2000) which, unusually for a scholarly work on historiography and thanks partly to some adroit promotion by the like-minded Norman Davies, received considerable public attention. England received satirical scrutiny in Julian Barnes's novel *England, England* (1999), while his fellow novelist Peter Vansittart preferred the reflective essay in his affectionate portrait, *In Memory of England* (1998), and the broadcaster Michael Wood eloquently interrogated landscape and history in his voyage of discovery, *In Search of England* (2000). A marked feature of much of this literature of Englishness were the frequent references to George Orwell's classic work of 1941, *The Lion and the Unicorn*, whose best-known first part, 'England your England', was described by Andrew Marr as 'perhaps the greatest, and certainly the most influential modern essay on identity' (Marr 2000: 9).

This recital can of course be no more than suggestive. It relates mainly to the thoughts and activities of what are unkindly called 'the chattering classes', the intellectuals, politicians, journalists and broadcasters who attempt to form 'public opinion'. What the vast mass of people feel about questions of national identity is, as usual, difficult to tap (partly because national identity is not on the minds of most people for most of the time). But there are distinct signs even here. The rise in national self-awareness – English, Scottish, Welsh – is clear from all the polls, even if it is unevenly distributed across the nations (McCrone et al. 1998; Marr 2000: x; McCrone 2001). The appearance of the cross of St George, replacing the Union Jack as the emblem of the English, at international football matches and other sporting events has been noted by all observers (e.g., Paxman 1999: 21; Marr 2000: 88; Pines 2001: 57) – a victory at least for logic, whatever else it might tell us about English nationalism. At a more complex level, it has been argued that a new 'English imaginary', as shown in areas such as fashion, pop art and pop music, is being elaborated, reflecting the rise of a new type of (hybrid) English identity (Davey 1999).

Popular consciousness calls for a different kind of inquiry from that attempted in this book. In all parts of the world, national identity historically has been a matter for scholars, intellectuals, artists and statesmen, who in their different ways have sought to shape it. Today, too, what is taking place in Britain is largely a debate among these groups. But that should not lead us to deprecate it. Intellectual and political discourse matters. It is not just some affair of the 'superstructure', of ideological posturing. It leads to visions and definitions which may be all we have when we need them – in a time of conflict or crisis, for instance (this was as clear in America after the attacks on New York and Washington DC on 11 September 2001 as it was, say, in Britain during the Second World War). National identity may be 'invented' – like everything else social – but if so it puts great power in the hands of those who do the inventing. If English identity is being vigorously debated today by intellectuals and politicians, this not only tells us that, to an unprecedented degree, it has been put on the public agenda, but it is also likely to influence the outcome. English identity will to some extent be shaped by the variable success of different groups in the debate.

Oversimplifying grotesquely, we can say that there are three main positions which are being argued, three strategies which are being urged on the English in this time of doubt and uncertainty. The first is to rally around Britishness – but Britishness of a new kind. This is the strategy being pursued by 'New Labour' under the leadership of Tony Blair, also by many artists and intellectuals on the left and in the liberal camp (Driver and Martell 2001). Britain, they all agree, cannot continue in the old way. The national aspirations of the Scots, Welsh and Northern Irish have to be respected and accepted. Hence devolution. So too must the claims of the 'new British', the people of Afro-Caribbean and Asian descent. Hence 'multiculturalism', in some form. The English too are not forgotten – they too must be allowed to express their own identity. Hence the restoration of the institution of the mayoralty to the English capital, London, the possibility of English regional councils or assemblies, and talk even of a separate English Parliament, on the model of the Scottish one. The proposal for a 'Council of the Isles', enshrined in the Belfast Agreement of 1998, suggests one far-reaching constitutional innovation whereby all national groups – including Channel Islanders and Manxmen and new immigrant groups if they so choose to define themselves – might find a place in a new Britain, indeed in something that goes beyond Britain in that the Council is to include representatives from the Republic of Ireland (Nairn 2001: 60–1).

Above all, the new Britain must be modern. It must shed its old primness and pomposity, its insularity and xenophobia. It must be outward-looking, open to new influences at home and those coming from abroad, from Europe and the world at large. 'New Labour', said the Labour chancellor of the exchequer Gordon Brown and one of the most vigorous campaigners for the new Britain, 'reflects the enduring traditions of Britain and the need to modernise our institutions'. He continued, in a magazine interview:

In the 1980s a very narrow view of Britishness was popularised by Margaret Thatcher, a Britain built on self-interested individualism, mistrust of foreigners and an unchanging constitution. I believe this was based on a misreading of our past. Our history shows Britain to be outward-looking and open. It is not true that British history is defined by mistrust of foreigners. The past shows Britain to have been internationalist and engaged.

(Richards 1999: 18)

Brown is Scottish by birth, and says he feels both Scottish and British. He shows – unlike some of his ministerial colleagues – little enthusiasm for an English Parliament or English regional assemblies. 'There are Yorkshire men and women, Cornish men and women, who are also British.' He is even cautious, again unlike many of his Labour colleagues, about defining himself as a 'European', though he does not see a conflict between Britishness and Europeanness. But he is passionate about what he calls the 'Great British Society', and what it can stand for in the future:

I see Britain as being the first country in the world that can be a multicultural, multi-ethnic and multinational state. America, at its best, is a multicultural and multi-ethnic society, but America does not have nationalities within identifiable political units in the way that Britain does. We have a chance to forge a unique pluralist democracy where diversity becomes a source of strength.

(Richards 1999: 19; see also Brown 1999; 2000; Marr 2000: 15)

Somewhat unwisely, New Labour sought to promote its vision of the new Britain under the adman's slogan, 'Cool Britannia'. Britain was to be hip, cool, youth-oriented, innovative and entrepreneurial – hyper-modern if not actually post-modern. The campaign drew upon the resources of the British Council and the British Tourist Authority as well as the Department of Trade and Industry and the No. 10 Policy Unit. Think-tanks such as Demos provided much of the background thinking. The aim, in the words of Demos author Mark Leonard, was to portray Britain as an 'outward-looking, diverse, creative hub in an increasingly open, global economy . . . Renewing Britain's identity . . . means galvanising excitement around Britain's core values – as a democratic and free society in an interconnected world, finding a better way of linking pride in the past with confidence in the future . . . Far from being unchanged or closed off, Britain is a country at ease with change, a place of coming and going, of import and export, of quickness and lightness . . . it is a peculiarly creative nation' (Leonard 1997: 17, 19; see also Dodd 1995; Smith 1998; Lloyd 1998; Edmunds and Turner 2001: 85; Driver and Martell 2001: 462).

Predictably, and perhaps rightly, such an exercise in image-building was widely mocked (see, e.g., Paxman 1999: 239–40; Marr 2000: 217).[10] But the intention was serious, and the goal – of a tolerant, humane, diverse Britain – as good as anything on offer. One problem noted by several commentators was the difficulty of fitting England into the picture of the new Britain. As long ago as 1982 Richard Rose had pointed to what he called the problem of 'asymmetrical commitment': the fact that while the Scots, Welsh and Irish were well aware that they belonged to a multinational state, and made a conscious commitment of loyalty to the Union, the English and most of their representatives at Westminster were 'indifferent Unionists', unthinkingly taking the Union for granted and lacking any emotional commitment to it. Rose noted that not only were the English people not consulted on the devolution proposals of the late 1970s – unlike Wales and Scotland, there was no referendum in England – they appeared singularly lacking in interest in them and made no protest at their exclusion. Had devolution gone into effect and the British state changed in character, the English would of course have been affected along with everybody else in the United Kingdom. But they did not seem to notice that (Rose 1982: 214–23).

Radical devolution has now taken place and the English, though taking a greater interest in the proceedings, have again not been formally consulted in a referendum. The 'question of England', as Tom Nairn says, remains to haunt the settlement. 'Now as then [in the late 1970s], what happens after Britain must depend very largely upon a redefinition of that majority identity – upon the people who, in the famous phrase, "have not spoken yet" or even acknowledged the need to do so as a separate political entity' (2000: 15; see also 84–8; cf. Marr 2000: 104, 226). One Labour politician, at least, is acutely aware of this 'English question', and the need to resolve it if Labour's vision of a new Britain is to be realized. Jack Straw, then Labour home secretary, caused quite a stir at the end of 2000 when he told the broadcaster Gavin Esler in the BBC Radio 4 programme 'Brits':

The English are potentially very aggressive, very violent and of course we have used that propensity to subjugate Ireland, Wales and Scotland and then we used it in Europe and without Empire. You have within the UK three small nations under the cosh of the English. These small nations have inevitably sought expression by a very explicit idea of nationhood. You have this very dominant other nation England, ten times bigger than the others, which is self-confident and therefore has no reason to be explicit about it. I think as we move into this new century people's sense of Englishness will become more articulated, and that's partly because of the mirror that devolution provides us and partly because we're becoming more European.   (Esler 2001: 8–9)

It was more likely the brutal frankness of the utterance, rather than the novelty of the thought, that caused the consternation. Unlike Gordon Brown, Jack Straw is English, very English. He hails from Essex, home of the famously truculent 'Essex man' – Norman Tebbit, equally plain-speaking, also represents the species – and bears the name of a legendary Essex rebel. He was probably therefore better placed than Brown to appreciate the 'English question' – both the need for the English to develop a more definite sense of themselves and their place in Britain, and the long-standing obstacles to such a change.

Another contributor to 'Brits', the cultural historian Sir Roy Strong, also put his finger on the problem when he remarked on the lack of any clear institutional definition of Englishness. The unthinking, unconsciously arrogant English habit of saying 'England' when they mean 'Britain' actually hides from them the fact that there are very few institutions which are clearly English as opposed to British. This is true of Parliament, the monarchy, the law courts, the civil service, the armed forces, the broadcasting system and practically every other important national institution. It is even true of the national anthem – unlike the Welsh, the English, like the Scots, lack their own (Robbins 1995: 170). 'In Scotland and Wales', Sir Roy observed, ' you have the National Museum of Scotland, the National Gallery of Scotland, the National Museum of Wales, the National Gallery of Wales, but there is no National Gallery of England. You see the word English attached to very little' (Esler 2001: 9; see also Robbins 1993d: 268).

There are, as we shall see, emerging efforts to mark out an English identity, one that might enable England to take its place – in Britain or outside it – alongside the other better-defined British nations. But before we consider that, we need to take account of the second main attempt to find a new definition of Englishness. This in fact might be considered a more radical version of Labour's 'New Britain', in that Englishness – as well as Welshness or Scottishness – in any traditional sense is downplayed and there is a vision instead of a Britain of a multiplicity of identities, many of them new or emergent. Fundamentally this vision derives from the experience and thinking of the new black and Asian communities in Britain, many of which now consist predominantly of young blacks and Asians born in Britain. But their place in British society, together with wider developments taking place in Britain and the world, have also stimulated certain native white thinkers to re-think the nature of their own identity and to formulate a view of national identity that departs radically from the traditional one (e.g., Cohen 1993; Davey 1999).

In 2000 the Runnymede Trust – 'an independent think-tank devoted to the cause of promoting racial justice in Britain', as it describes itself – published the report of its Commission on the Future of Multi-Ethnic Britain (Runnymede Trust 2000). Chaired by the eminent British Asian political theorist Bhikhu Parekh – hence known, as hereafter in the text, as the *Parekh Report* – the Commission included some of the most prominent black and Asian intellectuals, researchers and journalists in Britain, such as Stuart Hall, Tariq Modood (as adviser), Yasmin Alibhai-Brown and Trevor Phillips. It also included several well-known white academics, race relations experts and journalists, such as Sally Tomlinson, Bob Hepple, Peter Newsam and Andrew Marr. It was thus in a good position to draw upon not just the thinking but also the large body of empirical research on ethnic minorities conducted by several of its members (e.g., Modood *et al.* 1997; Alibhai-Brown 1999).

In words reminiscent of Labour's vision of the New Britain, the Commission's remit was not simply to examine 'the current state of multi-ethnic Britain' but also to suggest ways of 'making Britain a confident and vibrant multicultural society at ease with its rich diversity' (*Parekh Report*: viii). Individuals, the Report argued, were not to be seen simply as citizens holding individual rights, but also as members of particular communities – religious, ethnic, cultural, regional. 'Britain is both a community of citizens and a community of communities, both a liberal and a multicultural society' (*Parekh Report*: ix). What the Commission found was a disturbingly familiar picture of a Britain in which, especially for many of its black and Asian citizens, both the principles of liberalism and those of multiculturalism remained aspirations rather than realities. The Report detailed a distressing condition of 'racial discrimination, racial disadvantage, a racially oriented moral and political culture, an inadequate philosophy of government, a lack of carefully thought-out and properly integrated administrative structures at various levels of government, and a lack of political will' (*Parekh Report*: x). As if this were not enough, the Report noted a degree of rigidity and conservatism in the black and Asian communities that were also obstacles to the realization of a fully multicultural Britain.

What was to some extent novel about the Commission's approach, and the thing that brought it under fire from several quarters, was its view of national identity and its attempts to go beyond the usual language of 'majority' and 'minority', 'ethnic groups' and 'host culture', 'assimilation' and 'integration' (*Parekh Report*: xxiii–xxiv). All of these terms, it argued, suggested a misleading and illusory fixity and homogeneity of group culture that was as untrue for the 'national' culture of the 'majority' as it was for the 'ethnic' cultures of the 'minorities'. Fluidity and heterogeneity were the characteristics of all sections of British culture, white as well as black and Asian. If we are to recognize the diversity and changeability of immigrant communities, so we must recognize that the majority culture too is constantly evolving. The mutual interaction of older and newer communities changes them both. Far from being resisted, or regarded with regret or alarm, this condition should be seen as an enriching opportunity by both sets of groups. It should be an occasion for celebration, not hand-wringing (*Parekh Report*: 27–35, 103–4; see also Modood and others, 1997: 338, 356–9; Modood and Werbner, 1997).

An especially vexing problem, in the Commission's eyes, was how to relate this strategy to existing concepts of 'Englishness' and 'Britishness'. Past research had shown that while it was common for blacks and Asians to call themselves 'British' – as well as 'black', 'Asian', 'Muslim', etc. – they resisted an identification with 'English' (Eade 1994: 388–9; Modood and others 1997: 291–4; Modood 2001: 77). The Commision agreed that 'the concept of Englishness often seems inappropriate' to Asians, African-Caribbeans and Africans, 'since to be English, as the term is in practice used, is to be white'. But in a bold – and to their critics, extreme – move they rejected Britishness as well, as being also racially tainted:

> Britishness, as much as Englishness, has systematic, largely unspoken, racial connotations. Whiteness nowhere features as an explicit condition of being British, but it is widely understood that Englishness, and therefore by extension Britishness, is racially coded. "There ain't no black in the Union Jack", it has been said. Race is deeply entwined with political culture and with the idea of nation.
>
> (*Parekh Report*: 38; see also Gilroy 1987)

This was too much for the Labour establishment, which promptly repudiated the Report – as indeed in all conscience they had to, given their own commitment to a multiculturalism that was nevertheless unapologetically British.[11] Other critics, writing from a more conservative perspective, more predictably expressed their displeasure at this characterization of Britishness (see, e.g., 'Bagehot' 2000). In truth it is difficult to see precisely what kind of identity – apart from the stipulation that it should be non-racial – the Commission had in mind. Their reference to Paul Gilroy's work, and to that of certain other contemporary thinkers, seemed to suggest that they were contemplating some form of mongrel or hybridized identity, in which individuals draw upon all the elements of their inheritance – African, Indian, British, 'black', 'white', mixed-race – to construct new forms of identity which it is thought will be as liberating for the long-established white British as for the newer citizens of black or Asian descent (see, e.g., Rushdie 1992; Gilroy 1993; Kureishi 1995; Dodd 1995; Baumann 1998).[12] While such a free-wheeling, 'pick-and-mix' attitude to identity is attractive to certain cultural theorists, and certainly has some reality in the popular culture of contemporary Britain (Gates 1997; Davey 1999), it seems an unreal, and perhaps even undesirable, goal for the majority of people in both the old and the new communities. In a curious but not unfamiliar way, it may even lead to a new standardized identity: *all* minorities will be expected to conform to the new hybridized model chosen by certain elements in the youth culture and championed by cultural theorists. This may not appeal, say, to Muslim bankers or Hindu shopkeepers, who may prefer to retain at least in part the traditional identities of their respective 'ethno-religious communities' (Modood 1999: 13).

   The Commission, in its more cautious and carefully worded formulations, seemed to acknowledge the dangers of a too heady, voluntaristic, multiculturalism. Some sense of shared belonging, some notion of a national community, of the kind traditionally provided by the idea of national identity, seemed to be necessary. It put the problem as follows. 'How is a balance to be struck between the need to treat people equally, the need to treat people differently, and the need to maintain shared values and social cohesion?' (*Parekh Report*: 40). 'Proceduralists', liberals, nationalists, pluralists and 'separatists' all had their answers, depending on which part of that trinity they wished to stress. The Commission, seeking to avoid both the extremes of a rights-based, liberal individualism and a closed, conservative corporatism, tentatively advanced a position that was a synthesis of liberal and pluralist views. This rejects the hard and fast line between public and private spheres held to by liberals, but respects their defence of privacy and individual rights. At the same time it qualifies the pure 'community of communities' model it sees as implicit in the pluralist approach, as applied in such multicultural societies as Canada and Australia. This is likely to put too strong a stress on communal rights and customs, which can be oppressive to individuals trapped in traditional and sometimes authoritarian cultures. The goal has to be one that draws on both liberalism and pluralism; it has to be a Britain that is 'both a community of citizens and a community of communities' (*Parekh Report*: 47; cf. Modood 1999: 19).

This is undeniably appealing. The difficulty is the usual one: theoretical formulations have to map on to practical and concrete realities. Here the signs are not propitious. In the summer of 2001, just around the time of the general election, riots broke out in a number of northern English towns, notably Oldham, Bradford and Burnley. The main conflicts were between young whites and young Asians, primarily Pakistanis and Bangladeshis (*Financial Times* 27 June 2001). Observers have noted the rise of a relatively new phenomenon, 'culture racism', where the antagonism is not so much, or not only, that between white and black – 'colour racism' – but more that between groups of different cultures. Events such as 'the Rushdie affair' and the 1991 Gulf War were particularly important in highlighting the new 'culture wars' in Britain (Modood 2001: 75; Saeed and others 1999: 822; Favell 2001: 217–25). In the case of the summer riots of 2001, it was Asian Muslims (not, say, Asian Indians or Asians in general) who felt that the dominant white culture had singled them out for particular hostility. Far from groups interacting, learning from each other, being mutually shaped by each other's influence, we seemed to be in the presence of even greater estrangement and fragmentation than was previously thought.

In the wake of the Oldham and Bradford riots, the new Labour home secretary David Blunkett – successor to Jack Straw – commissioned an inquiry. Like the Runnymede Commission, the authors of the new report were dismayed by what they found, but the note was distinctly more disquieting and less hopeful. Britain, the report said, was a deeply divided country. Whites and ethnic minorities lead separate lives with no social and cultural contact and no sense of belonging to the same community:

Whilst the physical segregation of housing estates and inner-city areas came as no surprise, the team was particularly struck by the depth of polarization of our towns and cities, and the extent to which these physical divisions were compounded by so many other aspects of our daily lives. Many communities operate on the basis of a series of parallel lives. These lives often do not seem to touch at any point, let alone overlap and promote any meaningful interchanges . . . Segregation, albeit self-segregation, is an unacceptable basis for a harmonious community and it will lead to more serious problems if it is not tackled . . . [It is] essential to agree some common elements of "nationhood".

(Report, quoted in *New York Times*, 12 December 2001: A3)

Introducing the report, David Blunkett remarked that it showed that 'too many of our towns and cities lack any sense of civic identity or shared values'. While freely admitting the part played by persisting discrimination and disadvantage, Blunkett also put some of the blame for the high degree of segregation on the ethnic communities themselves. They were, he said, too attached to their traditional practices – some of them, like forced marriages and genital mutilation, reprehensible in the eyes of most Britons. Members of the ethnic communities needed to master the English language and adopt 'British norms' (*The Independent* 10 December 2001). In the face of the predictable outcry from some leaders and spokespersons for the ethnic communities, Blunkett stuck to his guns. He agreed with the authors of the Report that it was essential to forge a common Britishness, and that the insistence that people learn to speak English was in their best interest. 'This is not "linguistic colonialism"', he protested. 'This is not cultural conformity. There is no contradiction between retaining a distinct cultural identity and identifying with Britain' (*The Independent* 12 December 2001).

'No group, no community', declared the *Parekh Report*, 'owns Britain. It is no one's sole possession' (*Parekh Report*: 105). Hanif Kureishi similarly urges the white British to acknowledge that diversity and differentiation are now the hallmark of the national culture, and that they must not live off the kinds of myths of a unified 'British character' advanced by Orwell and his like-minded successors. 'It is the British, the white British, who have to learn that being British isn't what it was . . . There must be a fresh way of seeing Britain: a new way of being British' (quoted Lee 1995: 77; see also Paul 1997: 190; Modood and others 1997: 359; Davies 1999: 979–86). But, as Bernard Sharratt notes, this too may be too narrow, overprivileging the perspective of non-white groups and 'side-stepping the problem that the several varieties of non-white British may also have to extend their own notion of "British" to include a larger complexity' (2001: 306). There are, for instance, over 2 million Irish in Britain, making them easily the largest community of foreign origin. The black and Asian population is at most 7 per cent, perhaps as little as 5 per cent, of the total British population (*Parekh Report*: 104; see also 372). One has to compare this, in any realistic assessment of cultural impact, with the 25 per cent of the American population that is either black or Hispanic. In arguing that the black and Asian communities in Britain have the potential to transform British identity, we need to bear in mind the relative proportions of the populations concerned, and their markedly unequal distribution in the country as a whole (*Parekh Report*: 374). There has, so far, undoubtedly been a significant impact on food, youth styles and popular culture generally, especially in London and some of the larger cities; cinema, television, theatre and literature have also been increasingly influenced; but, as Yasmin Alibhai-Brown (2001) laments in her anguished and angry survey, large sections of British society remain relatively untouched.

There is, moreover, the cardinal question of what will unite the different groups, white and non-white, in Britain in a common Britishness. Even those, such as Bhikhu Parekh, who most wish to stress the multicultural character of Britain, warn of the need for an integrative and unifying identity. 'If a plural society is to hold together, it clearly needs a shared self-understanding, a conception of what it is and stands for, a national identity' (in Alibhai-Brown 2001: 273; see also Miller 1995b: 130–40, 174 n.29). Yet all studies emphasize not just the heterogeneity of the non-white groups but their clear and continuing attachments to their cultures of origin (Eade 1994; Acland and Siriwardena 1995; Modood *et al*. 1997: 328–38, 354–6; 1999: 5; Saeed *et al*. 1999: 831). They wish, at best, to be hyphenated Britons – and, in the case of a significant proportion of British-born African-Carribeans and Asians, even hyphenated Britishness is rejected in favour of a strong ethnic assertiveness (Modood *et al*. 1997: 329; 2001: 74). Taken with the evidence of a new 'cultural racism', of antagonisms between immigrant communities, and of isolation and segregation between them and white communities, this does not bode well for a common Britishness. If traditional British identities are to be significantly changed, if at the same time a new national identity is to emerge, there will have to be a far greater interpenetration and mutual influencing of groups than so far seems to have occurred. With Scots and Welsh also asserting their own distinctiveness, the main feature of the 'new Britain' of both Labour Party hopes and cultural theorists' aspirations would appear to be not so much unity-in-diversity as separation and fragmentation. The only people holding on desperately to a British identity seem to be the Protestants of Northern Ireland – technically not British at all, and the ones the mainland British themselves wish to be rid of.

Interestingly, while blacks and Asians appear increasingly disenchanted with Britishness, there is some evidence that they are prepared to identify with their fellow citizens in the respective parts of Britain as 'Scottish Pakistani', 'Welsh Muslim' and even 'Black English'.[13] Afro-Caribbeans, Pakistani Muslims and certain other ethnic minorities are, it is argued, like the Scots, Welsh and English in a 'post-British' phase of identity-formation (Saeed and others 1999: 835; see also Jacobson 1997; *Parekh Report*: 8; Pines 2001: 58). These findings are particularly relevant to England, since this is where nearly 98 per cent of all black and South Asian people live (*Parekh Report*: 373). Indeed one correspondent to the Runnymede Trust's Commission forcefully drew the Commission's attention to the fact that what was at stake was not so much the future of a multiethnic and multicultural Britain as that of a multicultural *England*:

> In the current climate [he wrote] . . . any failure to identify a positive multicultural English identity . . . will be an historic opportunity missed. More cheap shots about the conflation of England and Britain simply will not do as a means of avoiding the question of a separate civic identity for people living in England . . . The key issue is not fundamentally one of British identity. It is one of English identity and how previous conceptions of English identity have excluded so many people who live in and richly contribute to English society.   (quoted in *Parekh Report*: 8)

This does indeed seem to get to the heart of the matter – at least our matter, the question of English identity. If Britishness seems an increasingly unavailable or unattractive option for many non-English British, both white and black, where does this leave the English – the 'secret people', 'the people of England, that never have spoken yet', as G. K. Chesterton famously put it in his poem, 'The Secret People' (1915)? Englishness has for centuries slumbered unconsciously, and uncaringly, in the arms of Britishness (or the other way round, for all the English have cared). What happens when this shelter disappears? Can an English identity be excavated, or invented? 'Never before', says Jeremy Paxman, 'have the English had to think about what it really means to be English' (in Saeed and others 1999: 823; see also Paxman 1999: 1–23; Marr 2000: 84). In trying to do so now, what resources and traditions exist to help them in the task? It is here that the historical legacy proves most critical. It is here that English history catches up with itself, and shows the predicament in which it has landed the English.

English nationalism

During the soccer World Cup in 1998 observers were somewhat startled to find not only, as had already been noticed on several previous occasions, that the Cross of St George had replaced the Union Jack as the emblem of English national identity. They were also taken aback by the unexpected sight of many black and Asian fans, along with their white counterparts, adopting the St George's Cross. 'It was not uncommon to see . . . England fans from different ethnicities and cultural backgrounds with the red (or, alternatively, blue) cross painted across their faces and displaying the English flag with a degree of enthusiasm that often looked like good old-fashioned English patriotism' (Pines 2001: 58; see also Weight 1999).

Such a show of ethnic unity, not to say comity, in celebration of a common Englishness was as short lived as it was unexpected. By the time of Euro 2000 – the finals of the European football championship – the English flag was not available as an emblem of 'multicultural inclusiveness'. It had become powerfully associated with English racism, football hooliganism, violence and xenophobia (Pines 2001: 59). For a black or Asian fan to drape himself in it had become almost as unthinkable as wrapping himself in the Union Jack – the flag which earlier had been appropriated by far right racist groups such as the National Front and the British National Party. If non-white English groups had thought of replacing a declining Britishness with a local and more vibrant Englishness, this route seemed to be closed off almost as quickly as it had opened up. A multicultural England seemed as difficult of attainment as a multicultural Britain – more so, indeed, as the cultures to be integrated lacked the historic attachments to England enjoyed by Scots, Welsh and Irish while at the same time being in closer proximity to the dominant English culture.

'My name is Karim Amir, and I am an Englishman born and bred, almost.' So, ambiguously, begins Hanif Kureishi's novel, *The Buddha of Suburbia* (1990: 3). No doubt English culture will eventually be changed by the likes of his resourceful hero, as by people like Kureishi himself, a successful and influential writer and intellectual. But for the moment what one has to note is the resistance within English culture and society to such innovations, the difficulties that the English are finding in giving any account of themselves except such as they can dredge up from the past. There has never before been a time when some coherent account of English national identity was more needed. Equally there has never before been a time when the lack of a tradition of reflection on such identity has more glaringly revealed its consequences.

That has not stopped some politicians from seizing the moment. Just as the Labour Party has pinned a vision of New Britain to its masthead, so the Conservative Party has increasingly come to portray itself as 'the English party'. That neither slogan carries much conviction is not the issue. For the Conservatives it has become almost a matter of necessity, of what they need to do to survive. Ironically, the party that since Gladstone's attempt at Home Rule has called itself the Conservative and Unionist Party, is now faced with a future as an almost exclusively English party (cf. Marquand 1995: 289).

The shrinking of Conservative support to a narrow English base, as Liberals and Labour took Wales and Scotland, was becoming apparent as early as the beginning of the twentieth century (Cunningham 1986: 293). But in the middle decades the Conservatives rallied, especially in Scotland, and in the general election of 1955 the Conservatives took over 50 per cent of the Scottish vote – an achievement that Labour has never matched. Things went steadily downhill after that – by 1979 the Conservatives had less than a third of Welsh and Scottish votes (Rose and McAllister 1982: 92). It was the Thatcher years however that delivered the *coup de grâce*. It was she who made the Scots and Welsh feel that 'Britain' might no longer be a viable enterprise. Thatcher might speak about putting the 'Great' back in Great Britain, but her administration, and that of her successor John Major, massively undermined the principal remaining props of Britishness: the National Health Service, state education, trade unionism, British Rail, the Post Office, the BBC and the nationalized industries:

Of the 42 notable privatisations carried out by the Thatcher and Major administrations, 14 were of leading groups with the word "British" in their title, four had "National" and others, such as Rolls-Royce, Jaguar, Rover Group and the nuclear power industry, had mattered to the country's sense of itself... Because "British" was so associated after 1945 with the power and achievements of the state... the retreat of the state has also meant a retreat of Britishness. Indeed there is a case for saying that Margaret Thatcher, by privatising, deregulating and demolishing much of the old state apparatus, helped to undermine key aspects of British identity.
(Marr 2000: 30–1; see also Preston 1994: 193; Lynch 1999; McCrone 2001: 106; Osmond 2001: 113–17)

It was the Scots and Welsh, more than the English, who had the deepest attachment to the British welfare state and the nationalized economy, in the creation of which, from Lloyd George to Aneurin Bevan, many of them had played a key role. They now witnessed the systematic demolition of these structures during the eighteen years of Tory rule. Nothing could have been better calculated to turn the Scots and Welsh against the Conservatives and to boost the prospects of Scottish and Welsh nationalism. In successive elections – 1983, 1987, 1992 – the Conservative vote shrank to around a quarter in Scotland and Wales. In the 1997 general election, when Labour was returned, the Conservatives were wiped out in Scotland and Wales, gaining not a single seat. In the 2001 elections the rout was almost exactly repeated, though the Conservatives managed to regain one seat – Galloway – in the extreme south-west of Scotland (Bogdanor 2001: 194–5, 213, 234; Osmond 2001: 114; *The Independent* 9 June 2001).

The English, like the Scots and Welsh, do at least now have their own nationalist party. It is not any of the far right parties, such as the National Front or the British National Party. These groups are racist, not nationalist; they do not stand for an independent England and the break-up of Britain (Rose 1982: 29). It is the Conservative Party which, *faute de mieux*, finds itself holding the banner of English nationalism. It is a hard thing to accept for a party which has always staunchly defined itself as Unionist. Conservative rhetoric finds itself moving uneasily between boosting Britain – mainly in relation to Europe and the rest of the world – and in championing England against the claims of the Scots and Welsh. Thus William Hague, the former Conservative Party leader, can be found in the wake of devolution calling for an English Assembly to match those of Scotland and Wales; or, at the very least, restricting votes on English matters in the House of Commons to English MPs (*The Guardian* 12 October 1998; *The Times* 16 July 1999). Faced with a second thrashing in Scotland and Wales, and the suspicions of the immigrant communities that the Conservatives were the party of southern whites, the same Hague before the 2001 general election went out of his way to portray the Conservatives as a 'One Nation' party, 'which means that we will govern for all the people of Britain', Scots and Welsh as well as English, blacks and Asians as well as whites. At the same time he appealed to the common Britishness of the 'many decent, patriotic people' who shared his concern 'about preserving self-government' in the face of the European Union (*The Times* 2 June 2001).

It is a difficult balancing act, and it has led Conservative politicians and right-wing thinkers to hit out in all directions. On the one hand, there are those who wish to affirm the traditional Conservative attachment to Great Britain (even if, with the loss of empire, some of the traditional Tory fervour has abated). In their view it is Labour, not the Conservatives, who are destroying Britain. John Redmond, the former Conservative secretary of state for Wales, accuses Labour, through their devolution policies, of dismantling the Union and bringing about 'the death of Britain' (1999). Peter Hitchens, the right-wing journalist, sees Labour as responsible for the final 'abolition of Britain'. Labour has been executing a 'slow-motion *coup d'état*' through its comprehensive undermining of traditional institutions and its dominance by a 'liberal elite' (2000: 295). In a similar vein, Gordon Betts blames misguided aims of multiculturalism and a supine attitude to the European 'super-state' – both of which he associates predominantly with New Labour – as having lead to an erosion of British sovereignty and the subversion of British national identity: the 'twilight of Britain' (2001).

At the same time, some Conservative politicians and thinkers have entered the fray with what can only be seen as a defiant assertion of English national-ism. There was former cabinet minister Norman Tebbit's famous, or infamous, 'cricket test': when England plays India or the West Indies, whom do the black or Asian British support? Can they ever really be English if their cricketing hearts are set elsewhere? Following this up, a contributor to the bible of crick-eting, *Wisden Cricket Monthly*, wondered whether 'an Asian or negro raised in England will . . . feel exactly the same pride and identification with the place as a white man'. His own view was that 'a coloured England-qualified player' would not play for England with the same commitment as one who was 'unequivocally

English', and might actually undermine the 'team spirit' and 'camaraderie' of the English team (Malik 1996: 34–5; Paul 1997: 188).

For those Conservatives who were uncomfortable with this display of English – being cricket, it could scarcely be British – racism, a solider and more serious platform was provided by those who argued the case for a specifically English national identity, and a specifically English interest around which the party could rally. Writing in the right-wing journal *The Salisbury Review*, Raymond Tong insisted that 'there is no need for the English, whatever their political viewpoint, to be reticent about their nationality. They have, among other things, a long and remarkable history, a magnificent literature, and distinctive institutions expressing their Englishness' (Tong 1994: 14). Tong echoed Fowler's view that 'no Englishman calls himself a Briton without a sneaking sense of the ludicrous'. He noted that the Conservative Party had lost most of its support in 'the Celtic fringe', and would need to depend increasingly on its English majority. It should embrace this opportunity to put itself at the head of an emerging English national consciousness. The English needed to assert themselves, as the Scots and Welsh had; and just as it was likely that the Scots and Welsh would get their own parliaments, so too the English should not be fobbed off with regional assemblies but must demand their own national parliament (in which, without Welsh and Scottish support, it was unlikely that Labour would be able to form a majority) (1994: 17).

Tong's thoughts were strongly echoed by Paul Johnson, former editor of the *New Statesman* turned right-wing ideologue. National feeling depends on a feeling of oppression, he said, and the English, having for long been top nation, had not had to think about their national identity. That was now changing. 'Now that the English are themselves oppressed, for the first time since the Norman Conquest, by Continental bureaucrats and their fifth column and collaborators here – the Vichy regime in Westminster and Whitehall – the sense of Englishness is rising fast' (P. Johnson 1995: 21). Since Johnson was referring to the Conservative government of John Major, it is clear that he did not expect to convert the Conservative Party to English nationalism. Nor indeed would it be right to see claims on behalf of English nationalism solely in party terms. When, stung by the claims of Scottish nationalists and the establishment of a Scottish Parliament, the well-known right-wing journalist Simon Heffer called for 'the reinvention of England as an independent and proud nation' (1999: 3), he was not assuming that the English nation was the property of any political party. Nevertheless he drew pointed attention to the prominence of Scots in Tony Blair's Labour administration (including, of course, Blair himself).

Indeed if any party is to capitalize on the growth of English nationalism – so far still incoherent and relatively low-keyed – it is likely to be the Conservatives (Davies 1999: 1050; Marr 2000: 16).[14] This partly because of all British political parties it is the only one to have any tradition at all of reflecting on questions of national identity. This goes back to Burke and Disraeli, but more proximately it was expressed in the speeches and writings of the Conservative politician Enoch Powell: perhaps the only post-war politician to take questions of national identity seriously (Nairn 1981: 284).

Powell is popularly taken as a racist, and indeed there are a number of statements which seem clearly of this character, as when he says that 'the West Indian or Indian does not, by being born in England, become [ever?] an Englishman' (in Paul 1997: 178). But the general consensus among scholars of his thought is that, as he himself has consistently maintained, he is not so much a racist as an English nationalist (Nairn 1981: 256–90; Goulbourne 1991: 117; Marquand 1993: 212, 218; Fevre and others 1997: 18–19). That is, he believes that there a long-standing national culture which has persisted – unchanged in its essentials – over centuries. This is the culture of the 'old English' that he wishes to preserve against the threat of 'swamping' posed by large-scale immigration, with its non-English ways; by the same token, it is this very antiquity and solidity that make it virtually impossible for any but very small numbers of non-English people to be integrated or assimilated into English culture.

Powell's strength, and the basis of his widespread appeal to many ordinary English people, was his recognition that the imperial game was over, and that England had to find a new identity. But that identity could only be found in the past, in the old England that 'remained unaltered' despite 'the strange fantastic structure' of empire and all the other ventures that England had engaged in over the centuries. 'Our generation is like one which comes home again from years of distant wandering.' Here, in all its resplendent imagery and somewhat old-fashioned language, is how Powell put it in a speech to the Royal Society of St George on St George's Day, 1968:

Herodotus relates how the Athenians, returning to their city after it had been sacked and burned by Xerxes and the Persian army, were astonished to find, alive and flourishing in the midst of the blackened ruins, the sacred olive tree, the native symbol of their country. So we today, at the heart of a vanished empire, amid the fragments of a demolished glory, seem to find, like one of her own oak trees, standing and growing, the sap still rising from her ancient roots to meet the Spring, England herself.   (Powell 1969: 338–9)[15]

Powell, poet and classical scholar, had it in him to become the spokesman of an authentic English nationalism. Instead his obsession with immigrants and immigration drove him to the sidelines of British politics and destroyed his political career. But the legacy was not lost (Rich 1989a: 49–50). Conservative leaders such as Edward Heath may have turned their backs on him, but others such as Margaret Thatcher, John Major and William Hague have exploited what Phillip Lynch (1999) calls 'sub-Powellite' themes. Partly this is the race issue, also played up by other Conservative politicians such as Norman Tebitt. But race was not a concern of Major or Hague. As the Conservative base shrank in Wales and Scotland, as it became increasingly likely that the Northern Ireland problem would be solved by Irish reunification or some all-archipelagic 'Council of the Isles', English nationalism became increasingly the best card to play. When, in the wake of the establishment of the Scottish Parliament, Hague called for 'English votes on English laws' – that is, giving English MPs an exclusive say over English laws and English spending – he announced dramatically that 'the drums of English nationalism are starting to beat'. Referring to the 'sea of red-and-white flags and painted faces' at the 1998 World Cup, Hague argued that 'the signs of an emerging English consciousness' were all around, and that it was right that it should seek a legitimate political outlook. He warned that if 'we try to ignore this English consciousness, or bottle it up', it could take a dangerous or nasty turn (*The Times* 16 July 1999). It was clear that he was offering to make the Conservative Party the legitimate expression of this growing English nationalism.[16]

Once again though we should be careful of seeing English nationalism exclusively in terms of Conservative Party politics, or even of party politics in general. There are many in the Labour Party who are anxious that Labour may be presiding over a crumbling Britishness, and may see itself outflanked by the Conservatives on 'the English question'. In January 1999 Tony Blair revived the Commons 'Committee on the Regions' for English MPs, and a little later his Labour Cabinet colleague Margaret Beckett put forward her own more ambitious plan for a 'Standing Committee [of English MPs] on Regional affairs' – a modestly named affair that nevertheless, as Tom Nairn says, would be a '*de facto* English Parliament, convened on its own for the first time since 1546 (when Wales was formally incorporated)' (2000: 87; see also 270–1). In the same year the left-wing writer Richard Weight announced that 'the past – our past as a United kingdom – is becoming a foreign country'. The English people were feeling increasingly dislocated, increasingly isolated on an island that they had previously regarded as theirs. The flag of St George was everywhere. Anti-Scottish feeling was rising, especially among the young (in the 1998 World Cup, every goal scored against Scotland, whatever the match, was cheered by English supporters). Weight argued that the left should not let English nationalism be hijacked by the Tories. There was a tradition of radical English patriotism that was equally the inheritance of the left. The radical answer to the current English sense of disorientation should be to propose that 'England...become an independent nation-state once again.'

England was the driving force behind the British Empire and, as a result, the English, more than any other inhabitants of these islands, find it hard to discover a post-imperial identity. So they should take the initiative in the dismantling of the Union on which the empire was founded. If the English grasped independence within Europe now, it would be the making of modern England, a chance to rediscover and re-imagine themselves within a progressive framework.   (Weight 1999: 26; cf. Marr 2000: 231–46)[17]

This is a bold proposal; it has yet to receive official endorsement from any organ of the established left. But the race is clearly on. Parties of both the right and the left in England see a future as the vehicle of a burgeoning English nationalism. Symbolic victory may well go to the party that first clearly formulates a proposal for an English Parliament – within the existing United Kingdom, a new federation of the Isles, the European Union, or simply *tout court*. If Scotland secedes from the Union, as many think it will in the near future, that could be the signal for all-out competition for the mantle of 'the English party'. At any rate the important thing is to recognize that, as Andrew Marr says, 'Englishness exists' – now, at least, if not for the 'thousand years' that he credits it with. 'Unless England is recognized and given a new sense of its own security, then all hopes for a liberal, open, democratic and tolerant future are in danger. England cannot be ignored, tied down, balkanised or dissolved' (2000: 230).[18] In a similar vein Tom Nairn had written presciently in his *The Break-Up of Britain* on the need for 'some restoration of English political identity' after the centuries of incorporation in Union and empire. 'The English revolution is the most important element in the general upheaval of British affairs described in this book . . . Upon its character – conservative-nationalist reaction or socialist advance – will depend the future political re-arrangement of the British Isles' (1981: 305). He has seen no reason – apart from some tendency to change the 'socialist' to 'radical' or 'democratic' – to change this verdict in his more recent writings (see Nairn 2000: 15, 85, 128, 177, 215; 2001: 63–5).

England, Britain and Europe

The problem, as all commentators on 'the English question' have acknowledged, is the blankness of the English tradition on just this matter of English national identity. The Welsh, the Scots, the Irish, even the Ulster Protestants, all have something to fall back on, even if a considerable amount of inventiveness has gone into constructing their national cultures and traditions. The English, having for so long resolutely refused to consider themselves as a nation or to define their sense of nationhood, find themselves having to begin from scratch. All nations are, to a degree, invented, but the novelty of England's enterprise in that direction is startling and is bound to make the task especially hard. All that the English can really call upon is the highly selective, partly nostalgic and backward-looking version of 'cultural Englishness' elaborated in the late nineteenth century and continued into the next. This is not as feeble or class-ridden as many people say. It still has considerable appeal to all sections of the English (as the revolt against the banning of fox-hunting and the intense sympathy for the plight of the countryside during the ravages of foot-and-mouth disease vividly showed). But such a cultural definition of Englishness is only one side of the exercise and, in present circumstances, the less important. 'England', Richard Rose once remarked, 'is a state of mind, not a consciously organized political institution' (1982: 29). This did not matter, was indeed a source of strength, in the days when Britain was strong both internally and in the world at large. Neither of those conditions now applies. Now it is precisely a public, institutional definition of Englishness that is required; and it is precisely that that is found to be most lacking (cf. Miller 1995b: 172–3).

The result has been anxiety and bewilderment, amounting sometimes to panic, at least among those whose job it is to think about these things. David Starkey, the historian and public intellectual, bewails that 'England has become a sort of vile antithesis of a nation; we are similar to our neighbours and differ from each other' (*The Times* 20 April 1996). Peregrine Worsthorne, veteran journalist and former editor of the *Sunday Telegraph*, who once saw himself as a passionate British nationalist, now wants to wash his hands of English and British identity altogether. 'I care about my family, my friends, my village, my dogs – even my class – but about Great Britain itself very little' (1999a: 15; see also 1999b). Having Belgian roots he feels he can more easily than most in Britain settle for some kind of European citizenship.

Europe may certainly be one answer to the English predicament. If Scotland and Ireland and – to a lesser extent – Wales can see themselves as independent nations within the European Union, why not England? 'Under the umbrella of the European Union', writes Norman Davies, a "Scotland-in-Europe", a "Wales-in-Europe" and an "England-in- Europe" have every chance of doing as well as an "Ireland-in-Europe"' (1999: 1054). But everyone knows why it will not be so easy for the English (Marquand 1995: 290; Weale 1995). The Scots can recall their 'auld alliance' with France and the time, both before and after the Union of 1707, when Scotland had strong and flourishing relationships with continental Europe. The Irish found in Europe their escape from isolation in the British Isles, and have thrived within the European Union. Ulster might soon join them in this relationship. The English are the ones who, since the eighteenth century at least, have developed the strongest sense of themselves as a people who had not a continental but an imperial, oceanic, destiny. If their allegiances lay anywhere outside Britain, it was to the other English-speaking peoples of the world, especially, in the twentieth century, the United States. A strong tradition, from Dilke and Seeley through Churchill, Gaitskell and Thatcher, has affirmed this. When in 1946 Winston Churchill proposed the formation of 'United States of Europe', he made it clear that Britain itself would not be a member. 'Great Britain is not a part of Europe ... We are with Europe, not of it' (in Black 1994: 236). Margaret Thatcher has reiterated this position, even more emphatically, on numerous occasions, both during and after her time in office (see, e.g. Thatcher 1989; *New York Times* 7 October 1999; 6 October 2000).

T. C. Smout has remarked that, since Scotland managed to preserve a sense of national identity despite being deprived of a state and sovereignty at the time of the Union of 1707, it is able to view membership of the European Union with far greater equanimity than England. Scotland has learned that 'union does not mean that national identity disappears. England, however, has been riven since 1991 [Treaty of Maastsricht] with fears that if Britain surrenders any of her sovereignty to a federal Europe, her identity will go as well; her history has given her no experience of the loss of sovereignty, or of the possibility of survival of identity' (Smout 1994: 112; cf. Marquand 1995: 283). The debate, and promised referendum, over Britain's adoption of the common European currency of the euro, may well show where the English people stand on Europe. Current polls – including one taken on the eve of the day, 1 January 2002, when most countries in the European Union switched to the euro – show the English as deeply divided, for the most part resigned about integration in Europe but not enthusiastic at the prospect (Davies 1999: 1035–6; *New York Times* 9 December 2001).

We should remember that fear of Europe – 'Euro-scepticism' or Europhobia – is not confined to the right of the political spectrum. The current Labour Party may well be friendlier than the Conservatives to the European Union but it was a Labour leader, Hugh Gaitskell, who in a celebrated television interview in 1962 made the ringing declaration that entry into the European Economic Union 'means the end of Britain as an independent nation; we become no more than Texas or California in the United States of Europe. It means the end of a thousand years of history' (in Black 1994: 261). Gaitskell's grasp of history might be no sounder than John Major's, but the sentiment he expressed clearly has resonance among the English people, not least within his own party where there has always been a determined group of 'Little Englanders', mostly to the left of the leadership. No more than the Conservative right does the Labour left wish to abandon British sovereignty, and with it the ability, as they see it, to shape the future more readily in line with their ideologies.

Is Europe the touchstone for the future of Britain? 'Today', says the political scientist Vernon Bogdanor:

the crucial division of post-war British politics lies not so much between Right and Left, but between those who believe that British history since the late eighteenth century, for much of which we have been separated from the Continent, constitutes an aberrant period which ended when India acquired her independence in 1947; or whether, by contrast, the mind-set formed during this period remains fundamental to our understanding of ourselves as a nation. It is far too early to determine who is right, to determine whether Harold Macmillan, Edward Heath and Roy Jenkins have interpreted our historical experience more accurately than Hugh Gaitskell, Enoch Powell and Margaret Thatcher. What is clear is that, as the Continent has moved towards closer integration, so doubts as to whether Britain really belongs with Europe, far from being stilled, have grown in intensity.   (1997: 6)

Partly these doubts are based on a blissful ignorance, on the part of the British public, as to what is really going on in Europe, and what the European project is all about (see, e.g., Siedentop 2001). But 'British' here, as often, hides significant differences within Britain. It is the English – including, for obvious reasons, the black and Asian English – who seem most uncertain about Europe, most unsure whether it is their destiny. For some, such as Norman Davies, it represents a welcome return to the Continent from which England was severed nearly 500 years ago, at the time of the Protestant Reformation. For others, it would mark a sad end to England's special position in the world, as a broker between Europe and the wider Atlantic civilization of the West. Europe – a federal Europe, a Europe of the Regions – may well in the end resolve the current crisis of the British state. This could satisfy, Scottish, Welsh and Irish aspirations. The English are the ones who are most likely to find this a disconcerting and possibly highly divisive and disruptive experience.

But whatever England's future, whether in a federal Britain or a federal Europe or, looking much further ahead, even a global federation, it would be tragic if the English came to see themselves within the terms of a narrow English nationalism. This would be not simply to deny the whole of English history, it would also deprive England of the opportunity of providing a model of an open, expansive and diverse society. England's current difficulties in finding national self-definition are certainly owing to the absence of a tradition of reflection on such questions. But we should also remember its obverse, which is a history of remarkable openness to new peoples, cultures and ideas. The Liberal prime minister Lord Rosebery, himself a Scot, once told a Scottish audience that they should not feel unduly concerned when an Englishman says England when he evidently means Britain. This was understandable, he said, because the very wealth, power and population of England made it feel itself to be Great Britain, with Ireland and Scotland as 'lesser gems in her diadem'. The English presumption was no more than that 'notable self-possession' without which England would not be what it was. 'Rosebery', says J. H. Grainger, 'implied that not only did England accommodate other nations within her Ancient Constitution under skilled and experienced patrician rule, but also, without oppressing or annoying, had the capacity to absorb them within her consciousness...Englishness was not anything officiously mobilized in the island, not in any way a process of conversion' (1986: 52–3).

We might choose to put the matter rather differently from Rosebery these days, and no doubt the Scots, Irish and Welsh (whom Rosebery did not mention) might not be happy with being thought 'lesser gems' in the British crown. But there is an essential and important truth in Rosebery's observation. England has never been a homogeneous society – quite the opposite, as a succession of writers and thinkers from Daniel Defoe onwards have been at pains to point out (Lowenthal 1991: 208). It has absorbed a wide variety of peoples – Celts and Romans, Angles and Saxons, Danes, Scandinavians and Normans, Huguenots and Jews, Irish and Poles, Asians and Africans. It has never insisted on some primal or essential 'Englishness' that all must conform to – hence, as Rosebery put it, the 'more restricted patriotism' of the English as compared with the Scots or the Irish. It has not been introverted and self-absorbed, but has looked outward from itself to the world. England, a world-transforming force with its Industrial Revolution and its global empire, could not be 'just another nation'. 'As a long-sustained venture of character and will in the world, [England] had been such a success that she did not need to question what she was' (Grainger 1986: 53–4).

England has to find its place in a world where its former power and influence are much diminished. It no longer has the luxury of that unreflectiveness that these allowed it. They cannot any more protect it from the need to inquire more closely into its character as a nation, what it stands for and what face it wishes to display to the world. But in doing so the English should not allow themselves to forget what have been the strengths of their tradition of nonchalance towards nationhood and nationalism. Nationalism, especially in its 'ethnic' form, can be an ugly and murderous thing, as the world of the early twenty-first century shows us almost daily. If nations are still the substance of the world, if England too at last needs to see itself as a nation among other nations, it can by example still show the world that nationalism need not mean only narrowness and intolerance. English nationalism, that enigmatic and elusive thing, so long conspicuous by its absence, might newborn show what a truly civic nationalism can look like.

Notes

1 English or British? The question of English national identity

1. The mutual relationship of English and British is a central theme of this book, and so relevant references to the literature occur throughout. But there are helpful overviews of the problem in accounts by Birch (1977, 1989), Rose (1982), Steed (1986), Osmond (1988), Taylor (1991) and Langlands (1999). Susan Condor (1996) nicely explores the psychological consequences for the English of the English/British confusion.

2. We should remember that the same problem applies to 'America' or the USA, which also lacks a single, commonly accepted designation. See the witty discussion in de Grazia (1997), who quotes the lament of the New York Historical Society in 1845: 'Our condition is altogether anomalous. There never before has been a nation, of any consequence in the world, without its own appropriate distinctive name' (1997: 246). It would thus be quite wrong to see the problem as a uniquely English or British one, as many appear to think.

3. Cf. also Christopher Haigh's 'Preface' to the *Cambridge Historical Encyclopaedia of Great Britain and Ireland*, where the stated aim is 'to offer an account of the British past which is less anglo-centric' than in the traditional accounts (Haigh 1990: vii). Oxford had earlier led the way with *The Oxford Illustrated History of Britain* (Morgan 1984), in which Britain figured as prominently in the text as in the title. Many other publishers have now joined Penguin in producing a 'British history' series, e.g., Blackwell's *A History of the Modern British Isles*.

4. Conservative politicians, who appear to see themselves as the guardians of the nation's heritage, have a tendency to put their foot in it in this way. Norman Tebitt in the summer of 1992 described Britain's accession to the European Union's Treaty of Maastricht as an abandonment of '1,000 years of British Parliamentary history' – a statement, as Conrad Russell says, 'which runs at the high striking-rate of one howler every three words' (1993: 3).

5. For the following account I am indebted above all to the four-part gazetteer of the basic geo-political vocabulary of the English language by Tom McArthur (1985). I have also used the *Oxford English Dictionary* (*OED*) and the *Oxford Dictionary of English Etymology*.

274

6. The origin of the conflation or confusion of 'England' and 'Britain' goes back to Anglo-Saxon times (see chapter 5), and has had from the start evident imperial overtones. It continued steadily if intermittently in the succeeding centuries. John Morrill writes that 'the nasty English habit of using the terms English and British interchangeably can . . . readily be found in the historical works published around the turn of the sixteenth century and readers of both Camden's *Britannia* and Milton's *History of Great Britain* would be forgiven for wondering what the significance of the distinction is' (Morrill 1995b: 13).

7. The recent flaunting by the English of the St George's Cross at football matches presumably indicates a rise in specifically English as opposed to British national consciousness – or at least a recognition of the distinction between them.

8. Pocock modestly plays down his own influence, in comparison with 'the works of Conrad Russell, John Morrill, Linda Colley, Rees Davies and Robin Frame'. But he is glad to note that as the result of this work in the twenty years since he entered his plea for 'British history', 'we can now claim "British history" as a field of study well enough established to have both its paradigms and its critics' (Pocock 1995a: 292). David Cannadine is more inclined to attribute much of this success to Pocock's 'two seminal articles [Pocock 1975 and 1982]'; he too notes that 'today, there can scarcely be a historian left in these islands who would still unthinkingly interchange the words England and Britain, who is ignorant of the work done in Irish, Scottish and Welsh history, who pays no heed to connections and contrasts across the Channel, or who fails to recognise that "British history" is something substantively different from "English history" writ larger' (Cannadine 1995b: 22). For examples of the recent historiography employing a 'British' perspective, see the references in Evans (1988); Ellis (1988); R. R. Davies (1988b); Bailyn and Morgan (1991a); Pocock (1995); Cannadine (1995b); Robbins (1998: 345–9); Armitage (1999); Samuel (1999e). Neil Evans (1988: 196) notes the 'disappointing response' from English – though not Welsh and Scottish – historians to Pocock's earlier plea; and both he and Pocock (1995: 202) point out that Cannadine's earlier review and assessment of British history (Cannadine 1987) ignored it altogether. The change has indeed been largely a product of the last ten years. A symbolic marker might well be the conference organized by the Institute of Historical Research in London in 1994, whose theme was 'The Formation of the United Kingdom', and whose participants included many of the practitioners of the new British history (see Grant and Stringer 1995b). For other collections of historicals essays employing the 'British' framework, see R. R. Davies (1988a); Asch (1993a); Ellis and Barber (1995); Bradshaw and Morrill (1996); Brockliss and Eastwood (1997); Bradshaw and Roberts (1998); Connolly (1999); Burgess (1999). The preponderance of work on the early modern period is noticeable, and troubling. It seems to suggest that British history concludes with the Union of 1707, whereas of course that is merely the start.

9. In this connection it is instructive to note how many of the scholars involved in 'British Studies' are either not English or hail from the British peripheries, past and present. Pocock himself is a New Zealander by birth, who teaches in the United States. Michael Hechter, Richard Tompson and Gerald Newman are Americans. Hugh Kearney is a

Liverpudlian of Irish extraction who teaches in America; Richard Rose an American who teaches in Scotland. Linda Colley is a Welshwoman who until recently taught in the United States; Rees Davies and Neil Evans are both Welshmen. Tom Nairn is a Scotsman, Bernard Crick an Englishman living in Scotland. Wherever one looks in the burgeoning field of British Studies one encounters people from the peripheries. This is in one sense a familiar phenomenon: outsiders are always more fascinated by the workings of a culture than the natives themselves. It has been given new impetus by the unsettled political condition of the United Kingdom in the past twenty years – a period that coincides with the rise of British Studies.

2 Nations and nationalism: civic, ethnic and imperial

1. E.g., Hugh Seton-Watson: 'English nationalism never existed, since there was no need for either a doctrine or an independence struggle' (1977: 34). John Breuilly speaks of 'the absence of any distinctive English nationalist ideology' (1993: 87). John Armstrong considers that this denial applies not just to the English but to the whole English-speaking world: 'The plain fact is that a half-century of scholarship in the English-speaking world has tended to treat nationalism as something disturbing, alien, irrational, as contrasted to the healthy "patriotism" of the English and their overseas descendants' (1994: 83). Hugh Cunningham prefers 'patriotism' to nationalism in the English case because 'it is the word the English normally used to describe themselves' (1981: 28 n.1). Hans Kohn notes that for the English nationalism has never had a 'problematic character', and that 'English philosophical thought in the nineteenth century offers relatively little meditation upon nationalism, its theory and implications, compared with Italian, German or Russian thought, where the problem and the problematic character of nationalism occupied a central position' (1940: 91–2).
2. Cf. Bernard Crick: 'Every year some books of merit appear on what it is to be Scottish and Irish (dozens still on de Crevecoeur's vintage question, "what then is this American?"), but only a handful of serious reflections on Englishness, by Englishmen' (1991a: 92). Neil Evans notes the indifference of historians to 'the idea of Englishness', and remarks that 'perhaps there has always been more awareness of English nationalism in the Celtic fringe than in England itself, where the existence of the phenomenon has frequently been denied' (1988: 202). Eric Hobsbawm similarly remarks on 'the neglect, in Britain, of any problems connected with English nationalism – a term which in itself sounds odd to many ears – compared to the attention paid to Scots, Welsh, not to mention Irish nationalism' (1992: 11).
3. See, e.g., Greenfeld (1992, 1996a); Dumont (1994a); Llobera (1994: 151–74); Alter (1994: 8); Schöpflin (1994: 137); Ignatieff (1994: 3–9); Denitch (1996); Schnapper (1998). It is evident that the return of ethnic nationalism to Eastern Europe and the Balkans, especially in the case of Yugoslavia, has been a major stimulus to the renewed popularity of the contrast between civic and ethnic nationhood.
4. It is necessary to point out that since the Second World War Germany has been struggling to throw off, or at least modify, its legacy of an overwhelmingly ethnic

concept of nationhood – a matter that had become the more urgent as a result of massive post-war immigration that created a large pocket – nearly 10 per cent of the population – of resident aliens. But it was only with the coming of a new Social Democratic government to power in 1998 that – with the support of its coalition partners, the Greens – a serious attempt was made to change German citizenship law so that it came closer to a civic concept of nationality. In May 1999 a law was passed making it possible for any child born in Germany who has at least one parent who has lived in the country for eight years to gain automatic citizenship. On these developments, see Joppke (1999: 186–222); *New York Times* 22 May 1999: A3.

5. Some scholars, such as Kedourie (1993: 20–31) and Conor Cruise O'Brien (1988a: 43–4), wish to stress the prerevolutionary origins of the idea of the nation, in the writings of such thinkers as Kant, Herder, Montesquieu and Rousseau. But they too admit that it was the French Revolution that established the *ideology* of nationalism. See also Woolf 1992. Most accounts stress that nationalism first developed as a response of subject nations to the conquering armies of the French – but it was the nationalism of the French Revolution itself that provided the ideological weapons against it. See Kohn (1955: 29); Plamenatz (1973: 25); Llobera (1994: 179).

6. Though no-one sticks too closely to these labels. Irish nationalism, for instance, seems to belong clearly to the 'Eastern', cultural variety, while Russian nationalism, both in the Tsarist and the Communist periods, would – despite popular and some scholarly perceptions – seem to belong more to the 'Western', political kind.

7. For the distinction between nation and ethnic group, see Eriksen (1993: 97–120); see also Calhoun (1993); Connor (1994: 90–117); Miller (1995a: 155–6); Rex (1995: 27); Hastings (1997: 3); Oomen (1997); A. Smith (1998: 170–98); Hechter (2000: 14). Smith qualifies his account by arguing that ethnicity and nationalism are 'co-extensive, if not symbiotic' (1998: 201; see also 1986)). Richard Jenkins (1997: 74–87, 142–63) goes further and sees 'nation' (as well as 'race') as a historically specific facet or manifestation of the more general or universal phenomenon of ethnicity. He comments: 'It is now anthropological common sense to consider ethnicity and nationalism in the same analytical breath' (1997: 11). See also Armstrong (1982), whose impressive account of 'nations before nationalism' does not however distinguish sufficiently clearly between nations and ethnic groups.

8. As Robert Palmer says, ' France was glorious, in the eyes of the Revolutionary patriots, less because it was France than because it was the first nation to recognize certain universal and more than national principles' (1940: 110; see also Breuilly 1993: 91; Viroli 1995: 152; Billig 1995: 87–92). For – as it increasingly appeared to contemporaries outside France – the degeneration of this universalism into particularism, nationalism and French imperialism, see O'Brien (1988a: 36–43); Woolf (1989); Brubaker (1992: 44–48); Hont (1994: 222).

9. It was Jozef Pilsudski, the future leader of another supposedly classic ethnic nation, Poland, who made the similar remark, 'it is the state which makes the nation and not the nation the state' (in Hobsbawm 1992: 45). The view that politics or the state precede ethnicity, and are the basis of it, follows the classic and influential account of Max Weber: 'ethnic membership does not constitute a group; it only facilitates

group formation of any kind, particularly in the political sphere. On the other hand, it is primarily the political community, no matter how artificially organized, that inspires the belief in common ethnicity. This belief tends to persist even after the disintegration of the political community ... All history shows how easily political action can give rise to the belief in blood relationship...' (1978: 389, 393). Poland itself seems a perfect example of this, as it was for Meinecke in suggesting the difficulty of separating political and cultural concepts of the nation.

10. For the general characterization of state and nation in preindustrial empires, see Gellner (1983: 8–18; 1996: 99–105); Kautsky (1997: 72–5, 247–66). On the absence of nationalism specifically in the Roman Empire, see Brunt (1965: 270–84). On empire in general, see Lichtheim (1971); Doyle (1986); Pagden (1995); Motyl (1997, 1999); Lieven (2001).

11. In the sense, that is, of being ethnically heterogeneous. 'Multinational' might more strictly be reserved for those states – 'composite' states such as the United Kingdom, Spain or Canada – where groups claim or aspire to separate nationhood despite being contained within the same state formation. This does not apply to such cases as the United States or Germany despite their ethnic heterogeneity (I owe this distinction to Rogers Brubaker). Yet it is clear that depending on historical circumstances groups can move fairly readily from merely asserting ethnic distinctiveness to claiming full-blooded national identity (and perhaps back again). This seems to be the case, for instance, with the Flemings and Walloons of Belgium, and the Welsh and Cornish in Britain. On ethnic groups as 'potential nations', see Connor (1994: 103).

12. Strictly speaking I should perhaps write 'proto-nationalism' here and elsewhere when I discuss imperial or missionary nationalism. But, apart from the cumbersomeness of the term, I hope the context of use makes plain enough the type of collective identity to which I refer in those cases. It includes commitment, and pride, and a sense of belonging to a particular group endowed with a particular calling in the world. So much it shares with classic nationalism. The difference is that it does not see the nation-state as the exclusive framework for its existence; quite the contrary, its *raison d'être* is found in its role as the leader of a supranational entity with a potentially global reach.

13. One way of expressing this distinction might be to say that in all empires the carrier groups evince 'status closure', in a Weberian sense, but that only in some cases does this closure express itself it ethnic terms. The nineteenth-century Habsburg officer corps, for instance, displayed status closure – based mainly on military background and traditions of service to the monarchy – to a very high degree, but it was at the same time 'multitongued, multiconfessional, [and] supranational', open to all the educated strata of the monarchy's myriad nationalities. See Deak (1990: ix, 8 and *passim*). This distinction is useful, as long as one remembers that the dominant status groups in empires, even when they clearly reflect ethnic factors, are always careful to avoid a stress on ethnicity and are even prepared, on their own terms, to admit other ethnic groups to their circle. Such was the case of the English upper class in relation to the Scottish and Irish gentry in the eighteenth and nineteenth centuries, though the preeminence of the English 'style of life' was evident.

14. For a comparison of the types of missionary nationalism found in the Roman, Ottoman, Habsburg, Russian (Tsarist and Soviet) and British empires, see Kumar (2000).
15. For the reaction to Seeley see Burroughs (1973) and Bayly (1999: 57–59). And compare the disapproving remarks in Bailyn and Morgan (1991a: 1–2) and the disparaging remarks in Mehta (1999: *passim*). The tide though seems to be turning somewhat now. See the appreciation of Seeley as 'the founder of the field of Imperial history' by Wm. Roger Louis (1999: 8), and his recognition as a pioneer of British Studies by Norman Davies (1999: 865–7). David Armitage (2000: 21) sees his originality in the recognition that the study of the English (British) state and the English (British) Empire have to be integrated, and regrets the paucity of attempts to build on this insight. There is an earlier appreciation by the Dutch scholar Blaas (1978: 36–40). The *Expansion of England* remained continuously in print until 1956 (the year of the Suez crisis). It was reprinted in 1971, not by a British but an American publisher, the University of Chicago Press. It is not currently in print.
16. The term had been popularized by Charles Dilke, for very much the same purposes as Seeley wished to use it, in his *Greater Britain* (1868). 'If two small islands are by courtesy styled "Great", America, Australia, India, must form a Greater Britain' (1868: x). Seeley wrote: 'It is true that we in England have never accustomed our imaginations to the thought of Greater Britain. Our politicians, our historians still think of England not of Greater Britain as their country...' (1971: 241). On the use of the concept, and its possible usefulness, see Armitage (1999).

3 When was England?

1. For a list of references to this literature on the various continental European countries, see Kumar (2000: 594, n.3).
2. For a rare appreciation of Toynbee's contribution to British Studies, see N. Davies (1999: 1020). But then Davies is not professionally a historian of Britain.
3. 'As in the five books of Moses [the Pentateuch] Israel had become a people subject to Mosaic law, so in the five books of Bede's work the English became a people subject to the law of catholic Christianity' (Cowdrey 1981: 503, n.7). The *Catholic* purpose of Bede's *History*, the establishment of the hegemony of Latin Christian culture and all it stood for, is stressed throughout Cowdrey's very persuasive account.
4. But see Davis (1971) and Smyth (1995) for sceptical views of Alfred's supposedly nationalist accomplishments.
5. The fact of this disunity at the time of the Norman Conquest is suggested by the long-drawn-out resistance to William's rule. This was not because he was a 'foreign' king – the Danish King Cnut had been equally foreign, yet his rule had been accepted with equanimity. Moreover William's claim to the English throne was as good if not better than Harold Godwinson's (Gardiner and Wenborn 1995: 725; Clanchy 1998: 24). The resistance to his rule makes more sense if we see it as the consequence of William's definitive unification of a kingdom that was up to that time still divided and disunited, still an affair of *de facto* independent and autonomous regions ruled

by powerful families with only notional allegiance to 'England'. William struck at the heart of that condition; hence the violent resistance, especially in the north (A. Williams: 1997: 17, 27–44; see also Clanchy 1998: 26–7).

6. '[T]he fact remains', says Geoffrey Elton, 'that what the Normans took over was an English kingdom peopled by an English nation' (1992: 28). But nowhere does he tell us what he means by a nation, and by virtue of what features the English constituted a nation, rather than simply a state or kingdom. It is, as Gerald Aylmer (1990) rightly insists, the strength and continuity of the English *state*, from a remarkably early time, rather than the distinctiveness of the English as a *people*, that sets England apart from its continental neighbours – and indeed, it appears, from much of the rest of the world (see also Wormald 1997: 319). Susan Reynolds (1985) rightly warns us not to see an actually existing people behind the use of such terms as 'Anglo-Saxon' – this merely expressed the difference between the Saxons in England and their brethren on the Continent – but she seems perfectly happy to take 'the English' at its face value, as expressing the existence of a more or less unified community with 'a sense of solidarity'.

7. One should probably also include here the very popular *Hereward the Wake* (1866) by Charles Kingsley, which also circulated in simplified and abridged versions. Other works, in what seems to have been a veritable renaissance of the theme in Victorian England, include Edward Bulwer-Lytton's *Harold, Last of the Saxon Kings* (1848) and Tennyson's *Harold* (1876) (see Briggs 1985; Simmons 1990). Things are possibly changing now, as a result of a less confident feeling about 'Englishness' and its presumptive origins in Anglo-Saxon times. See the more judicious account of '1066' given by an 'average middle-class subject' in Julian Barnes's novel, *England, England* (1999: 80–2).

8. Macaulay was perhaps right in declaring that 'during the century and a half which followed the Conquest there is, to speak strictly, no English history'. What is more questionable is his further assertion that 'the history of the English nation' began in the thirteenth century (1979: 54).

9. ' "Foreignness" was as much a question of response to being an unwelcome newcomer to the charmed circle as a specific dissatisfaction with his place of origin' (Black 1994: 44).

10. Derek Pearsall rightly remarks that the kind of early fourteenth-century literature discussed in Turville-Petre's book is scant evidence for the growth of English national feeling in this period. The works are evidence 'only of fragmentary, sporadic, regional responses to particular circumstances, not of a wave of English nationalism sweeping the country. These writers are culturally under-capitalised: this is not where great changes will be initiated' (1999: 88–9).

11. For the complexities of the relationship between language and nationalism, see Fishman (1972) and Scaglione (1984). All scholars admit the association; most also stress its insufficiency (e.g., Hobsbawm 1992: 56–8; R. R. Davies 1997: 1–2; Pearsall 1999: 90). The current example of an English-speaking Scotland asserting its national identity against an English-speaking England is as good an example as any.

12. The issue of nationalism in the European middle ages is, like much else about nationalism, a hotly debated one. For a balanced survey of the question see Guenée (1985: ch. 3, esp. 58–62); Stringer (1994a); see also, more argumentatively, A. Smith (1994), R. R. Davies (1994a: 4–13); Johnson (1995a); and Reynolds (1997: 250–331). Tipton (1972) contains a very good collection of earlier views. As so often, much turns on the precise meanings attributed to 'nation', 'nationalism', etc.

4 The first English Empire?

1. For which see Hay (1955–56: 57–60); Ullman (1965); Thorpe (1966: 28–31); Mason (1987b); Johnson (1995b); Turville-Petre (1996: 79–89); R. R. Davies (2000: 39). Clanchy remarks that Geoffrey's *History* was 'the most popular work emanating from medieval Britain and perhaps the most popular of all medieval histories' (1998: 11–12).
2. For Edward's claims, see Hay (1955–56: 59–60); Ullman (1965: 264–8); R. R. Davies (1990: 4; 1995: 1–2); Reynolds (1997: 273). The claims based on Geoffrey were laid out in a letter to pope Boniface VIII in 1301. For the relevant passage in the *History*, see Geoffrey of Monmouth (1966: 75).
3. James the First too, on becoming king of England in 1603 and announcing himself king of 'Great Britain', drew on Geoffrey to support the antiquity of his claim. The Venetian secretary in England, Scaramelli, wrote to his government in 1603, following James's arrival in Berwick on his way to England, that 'it is said that he is disposed to abandon the titles of England and Scotland and to call himself King of Great Britain, and like that famous and ancient King Arthur to embrace under one name the whole circuit of one thousand and seven hundred miles, which includes the United Kingdom now possessed by his Majesty, in that one island' (in Bindoff 1945: 205–6). Despite James's failure to get the English and Scottish peoples to share his enthusiasm for 'Great Britain', there was a considerable irony in this Scottish king, who as an infant had seen his own mother, Mary Queen of Scots, executed by an English queen, drawing upon this revered standby of English kings in the renewed assertion of British unity.
4. Robert Bartlett (1994) has shown that the Norman conquest and colonization of the British Isles was part of a more general, Europe-wide pattern of conquest and colonization, whereby the 'core kingdoms' expanded into their Slavonic, Celtic and Iberian peripheries.
5. Peter Roberts however denies that the Tudors aimed at cultural annihilation of the Welsh. In fact, in some important respects their policies preserved the distinctiveness of Welsh culture. This was above all true of the decision to produce a Bible and a Book of Common Prayer in the Welsh vernacular, both of which appeared (in two parts) in 1567 and 1588. As Roberts says, 'without this official interest and the contribution of the translators, the [Welsh] language would surely not have survived the assimilation of Welsh to English society of which the legislation of "union" was so much a symptom as a cause. Without the vernacular Scriptures, Wales would have gone the way of Ireland, where Catholicism protected separatism at the expense of

the survival of Gaelic as a living tongue' (1972: 66; see also 1998: 19–20; and cf. Hastings 1997: 72–3). Equally important perhaps was the rehabilitation of 'British' history, in which the Welsh could take obvious pride. Tudor kings drew upon the tradition of the early Celtic Church in buttressing their claims to independence from Rome. 'In Wales as in England Protestantism came to be accepted as the final triumph which providence had ordained for a Celtic church whose virtues had been prematurely eclipsed.' The achievement, as Roberts notes, was paradoxical, since 'the Welsh sense of nationality was preserved at the same time, and with much the same argument, as the English national destiny was being expounded in a Protestant ideology naturalized, as it were, in the British tradition' (1972: 69; see also Kidd 1999: 99–122)). Nevertheless, it helped to reconcile the Welsh to their new Anglican culture so that, with the Reformation, the character of Wales was transformed: 'her modern identity was in the first instance both a British and an Anglican one – with all the ambivalence of allegiance which that suggests' (Roberts 1972: 69; see also Jenkins 1995).

6. The three Celtic peoples developed their own common stereotypes of the English, and on occasion tried to make common cause against their old enemy – most notably in the attempt by Edward Bruce, during the Scottish Wars of Independence, to become king of Ireland and unite the Scots and Irish against the English. The failure and short-lived nature of all such attempts betrayed a lack of any real feeling of unity between the peoples. 'In practice Celtic solidarity was ... a chimera' (Frame 1995a: 141; see also 209–12; Jones 1971: 164–5; Duncan 1988: 115).

5 The English nation: parent of nationalism?

1. Froude's essay was first published in 1852. Together with the patriotic fervour aroused by the Crimean War, it inspired Charles Kingsley's *Westward Ho!* (1855), Kingsley's own encomium on England's 'forgotten worthies', the 'Drakes and Hawkinses, Gilberts and Raleighs, Grenvilles and Oxenhams ... to whom [England] owes her commerce, her colonies, her very existence' (1947: 4).

2. As rightly noted in a number of appreciative reviews of her book, whatever their disagreements with Greenfeld. See, for example, Ignatieff (1993: 42); Hechter (1993: 504); Armstrong (1994: 94); Yack (1995: 167–8).

3. For a discussion, with full references to the literature up to 1960, see Hexter (1961b, 1961d). Hexter notes the importance of Pollard as a forerunner (1961d: 71; see also 1961e). As several scholars have pointed out, Geoffrey Elton's 'Tudor revolution in government' is also essentially an up-dating of Pollard's 'new monarchy'.

4. Greenfeld in fact largely makes use of the synthesis of earlier work on the rise of the gentry in such accounts as Stone (1986; 1st edn 1972). There are almost no references in her footnotes to any discussions after the mid-1960s – curiously for a book written in the 1990s.

5. In *Les Six Livres de la République* (1576) Jean Bodin made what is generally held to be the first claim in modern times for the untrammelled sovereignty of the state.

6. The growth of the sovereign territorial state, which undermined the universalism of the medieval world, needs to be distinguished from the growth of the *nation*-state, i.e., the idea of the state whose legitimacy derives from the nation. Cf. Kohn (1940: 70); Kiernan (1965).

7. For the mixture of old and new in Tudor ideas of sovereignty, see Yates (1975); Guy (1988: 132–4); Slavin (1993: 225); Mason (1994b: 169); Robertson (1995b: 9); A. G. R. Smith (1997: 21); Armitage (2000: 35–6). Much turns on the interpretation of the famous declaration in the 1533 Act of Appeals that England is an 'empire'. What the scholars cited argue is that the assertion of 'imperial' sovereignty did not mean that England turned in on itself, but that on the contrary its imperial claims meant that it shared in the general imperial ambitions – in the more conventional sense of outward expansion – of the age. This is shown especially by Tudor policy in relation to Scotland and Ireland, as well as by England's overseas ventures.

8. The mood of triumphant nationalism in Tudor England evoked by Pollard, Greenfeld and others writing in the traditional vein does not stand up to the scrutiny of more recent scholars. Susan Brigden (2001) in a recent account paints a dark picture of the last years of Elizabeth's reign, with the nation troubled by religious schism, internal threats of revolt and dire failures abroad, most notably in Ireland. The ambience of the English court resembled that of Shakespeare's Elsinore in *Hamlet*. 'The mood is of distrust, dissimulation and fear . . . The court was increasingly seen as a place of lies and spies, of "privy whispering", where intrigue and treachery flourished, and where the truth was not to be found' (2001: 364). This is hardly the atmosphere to encourage patriotic pride.

9. Gillian Brennan (1989) gives a quite different account of the effects and the official purposes of having a Bible in the English vernacular. English being the language of 'the common people' – the educated were still expected to read in Latin – it was thought that an English Bible would be an admirable way of instilling obedience and spreading respect for the authority of the crown. For a similar account of the purposes of the Lutheran reformers in Germany, see Gawthrop and Strauss (1984).

10. Patrick Wormald, who has most fully laid out this position, in fact claims that the Tudor idea of the elect nation is a direct inheritance from Bede, deriving from the interest of Tudor churchmen such as Matthew Parker in Bede's writings. 'The idea of England as "an elect nation enjoying God's special favour" was not a Tudor coinage' (1992: 27). For a concurrence with and a restatement of this view, see J. Clark (2000b: 270–1). Such a borrowing does not by itself necessarily undermine the claims of Haller, Greenfeld, Hastings and others, but it does throw doubt on the precise significance to be accorded to the idea of 'election'.

11. Most French historians have been content to wait until the eighteenth century for the invention of nationalism, though there are certainly some who argue strongly for the origins of nationalism – at least French nationalism – in the middle ages. See on this Church (1975: 44–46); Ranum (1975b: 3–4); Stringer 1994a: (23–8); L. Johnson (1995a: 6); Reynolds (1997: 276–89, and *passim*). Beaune (1991) gives an excellent account of 'national ideology' in France under the Capetians of the late middle ages, but stresses that such ideology – strongly monarchical and

state-centred – was very different from the nationalism of the French Revolution – 'a far more real demarcation point in the trajectory of this subject than the beginning of the sixteenth century', as the author herself says (1991: 316).

12. Patrick Collinson, in an examination of the 'prophetic mode' of English Protestant preachers in the Elizabethan and early Stuart period, has shown just how disunifying was the common practice of such preachers to appeal simply to the 'godly' English, the saving remnant among the English that they focused on in their constant analogizing between England and the Old Testament Israelites. If they constructed an English nation, it was a severely divided one, scarcely likely to develop a common sense of national membership:

> The preachers seemed to have known (for it was built into their biblical-prophetical sources) that they would *not* evoke a national response, that God's covenant would be honoured not by the whole nation but only by a remnant, a remnant which might for a time redeem and preserve the nation, but which would also survive the temporal ruin of the nation. For this was the experience in the Bible of Israel and Judah. Therefore such preaching was of necessity divisive . . . It was religiously but also socially divisive, insofar as its pathological rhetoric of moral outrage and alarm discriminated between supposedly godly and allegedly ungodly elements in society. And it was politically divisive, to the extent that the policies and actions of the royal government diverged from the preachers' prophetic imperatives, not only in specific content but in the absence of religious commitment, [in] lukewarmness and compromise . . .
>
> So the prophetic mode, which constructed and ostensibly united the nation in its shared religious relationship with God and moral responsibility before God, was almost designed to split, fragment, and, what was worse, dichotomize it, just as the protestant Reformation itself belied in its divisiveness its uniting affirmations and aspirations. The binary distinction between the better part and the worse part was instinctive to Protestantism, together with the conventional wisdom that the worse part would always constitute the greater part, the better the smaller.   (Collinson 1997: 20–1, 33–4; author's emphasis)

On the religious division and diversity, rather than unity or uniformity, of the Elizabethan age, see Collinson (1982: 189–241); Wrightson (1982: 212–21); Russell (1990a: xxvi); Haigh (1993: 285–95). On Elizabeth's policies towards the English Catholics ('Elizabeth I was soft on Catholics'), see Haigh (1988: 27–46); on English Catholics themselves, and their attempts to remain within the English nation, see Bossy (1965, 1975), Trimble (1964), and Haigh (1993: 251–67; see also 341 for further bibliographical references). Carol Wiener (1971) shows how the very fragmentation and division among the Protestants made them exaggerate the unity and power of the Catholic forces, producing a climate of pessimism in Elizabethan and early Jacobean England rather than the mood of triumphant apocalypticism, deriving from Foxe's Book of Martyrs, suggested by Haller and others.

Virulent anti-popery clearly had a unifying effect among English Protestants, even when the power and purpose of the papacy were misinterpreted and exaggerated. See

Clifton (1973); Lake (1980, 1989). But, as Lake emphasizes, anti-popery as often took on an international dimension – *all* Protestants were menaced by the Papacy and its machinations – as a national one.

13. 'Religion was a sixteenth-century word for nationalism', the historian Sir Lewis Namier is alleged to have said (Breuilly 1993: 50; cf. John Elliott on the 'aggressive religious nationalism' of the sixteenth century: 1992: 59). This is both helpful and misleading. It indicates the possible connections between religion and nationalism in general, but it tends to suggest, wrongly, that the religious conflicts of the sixteenth century were fundamentally nationalist.

14. On the cosmopolitanism of Renaissance humanism, including the English variety, see Kelley (1991: 55–73). There are many studies of the 'scientific revolution' of the seventeenth century which indicate England's relatively late rise to prominence: see, e.g., Butterfield (1957); Hall (1962). On the literary and intellectual struggle between 'Moderns' and 'Ancients' in England, and the victory *early in the eighteenth century* of the Moderns, see Jones (1982); see also Kohn (1940: 77–9).

15. Hans Kohn (1940: 74) remarks that 'it is characteristic that even at the end of the reign of Elizabeth, the greatest English poet in the infinite variety of his human types does not create for us a single English sailor' – and this in the era of Drake and Raleigh, and the naval defeat of the Spanish Armada. For a sceptical view of Shakespeare's nationalism, see also Breuilly (1993: 3–4); Hobsbawm (1992: 75).

    It seems fairly clear that for Shakespeare, 'nation' connoted *ethnicity* rather than nationhood as it generally figures in nationalist beliefs. Thus Shylock says of Antonio's attitude towards the Jews, 'He hates our sacred nation' (*Merchant of Venice*, Act 1, Scene 3); and the Irishman MacMorris asks the Welshman Fluellen, 'What ish my nation?' (*Henry the Fifth*, Act 3, Scene 2). It is interesting that, as appears especially in *Henry the Fifth*, *other* peoples – the Welsh, the Irish and the Scottish – are 'nations', often comic ones, but not the English – presumably because, as the dominant kingdom, they have no need of 'nationality'. See generally on state and nation in Tudor England, Guy (1988: 352–4), who notes a sharpening of the definition of 'Englishness' in the later part of Elizabeth's reign.

16. 'When men . . . spoke of their country', admits Geoffrey Elton, ' they meant their county. Most people's horizons did not in practice extend to the limits of the kingdom: they lived in and for a shire, a borough, a village, a manor; and for most of them the realities of social and political existence occurred within these narrower confines' (1986: 76; cf. Thomas 1978: 49). This was true even of the gentry and aristocracy, for the most part. Nevertheless, insists Elton, there was 'a national stage': 'People were quite capable of thinking of themselves as members of the English nation who also had particular local allegiances and concerns.' However, he continues, ' I agree that those local allegiances and concerns could at times be strong enough to override the attractions of the centre and thus disrupt the outward appearance of one nation conscious of its single nationhood' (1986: 76–7). Such national consciousness, he feels, was fortified by the clearly national institutions of the crown and Parliament. One senses, in this account, a distinct uneasiness about the claims for a national consciousness and an awareness of its precariousness.

6 The making of British identity

1. It is normal in these accounts to argue that only the common people of England were regarded as constituting the true nation: crown, Church, aristocracy and their allies, as at the time of the French Revolution, were seen as alien conquerors and tyrants, betrayers of the nation. Peter Furtado goes so far as to say that 'the Levellers' search for an untainted aboriginal national culture, free from the Norman yoke, seems to presage the forms of nineteenth-century nationalist theory' (1989: 45).

2. It is not only Kohn's language here that strongly recalls Greenfeld's, as discussed in chapter 5. It is the whole cast of the argument, the kind of contemporary sources used, the specific examples and quotations drawn upon. The difference of course is that Greenfeld employs them to argue for a sixteenth-century English nationalism, whereas for Kohn the important themes and sources belong squarely in the seventeenth century – and would, indeed, be unthinkable without the experience of what he chooses to call 'the Puritan Revolution'. But a comparison of the two accounts suggests that Greenfeld was closely guided in her thinking by Kohn's article of 1940 – which she certainly refers to at various points. Kohn's work, she says, 'was most useful as a pointer to primary sources' (1992: 497 n.2). There is even a close correspondence in their thinking about the relation between English and French nationalism. 'It was only a century later', says Kohn in a slightly later account (1944: 183), 'that, under the influence of English ideas, but on a much vaster scale, the French people opened a new chapter in the history of nationalism and of the liberation of the human mind.'

3. On the importance of religion as 'the master-code' of this period, 'the idiom in which the nation conversed with itself', see Shuger (1990: 5–6); Collinson (1997: 17–19). See also Christopher Hill (1993), though Hill continues to regard the biblical rhetoric as a means of addressing concerns that were basically secular.

4. Though the manner in which the proclamation of the sovereignty of the people was made – especially by the Levellers, the prime spokesmen for the doctrine – within the English Civil War itself furnished a further obstacle to the development of English nationalism in this period. See on this Pocock (1957); Skinner (1965); Hill (1986b); Seaberg (1981).

5. See on this Bindoff (1945); Trevor-Roper (1984d: 450–1); Levack (1987: 1–4, 27–28, 224–25).The new style was announced by royal proclamation in 1604; it was not ratified by the English Parliament, and the Scots, though using the new style, showed great resentment at the fact.

6. On this painting and its relation to James's vision of Great Britain, see Levack (1987: 224–5); J. Wormald (1992: 175–6); (1996); Robertson (1995b: 13–14). See also Galloway (1986); Lynch (1994: 132–3); Macinnes (1999); Brown (1999: 248–9), and W. Patterson (2000) for the grandiose nature of James's vision, involving not just the unity of the British kingdoms but the propagation of a British imperial identity abroad. Ultimately James looked to the community of all Christian nations of Europe living in a state of peace and concord.

7. Welsh opinion on this question is usually ignored, though it may well have been a Welshman, Sir William Maurice, who was responsible for actually suggesting – though in no way inventing – the style 'King of Great Britain' to James (Bindoff

1945: 203; Roberts 1996: 139). The Welsh throughout the Tudor period were among the most fervent supporters of a united kingdom, seeing in it some sort of resurrection of the old Arthurian empire of Britain and a rehabilitation of themselves as the direct descendants of the ancient Britons. The accession of James could be seen as a 'pan-Celtic' triumph, even a marginalization of the English, since James derived his title to the English throne through his descent from the Welsh Tudors: 'The triple empire of Britain was restored to British blood through James's descent from Henry VII' (Roberts 1998: 38; see also Jenkins 1998: 228; Macinnes 1999: 34).

8. See Robertson (1987; 1994: 238–46; 1995c); Trevor-Roper (1992: 292–6); Hayton (1995); Goldie (1996); Kidd (1993: 36–41; 1998: 331–4); N. Davies (1999: 681–96); Devine (1999: 3–16); Claydon (1999: 123–4). There was special resentment in Scotland at what was seen as deliberate English frustration of the Scottish attempt, in 1698–1700, to establish a base for an independent Scottish overseas trade – and a Scottish empire – by setting up a colony on the isthmus of Darien (see Armitage 1995a; 2000: 158–62; N. Davies 1999: 662–81).

9. See Bradshaw and Roberts (1998: 6–7); Bradshaw (1998: 94–5); Kiernan (1993: 9). As many people have pointed out, plantation policy in Ireland matched and perhaps was the model for plantation policies in the West Indies and the American colonies (see e.g. Rowse 1957: 315). For some scholars, therefore, sixteenth and seventeenth-century Ireland was England's first true colony – a theme developed especially by Nicholas Canny (Canny 1973, 1988, 1991, 1993; see also Colley 1992: 327; Lieven 1999: 181). We should remember, however, that as John Gillingham has often pointed out (1992, 1993), English colonial attitudes towards Ireland go back to the twelfth and thirteenth centuries, the time of the original invasions; they were not sixteenth-century inventions. For critiques of the treatment of Ireland as a colony, see Bartlett (1990: 14–15); Morgan (1991–92); Connolly (1992); Armitage (2000: 24–5).

10. From the mid-seventeenth to the early eighteenth centuries it was normal for the English Protestants in Ireland to insist on their Englishness, rather than their Britishness. 'British' was a term generally reserved for the Scots of Ulster, though the Anglo-Irish were prepared on occasion to use it when, as in 1688–90, they wished to stress pan-Protestant unity. On what Jim Smyth calls the 'amphibious' quality of the Protestant community in early eighteenth-century Ireland see Smyth (1993: 786–7, 791; 1998: 307–8, 320); Hayton (1987: 151–2); Connolly (1995: 197); Ford (1998: 185); Barnard (1998b: 208); Claydon (1999: 130–1). Later, by the mid-eighteenth century, 'the English in Ireland', or 'the English interest' in Ireland, came to think of themselves as 'Irish' or 'Anglo-Irish', and to see themselves as constituting the 'Irish interest' within a British context (Hayton 1987: 147; Smyth 1993: 787; McBride 1998: 245; Canny 1987: 201 n.78). Generally we should note Colin Kidd's comment that 'the vague sense of a shared Britishness in this period tended to be archipelagic, embracing Ireland, and was not narrowly confined to the nations of mainland Britain' (1998: 334).

11. See Smyth (1993: 789); Canny (1987: 205–6); Leersen (1988: 21); Hill (1995: 290); Connolly (1995: 197); Kidd (1996: 380; 1998: 334–5); McBride (1998: 241–2). As Jonathan Swift put it earlier, in the *Drapier's Letters* (1724) written during the affair

of Wood's Halfpence, 'Am I a freeman in England and do I become a slave in six hours by crossing the [Irish] Channel?' (in Bartlett 1995: 83).

12. We should note that elite Irish Protestant opinion on this question at this time chimed with that of the British state, which had its own reasons for overcoming its traditional anti-Catholicism. 'From the 1760s on, the manpower needs of the British army and navy would be increasingly met by Catholic recruits from Ireland: but the implication here was that such recruitment could be successfully undertaken only if the Catholic Irish were offered concessions in order to induce them to enlist' (Bartlett 1995: 86; see also 1990: 18–19; Bayly 1989: 126–7; Black 1998: 70–1; McBride 1998: 253). The hopes of Grattan and other liberal Irish Protestants were therefore not as unreal as often presented. On the 'more inclusionist' Irish nationalism of the late eighteenth century, 'a corporate Irishness embracing both colonized and colonizer', Catholics as well as Protestants, see Bartlett (1990: 17–180; see also Whelan 1995: 231–8; McBride 1998: 253–60). Joep Leersen has shown that it was Anglo-Irish patriots who were most active in the recovery of Gaelic culture and Gaelic history at the end of the eighteenth century. The Gaelic past which was invoked by the Young Irelanders of mid-nineteenth-century Irish nationalism had been 'familiarized by non-Gaelic cultural historians who could trace their endeavour back to the period of Grattan' (1988: 22, 24; see also 1997a: 315–76; Bartlett 1995: 82; McBride 1998: 247). On the Anglo-Irish patriotic movement as a species of 'colonial nationalism', with the patriots 'firmly' supporting the revolutionary actions of the North American colonies in the 1770s, see Canny (1987: 207–10).

13. Crick thus elaborates further on this distinction: ' "British" is a political and legal term, defining a culture of civil rights and duties, of protection and obligation, but not a culture in the full nationalistic sense of traditions, religions, rituals and customs – everything that Hegel called *sittlichkeit* or Montesquieu called *moeurs* . . . "British" describes the legal institutional framework and the specifically political allegiances that bind together . . . the British state . . . There is no British way of life, only a common political culture' (1995: 173). Jonathan Clark similarly argues that, in the eighteenth and nineteenth centuries, 'a shared British identity was appealed to only in specific contexts and for specific purposes, as a category inclusive of sectional identities, not as an identity which replaced its components' (2000b: 275; see also Robbins 1995: 1–28). We might say that what is at issue here is the extent to which a 'common political culture' – especially when it is underpinned by a common *religious* culture – can become 'a way of life', or at least generate a commitment and a feeling of belonging at least equal in intensity to that which we associate with nationalism.

14. Cf. Keith Brown, who calls the Church of Scotland 'the only truly national institution', 'the most effective institutional vehicle for a national identity', which uniquely involved the lives of ordinary people at every level (1998: 247; see also Patterson 1994: 38). On the importance of the courts and the legal profession in Scottish national self-conceptions, see Brown (1998: 240–2); Levack (1987: 68–101). Brown also emphasizes Scottish pride in their educational system, which had produced 'a level of literacy not surpassed anywhere else in the world', and which was the

springboard for the magnificent Scottish Enlightenment of the eighteenth century (1998: 251).

15. As Eric Richards notes, 'the winds of chauvinism in London were notoriously fickle. Fifteen years later [following the anti-Bute campaign] the Scots were themselves leading popular rampages against Papist chapels in London during the Gordon riots' (1991: 100).

16. Kidd (1996: 373, also 364, 370, 376); see also Kidd (1993, *passim*, esp. 205–15; 1997: 110–11; 1999: 250–1, 279–84); Mitchison (1978); Pocock (1983: 127–8); Phillipson (1987); Bayly (1989: 82–3); J. C. D. Clark (1989: 213); Wagner (1993: 154–7); Pittock (1997: 140–5); Allan (1997: 70–5); Claydon (1999: 118). See also Rebecca Langlands (1999: 59), who, basing herself on Anthony Smith's theories, argues that a 'core English ethnicity' – which had existed 'since at least the early modern period' – 'provided the basis for the state-aided development of the British "nation" during the eighteenth and nineteenth centuries'.

17. Nearly all commentators on Scottish identity agree that, whatever the degree of their Britishness, 'what Scots did not feel themselves to be was English' (Smout 1989: 5; see also, e.g., Janet Smith 1970; Phillipson 1970; Mitchison 1978; Armitage 1997: 49–50; Murdoch 1998: 96–9; Brown 1999: 251; Davis 1999). There can sometimes be some confusion owing to the practice of some Scots of referring, following the common English habit, to Britain as 'England' (Smout 1989: 4–5). But, generally, Scots, like several other peoples in similar situations – Bretons, Catalans – possessed what Anthony Smith calls 'concentric loyalties' (1981: 164), their Scottishness and Britishness overlapping and coexisting. In this respect James Bryce in 1887 made a pointed contrast between the English and the Scots: 'An Englishman has but one patriotism, because England and the United Kingdom are to him practically the same thing. A Scotchman has two, but he is sensible of no opposition between them' (quoted in Colley 1994: 413 n.18).

18. The Britishness of the Enlightenment in Scotland was expressed in its stones and streets as much as its thought. The great monument to this is Edinburgh's New Town, which not only reflects Enlightenment ideals of symmetry and rationality but, in the naming of its streets (George Street, Queen Street, Prince's Street, etc.) self-consciously identifies itself with the new Britain of the Union. 'Here we see Scottishness sublimated into a comprehensive Britishness' (Strong 2000: 471; see also Pittock 1997: 130, 136).

19. Murray Pittock argues that the promise of a joint Protestant-Catholic Irish Britishness continued well into the nineteenth century, and did not end with the famine of the 1840s. 'The Catholic middle class were in fact by the late nineteenth century moving towards British norms (Catholic Unionism is by no means an eccentric tradition)... Although Ireland's "Britishness" was perhaps less developed than Scotland's, and coalesced at a later date, to write Ireland out of Britain is to risk serious misrepresentation of the nature of Britain and its identities, not least the identities of its elites, right into the twentieth century' (1997: 132–3). This is a useful corrective to the Colley inspired view of Britishness as an almost exclusively Protestant identity.

20. It is true that the Dutch, a Protestant people, were for a time in the mid-seventeenth century seen as England's main commercial and imperial rival. But not only did the accession of a Dutch prince (William of Orange) to the English throne, securing the Protestant succession, still much of the anti-Dutch hostility, there was never any fear that, unlike the France of Louis the Fourteenth, the Dutch aimed at 'universal monarchy'. In the War of the Spanish Succession, Dutch and English fought together, as Protestant nations, against the universalist pretensions of the Bourbon monarchy.

21. As acknowledged by several of Colley's critics, e.g., Tony Claydon and Ian McBride (1998b: 3, 25–6, 28); Kidd (1998: 338–9).

22. The event that caused the most turmoil in the land in the middle years of the century was the papal decision in 1850 to divide England into Roman Catholic dioceses and to restore a regular Catholic hierarchy. This provoked a nationwide storm of protest – the biggest since the agitation over parliamentary reform in 1831–32 (Briggs 1965b: 32). Though anti-Catholicism abated considerably as a general force in the later nineteenth century, it remained potent in various parts of the kingdom, especially in those areas, such as Lancashire and the western Lowlands of Scotland, with the largest numbers of Catholic Irish immigrants. As late as 1909, Protestant–Catholic riots in Liverpool could leave one person dead and force 157 Catholic families and 110 Protestant families to flee their homes (McLeod 1999: 55; see also Wolfe 1998: 292); while Scotland in the 1920s and 1930s experienced an outbreak of anti-Catholicism, spearheaded by the Church of Scotland, that has been described as 'the most intense phase of sectarian bitterness in Scotland since the seventeenth century' (Devine 1999: 498; see also Robbins 1993b: 99). For attitudes towards Catholics in the later nineteenth and twentieth centuries see, for England, McLelland and Hodgetts (2000); and for Scotland, Devine (2000).

23. The crown did its part in the making of a unified British ruling class in a number of ways, but one tangible way was in the creation of new honours and orders – for instance, the addition of the (Scottish) Order of the Thistle and the (Irish) Order of St Patrick to the (English) Order of the Bath. In addition, 'there were unprecedented creations of peerages, as Scottish and Irish nobles were given United Kingdom titles' (Cannadine 2001: 21).

24. 'How far', queried Edward Thompson in his review of Colley's *Britons*, 'has she written a thesis on the making of the British ruling class, and how far is she entitled to incorporate the common people into the same thesis' (1993: 378)? It is a fair question. But Thompson himself admits that class and national identities do not always pull against each other (1993: 381–2). In any case, like other Marxist historians he tends to exaggerate the divisive affect of class in this period, and does not take the Gramscian concept of hegemony sufficiently seriously.

25. James Watt at least was highly conscious of his Scottish identity, in later life saying of his steam engine that 'if I merit it some of my countrymen, inspired by the *amor patriae* may say: *Hoc a Scoto factum fuit* [this was made by a Scot]' (Murdoch 1998: 96). But Watt was happy to live and work in Birmingham, doing his most creative work at Matthew Boulton's Soho works. Alexander Murdoch rightly notes that Watt saw no contradiction between his Scottish and British identity: he participated 'in

the new modern construction of Britishness in a way which did not exclude his traditional national identity as a Scot' (1998: 96; see also Colley 1994: 125).

26. For Owen's influence in the early English working-class movement, see Thompson (1964: *passim*, esp. 779–806; Davies 1994: 368); for the popularity among English, as well as Irish, workers of O'Brien and O'Connor, see Gammage ([1894] 1969: 13–17, 71–7). There is a blank spot among certain English writers in acknowledging the key role played by Irish radicals in the early British working-class movement. A starting point for tracing this prejudice might be Engels's notorious account ([1845] 1958: 104–7) of the Irish immigrants to England as 'uncivilised' and 'uncouth', a degrading influence on the respectable English workers who grow up amidst 'Irish filth'.

27. See also, for these activities, MacKenzie (1998: 221–25); and generally on Scottish success in the empire, Richards (1991); MacKenzie (1993: 721–8); Landsman (1994: 259–60, 266–7, 271); Robertson (1994: 224; 1995b: 3), Forsyth (1997); Murdoch (1998: 69–71); Devine (1999: 25–7); Fry (2001). Charles Dilke, in his travels through 'Greater Britain' in 1867–68, was struck by the unusual prominence of Scotsmen everywhere. 'In British settlements, from Canada to Ceylon, from Dunedin to Bombay, for every Englishman that you meet who has worked himself up to wealth from small beginnings without external aid you find ten Scotchmen. It is strange, indeed, that Scotland has not become the popular name for the United Kingdom' (1868: 511).

The Scots may have been the most ardent imperialists, but Irish (both Catholics and Protestants) and Welsh participation in the empire was also vigorous, in trade, missionary activity, colonial administration and the armed forces. See, for Ireland, Jones (1991); Jeffrey (1996); Bartlett (1998: 254–9, 272–4). For Wales, see G. Williams (1985: 156–7, 220–6); Davies (1994: 412–15); MacKenzie (1998: 220). It may be that the impression of lesser Welsh and Irish involvement in the British Empire simply reflects current historiography, which is heavily biased towards the Scottish case.

7 The moment of Englishness

1. See on this, for instance, Nairn (1981: 126–95); Bebbington (1982: 489–90); J. C. D. Clark (1989: 224); Paterson (1994: 46–102); Smout (1994: 101); Kidd (1993: 1–5; 1997: 118–24); Devine (1999: 285–98); Davidson (2000: 112–27).

2. The following is an incomplete listing of the pages where the confusion occurs: 68, 69, 75, *77*, 94, 96, 109, 111, 112, 113, 115, *117*, 118, 119, *135*, 148, 151, 152, *153*, *171*, 172, 175, 188, 196, 197, 203, 221, 230 (with italicized pages for particularly egregious or significant examples). It should also be noted that the frontispiece to the book is a copy of a print of 'Britannia in Distress', with the figures of 'Degenerate Britons' about to bury a trembling Britannia – this in a book on the rise of *English* nationalism!

The British/English confusion is of course pervasive in the literature, but it is particularly serious and misleading in that part of it dealing with the eighteenth century, the time when the new British state came into being. For other examples where it vitiates otherwise valuable accounts, see Breen (1997); Greene (1998); Evans 1994a).

3. What he doesn't do is indicate the distaste with which Wilkes's crude xenophobia was received by many educated Englishman. Samuel Johnson's famous definition of patriotism as 'the last refuge of scoundrels', in the 1775 edition of his *Dictionary*, was a deliberate riposte to Wilkes's rabble-rousing English chauvinism (Cunningham 1981: 12; Colley 1984: 110).

   The use of 'John Bull' (a figure invented in 1712 by a Scot, John Arbuthnot) as a symbol of English nationalism – by Newman as well as many others – is similarly misplaced, especially for the eighteenth century, as Miles Taylor (1992) has decisively shown. See also Hertz (1944: 27 n.1); Surel (1989).

4. The deliberately sustained Britishness of the monarchy (made easier by the fact that there has not been a purely English monarch on the throne since Harold Godwinson in 1066) can be seen simply in the range of titles held by the various 'royals'. Elizabeth the Second is of course 'of the United Kingdom of Great Britain and Northern Ireland and of Her Other Realms and Territories Queen'. Her consort, Philip, is earl of Merioneth, in Wales, and duke of Edinburgh, in Scotland (he also has an English title, as Baron Greenwich, of Greenwich in the county of London). Her eldest son, Charles, is not simply prince of Wales but earl of Chester, duke of Cornwall and Rothesay, earl of Carrick and Baron of Renfrew, lord of the Isles and great steward of Scotland (truly, after the queen, the most British of royals). The queen's second son, Andrew, is Baron Killyleagh (N. Ireland), earl of Inverness (Scotland), and duke of York (England). Various other royals are earl of Ulster (Alexander, eldest son of the duke of Gloucester), and earl of St Andrews (Scotland) and Baron Downpatrick (N. Ireland) (Edward, second duke of Kent). On his marriage to Princess Margaret, Anthony Armstrong-Jones was created earl of Snowdon (Wales). For these titles, see *Debrett's Peerage and Baronetage*. Jeremy Paxman goes so far as to say that 'the supreme embodiment of the idea of Britain is the country's royal family' (1999: 240).

5. There is, indeed, far more material of this kind in works written about the English by a succession of distinguished foreign visitors to its shores in the nineteenth century – observations such as Alexis de Tocqueville's *Journeys to England and Ireland* (*c*. 1833–57), Ralph Waldo Emerson's *English Traits* (1856), Hippolyte Taine's *Notes on England* (1860–70) and Henry James's *English Hours* (1905).

6. On 'the identification of nationalism with imperialism' in Europe in the later nineteenth century, see Mommsen (1978: 125–40). Mommsen quotes Joseph Chamberlain on imperialism as only 'a larger patriotism' (1978: 125); and MacKenzie also says that 'imperial ideology was a significant aspect of late-nineteenth-century nationalism' (1999a: 291). But Mommsen makes clear that this identification was a severe distortion of the principle of nationality as classically enunciated by Mazzini and other liberals. 'The imperialist ideology substantially devalued the principle of nationality, that is to say, the idea that all peoples had a right to live in a state of their own as well as the right to develop their own autonomous culture' (1978: 122).

7. Much of the recent historical research on the impact of 'the second empire' on British domestic culture has been published in the series 'Studies in Imperialism' edited by John MacKenzie for Manchester University Press. See especially MacKenzie's own volumes (1984, 1986). Several of the other volumes are reviewed in Thornton (1992). For references to other relevant literature on this topic see Burton (2000: 149–50, ns.9–11); see also Marshall (1993). Catherine Hall (2001: 29–32) gives a vivid picture of the interaction of empire and identity in the case of an ordinary middle-class family in mid-nineteenth-century Birmingham. Kathryn Tidrick (1982) shows entertainingly and instructively, through a series of portraits of imperial administrators and adventurers, how the idea of the imperial mission shaped the character of the English ruling classes. For an interesting literary and cultural study of empire and Englishness, indicating the importance of empire in the national culture and consciousness, see Baucom (1999); with a more specifically literary focus there is also the good study by Brantlinger (1990). For the impact of the 'first' North American empire on popular culture and consciousness in eighteenth century England, see Wilson (1998). See also Said (1994: 73–229) for the impact of empire on British literary culture, and on the wider culture more generally.

8. For comparisons between the Roman and British Empires in nineteenth-century England, see Brunt (1965: 267–70, 281–8); Faber (1966: 19, 24–6); Jenkyns (1981: 332); Hingley (2001).

9. Under the slogan, 'perfection . . . is finality, and finality is death', the same basic idea was masterfully worked out, in native English idiom, by C. Northcote Parkinson in his *Parkinson's Law* (1961: 91). Parkinson specifically applied this insight to the British Empire, noting that 'the decline of British imperialism actually began with the general election of 1906', and that the completion of the grand new imperial capital of New Delhi coincided with the beginning of the end of British rule in India (1961: 96–7).

10. Elgar's ceremonial music also, often regarded as an expression of imperial triumphalism and bombast, has come to be regarded by many as 'recessional', more accurately displaying, in Kiplingesque mode, an ironic sense of a coming downfall. This was clearer 'when the Empire disintegrated, and when people heard in the music what had always been there to hear; the funeral march of a civilisation, of a spiritual and artistic life which was decaying' (Michael Kennedy, quoted in Crump 1986: 183–4).

11. Disquieting comparisons with Rome could be found in all spheres of British society, from concerns with the empire as a whole to the condition of the new urban poor. London, especially, with its teeming East End and seemingly intractable social problems, was frequently compared with the imperial city of Rome. Fears of the mob, and of degeneration through contact with the 'dangerous classes', were common among the educated classes of both cities. It was a widely held view in Victorian Britain that Rome's decline and downfall could be attributed to this social degeneration. Its fate seemed to point to that of the British Empire if something were not done about the seething mass of poverty at its centre. See Hynes (1968:

24–7); Kiernan (1972); Jones (1976: 14–15, 281–314); Howkins (1986: 65–6); Pick (1989: 189–221); Harris (1993: 241–5).

12. In recognition of this, and in an attempt to identify the monarchy more closely with the nation during the First World War when anti-German feeling ran high, George the Fifth in 1917 changed the royal family's name from Saxe-Coburg und Gotha to Windsor (prompting his cousin Kaiser Wilhelm the Second to suggest that the well-known light opera by the German composer Nicolai should be re-named *The Merry Wives of Saxe-Coburg und Gotha* (James 1998: *s.v.* 'Windsor').

13. As Colin Kidd has said, 'Whig ideals remain at the core of English national consciousness, and "whiggism", broadly conceived in its non-partisan sense, is recognised as a viable intellectual scheme for organizing a study of English national identity' (1993: 6; and generally 12–15). See also, on the breadth of the Whig view, Butterfield (1945: 82); Pocock (1992: 365–6). Whig history, Hugh Trevor-Roper has said, 'is essentially English' (1979: 8).

14. This is of course a woefully incomplete account of the renaissance of English music in this period – the most creative since the age of Purcell. One would want, for instance, to include mention of composers such as Hubert Parry, a composer 'essentially English, not in the sense of using native folk-song themes, but in the sense that the typical national qualities markedly express themselves in his work' (Scholes 1942: *s.v.* 'Parry'). He is today perhaps best known for his setting of Blake's *Jerusalem*, a rousing choral work which by tradition has become the unofficial anthem that concludes the annual summer Promenade Concerts – a very *English* festival, significantly inaugurated in 1895– now organized by the BBC at the Royal Albert Hall, London (Elgar's *Land of Hope and Glory* forms the ritual companion piece). This is also the period, we should remember, of the even more quintessentially English works of William Gilbert and Arthur Sullivan ('the music of Sullivan is often described as typically and completely English' (Scholes 1942: *s.v.* 'Sullivan'). A string of their jointly composed operas – *Trial by Jury* (1875), *H.M.S. Pinafore* (1878), *The Pirates of Penzance* (1880), *The Yeoman of the Guard* (1888), *The Grand Duke* (1986), etc. – appeared in the last three decades of the century. It is impossible to imagine English life without them. One should note also that it was composers of this period – notably Vaughan Williams – who were responsible for rescuing Tudor and Stuart music from neglect, and for endowing it with the quality of Englishness with which it is associated to this day (despite Byrd and Tallis's very un-English Catholicism) (see Howkins 1989: 91–2).

15. The poster is reproduced in Blake (1982: 224). It shows a shepherd, with his dog, herding sheep over a sweeping view of low hills dotted with woods. He is returning home in the early evening – a small town or village nestles cosily in the valley beneath. In the distance is what looks like as ruined church or castle.

16. E. M. Forster gives a similar description of the English countryside, similarly meant to represent England, in the famous passage in chapter 19 of *Howard's End* (1910) which begins, 'If one wanted to show a foreigner England...' (1941: 156–7). For Forster as for Masterman it is the southern landscape – seen here from the Purbeck Hills above the Dorset coast – that best expresses the spirit of England.

Contemplating it, 'the imagination swells, spreads and deepens, until it becomes geographic and encircles England'.

17. Peter Mandler (1997a) has argued, as against writers like Martin Wiener and Alun Howkins, that the 'rural-nostalgic vision' of England elaborated before the First World War was the creation of a small *avant-garde* ('or rather a *derrière-garde*') of writers and intellectuals and did not reflect the attitudes of the great mass of urbanized English (nor indeed those of the dominant landowning class, intent on squeezing out the last remnants of the English peasantry). There was certainly a class and cultural component to this rural ideal, as in all such ideologies; but the evidence is that far more people were attracted to it, and continued to be for much of the following half century, than simply the writers most significant in articulating it, or thought to be doing so. The reception of Hardy as a celebrator of country life is a good indication of how popular perception turned his writing into an expression of their own desires. For the persistence of the rural idyll, at the deepest levels of English national life and consciousness, see Wright (1985: 33–92); for a response to Mandler, see Howkins (2001).

18. Another famous representation of this time of the Thames valley as a kind of utopia was of course Kenneth Grahame's *The Wind in the Willows* (1908). The enduring popularity of this story, among children of all classes, tells against Mandler's criticism, noted above, that such rural evocations had little appeal to ordinary people.

19. There was a particularly precipitous fall in the number of people working on the land in the second half of the century. In 1851 more than 21 per cent of the occupied population worked on the land; by 1891 this had shrunk to 10.5 per cent. 'By the end of the century, if not a little earlier, countrymen and women had ceased to be the representative figures they had been since time immemorial' (Hoppen 1998: 12). The same decline occurred in the importance of agriculture in the national economy. At mid century it accounted for 20 per cent of the gross national product, by the end of the century, around 6 per cent (Williams 1973: 186; Howkins 2001: 146). As Raymond Williams has said, 'there is almost an inverse proportion, in the twentieth century, between the importance of the working rural economy and the cultural importance of rural ideas' (1973: 248; see also Wiener 1981: 48–9; Howkins 2001: 146).

20. A theme much elaborated by a succession of thinkers – see Butterfield (1945: v–vi, 103–17); Stapleton (1994, 2000: 266) (discussing Sir Ernest Barker); Watson (1973: 26–47).

21. This was as true of this period – from the 1880s to the 1920s – as it was of the 1840s and 1850s, when Dickens, Disraeli, Gaskell and others debated 'the condition of England' in their novels. The question of England – its health, the threats to its prosperity and happiness, its future prospects – was the subject of many of the major works of fiction of this time: H. G. Wells's *The Time Machine* (1895) and *Tono-Bungay* (1909), Joseph Conrad's *The Secret Agent* (1907) and *Under Western Eyes* (1911), E. M. Forster's *Howard's End* (1910) and *A Passage to India* (1924), D. H. Lawrence's *Women in Love* (1921) and *Lady Chatterley's Lover* (1928), and

many of the plays of George Bernard Shaw. Thomas Hardy, of course, also contributed to this inquiry as did, in different ways, William Morris, George Gissing and Ford Maddox Ford. For brief discussions of this literature, which played an important part in the definition of Englishness in this period, see Brooker and Widdowson (1986); Trotter (1993: *passim*, esp. 154–66).

8 The English and the British today

1. Though typically Lady Thatcher mixed 'British' and 'English' with insouciance. For instance, in an interview with *Le Monde* in Paris in 1989 during the commemoration of the bicentennial of the French Revolution, Lady Thatcher, as 'a *British* Conservative', felt drawn to remind the French that 'human rights did not begin with the French Revolution . . . [We *English*] had 1688, our quiet revolution, where Parliament exerted its will over the King . . . It was not the sort of Revolution that France's was.' Expatiating on these crisp comments, Lady Thatcher observes that the 'abstract ideas' of the French Revolution were 'formulated by vain intellectuals', whereas 'the English tradition of liberty . . . grew over the centuries: its most marked features are continuity, respect for law and a sense of balance, as demonstrated by the Glorious Revolution of 1688'. To underline this Lady Thatcher pointedly presented President Mitterrand with a first edition of Charles Dickens's cautionary fable on the French Revolution, *A Tale of Two Cities* – 'which made somewhat more elegantly the same point as my interview' (1993: 753). It is clear that the Whig view of English history is strong and vibrant, and can be put to use in both an English and a British context. See also, for a similar sleight of hand, Thatcher's famous Bruges speech given at the College of Europe in September 1988 (Thatcher 1989: 257). On the essential Englishness of Thatcher's nationalism, see Letwin (1992: 336); Barnes (1995); Buruma (1996).

2. One should always remember the counter-currents as well. This was the period that saw the publication of Stella Gibbons's wicked satire on country life, *Cold Comfort Farm* (1932). There was also the scorching condemnation of the agricultural workers' conditions of life, and a grim recital of the realities of rural existence, in J. W. Robertson Scott's *England's Green and Pleasant Land* (1925, 2nd edn 1931) – somewhat ironically, as it was his magazine, *The Countryman*, begun in 1927, that did so much to spread – not necessarily intentionally – the idyllic image of the countryside for the townsman. There was often a similar misreading of Flora Thompson's sharply observed autobiographical study of country life, *Lark Rise* (1939; published with sequels as *Lark Rise to Candleford*, 1945). See Lowerson (1980: 261).

3. The 'Little England' of Priestley's imagination is redolent of the England of late nineteenth-century Englishness, and of such contemporary figures as Baldwin, most particularly in its rejection of industrialism and urbanism. But Priestley also knew that there was no going back to this England. On Priestley's complex view of Englishness, his attempt to combine the old and the new, see Wiener (1981: 123–5); Waters (1994); Miller (1995a: 99); Baxendale (2001).

4. On all these wartime and post-war expressions of Englishness, see Hopkins (1963: 271–88); Hopkinson (1970); Calder (1971: *passim*, esp 159–61, 413–31); Addison (1977: 118–20, 143–63); Richards and Aldgate (1983); Aldgate and Richards (1986); Samuel (1989d: xxiv–xxvi); Rich (1989a: 40–4); Waters (1997: 213–14).

5. The Scottish representation in the Labour government of Tony Blair is indeed remarkable. Before the changes following Labour's second victory in the 2001 general election, the Labour cabinet contained a prime minister who is Scottish by blood and went to school in Edinburgh, a Scottish chancellor of the exchequer, a Scottish lord chancellor, a Scottish foreign secretary, a Scottish secretary of state for social services, a Scottish defence secretary and, of course, a Scottish Scottish secretary. 'Outside the Home Office, dealing almost exclusively with English affairs, there [was] not a great office of state which [was] not held by a Scot' (Marr 2000: 83–4).

6. That popularity was for a while held to have been diminished by what was taken as an unacceptably cold demeanour on the royal family's part in the face of the death of Princess Diana in 1997. But the evidence is that royalty has not declined in popularity, simply that the nature of that popularity – based now more on media coverage and celebrity status than old-fashioned mystique – has changed. See Marr (2000: 52–3); Chaney (2001); Couldry (2001). See also, for a varied series of views on British royalty after Diana, Merck (1998).

7. The Scottish Parliament and the Assemblies of Wales and Northern Ireland have somewhat different powers. For the details, see Bogdanor (2001: 105–09, 201–64). On the Belfast Agreement see O'Leary (1999).

8. This is echoed by the self-perception of Northern Irish Catholics themselves, of whom (in a 1991 survey) 60 per cent described themselves as 'Irish' and only 2 per cent as 'Ulster'; a further 25 per cent termed themselves 'Northern Irish', and 10 per cent as 'British' (Boyle 1991: 72).

9. In the United Kingdom in the 1990s, fewer than 25 per cent of the population attended a church service at least once a month – the lowest figure in Western Europe except for the Scandinavian countries (Therborn 1995: 275). Since this includes Northern Ireland, as well as the more religious immigrant population, the figure for the majority white population of the British mainland is even lower.

10. One person who was distinctly unamused by Cool Britannia was Lady Thatcher. When, in emulation of the 'cool', anti-establishment Virgin Airways logo, British Airways removed the Union Jack from the tail-fins of its planes and replaced it with a colourful 'ethnic' pattern, Lady Thatcher publicly draped a Union Jack over the offending part on a model of a British Airways plane. British Airways, as if somewhat ashamed, later partly phased out its ethnic art tailfins in favour of the familiar Union Jack (Lloyd 1998: 11; Davies 1999: 1037; Marr 2000: 218).

11. Both the then home secretary, Jack Straw, and the prime minister, Tony Blair, distanced themselves from the Report, saying that they had no quarrel with Britishness and denying that it was 'racially coded' (*The Independent* 12 October 2000).

12. Writing of his novel, *The Satanic Verses*, Salman Rushdie says that it deals with the condition of contemporary British Muslims, and that it 'celebrates hybridity, impurity, intermingling, the transformation that comes of new and unexpected

combinations of human beings, cultures, ideas, politics, movies, songs. It rejoices in mongrelization and fears the absolute of the Pure. *Mélange*, hotchpotch, a bit of this and a bit of that is *how newness enters the world*. It is the great possibility that mass migration gives the world, and I have tried to embrace it. The Satanic Verses is for change-by-fusion, change-by-conjoining. It is a love-song to our mongrel selves' (1992: 394).

13. There are clearly ambivalent and contradictory feelings among non-white British on the loss of British identity. Some can welcome it on the grounds that it is, as the *Parekh Report* held, too closely tied to traditional white identities. Its decline, on this view, can be the springboard for the creation of new identities, scrambling Britishness and mixing it with cultural elements drawn from all the communities, new and old, of Britain. For others, while a change in the character of traditional Britishness is essential, the potential loss of a British identity as such is a threat. For these, the apparently liberating measures of devolution in 1997/98 have disquieting implications. Alibhai-Brown (2001: 271) writes: 'When Scotland has got kilted up and the English have established their homelands far from the Welsh and Irish, where do we, the black Britons, go? Perhaps we can put in a bid for London, please? When ethnicities are created on the back of bold political decentralization, and identity is tied to history and territory, the results are not always what you would want.' She notes that 'within the first months after the referendum in Scotland, racism there against blacks and the English appeared to be increasing' (see also Shields and Corbidge 1998; but cf. Nairn 2000: 204–8).

14. Polling evidence shows the English, as compared with the Scots and Welsh, to have a lower degree of national (i.e., specifically English) awareness. In one poll, for instance, nearly 50 per cent of the English identified themselves as 'equally English and British', compared with 27 per cent for Scotland and 26 per cent for Wales (McCrone 2001: 103; see also *The Guardian* 23 May 2001).

15. Powell once memorably said that 'the life of nations, no less than of men, is lived largely in the imagination' (1969: 245). It is obvious that the nation in Powell's imagination has always been England. For general discussions of Powellism, its nature and political impact, see Nairn (1981: 256–90); Foot (1969); Schoen (1977); Hedetoft (1985: 41–54); Gilroy (1987: 45–9); Rich (1989a: 48–50); Goulbourne (1991: 116–18); Hiro (1992: *passim*); Paul (1997: 170–9); Waters (1997: 236–7); A. Brown (1999). For the 'race relations industry' before Powell, and its conceptions of English/British identity, see Waters (1997); see also Joppke (1999) and Hansen (2000), on the impact of immigration on concepts of citizenship and nationality in Britain.

16. In January 1997 the Conservative MP Teresa Gorman placed a bill for an English Parliament before the House of Commons, proposing 'Home Rule for the English' within the Union. She later urged that English citizens should have English rather than British passports (Saeed *et al.* 1999: 823). It took Labour's crushing victory in the June 1997 elections, and the wiping out of the Tory vote in Wales and Scotland, to persuade her leaders that this might be the right way to go. By the autumn of 1998 William Hague too was raising the idea of an English Parliament at the

Conservative Party conference of that year (*The Guardian* 12 October 1998; *Sunday Times* 4 October 1998).

17. Tom Nairn has briefly traced the genealogy of a 'left-nationalist popular culture' in England, pointing especially to the work of Edward Thompson, Raymond Williams and the History Workshop group established by Raphael Samuel in both excavating and celebrating this tradition (1981: 303–4). See also Marr (2000: 231–2); Rich (1989b: 503–5). There is no doubt that a 'left' English patriotism can be uncovered that is every bit as convincing as that of the right. The problem for the Labour movement in recognizing this has been its historic privileging of class over nation, together with its ideological commitment to internationalism (see, e.g., M. Taylor 1990).

18. Cf. Bernard Crick: 'We English must feel secure in our Englishness if we are not to lapse back into a super-nationalism fuelled by rancid imperialist nostalgia' (quoted Alibhai-Brown 2001: 39).

References

Acland, Tony and Siriwardena, Shirley 1995. 'Changing Ethnic Identities in England: The South Asians', paper presented to the European Sociological Association conference, Budapest, 7–10 June.

Acton, John Emerich Edward Dalberg, First Baron (1862) 1956. 'Nationality', in G. Himmelfarb (ed.), *Essays on Freedom and Power*, pp. 141–70, London: Thames and Hudson.

Addison, Paul 1977. *The Road to 1945: British Politics and the Second World War*, London: Quartet Books.

Aldgate, Anthony and Richards, Jeffrey 1986. *Britain Can Take It: The British Cinema in the Second World War*, Oxford: Basil Blackwell.

Alibhai-Brown, Yasmin 1999. *True Colours*, London: Institute for Public Policy.

2000. 'Americans are shocked by the new faces of urban Britain', *The Independent*, 5 July.

2001. *Who Do We Think We Are? Imagining the New Britain*, with a new foreword, London: Penguin Books.

Allan, David 1997. '"The Inquisitive Age": Past and Present in the Scottish Enlightenment', *The Scottish Historical Review* 76, 1 (201): 69–85.

1998. 'Protestantism, Presbyterianism and National Identity in Eighteenth-Century Scottish History', in Claydon and McBride (eds.), pp. 182–205.

Allworth, Edward (ed.) 1971. *Soviet Nationality Problems*, New York and London: Columbia University Press.

Alter, Peter 1994. *Nationalism*, 2nd edn, London: Edward Arnold.

Anderson, Benedict 1991. *Imagined Communities: Reflections on the Origin and Spread of Nationalism*, revd. edn, London and New York: Verso.

Anderson, Perry 1974. *Lineages of the Absolutist State*, London: Verso.

Armes, Roy 1978. *A Critical History of the British Cinema*, London: Secker and Warburg.

Armitage, David 1995a. 'The Scottish Vision of Empire: Intellectual Origins of the Darien Venture', in Robertson (ed.), pp. 97–117.

1995b. 'The New World and British Historical Thought: From Richard Hakluyt to William Robertson', in Karen Ordahl Kupperman (ed.), *America in European Consciousness, 1493–1750*, Chapel Hill, NC and London: University of North Carolina Press.

1997. 'Making the Empire British: Scotland in the Atlantic World 1542–1707', *Past and Present* 155: 34–63.

1999. 'Greater Britain: A Useful Category of Historical Analysis?', *American Historical Review* 104: 427–45.

2000. *The Ideological Origins of the British Empire*, Cambridge: Cambridge University Press.

Armstrong, John A. 1982. *Nations before Nationalism*, Chapel Hill: University of North Carolina Press.

1994. 'Review Essay: Liah Greenfeld, *Nationalism: Five Roads to Modernity*', *History and Theory* 33 (1): 79–95.

1995. 'Towards a Theory of Nationalism: Consensus and Dissensus', in Periwal (ed.), pp. 34–43.

Arnold, Matthew (1867) 1905. *On the Study of Celtic Literature*, London: Smith Elder and Co.

Arnold-Baker, Charles 2001. *The Companion to British History*, revised edition, London and New York: Routledge.

Asad, Talal 1999. 'Religion, Nation-State, Secularism', in van der Veer and Lehman (eds.), pp. 178–96.

Asch, Ronald G. (ed.) 1993a. *Three Nations – A Common History? England, Scotland, Ireland and British History c. 1600–1920*, Bochum: Universitätsverlag Dr. N. Brockmeyer.

1993b. 'The Protestant Ascendancy in Ireland from the American Revolution to the Act of Union 1776–1801', in Asch (ed.), pp. 161–90.

Ashton, T. S. 1961. *The Industrial Revolution 1760–1830*, London: Oxford University Press.

Aston, Margaret 1965. 'John Wycliffe's *Reformation* Reputation', *Past and Present* 30: 23–51.

Aston, Trevor (ed.) 1965. *Crisis in Europe 1560–1660*, London: Routledge and Kegan Paul.

Aylmer, G. E. 1990. 'The Peculiarities of the English State', *Journal of Historical Sociology* 3 (2): 91–108.

'Bagehot' 2000. 'Don't Mention the B-Word', *The Economist*, 14 October: 72.

Bailyn, Bernard and Morgan, Philip D. 1991a. 'Introduction', in Bailyn and Morgan (eds.), pp. 1–31.

Bailyn, Bernard and Morgan, Philip D. (eds.) 1991b. *Strangers Within the Realm: Cultural Margins of the First British Empire*, Chapel Hill, NC, and London: University of North Carolina Press.

Balakrishnan, Gopal (ed.) 1996. *Mapping the Nation*, London and New York: Verso.

Baldick, Chris 1983. *The Social Mission of English Criticism 1848–1932*, Oxford: Oxford University Press.

Baldwin, Stanley 1926. *On England, and Other Addresses*, London: Philip Allan.

Banks, J. C. 1971. *Federal Britain*, London: George Harrap and Co.

Banton, Nicholas 1982. 'Monastic Reform and the Unification of Tenth-Century England', in Mews (ed.), pp. 71–85.

Barber, Sarah 1995. 'A State of Britishness?', in Ellis and Barber (eds.), pp. 306–11.

Barczewski, Stephanie L. 2000. *Myth and National Identity in Nineteenth-Century Britain: The Legends of King Arthur and Robin Hood*, Oxford: Oxford University Press.

Barker, Ernest (ed.) 1947. *The Character of England*, Oxford: Oxford University Press.

Barker, Paul 1997. 'Land of the Lost', *The Guardian*, 22 December.

Barkey, Karen 1997. 'Thinking about Consequences of Empire', in Barkey and von Hagen (eds.), pp. 99–114.

Barkey, Karen and von Hagen, Mark (eds.) 1997. *After Empire: Multiethnic Societies and Nation-Building. The Soviet Union and the Russian, Ottoman and Habsburg Empires*, Boulder, CO: Westview Press.

Barnard, F. M. (ed.) 1969. *J. G. Herder on Social and Political Culture*, Cambridge: Cambridge University Press.

Barnard, T. C. 1998a. 'New Opportunities for British Settlements: Ireland, 1650–1700', in Canny (ed.), pp. 309–27.

[T. C.] 1998b. 'Protestantism, Ethnicity and Irish Identities, 1660–1760', in Clyadon and McBride (eds.), pp. 206–35.

Barnes, Julian 1995. 'Mrs Thatcher Remembers', in *Letters from London 1990–1995*, pp. 241–56, London: Picador.

1999. *England, England*, London: Picador.

Barnett, Anthony 1997. *This Time: Our Constitutional Revolution*, London: Vintage.

Barnett, Corelli (1972) 1984. *The Collapse of British Power*, Gloucester: Alan Sutton Publishing.

1986. *The Audit of War: The Illusion and Reality of Britain as a Great Nation*, London: Macmillan.

Barrow, G. W. S. 1980. *The Anglo-Norman Era in Scottish History*, Oxford: Oxford University Press.

Barth, Fredrik (ed.) 1969. *Ethnic Group and Boundaries: The Social Organization of Culture*, Boston: Little, Brown and Co.

Bartlett, Robert 1994. *The Making of Europe: Conquest, Colonization and Cultural Change 950–1350*, London: Penguin Books.

Bartlett, Thomas 1990. ' "A People Made Rather for Copies than Originals": The Anglo-Irish, 1760–1800', *The International History Review* 12 (1): 11–25.

1995. 'Protestant Nationalism in Eighteenth-Century Ireland', in O'Dea and Whelan (eds.), pp. 79–88.

1998. ' "This Famous Island Set in a Virginian Sea": Ireland in the British Empire, 1690–1801', in Marshall (ed.), pp. 253–75.

Bashford, Christina and Langley, Leanne (eds.) 2001. *Music and British Culture 1785–1914*, Oxford: Oxford University Press.

Bates, David 1990. 'Government and Politics 1042–1154: the Norman Conquest and the Anglo-Norman Realm', in Haigh 1990: 66–70.

Baucom, Ian 1999. *Out of Place: Englishness, Empire and the Locations of Identity*, Princeton: Princeton University Press.

Bauer, Clemens, Boehm, Laetitia and Müller, Max (eds.) 1965. *Speculum Historiale: Geschichte in Spiegel von Geschichtsschreibung und Geschichtsdeutung*, Freiburg/Munich: Verlag Karl Alber.

Bauman, Zygmunt 1998. 'Allosemitism: Premodern, Modern, Postmodern', in Cheyette and Marcus (eds.), pp. 143–56.

Baumann, Gerd 1998. *Contesting Culture: Discourses of Identity in Multi-ethnic London*, Cambridge: Cambridge University Press.

Baxandale, John 2001. ' "I had seen a lot of Englands": Priestley's English Journey', *History Workshop Journal* 51: 87–111.

Bayly, C. A. 1989. *Imperial Meridian: The British Empire and the World 1780–1830*, London: Longman.

1999. 'The Second British Empire', in Winks (ed.), pp. 54–72.

Beaune, Colette 1991. *The Birth of an Ideology: Myth and Symbols of Nation in Late-Medieval France*, trans. Susan Ross Huston, Berkeley, CA: University of California Press.

Bebbington, D. W. 1982. 'Religion and National Feeling in Nineteenth-Century Wales and Scotland', in Mews (ed.), pp. 489–503.

Beckett, J. V. 1986. *The Aristocracy in England 1660–1914*, Oxford: Basil Blackwell.

Bede (731 AD) 1990. *Ecclesiastical History of the English People*, trans. Leo Shirley-Price, ed. and introduced D. H. Farmer, London: Penguin Books.

Bell, Philip 1996. 'A Historical Cast of Mind. Some Eminent English Historians and Attitudes to Continental Europe in the Middle of the Twentieth Century', *Journal of European Integration History* 2: 5–19.

Bellah, Robert 1967. 'Civil Religion in America', *Daedalus* 96: 1–21.

Benbassa, Esther 2000. *The Jews of France: A History from Antiquity to the Present*, Princeton: Princeton University Press.

Berdyaev, Nikolai (1947) 1992. *The Russian Idea*, trans. R. M. French, Hudson, NY: Lindisfarne Press.

Berg, Maxine 1985. *The Age of Manufactures: Industry, Innovation and Work in Britain 1700–1820*, London: Fontana Press.

Berlin, Isaiah 2001. 'Notes on Prejudice', *New York Review of Books*, 18 October: 12.

Bernard, G. W. (ed.) 1992. *The Tudor Nobility*, Manchester: Manchester University Press.

Best, Geoffrey (ed.) 1988. *The Permanent Revolution: The French Revolution and its Legacy, 1789–1989*, London: Fontana Press.

Betts, G. Gordon 2001. *The Twilight of Britain: Cultural Nationalism, Multi-Culturalism and the Politics of Toleration*, New Brunswick, NJ: Transaction Books.

Bew, Paul 2001. 'Where is Burke's Vision of the Union?', *Times Literary Supplement*, 16 March: 6–7.

Bhabha, Homi K. (ed.) 1990. *Nation and Narration*, London and New York: Routledge.

Billig, Michael 1992. *Talking of the Royal Family*, London and New York: Routledge.

1995. *Banal Nationalism*, London and Thousand Oaks, CA: Sage Publications.

Bindoff, S. T. 1945. 'The Stuarts and their Style', *English Historical Review* 60 (237): 192–216.

Birch, Anthony H. (1977) *Political Integration and Disintegration in the British Isles*, London: Allen and Unwin.

1989. *Nationalism and National Integration*, London: Unwin Hyman.

Bjørn, Claus, Grant, Alexander and Stringer, Keith J. (eds.) 1994a. *Nations, Nationalism and Patriotism in the European Past*, Copenhagen: Academic Press.

(eds.) 1994b. *Social and Political Identities in Western History*, Copenhagen: Academic Press.

Blaas, P. B. M. 1978. *Continuity and Anachronism: Parliamentary and Constitutional Development in Whig Historiography and in the Anti-Whig Reaction Between 1890 and 1930*, The Hague: Martinus Nijhoff.

Black, Jeremy 1994. *Convergence or Divergence? Britain and the Continent*, Basingstoke: Macmillan.

1996. *A History of the British Isles*, Basingstoke: Macmillan.

1998. 'Confessional State or elect nation? Religion and Identity in Eighteenth-Century England', in Claydon and McBride (eds.), pp. 206–35.

2000. *A New History of England*, Thrupp, Gloucestershire: Sutton Publishing.

Blackbourn, David and Eley, Geoff 1984. *The Peculiarities of German History: Bourgeois Society and Politics in Nineteenth-Century Germany*, Oxford and New York: Oxford University Press.

Blake, Robert 1972. *The Conservative Party from Peel to Churchill*, London: Fontana.

(ed.) 1982. *The English World: History, Character and People*, New York: Harry N. Abrams Publishers.

Blatchford, Robert (1893) 1976. *Merrie England*, London: The Journeymen Press.

Bogdanor, Vernon 1997. 'Sceptred Isle – or Isles?', *Times Literary Supplement*, 27 September: 5–6.

2001. *Devolution in the United Kingdom*, Oxford: Oxford University Press.

Bossy, John 1965. 'The Character of Elizabethan Catholicism', in Aston (ed.), pp. 223–46.

1975. *The English Catholic Community 1570–1850*, London: Darton, Longman and Todd.

Boyce, D. G. 1986. ' "The Marginal Britons": The Irish', in Colls and Dodd (eds.), pp. 230–53.

1995. *Nationalism in Ireland*, 3rd edn, London and New York: Routledge.

Boyle, Kevin 1991. 'Northern Ireland: Allegiances and Identities', in Crick (ed.), pp. 68–78.

Bradbury, Jonathan and Mawson, John (eds.) 1997. *British Regionalism and Devolution: The Challenges of State Reform and European Integration*, London: Jessica Kingsley Publishers.

Bradshaw, Brendan 1996. 'The Tudor *Reformation* and Revolution in Wales and Ireland: the Origins of the British Problem', in Bradshaw and Morrill (eds.), pp. 39–65.

1998. 'The English Reformation and Identity Formation in Wales and Ireland', in Bradshaw and Roberts (eds.), pp. 43–111.

Bradshaw, Brendan and Morrill, John (eds.) 1996. *The British Problem, c. 1534–1707: State Formation in the Atlantic Archipelago*, London: Macmillan.

Bradshaw, Brendan and Roberts, Peter (eds.) 1998. *British Consciousness and Identity: The Making of Britain, 1533–1707*, Cambridge: Cambridge University Press.

Bradshaw, Brendan, Hadfield, Andrew and Maley, Willy (eds.) 1993. *Representing Ireland: Literature and the Origins of Conflict, 1534–1660*, Cambridge: Cambridge University Press.

Brantlinger, Patrick 1990. *Rule of Darkness: British Literature and Imperialism, 1830–1914*, Ithaca, NY and London: Cornell University Press.

Breen, T. H. 1997. 'Ideology and Nationalism on the Eve of the American Revolution: Revisions *Once More* in Need of Revising', *The Journal of American History* 84 (1): 13–39.

Bremmer, Ian and Taras, Ray (eds.) 1997. *New States, New Politics: Building the Post-Soviet Nations*, Cambridge: Cambridge University Press.

Brennan, Gillian 1989. 'Patriotism, Language and Power: English Translations of the Bible, 1520–1580', *History Workshop Journal* 27: 18–36.

Breuilly, John 1993. *Nationalism and the State*, 2nd edn, Chicago: University of Chicago Press.

Brigden, Susan 2001. *New Worlds, Lost Worlds: The Rule of the Tudors 1485–1603*, London: Penguin Books.

Briggs, Asa 1965a. *Victorian People: A Re-assessment of Persons and Themes 1851–67*, Harmondsworth: Penguin Books.

1965b. 'The Crystal Palace and the Men of 1851', in Briggs 1965a, pp. 23–59.

1965c. 'Thomas Hughes and the Public Schools', in Briggs 1965a, pp. 148–75.

1985. 'Saxons, Normans and Victorians', in *The Collected Essays of Asa Briggs*, 2 vols., vol. II, pp. 213–35, Brighton: The Harvester Press.

Brockliss, Laurence and Eastwood, David (eds.) 1997. *A Union of Multiple Identities: The British Isles, c. 1750–1850*, Manchester and New York: Manchester University Press.

Brooker, Peter and Widdowson, Peter 1986. 'A Literature for England', in Colls and Dodd (eds.), pp. 116–63.

Broun, Dauvit 1994. 'The Origins of Scottish Identity', in Bjørn, Grant and Stringer (eds.), pp. 35–55.

Brown, Andy R. 1999. *Political Languages of Race and the Politics of Exclusion*, Brookfield, VT: Ashgate Publishers.

Brown, Gordon 1999. 'New Britannia', *The Guardian*, 6 May.

2000. 'This is the Time to Start Building a Greater Britain', *The Times*, 10 January.

Brown, Judith M. and Louis, Wm. Roger (eds.) 1999. *The Oxford History of the British Empire: The Twentieth Century*, Oxford and New York: Oxford University Press.

Brown, Keith M. 1995. 'The Origins of a British Aristocracy: Integration and its Limitations Before the Treaty of Union', in Ellis and Barber (eds.), pp. 222–49.

1998. 'Scottish Identity in the Seventeenth Century', in Bradshaw and Roberts (eds.), pp. 236–58.

'Seducing the Scottish Clio: Has Scottish *History* Anything to Fear from the New British History?', in Burgess (ed.), pp. 238–65.

Brubaker, Rogers 1992. *Citizenship and Nationhood in France and Germany*, Cambridge, MA: Harvard University Press.

1996a. *Nationalism Reframed: Nationhood and the National Question in the New Europe*, Cambridge: Cambridge University Press.

1996b. 'Nationhood and the National Question in the Soviet Union and its Successor States: An Institutionalist Account', in Brubaker 1996a, pp. 23–54.

1996c. 'Aftermath of Empires and the Unmixing of Peoples', in Brubaker 1996a, pp. 148–78.

Brubaker, Rogers and Cooper, Frederick 2000. 'Beyond "Identity" ', *Theory and Society* 29: 1–47.

Bruce, Steve 1987. *God Save Ulster! The Religion and Politics of Paisleyism*, Oxford: Oxford University Press.

Bruce, S. and Yearley, S. 1989. 'The Social Construction of Tradition: The Restoration Portraits of the Kings of Scotland', in McCrone, Kendrick and Straw (eds.), pp. 175–88.

Brunt, P. A. 1965. 'Reflections on British and Roman Imperialism', *Comparative Studies in Society and History* 7 (3): 267–88.

Bulpitt, Jim 1983. *Territory and Power in the United Kingdom*, Manchester: Manchester University Press.

Bulwer, Edward Lytton (1833) 1970. *England and the English*, ed. and introduced Standish Meacham, Chicago and London: University of Chicago Press.

Burgess, Glenn (ed.) 1999. *The New British History: Founding a Modern State 1603–1715*, London and New York: I. B. Tauris.

Burgess, Michael 1989. 'The Roots of British Federalism', in Patricia L. Garside and Michael Hibbert (eds.), *British Regionalism 1900–2000*, pp. 20–39, London and New York: Mansell Publishing.

Burke, Peter 1979. *Popular Culture in Early Modern Europe*, London: Maurice Temple Smith.

Burroughs, Peter 1973. 'John Robert Seeley and British Imperial History', *Journal of Imperial and Commonwealth History* 1 (2): 191–211.

Burrow, J. W. 1966. *Evolution and Society: A Study in Victorian Social Theory*, Cambridge: Cambridge University Press.

1974. 'The "Village Community" and the Uses of History in Late Nineteenth-Century England', in Neil McKendrick (ed.), *Historical Perspectives: Studies in English Thought and Society in Honour of J. H. Plumb*, pp. 255–84, London: Europa Publications.

1983. *A Liberal Descent: Victorian Historians and the English Past*, Cambridge: Cambridge University Press.

Burton, Antoinette 2000. 'Who Needs the Nation? Interrogating "British History"', in Hall (ed.), pp. 137–53.

Buruma, Ian 1996. 'Mrs. Thatcher's Revenge', *New York Review of Books*, 21 March: 22–7.

1998. *Anglomania: A European Love Affair*, New York: Vintage Books.

Butterfield, Herbert (1931) 1951. *The Whig Interpretation of History*, London: G. Bell and Sons.

1945. *The Englishman and His History*, London: Cambridge University Press.

1957. *The Origins of Modern Science, 1300–1800*, new edn, London: Bell.

Bury, J. B. (1923) 1955. *The Idea of Progress: An Inquiry into its Growth and Origin*, New York: Dover Publications.

Caball, Marc 1998. 'Faith, Culture and Sovereignty: Irish Nationality and its Development, 1558–1625', in Bradshaw and Roberts (eds.), pp. 112–39.

Cable, Thomas 1984. 'The Rise of Written Standard English', in Scaglione (ed.), pp. 75–94.

Caglar, Ayse 1997. 'Hyhenated Identities and the Limits of "Culture"', in Modood and Werber (eds.), pp. 169–85.

Cain, P. J. and Hopkins, A. G. 1993. *British Imperialism*, 2 vols., London and New York: Longman.

Cairns, John W. 1995. 'Scottish Law, Scottish Lawyers and the Status of the Union', in Robertson (ed.), pp. 243–68.

Calder, Angus 1971. *The People's War: Britain 1939–1945*, London: Panther Books.

1981. *Revolutionary Empire: The Rise of the English-Speaking Empires from the Fifteenth Century to the 1780s*, New York: R. P. Dutton.

Calhoun, Craig 1993. 'Nationalism and Ethnicity', *Annual Review of Sociology* 19: 211–39.

1997. *Nationalism*, Buckingham: Open University Press.

Campbell, James 1986. 'Some Twelfth-Century Views of the Anglo-Saxon Past', in *Essays in Anglo-Saxon History*, pp. 209–28, London and Ronceverte: The Hambledon Press.

1995a. 'The United Kingdom of England: The Anglo-Saxon Achievement', in Grant and Stringer (eds.), pp. 31–47.

1995b. 'The Late Anglo-Saxon State: A Maximum view', *Proceedings of the British Academy* 87: 39–65.

Cannadine, David 1984. 'The Context, Performance and Meaning of Ritual: The British Monarchy and the "Invention of Tradition", *c.* 1820–1977', in Hobsbawm and Ranger (eds.), pp. 101–64.

1987. 'British History: Past, Present – And Future?', *Past and Present* 116: 169–91.

1993. 'Penguin Island Story: Planning a New History of Britain', *Times Literary Supplement*, 12 March: 4–5.

1995a. *Creating a New Penguin History: A Series Introduction*, London: Penguin Books.

1995b. 'British History as a "New Subject": Politics, Perspectives and Prospects', in Grant and Stringer (eds.), pp. 12–28.

2001. *Ornamentalism: How the British Saw Their Empire*, Oxford: Oxford University Press.

Cannon, John and Griffiths, Ralph 1998. *The Oxford Illustrated History of the British Monarchy*, Oxford: Oxford University Press.

Canny, Nicholas 1973. 'The Ideology of English Colonization: From Ireland to America', *William and Mary Quarterly* 30: 575–98.

1987. 'Identity Formation in Ireland: The Emergence of the Anglo-Irish', in Canny and Pagden (eds.), pp. 159–212.

1988. *Kingdom and Colony: Ireland in the Atlantic World 1560–1800*, Baltimore, MD: Johns Hopkins University Press.

1991. 'The Marginal Kingdom: Ireland as a Problem in the First British Empire', in Bailyn and Morgan (eds.), pp. 35–66.

1993. 'The Attempted Anglicization of Ireland in the Seventeenth Century: An Exemplar of "British History" ', in Asch (ed.), pp. 49–82.

(ed.) 1998. *The Origins of Empire: British Overseas Enterprise to the Close of the Seventeenth Century*, Oxford and New York: Oxford University Press.

Canny, Nicholas and Pagden, Anthony (eds.) 1987. *Colonial Identity in the Atlantic World, 1500–1800*, Princeton: Princeton University Press.

Capp, Bernard 1986. 'The Fifth Monarchists and Popular Millenarianism', in McGregor and Reay (eds.), pp. 165–89.

Carlyle, Thomas (1840) 1971. 'Chartism', in Alan Shelston (ed.), *Thomas Carlyle: Selected Writings*, pp. 151–232, Harmondsworth: Penguin Books.

(1843) 1910. *Past and Present*, London: Ward, Lock and Co.

Castells, Manuel 1998. *End of Millennium*, Oxford and Malden, MA: Blackwell.

Chadwick, Owen 1990. *The Secularization of the European Mind in the 19th Century*, Canto edn, Cambridge: Cambridge University Press.

Chamberlin, Russell 1986. *The Idea of England*, London: Thames and Hudson.

Chaney, David 2001. 'The Mediated Monarchy', in Morley and Robins (eds.), pp. 207–19.

Cheyette, Brian and Marcus, Laura (eds.) 1998. *Modernity, Culture and "the Jew"*, Palo Alto, CA: Stanford University Press.

Chitnis, Anand C. 1976. *The Scottish Enlightenment: A Social History*, London: Croom Helm.

1986. *The Scottish Enlightenment and Early Victorian English Society*, London: Croom Helm.

Christiansen, Paul 1978. *Reformers and Babylon: English Apocalyptic Visions from the Reformation to the Eve of the Civil War*, Toronto: University of Toronto Press.

Church, William F. 1975. 'France', in Ranum (ed.), pp. 43–66.

Cipolla, Carlo M. 1969. *Literacy and Development in the West*, Harmondsworth: Penguin Books.

Clanchy, M. T. 1998. *England and its Rulers 1066–1272*, 2nd edn, Oxford: Blackwell.

Clark, G. N. (Sir George) 1960a. *The Seventeenth Century*, 2nd edn, London: Oxford University Press.

Clark, George [Sir] 1960b. *Early Modern Europe: From about 1450 to about 1720*, New York: Oxford University Press.

1971. *English History: A Survey*, Oxford: Clarendon Press.

Clark, J. C. D. 1986. *Revolution and Rebellion: State and Society in England in the Seventeenth and Eighteenth Centuries*, Cambridge: Cambridge University Press.

1989. 'English History's Forgotten Context: Scotland, Ireland, Wales', *The Historical Journal* 32 (1): 211–28.

1994. *The Language of Liberty, 1660–1832: Political Discourse and Social Dynamics in the Anglo-American World*, Cambridge: Cambridge University Press.

2000a. *English Society 1660–1832: Religion, Ideology and Politics during the Ancien Règime*, 2nd edn, Cambridge: Cambridge University Press.

2000b. 'Protestantism, Nationalism and National Identity, 1660–1832', *The Historical Journal* 43 (1): 249–76.

Clarke, Aidan 1978. 'Colonial Identity in Early Seventeenth-Century Ireland', in Moody (ed.), pp. 57–71.

Clarke, I. F. 1970. *Voices Prophesying War 1763–1984*, London: Panther Books.

Claydon, Tony 1999. ' "British History" in the Post-Revolutionary World 1690–1715', in Burgess (ed.), pp. 115–37.

Claydon, Tony and McBride, Ian (eds.) 1998a. *Protestantism and National Identity: Britain and Ireland, c. 1650–1850*, Cambridge: Cambridge University Press.

1998b. 'The Trials of the Chosen Peoples: Recent Interpretations of Protestantism and National Identity in Britain and Ireland', in Claydon and McBride (eds.), pp. 3–29.

Clifton, Robin 1973. 'Fear of Popery', in Russell (ed.), pp. 144–67.

Clive, John 1970. 'The Social Background of the Scottish Renaissance', in Phillipson and Mitchison (eds.), pp. 225–44.

1975. *Macaulay: The Shaping of the Historian*, New York: Vintage Books.

Cohen, Phil 1993. *Home Rules: Some Reflections on Racism and Nationalism in Everyday Life*, London: New Ethnicities Unit, University of East London.

Cohen, Robin 1994. *Frontiers of Identity: The British and the Others*, London and New York: Longman.

Coleman, Christopher and Starkey, David (eds.) 1986. *Revolution Reassessed: Revisions in the History of Tudor Government and Administration*, Oxford: Clarendon Press.

Coleman, Janet 1981. *English Literature in History 1350–1400: Medieval Readers and Writers*, London: Hutchinson.

Collette, C. P. 1989. 'Chaucer and Victorian Medievalism: Culture and Society', *Poetica* 29–30: 115–25.

Colley, Linda 1984. 'The Apotheosis of George III: Loyalty, Royalty and the British Nation 1760–1820', *Past and Present* 102: 94–129.

1986. 'Whose Nation? Class and National Consciousness in Britain 1750–1830', *Past and Present* 113: 97–117.

1989. 'Radical Patriotism in Eighteenth-Century England', in Samuel (ed.), vol. I, pp. 169–87.

1992. 'Britishness and Otherness: An Argument', *Journal of British Studies* 31: 309–29.

(1992) 1994. *Britons: Forging the Nation 1707–1837*, London: Pimlico.

Collini, Stefan 1993. *Public Moralists: Political Thought and Intellectual Life in Britain 1850–1930*, Oxford: Clarendon Press.

Collini, Stefan, Winch, Donald and Burrow, John (eds.) 1983. *That Noble Science of Politics: A Study in Nineteenth-Century Intellectual History*, Cambridge: Cambridge University Press.

Collini, Stefan, Whatmore, Richard and Young, Brian (eds.) 2000. *History, Religion and Culture: British Intellectual History 1750–1950*, Cambridge: Cambridge University Press.

Collinson, Patrick 1982. *The Religion of Protestants: The Church in English Society 1559–1625*, Oxford: Clarendon Press.

1997. 'Biblical Rhetoric: The English Nation and National Sentiment in the Prophetic Mode', in McEachern and Shuger (eds.), pp. 15–45.

Colls, Robert 1986. 'Englishness and Political Culture', in Colls and Dodd (eds.) pp. 29–61.

Colls, Robert and Dodd, Philip (eds.) 1986. *Englishness: Politics and Culture 1880–1920*, London: Croom Helm.

Condor, Susan 1996. 'Unimagined Community? Some Social Psychological Issues Concerning English National Identity', in Glynis M. Breakwell and Evanthia Lyons (eds.), *Changing European Identities: Social Psychological Analyses of Social Change*, pp. 41–68, Oxford: Butterworth-Heinemann.

Connolly, S. J. 1992. *Religion, Law and Power: The Making of Protestant Ireland, 1660–1760*, Oxford: Oxford University Press.

1995. 'Varieties of Britishness: Ireland, Scotland and Wales in the Hanoverian State', in Grant and Stringer (eds.), pp. 193–207.

Connolly, S. J. (ed.) 1999. *Kingdoms United? Great Britain and Ireland Since 1500: Integration and Diversity*, Dublin: Four Courts Press.

Connor, Walker 1994. *Ethnonationalism: The Quest for Understanding*, Princeton: Princeton University Press.

Conrad, Joseph (1902) 1995. *Heart of Darkness, with The Congo Diary*, ed. Robert Hampson, London: Penguin Books.

Coombes, David 1991. 'Europe and the Regions', in Crick (ed.), pp. 134–50.

Corrigan, Philip and Sayer, Derek 1985. *The Great Arch: English State Formation and Cultural Revolution*, Oxford: Basil Blackwell.

Cottle, Basil 1969. *The Triumph of English 1350–1400*, London: Blandford Press.

Couldry, Nick 2001. 'Everyday Royal Celebrity', in Morley and Robins (eds.), pp. 221–33.

Coulton, G. G. (1935) 1972. 'Nationalism in the Middle Ages', in Tipton (ed.), pp. 70–4 (reprinted as 'The Papacy').

Cowdrey, H. E. J. 1981. 'Bede and the "English People" ', *Journal of Religious History* 11 (4): 501–23.

Cox, Jeffrey N. and Reynolds, Larry J. (eds.), 1993. *New Historical Literary Study: Essays on Reproducing Texts, Representing History*, Princeton: Princeton University Press.

Cox, W. Harvey 1989. 'On Being an Ulster Protestant', in Evans (ed.), pp. 35–45.

Cressy, David 1980. *Literacy and the Social Order: Reading and Writing in Tudor and Stuart England*, Cambridge: Cambridge University Press.

1990. *Bonfires and Bells: National Memory and the Protestant Calendar in Elizabethan and Stuart England*, Berkeley and Los Angeles, CA: University of California Press.

1994. 'National Memory in Early Modern England', in Gillis (ed.), pp. 61–74.

Crick, Bernard 1989. 'An Englishman Considers his Passport', in Evans (ed.), pp. 23–34.

1991a. 'The English and the British', in Crick (ed.), pp. 90–104.

(ed.) 1991b. *National Identities: The Constitution of the United Kingdom*, Oxford: Blackwell.

Crick, Bernard 1995. 'The Sense of Identity of the Indigenous British', *New Community* 21 (2): 167–82.

Crozier, Maurna (ed.) 1989. *Cultural Traditions in Northern Ireland*, Belfast: Institute of Irish Studies, The Queen's University of Belfast.

Crump, Jeremy 1986. 'The Identity of English Music: The Reception of Elgar 1898–1935', in Colls and Dodd (eds.), pp. 164–90.

Cullen, L. M. 1989. 'Scotland and Ireland, 1600–1800: Their Role in the Evolution of British Society', in R. A. Houston and I. D. Whyte (eds.), *Scottish Society 1500–1800*, pp. 226–44, Cambridge: Cambridge University Press.

Cunningham, Hugh 1981. 'The Language of Patriotism, 1750–1914', *History Workshop Journal* 15: 8–33.

1986. 'The Conservative Party and Patriotism', in Colls and Dodd (eds.), pp. 283–307.

1989. 'The Language of Patriotism', in Samuel (ed.), vol. I, pp. 57–89.

Curran, James and Seaton, Jean 1991. *Power Without Responsibility: The Press and Broadcasting in Britain*, 4th edn, London: Routledge.

Curtis, Jr, L. P. 1968. *Anglo-Saxons and Celts: A Study of Anti-Irish Prejudice in Victorian England*, Bridgeport, CT: Conference on British Studies, University of Bridgeport.

Davey, Kevin 1999. *English Imaginaries: Six Studies in Anglo-British Modernity*, London: Lawrence and Wishart.

2001. 'No Longer "Ourselves Alone" in Northern Ireland', in Morley and Robins (eds.), pp. 79–95.

Davidson, Neil 2000. *The Origins of Scottish Nationhood*, London: Pluto Press.

Davies, John 1994. *A History of Wales*, London: Penguin Books.

Davies, Norman 1998. 'Britain is breaking up faster than you think', *Sunday Times*, 31 May.

1999. *The Isles: A History*, New York: Oxford University Press.

Davies, R. R. 1974. 'Colonial Wales', *Past and Present* 65: 3–23.

1987. *The Age of Conquest: Wales 1063–1415*, Oxford: Oxford University Press.

(ed.). 1988a. *The British Isles 1100–1500: Comparisons, Contrasts and Connections*, Edinburgh: John Donald.

1988b. 'In Praise of British *History*', in Davies (ed.), pp. 9–26.

1990. *Domination and Conquest: The Experience of Ireland, Scotland and Wales 1100–1300*, Cambridge: Cambridge University Press.

1993. 'The English State and the "Celtic" Peoples, 1100–1400', *Journal of Historical Sociology* 6 (1): 1–14.

1994a. 'The Peoples of Britain and Ireland 1100–1400, I: Identities', *Transactions of the Royal Historical Society*, 6th series, 4: 1–20.

1994b. 'The Failure of the First British Empire? England's Relations with Ireland, Scotland and Wales, 1066–1500', in Saul (ed.), pp. 121–32.

1995. 'The Peoples of Britain and Ireland 1100–1400, II: Names, Boundaries and Regnal Solidarities', *Transactions of the Royal Historical Society*, 6th series, 5: 1–20.

1996. 'The Peoples of Britain and Ireland 1100–1400, III: Laws and Customs', *Transactions of the Royal Historical Society*, 6th series, 6: 1–23.

1997. 'The Peoples of Britain and Ireland 1100–1400, IV: Language and Historical Mythology', *Transactions of the Royal Historical Society*, 6th series, 7: 1–24.

2000. *The First English Empire: Power and Identities in the British Isles 1093–1343*, Oxford: Oxford University Press.

Davies, Wendy 1984. 'Picts, Scots and Britons', in L. Smith (ed.), pp. 63–76.

Davis, Leith 1999. *Acts of Union: Scotland and the Literary Negotiation of the British Nation 1707–1830*, Palo Alto, CA: Stanford University Press.

Davis, R. H. C. 1971. 'Alfred the Great: Propaganda and Truth', *History* 56: 169–82.

Dawson, Jennifer 1995. 'Anglo-Scottish Protestant Culture and Integration in Sixteenth-Century Britain', in Ellis and Barber (eds.), pp. 87–114.

Déak, Istvan 1990. *Beyond Nationalism: A Social and Political History of the Habsburg Officer Corps, 1848–1918*, New York and Oxford: Oxford University Press.

1997. 'The Habsburg Empire', in Barkey and von Hagen (eds.), pp. 129–41.

De Grazia, Sebastian 1997. *A Country with No Name: Tales from the Constitution*, New York: Pantheon Books.

Deansley, Margaret 1954. *A History of the Medieval Church, 590–1500*, 8th edn, London: Methuen.

Denitch, Bogdan 1996. *Ethnic Nationalism: The Tragic Death of Yugoslavia*, revd. edn, Minneapolis: University of Minnesota Press.

Dennis, Nigel 1955. *Cards of Identity*, Harmondsworth: Penguin Books.

Devine, T. M. (ed.) 1991. *Irish Immigrants and Scottish Society in the Nineteenth and Twentieth Centuries*, Edinburgh: J. Donald.

Devine, T. M. 1999. *The Scottish Nation: A History, 1700–2000*, New York: Viking.

2000. *Scotland's Shame*, Edinburgh: J. Donald.

Dilke, Charles Wentworth 1868. *Greater Britain: A Record of Travel in English-Speaking Countries During 1866 and 1867*, New York: Harper and Row.

Dodd, Philip 1986. 'Englishness and the National Culture', in Colls and Dodd (eds.), pp. 1–28.

1995. *The Battle over Britain*, London: Demos.

Doyle, Brian 1986. 'The Invention of English', in Colls and Dodd (eds.), pp. 89–115.

1986. *Empires*, Ithaca, NY: Cornell University Press.

Doyle, Michael 1989. *English and Englishness*, London: Routledge.

Dresser, Madge 1989. 'Britannia', in Samuel (ed.), vol. III, pp. 26–49.

Driver, Stephen and Martell, Luke 2001. 'Blair and "Britishness"', in Morley and Robins (eds.), pp. 461–72.

Dukes, Paul (ed.) 1991. *Russia and Europe*, London: Collins and Brown.

Dumont, Louis 1986a. *Essays on Individualism: Modern Ideology in Anthropological Perspective*, Chicago and London: University of Chicago Press.

1986b. 'German Identity: Herder's *Volk* and Fichte's *Nation*', in Dumont 1986a, pp. 113–32.

1994a. *German Ideology: From France to Germany and Back*, Chicago: University of Chicago Press.

1994b. 'French Political Ideology Seen in the Light of the Incipient Comparison of National Cultures', in Dumont 1994a, pp. 199–235.

Duncan, A. A. M. 1975. *Scotland: The Making of a Kingdom*, Edinburgh: Oliver and Boyd.

1984. 'The Kingdom of the Scots', in Lesley Smith (ed.), pp. 131–45.

1988. 'The Scots' Invasion of Ireland, 1315', in R. R. Davies (ed.), pp. 100–17.

Eade, John 1994. 'Identity, Nation and Religion: Educated Young Bangladeshi Muslims in London's East End', *International Sociology* 9 (3): 377–94.

The Economist 1999. 'Undoing Britain?', 6 November.

Edmunds, June and Turner, Bryan 2001. 'The Re-invention of a National Identity? Women and "cosmopolitan" Englishness', *Ethnicities* 1 (1): 377–94.

Einstein, Lewis 1921. *Tudor Ideals*, New York: Harcourt, Brace and Company.

Eley, Geoff and Suny, Ronald Grigor (eds.) 1996. *Becoming National: A Reader*, New York and Oxford: Oxford University Press.

Eliot, T. S. 1962. *Notes Towards the Definition of Culture*, 2nd edn, London: Faber and Faber.

Eliott, J. H. 1992. 'A Europe of Composite Monarchies', *Past and Present* 137: 48–71.

Ellis, Steven G. 1988. '"Not Mere English": The British Perspective 1400–1650', *History Today* 38: 41–8.

Ellis, Steven G. and Barber, Sarah (eds.) 1995. *Conquest and Union: Fashioning a British State, 1485–1725*, London and New York: Longman.

Elton, Geoffrey 1953. *The Tudor Revolution in Government*, London and New York: Cambridge University Press.

(ed.) 1960. *The Tudor Constitution: Documents and Commentary*, Cambridge: Cambridge University Press.

1986. 'English National Self-Consciousness and the Parliament in the Sixteenth Century', in Otto Dann (ed.), *Nationalismus in vorindustrieller Zeit*, pp. 73–82, Munich: R. Oldenbourg Verlag.

1992. *The English*, Oxford: Blackwell.

Emerson, Ralph Waldo (1856) 1966. *English Traits*, ed. Howard Mumford Jones, Cambridge, MA: Harvard University Press.

Engels, Friedrich (1845) 1958. *The Condition of the Working Class in England*, trans. W. O. Henderson and W. H. Chaloner, Oxford: Basil Blackwell.

Eriksen, Thomas Hylland 1993. *Ethnicity and Nationalism: Anthropological Perspectives*, London and Sterling, VA: Pluto Press.

Esler, Gavin 2001. 'What British Means', *University of Kent Bulletin* 36: 8–10.

Evans, Eric 1994a. 'National Consciousness? The Ambivalences of English Identity in the Eighteenth Century', in Bjørn, Grant and Stringer (eds.), pp. 145–60.

1994b. 'From English to Britons? Nationhood in the Nineteenth Century', in Bjørn, Grant and Stringer (eds.), pp. 195–213.

1995. 'Englishness and Britishness: National Identities, *c.* 1790–*c.* 1870', in Grant and Stringer (eds.), pp. 223–43.

Evans, Neil (ed.) 1988. 'Debate: British History – Past, Present – and Future?', *Past and Present* 119: 194–203.

(ed.) 1989. *National Identity in the British Isles*, Harlech, Gwynedd: Centre for Welsh Studies, Coleg Harlech.

Evans, R. J. W. 1994. 'Austrian Identity in Hungarian Perspective', in Robertson and Timms (eds.), pp. 27–36.

Faber, Richard 1966. *The Vision and the Need: Late Victorian Imperialist Aims*, London: Faber and Faber.

Facey, Jane 1987. 'John Foxe and the Defence of the English Church', in Lake and Dowling (eds.), pp. 162–92.

Faulkner, Peter 1992. *William Morris and the Idea of England*, London: William Morris Society.

Favell, Adrian 2001. *Philosophies of Integration: Immigration and the Idea of Citizenship in France and Britain*, 2nd edn, Basingstoke and New York: Palgrave.

Fawtier, Robert 1960. *The Capetian Kings of France: Monarchy and Nation (987–1328)*, trans. Lionel Butler and R. J. Adam, London: Macmillan.

Feldman, David 1998. 'Was Modernity Good for the Jews?', in Cheyette and Marcus (eds.), pp. 171–87.

Ferguson, Arthur B. 1965. *The Articulate Citizen and the English Renaissance*, Durham, NC: Duke University Press.

Ferguson, William 1998. *The Identity of the Scottish Nation: An Historic Quest*, Edinburgh: Edinburgh University Press.

Fevre, Ralph, Borland, John and Denney, David 1997. 'Nation, Identity and Immigration in England and Wales 1967–1989', paper presented to the Annual Meeting of the American Sociological Association, Toronto, August 1997.

Fideler, Paul A. and Mayer, T. F. (eds.) 1992. *Political Thought and the Tudor Commonwealth: Deep Structure, Discourse and Disguise*, London and New York: Routledge.

Finley, M. I. 1976. 'Colonies – An Attempt at a Typology', *Transactions of the Royal Historical Society*, 5th series, 26: 167–88.

Firth, Sir Charles 1953. *Oliver Cromwell and the Rule of the Puritans in England*, London: Oxford University Press.

Firth, Katharine 1979. *The Apocalyptic Tradition in Reformation Britain, 1530–1645*, Oxford: Oxford University Press.

Fisher, J. H. 1992. 'A Language Policy for Lancastrian England', *Proceedings of the Modern Languages Association [PMLA]*107: 1168–80.

Fishman, Joshua A. 1972. *Language and Nationalism*, Rowley, MA: Newbury House Publishers.

Fletcher, Anthony 1982. 'The First Century of English Protestantism and the Growth of National Identity', in Mews (ed.), pp. 309–17.

Foot, Paul 1969. *The Rise of Enoch Powell: An Examination of Enoch Powell's Attitudes to Immigration and Race*, Harmondsworth: Penguin Books.

Foot, Sarah 1996. 'The Making of *Angelcynn*: English Identity Before the Norman Conquest', *Transactions of the Royal Historical Society*, 6th series, 6: 25–49.

Forde, Simon, Johnson, Lesley and Murray, Alan V. (eds.) 1995. *Concepts of National Identity in the Middle Ages*, Leeds: Leeds Texts and Monographs, new series 14, University of Leeds.

Forster, E. M. (1910) 1941. *Howard's End*, Harmondsworth: Penguin Books.

Forster, Robert and Greene, Jack P. (eds.) 1970. *Preconditions of Revolution in Early Modern Europe*, Baltimore, MD and London: The Johns Hopkins University Press.

Forsyth, David S. 1997. 'Empire and Union: Imperial and National Identity in Nineteenth-Century Scotland', *Scottish Geographical Magazine* 113 (1): 6–12.

Foster, R. F. 1989a. *Modern Ireland 1600–1972*, London: Penguin Books.
  1989b. 'Varieties of Irishness', in Crozier (ed.), pp. 5–24.
  1993. 'Commentary', in Asch (ed.), pp. 265–71.

Fowler, H. W. 1983. *A Dictionary of Modern English Usage*, 2nd edn, revised Sir Ernest Gowers, Oxford: Oxford University Press.

Frame, Robin 1977. 'Power and Society in the Lordship of Ireland 1272–1377', *Past and Present* 76: 3–33.

1981. *Colonial Ireland 1169–1369*, Dublin: Helicon.

1993. ' "Les Engleys Nées En Irelande": The English Political Identity in Medieval Ireland', *Transactions of the Royal Historical Society*, 6th series, 3: 83–103.

1995a. *The Political Development of the British Isles 1100–1400*, 2nd edn, Oxford and New York: Oxford University Press.

1995b. 'Overlordship and Reaction, *c.* 1200–*c.* 1450', in Grant and Stringer (eds.), pp. 65–84.

Freeden, Michael 1986. *The New Liberalism: An Ideology of Social Reform*, Oxford: Clarendon Press.

(ed.) 1988. *J. A. Hobson: A Reader*, London: Unwin Hyman.

1998. 'Is Nationalism a Distinct Ideology?', *Political Studies* 46: 748–65.

Freud, Sigmund 1963. *Civilization and Its Discontents*, trans. Joan Riviere, London: The Hogarth Press.

Froude, James Anthony (1852) 1876. 'England's Forgotten Worthies', in *Short Studies on Great Subjects*, 2 vols, vol. I: 443–501, London: Longman, Greem and Co.

Fry, Michael 2001. *The Scottish Empire*, East Linton, East Lothian: Tuckwell Press.

Furtado, Peter 1989. 'National Pride in Seventeenth-Century England', in Samuel (ed.), vol. I: 44–56.

Fussell, Paul 1977. *The Great War and Modern Memory*, New York and London: Oxford University Press.

Galbraith, Vivian H. (1941) 1972. 'Nationality and Language in Medieval England', in Tipton (ed.), pp. 45–53.

Galloway, Bruce 1986. *The Union of England and Scotland 1603–1608*, Edinburgh: Edinburgh University Press.

Gammage, R. C. (1894) 1969. *History of the Chartist Movement 1837–1854*, London: The Merlin Press.

Gardiner, Juliet and Wenborn, Neil (eds.) 1995. *The Companion to British History*, London: Collins and Brown.

Gates, Jnr, Henry L. 1997. 'Black London', *New Yorker*, 28 April–5 May: 32–41.

Gawthrop, Richard and Strauss, Gerald 1984. 'Protestantsim and Literacy in Early Modern Germany', *Past and Present* 104: 31–55.

Gellner, Ernest 1983. *Nations and Nationalism*, Oxford: Basil Blackwell.

1996. 'The Coming of Nationalism and Its Interpretation', in Balakrishnan (ed.), pp. 98–145.

1998. *Nationalism*, London: Phoenix.

Genet, J.-P. 1984. 'English Nationalism: Thomas Poulton at the Council of Constance', *Nottingham Medieval Studies* 28: 60–78.

Geoffrey of Monmouth (*c.* 1136) 1966. *The History of the Kings of Britain*, trans. and ed. Lewis Thorpe, London: Penguin Books.

Gilbert, Felix 1975. 'Italy', in Ranum (ed.), pp. 21–42.

Giles, Judy and Middleton, Neil (eds.) 1995. *Writing Englishness 1900–1950: An Introductory Sourcebook on National Identity*, London and New York: Routledge.

Gilley, Sheridan 1978. 'English Attitudes to the Irish in Ireland, 1780–1900', in C. Holmes (ed.), *Immigrants and Minorities in British Society*, 87–105, London: Allen and Unwin.

Gillingham, John 1990–91. 'The Context and Purposes of Geoffrey of Monmouth's *History of the Kings of Britain*', *Anglo-Norman Studies* 13: 99–118.

     1992. 'The Beginnings of English Imperialism', *Journal of Historical Sociology* 5 (4): 392–409.

     1993. 'The English Invasion of Ireland', in Bradshaw, Hadfield and Maley (eds.), pp. 24–42.

     1995a. 'Henry of Huntingdon and the Twelfth-Century Revival of the English Nation', in Forde, Johnson and Murray (eds.), pp. 75–101.

     1995b. 'Foundations of a Disunited Kingdom', in Grant and Stringer (eds.), pp. 48–64.

     2000. *The English in the Twelfth Century: Imperialism, National Identity and Political Values*, Woodbridge: The Boydell Press (includes essays cited above).

Gillis, John (ed.) 1994. *Commemorations: The Politics of National Identity*, Princeton: Princeton University Press.

Gilroy, Paul 1987. *'There Ain't No Black in the Union Jack': The Cultural Politics of Race and Nation*, London: Hutchinson.

     1993. *The Black Atlantic: Modernity and Double Consciousness*, Cambridge, MA: Harvard University Press.

Godechot, Jacques 1971. 'Nation, Patrie, Nationalisme et Patriotisme en France au XVIIIe siècle', *Annales Historiques De La Révolution Francaise* 43 (206): 481–501.

Goldie, Mark 1996. 'Divergence and Union: Scotland and England, 1660–1707', in Bradshaw and Morrill (eds.), pp. 220–45.

Gott, Richard 1989. 'Little Englanders', in Samuel (ed.), vol. I, pp. 90–102.

Goulbourne, Harry 1991. *Ethnicity and Nationalism in Post-Imperial Britain*, Cambridge: Cambridge University Press.

Grainger, J. H. 1986. *Patriotisms: Britain 1900–1939*, London: Routledge and Kegan Paul.

Grant, Alexander 1987. 'Crown and Nobility in Late Medieval Britain', in Mason (ed.), pp. 34–59.

1988. 'Scotland's "Celtic Fringe" in the Late Middle Ages: The Macdonald Lords of the Isles and the Kingdom of Scotland', in R. R. Davies (ed.), pp. 118–41.

1994. 'Aspects of National Consciousness in Medieval Scotland', in Bjørn, Grant and Stringer (eds.) (1994a), pp. 68–95.

1995. 'Scottish Foundations: Late Medieval Contributions', in Grant and Stringer (eds.), pp. 97–108.

Grant, Alexander and Stringer, Keith J. 1995a. 'Introduction: The Enigma of British History', in Grant and Stringer (eds.), pp. 3–11.

(eds.) 1995b. *Uniting the Kingdom? The Making of British History*, London and New York: Routledge.

Green, E. and Taylor, M. 1989. 'Further Thoughts on Little Englandism', in Samuel (ed.), vol. I, pp. 103–9.

Green, John Richard 1893. *A Short History of the English People*, revd. edn, New York: American Book Company.

Greene, Jack P. 1998. 'Empire and Identity from the Glorious Revolution to the American Revolution', in Marshall (ed.), pp. 208–30.

Greenfeld, Liah 1992. *Nationalism: Five Roads to Modernity*, Cambridge, MA: Harvard University Press.

1996a. 'Foreword' to Lukic and Lynch, pp. x–xiv.

1996b. 'The Modern Religion?', *Critical Review* 10 (2): 169–91.

Greengrass, Mark (ed.) 1991. *Conquest and Coalescence: The Shaping of the State in Early Modern Europe*, London: Edward Arnold.

Grew, Raymond (ed.) 1978. *Crises of Political Development in Europe and the United States*, Princeton: Princeton University Press.

Gross, John 1973. *The Rise and Fall of the Man of Letters: English Literary Life since 1800*, Harmondsworth: Penguin Books.

Guenée, B. 1985. *States and Rulers in Later Medieval Europe*, trans. J. Vale, Oxford: Oxford University Press.

Guth, Delloyd J. and McKenna, John W. (eds.) 1982. *Tudor Rule and Revolution*, Cambridge: Cambridge University Press.

Guy, John 1988. *Tudor England*, Oxford and New York: Oxford University Press.

Habermas, Jürgen 1995. 'Citizenship and National Identity: Some Reflections on the Future of Europe', in Ronald Beiner (ed.), *Theorizing Citizenship*, pp. 255–81, Albany, NY: State University of New York Press.

Hadfield, Andrew 1994. *Literature, Politics and National Identity: Reformation to Renaissance*, Cambridge: Cambridge University Press.

Hadfield, Andrew and Maley, Willy 1993. 'Irish Representations and English Alternatives', in Bradshaw, Hadfield and Malley (eds.), pp. 1–23.

Haigh, Christopher 1988. *Elizabeth I*, London and New York: Longman.

(ed.) 1990. *The Cambridge Historical Encyclopaedia of Great Britain and Ireland*, Cambridge: Cambridge University Press.

1993. *English Reformation: Religion, Politics and Society under the Tudors*, Oxford: Clarendon Press.

Hall, A. Rupert. 1962. *The Scientific Revolution 1500–1800*, 2nd edn, London: Longmans.

Hall, Catherine (ed.) 2000a. *Cultures of Empire: Colonizers in Britain and the Empire in the Nineteenth and Twentieth Centuries*, Manchester: Manchester University Press.

2000b. 'Introduction: Thinking the Postcolonial, Thinking the Empire', in Hall (ed.), pp. 1–33.

2001. 'British Cultural Identities and the Legacy of the Empire', in Morley and Robins (eds.), pp. 27–39.

Hall, John A. 1995. 'Nationalisms, Classified and Explained', in Periwal (ed.), pp. 8–33.

Hall, Stuart 1996. 'Introduction: Who Needs "Identity"?', in Stuart Hall and Paul du Gay (eds.), *Questions of Cultural Identity*, pp. 1–18, London: Sage Publications.

1997. 'Old and New Identities, Old and New Ethnicities', in Anthony D. King (ed.), *Culture, Globalization and the World System*, pp. 41–68, Minneapolis: University of Minnesota Press.

Haller, William 1963. *Foxe's Book of Martyrs and the Elect Nation*, London: Jonathan Cape.

Hammond, Gerald 1996. 'How They Brought the Good News to Halifax: Tyndale's Bible and the Emergence of the English Nation State', *Reformation* 1: 11–28.

Hansen, Randall 2000. *Citizenship and Immigration in Postwar Britain: The Institutional Foundations of a Multicultural Nation*, Oxford: Oxford University Press.

Hargreaves, Alec G. 1995. *Immigration, 'Race' and Ethnicity in Contemporary France*, London and New York: Routledge.

Harris, Jose 1993. *Private Lives, Public Spirit: Britain 1870–1914*, London: Penguin Books.

Harris, Tim 1999. 'Critical Perspectives: The Autonomy of English History', in Burgess (ed.), pp. 266–86.

Hartz, Louyis (ed.) 1964. *The Founding of New Societies*, New York: Harcourt, Brace and World.

Harvie, Christopher 1991. 'English Regionalism: The Dog that Never Barked', in Crick (ed.), pp. 105–18.

1993. 'Nineteenth-Century Scotland: Political Unionism and Cultural Nationalism, 1843–1906', in Asch (ed.), pp. 191–228.

1994a. 'Enlightenment to Renaissance: Scottish Cultural Life in the Nineteenth Century', in Bjørn, Grant and Stringer (eds.) (1994b), pp. 214–43.

1994b. *The Rise of Regional Europe*, London and New York: Routledge.

1995. *Scotland and Nationalism: Scottish Society and Politics 1707–1994*, 2nd edn, London and New York: Routledge.

1999. 'Uncool Britannia: Linda Colley's *Britons* Reconsidered', *Times Literary Supplement*, 8 January: 12.

Haseler, Stephen 1996. *The English Tribe*, London: Macmillan.

Hastings, Adrian 1997. *The Construction of Nationhood: Ethnicity, Religion and Nationalism*, Cambridge: Cambridge University Press.

Hay, Denys 1955–56. 'The Term "Great Britain" in the Middle Ages', *Proceedings of the Society of Antiquaries of Scotland* 89: 55–66.

1975. 'England, Scotland and Europe: The Problem of the Frontier', *Transactions of the Royal Historical Society*, 5th series, 25: 77–91.

Haydon, Colin 1993. *Anti-Catholicism in Eighteenth-Century England, c. 1714–80*, Manchester: Manchester University Press.

1998. ' "I Love my King and Country, but a Roman Catholic I Hate": Anti-Catholicism, Xenophobia and National Identity in Eighteenth-Century England', in Claydon and McBride (eds.), pp. 33–52.

Hayton, David 1987. 'Anglo-Irish Attitudes: Changing Perceptions of National Identity Among the Protestant Ascendancy in Ireland, *ca.* 1690–1750', *Studies in Eighteenth-Century Culture* 17: 145–57.

1995. 'Constitutional Experiments and Political Expediency, 1689–1725', in Ellis and Barber (eds.), pp. 276–305.

Hazareesingh, Sudhir 1994. *Political Traditions in Modern France*, Oxford: Oxford University Press.

Heal, Felicity and Holmes, Clive (eds.) 1994. *The Gentry in England and Wales, 1500–1700*, Basingstoke: Macmillan.

Hechter, Michael 1993. 'Nationalism Redux', *Contemporary Sociology* 22 (4): 502–5.

1999. *Internal Colonialism: The Celtic Fringe in British National Development*, 2nd edn, New Brunswick, NJ and London: Transaction Books.

2000. *Containing Nationalism*, Oxford and New York: Oxford University Press.

Hedetoft, Ulf 1985. *British Colonialism and Modern Identity*, Aalborg: Aalborg Universitetsforlag.

Heffer, Simon 1999. *Nor Shall My Sword: The Reinvention of England*, London: Weidenfeld and Nicolson.

Hegel, Georg Wilhelm Friedrich (1830–31) 1956. *The Philosophy of History*, trans. J. Sibree, New York: Dover Publications.

Helgerson, Richard 1992. *Forms of Nationhood: The Elizabethan Writing of England*, Chicago and London: University of Chicago Press.

Hennegan, Alison 1990. 'Personalities and Principles: Aspects of Literature and Life in *Fin-de-Siècle* England', in Teich and Porter (eds.), pp. 170–215.

Herman, Peter C. 1995. ' "O, 'tis a gallant king": Shakespeare's *Henry V* and the Crisis of the 1590s', in Hoak (ed.), pp. 204–25.

Hernan, Joseph M. 1976. 'The Last Whig Historian and Consensual History: George Macaulay Trevelyan 1876–1962', *American Historical Review* 81: 66–97.

Hertz, Frederick 1944. *Nationality in History and Politics*, London: Routledge and Kegan Paul.

Hexter, J. H. 1961a. *Reappraisals in History*, London: Longmans.

1961b. 'Storm over the Gentry', in Hexter 1961a, pp. 117–62.

1961c. 'The Education of the Aristocracy in the Renaissance', in Hexter 1961a, pp. 45–70.

1961d. 'The Myth of the Middle Class in Tudor England', in Hexter 1961a, pp. 71–116.

1961e. 'Factors in Modern History', in Hexter 1961a, pp. 26–44.

Heyck, T. W. 1982. *The Transformation of Intellectual Life in Victorian England*, London: Croom Helm.

Higham, N. J. 1995. *An English Empire: Bede and the Early Anglo-Saxon Kings*, Manchester and New York: Manchester University Press.

Hill, Christopher 1970. *God's Englishman: Oliver Cromwell and the English Revolution*, London: Weidenfeld and Nicolson.

1973. *The World Turned Upside Down: Radical Ideas During the English Revolution*, New York: The Viking Press.

1986a. *Puritanism and Revolution: Studies in Interpretation of the English Revolution of the 17th Century*, Harmondsworth: Penguin Books.

1986b. 'The Norman Yoke', in Hill 1986a, pp. 58–125.

1989a. 'History and Patriotism', in Samuel (ed.), vol. I, pp. 3–8.

1989b. 'The English Revolution and Patriotism', in Samuel (ed.), vol. I, pp. 159–67.

1990. *Antichrist in Seventeenth-Century England*, revd. edn, London and New York: Verso.

1993. *The English Bible and the Seventeenth-Century Revolution*, London: Allen Lane.

Hill, Jacqueline 1995. 'Ireland without Union: Molyneaux and His Legacy', in Robertson (ed.), pp. 271–96.

Hilton, Rodney 1989. 'Were the English English?', in Samuel (ed.), vol. I, pp. 39–43.

Hingley, Richard 2001. *Roman Officers and English Gentlemen: The Imperial Origins of Roman Archaeology*, London and New York: Routledge.

Hiro, Dilip 1992. *Black British, White British: A History of Race Relations in Britain*, revd. edn, London: Paladin.

Hirst, Derek 1996. 'The English Republic and the Meaning of Britain', in Bradshaw and Morrill (eds.), pp. 192–219.

Hirst, Paul 1994. *Associative Democracy: New Forms of Economic and Social Governance*, Cambridge: Polity Press.

Hitchens, Peter 2000. *The Abolition of Britain: From Winston Churchill to Princess Diana*, 2nd edn, San Francisco: Encounter Books.

Hoak, Dale (ed.) 1995. *Tudor Political Culture*, Cambridge: Cambridge University Press.

Hobsbawm, Eric 1984. 'Mass-Producing Traditions: Europe, 1870–1914', in Hobsbawm and Ranger (eds.), pp. 263–307.

1992. *Nations and Nationalism Since 1780: Programme, Myth, Reality*, 2nd edn, Cambridge: Cambridge University Press.

1997. 'The End of Empires', in Barkey and von Hagen (eds.), pp. 12–16.

Hobsbawm, Eric and Ranger, Terence (eds.) 1984. *The Invention of Tradition*, Cambridge: Cambridge University Press.

Hobson, J. A. (1938) 1988. *Imperialism: A Study*, 3rd edn, London: Unwin Hyman (1st edn 1902).

Hont, Istvan 1994. 'The Permanent Crisis of a Divided Mankind: "Contemporary Crisis of the Nation State" in Historical Perspective', *Political Studies* 42: 166–231.

Hopkins, Harry 1963. *The New Look: A Social History of the Forties and Fifties in Britain*, London: Secker and Warburg.

Hopkinson, Tom (ed.) 1970. *Picture Post 1938–1950*, Harmondsworth: Penguin Books.

Hoppen, K. Theodore 1998. *The Mid-Victorian Generation 1846–1886*, Oxford: Oxford University Press.

Horsman, Reginald 1976. 'Origins of Racial Anglo-Saxonism in Great Britain Before 1850', *Journal of the History of Ideas* 37 (3): 387–410.

Houghton, Walter E. 1957. *The Victorian Frame of Mind*, New Haven, CT and London: Yale University Press.

Howes, Frank 1966. *The English Musical Renaissance*, London: Secker and Warburg.

Howkins, Alun 1986. 'The Discovery of Rural England', in Colls and Dodd (eds.), pp. 62–88.

1989. 'Greensleaves and the Idea of National Music', in Samuel (ed.), vol. III, pp. 89–98.

2001. 'Rurality and English Identity', in Morley and Robins (eds.), pp. 145–56.

Hudson, Anne 1982. 'Lollardy: The English Heresy?', in Mews (ed.), pp. 261–83.

Hudson, Pat 1992. *The Industrial Revolution*, London: Edward Arnold.

Hughes, Thomas (1857) 1986. *Tom Brown's Schooldays*, New York: New American Library.

Huizinga, Johan 1959a. *Men and Ideas: History, the Middle Ages, the Renaissance*, trans. James S. Holmes and Hans van Marle, New York: Meridian Press.

1959b. 'Patriotism and Nationalism in European History', in Huizinga 1959a, pp. 97–155.

Hume, David (1741) 1987. 'Of National Character', in *Essays, Moral, Political, and Literary*, ed. Eugene F. Miller, Indianapolis: Liberty Classics.

Hussey, Stanley 1994. 'Nationalism and Language in England, *c.* 1300–1500', in Bjørn, Grant and Stringer (eds.), 1994a, pp. 96–108.

Hutchinson, John and Smith, Anthony D. (eds.) 1994. *Nationalism*, Oxford and New York: Oxford University Press.

Hyam, Ronald 1999. 'The British Empire in the Edwardian Era', in Brown and Louis (eds.), pp. 47–63.

Hyman, Paula E. 1998. *The Jews of Modern France*, Berkeley and Los Angeles: University of California Press.

Hynes, Samuel 1968. *The Edwardian Turn of Mind*, Princeton: Princeton University Press.

Ignatieff, Michael 1993. 'Strange Attachments', *The New Republic*, 29 March: 42–6.

1994. *Blood and Belonging: Journeys into the New Nationalism*, London: Vintage.

Jacobson, Jessica 1997. 'Perceptions of Britishness', *Nations and Nationalism* 3 (2): 181–1999.

James, Ewart 1998. *NTC's Dictionary of the United Kingdom*, Chicago, IL: NTC Publishing Company.

James, Henry (1905) 1981. *English Hours*, Oxford: Oxford University Press.

Jaszi, Oscar (1929) 1961. *The Dissolution of the Habsburg Monarchy*, Chicago: Chicago University Press.

Jeffrey, Keith (ed.) 1996. *An Irish Empire? Aspects of Ireland and the British Empire*, Manchester: Manchester University Press.

Jenkins, Brian and Sofos, Spyros A. (eds.), 1996. *Nation and Identity in Contemporary Europe*, London and New York: Routledge.

Jenkins, Philip 1983. *The Making of a Ruling Class: The Glamorgan Gentry 1640–1790*, Cambridge: Cambridge University Press.

1995. 'The Anglican Church and the Unity of Britain: the Welsh Experience, 1560–1714', in Ellis and Barber (eds.), pp. 115–38.

1998. 'Seventeenth-Century Wales: Definition and Identity', in Bradshaw and Roberts (eds.), pp. 213–35.

Jenkins, Richard 1997. *Rethinking Ethnicity: Arguments and Explorations*, London and Thousand Oaks, CA: Sage Publications.

Jenkyns, Richard 1981. *The Victorians and Ancient Greece*, Oxford: Basil Blackwell.

Johnson. Lesley 1995a. 'Imagining Communities: Medieval and Modern', in Forde, Johnson and Murray (eds.), pp. 1–10.

1995b. 'Etymologies, Genealogies, and Nationalities (Again)', in Forde, Johnson and Murray (eds.), pp. 125–36.

Johnson, Paul 1995. 'Being English is getting a lot of laughs', *The Spectator*, 5 August: 21.

Jones, Barry and Keating, Michael (eds.) 1995. *The European Union and the Regions*, Oxford: Oxford University Press.

Jones, Edwin 2000. *The English Nation: The Great Myth*, Thrupp, Glos.: Sutton Publishing.

Jones, Gareth Stedman 1976. *Outcast London: A Study in the Relationship Between Classes in Victorian Society*, Harmondsworth: Penguin Books.

Jones, Maldwyn A. (1991). 'The Scotch-Irish in British America', in Bailyn (ed.), pp. 284–313.

Jones, R. F. 1982. *Ancients and Moderns: A Study of the Rise of the Scientific Movement in England*, New York: Dover.

Jones, W. R. 1971. 'England Against the Celtic Fringe: A Study in Cultural Stereotypes', *Journal of World History* 13: 155–71.

Joppke, Christian 1994. 'Revisionism, dissidence, nationalism: opposition in Leninist regimes', *British Journal of Sociology* 45 (4): 544–61.

1999. *Immigration and the Nation State: The United States, Germany, and Great Britain*, Oxford and New York: Oxford University Press.

Judd, Denis 1996. *Empire: The British Imperial Experience from 1765 to the Present*, New York: Basic Books.

Junor, Penny 1993. *The Major Enigma*, London: Michael Joseph.

Kamen, Henry 1984. *European Society 1500–1700*, London: Hutchinson.

Kamenka, Eugene (ed.) 1973a. *Nationalism: The Nature and Evolution of an Idea*, Canberra: Australian National University Press.

1973b. 'Political Nationalism – The Evolution of an Idea', in Kamenka (ed.), pp. 3–20.

Kates, Gary 1989. 'Jews into Frenchmen: Nationality and Representation in Revolutionary France', *Social Research* 56 (1): 213–32.

Kautsky, John H. 1997. *The Politics of Aristocratic Empires*, 2nd edn, New Brunswick, NJ and London: Transaction Books.

Keane, John 1995. 'Nations, Nationalism and European Citizens', in Periwal (ed.), pp. 182–207.

Kearney, Hugh 1995. *The British Isles: A History of Four Nations*, 2nd edn, Cambridge: Cambridge University Press.

Kedourie, Elie 1993. *Nationalism*, 4th edn, Oxford: Blackwell.

Keeney, Baranaby C. (1947) 1972. 'Military Service and the Development of Nationalism in England, 1272–1327', as 'England' in Tipton (ed.), pp. 87–97.

Kelley, Donald R. 1991. *Renaissance Humanism*, Boston, MA: Twayne Publishers.

Kelly, James 1987. 'The Origins of the Act of Union: an Examination of Unionist Opinion in Britain and Ireland', *Irish Historical Studies* 25 (99): 236–63.

Kendle, John 1997. *Federal Britain: A History*, London: Routledge.

Keyder, Calgar 1997. 'The Ottoman Empire', in Barkey and von Hagen (eds.), pp. 30–44.

Khilnani, Sunil 1998. *The Idea of India*, London: Penguin Books.

Kidd, Colin 1993. *Subverting Scotland's Past: Scottish Whig Historians and the Creation of an Anglo-British Identity, 1689–c. 1830*, Cambridge: Cambridge University Press.

  1996. 'North Britishness and the Nature of Eighteenth-Century British Patriotisms', *The Historical Journal* 39 (2): 361–82.

  1997. 'Sentiment, Race and Revival: Scottish Identities in the Aftermath of Enlightenment', in Brockliss and Eastwood (eds.), pp. 110–25.

  1998. 'Protestantism, Constitutionalism and British Identity under the Later Stuarts', in Bradshaw and Roberts (eds.), pp. 321–42.

  1999. *British Identities Before Nationalism: Ethnicity and Nationhood in the Atlantic World 1600–1800*, Cambridge: Cambridge University Press.

Kiernan, V. G. 1965. 'State and Nation in Western Europe', *Past and Present* 31: 20–38.

Kiernan, Victor 1972. 'Victorian London: Unending Purgatory', *New Left Review* 76: 73–90.

  1993. 'The British Isles: Celt and Saxon', in Teich and Porter (eds.), pp. 1–34.

Kingsley, Charles (1855) 1947. *Westward Ho!*, New York: The Heritage Press.

Kipling, Rudyard 1940. 'The Glory of the Garden', in *Rudyard Kipling's Verse: Definitive Edition*, London: Hodder and Stoughton.

Kirkland, Dorothy 1938–39. 'The Growth of National Sentiment in France Before the Fifteenth Century', *History* 23: 12–24.

Knowles, David 1962. 'Bede the Venerable', in *Saints and Scholars*, pp. 12–18, London: Cambridge University Press.

Koenigsberger, Helmut 1975. 'Spain', in Ranum (ed.), pp. 144–72.

    1987. '*Dominum Regale* or *Dominium Politicum et regale*: Monarchies and Parliaments in Early Modern History', in *Politicians and Virtuosi: Essays in Early Modern History*, pp. 1–25, London and Roncerverte: The Hambledon Press.

Kohn, Hans 1940. 'The Genesis and Character of English Nationalism', *Journal of the History of Ideas* 1: 69–94.

    1944. *The Idea of Nationalism: A Study in Its Origins and Background*, New York: Macmillan.

    1955. *Nationalism: Its Meaning and History*, Princeton, NJ: D. Van Nostrand Company.

    1961. *The Habsburg Empire, 1804–1918. Text and Documents*, Princeton, NJ: D. Van Nostrand Company.

Krieger, Leonard 1975. 'Germany', in Ranum (ed.), pp. 67–97.

Kumar, Krishan 1988. 'Thoughts on the Present Discontents in Britain', in *The Rise of Modern Society*, pp. 290–328, Oxford: Basil Blackwell.

    1994. 'A Pilgrimage of Hope: William Morris's Journey to Utopia', *Utopian Studies* 5 (1): 89–106.

    1995. 'Versions of the Pastoral: Poverty and the Poor in English Fiction from the 1840s to the 1950s', *Journal of Historical Sociology* 8 (1): 1–35.

    1998. 'Morris and Englishness', in Adriana Corrado (ed.), *Pellegrini Della Speranza*, pp. 189–207, Naples: CUEN.

    2000. 'Nation and Empire: English and British National Identity in Comparative Perspective', *Theory and Society* 29 (5): 575–608.

    2001. 'Sociology and the Englishness of English Social Theory', *Sociological Theory* 19 (1): 41–64.

Kureishi, Hanif 1990. *The Buddha of Suburbia*, London: Faber and Faber.

    1995. *The Black Album*, London: Faber and Faber.

Lake, Peter 1980. 'The Significance of the Elizabethan Identification of the Pope as Antichrist', *Journal of Ecclesiastical History* 31: 161–71.

    1989. 'Anti-popery: the structure of a prejudice', in Richard Cust and Ann Hughes (eds.), *Conflict in Early Stuart England*, pp. 72–106, London: Longman.

Lake, Peter and Dowling, Maria (eds.) 1987. *Protestantism and the National Church in Sixteenth-Century England*, London: Croom Helm.

Lamont, William 1969. *Godly Rule: Politics and Religion 1603–1660*, London: Macmillan.

Landsman, Ned C. 1994. 'The Provinces and the Empire: Scotland, the American Colonies and the Development of British Provincial Identity', in Stone (ed.), pp. 258–87.

Langford, Paul 1992. *A Polite and Commercial People: England 1727–1783*, Oxford: Oxford University Press.

2000. *Englishness Identified: Manners and Character 1650–1850*, Oxford: Oxford University Press.

Langlands, Rebecca 1999. 'Britishness or Englishness? The Historical Problem of National Identity in Britain', *Nations and Nationalism* 5 (1): 53–69.

Lawrence, D. H. (1930) 1950. 'Nottingham and the Mining Country', in *D. H. Lawrence: Selected Essays*, pp. 114–22, Harmondsworth: Penguin Books.

Leckie, R. William Jr. 1981. *The Passage of Dominion: Geoffrey of Monmouth and the Periodization of Insular History in the Twelfth Century*, Toronto and London: University of Toronto Press.

Lee, A Robert (ed.) 1995. *Other Britain, Other British: Contemporary Multicultural Fiction*, London: Pluto Press.

Leersen, Joep 1988. 'Anglo-Irish Patriotism and Its European Context: Notes Towards a Reassessment', *Eighteenth-Century Ireland* 3: 7–24.

1997a. *Mere Irish and Fíor-Ghael: Studies in the Idea of Irish Nationality, its Development and Literary Expression prior to the Nineteenth Century*, 2nd edn, Notre Dame: University of Notre Dame Press/Cork: Cork University Press.

1997b. *Remembrance and Imagination: Patterns in the Historical and Literary Representation of Ireland in the Nineteenth Century*, Notre Dame: University of Notre Dame Press/Cork: Cork University Press.

LeMahieu, D. L. 1988. *A Culture for Democracy: Mass Communication and the Cultivated Mind in Britain Between the Wars*, Oxford: Clarendon Press.

Lenman, Bruce 1981. *Integration, Enlightenment, and Industrialization: Scotland 1746–1832*, Toronto: University of Toronto Press.

Leonard, Mark 1997. *Britain TM: Renewing Our Identity*, London: Demos and The Design Council.

Le Rider, Jacques 1994. 'Hugo von Hofmannsthal and the Austrian Idea of Central Europe', in Robertson and Timms (eds.), pp. 121–35.

Letwin, Shirley 1992. *The Anatomy of Thatcherism*, London: Fontana.

Levack, Brian P. 1987. *The Formation of the British State: England, Scotland and the Union 1603–1707*, Oxford: Clarendon Press.

Lewis, Anthony 1995. 'Henry V: Two Films', in Ted Mico, John Miller-Monzon and *David Rubel (eds.), Past Imperfect: History According to the Movies*, pp. 48–53, New York: Henry Holt and Company.

Lichtheim, George 1971. *Imperialism*, Harmondsworth: Penguin Books.

Lieven, Dominic 1992. *The Aristocracy in Europe 1815–1914*, London: Macmillan.

1995. 'The Russian Empire and the Soviet Union as Imperial Polities', *Journal of Contemporary History* 30 (4): 607–36.

1998. 'Russian, Imperial and Soviet Identities', *Transactions of the Royal Historical Society*, 6th series, 8: 253–69.

1999. 'Dilemmas of Empire 1850–1918: Power, Territory, Identity', *Journal of Contemporary History* 34 (2): 163–200.

2001. *Empire: The Russian Empire and its Rivals*, New Haven, CT and London: Yale University Press.

Light, Alison 1991. *Forever England: Femininity, Literature and Conservatism Between the Wars*, London and New York: Routledge.

Llobera, Josep R. 1994. *The God of Modernity: The Development of Nationalism in Western Europe*, Oxford and Providence, RI: Berg Publishers.

Lloyd, John 1998. 'Cool Britannia Warms Up', *New Statesman and Society*, 13 March: 10–11.

1999. 'Goodbye to All That', *Financial Times*, 24/25 April: v.

Lloyd, T. O. 1996. *The British Empire, 1558–1995*, 2nd edn, Oxford: Oxford University Press.

Loades, David 1982. 'The Origins of English Protestant Nationalism', in Mews (ed.), pp. 297–307.

1997a. *Tudor Government: Structures of Authority in the Sixteenth Century*, Oxford and Malden, MA: Blackwell.

1997b. *Power in Tudor England*, New York: St. Martin's Press.

Louis, Wm. Roger 1999. 'Introduction', in Winks (ed.), pp. 1–53.

Lowenthal, David 1991. 'British National Identity and the English Landscape', *Rural History* 2 (2): 205–30.

Lowerson, John 1980. 'Battles for the Countryside', in Frank Gloversmith (ed.), *Class, Culture and Social Change: A New View of the 1930s*, pp. 258–80, Brighton, Sussex: The Harvester Press.

Loyn, H. R. 1991. *The Making of the English Nation: From the Anglo-Saxons to Edward I*, London: Thames and Hudson.

Lydon, James F. 1995. 'Nation and Race in Medieval Ireland', in Forde, Johnson and Murray (eds.), pp. 103–24.

Lynch, Michael 1994. 'National Identity in Ireland and Scotland, 1500–1640', in Bjørn, Grant and Stringer (eds), 1994a, pp. 109–36.

Lynch, Phillip 1999. *The Politics of Nationhood: Sovereignty, Britishness and Conservative Politics*, Basingstoke: Macmillan.

Macaulay, Thomas Babington (1835) 1907a. 'Sir James MacKintosh', in *Critical and Historical Essays*, 2 vols., vol. I: 109–31, London: Dent and Sons.

Macaulay, Lord (1848–55) 1979. *The History of England*, ed. abridged with Introduction by Hugh Trevor-Roper, Harmondsworth: Penguin.

MacCabe, Colin and Stewart, Olivia (eds.) 1986. *The BBC and Public Service Broadcasting*, Manchester: Manchester University Press.

MacCaffrey, W. T. 1965. 'England: The Crown and the New Aristocracy', *Past and Present* 30: 52–64.

Macdonnell, A. G. (1933) 1949. *England, Their England*, London: Pan Books.

MacDougall, Hugh A. 1982. *Racial Myth in English History: Trojans, Teutons, and Anglo-Saxons*, Montreal: Harvest House and Hanover, NH: University Press of New England.

Macinnes, Allan, I. 1999a. 'Politically Reactionary Brits? The Promotion of Anglo-Scottish Union, 1603–1707', in Connolly (ed.), pp. 43–55.

1999b. 'Regal Union for Britain, 1603–38', in Burgess (ed.), pp. 33–64.

Mackenzie, John M. 1984. *Propaganda and Empire: The Manipulation of British Public Opinion 1880–1960*, Manchester and New York: Manchester University Press.

(ed.) 1986. *Imperialism and Popular Culture*, Manchester: Manchester University Press.

1993. 'On Scotland and the Empire', *International History Review* 15 (4): 714–39.

1998. 'Empire and National Identities: The Case of Scotland', *Transactions of the Royal Historical Society*, 6th series, 8: 215–31.

1999a. 'Empire and Metropolitan Cultures', in Porter (ed.), pp. 270–93.

1999b. 'The Popular Culture of Empire in Britain', in Brown and Louis (eds.), pp. 212–31.

Mackie, J. D. 1978. *A History of Scotland*, revised and ed. Bruce Lenman and Geoffrey Parker, Harmondsworth: Penguin.

Madgwick, Peter and Rose, Richard (eds.) 1982. *The Territorial Dimension in United Kingdom Politics*, London: Macmillan.

Malik, Kenan 1996. *The Meaning of Race: Race, History and Culture in Western Society*, London: Macmillan.

Mandler, Peter 1997a. 'Against "Englishness": English Culture and the Limits to Rural Nostalgia, 1850–1940', *Transactions of the Royal Historical Society*, 6th series, 7: 155–75.

1997b. ' "In the Olden Time": Romantic History and English National Identity, 1820–50', in Brockliss and Eastwood (eds.), pp. 78–92.

2000. ' "Race" and "Nation" in Mid-Victorian Thought', in Collini, Whatmore and Young (eds.), pp. 224–44.

2001. 'The Consciousness of Modernity:? Liberalism and the English National Character, 1870–1940', in Martin Daunton and Bernhard Rieger (eds.), *Meanings of Modernity: Britain from the Late-Victorian Era to World War II*, pp. 119–44, Oxford and New York: Berg.

Mann, Michael 1986. *The Sources of Social Power, volume one: A History of Power from the Beginning to A.D. 1760*, Cambridge: Cambridge University Press.

1995. 'A Political Theory of Nationalism and its Excesses', in Periwal (ed.), pp. 44–64.

Marcu, E. D. 1976. *Sixteenth Century Nationalism*, New York: Abaris Books.

Marquand, David 1993. 'The Twilight of the British State? Henry Dubb versus Sceptred Awe', *The Political Quarterly* 64 (2): 210–21.

1995. 'How United is the Modern United Kingdom?', in Grant and Stringer (eds.), pp. 277–91.

Marr, Andrew 2000. *The Day Britain Died*, London: Profile Books.

Marsh, Jan 1982. *Back to the Land: The Pastoral Impulse in Victorian England from 1880–1914*, London: Quarter Books.

Marshall, P. J. 1993. 'No Fatal Impact? The Elusive History of Imperial Britain', *Times Literary Supplement*, 12 March: 8–10.

(ed.) 1998. *The Eighteenth Century*, The Oxford History of the British Empire, vol. II, Oxford and New York: Oxford University Press.

Martines, Lauro 1980. *Power and Imagination: City-States in Renaissance Italy*, New York: Vintage Books.

Mason, Roger A. (ed.) 1987a. *Scotland and England 1286–1815*, Edinburgh: John Donald Publishers.

1987b. 'Scotching the Brut: Politics, History and National Myth in Sixteenth-Century Britain', in Mason (ed.), pp. 60–84.

(ed.) 1994a. *Scots and Britons: Scottish Political Thought and the Union of 1603*, Cambridge: Cambridge University Press.

1994b. 'The Scottish Reformation and the Origins of Anglo-British Imperialism', in Mason (ed.), pp. 161–86.

Masterman, C. F. G. (1909) 1960. *The Condition of England*, ed., J. F. Boulton, London: Methuen.

Masur, Gerhard 1966. *Prophets of Yesterday: Studies in European Culture 1890–1914*, New York: Harper Colophon.

Matless, David 1998. *Landscape and Englishness*, London: Reaktion Books.

Mayer, Arno J. 1981. *The Persistence of the Old Regime: Europe to the Great War*, New York: Pantheon Books.

McArthur, Tom 1985. 'An ABC of World English', *English Today* 1 (January): 11–17; 2 (April): 21–7; 3 (July): 27–33; 4 (October): 31–6.

McBride, Ian 1998. 'Protestantism and Patriotism in Eighteenth-Century Ireland', in Claydon and McBride (eds.), pp. 236–61.

McCrone, David 1992. *Understanding Scotland: The Sociology of a Stateless Nation*, London and New York: Routledge.

1997. 'Unmasking Britannia: The Rise and Fall of British National Identity', *Nations and Nationalism* 3 (4): 579–96.

2000. 'National Identity', in Geoff Payne (ed.), *Social Divisions*, pp. 115–32, London: Macmillan.

2001. 'Scotland and the Union: Changing Identities in the British State', in Morley and Robins (eds.), pp. 97–108.

McCrone, David, Kendrick, Stephen and Straw, Pat (eds.) 1989. *The Making of Scotland: Nation, Culture and Social Change*, Edinburgh: Edinburgh University Press.

McCrone, David, Stewart, Robert, Kiely, Richard and Bechhofer, Frank 1998. 'Who Are We? Problematising National Identity', *The Sociological Review* 46 (4): 629–52.

McEachern, Claire 1996. *The Poetics of English Nationhood, 1590–1612*, Cambridge: Cambridge University Press.

McEachern, Claire and Shuger, Deborah (eds.) 1997. *Religion and Culture in Renaissance England*, Cambridge: Cambridge University Press.

McGiffert, Michael 1982. 'God's Controversy with Jacobean England', *American Historical Review* 88: 1151–76.

McGregor, J. F. and Reay, B. (eds.) 1986. *Radical Religion in the English Revolution*, Oxford: Oxford University Press.

McKenna, John W. 1982. 'How God Became an Englishman', in Guth and McKenna (eds.), pp. 25–43.

McLaren, A. N. 1999. *Political Culture in the Reign of Elizabeth: Queen and Commonwealth 1558–1585*, Cambridge: Cambridge University Press.

McLelland, V. Alan and Hodgetts, Michael (eds.) 2000. *From Without the Flaminian Gate: 150 Years of Roman Catholicism in England and Wales, 1850–2000*, London: Darton, Longman and Todd.

McLeod, Hugh 1999. 'Protestantism and British National Identity', in van der Veer and Lehman (eds.), pp. 44–70.

Mehta, Uday Singh 1999. *Liberalism and Empire: A Study in Nineteenth-Century British Liberal Thought*, Chicago and London: University of Chicago Press.

Meinecke, Friedrich (1907) 1970. *Cosmopolitanism and the National State*, trans. Robert B. Kimber, Princeton: Princeton University Press.

Melman, Billie 1991. 'Claiming the Nation's Past: The Invention of an Anglo-Saxon Tradition', *Journal of Contemporary History* 26 (3–4): 575–95.

Merck, Mandy (ed.) 1998. *After Diana: Irreverent Elegies*, London: Verso.

Merriman, Marcus 1995. 'Stewarts and Tudors in the Mid-Sixteenth Century', in Grant and Stringer (eds.), pp. 111–22.

Mews, Stuart (ed.) 1982. *Religion and National Identity*, Oxford: Basil Blackwell.

Milbank, Alison 2000. 'People in Glass Houses: Queen Victoria, the Sensation Novel Heroine and the Crystal Palace', paper given at the British Studies Seminar, University of Virginia, May.

Miller, David 1995a. 'Reflections on British National Identity', *New Community* 21 (2): 153–66.

1995b. *On Nationality*, Oxford: Clarendon Press.

Miller, Simon 1995a. 'Urban Dreams and Rural Reality: Land and Landscape in English Culture, 1920–45', *Rural History* 6 (1): 89–102.

1995b. 'Land, Landscape and the Question of Culture: English Urban Hegemony and Research Needs', *Journal of Historical Sociology* 8 (1): 94–107.

Milton, John 1990. *Complete English Poems, of Education, Areopagitica*, ed. Gordon Campbell, London: J. M. Dent and Sons.

Mitchison, Rosalind 1978. 'Patriotism and National Identity in Eighteenth-Century Scotland', in Moody (ed.), pp. 73–95.

Modood, Tariq 1999. 'New Forms of Britishness: Post-Immigration Ethnicity and Hybridity in Britain', in R. Lentin (ed.), *The Expanding Nation: Towards a Multi-Ethnic Ireland* (Conference Proceedings), Dublin: Trinity College.

2001. 'British Asian Identities: Something Old, Something Borrowed, Something New', in Morley and Robins (eds.), pp. 67–78.

Modood, Tariq and Werbner, Pnina (eds.) 1997. *The Politics of Multiculturalism in the New Europe: Racism, Identity and Community*, London and New York: Zed Books.

Modood, Tariq, Berthoud, Richard, Lakey, Jane, Nazroo, James, Smith, Patten, Virdee, Satnam, Beishon, Sharon 1997. *Ethnic Minorities in Britain: Diversity and Disadvantage*, London: Policy Studies Institute.

Mommsen, Wolfgang J. 1978. 'Power Politics, Imperialism and National Emancipation, 1870–1914', in Moody (ed.), pp. 121–40.

Montesquieu, Baron de (1748) 1949. *The Spirit of the Laws*, 2 vols., trans. Thomas Nugent, New York: Hafner Publishing Company.

Moody, T. W. (ed.) 1978. *Nationality and the Pursuit of National Independence*, Belfast: The Appletree Press.

Morgan, Hiram 1991–92. 'Mid-Atlantic Blues', *Irish Review* 11: 50–5.

1996. 'British Policies before the British State', in Bradshaw and Morrill (eds.), pp. 66–88.

Morgan, Kenneth O. 1982. *Rebirth of a Nation: A History of Modern Wales*, Oxford: Oxford University Press.

(ed.) 1984. *The Oxford Illustrated History of Britain*, Oxford: Oxford University Press.

Morley, David and Robins, Kevin (eds.) 2001a. *British Cultural Studies: Geography, Nationality, and Identity*, Oxford: Oxford University Press.

2001b. 'The National Culture and its Global Context', in Morley and Robins (eds.), pp. 1–15.

Morrill, John 1993a. *The Nature of the English Revolution*, London and New York: Longman.

1993b. 'The Religious Context of the English Civil War', in Morill 1993a, pp. 45–68.

1993c. 'The Scottish National Covenant of 1638 in its British Context', in Morrill 1993a, pp. 91–117.

1993d. 'The Causes of Britain's Civil Wars', in Morrill 1993a, pp. 252–72.

1993e. 'The Britishness of the English Revolution 1640–1660', in Asch (ed.), pp. 83–115.

1995a. 'Three Kingdoms and One Commonwealth? The Enigma of Mid-Seventeenth-Century Britain and Ireland', in Grant and Stringer (eds.), pp. 170–90.

1995b. 'The Fashioning of Britain', in Ellis and Barber (eds.), pp. 8–39.

1996. 'The British Problem, *c.* 1534–1707', in Bradshaw and Morrill (eds.), pp. 1–38.

Morris, William (1890) 1995. *News from Nowhere*, ed. and introduced Krishan Kumar, Cambridge: Cambridge University Press.

Morton, A. V. 1927. *In Search of England*. London: Methuen.

Motyl, Alexander 1992. 'From Imperial Decay to Imperial Collapse: The Fall of the Soviet Union in Comparative Perspective', in Rudolf and Good (eds.), pp. 15–43.

1997. 'Thinking About Empire', in Barkey and von Hagen (eds.), pp. 19–29.

1999. *Revolutions, Nations, Empires: Conceptual Limits and Theoretical Possibilities*, New York: Columbia University Press.

Murdoch, Alexander 1998. *British History 1660–1832: National Identity and Local Culture*, London: Macmillan.

Nairn, Tom 1981. *The Break-Up of Britain*, 2nd edn, London: Verso.

1994. *The Enchanted Glass: Britain and its Monarchy*, 2nd edn, New York: Vintage.

1997. *Faces of Nationalism: Janus Revisited*, London: Verso.

2000. *After Britain: New Labour and the Return of Scotland*, London: Granta Books.

2001. 'Farewell Britannia: Break-Up or New Union?', *New Left Review*, 2nd series, 7: 55–74.

Newman, Gerald 1987. *The Rise of English Nationalism: A Cultural History 1740–1830*, London: Weidenfeld and Nicolson.

New Statesman and Society 1995. 'England, Whose England?', 24 February.

Nicholls, Mark 1999. *A History of the Modern British Isles 1529–1603: The Two Kingdoms*, Oxford and Malden, MA: Blackwell Publishers.

Noiriel, Gérard 1996. *The French Melting Pot: Immigration, Citizenship, and National Identity*, trans. Geoffrey de Laforcade, Minneapolis: University of Minnesota Press.

Noonkester, Myron C. 1997. 'The Third British Empire: Transplanting the English Shire to Wales, Scotland, Ireland and America', *Journal of British Studies* 36 (3): 251–84.

Nordau, Max (1892) 1993. *Degeneration*, translated from the second German edition and introduced by George L. Mosse, Lincoln, NE: University of Nebraska Press.

O'Brien, Conor Cruise 1988a. 'Nationalism and the French Revolution', in Best (ed.), pp. 17–48.

    1988b. *God-Land: Reflections on Religion and Nationalism*, Cambridge, MA: Harvard University Press.

    1993. 'Inventing Britain', *The New Republic*, 8 March: 37–9.

O'Dea, Michael and Whelan, Kevin (eds.) 1995. *Nations and Nationalism: France, Britain, Ireland and the Eighteenth-Century Context*, Oxford: Voltaire Foundation.

Ohlmeyer, Jane H. 1998. ' "Civilizing of those Rude Partes": Colonization within Britain and Ireland, 1580s–1640s', in Canny (ed.), pp. 124–47.

O'Leary, Brendan 1999. 'The Nature of the British–Irish Agreement', *New Left Review*, 1st series, 233: 5–20.

Oomen, T. K. 1997. *Citizenship, Nationality and Ethnicity*, Cambridge: Polity Press.

Orwell, George (1941) 1970a. 'The Lion and the Unicorn: Socialism and the English Genius', in Orwell and Angus (eds.), II, pp. 74–134.

    (1947) 1970b. 'The English People', in Orwell and Angus (eds.), III, pp. 15–56.

    (1945) 1970c. 'Notes on Nationalism', in Orwell and Angus (eds.), III, pp. 410–431.

Orwell, Sonia and Angus, Ian (eds.) 1970. *The Collected Essays, Journalism and Letters of George Orwell*, 4 vols., Harmondsworth: Penguin Books.

Osmond, John 1988. *The Divided Kingdom*, London: Constable.

    2001. 'Welsh Politics in the New Millennium', in Morley and Robins (eds.), pp. 109–25.

Owen, Nicholas 1999. 'Critics of Empire in Britain', in Brown and Louis (eds.), pp. 188–211.

Pagden, Anthony 1995. *Lords of All the World: Ideologies of Empire in Spain, Britain and France, c. 1500–c. 1800*, New Haven, CT and London: Yale University Press.

Palmer, Robert R. 1940. 'The National Idea in France Before the Revolution', *Journal of the History of Ideas* 1 (1): 95–111.

Parkinson, C. Northcote 1961. *Parkinson's Law, or The Pursuit of Progress*, London: John Murray.

Paterson, Lindsay 1994. *The Autonomy of Modern Scotland*, Edinburgh: Edinburgh University Press.

Patterson, L. 1993. 'Making Identities in Fifteenth-Century England: Henry V and John Lydgate', in Cox and Reynolds (eds.), pp. 69–107.

Patterson, W. B. 1982. 'King James I and the Protestant Cause in the Crisis of 1618–22', in Mews (ed.), pp. 319–34.

2000. *King James VI and I and the Reunion of Christendom*, Cambridge: Cambridge University Press.

Paul, Kathleen 1997. *Whitewashing Britain: Race and Citizenship in the Postwar Era*, Ithaca, NY and London: Cornell University Press.

Paxman, Jeremy 1999. *The English: A Portrait of a People*, London: Penguin Books.

Paz, D. G. 1992. *Popular Anti-Catholicism in Mid-Victorian England*, Stanford, CA: Stanford University Press.

Pearsall, Derek 1999. 'Chaucer and Englishness', *Proceedings of the British Academy* 101: 77–99.

Penovich, Katherine R. 1995. 'From "Revolution Principles" to Union: Daniel Defoe's Intervention in the Scottish Debate', in Robertson (ed.), pp. 228–42.

Periwal, Sukumar (ed.) 1995. *Notions of Nationalism*, Budapest: Central European University Press.

Phillips, Trevor and Worsthorne, Peregrine 1996. 'England's On the Anvil', *Prospect*, March: 16–19.

Phillipson, N. T. 1970. 'Scottish Public Opinion and the Union in the Age of the Association', in Phillipson and Mitchison (eds.), pp. 125–47.

Phillipson, Nicholas 1981. 'The Scottish Enlightenment', in Roy Porter and Mikulás Teich (eds.), *The Enlightenment in National Context*, pp. 19–40, Cambridge: Cambridge University Press.

1987. 'Politics, Politeness and the Anglicisation of Early Eighteenth-Century Scottish Culture', in Mason (ed.), pp. 226–46.

Phillipson, N. T. and Mitchison, Rosalind (eds.) 1970. *Scotland in the Age of Improvement: Essays in Scottish History in the Eighteenth Century*, Edinburgh: Edinburgh University Press.

Pick, Daniel 1989. *Faces of Degeneration: A European Disorder, c. 1848–1918*, Cambridge: Cambridge University Press.

Pincus, Steven 1995. 'The English Debate Over Universal Monarchy', in Robertson (ed.), pp. 37–62.

1998. ' "To Protect English Liberties": The English Nationalist Revolution of 1688–89', in Claydon and McBride (eds.), pp. 75–104.

Pines, Jim 2001. 'Rituals and Representations of Black "Britishness" ', in Morley and Robins (eds.), pp. 57–66.

Pittock, Murray G. H. 1997. *Inventing and Resisting Britain: Cultural Identities in Britain and Ireland, 1685–1789*, London: Macmillan.

Plamenatz, John 1973. 'Two Types of Nationalism', in Kamenka (ed.), pp. 22–36.

Pocock, J. G. A. 1957. *The Ancient Constitution and the Feudal Law*, Cambridge: Cambridge University Press.

1975a. 'British History: A Plea for a New Subject', *Journal of Modern History* 47 (4): 601–28 (includes comments, pp. 622–8, by A. J. P. Taylor, Gordon Donaldson and Michael Hechter, with reply by Pocock).

1975b. 'England', in Ranum (ed.), pp. 98–117.

(ed.) 1980. *Three British Revolutions: 1641, 1688, 1776*, Princeton: Princeton University Press.

1982. 'The Limits and Divisions of British History: In Search of the Unknown Subject', *American Historical Review* 87 (2): 311–36.

1983. 'Hume and the American Revolution: The Dying Thoughts of a North Briton', in *Virtue, Commerce and History*, pp. 125–41, Cambridge: Cambridge University Press.

1992. 'History and Sovereignty: The Historiographical Response to Europeanization in Two British Cultures', *Journal of British Studies* 31: 358–89.

1995. 'Conclusion: Contingency, Identity, Sovereignty', in Grant and Stringer (eds.), pp. 292–302.

1996. 'The Atlantic Archiepelago and the War of the Three Kingdoms', in Bradshaw and Morrill (eds.), pp. 172–91.

Pollard, A. F. 1907. *Factors in Modern History*, New York: G. P. Putnam's Son.

'Pont' 1940. *The British Character, Studied and Revealed*, Introduced E. M. Delafield, Leipzig: Albatross Verlag.

Porter, Andrew (ed.) 1999a. *The Nineteenth Century*, The Oxford History of the British Empire, vol. III, Oxford and New York: Oxford University Press.

1999b. 'Religion, Missionary Enthusiasm, and Empire', in Porter (ed.), pp. 222–46.

Porter, Bernard 1987. *Britain, Europe and the World 1850–1986*, 2nd edn, London: George Allen and Unwin.

Porter, Roy 2000. *Enlightenment: Britain and the Creation of the Modern World*, London: Allen Lane the Penguin Press.

Powell, J. Enoch 1969. *Freedom and Reality: Selected Speeches*, ed. John Wood, Kingswood, Surrey: Elliott Rightway Books.

Preston, P. W. 1994. 'The Dissolution of Britain?', *The Political Quarterly* 65 (2): 191–202.

Prestwich, Michael 1987. 'Colonial Scotland: The English in Scotland under Edward I', in Mason (ed.), pp. 6–17.

Prestwich, Minna 1985. *International Calvinism, 1541–1715*, Oxford: Oxford University Press.

Priestley, J. B. 1973. *The English*, London: Heinemann.

(1934) 1977. *English Journey*, Harmondsworth: Penguin Books.

Ranum, Orest (ed.) 1975a. *National Consciousness, History and Political Culture in Early-Modern Europe*, Baltimore, MD and London: The Johns Hopkins University Press.

1975b. 'Introduction', in Ranum (ed.), pp. 1–19.

Redwood, John 1999. *The Death of Britain*, Basingstoke: Macmillan.

Reeve, John 1999. 'Britain or Europe? The Context of Early Modern English History', in Burgess (ed.), pp. 287–312.

Reith, J. C. W 1924. *Broadcast over Britain*, London: Hodder and Stoughton.

1949. *Into the Wind*, London: Hodder and Stoughton.

Renan, Ernest (1889) 1990. 'What is a Nation?', in Bhabha (ed.), pp. 8–22.

Reynolds, Susan 1985. 'What Do We Mean by "Anglo-Saxon" and "Anglo-Saxons"'?, *Journal of British Studies* 24: 395–414.

1997. *Kingdoms and Communities in Western Europe 900–1300*, 2nd edn, Oxford: Clarendon Press.

1999. 'How Different was England?', *Thirteenth Century England VII*, Proceedings of the Durham Conference 1997, ed. Michael Prestwich, Richard Britnell and Robin Frame, pp. 1–16, Woodbridge: The Boydell Press.

Rex, John 1995. 'Ethnic Identity and the Nation State: the Political Sociology of Multicultural Societies', *Social Identities* 1 (1): 21–34.

Rich, Paul B. 1989a. 'Imperial Decline and the Resurgence of English National Identity, 1918–1979', in Tony Kushner and Kenneth Lunn (eds.), *Traditions of Intolerance: Historical Perspectives on Fascism and Race Discourse in Britain*, pp. 33–52, Manchester: Manchester University Press.

1989b. 'A Question of Life and Death to England: Patriotism and the British Intellectuals', *New Community* 15 (4): 491–508.

1990. *Race and Empire in British Politics*, 2nd edn, Cambridge: Cambridge University Press.

Richards, Eric 1991. 'Scotland and the Uses of the Atlantic Empire', in Bailyn and Morgan (eds.), pp. 67–114.

Richards, Jeffrey and Aldgate, Anthony 1983. *Best of British: Cinema and Society 1930–1970*, Oxford: Basil Blackwell.

Richards, Steve 1999. 'The NS Interview: Gordon Brown', *New Statesman and Society*, 19 April: 18–19.

Robbins, Keith 1993a. *History, Religion and Identity in Modern Britain*, London and Rio Grande: The Hambledon Press.

1993b. 'Religion and Identity in Modern British History', in Robbins 1993a, pp. 85–103.

1993c. 'History, the Historical Association and the "National Past"', in Robbins 1993a, pp. 1–14.

19993d. 'Varieties of Britishness', in Robbins 1993a, pp. 259–69.

1995. *Nineteenth-Century Britain: Integration and Diversity*, Oxford: Clarendon Press.

1998. *Great Britain: Identities, Institutions and the Idea of Britishness*, London and New York: Longman.

Roberts, Peter 1972. 'The Union with England and the Identity of "Anglican" Wales', *Transactions of the Royal Historical Society*, 5th series, 22: 49–70.

1996. 'The English Crown, the Principality of Wales and the Council in the Marches, 1534–1641', in Bradshaw and Morrill (eds.), pp. 118–47.

1998. 'Tudor Wales, National Identity and the British Inheritance', in Bradshaw and Roberts (eds.), pp. 8–42.

Robertson, John 1987. 'Andrew Fletcher's Vision of Union', in Mason (ed.), pp. 203–225.

1994. 'Union, State and Empire: The Britain of 1707 in its European Setting', in Stone (ed.), pp. 224–57.

(ed.) 1995a. *A Union for Empire: Political Thought and the British Union of 1707*, Cambridge: Cambridge University Press.

1995b. 'Empire and Union: Two Concepts of the Early Modern European Political Order', in Robertson (ed.), pp. 3–36.

1995c. 'An Elusive Sovereignty: The Course of the Union Debate in Scotland 1698–1707', in Robertson (ed.), pp. 198–227.

Robertson, Richie and Timms, Edward (eds.) 1994. *The Habsburg Legacy: National Identity in Historical Perspective*, Edinburgh: Edinburgh University Press.

Rose, Richard 1976. 'The United Kingdom as a Multi-National State', in R. Rose (ed.), *Studies in British Politics*, 3rd edn, pp. 115–50, New York: St. Martin's Press.

1982. *Understanding the United Kingdom: The Territorial Dimension in Government*, London: Longman.

Rose, Richard and McAllister, Ian 1982. *United Kingdom Facts*, London: Macmillan.

Rowell, Geoffrey (ed.) 1992. *The English Religious Tradition and the Genius of Anglicanism*, Nashville, TN: Abingdon Press.

Rowse, A. L. 1943. *The Spirit of English History*, London: Jonathan Cape.

1957. 'Tudor Expansion: The Transition from Medieval to Modern History', *The William and Mary Quarterly* 14 (3): 309–16.

Rudolf, Richard L. and Good, David F. (eds.) 1992. *Nationalism and Empire: The Habsburg Empire and the Soviet Union*, New York: St. Martin's Press.

Runnymede Trust 2000. *The Future of Multi-Ethnic Britain: The Parekh Report*, London: Profile Books.

Rushdie, Salman 1992. 'In Good Faith', in *Imaginary Homelands: Essays and Criticism 1981–1991*, pp. 393–414, London: Granta Books.

Russell, Conrad (ed.) 1973. *The Origins of the English Civil War*, Oxford: Clarendon Press.

1987. 'The British Problem and the English Civil War', *History* 72: 394–415.

1990a. *Unrevolutionary England, 1603–42*, London: The Hambledon Press.

1990b. *The Causes of the English Civil War*, Oxford: Clarendon Press.

1991. *The Fall of the British Monarchies 1637–1642*, Oxford: Clarendon Press.

1993. 'John Bull's Other Nations', *Times Literary Supplement*, 12 March: 3–4.

1995. 'Composite Monarchies in Early Modern Europe: The British and Irish Examples', in Grant and Stringer (eds.), pp. 133–46.

Saeed, Amir, Blain, Neil and Forbes, Douglas 1999. 'New Ethnic and National Questions in Scotland: post-British identities among Glasgow Pakistani teenagers', *Ethnic and Racial Studies* 22 (5): 821–44.

Sahlins, Peter 1989. *Boundaries: The Making of France and Spain in the Pyrenees*, Berkeley and Los Angeles: University of California Press.

Said, Edward W. 1994. *Culture and Imperialism*, London: Vintage.

Salter, Elizabeth 1980. 'Chaucer and Internationalism', *Studies in the Age of Chaucer* 2: 71–79.

Samuel, Raphael (ed.) 1989a. *Patriotism: The Making and Unmaking of British National Identity*, 3 vols., London and New York: Routledge.

1989b. 'Preface', in Samuel (ed.), I, pp. x–xvii.

1989c. 'Continuous National History', in Samuel (ed.), I, pp. 9–17.

1989d. 'Introduction: Exciting to be English', in Samuel (ed.), I, pp. xviii–lxvii.

1994. *Theatres of Memory, volume 1: Past and Present in Contemporary Culture*, London and New York: Verso.

1999a. *Island Stories: Unravelling Britain* (*Theatres of Memory*, vol. 2), ed. Alison Light, London: Verso.

1999b. 'Empire Stories: The Imperial and the Domestic', in Samuel 1999a, pp. 74–97.

1999c. 'The Voice of Britain', in Samuel 1999a, pp. 172–93.

1999d. 'Unravelling Britain', in Samuel 1999a, pp. 41–73.

1999e. 'Four Nations History', in Samuel 1999a, pp. 21–40.

Santayana, George 1922. *Soliloquies in England, and Later Soliloquies*, New York: Charles Scribner's Sons.

Saul, Nigel (ed.) 1994. *England in Europe 1066–1453*, New York: St. Martin's Press.

Scaglione, Aldo (ed.) 1984. *The Emergence of National Languages*, Ravenna: Longo Editore.

Scannell, Paddy and Cardiff, David 1982. 'Serving the Nation: Public Service Broadcasting Before the War', in Bernard Waites, Tony Bennett and Graham Martin (eds.), *Popular Culture: Past and Present*, pp. 160–75, London: Croom Helm.

Schama, Simon 1988. *The Embarrassment of Riches: An Interpretation of Dutch Culture in the Golden Age*, Berkeley and Los Angeles: University of California Press.

2000. *A History of Britain: At the Edge of the World? 3000 BC–AD 1603*, New York: Hyperion.

Schnapper, Dominique 1998. *Community of Citizens: On the Modern Idea of Nationality*, translated from the French by Séverine Rosée, New Brunswick, NJ: Transaction Publishers.

Schoen, R. 1977. *Enoch Powell and the Powellites*, London: Macmillan.

Scholes, Percy A. 1942. *The Oxford Companion to Music*, 4th edn, London: Oxford University Press.

Schöpflin, George 1994. 'Postcommunism: The Problems of Democratic Construction', *Daedalus*, summer: 127–41.

Schwarz, Bill (ed.) 1996a. *The Expansion of England: Race, Ethnicity and Cultural History*, London and New York: Routledge.

1996b. 'Introduction: The Expansion and Contraction of England', in Schwarz (ed.), pp. 1–8.

Scott, Peter 1990. *Knowledge and Nation*, Edinburgh: Edinburgh University Press.

Seaberg, R. B. 1981. 'The Norman Conquest and the Common Law: The Levellers and the Argument from Continuity', *The Historical Journal* 24 (4): 791–806.

Seeley, J. R. (1883) 1971. *The Expansion of England*, Chicago: University of Chicago Press.

Sellar, W. C. and Yeatman, R. J. (1930) 1960. *1066 and All That*, Harmondsworth: Penguin Books.

Sellar, W. David H. 1988. 'The Common Law of Scotland and the Common Law of England', in R. R. Davies (ed.), pp. 82–99.

Seton-Watson, Hugh 1977. *Nations and States: An Inquiry into the Origins of Nations and the Politics of Nationalism*, London: Methuen.

Shannon, Richard 1976. *The Crisis of Imperialism, 1865–1915*, St Albans: Paladin.

Sharpe, L. J. (ed.) 1993. *The Rise of Meso Government in Europe*, London: Sage Publications.

Sharratt, Bernard 2001. 'Writing Britains', in Morley and Robins (eds.), pp. 305–16.

Sheehan, James J. 1999. 'A People Apart?', *Times Literary Supplement*, 24 December: 6.

Shields, Jenny and Corbidge, Rob 1998. 'Anti-English Feeling Grows in Scotland', *The Sunday Times*, 28 June.

Shuger, Deborah 1990. *Habits of Thought in the English Renaissance: Religion, Politics, and the Dominant Culture*, Berkeley and Los Angeles: University of California Press.

Siedentop, Larry 2001. *Democracy in Europe*, London: Penguin Books.

Sièyes, Emmanuel Joseph (1789) 1963. *What is the Third Estate?*, trans. M. Blondel, London and Dunmow: Pall Mall Press.

Simmons, Clare A. 1990. *Reversing the Conquest: History and Myth in 19th-Century British Literature*, New Brunswick, NJ and London: Rutgers University Press.

Simpson, David 1993. *Romanticism, Nationalism and the Revolt Against Theory*, Chicago: University of Chicago Press.

Sked, Alan 1981. 'Historians, The Nationality Question, and the Downfall of the Habsburg Empire', *Transactions of the Royal Historical Society*, 5th series, 31: 175–93.

Skinner, Quentin 1965. 'History and Ideology in the English Revolution', *The Historical Journal* 8 (2): 151–78.

Slavin, A. J. 1993. 'The Tudor State, Reformation and Understanding Change', in *Political Thought and the Tudor Commonwealth*, pp. 223–53. London: Routledge.

Smith, Alan G. R. 1997. *The Emergence of a Nation State: The Commonwealth of England 1529–1660*, 2nd edn, London and New York: Longman.

Smith, Anthony 1973. *The Shadow in the Cave: The Broadcaster, the Audience and the State*, London: George Allen and Unwin.

Smith, Anthony D. 1981. *The Ethnic Revival in the Modern World*, Cambridge: Cambridge University Press.

  1986. *The Ethnic Origins of Nations*, Oxford: Basil Blackwell.

  1992. 'National Identity and the Idea of European unity', *International Affairs* 68 (1): 55–76.

  1994. 'The Problem of National Identity: Ancient, Medieval and Modern', *Ethnic and Racial Studies* 17 (3): 375–99.

  1995. *Nations and Nationalism in A Global Era*, Cambridge: Polity Press.

  1998. *Nationalism and Modernism*, London and New York: Routledge.

Smith, Chris 1998. *Creative Britain*, London: Faber and Faber.

Smith, David L. 1998. *A History of the Modern British Isles, 1603–1707*, Oxford and Malden, MA: Blackwell Publishers.

Smith, Dennis 1986. 'Englishness and the Liberal Inheritance After 1886', in Colls and Dodd (eds.), pp. 254–82.

Smith, Janet Adam 1970. 'Some Eighteenth-Century Ideas of Scotland', in Phillipson and Mitchison (eds.), pp. 107–24.

Smith, Lesley M. (ed.) 1984. *The Making of Britain: The Dark Ages*, Basingstoke: Macmillan.

Smith, Paul 1967. *Disraelian Conservatism and Social Reform*, London: Routledge and Kegan Paul.

Smith, Zadie 2001. *White Teeth*, London: Penguin Books.

Smout, T. C. 1980. 'Scotland and England: Is Dependency a Symptom or a Cause of Underdevelopment?', *Review* 3 (4): 601–30.

1989. 'Problems of Nationalism, Identity and Improvement in Later Eighteenth-Century Scotland', in T. M. Devine (ed.), *Improvement and Enlightenment*, pp. 1–21, Edinburgh: John Donald Publishers.

1994. 'Perspectives on the Scottish Identity', *Scottish Affairs* 6: 101–13.

Smyth, Alfred P. 1995. *King Alfred the Great*, Oxford: Oxford University Press.

(ed.) 1998a. *Medieval Europeans: Studies in Ethnic Identity and National Perspectives in Medieval Europe*, London: Macmillan.

1998b. 'The Emergence of English Identity, 700–1000', in Smyth (ed.), pp. 24–52.

Smyth, Jim 1993. ' "Like Amphibious Animals": Irish Protestants, Ancient Britons, 1691–1707', *The Historical Journal* 36 (4): 785–97.

1996. 'The Communities of Ireland and the British State, 1660–1707', in Bradshaw and Morrill (eds.), pp. 246–61.

1998. ' "No Remedy More Proper": Anglo-Irish Unionism before 1707', in Bradshaw and Roberts (eds.), pp. 301–20.

Snyder, Louis L. 1990 *Encyclopedia of Nationalism*, Chicago, IL and London: St. James Press.

Soffer, Reba N. 1987. 'Nation, Duty, Character and Confidence: History at Oxford, 1850–1914', *Historical Journal* 30: 77–104.

Southern, R. W. 1970a. *Medieval Humanism and Other Studies*, Oxford: Basil Blackwell.

1970b. 'England's First Entry into Europe', in Southern 1970a, pp. 135–57.

1970c. 'The Place of England in the Twelfth Century Renaissance', in Southern 1970a, pp. 158–80.

1970d. *Western Society and the Church in the Middle Ages*, Harmondsworth: Penguin Books.

1973. 'Aspects of the European Tradition of Historical Writing: 4. The Sense of the Past', *Transactions of the Royal Historical Society*, 5th series, 23: 243–63.

Stafford, Pauline 1984. 'One English Nation', in L. Smith (ed.), pp. 117–29.

1989. *Unification and Conquest: A Political and Social History of England in the Tenth and Eleventh Centuries*, London: Edward Arnold.

Stafford, William 1982. 'Religion and the Doctrine of Nationalism in England at the Time of the French Revolution and Napoleonic Wars', in Mews (ed.), pp. 381–95.

Stapleton, Julia 1994. *Englishness and the Study of Politics: The Social and Political Thought of Ernest Barker*, Cambridge: Cambridge University Press.

2000. 'Political Thought and National Identity in Britain, 1850–1950', in Collini, Whatmore and Young (eds.), pp. 245–69.

Steed, Michael 1986. 'The Core–Periphery Dimension of British Politics', *Political Geography Quarterly*, supplement to vol. V (4): S91–S103.

Stevenson, John 1984. *British Society 1914–45*, Harmondsworth: Penguin Books.

Stone, Lawrence 1964. 'The Educational Revolution in England, 1560–1640', *Past and Present* 28: 41–80.

1969. 'Literacy and Education in England 1640–1900', *Past and Present* 42: 69–139.

1986. *The Causes of the English Revolution 1529–1642*, 2nd edn, London: Ark Paperbacks.

Stone, Lawrence (ed.) 1994. *An Imperial State at War: Britain from 1689–1815*, London and New York: Routledge.

Strayer, Joseph R. 1971. 'France: The Holy Land, the Chosen People, and the Most Christian King', in *Medieval Statecraft and the Perspectives of History*, pp. 300–14, Princeton: Princeton University Press.

Stringer, Keith J. 1994a. 'Social and Political Communities in European History: Some Reflections on Recent Studies', in Bjørn, Grant and Stringer (eds), 1994a, pp. 9–34.

1994b. 'Identities in Thirteenth-Century England: Frontier Society in the Far North', in Bjørn, Grant and Stringer (eds.), 1994b, pp. 28–66.

1995. 'Scottish Foundations: Thirteenth-Century Perspectives', in Grant and Stringer (eds.), pp. 85–96.

Strong, Roy 1978. *And When Did You Last See Your Father? The Victorian Painter and British History*, London: Thames and Hudson.

2000. *The Spirit of Britain: A Narrative History of the Arts*, New York: Fromm International.

Sullivan, Andrew 1999. 'There Will Always Be an England', *The New York Times Magazine*, 21 February: 39–48.

Suny, Ronald Grigor 1995. 'Ambiguous Categories: States, Empires and Nations', *Post-Soviet Affairs* 11 (2): 185–96.

1996. 'Making and Unmaking Nations: The Legacies of Empire', paper given at the conference, 'Recasting Social and Political Boundaries in Eastern Europe', University of Colorado, Boulder, 25–26 October.

Surel, Jeannine 1989. 'John Bull', in Samuel (ed.), vol. III, pp. 3–25.

Swift, Roger and Gilley, Sheridan (eds.) 1989. *The Irish in Britain*, London: Pinter Publishers.

Szechi, David 1991. 'The Hanoverians and Scotland', in Greengrass (ed.), pp. 116–33.

Szporluk, Roman (ed.) 1994a. *National Identity and Ethnicity in Russia and the New States of Eurasia*, Armonk, NY: M. E. Sharpe.

1994b. 'After Empire, What?', *Daedalus* 123 (3): 21–39.

Taine, Hippolyte (1860–1870) 1958. *Notes on England*, trans. and introduced Edward Hyams, Fair Lawn, NJ: Essential Books.

Tamir, Yael 1993. *Liberal Nationalism*, Princeton: Princeton University Press.

Taylor, A. J. P. 1945. *The Course of German History*, London: Hamish Hamilton.

1965. *English History 1914–1945*, Oxford: Clarendon Press.

1975. 'Comment' on Pocock's 'British History: A Plea for a New Subject', *Journal of Modern History* 47 (4): 622.

Taylor, Miles 1990. 'Patriotism, History and the Left in Twentieth-Century Britain', *Historical Journal* 33 (3): 981–7.

1992. 'John Bull and the Iconography of Public Opinion in England, *c.* 1712–1929', *Past and Present* 134: 93–128.

Taylor, P. J. 1991. 'The English and their Englishness: "A Curiously Mysterious, Elusive and little Understood People" ', *Scottish Geographical Magazine* 107 (3): 146–61.

2001. 'Which Britain? Which England? Which North?', in Morley and Robins (eds.), pp. 127–44.

Teich, Mikulás and Porter, Roy (eds.) 1990. *Fin-de-Siècle and its Legacy*, Cambridge: Cambridge University Press.

(eds.) 1993. *The National Question in Europe in Historical Context*, Cambridge: Cambridge University Press.

Thatcher, Margaret 1989. 'Speech at the College of Europe, Bruges 20 September 1988', in *The Revival of Britain: Speeches on Home and European Affairs 1975–1988*, pp. 256–66, London: Aurum Press.

1993. *The Downing Street Years*, New York: HarperCollins.

Therborn, Göran 1995. *European Modernity and Beyond: The Trajectory of European Societies 1945–2000*, London: Sage Publications.

Thomas, Dafydd Elis 1991. 'The Constitution of Wales', in Crick (ed.), pp. 57–67.

Thomas, Edward (1917) 1980. *A Literary Pilgrim in England*, Oxford: Oxford University Press.

Thomas, Keith 1978. 'The United Kingdom', in Grew (ed.), pp. 41–97.

Thompson, E. P. 1964. *The Making of the English Working Class*, London: Victor Gollancz.

1978. 'The Peculiarities of the English', in *The Poverty of Theory and Other Essays*, pp. 35–91, London: The Merlin Press.

1993. 'The Making of a Ruling Class', *Dissent*, summer: 377–82.

Thompson, F. M. L. 1971. *English Landed Society in the Nineteenth Century*, London: Routledge and Kegan Paul.

1986. *The Rise of Respectable Society: A Social History of Victorian Britain, 1830–1900*, London: Fontana Press.

Thornton, A. P. 1968. *The Imperial Idea and its Enemies*, New York: Anchor Books.

1992. 'Empire: The View from Beyond', *International History Review* 14 (3): 441–60.

Thorpe, Lewis 1966. 'Introduction', in Geoffrey of Monmouth 1966, pp. 9–37.

Tidrick, Kathryn 1982. *Empire and the English Character*, London: I. B. Tauris.

The Times 1997. 'Our Island Story' (editorial), December 18.

Timms, Edward 1991. 'National Memory and the "Austrian idea" from Metternich to Waldheim', *The Modern Language Review* 86 (4): 898–910.

Tipton, C. Leon (ed.) 1972. *Nationalism in the Middle Ages*, New York: Holt, Rinehart and Winston.

Tocqueville, Alexis de (1833–57) 1958. *Journeys to England and Ireland*, trans. George Lawrence and K. P. Mayer, ed. J. P. Mayer, London: Faber and Faber.

(1835) 1988. *Democracy in America*, trans. George Lawrence, New York: Harper and Row.

Tompson, Richard S. 1986. *The Atlantic Archipelago: A Political History of the British Isles*, Lewiston, NY and Queenston, Ont.: The Edwin Mellen Press.

Tong, Raymond 1994. 'The English Dimension', *The Salisbury Review* 13 (1): 14–17.

Toynbee, Arnold 1962a. *A Study of History*, vol. I: *Introduction. The Geneses of Civilizations, Part One*, London: Oxford University Press.

1962b. *A Study of History*, vol. II: *The Geneses of Civilizations, Part Two*, London: Oxford University Press.

1962c. *A Study of History*, vol. III: *The Growth of Civilizations*, London: Oxford University Press.

Trentmann, Frank 1994. 'Civilization and its Discontents: English Neo-Romanticism and the Transformation of Anti-Modernism in Twentieth-Century Western Culture', *Journal of Contemporary History* 29 (4): 583–625.

Trevor-Roper, H. R. 1965. 'The General Crisis of the Seventeenth Century', in Aston (ed.), pp. 59–95.

1979. 'Lord Macaulay: Introduction', in Macaulay 1979, pp. 7–48.

1984a. *Religion, Reformation and Social Change, and Other Essays*, revised 3rd edn, London: Secker and Warburg.

1984b. 'Three Foreigners: The Philosophers of the Puritan Revolution', in Trevor-Roper 1984a, pp. 237–96.

1984c. 'Scotland and the Puritan Revolution', in Trevor-Roper 1984a, pp. 392–444.

1984d. 'The Union of Britain in the Seventeenth Century', in Trevor-Roper 1984a, pp. 445–67.

1984e. 'The Invention of Tradition: The Highland Tradition of Scotland', in Hobsbawm and Ranger (eds.), pp. 15–41.

1992. 'The Anglo-Scottish Union', in *From Counter-Reformation to Glorious Revolution*, pp. 287–302, Chicago: University of Chicago Press.

Trimble, David 1989. 'Discussion' of Roy Foster, 'Varieties of Irishness', in Crozier (ed.). pp. 45–50.

Trimble, William 1964. *The Catholic Laity in Elizabethan England 1558–1603*, Cambridge, MA: Harvard University Press.

Trotter, David 1993. *The English Novel in History 1895–1920*, London and New York: Routledge.

Trumpener, Katie 1997. *Bardic Nationalism: The Romantic Novel and the British Empire*, Princeton: Princeton University Press.

Turville-Petre, Thorlac 1996. *England the Nation: Language, Literature, and National Identity, 1290–1340*, Oxford: Clarendon Press.

Ullman, Walter 1965. 'On the Influence of Geoffrey of Monmouth in English History', in Bauer, Boehm and Müller (eds.), pp. 257–76.

van der Veer, Peter and Lehmann, Hartmut (eds.) 1997. *Nation and Religion: Perspectives on Europe and Asia*, Princeton: Princeton University Press.

Vansittart, Peter 1998. *In Memory of England*, London: John Murray.

Viroli, Maurizio 1995. *For Love of Country: An Essay on Patriotism and Nationalism*, Oxford: Clarendon Press.

von Hagen, Mark 1997. 'The Russian Empire', in Barkey and von Hagen (eds.), pp. 58–72.

Von Schierbrand, Wolf 1917. *Austria-Hungary: The Polyglot Empire*, New York: Frederick A. Stokes.

Wagner, Michael 1993. 'Scotland in the Late Eighteenth Century: Integration, Modernization and Opposition', in Asch (ed.), pp. 147–59.

Walzer, Michael 1968. *The Revolution of the Saints: A Study in the Origins of Radical Politics*, New York: Atheneum.

Waters, Chris 1994. 'J. B. Priestley 1894–1984: Englishness and the Politics of Nostalgia', in Susan Pederson and Peter Mandler (eds.), *After the Victorians: Private Conscience and Public Duty in Modern Britain*, pp. 209–26, London and New York: Routledge.

1997. ' "Dark Strangers" in Our Midst: Discourses of Race and Nation in Britain, 1947–1963', *Journal of British Studies* 36 (2): 207–38.

Watson, Fiona J. 1999. *Under the Hammer: Edward I and Scotland, 1286–1306*, East Linton: Tuckwell.

Watson, George 1973. *The English Ideology: Studies in the Language off Victorian Politics*, London: Allen and Unwin.

Weale, Albert 1995. 'From Little England to Democratic Europe?', *New Community* 21 (2): 215–25.

Weber, Eugen 1976. *Peasants into Frenchmen: The Modernization of Rural France, 1870–1914*, Stanford, CA: Stanford University Press.

Weber, Max 1978. *Economy and Society: An Outline of Interpretive Sociology*, 2 vol., ed. Guenther Roth and Claus Wittich, Berkeley, CA: University of California Press.

(1904–5) 1998. *The Protestant Ethic and the Spirit of Capitalism*, trans. Talcott Parsons, ed. Randall Collins, Los Angeles: Roxbury Publishing.

Webster, Bruce 1997. *Medieval Scotland: The Making of an Identity*, Basingstoke: Macmillan.

Weight, Richard 1999. 'Raise St George's Standard High', *New Statesman and Society*, 8 January: 25–7.

Weinbrot, Howard D. 1993. *Britannia's Issue: The Rise of British Literature from Dryden to Ossian*, Cambridge: Cambridge University Press.

Werbner, Pnina and Modood, Tariq (eds.) 1997. *Debating Cultural Hybridity: Multi-Cultural Identities and the Politics of Anti-Racism*, London and New York: Zed Books.

Whaley, Joachim 1994. 'Austria, "Germany", and the Dissolution of the Holy Roman Empire', in Robertson and Timms (eds.), pp. 3–12.

Whelan, Kevin 1995. 'United and Disunited Irishmen: the Discourse of Sectarianism in the 1790s', in O'Dea and Whelan (eds.), pp. 231–47.

White, J. D. 1994. *The Russian Revolution 1917–21*, London: Edward Arnold.

Whyte, John 1990. *Interpreting Northern Ireland*, Oxford: Clarendon Press.

Widdowson, Peter 1989. *Hardy in History: A Study in Literary Sociology*, London and New York: Routledge.

Wiener, Carol Z. 1971. 'The Beleagured Isle: A Study of Elizabethan and Early Jacobean Anti-Catholicism', *Past and Present* 51: 27–62.

Wiener, Martin J. 1981. *English Culture and the Decline of the Industrial Spirit 1850–1980*, Cambridge: Cambridge University Press.

Williams, Ann 1997. *The English and the Norman Conquest*, Woodbridge: The Boydell Press.

Williams, Emyr W. 1989. 'The Dynamics of Welsh Identity', in Evans (ed.), pp. 46–59.

Williams, Gwyn A. 1982. 'When Was Wales?', in *The Welsh in their History*, pp. 189–201, London and Canberra: Croom Helm.

  1985. *When Was Wales? A History of the Welsh*, London: Penguin Books.

Williams, Merryn 1972. *Thomas Hardy and Rural England*, London: Macmillan.

Williams, Neville 1972. *The Life and Times of Elizabeth I*, New York: Doubleday and Company.

Williams, Penry 1979. *The Tudor Regime*, Oxford: Clarendon Press.

Williams, Raymond 1963. *Culture and Society 1760–1950*, Harmondsworth: Penguin Books.

  1973. *The Country and the City*, London: Chatto and Windus.

Williamson, Arthur H. 1983. 'Scotland, Antichrist and the Invention of Britain', in John Dwyer, Roger A. Mason and Alexander Murdoch (eds.), *New Perspectives on the Politics and Culture of Early Modern Scotland*, pp. 34–58, Edinburgh: John Donald Publishers.

Williamson, Arthur 1999. 'Patterns of British Identity: "Britain" and its Rivals in the Sixteenth and Seventeenth Centuries', in Burgess (ed.), pp. 138–73.

Williamson, Bill 1990. *The Temper of the Times: British Society Since World War II*, Oxford: Basil Blackwell.

Wilson, Kathleen 1998. *The Sense of the People: Politics, Culture and Imperialism in England, 1715–1785*, Cambridge: Cambridge University Press.

Winks, Robin W. (ed.) 1999. *Historiography*, The Oxford *History* of the British Empire, vol. V, Oxford and New York: Oxford University Press.

Winter, J. M 1996. 'British National Identity and the First World War', in S. J. D. Green and R. C. Whting (eds.), *The Boundaries of the State in Modern Britain*, pp. 261–77, Cambridge: Cambridge University Press.

Wolfe, John 1998. 'A Transatlantic Perspective: Protestantism and National Identities in Mid-Nineteenth-Century Britain and the United States', in Claydon and McBride (eds.), pp. 291–309.

Wood, Michael 2000. *In Search of England: Journeys Into the English Past*, London: Penguin Books.

Wood, Neal 1992. 'Foundations of Political Economy: The New Moral Philosophy of Sir Thomas Smith', in Fideler and Mayer (eds.), pp. 140–68.

Woolf, Stuart 1989. 'French Civilization and Ethnicity in the Napoleonic Empire', *Past and Present* 124: 96–120.

1992. 'The Construction of a European World-View in the Revolutionary-Napoleonic Years', *Past and Present* 137: 72–101.

Wormald, Jenny 1992. 'The Creation of Britain: Multiple Kingdoms or Core and Colonies?', *Transactions of the Royal Historical Society*, 6th series, 2: 175–94.

1994. 'The Union of 1603', in Mason (ed.), pp. 17–40.

1995. 'One King, Two Kingdoms', in Grant and Stringer (eds.), pp. 123–32.

1996. 'James VI, James I and the Identity of Britain', in Bradshaw and Morrill (eds.), pp. 148–71.

Wormald, Patrick 1983. 'Bede, the *Bretwaldas* and the Origins of the *Gens Anglorum*', in Patrick Wormald, Donald Bullough and Roger Collins (eds.), *Ideal and Reality in Frankish and Anglo-Saxon Society*, pp. 99–129, Oxford: Basil Blackwell.

1984. 'The Emergence of Anglo-Saxon Kingdoms', in L. Smith (ed.), pp. 49–62.

1992. 'The Venerable Bede and the "Church of the English"', in Rowell (ed.), pp. 13–32.

1994. '*Engla Lond*: the Making of an Allegiance', *Journal of Historical Sociology* 7 (1): 1–24.

1997. 'Sir Geoffrey Elton's *English*: A View from the Early Middle Ages', *Transactions of the Royal Historical Society*, 6th series, 7: 318–25.

2000. *The Making of English Law: King Alfred to the Twelfth Century*, Oxford: Blackwell.

Worsthorne, Peregrine 1999a. 'Why I'm No Longer a Nationalist', *New Statesman and Society*, 16 August: 15–16.

1999b. 'Land of Concrete and Wapping Lies, I Love You No More', *The Spectator*, 20 February: 34.

Wright, Patrick 1985. *On Living in an Old Country: The National Past in Contemporary Britain*, London: Verso.

1994. 'Wrapped in the Tatters of the Flag', *The Guardian*, 31 December.

1996. 'England as Lost Idyll', *The Independent on Sunday*, 16 June.

Wrightson, Keith 1982. *English Society, 1580–1680*, London: Hutchinson.

Xenos, Nicholas 1996. 'Civic Nationalism: Oxymoron?', *Critical Review* 10 (2): 213–231.

Yack, Bernard 1995. 'Reconciling Liberalism and Nationalism', *Political Theory* 23 (1): 166–82.

1996. 'The Myth of the Civic Nation', *Critical Review* 10 (2): 193–211.

Yates, Frances A. 1975. 'Queen Elizabeth as Astraea', in *Astraea: The Imperial Theme in the Sixteenth Century*, pp. 29–87, London: Routledge and Kegan Paul.

Yeo, Stephen 1986. 'Socialism, the State, and Some Oppositional Englishness', in Colls and Dodd (eds.), pp. 308–69.

Young, Robert J. C. 1995. *Colonial Desire: Hybridity in Theory, Culture and Race*, London and New York: Routledge.

Zaslavsky, Victor 1996. 'The Soviet Union', in Barkey and von Hagen (eds.), pp. 73–96.

Zeldin, Theodore 1984. *The French*, London: Fontana.

Zernatto, Guido 1944. 'Nation: The History of a Word', *The Review of Politics* 6 (3): 351–66.

Index

Location references in **bold type** indicate more extensive treatment of a topic.

Aberystwyth 73
absentee kings 44, 51
Act of Appeals (1533) 95, 100, 283
Act of Toleration 153, 154
Acts of Union
    Scotland 5, 135, 145, 146, 156
    Wales 73, 74
Adderley, Charles 189
Adrian IV 82
Aetheling, Edgar 51
Aethelred the Unready 70
Aethelstan 42
After Britain (Nairn) 240
agriculture 295, 296
Albert the Prince Consort 192
Alfred the Great 42, 47, 48
Alibhai-Brown, Yasmin 242, 256
anachronisms 90, 100, 119, 178
1066 and All That (Sellar and Yeatman) 219
Angles 5, 45, 46, 70, 78
anglicization **77–81**, 166
Anglo- **11–12**
Anglo-British identity **155–156**
Anglo-Indian 11
Anglo-Irish 11, 75, 77, **87–88**, 288
Anglo-Norman aristocracy 75, 81
Anglo-Norman historians 51
Anglo-Norman identity 50, 72, 79
Anglo-Norman state 49
Anglo-Saxon 11, 100, 280
Anglo-Saxon period **41–48**
Anglo-Saxonism **205–207**, 206
Anglo-Scottish Borders 80
Anglocentrism 13
anthems 148

anti-Catholicism (anti-Popery) 113, 163, 164,
    284, 288, 290
anti-urbanism 212, 296
Arbuthnot, John 137
architecture 54
Areopagitiga (Milton) 107
Argyll 69
aristocracy 166, 171, 177, 286
armed services 173
Arthur, King 66, 138
associationism 214
Athelstan 71
Atlantic Archipelago 6, 13
Australia 14, 259
Aylmer, Bishop 114

backward civilizations 190
Bacon, Sir Francis 134
Bagehot, Walter 188
Baldwin, Stanley **229–230**, 231
Bale, John 205
Balkans 276
Balliol, John 80, 83
Balliol, John (the First) 80
Balmoral Castle 181
Bamburgh 70
Barnard Castle 80
Barth, Frederick 61
Battle of the Boyne 141
Battle of Britain 234
Bayly, Christopher 197
Beckett, Margaret 268
Bede, the Venerable
    Ecclesiastical History of the English People
        (Bede) 41, 46, 71, 205

Bede, the Venerable (*cont.*)
   elect nation 283
   ideology of Englishness 44
   imperialism 47
Belfast Agreement 1998 240
Berkeley, Bishop 143
Bernicia 70
Betjeman, John 228
Bible **103–104**, 283
black and Asian communities 256, 257, 260, 261, 262
Black Death 86
Blair, Tony 253, 266, 268, 297
Blatchford, Robert 215
Blunkett, David 259
Boer War 198
Bogdanor, Vernon 240, 271
Book of Martyrs (Foxe) **105–107**, 112
Book of Revelation 126
Boru, Brian, of Munster 68
boundaries **61**, 68
'The Boyhood of Raleigh' (Millais) 188
Boyle earls of Cork 165
Braham, J. 8
The Break-Up of Britain (Nairn) 240, 269
Britain **5–6**, 9, 19, **239–249**
   v. England 234, 275
Britannia 5, 47, 134, 291
British **6**, 37, 47, 85, 288
   v. English **1–2**, 16
British Airways 297
British Broadcasting Corporation (BBC) 237
'the British disease' 236
British economy **167–169**
British Empire 9, 36, 145, **170–172**, 173
   decline **196–202**
   and English identity 187–196
   in Europe **180–187**
   post-World War I 235
British history **12–15**, 275
British identity 38, **121–174**, 200, 298
British Isles 6
British monarchy 200, 238
British nation **172–174**
British National Party 263, 264
British Regiments 170
British ruling class 166, 167, 170
British Social Attitudes Survey 1990 247
British society **165–167**, 184
British state 145, 172
British Studies **12–17**, 19, 40, 275, 279
Britishness 38, 173
   Catholic Unionism 289
   hyphenated 261
   New Labour 253
   Parekh Report 258

persistance of **233–239**
Thatcher, Margaret 254, 264
Ulster Protestants 245
   v. Englishness **35–38**, **154–157**
   v. Scottishness 146–147, 289
Britons 5, 71, 81
   Geoffrey of Monmouth **62–66**
   Irish **140–145**
   Scotland **145–154**
   Welsh **136–140**
Britons (Colley) 18, 146, 290
'Brits' (Esler) 239, 255
Brittones 42
Brown, Gordon 253
Brown, Keith 288
Brubaker, Rogers 22
Bruce, Edward 282
Bruce, Robert de 80, 81
Brussels 249
Brut legend 77; tradition 64, 66
Bryce, James 289
Buchanan, Francis 170
Buckle, Thomas 192
The Buddha of Suburbia (Kureishi) 243, 263
Bulwer, Edward Lytton 185, 201
Burke, Edmund 143, 144, 145
Bute, Lord 150
Butler earls of Ormond 165
Butterfield, Herbert **202–203**
Byrd, William 111

Caernarvon Castle 182
Caird, Edward 202
Caledonia 70
Calvinism 112, 125, 153
Campbell-Bannerman, Sir Henry 183
Canada 259
Cannadine, David 4, 275
Canterbury Tales (Chaucer) 56
capitalism 97
Carham 70
Carlyle, Thomas 185, 189, 196, 207
Carmarthen 72
Carson, Sir Edward 245
The Case of Ireland . . . Stated (Molyneux) 141, 142
Castlereagh, Viscount 182
Catalan community 61
Catholic Church 43, 46, **58–59**
Catholic cultures 165
Catholic Emancipation Act (1829) 158, 160
Catholic Unionism 289
Catholicism 37, 141, 153, 181
   v. Protestantism **158–165**
Caxton, William 54, 56
Cecil, Lord Hugh 191

Celtic church 139
Celtic fringe 13, 81, 82, 86, 183, 250
Celts 5, **66–71**, 82, 85, 207
Cerdanya 61
Chamberlain, Joseph 199, 206, 292
chapel 160
Charke, William 113
Charles I 131
Charles II 134
Chartism (Carlyle) 189, 236; Chartists 169,
    183
chattering classes 252
Chaucer, Geoffrey 55, **56–57**
Chesterton, G. K. 262
Christianity 41, 47
Church of England 153
Church (Kirk) of Scotland **153–154**, 160, 288,
    290
Churchill, Winston 234, 270
citizenship 22, 23, 96
civic nation 27
civic nationalism 25, 26, 147, 149
civic nationhood 25, 27, 100
Clare, Richard de, second earl of Pembroke
    (Strongbow) 75
The Clarion (Blatchford) 215
classic nationalism x
Cnut 44, 70
Cold Comfort Farm (Gibbons) 296
collective identities 61, 199
Colley, Linda ix, 18, 146, 289, 290
Collinson, Patrick 284
colonial empire 87, 190
colonial nationalism 288
colonization **71–77**, 83, 84, 87, 281
commonwealth 95, 96
community of communities model 259
composite states 278
The Condition of England (Masterman) 210,
    212
conquest **71–77**, 83, 84, 87, 281
Conrad, Joseph 193
Conservatism 213, 214
Conservative Party 214, 236, 263–265, 266,
    268
constitutional change 240
continental thought **216–217**
'Cool Britannia' 254, 297
Cornwall 71
cosmopolitanism 120, 127, 166, 177
Cosmopolitanism and the National State
    (Meinecke) 21
Cotton, Sir Robert 134
Council of Constance 74
'Council of the Isles' 253, 268
country 95, 123, 285

The Countryman (Roberston-Scott) 296
court 123
Covenanter Revolution 135
Cramb, J. A. 198
Crick, Bernard 181
Cromarty, earl of 136
Cromwell, Oliver **128–129**, 130, 131, 135
Cross of St George 9, 252, 262, 275
cultural (ethnic) nationalism 24–**25**, 26, 31, 33
    Europe 201, 276
    force for evil 273
    v. civic/political nationalism 147
    see also ethnicity
cultural inheritance 26, 29
cultural nations 21, **23–24**
cultural racism 259, 261
culture
    Gaelic 288
    group 257
    and identity 26
    left-nationalist popular 299
    political 288
    and religion 157–165
    Wales 138, 281
Cumbria 69, 70

Dafydd ap Gruffydd 83
Dalriada 69
Danes 44, 70
Darwin, Charles 215
David I 79, 80
Davies, Rees 180
The Day Britain Died (Marr) 239
de Montfort, Simon 50
De Republica Anglorum (Smith) 101
deindustrialization 249
Declaration of Arbroath (1320) 81
Declaration of the Rights of Man 30
Declaratory Act (1720) 140
Dee, John 138
Defoe, Daniel 150, 273
Deira 70
democracy 99, 100
Demos 254
denizenship 83
despotism 196
devolution
    'asymmetrical commitment' (Rose) 255
    black Britons 298
    national aspirations 253
    Northern Ireland **240–249**
        Belfast agreement 1998 240
    radical measures 244
    Redmond, John on 265
    Scotland **247–249**
    Wales **243–244**

Dickens, Charles 296
Dilke, Charles 291
dilution 242
A Discourse of the Commonwealth of This Realm of England (Smith) 101
discursive foundations 116
dissenters 160
dissolution of the monasteries 96
divided nation **121–130**
Doherty, John 183
Domesday Book 42
dominant ideologies 167
Donald II 70
Drapier's Letters (Swift) 287
Dreyfus Affair 27
Dublin 75, 144
Dunedin (Edinburgh) 70
Dury, John 126
Dutch 290
Dyfed 72
dynastic marriages 133

Ealing film comedies 216, 233
Eboracum (York) 70
Ecclesiastical History of the English People (Bede) 41, 46, 205
Edgar, king of Mercia and Northumbria 44
Edinburgh 70, 78, 289
education 105, **222–223**
   see also public schools
Edward I 66, 72, 79, 82, 132
Edward VII 197
Edward the Black Prince
Edward the Confessor 44
Edwin, king of Northumbria 70
elect nation
   Bede, the Venerable 283
   Calvinist doctrine **112–113**
   derivation 283
   France 108, **109–110**
   Milton, John 127
   nineteenth century 196
   Shakespeare, William 118
electoral reform 160
Elgar, Edward 209, 293
Eliot, T. S. 228
elites 166, 182, 183
elitism 102
Elizabeth I
   Book of Martyrs (Foxe) 106
   division and diversity **284**
   political nation 102
   popularity 93–94, 102
   religion 111
Elizabethan literature 114, **116–119**

'the Elizabethan writing of England' (Helgerson) 116
Elton, Geoffrey 285
Empire, of Great Britain 180
empires **32–35**, 180
   colonial 87, 190
   decline of **196–202**
   English **81–88**
   external 36, 132, 250
   Great Britain 180
   Greek 190
   internal 36, 63, 85, 250
   Oriental 190
   Orwell, George 195
   Roman 190, 196, 198
   see also British Empire
empiricism 215
The Enchanted Glass (Nairn) 18
enclosures 96
Engla Land 41
England **7–8**, 19, 227, 270
   as first nation **93–103**
   forever **226–233**
   'Little Englandism' 213, 271, 296
   origins 40, 53
   unification 42
   v. Britain 234, 275
England and the English (Bulwer) 185, 201
England Speaks (Gibb) 231
England, Their England (Macdonell) 232
'England's Forgotten Worthies' (Froude) 188
England's Green and Pleasant Land (Robertson Scott) 296
English **8–10**, 46, 81
   and others **60–62**
   v. British **1–2**, 16
English Assembly 265
English Association 222
English Church 46, 204, 286
English Civil War 14, 97, **122–130**, 131, 132, 286
English common law 54
The English Constitution (Bagehot) 188
English countryside 209–212, 213, **230–231**
   see also rural ideology
The English Flag (Kipling) 8
English Folk Song (Sharp) 208
English history 14, 203, 275
English Journey (Priestley) 231
English kingdom 46, 82
English kings 63, 66, 84, 109
   English language **10–11**; and literature teaching 222
   fourteenth century **54, 55, 56**
   standardization and national consciousness **221–222**

English law 152
English literature 54, 55, **114–120, 219–221,**
    295
'English Men of Letters' (Morley) 220
English moralism 178
English music 294
'English Musical Renaissance' (Sharp)
    208–209
English nation 47, **48–59**
English national character 216
    Baldwin, Stanley 229
    and nationalism x
    Priestley, J. B. 234
    superiority 62
    writings 16, 18, 20, 232, 233
English national consciousness 48
English national identity, major themes 36
English nationalism **18–21**, 34, 175–179,
    262–269, 276
English nationhood 48
English Parliament 269, 298
English political nationalism 239
English question **1–17,** 255, 268
English Revolution **124–130**
English state 43, 47, 280
The Englishman and his History (Butterfield)
    202
Englishness 10, 16, **175–225**
    discovery of **202–217**
    as history **217–219**
    identification of **224–225**
    identity crisis **249–262**
    indifference of historians 276
    interwar period 232
    literary **114–120**
    v. Britishness **35–38**, 154–157
Englishness Identified (Langford) 224
Enlightenment 92
Episcopalians 154, 160
equality 125
Esler, Gavin 239, 255
Essex man 255
ethnic (cultural) nationalism *see* cultural
    (ethnic) nationalism
ethnic identities 26, 27
ethnic nationalism *see* cultural (ethnic)
    nationalism
ethnic nationhood 27
ethnic–civic distinction 238
ethnicity 26, 33, 246
    boundary approach 61
    and nationalism 200, 277
Euro-scepticism 271
Europe 38, 52, 57, 58, **180–187, 270–272**
European Union 241, 249, 265
Evangelical movement 178

exclusion ix, 60
The Expansion of England (Seeley) 35, 187,
    279
external empires 36, 132, 250

Factors in Modern History (Pollard) 97
fascism 25
federalism 240
feminization 232
first English empire **81–88**
The First English Empire (Davies) 180–182
Firth, Katherine 125
Fitzgerald earls of Kildare 166
fitzGerald, Maurice 75, 76
fitzMalcolm, David 79
Fletcher, Andrew 136
folk mania 208
foreignness 280
Forster, E. M. 213
Forz, Willima de 80
four nations 14
Fowler, H. W. 2
Foxe, John 105, 112, 125
France
    Catholic bogey 162, 201
    elect nation 108, **109–110**
    English perspective on 216
    language 55, 58
    monarchies 92, 101
    national identity 20
    nationhood 22, 27, **91–93,** 123
    patriotism 101
    political nation 23
    universalism 277
    see also French Revolution
Francophobia 201
Free Presbyterian Church 246
freedom 125
Freeman, Edward 204
French Revolution 23
    imperialism 130
    Jewish emancipation 27
    missionary nationalism 31
    nation and state 92
    and nationalism 29, 277, 284
    Thatcher, Margaret on 296
From the Four Corners (Howard) 234
Froude, J. A. 93, 188, 282
Future of Multi-Ethnic Britain (Runnymede
    trust), *see Parekh Report*

Gaelic culture 288
Gaelic dialect 78
Gaelicization 87
Gaitskell, Hugh 271
Gallophobia 162

gens Anglorum 46
gentlemen 102
Geoffrey of Monmouth 13, 204, 205, 281
  Britons **62–66**
  Germania 205
  History of the Kings of Britain **63–66**, 204, 281
  Wales 64, **67–68**
George III 148
George IV 181
George V 182, 197, 294
Gerald of Wales 72, 82
German citizenship law 277
German national identity 20, 60
German nationalism 18, 91, 100
German nationhood 22
German reunification 25, 26
German unity 60
Germania (Geoffrey of Monmouth) 205
Gibbons, Stella 296
Gibbs, Philip 231
Gilbert and Sullivan 294
Gilroy, Paul 258
Gladstone, William Ewart 183
Glamorgan 72
Glasgow 168, 171
globalization 249
Gododdin 70
Godwine Earl of Wessex 44
Golden Treasury of English Verse (Palgrave) 220
Goldsmith, Oliver 180
Gordon, Lord George 163
Gordon riots 163, 289
Gorman, Teresa 298
Grahame, Kenneth 295
Grainger, Percy 208
Grattan, Henry 143, 288
Great Britain 5, **130–136**, 180, 187
Great Depression 236
Great Exhibition 1851 192, 193
'Greater Britain' 36, 38, 188, 279
Greater England 63
Greek empire 190
Green, J. R. 93, 117, 206, 218
Green, T. H. 214
Greenfeld, Liah
  literary Englishness 114
  nation **122–123**
  nationalism
    seventeenth century 122, 124, 125, 126
    sixteenth century 18, **95–100**, 102
  Protestant nation **103–108**, **109–111**
Gregory the Great, Pope 45
group culture 257

guidebooks 230
Guild Socialism 214
Gwynedd 72

Habermas, Jürgen 25, 26
Hague, William 265, 267, 268, 298
Hakluyt, Richard 93
Hall, Stuart 256
Haller, William 106, 112
Hamilton family 165
Hanoverians 154
Hardie, James Keir 169, 183
Hardy, Thomas 210, 295
Harlech 73
Hartlib, Samuel 126
Hartz, Louis 14
Hastings, Adrian 124, 126
Hazareesingh, Sudhir 31
Hazlitt, William 185
Heart of Darkness (Conrad) 193
Heath, Edward 267
Hebrew nationalism 125
Heffer, Simon 266
Hegel, G. W. F. 197, 288
hegemony 167
Helgerson, Richard **116–119**
Henry the Fifth (Shakespeare) 118, 285
Henry I 72, 79
Henry II 72, 75, 76, 82
Henry III 52, 53, 72
Henry IV 73
Henry V **57–58**, 59
Henry VI 58
Henry VII 73
Henry VIII 75
Hepple, Bob 256
Herder, Johann Gottfried von 23, 24, 25
Highlands 70, 81, 135, 181
Historia Regum Britanniae, History of the Kings of Britain (Geoffrey of Monmouth) **63–66**, 204, 281
historians 59
Historical Association 219
historical inquiries **251–252**
histories 4, 7, 14, 40, 50, 274
  see also Bede, the Venerable
historiography 36, 46, 218, 275
History of Greater Britain (Mair) 133
history plays (Shakespeare) 118, 119
history teaching **218–219**
History of the Union of Great Britain (Defoe) 150
Hitchins, Peter 265
Hobsbawm, Eric 199, 276
Hobson, J. A. 198
Holst, Gustav 209

Home Rule *see* devolution
honours and orders 290
House of Lords 152
Howard, Leslie 234
Howard's End (Forster) 213
Hughes, Thomas 191
Hundred Years War 54
Huskisson, William 194
Hyndman, H. M. 215
hyphenated Britishness 261
Hywel Dda, high king of Wales 71

identity crisis **241–243**, 250
   see also Parekh Report
Ignatieff, Michael 26
image-building 254
immigrants 241, 290
imperial history 279
imperial (missionary) nationalism x, 34, 278
imperial nations *see* empires
imperialism 292
   Bede, the Venerable 47
   and class 194
   French Revolution 130
   the mission 196
   Napoleon 32
   v. nationalism 30, 193
Imperialism (Hobson) 198
independence 24, 269
individual human rights 96
Industrial Revolution **167–169**
'Inglis' 78
Institute of Historical Research 275
institutions
   Anglo-Saxon 42
   British 37
   crown 286
   eighteenth, nineteenth centuries 167
   eleventh to thirteenth centuries 52, 53
   fourteenth century 54
   Scotland 149, 151
internal colonialism 13, 36
internal empires 36, 63, 85, 250
internationalism 57, 113, 114
interwar period 231, 232, 233
inventors 168
Iona 69
Ireland **68**
   British identity **140–145**
   as Catholic Other 163
   conquest and colonization **74–77**, 83, 84, 87, 287
   nationalism 18, 143, 144, 200, 277
   Northern Ireland **240–249**
   Protestantism 141, 142, 144, 261, 287
   union with England **142–144**, 145, 202

Irish 69, 81, **140–145**, 260
   British Empire 170, 171
   Irish Catholics 159, 170, 245, 288, 290, 297
   Irish Chartists 169
   Irish Free State 247
   Irish radicals 291
   Irish Revival 158
Israel 128, 284
Italian Renaissance 58
ius sanguinis (law of blood) 24
ius soli (law of the soil) 23
Ivanhoe (Scott) 48, 49

Jacobite rebellion 152, 158
James, duke of York 135
James, Henry 218
James II 141
James IV of Scotland 133
James VI (I of England) 5, 86
   Ireland 140
   king of 'Great Britain' 281, 286
   multiple kingdoms 130, 131
   Union with England 132, 133
Jenkins, Lord, of Hillhead 228
Jews 27, 28, 158
'John Bull' symbol 292
Johnson, Paul 266
Johnson, Samuel 292

Kambria 67
Kant, Immanuel 23
Kidd, Colin 155
King's English 10, 57
Kingsley, Charles 192, 282
Kipling, Rudyard 8
Knox, Robert 207
Kohn, Hans 18, 23, **124–125**, 285, 286
Kureishi, Hanif 243, 260, 263

labour movement 169, 184, 236
Labour Party 236, 237, 263, 265, 268, 271
Langford, Paul 224
Lark Rise (Thompson) 296
Latin 55, 58
Laudabiliter 82
law of blood (*ius sanguinis*) 24
law of the soil (*ius soli*) 23
Lawrence, D. H. 212
left-nationalist popular culture 299
Leonard, Mark 254
Levellers 286
Lewis, Saunders 243
Lhuyd, Humphrey 138
liberal contractualism 26
Liberal Party 237
liberalism *see* new liberalism

liberty 124, 127
Light, Alison 232
The Lion and the Unicorn (Orwell) 227–228, 252
Lipton, Thomas 171
literacy 104
literary Englishness **114–120**
'Little Englandism' 213, 271, 296
Livingstone, David 171
Llewelyn ap Gruffudd 68, 72
Lloyd George, David 169, 182, 183
localism 120
Lollards 54
long bow 54
Lothian 70, 78
Louis XIV 92
Lowlands 70, 81, 135
Lugard, Frederick 194

Mac Alpin, Kenneth 69
Mac Murrough, Art, king of Leinster 76
Mac Murrough, Dermot, of Leinster 75
Macaulay, Thomas Bebington 190, 191, 280
MacDonald, Ramsay 169
Macdonell, G. 232
McNeil, Hugh 176
Madoc, Prince 138
Mafeking 198
Magna Carta 50, 143
Mair (Major), John 133
Major, John 230, 267, 271
  comment; (*The Guardian*) **226–228**;
    (*The Times*) 4
  Middle England 228
  privatisation 264
Malcolm I 70
Malcolm II 70, 71
Malcolm III (Canmore) 78, 79
Marcher lordships 72, 73
Marches 72, 138
Margaret 'Maid of Norway' 79
Margaret Tudor 133
Marian exiles 105, 107
Marr, Andrew 238, 239, 256, 269
Marten, C. H. K. 219
Mary I 140
Masterman, C. F. G. 210, 212
mayoralty 253
medieval English kingdom 82
medieval English rule 84
medieval universities 28
Meinecke, Friedrich 21, 22
Merchant of Venice (Shakespeare) 285
Mercian kingdom 44
Merrie England (Blatchford) 215
Methodism 153, 160, 178

Middle Ages 58
middle class 56, 96, 97
Middle England 227
middle nations 83
Mill, John Stuart 190
Millais, Everett 188
millenialism 126, 128
Miller, David 194
Milner, Alfred 206, 213
Milton, John 8, 107, 112, **127–128**
'Minute on Indian Education' (Macaulay) 190
missionary (imperial) nationalism x, **30–32**, 34, 278
Modern English Usage (Fowler) 2
modernists 29, 30
Modood, Tariq 256
Molyneux, William 141, 142, 143
moment of Englishness 224
monarchies
  Britishness 292
  France 92, 101
  nation-building 22, 23
  non-national nationalism 20
  Tudor England 97, 101, 102
monastic movement 43
Monmouth 72
Montesquieu 102, 288
Montfort, Simon de 72
More, Sir Thomas 95
Morgann-Gwent 72
Morris, William 211, 215
Morton, H. V. 230
multiculturalism 242, 253, 258
multidisciplinary studies 15
multinational state 150; multinationalism 278
multiple identities 145, 149, 179
multiple kingdoms 130
Murray, William 150
My Beautiful Launderette (Kureishi) 243

Nairn, Tom 3, 18, 20, 240, 255, 268, 269, 299
narcissism 21, 61
natio 28, 51
'The Nation as an Ethical Ideal' (Caird) 202
nation-building 45
nation-states 23, 30, 33, 43, 47, 116, 283
national awakening 125
national character 40, 84
national churches 43, 54
national conglomerates 235
national consciousness x, 28, 29, 34
national curriculum 223
National Front 263, 264
national identity 34, 40
national portraits 10
national sovereignty 95

nationalism 23, **28–30**
  civic 25, 26, 147, 149
  classic x
  colonial 288
  English **18–21**, 34, **175–179**, 239, **262–269**,
    276
  and English national character x
  and ethnicity 200, 277
  French Revolution 29, 277, 284
  German 18, 91, 100
  Hebrew 125
  as mass force 199
  medieval 89
  missionary (imperial) x, **30–32**, 34, 278
  nineteenth century 33
  Old Testament 103, 125
  origins 283
  Orwell, George 20
  political 31, 147, 239
  and Protestantism **108–114**, 125, 201
  and religion 125, 127, 285
  rise of 176, 177
  sixteenth century **89–103**
  as subject of study 41
  v. national identity 33
  v. patriotism 276
  Welsh 243
  see also cultural (ethnic) nationalism
Nationalism in Religion (McNeil) 176
nationalist movements 184, 200, 236, 242
nationality 24, 233, 292
nationalization 237
nationes 28
nationhood 23, 29, 30
  ambiguities **25–28**
  America 25
  boundary maintenance **61**
  civic 25, 27, 100
  and decline of empire **196–202**
  English 48
  ethnic 27
  France 22, 27, **91–93**, 123
  Germany 22
  medieval 89, 90
  political 28
  segregation of communities in England
    260
nation(s)
  (and) nationalism **28–30**
  British 172–174
  civic 27
  cultural 21, **23–24**
  divided **121–130**
  and empires **32–35**
  English 47, **48–59**, **93–103**
  Greenfeld, Liah **122–123**

middle 83
  political **21–25**, 33, **102**
  and states 92, 277
  see also elect nation
Nazism 25
Nelson, Admiral 187
new aristocracy 98
'New English' 76, 140, 141, 142
New Irish 141
New Labour 253, 254
new liberalism **213–214**
Newbolt Report 223
Newbould, Frank 209
Newman, Gerald 18, **176–178**
News from Nowhere (Morris) 211
Newsam, Peter 256
Nine Years War 140
nomenclature **3–4**, **5–7**, 12, 45
Norman Conquest 9, 42, 48, 49, 50
  Anglo-Norman expansion 67, 77
Norman kings **65**
Norman Yoke 48, 49
Normandy 51
Normanization 78, 79
Normans 81
Norse 81
North Britons **145–154**, 155
North Sea Oil 248
Northern Ireland **240–249**
Northern Ireland Assembly 240
Northumbria 44, 70, 78
'Notes on Nationalism' (Orwell) 20

O'Brien, James Bronterre 169
O'Connell, Daniel 144, 183
O'Connor, Feargus 169
O'Connor, Rory, of Connacht 75
'Old English' 76, 140
Old Testament nationalism 103, 125
Oldham and Bradford riots 2001 259
O'Neill, Hugh 140
opposition between familiars ix, 60, 61
orders *see* honours and orders
Oriental empires 190
origins 40
Origins and Destiny of Imperial Britain
    (Cramb) 198
Orwell, George
  Empire 195
  The English People 16
  The Lion and the Unicorn (Orwell)
    227–228, 252
  nomenclature 12
  'Notes on Nationalism' 20
Owain Glyn Dwr (Owen Glendower) 73
Owen, Robert 169, 183

Oxford Book of English Verse (Quiller-Couch)
    220, 223
Oxford English Dictionary on Historical
    Principles (Murray) 221
The Oxford History of England (Taylor) 3

Paisley, Dr Ian 246
Palmerston, Viscount 183
parallel societies 83
Parekh, Bhikhu *see Parekh Report*
Parekh Report **256–262**
Parker, Matthew 205
Parkinson, C. Northcote 293
Parkinson's Law 293
Parliament 54, 96, 151
    parliamentary sovereignty 241
Parnell, Charles 183
Parry, Hubert 294
Past and Present (Carlyle) 189
patriotism
    English 50, 268
    France 101
    Germany 25
    Jacobin thinking 31
    Johnson, Samuel 292
    v. nationalism 124, 276
Patriotism The Making and Unmaking of
    British National Identity (History
    Workshop) 15, 19
Paxman, Jeremy 262, 292
'peculiarities of the English' (Thompson)
    20
peerages 290
Penguin History of Britain 4
Philip II 140
Picts 69, 70, 81
Picture Post 233
Pilsudski, Jozef 277
Pitt, William, the Younger 187
Pittock, Murray 289
Plaid Cymru 243
plantation policy 140, 287
pluralism 150, 154, 254, 259, 261
Pocock, J. G. A. **12–14**, 275
Poitevins 52, 53
Poland 277
political culture 288
political elite 183
political nationalism 31, 147, 239
political nationhood 28
political nations **21–25**, 33, **102**
political science studies 15
political theology 109, 110
political unification 24
Pollard, A. F. 97, 219
Pope Clement V 108

popular consciousness 252
popular sovereignty 124
Portugal 90
postmodernism 242
'Postscript' broadcasts 234
potato famine 159
Powell, Enoch **267**, 298
Poyning's Law (1495) 140
pre-modern societies 58
Presbyterianism 135, 153, 154
The Present State of the British Empire in
    Europe, America, Africa and Asia
    (Goldsmith) 180
Priestley, J. B. 16, 231, 234, 296
Priestley, Joseph 160
'primordialists' 29
Prince of Wales 139, 182
The Principal Navigations, Voyages and
    Discoveries of the English Nation
    (Hakluyt) 93
privatisations 264
progress 190, 191, 204
'Prologue' (Chaucer) 55
Protector Somerset *see* Seymour, Edward
    (Protector Somerset)
Protestant Church **284**
Protestant–Catholic riots (Liverpool) 290
Protestantism **37–38**, **103**, 146
    England 153, **157–165**, 249
    Greenfeld, Liah **103–108**, **109–111**
    Ireland 141, 142, 144, 261, 287
    and nationalism **108–114**, 125, 201
    v. Catholicism **158–165**
    Wales 139
proto-nationalism 29, 278
public schools 221
Puritanism 105, 124, 125, 127, 130

quasi-federalist state 150
Queen Victoria 146, 181, 197
Quiller-Couch, Sir Arthur 220

race 24, 206, 258
    racism 242, 259
    racist groups 263
Raleigh, Walter 188
Ranke, Leopold von 24
Redmond, John 265
Reformation 74, 76, 111, 119, 133, 139,
    141
regionalism 240
Reith, John 237
religion
    and culture 157–165
    decline 38, 249, 297
    disunity 131, 160, 201

Elizabeth I 111
and nationalism 125, 127, 285
wars of 114
responsibility 194
Restoration 123, 135
Rex gloriae 108
Rheged 70
Rhodes, Cecil 206
Rhys ap Tewdwr 72
Richard II 8
The Rise of English Nationalism (Newman)
    176
rise of the gentry 98
Robert, earl of Gloucester 65
Robert II 80
Robert VIII de Bruce *see* Bruce, Robert
Robertson Scott, J. W. 296
Roman Britain 47
Roman Empire 190, 196, 198
Romanticism 178, 209, 215
Rome 293
Ros, Robert de 80
Rosebery, earl of 183, 191, 272
Roxburghe, earl of 136
royal family 238, 292, 297
royalism 92
Rubens, Peter Paul 132
'Rule Britannia' 148
Runnymede Trust 256
rural economy 295, 296
rural ideology 213, 215, 230
    see also English countryside
Rushdie, Salman 297
Russia 21, 100

Sacheverell riots 160
St George's Cross 9, 252, 262, 275
St Thomas Aquinas 58
The Salisbury Review 266
Santayana, George 231
The Satanic Verses (Rushdie) 297
satirical portraits 9
Savoyards 53
Saxons 5, 65
science **115–116**
Scone Abbey 69
Scotia 69
Scotland 40
    Anglicization **77–81**, 84
    Britons **145–154**
    Church (Kirk) of Scotland **153–154**, 160,
        288, 290
    colonization 86
    devolution **247–249**
    diversity **68–71**
    Enlightenment 289

identity **148–154**, **155–156**, 289
    institutions 149, 151
    law **151–153**
    Parliament 240, 248
    union with England **132–135**, 142, 148, 150
        Acts of Union 5, 135, 145, 146, 156
        convergence and divergence **135–136**,
            287
Scots 69, 170, 171, 236, 266, 291
Scott, David 186
Scott, Sir Walter 48, 181
Scotti (Irish) 69
'Scottis' 78
Scottish National Party (SNP) 248
Scottish nationalist movement 240
Scottish Office 248
Scottishness 80, 146–147, 248, 289
'The Secret People' (Chesterton) 262
secularism 154, 201
Seeley, Sir John 35–36, 38, 187, 189, 206, 219,
    279
segregation 260, 261
self-absorption 21
self-images ix, 62, 85
Seton, William 137
Seymour, Edward (Protector Somerset) 133,
    136
Shakespeare, William 8, **118–119**, 285
Sharp, Cecil 208
Short History of the English People (Green)
    93, 117, 206, 218
'Signs of the Time' (Carlyle) 185
Slessor, Mary 171
Smith, Anthony 26
Smith, Goldwin 217
Smith, Sir Thomas 101
Smith, Zadie 243
Smout, T. C. 271
social mobility **95–96**, 98
social revolution 184
socialism 214
society *see* British society
sociological studies 15
Soliloquies in England (Santayana) 231
Somerville, William 5
'south country' **209–212**, 218, 231
'The South Downs' (Newbould) 209
Southern, R. W. 217
sovereign territorial state 283
    sovereignty 95, 101, 124, 241, 271, 283, 286
Spain 90, 131, 290
Spencer, Herbert 192
Spirit of the Age (Hazlitt) 185
Staatsvölker 34
Starkey, David 270
state-nations *see* political nations

state–people rupture 53
statehood 22, 91
state(s) 29, 43, 90, 92, 101, 277, 278
status closure 278
Statute of Rhuddlan 73
Statutes of Kilkenny 76
Stone of Destiny 69, 83
Strathclyde 69, 70
Straw, Jack 255
Strong, Sir Roy 256
Strongbow (Richard de Clare, second earl of
    Pembroke) 75, 84
Stuart, Charles Edward 162
Stuart dynasty 35, 86, 154, 163, 165
Stuart, James Edward 162
Stubbs, William 204, 216
superiority 53, 179, 194
'swamping' 242, 267
Swift, Dean 143, 145
Swift, Jonathan 143, 287

A Tale of Two Cities (Dickens) 296
Tallis, Thomas 111
Tara 68
Taylor, A. J. P. **3–4**, 12
Taylor, William, of Norwich 224
The Teaching of English in England (Newbolt)
    223
Tebbit, Norman 255, 265, 268, 274
television 238
Tennyson, Alfred Lord 8
Teutonic dialect 78
Thatcher, Margaret
    Britishness 254, 264
    on Cool Britannia 297
    Europe 271
    on the French Revolution 296
    Middle England 227, 228
    race issue 267
Thirty Years War 126
thistle and rose 133
Thompson, Edward 290
Thompson, Flora 296
Thomson, James 5, 148
Thornton, A. P. 194
three kingdoms 14, 130, 131
toleration 153, 154
Tom Brown's Schooldays (Hughes) 191
Tomlinson, Sally 256
Tone, Wolfe 143
Tong, Raymond 266
Toynbee, Arnold 40
trade unionism 183, 236
Trades Union Congress 237
The Tragic Muse (James) 218
travel literature 291

Treaty of Maastricht 226, 271, 274
Tudor England **97–98**, 283
Tudor state 101
Tudors 73, 74, 86, 98, 133
    Anglo-Welsh relations 138, 281
    Margaret Tudor 133
Turville-Petre, T. 280
Tyndale, William 103

Ulster 140, 144, 246
Ulster Protestants **245–247**
unification of England 42
Union Jack 9, 132, 297
unitary state 150
United Kingdom 6, 7, **39–41**, 170
United Kingdom of Great Britain 5, 137
United Kingdom of Great Britain and Ireland
    6, 137
United Kingdom of Great Britain and
    Northern Ireland 6
United States of America 14, 20, 26, 96, 274
unity 43, 50
universalism 31, 277, 283
utopianism 91, 128

Vaughan Williams, Ralph 209, 294
vernacular 54, 56, 57, 283
Vescy, Eustace de 80
Vikings 42, 70

Wales 6, 202
    Acts of Union 73, 74
    conquest and colonization **71–77**, 83, 84, 86
    culture 138, 281
    devolution **243–244**
    Geoffrey of Monmouth 64, **67–68**
    Gladstone, William Ewart 183
    identity **137–140**, 168, 174
    Labour Party 236
    language 137
    Prince Madoc 138
    Prince of Wales 68, 139, 182
    Protestantism 139
Wallace, William 81
wars 38, 54, 57, 60, 173
Wars of Independence (1296–1371) 77, 79,
    80
Waterford 75
Watt, James 290
Weber, Max 277
welfare state 237
Wellesley, Richard 170
Wellesley, Richard, Baron 159
Wellington, duke of 170
Welsh 64, 65, 86, **136–140**
Welsh Assembly 240

Welsh nationalism 243
Welsh Nationalist Party 243
Wessex kings 4, 42, 43, 51, 67, 70
Westward Ho! (Kingsley) 192, 282
Whig interpretation of history **202–207**, 219, 294
White Man's Burden 194
White Teeth (Smith) 243
Who Do We Think We Are? (Alibhai-Brown) 243
Widley, George 113
Wilkes, John 150, 292
William I 'the Conqueror' 42, 43, 49, 279
William III 141, 142
William of Malmesbury 50, 51, 55, 82
William of Newburgh 82
William of Orange 290
Williams, Glyn 168

Williams, Gwyn 174
The Wind in the Willows (Grahame) 295
Wisden Cricket Monthly 265
Wolfe, John 176
women writers 232
Woolf, Stuart 31
working class 169
World War I 230, 232, 294
World War II 233
Worsthorne, Peregrine 270
Wyclif, John 54, 59

xenophobia x, 53, 97, 292

Yack, Bernard 25
York (Eboracum) 70
You ask me, why, tho' ill at ease (Tennyson) 8
Young Pretender 163

MICHAEL MULKAY, *The Embryo Research Debate*
0 521 57180 4 hardback 0 521 57683 0 paperback

LYNN RAPAPORT, *Jews in Germany after the Holocaust*
0 521 58219 9 hardback 0 521 58809 X paperback

CHANDRA MUKERJI, *Territorial Ambitions and the Gardens of Versailles* 0 521 49675 6 hardback 0 521 59959 8 paperback

LEON H. MAYHEW, *The New Public* 0 521 48146 5 hardback 0 521 48493 6 paperback

VERA L. ZOLBERG AND JONI M. CHERBO (eds.), *Outsider Art* 0 521 58111 7 hardback 0 521 58921 5 paperback

SCOTT BRAVMANN, *Queer Fictions of the Past*
0 521 59101 5 hardback 0 521 59907 5 paperback

STEVEN SEIDMAN, *Difference Troubles* 0 521 59043 4 hardback 0 521 59970 9 paperback

RON EYERMAN AND ANDREW JAMISON, *Music and Social Movements* 0 521 62045 7 hardback 0 521 62966 7 paperback

MEYDA YEGENOGLU, *Colonial Fantasies* 0 521 48233 X hardback 0 521 62658 7 paperback

LAURA DESFOR EDLES, *Symbol and Ritual in the New Spain* 0 521 62140 2 hardback 0 521 62885 7 paperback

NINA ELIASOPH, *Avoiding Politics* 0 521 58293 8 hardback 0 521 58759 X paperback

BERNHARD GIESEN, *Intellectuals and the German Nation* 0 521 62161 5 hardback 0 521 63996 4 paperback

PHILIP SMITH (ed.), *The New American Cultural Sociology* 0 521 58415 9 hardback 0 521 58634 8 paperback

S. N. EISENSTADT, *Fundamentalism, Sectarianism and Revolution* 0 521 64184 5 hardback 0 521 64586 7 paperback

MARIAM FRASER, *Identity without Selfhood* 0 521 62357 X hardback 0 521 62579 3 paperback

LUC BOLTANSKI, *Distant Suffering* 0 521 57389 0 hardback 0 521 65953 1 paperback

PYOTR SZTOMPKA, *Trust* 0 521 59144 9 hardback 0 521 59850 8 paperback

SIMON J. CHARLESWORTH, *A Phenomenology of Working Class Culture* 0 521 65066 6 hardback 0 521 65915 9 paperback

ROBIN WAGNER-PACIFICI, *Theorizing the Standoff* 0 521 65244 8 hardback 0 521 65479 3 paperback

RONALD R. JACOBS, *Race, Media and the Crisis of Civil Society* 0 521 62360 X hardback 0 521 62578 5 paperback

ALI MIRSEPASSI, *Intellectual Discourse and the Politics of Modernization* 0 521 65000 3 hardback 0 521 65997 3 paperback

RON LEMBO, *Thinking Through Television* 0 521 58465 5 hardback 0 521 58577 5 paperback

MICHÈLE LAMONT AND LAURENT THÉVENOT (eds.), *Rethinking Comparative Cultural Sociology* 0 521 78263 5 hardback 0 521 78794 7 paperback

STEPHEN M. ENGEL, *The Unfinished Revolution: Social Movement Theory and the Gay and Lesbian Movement* 0 521 80287 3 hardback 0 521 00377 6 paperback

RON EYERMAN, *Cultural Trauma: Slavery and the Formation of African American Identity* 0 521 80828 6 hardback 0 521 00437 3 paperback